The Magazine Novels
of Pauline Hopkins

THE SCHOMBURG LIBRARY OF
NINETEENTH-CENTURY BLACK WOMEN WRITERS

General Editor, Henry Louis Gates, Jr.

Titles are listed chronologically; collections that include works published over a span of years are listed according to the publication date of their initial work.

The Magazine Novels

of

Pauline Hopkins

With an Introduction by
HAZEL V. CARBY

❧ ❧ ❧

❧ ❧ ❧

OXFORD UNIVERSITY PRESS
New York   Oxford

Oxford University Press

Oxford   New York   Toronto
Delhi   Bombay   Calcutta   Madras   Karachi
Petaling Jaya   Singapore   Hong Kong   Tokyo
Nairobi   Dar es Salaam   Cape Town
Melbourne   Auckland

and associated companies in
Berlin   Ibadan

Library of Congress Cataloging-in-Publication Data

Hopkins, Pauline E. (Pauline Elizabeth)
[Novels, Selections]
The magazine novels of Pauline Hopkins / introduction by Hazel V. Carby.
p. cm.—(The Schomburg library of nineteenth-century black
women writers)
Contents: Hagar's daughter—Winona—Of one blood.
1. Afro-Americans—Fiction. I. Title. II. Series.
PS1999.H4226A6   1988   813'.4—dc19   87-21182
ISBN 0-19-505248-X
ISBN 0-19-505267-6 (set)
ISBN 0-19-506325-2 (pbk.)

2 4 6 8 10 9 7 5 3 1

Printed in the United States of America

The
Schomburg Library
of
Nineteenth-Century
Black Women Writers
is
Dedicated
in Memory
of
PAULINE AUGUSTA COLEMAN GATES

1916–1987

PUBLISHER'S NOTE

FOREWORD
In Her Own Write

Henry Louis Gates, Jr.

One muffled strain in the Silent South, a jarring chord and a
vague and uncomprehended cadenza has been and still is the
Negro. And of that muffled chord, the one mute and voiceless note has been the sadly expectant Black Woman, ...

The "other side" has not been represented by one who "lives
there." And not many can more sensibly realize and more
accurately tell the weight and the fret of the "long dull pain"
than the open-eyed but hitherto voiceless Black Woman of
America.

. . . as our Caucasian barristers are not to blame if they
cannot *quite* put themselves in the dark man's place, neither
should the dark man be wholly expected fully and adequately
to reproduce the exact Voice of the Black Woman.

—ANNA JULIA COOPER, *A Voice From the South* (1892)

The birth of the Afro-American literary tradition occurred
in 1773, when Phillis Wheatley published a book of poetry.
Despite the fact that her book garnered for her a remarkable
amount of attention, Wheatley's journey to the printer had
been a most arduous one. Sometime in 1772, a young African girl walked demurely into a room in Boston to undergo
an oral examination, the results of which would determine
the direction of her life and work. Perhaps she was shocked
upon entering the appointed room. For there, perhaps gath-

ered in a semicircle, sat eighteen of Boston's most notable citizens. Among them were John Erving, a prominent Boston merchant; the Reverend Charles Chauncy, pastor of the Tenth Congregational Church; and John Hancock, who would later gain fame for his signature on the Declaration of Independence. At the center of this group was His Excellency, Thomas Hutchinson, governor of Massachusetts, with Andrew Oliver, his lieutenant governor, close by his side.

Why had this august group been assembled? Why had it seen fit to summon this young African girl, scarcely eighteen years old, before it? This group of "the most respectable Characters in *Boston*," as it would later define itself, had assembled to question closely the African adolescent on the slender sheaf of poems that she claimed to have "written by herself." We can only speculate on the nature of the questions posed to the fledgling poet. Perhaps they asked her to identify and explain—for all to hear—exactly who were the Greek and Latin gods and poets alluded to so frequently in her work. Perhaps they asked her to conjugate a verb in Latin or even to translate randomly selected passages from the Latin, which she and her master, John Wheatley, claimed that she "had made some Progress in." Or perhaps they asked her to recite from memory key passages from the texts of John Milton and Alexander Pope, the two poets by whom the African claimed to be most directly influenced. We do not know.

We do know, however, that the African poet's responses were more than sufficient to prompt the eighteen august gentlemen to compose, sign, and publish a two-paragraph "Attestation," an open letter "To the Publick" that prefaces Phillis Wheatley's book and that reads in part:

> We whose Names are under-written, do assure the World, that the Poems specified in the following Page, were (as we

verily believe) written by Phillis, a young Negro Girl, who
was but a few Years since, brought an uncultivated Barbarian
from *Africa*, and has ever since been, and now is, under the
Disadvantage of serving as a Slave in a Family in this Town.
She has been examined by some of the best Judges, and is
thought qualified to write them.

So important was this document in securing a publisher for
Wheatley's poems that it forms the signal element in the
prefatory matter preceding her *Poems on Various Subjects, Religious and Moral*, published in London in 1773.

Without the published "Attestation," Wheatley's publisher
claimed, few would believe that an African could possibly
have written poetry all by herself. As the eighteen put the
matter clearly in their letter, "Numbers would be ready to
suspect they were not really the Writings of Phillis." Wheatley and her master, John Wheatley, had attempted to publish
a similar volume in 1772 in Boston, but Boston publishers
had been incredulous. One year later, "Attestation" in hand,
Phillis Wheatley and her master's son, Nathaniel Wheatley,
sailed for England, where they completed arrangements for
the publication of a volume of her poems with the aid of the
Countess of Huntington and the Earl of Dartmouth.

This curious anecdote, surely one of the oddest oral ex-
aminations on record, is only a tiny part of a larger, and
even more curious, episode in the Enlightenment. Since the
beginning of the sixteenth century, Europeans had wondered aloud whether or not the African "species of men," as
they were most commonly called, *could* ever create formal
literature, could ever master "the arts and sciences." If they
could, the argument ran, then the African variety of humanity was fundamentally related to the European variety. If not,
then it seemed clear that the African was destined by nature

to be a slave. This was the burden shouldered by Phillis
Wheatley when she successfully defended herself and the au-
thorship of her book against counterclaims and doubts.

Indeed, with her successful defense, Wheatley launched
two traditions at once—the black American literary tradition
and the black woman's literary tradition. If it is extraordinary
that not just one but both of these traditions were founded
simultaneously by a black woman—certainly an event unique
in the history of literature—it is also ironic that this important fact of common, coterminous literary origins seems to
have escaped most scholars.

That the progenitor of the black literary tradition was a
woman means, in the most strictly literal sense, that all subsequent black writers have evolved in a matrilinear line of
descent, and that each, consciously or unconsciously, has extended and revised a canon whose foundation was the poetry
of a black woman. Early black writers seem to have been
keenly aware of Wheatley's founding role, even if most of
her white reviewers were more concerned with the implica-
tions of her race than her gender. Jupiter Hammon, for example, whose 1760 broadside "An Evening Thought. Salvation by Christ, With Penitential Cries" was the first
individual poem published by a black American, acknowledged Wheatley's influence by selecting her as the subject of
his second broadside, "An Address to Miss Phillis Wheatly
[*sic*], Ethiopian Poetess, in Boston," which was published at
Hartford in 1778. And George Moses Horton, the second
Afro-American to publish a book of poetry in English (1829),
brought out in 1838 an edition of his *Poems By A Slave*
bound together with Wheatley's work. Indeed, for fifty-six
years, between 1773 and 1829, when Horton published *The
Hope of Liberty*, Wheatley was the *only* black person to have
published a book of imaginative literature in English. So

central was this black woman's role in the shaping of the Afro-American literary tradition that, as one historian has maintained, the history of the reception of Phillis Wheatley's poetry *is* the history of Afro-American literary criticism. Well into the nineteenth century, Wheatley and the black literary tradition were the same entity.

But Wheatley is not the only black woman writer who stands as a pioneering figure in Afro-American literature. Just as Wheatley gave birth to the genre of black poetry, Ann Plato was the first Afro-American to publish a book of essays (1841) and Harriet E. Wilson was the first black person to publish a novel in the United States (1859).

Despite this pioneering role of black women in the tradition, however, many of their contributions before this century have been all but lost or unrecognized. As Hortense Spillers observed as recently as 1983,

> With the exception of a handful of autobiographical narratives from the nineteenth century, the black woman's realities are virtually suppressed until the period of the Harlem Renaissance and later. Essentially the black woman as artist, as intellectual spokesperson for her own cultural apprenticeship, has not existed before, for anyone. At the source of [their] own symbol-making task, [the community of black women writers] confronts, therefore, a tradition of work that is quite recent, its continuities, broken and sporadic.

Until now, it has been extraordinarily difficult to establish the formal connections between early black women's writing and that of the present, precisely because our knowledge of their work has been broken and sporadic. Phillis Wheatley, for example, while certainly the most reprinted and discussed poet in the tradition, is also one of the least understood. Ann Plato's seminal work, *Essays* (which includes biographies and poems), has not been reprinted since it was published a century and a half ago. And Harriet Wilson's *Our Nig*, her compelling novel of a black woman's expanding consciousness in a racist Northern antebellum environment, never received even *one* review or comment at a time when virtually *all* works written by black people were heralded by abolitionists as salient arguments against the existence of human slavery. Many of the books reprinted in this set experienced a similar fate, the most dreadful fate for an author: that of being ignored then relegated to the obscurity of the rare book section of a university library. We can only wonder how many other texts in the black woman's tradition have been lost to this generation of readers or remain unclassified or uncatalogued and, hence, unread.

This was not always so, however. Black women writers dominated the final decade of the nineteenth century, perhaps spurred to publish by an 1886 essay entitled "The Coming American Novelist," which was published in *Lippincott's Monthly Magazine* and written by "A Lady From Philadelphia." This pseudonymous essay argued that the "Great American Novel" would be written by a black person. Her argument is so curious that it deserves to be repeated:

> When we come to formulate our demands of the Coming American Novelist, we will agree that he must be native-born. His ancestors may come from where they will, but we must give him a birthplace and have the raising of him. Still, the longer his family has been here the better he will represent us. Suppose he should have no country but ours, no traditions but those he has learned here, no longings apart from us, no future except in our future—the orphan of the world, he finds with us his home. And with all this, suppose he refuses to be fused into that grand conglomerate we call the "American type." With us, he is not of us. He is original, he has humor, he is tender, he is passive and fiery, he has been

taught what we call justice, and he has his own opinion about it. He has suffered everything a poet, a dramatist, a novelist need suffer before he comes to have his lips anointed. And with it all he is in one sense a spectator, a little out of the race. How would these conditions go towards forming an original development? In a word, suppose the coming novelist is of African origin? When one comes to consider the subject, there is no improbability in it. One thing is certain,—our great novel will not be written by the typical American.

An atypical American, indeed. Not only would the great American novel be written by an African-American, it would be written by an African-American *woman:*

> Yet farther: I have used the generic masculine pronoun because it is convenient; but Fate keeps revenge in store. It was a woman who, taking the wrongs of the African as her theme, wrote the novel that awakened the world to their reality, and why should not the coming novelist be a woman as well as an African? She—the woman of that race—has some claims on Fate which are not yet paid up.

It is these claims on fate that we seek to pay by publishing The Schomburg Library of Nineteenth-Century Black Women Writers.

This theme would be repeated by several black women authors, most notably by Anna Julia Cooper, a prototypical black feminist whose 1892 *A Voice From the South* can be considered to be one of the original texts of the black feminist movement. It was Cooper who first analyzed the fallacy of referring to "the Black man" when speaking of black people and who argued that just as white men cannot speak through the consciousness of black men, neither can black *men* "fully and adequately . . . reproduce the exact Voice of the Black Woman." Gender and race, she argues, cannot be conflated, except in the instance of a black woman's voice, and it is this voice which must be uttered and to which we must listen. As Cooper puts the matter so compellingly:

> It is not the intelligent woman vs. the ignorant woman; nor the white woman vs. the black, the brown, and the red,—it is not even the cause of woman vs. man. Nay, 'tis woman's strongest vindication for speaking that *the world needs to hear her voice*. It would be subversive of every human interest that the cry of one-half the human family be stifled. Woman in stepping from the pedestal of statue-like inactivity in the domestic shrine, and daring to think and move and speak,— to undertake to help shape, mold, and direct the thought of her age, is merely completing the circle of the world's vision. Hers is every interest that has lacked an interpreter and a defender. Her cause is linked with that of every agony that has been dumb—every wrong that needs a voice.
>
> It is no fault of man's that he has not been able to see truth from her standpoint. It does credit both to his head and heart that no greater mistakes have been committed or even wrongs perpetrated while she sat making tatting and snipping paper flowers. Man's own innate chivalry and the mutual interdependence of their interests have insured his treating her cause, in the main at least, as his own. And he is pardonably surprised and even a little chagrined, perhaps, to find his legislation not considered "perfectly lovely" in every respect. But in any case his work is only impoverished by her remaining dumb. The world has had to limp along with the wobbling gait and one-sided hesitancy of a man with one eye. Suddenly the bandage is removed from the other eye and the whole body is filled with light. It sees a circle where before it saw a segment. The darkened eye restored, every member rejoices with it.

The myopic sight of the darkened eye can only be restored when the full range of the black woman's voice, with its own special timbres and shadings, remains mute no longer.

Similarly, Victoria Earle Matthews, an author of short stories and essays, and a cofounder in 1896 of the National Association of Colored Women, wrote in her stunning essay, "The Value of Race Literature" (1895), that "when the literature of our race is developed, it will of necessity be different in all essential points of greatness, true heroism and real Christianity from what we may at the present time, for convenience, call American literature." Matthews argued that this great tradition of Afro-American literature would be the textual outlet "for the unnaturally suppressed inner lives which our people have been compelled to lead." Once these "unnaturally suppressed inner lives" of black people are unveiled, no "grander diffusion of mental light" will shine more brightly, she concludes, than that of the articulate Afro-American woman:

> And now comes the question, What part shall we women play in the Race Literature of the future? . . . within the compass of one small journal ["Woman's Era"] we have struck out a new line of departure—a journal, a record of Race interests gathered from all parts of the United States, carefully selected, moistened, winnowed and garnered by the ablest intellects of educated colored women, shrinking at no lofty theme, shirking no serious duty, aiming at every possible excellence, and determined to do their part in the future uplifting of the race.
> If twenty women, by their concentrated efforts in one literary movement, can meet with such success as has engendered, planned out, and so successfully consummated this convention, what much more glorious results, what wider spread success, what grander diffusion of mental light will not come forth at the bidding of the enlarged hosts of women writers, already called into being by the stimulus of your efforts?
> And here let me speak one word for my journalistic sisters

who have already entered the broad arena of journalism. Before the "Woman's Era" had come into existence, no one except themselves can appreciate the bitter experience and sore disappointments under which they have at all times been compelled to pursue their chosen vocations.

If their brothers of the press have had their difficulties to contend with, I am here as a sister journalist to state, from the fullness of knowledge, that their task has been an easy one compared with that of the colored woman in journalism.

Woman's part in Race Literature, as in Race building, is the most important part and has been so in all ages. . . . All through the most remote epochs she has done her share in literature. . . .

One of the most important aspects of this set is the republication of the salient texts from 1890 to 1910, which literary historians could well call "The Black Woman's Era." In addition to Mary Helen Washington's definitive edition of Cooper's *A Voice From the South*, we have reprinted two novels by Amelia Johnson, Frances Harper's *Iola Leroy*, two novels by Emma Dunham Kelley, Alice Dunbar-Nelson's two impressive collections of short stories, and Pauline Hopkins's three serialized novels as well as her monumental novel, *Contending Forces*—all published between 1890 and 1910. Indeed, black women published more works of fiction in these two decades than black men had published in the previous half century. Nevertheless, this great achievement has been ignored.

Moreover, the writings of nineteenth-century Afro-American women in general have remained buried in obscurity, accessible only in research libraries or in overpriced and poorly edited reprints. Many of these books have never been reprinted at all; in some instances only one or two copies are extant. In these works of fiction, poetry, autobiography, biography, essays, and journalism resides the mind of the nineteenth-century Afro-American woman. Until these works are made readily available to teachers and their students, a significant segment of the black tradition will remain silent.

Oxford University Press, in collaboration with the Schomburg Center for Research in Black Culture, is publishing thirty volumes of these compelling works, each of which contains an introduction by an expert in the field. The set includes such rare texts as Johnson's *The Hazeley Family* and *Clarence and Corinne*, Plato's *Essays*, the most complete edition of Phillis Wheatley's poems and letters, Emma Dunham Kelley's pioneering novel *Megda*, several previously unpublished stories and a novel by Alice Dunbar-Nelson, and the first collected volumes of Pauline Hopkins's three serialized novels and Frances Harper's poetry. We also present four volumes of poetry by such women as Mary Eliza Tucker Lambert, Adah Menken, Josephine Heard, and Maggie Johnson. Numerous slave and spiritual narratives, a newly discovered novel—*Four Girls at Cottage City*—by Emma Dunham Kelley (-Hawkins), and the first American edition of *Wonderful Adventures of Mrs. Seacole in Many Lands* are also among the texts included.

In addition to resurrecting the works of black women authors, it is our hope that this set will facilitate the resurrection of the Afro-American woman's literary tradition itself by unearthing its nineteenth-century roots. In the works of Nella Larsen and Jessie Fauset, Zora Neale Hurston and Ann Petry, Lorraine Hansberry and Gwendolyn Brooks, Paule Marshall and Toni Cade Bambara, Audre Lorde and Rita Dove, Toni Morrison and Alice Walker, Gloria Naylor and Jamaica Kincaid, these roots have branched luxuriantly. The eighteenth- and nineteenth-century authors whose works are presented in this set founded and nurtured the black women's literary tradition, which must be revived, explicated, analyzed, and debated before we can understand more completely the formal shaping of this tradition within a tradition, a coded literary universe through which, regrettably, we are only just beginning to navigate our way. As Anna Cooper said nearly one hundred years ago, we have been blinded by the loss of sight in one eye and have therefore been unable to detect the full *shape* of the Afro-American literary tradition.

Literary works configure into a tradition not because of some mystical collective unconscious determined by the biology of race or gender, but because writers read other writers and *ground* their representations of experience in models of language provided largely by other writers to whom they feel akin. It is through this mode of literary revision, amply evident in the *texts* themselves—in formal echoes, recast metaphors, even in parody—that a "tradition" emerges and defines itself.

This is formal bonding, and it is only through formal bonding that we can know a literary tradition. The collective publication of these works by black women now, for the first time, makes it possible for scholars and critics, male and female, black and white, to *demonstrate* that black women writers read, and revised, other black women writers. To demonstrate this set of formal literary relations is to demonstrate that sexuality, race, and gender are both the condition and the basis of *tradition*—but tradition as found in discrete acts of language use.

A word is in order about the history of this set. For the past decade, I have taught a course, first at Yale and then at Cornell, entitled "Black Women and Their Fictions," a course that I inherited from Toni Morrison, who developed it in the mid-1970s for Yale's Program in Afro-American Studies. Although the course was inspired by the remarkable accomplishments of black women novelists since 1970, I gradually extended its beginning date to the late nineteenth century, studying Frances Harper's *Iola Leroy* and Anna Julia Cooper's *A Voice From the South,* both published in 1892. With the discovery of Harriet E. Wilson's seminal novel, *Our Nig* (1859), and Jean Yellin's authentication of Harriet Jacobs's brilliant slave narrative, *Incidents in the Life of a Slave Girl* (1861), a survey course spanning over a century and a quarter emerged.

But the discovery of *Our Nig,* as well as the interest in nineteenth-century black women's writing that this discovery generated, convinced me that even the most curious and diligent scholars knew very little of the extensive history of the creative writings of Afro-American women before 1900. Indeed, most scholars of Afro-American literature had never even read most of the books published by black women, simply because these books—of poetry, novels, short stories, essays, and autobiography—were mostly accessible only in rare book sections of university libraries. For reasons unclear to me even today, few of these marvelous renderings of the Afro-American woman's consciousness were reprinted in the late 1960s and early 1970s, when so many other texts of the Afro-American literary tradition were resurrected from the dark and silent graveyard of the out-of-print and were reissued in facsimile editions aimed at the hungry readership for canonical texts in the nascent field of black studies.

So, with the help of several superb research assistants—including David Curtis, Nicola Shilliam, Wendy Jones, Sam Otter, Janadas Devan, Suvir Kaul, Cynthia Bond, Elizabeth Alexander, and Adele Alexander—and with the expert advice of scholars such as William Robinson, William Andrews, Mary Helen Washington, Maryemma Graham, Jean Yellin, Houston A. Baker, Jr., Richard Yarborough, Hazel Carby, Joan R. Sherman, Frances Foster, and William French, dozens of bibliographies were used to compile a list of books written or narrated by black women mostly before 1910. Without the assistance provided through this shared experience of scholarship, the scholar's true legacy, this project could not have been conceived. As the list grew, I was struck by how very many of these titles that I, for example, had never even heard of, let alone read, such as Ann Plato's *Essays*, Louisa Picquet's slave narrative, or Amelia Johnson's two novels, *Clarence and Corinne* and *The Hazeley Family*. Through our research with the Black Periodical Fiction and Poetry Project (funded by NEH and the Ford Foundation), I also realized that several novels by black women, including three works of fiction by Pauline Hopkins, had been serialized in black periodicals, but had never been collected and published as books. Nor had the several books of poetry published by black women, such as the prolific Frances E. W. Harper, been collected and edited. When I discovered still another "lost" novel by an Afro-American woman (*Four Girls at Cottage City*, published in 1898 by Emma Dunham Kelley-Hawkins), I decided to attempt to edit a collection of reprints of these works and to publish them as a "library" of black women's writings, in part so that I could read them myself.

Convincing university and trade publishers to undertake this project proved to be a difficult task. Despite the commercial success of *Our Nig* and of the several reprint series of women's works (such as Virago, the Beacon Black Women Writers Series, and Rutgers' American Women Writers Series), several presses rejected the project as "too large," "too limited," or as "commercially unviable." Only two publishers recognized the viability and the import of the project and, of these, Oxford's commitment to publish the titles simultaneously as a set made the press's offer irresistible.

While attempting to locate original copies of these exceedingly rare books, I discovered that most of the texts were housed at the Schomburg Center for Research in Black Culture, a branch of The New York Public Library, under the direction of Howard Dodson. Dodson's infectious enthusiasm for the project and his generous collaboration, as well as that of his stellar staff (especially Diana Lachatanere, Sharon Howard, Ellis Haizip, Richard Newman, and Betty Gubert), led to a joint publishing initiative that produced this set as part of the Schomburg's major fund-raising campaign. Without Dodson's foresight and generosity of spirit, the set would not have materialized. Without William P. Sisler's masterful editorship at Oxford and his staff's careful attention to detail, the set would have remained just another grand idea that tends to languish in a scholar's file cabinet.

I would also like to thank Dr. Michael Winston and Dr. Thomas C. Battle, Vice-President of Academic Affairs and the Director of the Moorland-Spingarn Research Center (respectively) at Howard University, for their unending encouragement, support, and collaboration in this project, and Esme E. Bhan at Howard for her meticulous research and bibliographical skills. In addition, I would like to acknowledge the aid of the staff at the libraries of Duke University, Cornell University (especially Tom Weissinger and Donald Eddy), the Boston Public Library, the Western Reserve Historical Society, the Library of Congress, and Yale University. Linda Robbins, Marion Osmun, Sarah Flanagan, and Gerard Case, all members of the staff at Oxford, were

extraordinarily effective at coordinating, editing, and producing the various segments of each text in the set. Candy
Ruck, Nina de Tar, and Phillis Molock expertly typed reams
of correspondence and manuscripts connected to the project.

I would also like to express my gratitude to my colleagues
who edited and introduced the individual titles in the set.
Without their attention to detail, their willingness to meet
strict deadlines, and their sheer enthusiasm for this project,
the set could not have been published. But finally and ulti-
mately, I would hope that the publication of the set would
help to generate even more scholarly interest in the black
women authors whose work is presented here. Struggling
against the seemingly insurmountable barriers of racism *and*
sexism, while often raising families and fulfilling full-time
professional obligations, these women managed nevertheless
to record their thoughts and feelings and to *testify* to all who
dare read them that the will to harness the power of collective
endurance and survival is the will to write.

The Schomburg Library of Nineteenth-Century Black
Women Writers is dedicated in memory of Pauline Augusta
Coleman Gates, who died in the spring of 1987. It was she
who inspired in me the love of learning and the love of literature. I have encountered in the books of this set no will
more determined, no courage more noble, no mind more
sublime, no self more celebratory of the achievements of all
Afro-American women, and indeed of life itself, than her
own.

A NOTE FROM
THE SCHOMBURG CENTER

Howard Dodson

The Schomburg Center for Research in Black Culture, The New York Public Library, is pleased to join with Dr. Henry Louis Gates and Oxford University Press in presenting The Schomburg Library of Nineteenth-Century Black Women Writers. This thirty-volume set includes the work of a generation of black women whose writing has only been available previously in rare book collections. The materials reprinted in twenty-four of the thirty volumes are drawn from the unique holdings of the Schomburg Center.

A research unit of The New York Public Library, the Schomburg Center has been in the forefront of those institutions dedicated to collecting, preserving, and providing access to the records of the black past. In the course of its two generations of acquisition and conservation activity, the Center has amassed collections totaling more than 5 million items. They include over 100,000 bound volumes, 85,000 reels and sets of microforms, 300 manuscript collections containing some 3.5 million items, 300,000 photographs and extensive holdings of prints, sound recordings, film and videotape, newspapers, artworks, artifacts, and other book and nonbook materials. Together they vividly document the history and cultural heritages of people of African descent worldwide.

Though established some sixty-two years ago, the Center's book collections date from the sixteenth century. Its oldest item, an Ethiopian Coptic Tunic, dates from the eighth or ninth century. Rare materials, however, are most available

for the nineteenth-century African-American experience. It is
from these holdings that the majority of the titles selected for
inclusion in this set are drawn.

The nineteenth century was a formative period in African-
American literary and cultural history. Prior to the Civil
War, the majority of black Americans living in the United
States were held in bondage. Law and practice forbade teaching them to read or write. Even after the war, many of the
impediments to learning and literary productivity remained.
Nevertheless, black men and women of the nineteenth century
persevered in both areas. Moreover, more African-Americans
than we yet realize turned their observations, feelings, social
viewpoints, and creative impulses into published works. In
time, this nineteenth-century printed record included poetry,
short stories, histories, novels, autobiographies, social criticism, and theology, as well as economic and philosophical
treatises. Unfortunately, much of this body of literature
remained, until very recently, relatively inaccessible to twentieth-
century scholars, teachers, creative artists, and others interested in black life. Prior to the late 1960s, most Americans
(black as well as white) had never heard of these nineteenth-
century authors, much less read their works.

The civil rights and black power movements created un-
precedented interest in the thought, behavior, and achievements of black people. Publishers responded by revising
traditional texts, introducing the American public to a new
generation of African-American writers, publishing a variety
of thematic anthologies, and reprinting a plethora of "classic
texts" in African-American history, literature, and art. The
reprints usually appeared as individual titles or in a series of
bound volumes or microform formats.

The Schomburg Center, which has a long history of supporting publishing that deals with the history and culture of Africans in diaspora, became an active participant in many of the reprint revivals of the 1960s. Since hard copies of original printed works are the preferred formats for producing facsimile reproductions, publishers frequently turned to the Schomburg Center for copies of these original titles. In addition to providing such material, Schomburg Center staff members offered advice and consultation, wrote introductions, and occasionally entered into formal copublishing arrangements in some projects.

Most of the nineteenth-century titles reprinted during the 1960s, however, were by and about black men. A few black women were included in the longer series, but works by lesser known black women were generally overlooked. The Schomburg Library of Nineteenth-Century Black Women Writers is both a corrective to these previous omissions and an important contribution to Afro-American literary history in its own right. Through this collection of volumes, the thoughts, perspectives, and creative abilities of nineteenth-century African-American women, as captured in books and pamphlets published in large part before 1910, are again being made available to the general public. The Schomburg Center is pleased to be a part of this historic endeavor.

I would like to thank Professor Gates for initiating this project. Thanks are due both to him and Mr. William P. Sisler of Oxford University Press for giving the Schomburg Center an opportunity to play such a prominent role in the set. Thanks are also due to my colleagues at The New York Public Library and the Schomburg Center, especially Dr. Vartan Gregorian, Richard De Gennaro, Paul Fasana, Betsy

Pinover, Richard Newman, Diana Lachatanere, Glenderlyn Johnson, and Harold Anderson for their assistance and support. I can think of no better way of demonstrating than in this set the role the Schomburg Center plays in assuring that the black heritage will be available for future generations.

CONTENTS

limits of genre

1859 – 1930

rel'n to Colored American magazine – a project
critic Harlem periy 20's – create a cult alan
+ say audience

job

ry | 80 – archetypal western pioneer – Zekas Bowen
who | 84 metaphor of yankee "culture"
       135

INTRODUCTION

Hazel V. Carby

This volume of Pauline Hopkins's three magazine novels, published for the first time since they appeared serially in the *Colored American Magazine* between March 1901 and November 1903, is a significant contribution to the history of Afro-American cultural production. It is of particular importance to feminist scholars that this volume provides evidence of the formal and political direction of Hopkins's writing after her historical romance, *Contending Forces* (1900). These magazine novels also represent a sustained attempt to develop an Afro-American popular fiction. Hopkins both utilizes the strategies and formulas of nineteenth-century dime novels and story papers and reveals the limits of these popular American narrative forms for black characterization. The novels—*Hagar's Daughter. A Story of Southern Caste Prejudice; Winona. A Tale of Negro Life in the South and Southwest;* and *Of One Blood. Or, the Hidden Self*—can now be situated between the earlier work of William Wells Brown and Victoria Earle Matthews (Brown's *Clotel* [1853] was republished as *Clotelle* in a dime novel series in 1864; Matthews wrote for story papers in the 1890s) and the later detective fiction of Chester Himes. Collectively these texts provide the foundation for understanding the development of a black popular fiction in the United States.

Pauline Elizabeth Hopkins was born in Portland, Maine in 1859 but lived most of her life in Boston. When she died in 1930, she was working as a stenographer for the Massachusetts Institute of Technology. As a high school student,

Hopkins won a prize for an essay entitled "Evils of Intemperance and Their Remedy," which had been submitted to a competition organized by William Wells Brown and the Congregational Publishing Society of Boston. As a young writer, Hopkins authored musical dramas, two of which, *Colored Aristocracy* (1877) and *Slaves' Escape; or the Underground Railroad* (1879), were performed by various groups, including the Hyers Sisters Concert Company. But Hopkins was unable to make a living as an author, and throughout the 1890s she worked as a stenographer, at first for Republican politicians and then for the Massachusetts Bureau of Statistics. It was not until Hopkins was forty years old that she became a published author of narrative fiction. Her first novel, *Contending Forces*, was published in 1900 by the Colored Co-operative Publishing Company of Boston, which also published the *Colored American Magazine* where Hopkins's next three novels were serialized.

The first issue of the *Colored American Magazine* appeared in May 1900, and during the next four years the journal became the central focus for Hopkins's intellectual activity. Within its pages, Hopkins published her three novels, seven short stories, two major biographical series of articles on famous black men and women, and numerous political and social commentaries and editorials. Hopkins was not only a prolific writer for the journal but was also a powerful editorial force within it until, under the increasing influence of Booker T. Washington, the *Colored American Magazine* moved from Boston to New York in June 1904 and became an organ of the National Negro Business League.

There is a great deal of ambiguity in the history of the official editorial offices held by Hopkins, although a consensus exists among scholars of the black periodical press that Hopkins's influence has been vastly underestimated. In 1947 William Braithwaite wrote an article called "Negro America's First Magazine" in which he refers to Hopkins as if she were the editor of the *Colored American Magazine* for the first few years of its publication. Braithwaite was a contributor to the magazine and makes it clear that he resented Hopkins's editorial power. He implies that Hopkins should have remained in silent and grateful submission for having had the opportunity to publish in the magazine, and he reserves his praise for her male colleagues. Perhaps it was precisely because Hopkins was a woman that her editorial influence was not publicly recognized; her name did not actually appear on the masthead until 1903. But despite this confusion over official recognition, the textual evidence of the *Colored American Magazine* confirms the significance of Hopkins's editorial contributions.

In its early years, the *Colored American Magazine* tried to create the literary and political climate for a black renaissance in Boston two decades before the emergence of what we now refer to as the "Harlem Renaissance." The fiction that Hopkins contributed to the magazine was part of a wider intellectual project that was described in the first editorial as offering "the colored people of the United States, a medium through which they can demonstrate their ability and tastes, in fiction, poetry and art, as well as in the arena of historical, social and economic literature." The ambition of Hopkins and her colleagues was demonstrated in their pledge to introduce "a monthly magazine of merit into every Negro family." The *Colored American Magazine* was an attempt to create a cultural renaissance that would not be limited to a Northern black elite but that would encourage the flowering of any black talent which had been suppressed by a lack of encour-

agement and opportunity to be published. The journal promised to be the vehicle for the nurturing and expression of that
talent.

The political aims of the journal were also clear from the
first editorials. Hopkins argued that it was the duty of
Northern black intellectuals like herself to revive a neglected
New England tradition of radical politics. In Hopkins's
imagination, the city of Boston could be recreated as the
center of black and white political agitation that it was at the
height of abolitionism. The *Colored American Magazine* was
a direct response to the political climate of the turn of the
century—that is, to black disenfranchisement, Jim Crow laws,
the widespread murder of black people in the South, and
political apathy in the North. Hopkins viewed the journal as
a vehicle for social intervention, as an attempt to replace the
politics of compromise with political demands for changes in
social relations. The first editorial asserted that the *Colored
American Magazine* "aspire[d] to develop and intensify the
bonds of that racial brotherhood, which alone can enable a
people, to assert their racial rights as men, and demand their
privileges as citizens."

The members of the Colored Co-operative Publishing
Company clearly intended to produce a popular magazine
that would capture both a black readership and a black
advertising market. In structure, the *Colored American Magazine* can be regarded as a product of the magazine "revolution" that had started in the 1880s when journals first began
to establish a mass audience and a large advertising business.
In the following decade, low prices, mass circulation, and
advertising revenues became the cornerstones of the magazine
industry, and the *Colored American Magazine* tried to sell at
a competitive price, fifteen cents, and to make enough money

from advertising to cover much of the cost of production. The precarious financial history of the journal would indicate, however, that the magazine failed to attract enough subscribers and thereby to establish a secure basis of advance capital. There was a transfer of management in May 1903, but the *Colored American Magazine* remained financially vulnerable until bought out by Booker T. Washington.

Two aspects of the structural organization of the journal made it a very different publishing venture from the white journals that dominated the magazine market. First, the *Colored American Magazine* was a key element in the attempt to establish cooperative publishing. Both readers of and contributors to the journal could become full members of the cooperative: Readers were asked to become members by investing five dollars, and contributors were made members through a system that gave them a cash evaluation of their articles which equated to certificates of deposit. What also clearly differentiated the *Colored American Magazine* from other monthly journals was its intended readership; the editorial staff tried to define as well as create a black magazine reading public. Indeed, their stated intention "to offer the colored people of the United States, a medium through which they can demonstrate their ability and tastes" was followed by a declaration that the journal awaited "its success or failure on the proposition that there is a demand for such a magazine."

The intention to establish a mass or popular black magazine makes the *Colored American Magazine* a pioneer of the contemporary black magazine market, but there were historical limitations to what could be achieved. Its potential audience was a possible 12 percent of the population, but in 1900, out of a total black population of 6,415,581, 45 percent aged ten years and over were illiterate. Regional statistics indicate that just over 18 percent of the black population of the North were illiterate, while in the Southern regions the figures were between 47 and 49 percent. Rural illiteracy was much greater than urban illiteracy, and consequently agents for the *Colored American Magazine* were situated in major cities.

But the use of statistical accounts of the rates of illiteracy is not the most illuminating method of determining a constituency for a particular magazine. It is more interesting, perhaps, to speculate about the potential readership of the *Colored American Magazine* in light of the investigations of W. E. B. Du Bois into black training and occupation. By the turn of the century, there were only 2,500 black college graduates, so a black college-educated elite could not possibly have sustained a journal. Clearly the audience that the *Colored American Magazine* tried to address would have included those in professional service, the majority of whom were teachers and clergy, and the literate among those categorized by Du Bois as "negro artisans." The category of artisan included male and female tobacco factory operatives, male blacksmiths, wheelwrights, boot and shoe makers, butchers, carpenters and joiners, cotton and textile mill operatives, machinists, masons, miners and quarrymen, printers, and railroad workers, as well as female dressmakers, milliners, seamstresses, and tailoresses. Although Du Bois excluded domestic servants from the skilled and semi-skilled categories of workers, books like Mamie Fields's *Lemon Swamp* have revealed the significant influence of domestic workers in urban communities, especially in the South, and they should be included in the constituency of a target readership.

Hopkins and her colleagues clearly defined a pedagogic role for the *Colored American Magazine* in relation to its potential readers, and Hopkins regarded fiction as a particularly effective vehicle of instruction as well as entertainment. Fiction, Hopkins thought, could reach the many classes of citizens who never read history or biography, and thus she created fictional histories with a pedagogic function: narratives of the relations between the races that challenged racist ideologies. The social separation of the races—disenfranchisement, lynching, and the institutionalization of Jim Crow—was challenged by her alternative history of close blood ties through miscegenation. As can be seen in her first novel, *Contending Forces*, Hopkins created histories that rewrote definitions of American culture. Questions of heritage and inheritance shape the political direction of all her stories. The actions and destinies of Hopkins's characters are related to the ways in which their ancestors acted upon their own social conditions; the contemporary moments of the tales are shaped and determined by the history of the social relations between white and black.

In her preface to *Contending Forces*, Hopkins stated that she wanted the novel to "raise the stigma of degradation from my race." She believed that writing fiction was an especially effective means of intervening politically in the social order. It is the "simple, homely tale, unassumingly told," she argued, "which cements the bond of brotherhood among all classes and all complexions." Her pedagogic and political intent was that her fiction enter "these days of mob violence" and "lynch-law" and inspire her readers to political action. To a contemporary readership, which is cynical about the possibilities of narrative contributions to social change, it is important to stress Hopkins's belief in the historical and political significance of fiction. She considered fiction to be "of great value to any people as a preserver of manners and customs—religious, political and social" and to be a "record of growth and development from generation to generation." Black intellectuals had a crucial role to play as writers, for only they, Hopkins thought, could *"faithfully portray the inmost thoughts and feelings of the Negro with all the fire and romance which lie dormant in our history"* (italics in original).

Hopkins's fictional histories provide her readers with an understanding of the source of contemporary forms of oppression. "Mob-law is nothing new," she argued in *Contending Forces*. "Southern sentiment has not been changed . . . . acts committed one hundred years ago are duplicated today, when slavery is supposed no longer to exist." What she feared most was that mob-rule and lynch-law would become acceptable practices throughout all the states. Hopkins saw the black inhabitants of the North as the inheritors of a New England tradition of liberty, and as a Northern black intellectual she thought the culture that she could produce could contribute to, if not create, a political climate of agitation, a new abolitionist fervor.

Although Hopkins's *Contending Forces* gives considerable insight into her construction of fictional histories, there are significant differences between this novel and her magazine fiction. Within the pages of the *Colored American Magazine*, Hopkins made a decision to incorporate some of the narrative formulas of the sensational fiction of dime novels and story papers. Consequently, her magazine fiction shows an increased emphasis on such narrative elements as suspense, action, adventure, complex plotting, multiple and false identities, and the use of disguise. The representation of social and intellectual conflict is more frequently accompanied by physical action and confrontation. Hopkins's didactic intent remains but is shaped by the attempt to combine these elements of a popular fiction with stories of political and social critique. In *Hagar's Daughter*, which she wrote under the pseudonym of Sarah A. Allen, the physical action includes murder, kidnappings, and escapes, if not actual fights, and concludes with a spectacle, a confrontation in open court that brings together the entire community of the novel. The use of more popular fictional formulas in all three of Hopkins's magazine novels was also a consequence of the demands of serial publication, as can be seen in each novel's episodic structure. Each episode ends in a state of suspense that is not relieved until the next issue, which in turn ends in suspense. Fictional resolutions to the overall narrative structure and history occur only in the concluding episodes to each of the novels.

Hopkins's magazine fiction also differs from *Contending Forces* in terms of setting; the serialized novels are situated within a white rather than a black social order, although the conclusion in *Of One Blood* does assert a Pan-African history. In *Contending Forces*, a black family's boarding house and the black church are the central focus of the consequences of Hopkins's fictional history, and the representation of the black community is as a fairly autonomous locus of alternative possibilities for American culture. White society is represented indirectly, as a systemic set of social forces, through accounts of the experiences of Hopkins's black characters. But in *Hagar's Daughter* and *Winona*, the white world is represented directly through white villians as individual figures of greed who symbolize the power of white society to oppress. *Hagar's Daughter* contains three black female characters who exist within the context of a white community and are believed to be white; for each, blackness is a secret and a means of their victimization.

The history of *Hagar's Daughter* is present in an introductory plot (Chapters I–VIII) that is a direct imitation of

William Wells Brown's *Clotelle*. The main body of the
narrative takes place twenty years later and is situated securely
within the high society of Washington. The relation between
the two histories is the key to understanding the plot, but as
the Washington narrative opens the histories appear unrelated
because the drama involves various levels of disguise, from
the simple change of names to more complex changes in
identity. Changes in names are accompanied by changes in
appearance; all characters are, of course, twenty years older.
The use of disguise hides the evil intentions of villains from
their potential victims. While the villains are empowered by
their knowledge of the secret pasts of others, the victims
remain ignorant of their blackmailers' true identities until the
end of the story. But while this use of disguise is conventional
and formulaic, Hopkins also complicates questions of hidden
identity through her three heroines who are disguised as
white.

The disguise of whiteness enabled Hopkins to write a
"black" story that unravels in the heart of elite Washington
society. In conventional terms, if an elite was to be the subject
of fiction, black characters would have to remain on the
periphery as servants. And, indeed, as the story begins, the
only characters that are obviously black are the servants.
Popular fiction formulas allowed a white character to darken
his skin and move into and out of black communities. "Black
Tom the Negro Detective" was such a character in dime
novels, and the disguise of blackness in popular fiction was
directly related to "blacking-up" in vaudeville and minstrel
shows. But American popular culture offered no equivalent
convention that would allow black characters access to a
fictional or theatrical white society. At the height of the era
of Jim Crow, narratives of "passing" appeared to offer the

still passing

only fictional mechanism that could enable representation of the relation between the races. But Hopkins does not offer her readers narratives of "passing." The "whiteness" of her major female figures is constructed in response to the formal prerequisites of popular fictional formulas of disguises and double identities.

The characterization of Aurelia is particularly interesting in relation to conventional representations of women. Aurelia is a woman who compromises her sexuality by using her "charms" to lure men to gamble against, and lose money to, her father. Aurelia is an example of the masculinized female character first found in popular fiction in the 1860s. As General Benson states, what he admires about Aurelia is her ability to be like a man: "It's a relief to be with a woman who can join a man in a social glass, have a cigar with him, or hold her own in winning or losing a game with no Sunday-school nonsense about her." Aurelia exists as, but is not condemned for, being a villain. She is a central figure in the attempt to gain control over Senator Bowen's financial fortunes but is not punished for her role in the conspiracy. Aurelia is a fighter, courageous and defiant. Her masculinity and her courage disguise a feminine weakness: the love for a man who was her prey. But this love is not her downfall, for Aurelia embodies all the elements of the popular figure of the "adventuress": the woman who uses her sexuality for her own ends and threatens men with her ambition. Hopkins extends her use of the masculinized female to the character of Venus who evolves from being a black maid to becoming a heroine of the story. Not only does Venus make the transition from minor to major character, but disguised as a man named "Billy," she is employed as an assistant detective and saves Jewel, her mistress, from kidnappers.

At the time Hopkins was writing, the figure of the detective was a recent invention in popular fiction. The first dime novel series that was entirely detective fiction was the Old Cap. Collier Library, which started in the 1880s. The first detective agency in the United States was founded by Allan Pinkerton, who became famous for foiling an assassination plot against Abraham Lincoln. In the denouement to *Hagar's Daughter,* the history of the Pinkerton Agency and the fictional heroic status of the detective are woven together in the figure of J. Henson as the two villains he is responsible for capturing are themselves implicated in the presidential assassination plot. But there again Hopkins both adopts and adapts popular fiction formulas. As J. Randolph Cox has argued, in the classic dime novel detective story, the detective had no family background and was separated "both physically and psychically from his cases and from the individuals whose destinies he corrects." Critics of detective fiction insist that this detachment is central to the success of the figure; the detective is "the only one who can read the riddle because he is never personally involved." And indeed, personal involvement with clients in a popular fictional format means that the detective is unable to function as a detective. As for Henson, he appears completely detached from his clients, but the series of exposures of identity in the court scene reveal his familial ties to his clients and end his days as a detective. Henson's function in the narrative changes as he is renamed husband, landowner, and eventually, father.

A number of magical resolutions conclude *Hagar's Daughter*. The most magical of all is the rediscovery of a lost child through a locket (such magical signs were common popular fictional narrative devices for returning an orphan to his or her true parents). The secrets of the "little hair trunk" lead to the discovery of Hagar's daughter but not to the restoration of a moral order. Conventional popular fictional use of disguise and double identities indicates a disruption of the natural order of events in a society or community. The revelations and fictional resolutions of popular fiction signal the reestablishment of the disrupted moral and social order in the characters' lives. But the resolutions to *Hagar's Daughter* reveal the contradictions inherent in Hopkins's attempt to use popular and easily accessible narrative forms to question the morality of, rather than to restore faith in, the social formation. The capture and imprisonment of the villains do not return Hopkins's fictional society to happiness. Nor are the heroes and heroines secured in their social positions when threats to expose them cease. Blackness is the source of their vulnerability.

A key to understanding this contradictory use of popular narrative forms is the denial of heroic status to Cuthbert Sumner. Sumner's family history of links to the abolition movement apparently establish his sympathy for black people and the fight for black equality. But Hopkins uses this figure as a representation of the ambivalence and limits of white liberalism and New England philanthropy. Sumner becomes an embodiment of the inherent and thinly disguised racism beneath a professed sympathy for black people. When Hagar's identity as a black woman is revealed, Sumner tells his wife Jewel that she can no longer have any contact with her stepmother. In the passages that follow this revelation, Hopkins's text is a searing indictment of "the limits of New England philanthropy." The final revelation, that Jewel herself is black, is aimed directly at Sumner's hypocrisy. Jewel dies rapidly, virtually off-stage, and the tale ends with the tragic consequences of Sumner's racism. His regret at his desertion and repulsion comes too late, and Hopkins rapidly shifts her readers' attention from the individual consequences of racism to systemic oppression. "Sumner questioned wherein he had sinned and why he was so severly punished. Then it was borne in upon him: the sin is the nation's." This shift from individual to nation indicates Hopkins's rejection of a return to an acceptable moral order at the end of her tale that a simple "happy ending" would have imposed. Her refusal to resolve *Hagar's Daughter* within the terms of the popular conventions that structured her narrative is symptomatic of the tension between her political and didactic intent and the desire to write popular fiction. Through the use of direct authorial address, Hopkins forces her readers to contemplate the cultural and political separation of the races by means of the political disruption to conventional imaginary resolutions.

Winona uses the historical landscape of slavery to represent a contemporary social order. Hopkins adapts stories about John Brown and the Free Soil Movement in Kansas and focuses on the organized and individual acts of resistance and self-defense against oppression. The theme of revenge is pivotal to the text, which contains Hopkins's first aggressively active black male hero. Judah, who is described as "a living statue of a mighty Vulcan," is an orphaned son of an escaped slave who grew up in a "mixed community of Anglo-Saxons, Indians and Negroes." Judah's stoicism enables him to bear his punishment as a slave "without murmur," but each beating stimulates his desire for vengeance. In the novel, Hopkins creates Judah as "the true expression of the innate nature of the Negro when given an opportunity equal with the white man," and she uses him as a figure of mediation for her own reflections on structures of subordination. The text poses a series of questions: "Is there such a thing as social equality. . . ? Who is my social equal . . . who is my brother in the spirit of the scriptural text?" Judah becomes a warrior who achieves his revenge while fighting with John Brown. His heroism is rewarded in the fictional world by his being transported from the United States to Britain where Hopkins imagines him being honored as a soldier and living his life as a revered citizen.

Winona is transparently a call for organized political resistance against contemporary persecution displaced to a fictional history. It is Hopkins's only long piece of fiction set entirely before the Civil War. However, her most extensive revision of black history occurred in her next serialized novel, *Of One Blood. Or, the Hidden Self*, which clearly indicates the ultimate political trajectory of her fiction for the *Colored American Magazine*.

In *Of One Blood*, Hopkins returns to the themes of inheritance and heritage but with a very different political motivation. In *Contending Forces*, Hopkins's black characters are revealed to be related to the British aristocracy. In *Hagar's Daughter*, the threads of black inheritance and heritage extend to the Washington elite, to the heart of the white power structure. But in *Of One Blood*, Hopkins transcends her preoccupation with miscegenation as a device for establishing that the concepts of racial purity and racial separation are mythical, and she incorporates a Pan-African perspective into her narrative framework.

The popular formulaic conventions that undermine as well as reveal the contradictory aspect of appearance remain; none of the characters are what they seem to be. But the movement of the novel takes the reader away from the American consequences of secret histories and toward an Africa that embodies both the history and future possibilities of black people.

The archeological expedition of Reuel is a journey toward the knowledge of a black heritage for the protagonist and the reader. The past that is found in the city of Meroe represents Hopkins's vision of black history and her challenge to the mythology of Europe as the source of civilization.

Five months before *Of One Blood*'s first installment appeared, Hopkins outlined the premise of the serial in an article on Afro-American women educators in her series "Famous Women of the Negro Race":

> Rome got her civilization from Greece; Greece borrowed hers from Egypt, thence she derived her science and beautiful mythology. Civilization descended the Nile and spread over the delta, as it came down from Thebes. Thebes was built and settled by the Ethiopians. As we ascend the Nile we come to Meroe the queen city of Ethiopia and the cradle of learning into which all Africa poured its caravans. So we trace the light of civilization from Ethiopia to Egypt, to Greece, to Rome, and thence diffusing its radiance over the entire world.

Hopkins hoped to teach her black readership, in a popular narrative form, that they were the descendants of a great and ancient civilization. The leader of the expedition to Meroe, Professor Stone, is a historian of ancient civilizations who acts to authenticate the theories that Ethiopia was the original source of civilization and "black . . . the original color of man." For white readers, Hopkins poses two questions. The first is a direct challenge: "How can the Anglo-Saxon World bear the establishment of such a theory?" But the second tries to reverse contemporary debates about the origins of black people and thus seeks to question and undermine the racist ideologies of social Darwinism. "What puzzles me," says Professor Stone, "is not the origin of the Blacks, but of the Whites."

This story of origins is used by Hopkins to elaborate the Afro-American literary convention of the search for and the discovery of family, a metaphor for the black diaspora. In returning to Africa, Reuel is reborn as the descendant of a line of African kings and is destined to "restore the former glory of the race." Reuel is initiated not only into his previously unknown family heritage but also into the heritage of black people throughout the diaspora. The narrative asserts that contemporary black Americans are Ethiopians, and the fiction was externally authenticated by a series of documentary articles written by A. Kirkland Soga and entitled "Ethiopians of the Twentieth Century," which ran concurrently with the novel.

The figure of Reuel should be seen as the mediator of the meaning of the historic link to Ethiopia and Ethiopianism for Afro-American readers. The discovery of his heritage is the discovery of a Pan-Africanist political philosophy. A Pan-African conference had been convened in London in 1900 by a West Indian, Henry Sylvester Williams, both as a protest against European imperialism and as an appeal for support for Africans fighting the aggressive colonization of their lands. *Of One Blood* is an early fictional response to the philosophy of Pan-Africanism in the United States, a philosophy that was always thought to have lain dormant until W. E. B. Du Bois revived it and organized the First Pan-African Congress to address the Peace Conference at Versailles after World War I. At the end of the novel, Reuel returns to rule his African empire and to fight "the advance of Mighty nations penetrating the dark, mysterious forces of his native land."

Until he reached Africa, Reuel had denied his blackness. In her fiction, Hopkins herself first directly confronted the

consequences of passing in a short story, "The Test of Manhood." In this story, the protagonist purposefully and deliberately determines to "become" white. His material success,
which includes a white woman's promise to be his wife,
depends on the denial of his black mother as his mother. The
test of his manhood is his willingness to renounce the rewards
of a white society and to leave his wife. Reuel also has to
confront the denial of his blackness, but in *Of One Blood* it
is not only the denial of an immediate black family that is
questioned but the denial of an African heritage. Reuel comes
to be ashamed of his isolation from his race and feels "that
he had played a coward's part in hiding his origin. What
though obstacles were many, some way would have been
shown him to surmount the difficulties of caste prejudice."

One of the "difficulties" that Hopkins confronts in *Of One
Blood* is the dominant Western ideology of beauty:

> Is there ever a flock or herd without its black member? What
> more beautiful than the satin gloss of the raven's wing, the
> soft glitter of eyes of blackest tint or the rich black fur of
> your own native animals? Fair-haired worshippers of Mam-
> mon, do you not know that you have been weighed in the
> balance and found wanting?

But the idealization of black beauty in the novel is contradictory and retains classically European pretensions. Hopkins
selects black skin, eyes, brows, and "crisp" black hair for
praise, but profiles and bone structure remain Athenian. As
with the assertions of Ethiopianism, Hopkins sought to externally authenticate her fictional representation of black as
beautiful. An anonymous article, which was probably written
by Hopkins herself and which was entitled "Venus and the
Apollo Modelled from Ethiopians," was published in the

May/June 1903 issue of the *Colored American Magazine*. It cited scientific proof that "the most famous examples of classic beauty in sculpture . . . were chiselled from Ethiopian slave models." This network of relationships between *Of One Blood* and other, nonfictional articles in the journal indicates not only the extent of an intertextual coherence achieved under Hopkins's editorship but also the extent of her political commitment to the development of pride in and allegiance toward an African heritage.

Popular conventions of narrative fiction structure the revelations of kinship in the novel. Babies are switched at birth, and the history of kinship between characters is confirmed by magical signs: Family members bear a lotus birthmark on their breasts. But the impossibility of resolving *Of One Blood* within the framework of popular formulas dominates the conclusion. The social relations of the institution of slavery determine the relations of contemporary society, and Hopkins offers no possibility that these contradictions can be resolved within the boundaries of the United States. The social and moral order of American society is revealed to be based on incest, and thus no happy endings are possible. The tangle of incestuous relationships represents Hopkins's vision of a hell in which the "laws of changeless justice bind Oppressor and oppressed."

Hopkins shaped her work as testimony to a black presence in history. She wrote out of fear that black people in the United States faced annihilation, and she responded with a fiction that could represent a history that challenged contemporary racist ideologies. But the political trajectory of the history that she recreated developed from an assertion of the presence of Afro-Americans within an Anglo-Saxon context, as represented in *Contending Forces*, and moved toward a reinterpretation of the meaning of an African heritage, as represented in *Of One Blood*. This shift allowed Hopkins to see that it was not only the American black community that faced a crisis but that the "dawn of the twentieth century finds the Black race fighting for existence in every quarter of the globe. . . . Africa stretches her hands to the American Negro and cries aloud for sympathy in her hour of trial." Thus the establishment of an African genealogy in *Of One Blood* is a climax to Hopkins's consistent concern with the questions of inheritance and heritage. The publication of this volume of her magazine novels allows us to understand more deeply the political direction of Hopkins's fiction after *Contending Forces* and provides us with the critical tools for reassessing the significance of her first novel.

Pauline Hopkins was a black intellectual whose writing was part of, not separate from, the politics of oppression. In an article called "Heroes and Heroines in Black," she appealed to her readers to exhibit a "wild courage." Fiction, she thought, needed to be of "cathartic virtue" to stimulate political resistance, and we can now read this collection as her cathartic response to black oppression.

SELECTED BIBLIOGRAPHY

Braithwaite, William Stanley. "Negro America's First Magazine." *Negro Digest* (December 1947):21–26. Reprinted in Philip Butcher, ed. *The William Stanley Braithwaite Reader*. Ann Arbor: University of Michigan Press, 1972, pp. 114–21.

Brown, William Wells. *Clotelle*. Boston: James Redpath, 1864.

Bullock, Penelope L. *The Afro-American Periodical Press, 1838–1909*. Baton Rouge: Louisiana State University Press, 1981.

Carby, Hazel V. *Reconstructing Womanhood: The Emergence of the Afro-American Woman Novelist*. New York: Oxford University Press, 1987.

Cawelti, John G. *Adventure, Mystery, and Romance: Formula Stories as Art and Popular Culture*. Chicago: University of Chicago Press, 1976.

Collier, Old Cap. *Black Tom the Negro Detective, or, Solving a Thompson Street Mystery*. Old Cap. Collier Library 486 (April 22, 1893).

Cox, J. Randolph. "The Detective Hero in the American Dime Novel." *Dime Novel Roundup* 50 (February 1981):2–18.

Daniel, Walter C. *Black Journals of the United States*. Westport, Ct.: Greenwood Press, 1982.

Elliot, R. S. "The Story of Our Magazine." *Colored American Magazine* 3 (May 1901):47.

Hopkins, Pauline Elizabeth. *Contending Forces: A Romance Illustrative of Negro Life North and South*. Boston: Colored Co-operative Publishing Company, 1900.

———. "Famous Women of the Negro Race 7. Educators." *Colored American Magazine* 5 (June 1902):125–30.

———. "The First Pan-African Conference of the World." *Colored American Magazine* 1 (September 1900):223–31.

———. "Heroes and Heroines in Black." *Colored American Magazine* 5 (January 1903):206–11.

——— [Sarah A. Allen]. "Latest Phases of the Race Problem in America." *Colored American Magazine* 6 (February 1903):244–51.

———. *A Primer of Facts Pertaining to the Early Greatness of the African Race and the Possibility of Restoration by its Descendents*. Cambridge, Mass.: P. E. Hopkins & Company, 1905.

———. "The Test of Manhood." *Colored American Magazine* 6 (December 1902):113–19.

———. "Venus and Apollo Modelled from Ethiopians." *Colored American Magazine* 6 (May/June 1903):465.

Johnson, Abby A., and Ronald M. Johnson. "Away From Accom-

modation: Radical Editors and Protest Journalism, 1900–
1910." *Journal of Negro History* 52 (October 1977):325–
38.

―――. *Propaganda and Aesthetics: The Literary Politics of Afro-
American Magazines in the Twentieth Century.* Amherst:
University of Massachusetts Press, 1979.

Meier, August. "Booker T. Washington and the Negro Press with
Special Reference to the Colored American Magazine."
Journal of Negro History 38 (January 1953):67–90.

Mitchell, Sally. *The Fallen Angel: Chastity, Class and Women's Reading
1835–1880.* Bowling Green, Ohio: Bowling Green University Popular Press, 1981.

Ohmann, Richard. "Where Did Mass Culture Come From? The
Case of Magazines." *Berkshire Review* 16 (1981):85–101.

Padmore, George. *Pan-Africanism or Communism.* Garden City, N.Y.:
Doubleday & Company, 1971.

Penn, I. Garland. *The Afro-American Press and Its Editors.* New
York: Arno Press and The New York Times, 1969.

Shockley, Ann Allen. "Pauline Elizabeth Hopkins: A Biographical
Excursion into Obscurity." *Phylon* 33 (Spring 1972):22–
26.

Southern, Eileen. *The Music of Black Americans.* New York:
W. W. Norton & Company, 1983.

HAGAR'S DAUGHTER

A Story of Southern Caste Prejudice

CHAPTER I

In the fall of 1860 a stranger visiting the United States would
have thought that nothing short of a miracle could preserve
the union of states so proudly proclaimed by the signers of
the Declaration of Independence, and so gloriously maintained
by the gallant Washington.

The nomination of Abraham Lincoln for the presidency
by the Republican party was inevitable. The proslavery Democracy was drunk with rage at the prospect of losing control
of the situation, which, up to that time, had needed scarcely
an effort to bind in riveted chains impenetrable alike to the
power of man or the frowns of the Godhead; they had
inaugurated a system of mob-law and terrorism against all
sympathizers with the despised party. The columns of partisan
newspapers teemed each day in the year with descriptions of
disgraceful scenes enacted North and South by pro-slavery
men, due more to the long-accustomed subserviency of Northern people to the slaveholders than to a real, personal hatred
of the Negro.

The free negroes North and South, and those slaves with
the hearts of freemen who had boldly taken the liberty denied

[*Hagar's Daughter* originally appeared in serial form in the *Colored American
Magazine* in the following issues: vol. 2, nos. 5, 6 (March and April 1901);
vol. 3, nos. 1–6 (May–October 1901); vol. 4, nos. 1–4 (November–
December 1901; January, March 1902). In the original publication, each
episode was preceded by a synopsis, which I have deleted. "(To be continued)" lines, however, have been retained in the body of the text to indicate
for the reader the serialized structure of the novel.—H.V.C.]

by man, felt the general spirit of unrest and uncertainty which was spreading over the country to such an alarming extent. The subdued tone of the liberal portion of the press, the humiliating offers of compromise from Northern political leaders, and the numerous cases of surrendering fugitive slaves to their former masters, sent a thrill of mortal fear into the very heart of many a household where peace and comfort had reigned for many years. The fugitive slave had perhaps won the heart of some Northern free woman; they had married, prospered, and were happy. Now came the haunting dread of a stealthy tread, an ominous knock, a muffled cry at midnight, and the sunlight of the new day would smile upon a broken-hearted woman with baby hands clinging to her skirts, and children's voices asking in vain for their father lost to them forever. The Negro felt that there was no safety for him beneath the Stars and Stripes, and, so feeling, sacrificed his home and personal effects and fled to Canada.

The Southerners were in earnest, and would listen to no proposals in favor of their continuance in the Union under existing conditions; namely, Lincoln and the Republican party. The vast wealth of the South made them feel that they were independent of the world. Cotton was not merely king; it was God. Moral considerations were nothing. Drunk with power and dazzled with prosperity, monopolizing cotton and raising it to the influence of a veritable fetich, the authors of the Rebellion did not admit a doubt of the success of their attack on the Federal government. They dreamed of perpetuating slavery, though all history shows the decline of the system as industry, commerce, and knowledge advance. The slaveholders proposed nothing less than to reverse the currents of humanity, and to make barbarism flourish in the bosom of civilization.

The South argued that the principle of right would have no influence over starving operatives; and England and France, as well as the Eastern States of the Union, would stand aghast, and yield to the master stroke which should deprive them of the material of their labor. Millions of the laboring class were dependent upon it in all the great centers of civilization; it was only necessary to wave this sceptre over the nations and all of them would acknowledge the power which wielded it. But, alas! the supreme error of this anticipation was in omitting from the calculation the power of principle. Right still had authority in the councils of nations. Factories might be closed, men and woman out of employment, but truth and justice still commanded respect among men. The proslavery men in the North encouraged the rebels before the breaking out of the war. They promised the South that civil war should reign in every free state in case of an uprising of the Southern oligarchy, and that men should not be permitted to go South to put down their brothers in rebellion.

Weak as were the Southern people in point of numbers and political power, compared with those of the North, yet they easily persuaded themselves that they could successfully cope in arms with a Northern foe, whom they affected to despise for his cowardly and mercenary disposition. They indulged the belief, in proud confidence, that their great political prestige would continue to serve them among party associates at the North, and that the counsels of the adversary would be distracted and his power weakened by the effects of dissension.

When the Republican banner bearing the names of Abraham Lincoln for President and Hannibal Hamlin for Vice-President flung its folds to the breeze in 1860, there was a panic of apprehension at such bold manœuvering; mob-law reigned in Boston, Utica and New York City, which witnessed the greatest destruction of property in the endeavor to put down the growing public desire to abolish slavery. Elijah Lovejoy's innocent blood spoke in trumpet tones to the reformer from his quiet grave by the rolling river. William Lloyd Garrison's outraged manhood brought the blush of shame to the cheek of the honest American who loved his country's honor better than any individual institution. The memory of Charles Sumner's brutal beating by Preston Brooks stamped the mad passions of the hour indelibly upon history's page. Debate in the Senate became fiery and dangerous as the crisis approached in the absorbing question of the perpetuation of slavery.

At the South laws were enacted abridging the freedom of speech and press; it was difficult for Northerners to travel in slave states. Rev. Charles T. Torrey was sentenced to the Maryland penitentiary for aiding slaves to escape; Jonathan Walker had been branded with a red-hot iron for the same offense. In the midst of the tumult came the "Dred Scott Decision," and the smouldering fire broke forth with renewed vigor. Each side waited impatiently for the result of the balloting.

In November the Rubicon was passed, and Abraham Lincoln was duly elected President contrary to the wishes and in defiance of the will of the haughty South. There was much talk of a conspiracy to prevent by fraud or violence a declaration of the result of the election by the Vice-President before the two Houses, as provided by law. As the eventful day drew near patriotic hearts were sick with fear or filled with forebodings. Would the certificates fail to appear; would they be wrested by violence from the hands ordered to bear them across the rotunda from the Senate Chamber to the hall of the House, or would they be suppressed by the only official who could open them, John C. Breckenridge of Kentucky, himself a candidate and in full sympathy with the rebellion.

A breathless silence, painfully intense, reigned in the crowded chamber as the Vice-President arose to declare the result of the election. Six feet in height, lofty in carriage, youthful, dashing, he stood before them pale and nervous. The galleries were packed with hostile conspirators. It was the supreme moment in the life of the Republic. With unfaltering utterance his voice broke the oppressive stillness:

"I therefore declare Abraham Lincoln duly elected President of the United States for the term of four years from the fourth of March next."

It was the signal for secession, and the South let loose the dogs of war.

CHAPTER II

During the week preceding the memorable 20th of December, 1860, the streets of Charleston, S. C., were filled with excited citizens who had come from all parts of the South to participate in the preparations for seceding from the Union. The hotels were full; every available space was occupied in the homes of private citizens. Bands paraded the streets heading processions of excited politicians who came as delegates from every section south of Mason and Dixon's line; there was shouting and singing by the populace, liberally mingled with barrelhead orations from excited orators with more zeal than worth; there were cheers for the South and oaths for the government at Washington.

Scattered through the crowd traders could be seen journeying to the far South with gangs of slaves chained together like helpless animals destined for the slaughter-house. These slaves were hurriedly sent off by their master in obedience to orders from headquarters, which called for the removal of all human property from the immediate scene of the invasion so soon to come. The traders paused in their hurried journey to participate in the festivities which ushered in the birth of the glorious Confederate States of America. Words cannot describe the scene.

> "The wingèd heralds by command
> Of sovereign power, with awful ceremony
> And trumpet sound, proclaimed
> A solemn council forthwith to be held
> At Pandæmonium, the high capital
> Of Satan and his peers."

Among the traders the most conspicuous was a noted man from St. Louis, by the name of Walker. He was the terror of the whole Southwest among the Negro population, bond and free; for it often happened that free persons were kidnapped and sold to the far South. Uncouth, ill-bred, hardhearted, illiterate, Walker had started in St. Louis as a draydriver, and now found himself a rich man. He was a repulsive-looking person, tall, lean and lank, with high cheekbones and face pitted with the small-pox, gray eyes, with red eyebrows and sandy whiskers.

Walker, upon his arrival in Charleston, took up his quarters with his gang of human cattle in a two-story flat building, surrounded by a stone wall some twelve feet high, the top of which was covered with bits of glass, so that there could be no passage over it without great personal injury. The rooms in this building resembled prison cells, and in the office were to be seen iron collars, hobbles, handcuffs, thumbscrews, cowhides, chains, gags and yokes.

Walker's servant Pompey had charge of fitting the stock for the market-place. Pompey had been so long under the instructions of the heartless speculator that he appeared perfectly indifferent to the heart-rending scenes which daily confronted him.

On this particular morning, Walker brought in a number of customers to view his stock; among them a noted divine, who was considered deeply religious. The slaves were congregated in a back yard enclosed by the high wall before referred to. There were swings and benches, which made the place very much like a New England schoolyard.

Among themselves the Negroes talked. There was one woman who had been separated from her husband, and another woman whose looks expressed the anguish of her heart. There was old "Uncle Jeems," with his whiskers off, his face clean shaven, and all his gray hairs plucked out, ready to be sold for ten years younger than he was. There was Tobias, a gentleman's body servant educated at Paris, in medicine, along with his late master, sold to the speculator because of his intelligence and the temptation which the confusion of the times offered for him to attempt an escape from bondage.

"O, my God!" cried one woman, "send dy angel down once mo' ter tell me dat you's gwine ter keep yer word, Massa Lord."

"O Lord, we's been a-watchin' an' a-prayin', but de 'liverer done fergit us!" cried another, as she rocked her body violently back and forth.

It was now ten o'clock, and the daily examination of the stock began with the entrance of Walker and several customers.

"What are you wiping your eyes for?" inquired a fat, red-faced man, with a white hat set on one side of his head and a cigar in his mouth, of the woman seated on a bench.

" 'Cause I left my mon behin'."

"Oh, if I buy you, I'll furnish you with a better man than you left. I've got lots of young bucks on my farm," replied the man.

"I don't want anudder mon, an' I tell you, massa, I nebber will hab anudder mon."

"What's your name?" asked a man in a straw hat, of a Negro standing with arms folded across his breast and leaning against the wall.

"Aaron, sar."

"How old are you?"

"Twenty-five."

"Where were you raised?"

"In Virginny, sar."

"How many men have owned you?"

"Fo."

"Do you enjoy good health?"

"Yas, sar."

"Whipped much?"

"No, sar. I s'pose I didn't desarve it, sar."

"I must see your back, so as to know how much you've been whipped, before I conclude a bargain."

"Cum, unharness yoseff, ole boy. Don't you hear the gemman say he wants to zammin yer?" said Pompey.

The speculator, meanwhile, was showing particular attention to the most noted and influential physician of Charleston.
The doctor picked out a man and a woman as articles that he
desired for his plantation, and Walker proceeded to examine
them.

"Well, my boy, speak up and tell the doctor what's your
name."

"Sam, sar, is my name."

"How old are you?"

"Ef I live ter see next corn plantin' I'll be twenty-seven,
or thirty, or thirty-five, I dunno which."

"Ha, ha, ha! Well, doctor, this is a green boy. Are you
sound?"

"Yas, sar; I spec' I is."

"Open your mouth, and let me see your teeth. I allers
judge a nigger's age by his teeth, same as I do a hoss. Good
appetite?"

"Yas, sar."

"Get out on that plank and dance. I want to see how supple
you are."

"I don't like to dance, massa; I'se got religion."

"Got religion, have you? So much the better. I like to deal
in the gospel, doctor. He'll suit you. Now, my gal, what's
your name?"

"I is Big Jane, sar."

"How old are you?"

"Don' know, sar; but I was born at sweet pertater time."

"Well, do you know who made you?"

"I hev heard who it was in de Bible, but I done fergit de
gemman's name."

"Well, doctor, this is the greenest lot of niggers I've had
for some time, but you may have Sam for a thousand dollars

and Jane for nine hundred. They are worth all I ask for them."

"Well, Walker, I reckon I'll take them," replied the doctor.

"I'll put the handcuffs on 'em, and then you can pay me."

"Why," remarked the doctor, "there comes Reverend Pinchen."

"It is Mr. Pinchen as I live; jest the very man I want to see." As the reverend gentleman entered the enclosure, the trader grasped his hand, saying: "Why, how do you do, Mr. Pinchen? Come down to Charleston to the Convention, I s'pose? Glorious time, sir, glorious; but it will be gloriouser when the new government has spread our institootions all over the conquered North. Gloriouser and gloriouser. Any camp-meetin's, revivals, death-bed scenes, or other things in your line going on down here? How's religion prospering now, Mr. Pinchen? I always like to hear about religion."

"Well, Mr. Walker, the Lord's work is in good condition everywhere now. Mr. Walker, I've been in the gospel ministry these thirteen years, and I know that the heart of man is full of sin and desperately wicked. Religion is a good thing to live by, and we'll want it when we die. And a man in your business of buying and selling slaves needs religion more than anybody else, for it makes you treat your people well. Now there's Mr. Haskins—he's a slave-trader like yourself. Well, I converted him. Before he got religion he was one of the worst men to his niggers I ever saw; his heart was as hard as a stone. But religion has made his heart as soft as a piece of cotton. Before I converted him he would sell husbands from their wives and delight in doing it; but now he won't sell a man from his wife if he can get anyone to buy them together. I tell you, sir, religion has done a wonderful work for him."

"I know, Mr. Pinchen, that I ought to have religion, and that I am a great sinner; and whenever I get with good, pious people, like you and the doctor, I feel desperate wicked. I know that I would be happier with religion, and the first spare time I have I'm going to get it. I'll go to a protracted meeting, and I won't stop till I get religion."

Walker then invited the gentlemen to his office, and Pompey was dispatched to purchase wine and other refreshments for the guests.

Within the magnificent hall of the St. Charles Hotel a far different scene was enacted in the afternoon. The leading Southern politicians were gathered there to discuss the election of Lincoln, the "sectional" candidate, and to give due weight and emphasis to the future acts of the new government. There was exaltation in every movement of the delegates, and they were surrounded by the glitter of a rich and powerful assemblage in a high state of suppressed excitement, albeit this meeting was but preliminary to the decisive acts of the following week.

The vast hall, always used for dancing, was filled with tables which spread their snow-white wings to receive the glittering mass of glass, plate and flowers. The spacious galleries were crowded to suffocation by beautiful Southern belles in festive attire. Palms and fragrant shrubs were everywhere; garlands of flowers decorated the walls and fell, mingled with the new flaw—the stars and bars—gracefully above the seat of the chairman. In the gallery opposite the speaker's desk a band was stationed; Negro servants in liveries of white linen hurried noiselessly to and fro. The delegates filed in to their places at table to the crashing strains of "Dixie"; someone raised the new flag aloft and waved it furiously; the whole assembly rose *en masse* and cheered

vociferously, and the ladies waved their handkerchiefs. Mirth
and hilarity reigned. The first attention of the diners was
given to the good things before them. After cigars were
served the music stopped, and the business of the day began
in earnest.

There was the chairman, Hon. Robert Toombs of Georgia;
there was John C. Breckenridge of Kentucky, Stephen A.
Douglas, Alexander H. Stevens, and Jefferson Davis.

"Silence!" was the cry, as Hon. Robert Toombs, the
chairman, arose.

"Fellow Delegates and Fellow Citizens: I find myself in a
most remarkable situation, and I feel that every Southern
gentleman sympathizes with me. Here am I, chairman of a
meeting of the most loyal, high-spirited and patriotic body
of men and their guests and friends, that ever assembled to
discuss the rights of humanity and Christian progress, and
yet unable to propose a single toast with which we have been
wont to sanction such a meeting as this. With grief that
consumes my soul, I am compelled to bury in the silence of
mortification, contempt and detestation the name of the government at Washington.

"I can only counsel you, friends, to listen to no vain
babbling, to no treacherous jargon about overt acts; they have
already been committed. Defend yourselves; the enemy is at
your door; wait not to meet him at the hearthstone,—meet
him at the door-sill, and rive him from the temple of liberty,
or pull down its pillars and involve him in a common ruin.
Never permit this federal government to pass into the trai-
torous hands of the black Republican party.

"My language may appear strong; but it is mild when we
consider the attempt being made to wrest from us the exclusive
power of making laws for our own community. The repose

of our homes, the honor of our color, and the prosperity of
the South demand that we resist innovation.

"I rejoice to see around me fellow-laborers worthy to lead
in the glorious cause of resisting oppression, and defending
our ancient privileges which have been set by an Almighty
hand. We denounce once and for all the practices proposed
by crazy enthusiasts, seconded by designing knaves, and
destined to be executed by demons in human form. We shall
conquer in this pending struggle; we will subdue the North,
and call the roll of our slaves beneath the very shadow of
Bunker Hill. 'It is a consummation devoutly to be wished.'

"And now, I call upon all true patriots in token of their
faith, to drink deep of one deserving their fealty,—the
guardian and savior of the South, Jefferson Davis."

Vociferous cheers broke forth and shook the building. The
crowd surrounding the hotel took it up, and the name "Davis!"
"Davis!" was repeated again and again. He arose in his seat
and bowed profoundly; the band played "See the Conquering
Hero Comes"; a lady in the gallery back of him skilfully
dropped a crown of laurel upon his head. The crowd went
mad; they tore the decorations from the walls and pelted their
laurel-crowned hero until he would gladly have had them
cease; but such is fame. When the cheers had somewhat
subsided, Mr. Davis said:

"I must acknowledge, my fellow-citizens, the truth of the
remarks just made by our illustrious friend, Senator Toombs.
I was never more satisfied with regard to the future history
of our country than I am at present. I believe in state rights,
slavery, and the Confederacy that we are about to inaugurate.

"The principle of slavery is in itself right, and does not
depend upon difference of complexion. Make the laboring
man the slave of *one* man, instead of the slave of society, and

16   *The Magazine Novels of Pauline Hopkins*

he would be far better off. Slavery, black or white, is
necessary. Nature has made the weak in mind or body for
slaves.

"In five days your delegates from all the loyal Southern
States will meet here in convention. I feel the necessity that
every eye be fixed upon the course which will be adopted by
this assembly of patriots. You know our plans. South Carolina
will lead the march of the gallant band who will give us the
liberty we crave. We are all united in will and views, and
therefore powerful. I see before me in my colleagues men to
whom the tranquility of our government may be safely
confided—men devoted and zealous in their interest—senators
and representatives who have managed everything for our aid
and comfort. Few of the vessels of the navy are available at
home; the army is scattered on the Western frontier, while
all the trained officers of the army are with us. Within our
limits we have control of the entire government property—
mints, custom-houses, post-offices, dock-yards, revenue-cutters,
arsenals and forts. The national finances have been levied
upon to fill our treasury by our faithful Southern members
of the late cabinet. Yes, friends, all is ready; every preparation
is made for a brief and successful fight for that supremacy in
the government of this nation which is our birthright. (Tremendous applause.)

"By the election just thrust upon us by the Republican
party the Constitution is violated; and were we not strong to
sustain our rights, we should soon find ourselves driven to
prison at the point of the bayonet (cries of 'Never, never!'),
ousted from the council of state, oblivion everywhere, and
nothing remaining but ourselves to represent Truth and
Justice. We believe that our ideas are the desires of the
majority of the people, and the people represent the supreme

and sovereign power of Right! (Hear! hear! cheer
Abraham Lincoln (hisses) nothing is inviolate, nothing
he menaces, in his election, our ancient ideas and privileges.
The danger grows greater. Let us arise in our strength and
meet it more than half way. Are you ready, men?"

"We are ready!" came in a roar like unto the waters of the
mighty Niagara. What shall we do?"

"No half measures; let it be a deed of grandeur!"

"It shall be done!" came in another mighty chorus.

"In such a crisis there must be no vacuum. There must be
a well-established government before the people. You, citizens, shall take up arms; we will solicit foreign re-enforcements;
we will rise up before this rail-splitting ignoramus a terrible
power; we will overwhelm this miserable apology for a
gentleman and a statesman as a terrible revolutionary power.
Do you accept my proposition?"

"Yes, yes!" came as a unanimous shout from the soul of
the vast assembly.

"Our Northern friends make a great talk about free society.
We sicken of the name. What is it but a conglomeration of
greasy mechanics, filthy operatives, small-fisted farmers, and
moonstruck Abolitionists? All the Northern States, and particularly the New England States, are devoid of society fitted
for well-bred gentlemen. The prevailing class one meets with
is that of mechanics struggling to be genteel, and farmers
who do their own drudgery, and yet who are hardly fit for
association with a gentleman's slave.

We have settled this matter in the minds of the people of
the South by long years of practice and observation; and I
believe that when our principles shall have been triumphantly
established over the entire country—North, South, West—a
long age of peace and prosperity will ensue for the entire

country. Under our jurisdiction wise laws shall be passed for the benefit of the supreme and subordinate interests of our communities. And when we have settled all these vexed questions I see a season of calm and fruitful prosperity, in which our children's children may enjoy their lives without a thought of fear or apprehension of change."

Then the band played; there was more cheering and waving of handkerchiefs, in the midst of which John C. Breckenridge arose and gracefully proposed the health of the first President of the Confederate States of America. It was drunk by every man, standing. Other speakers followed, and the most intemperate sentiments were voiced by the zealots in the great cause. The vast crowd went wild with enthusiasm.

St. Clair Enson, one of the most trusted delegates, and the slave-trader Walker sat side by side at the table, and in the excitement of the moment all the prejudices of the Maryland aristocrat toward the vile dealer in human flesh were forgotten.

The convention had now passed the bounds of all calmness. Many of the men stood on chairs, gesticulating wildly, each trying to be heard above his neighbor. In vain the Chair rapped for order. Pandemonium reigned. At one end of the long table two men were locked in deadly embrace, each struggling to enforce his views upon the other by brute strength.

One man had swept the dishes aside, and was standing upon the table, demanding clamorously to be heard, and above all the band still crashed its brazen notes of triumph in the familiar strains of "Dixie."

A Negro boy handed a letter to Mr. Enson. He turned it over in his hand, curiously examining the postmark.

"When did this come, Cato?"

"More'n a munf, massa," was the reply.

Mr. Enson tore open the envelope and glanced over its contents with a frowning face.

"Bad news?" ventured Walker, with unusual familiarity.

"The worst possible for me. My brother is married, and announces the birth of a daughter."

"Well, daughters are born every day. I don't see how that can hurt you."

"It happens in this case, however, that this particular daughter will inherit the Enson fortune," returned Enson with a short laugh.

Walker gave a long, low whistle. "Who was your brother's wife? Any money?"

"Clark Sargeant's daughter. Money enough on both sides; but the trouble is, it will never be mine." Another sharp, bitter laugh.

"Sargeant, Sargeant," said Walker, musingly. " 'Pears to me I've had business with a gentleman of the same name years ago, in St. Louis. However, it can't be the same one, 'cause this man hadn't any children. Leastways, I never heard on eny."

"Perhaps it is the same man. Clark Sargeant was from St. Louis; moved to Baltimore when the little girl was five years old. Mr. and Mrs. Sargeant are dead."

"Same man, same man. Um, um," said Walker, scratching the flesh beneath his sandy whiskers meditatively, as he gazed at the ceiling. "Both dead, eh? Come to think of it, I moight be mistaken about the little gal. Has she got black hair and eyes and a cream-colored skin, and has she growed up to be a all-fired pesky fine woman?"

"Can't say," replied Enson, with a yawn as he rose to his feet. "I've never had the pleasure of meeting my sister-in-law."

"When you going up to Baltimore?" asked Walker.

"Next week, on 'The Planter.' "

"Think I'll take a trip up with you. You don't mind my calling with you on your brother's family, do you, Mr. Enson? I would admire to introduce myself to Clark Sargeant's little gal. She moight not remember me at first, but I reckon I could bring back recollections of me to her mind, ef it's jes' the same to you, Mr. Enson."

"O, be hanged to you. Go where you please. Go to the devil," replied Enson, as he swung down the hall and elbowed his way out.

"No need of goin' to the devil when he's right side of you, Mr. Enson," muttered Walker, as he watched the young man out of sight. "You d—d aristocrats carry things with a high hand; I'll be glad to take a reef in your sails, and I'll do it, too, or my name's not Walker."

CHAPTER III

St. Clair Enson was the second son of an aristocratic Maryland family. He had a fiery temper that knew no bounds when once aroused. Motherless from infancy, and born at a period in the life of his parents when no more children were expected, he grew up wild and self-willed. As his character developed it became evident that an unsavory future was before him. There was no malicious mischief in which he was not found, and older heads predicted that he would end on the gallows. Sensual, cruel to ferocity, he was a terror to the God-fearing community where he lived. With women he was successful from earliest youth, being possessed of the diabolical beauty of Satan himself. There was great rejoicing in the quiet village near which Enson Hall was situated when it was known that the young scapegrace had gone to college.

The atmosphere of college life suited him well, and he was soon the leader of the fastest set there. He was the instigator of innumerable broils, insulted his teachers, and finally fought a duel, killing his man instantly. According to the code of honor of the time, this was not murder; but expulsion from the halls of learning followed for St. Clair, and much to his surprise and chagrin, his father, who had always indulged and excused his acts as the thoughtlessness of youth's high spirits, was thoroughly enraged.

There was a curious scene between them, and no one ever knew just what passed, but it was ended by his father's saying:

"You have disgraced the name of Enson, and now you dare make a joke to me of your wickedness. Let me not see your face in this house again. Henceforth, until you have redeemed yourself by an honest man's career, I have but one son, your brother Ellis."

"As you please, sir," replied St. Clair nonchalantly, as he placed the check his father handed him in his pocket, bowed, and passed from the room.

That was the last heard of him for five years, when at his father's death he went home to attend the funeral.

By the terms of the will St. Clair received a small annuity, to be enlarged at the discretion of his brother, and in event of the latter's death without issue, the estate was to revert to St. Clair's heirs "if any there be who are an honor to the name of Enson," was the wording of the will. In the event of St. Clair's continuing in disgrace and "having no honorable and lawful issue," the property was to revert to a distant branch of cousins, "for I have no mind that debauchery and crime shall find a home at Enson Hall."

After this St. Clair seemingly dropped his wildest habits, but was still noted on all the river routes of the South as a reckless and daring gambler.

His man Isaac was as much of a character as himself, and many a game they worked together on the inexperienced, and many a time but for Isaac, St. Clair would have fared ill at the hands of his victims. Isaac was given to his young master at the age of ten years. The only saving grace about the scion of aristocracy appeared in his treatment of Isaac. Master and slave were devoted to each other.

As a last resource young Enson had gone in for politics, and the luck that had recently deserted him at cards and dice, favored him here. The unsettled state of the country and the threatening war-clouds were a boon to the tired child of chance, which he hailed as harbingers of better times for recreant Southern sons. He would gain fame and fortune in the service of the new government.

All through the dramatic action of the next week when history made so fast in the United States, when the South Carolina convention declared that "the union then subsisting between herself and other states of America, was dissolved" and her example followed by Mississippi, Florida, Alabama, Georgia, Louisiana, Texas, Virginia, Arkansas, North Carolina and Tennessee, all through that time when politics reached the boiling point, St. Clair, although in the thickest of the controversy, busy making himself indispensable to the officials of the new government, was thinking of the heiress of Enson Hall. He was bitter over his loss, and ready to blame anyone but himself.

In his opinion, Ellis was humdrum; he was mild and peaceful in his disposition, because his blood was too sluggish and his natural characteristics too womanish for the life of a gentleman. Then, too, Ellis was old, fifteen years his senior, and he was twenty-five.

St. Clair shared the universal opinion of his world (and to him the world did not exist north of Mason and Dixon's line), that a reckless career of gambling, wine and women was the only true course of development for a typical Southern gentleman. As he thought of the infant heiress his face grew black with a frown of rage that for the time completely spoiled the beauty women raved over. His man Isaac, furtively watching him from the corner of his eye, said to himself:

"I know dat dar's gwine to be a rippit; Marse St. Clair never look dat a way widout de debbil himself am broked loose." In which view of the case Isaac was about right.

St. Clair made up his mind to go home and see this fair woman who had come to blast his hopes and steal his patrimony for her children. Perhaps as she was young, and presumably susceptible, something might be done. He was handsome—Ah, well! and he laughed a wicked laugh at his reflection in the mirror; he would trust to luck to help him out. He ordered Isaac to pack up.

"Good Lawd, Marse St. Clair! I thought you'd done settled here fer good. How comes we go right off?"

"We're going home, Isaac, to see the new mistress Enson and my niece. Haven't I told you that your master, Ellis was married, and had a daughter?"

"Bress my soul! no sar!" replied Isaac, dropping the clothes he held upon the floor. His master left the room.

"Now de Lawd help de mistress an' de little baby. I love

my master, but he's a borned debbil. He's jes' gwine home
to tare up brass, dat's de whole collusion ob de mystery."

St. Clair Enson took passage on board "The Planter,"
which was ready to start upon its last trip up Chesapeake Bay
before going into the service of the Confederate government.
At that time this historic vessel was a side-wheel steamer
storing about fourteen hundred bales of cotton as freight, but
having accommodations for a moderate number of passengers.
No one of the proud supporters of the new government
dreamed of her ultimate fate. The position of the South was
defined, and given to the world with a loud flourish of
trumpets. By their reasoning, a few short months would make
them masters of the entire country. Wedded to their idols,
they knew not the force of the "dire arms" which Omnipotence would wield upon the side of Right. One of the most
daring and heroic adventures of the Civil War was successfully accomplished by a party of Negroes, Robert Small
commanding, when the rebel gunboat "The Planter" ran by
the forts and batteries of Charleston Harbor, and reaching
the flagship "Wabash" was duly received into the service of
the United States government.

St. Clair Enson went on board the steamer with mixed
feelings of triumph and chagrin—triumph because of the
place he had made for himself in the councils of the new
government and the adulation meted out to him by the public;
chagrin because of his brother's new family ties and his own
consequent poverty.

For a while he wandered aimlessly about, resisting all the
tempting invitations extended by his numerous admirers in
the sporting and political world to "have something" at the
glittering bar. But his pockets were empty—they always

were—and he finally allowed himself to be cajolled to join in a quiet game in the hope of replenishing his purse, where he saw the chances were all in his favor.

The saloon was alight with music and gaiety; the jolly company of travelers and the gaudy furniture were reflected many times over in the gilded mirrors that caught the rays of a large chandelier depending from the center of the ceiling. To the eye and ear merriment held high carnival; some strolled about, many sought the refreshment bar, but a greater number—men and even women—took part in the play or bet lightly on the players, sotto voce, for pastime. The clink and gleam of gold was there as it passed from hand to hand. Six men at a table played baccarat; farther on, a party of very young people—both sexes—played loo for small stakes. There were quartets of whist players, too; but the most popular game was poker, for high stakes made by reckless and inveterate gamblers.

St. Clair and his party found an empty table, and Isaac, obedient to a sign from his master, brought him the box containing implements for a game of poker. All the men were inveterate gamblers, but Enson was an expert. Gradually the on-lookers gathered about that one particular table. Not a word was said; the men gripped their cards and held their breaths, with now and then an oath to punctuate a loss more severe than usual.

The slaver-trader Walker sauntered up to the place where St. Clair sat, and stood behind him.

"What's the stakes?" he asked of his next neighbor. The man addressed smiled significantly: "Not a bagatelle to begin with; they've raised them three times."

"Whew!" with a whistle. "And who is winning?"

"Oh, Enson, of course."

"Why 'of course?' " asked Walker with a wicked smile on his ugly face.

"He always wins."

"I reckon not now," returned Walker, as he pointed to the play just made.

"He's dealing above board and square, and luck's agin him."

It was true. From this time on Enson played again and again, and lost. The other players left their seats and stood near watching the famous gambler make his play. Finally, with a muttered curse, he staggered up from his chair and started to leave the table with desperate eyes and reeling gate. But he stopped as if struck by a sudden inspiration, and resumed his seat.

"What will he do now?" was the unspoken thought of the crowd.

"Isaac, come here," called out Enson. "I will see you and five hundred better," he continued, addressing his opponent, as the boy approached, and at a signal from him climbed upon the table. The crowd watched the strange scene in breathless silence.

"What price do you set on the boy?" asked the winner, whose name was Johnson, taking a large roll of bills from his pocket.

"He will bring eighteen hundred dollars any day in the New Orleans market."

"I reckon he ain't noways vicious?" asked Johnson, looking in the Negro's smiling face.

"I've never seen him angry."

"I'll give you fifteen hundred for him."

"Eighteen," returned Enson, with an ominous tightening about the mouth.

"Well, I'll tell you what I'll do, the very best; I'll make it sixteen hundred, no more, no less. That's fair. Is it a bargain?"

Enson nodded assent. The crowd heaved a sigh of relief.

"Then you bet the whole of this boy, do you?" continued Johnson.

"Yes."

"I call you, then," said Johnson.

"I've got three queens," replied Enson.

"Not enough," said the other.

"Then if you beat three queens, you beat me."

"I have four jacks, and the boy is mine." The crowd heaved another sigh as one man.

"Hold on! Not so fast!" shouted Enson. "You don't take him till you *show* me that you beat three queens." Johnson threw his five cards upon the table, and four of them were jacks! "Sure," said Johnson, as he looked at Enson and then at the crowd.

"Sure!" came in a hoarse murmur from many throats. For a moment all things whirled and danced before Enson's eyes as he realized what he had lost. The lights from the chandelier shot out sparkles from piles of golden coin, the table heaved, faces were indistinct. He seemed to hear his father's voice again in stern condemnation, as he had heard it for the last time on earth. His face was white and set. He was a man ready for desperate needs. It seemed an hour to him, that short second. Then he turned to the winner:

"Mr. Johnson, I quit you."

Isaac was standing upon the table with the money at his feet. As he stepped down, Johnson said:

"You will not forget that you belong to me."

"No, sir."

"Be up in time to brush my clothes and clean my boots; do you hear?"

"Yas, sir," responded Isaac, with a good-natured smile and a long side-glance at Enson, in which one might have seen the lurking deviltry of a spirit kindred to his master's. Enson turned to leave the saloon, saying:

"I claim the right of redeeming that boy, Mr. Johnson. My father gave him to me when I was a lad. I promised never to part with him."

"Most certainly, sir; the boy shall be yours whenever you hand me over a cool sixteen hundred," returned Johnson. As Enson moved away, chewing the bitter curd of disappointment, Walker strolled up to him.

"That's a bad bargain Johnson's got in your man, Mr. Enson."

"How? Explain yourself."

"If he finds him after tomorrow morning, it's my belief it won't be the fault of Isaac's legs."

"Do you mean to say, sir, that I would connive at robbing a gentleman in fair play?"

"Oh, no; it won't be your fault," replied Walker with a familiar slap on Enson's back, that made the latter wince; "but he's a cute darkey that you can sell in good faith to a man, but he won't stay with him. Bet you the nigger'll be in Baltimore time you are."

"I'll take you. Make your bet."

Walker shook his head. "No, don't you do it. Luck's agin you, an' I won't rob you. That nigger'll lose you, sure."

Enson made no reply, but stood gazing moodily out upon the dark waters of the Atlantic, through which the steamer swiftly ploughed her way. Finally Walker continued:

"Why don't you try another game? Keep it up; luck may change. I'll lend you."

Enson waved his hand impatiently and said: "No; no more tonight. I have not a cent in the world until I eat humble pie and beg money from my brother."

"Tough!"

"Thank you. I do not want your sympathy."

"My help, then. Perhaps I can help you. Enson smiled derisively at the endless black waves and the moonless sky.

"No man can do that. I have made my bed hard and must abide the issue."

"Oh, rot! Be a man, and keep on fighting 'em. You'll be all right presently. Never say die."

"Perhaps you have a plan to compass the impossible," returned Enson with a sneer.

"I should say so. I've been thinking a good deal about your brother's marriage, and my old friends, the Sargeants. What would it be worth to you now to find a way to break off this marriage?"

"Break it off! Why, man, that can't be done. What are you driving at?"

"Easy there, now. I said 'break it off,' and I meant 'break if off.' They used to tell me when I was a boy that two heads was better'n one ef one was a sheep's head. Same case here. Job's worth ten thou. I can see three thou right in sight, that would make your bill about seven thou." Walker settled his hat at the back of his head, thrust his hands deep in his hip pockets, and gazed out over the dark waters with a glance from his ferret-like gray eyes that seemed to pierce the blackness.

"I don't understand you, Walker; explain yourself."

"I understand myself, and that's enough. All you've got to do is to put your I O U to a paper calling for seven thousand dollars conditional on my rendering you valuable service in a financial matter. Savey?"

"I'd do anything that would break this cursed luck I'm having. Can you do anything? What do you mean, anyhow, Walker?"

"Never mind what I mean. You meet me at Enson Hall. Wait for me if you get there first. Be ready to sign the paper, and I'll show you as neat a job as was ever put up by any man on earth. That's all." Walker turned as he finished speaking and walked away. St. Clair looked after him, uncertain what to think of his strange words and actions.

(To be continued.)

CHAPTER IV

The morning sun poured its golden light upon the picturesque old house standing in its own grounds in one of the suburban towns adjacent to Baltimore—the Baltimore of 1858 or 1860.

The old house seemed to command one to render homage to its beauty and stateliness. It was a sturdy brick building flanked with offices and having outbuildings touching the very edge of the deep, mysterious woods where the trees waved their beckoning arms in every soft breeze that came to revel in their rich foliage. This was Enson Hall. The Hall was reached through a long dim stretch of these woods—locusts and beeches—from ten to twelve acres in extent; its mellow, red-brick walls framed by a background of beechtrees reminded one of English residences with their immense extent of private grounds. In the rear of the mansion was the garden, with its huge conservatories gay with shrubs and flowers. Piazzas and porticoes promised delightful retreats for sultry weather. The interior of the house was in the style that came in after the Revolution. An immense hall with outer door standing invitingly open gave greeting to the guest. The stairs wound from the lower floor to the rooms above. The grand stairway was richly embellished with carving, and overhead a graceful arch added much to the impressive beauty which met the stranger's first view. The rooms, spacious and designed for entertaining largely, had panelled wainscotting and carved chimney-pieces.

Ellis Enson, the master of the Hall, was a well-made man, verging on forty. "Born with a silver spoon in his mouth," for the vast estate and all invested money was absolutely at his disposal, he was the envy of the men of his class and the despair of the ladies. He was extremely good-looking, slight, elegant, with wavy dark hair, and an air of distinction. Since his father's death he had lived at the Hall, surrounded by his slaves in lonely meditation, fancy free. This handsome recluse had earned the reputation of being morose, so little had he mixed with society, so cold had been his politeness to the fair sex. His farms, his lonely rides, his favorite books, had sufficed for him. He was a good manager, and what was more wonderful, considering his Southern temperament, a thorough man of business. His crops, his poultry, his dairy products, were of the very first quality. Sure it was that his plantation was a paying investment. Meanwhile the great house, with all its beautiful rooms and fine furniture, remained closed to the public, and was the despair of managing mammas with many daughters to provide with eligible husbands. Enson was second to none as a "catch," but he was utterly indifferent to women.

Just about this time when to quarry the master of Enson Hall seemed a hopeless task, Hagar Sargeant came home from a four years' sojourn at the North in a young ladies' seminary.

The Sargeant estate was the one next adjoining Enson Hall; not so large and imposing, but a valuable patrimony that had descended in a long line of Sargeants and was well preserved. For many years before Hagar's birth the estate had been rented because of financial misfortunes, and they had lived in St. Louis, where Mr. Sargeant had engaged in trade so successfully that when Hagar was six years old they were enabled to return to their ancestral home and resume a life of luxurious leisure. Since that time Mr. Sargeant had died. On a trip to St. Louis, where he had gone to settle his business affairs, he contracted cholera, then ravaging many large cities of the Southwest, and had finally succumbed to the scourge. Hagar, their only child, then became her mother's sole joy and inspiration. Determined to cultivate her daughter's rare intellectual gifts, she had sent her North to school when every throb of her heart demanded her presence at home. She had developed into a beautiful girl, the admiration and delight of the neighborhood to which she returned, almost a stranger after her long absence.

A golden May morning poured its light through the open window of the Sargeant breakfast-room. A pleasanter room could scarcely be found, though the furniture was not of latest fashion, and the carpet slightly faded. There was a bay window that opened on the terrace, below which was a garden; there was a table in the recess spread with dainty china and silver, and the remains of breakfast; honeysuckles played hide-and-seek at the open window. Aunt Henny, a coal-black Negress of kindly face, brought in the little brass-bound oaken tub filled with hot water and soap, and the linen towels. Hagar stood at the window contemplating the scene before her. It was her duty to wash the heirlooms of colonial china and silver. From their bath they were dried only by her dainty fingers, and carefully replaced in the corner cupboard. Not for the world would she have dropped one of these treasures. Her care for them, and the placing of every one in its proper niche, was wonderful to behold. Not the royal jewels of Victoria were ever more carefully guarded than these family heirlooms.

This morning Hagar was filled with a delicious excitement, caused by she knew not what. The china and silver were an anxiety unusual to her. She felt a physical exhilaration, inspired, no doubt, by the delicious weather. She always lamented at this season of the year the lost privileges of the house of Sargeant, when their right of way led directly from the house to the shining waters of the bay. There was a path that led to the water still, but it was across the land of their neighbor Enson. Sometimes Hagar would trespass; would cross the parklike stretch of pasture, bordered by the woodland through which it ran, and sit on the edge of the remnant of a wharf, by which ran a small, rapid river, an arm of Chesapeake Bay, chafing among wet stones and leaping gaily over rocky barriers. There she would dream of life before the Revolution, and in these dreams participate in the joys of the colonial dames. She longed to mix and mingle with the gay world; she had a feeling that her own talents, if developed, would end in something far different from the calm routine, the housekeeping and churchgoing which stretched before her. Sometimes softer thoughts possessed her, and she speculated about love and lovers. This peaceful life was too tranquil and uneventful. Oh, for a break in the humdrum recurral of the same events day after day.

She had never met Ellis Enson. He was away a great part of the time before she left home for school, and since she had returned. If she remembered him at all, it was with the thought of a girl just past her eighteenth birthday for a man forty.

This morning Hagar washed the silver with the sleeves of her morning robe turned up to the shoulder, giving a view of rosy, dimpled arms. "A fairer vision was never seen," thought the man who paused a moment at the open window to gaze again upon the pretty, homelike scene. As Hagar turned from replacing the last of the china, she was startled out of her usual gay indifference at the sight of a handsome pair of dark eyes regarding her intently from the open window. A quick wonder flashed in the eyes that met hers; the color deepened in his face as he saw he was observed. The girl's beauty startled him so, that for a moment he lost the self-control that convention dictates. Then he bared his head in courteous acknowledgment of youth and beauty, with an apology for his seeming intrusion.

"I beg pardon," Enson said in his soft, musical tones; "is Mrs. Sargeant at home? I did not know she had company."

"I am not company; I am Hagar. Yes, mamma is at home; if you will come in, I will take you to her."

He turned and entered the hall door and followed her through the dark, cool hall to the small morning-room, where Mrs. Sargeant spent her mornings in semi-invalid fashion. Then a proper introduction followed, and Ellis Enson and Hagar Sargeant were duly acquainted.

At forty Enson still retained his faith in womanhood,

although he had been so persistently pursued by all the women of the vicinity. He believed there were women in the world capable of loving a man for himself alone without a thought of worldly advantage, only he had not been fortunate enough to meet them.

He had a very poor opinion of himself. Adulation had not made him vain. His face indicated strong passions and much pride; but it was pride of caste, not self. There was great tenderness of the eye and lip, and signs of a sensitive nature that could not bear disgrace or downfall that might touch his ancient name. After he left the Sargeant home Hagar's face haunted him; the pure creamy skin, the curved crimson lips ready to smile,—lips sweet and firm,—the broad, low brow, and great, lustrous, long-lashed eyes of brilliant black—soft as velvet, and full of light with the earnest, cloudless gaze of childhood; and there was heart and soul and mind in this countenance of a mere girl. Such beauty as this was a perpetual delight to feast the eyes and charm the senses—aye, to witch a man's heart from him; for here there was not only the glory of form and tints, but more besides,—heart that could throb, soul that could aspire, mind that could think. She was not shy and self-conscious as young girls so often are; she seemed quite at her ease, as one who has no thought of self. He was conscious of his own enthralment. He knew that he had set his feet in the perilous path of love at a late day, but knowing this, he none the less went forward to his fate.

After that the young girl and the man met frequently. She did not realize when the time came that she had grown to look for his coming. There were walks and drives and accidental meetings in the woods. The sun was brighter and the songs of the birds sweeter that summer than ever before.

Ellis fell to day-dreaming, and the dreams were tinged

with gold, bringing a flush to his face and a thrill to his heart. Still he would have denied, if accused, that this was love at first sight—bah! That was a well-exploded theory. And yet if it was not love that had suddenly come into his being for this slender, dark-eyed girl, what was it? A change had come into Ellis Enson's life. The greatest changes, too, are always unexpected.

It was a sultry day; there was absolutely no chance to catch a refreshing breeze within four walls. It was one of the rare occasions when Mrs. Sargeant felt obliged to make a business call alone. From the fields came the sound of voices singing: the voices of slaves. Aunt Henny's good-natured laugh occasionally broke the stillness.

"Now I shall have a nice quiet afternoon," thought Hagar, as she left the house for the shadow of the trees. Under the strong, straight branches of a beech she tied three old shawls, hammock-like, one under another, for strength and safety. It was not very far from the ground. If it should come down, she might be bruised slightly, but not killed. She crawled cautiously into her nest; she had let down the long braids of her hair, and as she lolled back in her retreat, they fell over the sides of the hammock and swept the top of the long, soft grass. Lying there, with nothing in sight but the leafy branches of the trees high above her head, through which gleams of the deep blue sky came softly, she felt as if she had left the world, and was floating, Ariel-like, in midair.

After an hour of tranquility, footsteps were audible on the soft grass. There was a momentary pause, then someone came to a standstill beside her fairy couch.

"Back so soon, mamma? I wish you could come up here with me; it is just heavenly."

"Then I suppose you must be one of the heavenly inhabitants, an angel, but I never can pay compliments as I ought," said a voice.

"Mr. Enson!" Hagar was conscious of a distinct quickening of heart-action and a rush of crimson to her cheeks; with a pretty, hurried movement she rose to a sitting position in her hammock; "I really am ashamed of myself. I thought you were mamma."

"Yes," he answered, smiling at her dainty confusion.

"Mr. Enson," she said again, this time gravely, "politeness demands that I receive you properly, but decency forbids I should do it unless you will kindly turn your back to me while I step to earth once more."

The man was inwardly shaking with laughter at the grave importance with which she viewed the business in hand, but not for worlds would he have had her conscious of his mirth.

"I can help you out all right," he said.

"No, I am too heavy. I think I will stay here until you go."

"Oh—but—say now, Miss Hagar, that is hard to drive me away when I have just come; and such an afternoon, too, hot enough to kill a darkey. Do let me help you down."

"No; I can get out myself if I must. Please turn your back."

Thus entreated, he turned his back and commenced an exhaustive study of the landscape. Hagar arose; the hammock turned up, and Ellis was just in time to receive her in his arms as she fell.

"Hagar—my darling—you are not hurt?" he asks anxiously, still holding her in a close embrace.

"No; of course not. It is so good of you to be by to care for me so nicely," she said in some confusion.

"Hagar—my darling," he said again, with a desperate

resolve to let her know the state of his feelings, "will you marry me?" She trembled as his lips pressed passionate kisses on hers. The veil was drawn away. She understood—this was the realization of the dreams that had come to her dimly all the tender springtime. Never in all her young life had she felt so happy, so strangely happy. A soft flush mounted to cheek and brow under his caresses.

"I don't understand," murmured the girl, trembling with excitement.

"My darling, I think I have said it more plainly than most men do. Hagar, I think you must know it; I have made no secret of my love for you. Have you not understood me all the days of the spring and summer?"

"Are you quite sure that you love me? You are so old and wise, and I so ignorant to be the wife of so grand a man as you."

She glanced up fleetingly, and flushed more deeply under the look she met. He folded her closer still in his arms. His next words were whispered:

"My love! lift your eyes to mine, and say you love me."

Hagar had not dreamed that such passion as this existed in the world. It seemed to take the breath of her inner life and leave her powerless, with no separate existence, no distinct mental utterance.

Gently Ellis drew back the bright head against him, and bent over the sweet lips that half sought his kiss; and so for one long moment he knew a lifetime of happiness. Then he released her.

"Heaven helping me, you shall be so loved and shielded that sorrow shall never touch you. You shall never repent trusting your young life to me. May I speak to your mother tonight?"

"Yes," she whispered.

And so they were betrothed. Ellis felt and meant all that he said under the stress of the emotion of the moment; but who calculates the effect of time and cruel circumstance? Mrs. Sargeant was more than pleased at the turn of events. Soon Ellis was taking the bulk of the business of managing her estates upon his own strong shoulders. These two seemed favored children of the gods all that long, happy summer. She was his, and he was hers.

The days glided by like a dream, and soon brought the early fall which was fixed for the wedding festivities. All was sunshine. The wedding day was set for October. On the morning of the day before, Hagar entered her mother's room as was her usual custom, to give her a loving morning greeting, and found nothing but the cold, unresponsive body, from which the spirit had fled. Then followed days that were a nightmare to Hagar, but under Ellis' protecting care the storm of grief spent itself and settled into quiet sadness. There was no one at the Sargeant home but the bereaved girl and her servants. At the end of a month Ellis put the case plainly before her, and she yielded to his persuasions to have the marriage solemnized at once, so that he might assume his place as her rightful protector. A month later than the time originally set there was a quiet wedding, very different from the gay celebration originally planned by a loving mother, and the young mistress took her place in the stately rooms of Enson Hall. When a twelve-month had passed there was a little queen born—the heiress of the hall. Ellis' happiness was complete.

CHAPTER V

It was past the breakfast hour in the Hall kitchen, but Marthy still lingered. It was cold outside; snow had fallen the night before; the clouds were dull and threatening. The raw north-ern blasts cut like bits of ice; the change was very sudden from the pleasant coolness of autumn. The kitchen was an inviting place; the blaze shot up gleefully from between the logs, played hide-and-seek in dark corners and sported mer-rily across the faces of the pickaninnies sprawling on the floor and constantly under Aunt Henny's feet.

Aunt Henny now reigned supreme in the culinary depart-ment of the Hall. Her head was held a little higher, if possible, in honor of the new dignity that had come to the family from the union of the houses of Enson and Sargeant.

" 'Twarn't my 'sires fer a weddin' so close to a fun'ral, but Lor', chile, dars a diffurunce in doin' things, an' it 'pears dis weddin's comin' out all right. Dem two is a sight fer sore eyes, an' as fer de baby"—Aunt Henny rolled up her eyes in silent ecstasy.

"Look hyar, mammy," said Marthy, Mrs. Enson's maid and Aunt Henny's daughter, "why don' you see Unc' Demus? He'd guv you a charm fer Miss Hagar to wear; she needn't know nuthin' 'bout it."

"Sho, honey, wha' you take me fo'? I done went down to Demus soon as dat weddin' wus brung up."

"Wha' he say, mammy?"

"Let me 'lone now tell I tells you." Aunt Henny was singeing pin-feathers from a pile of birds on the floor in front of the fire. She dropped her task to give emphasis to her words. "I carried him Miss Hagar's pocket-hankercher and he guv me a bag made outen de skin ob a rattlesnake, an' he put in it a rabbit's foot an' er sarpint's toof, an' er squorerpin's tail wid a leetle dust outen de graveyard an' he sewed up de bag. Den he tied all dat up in de hankercher an' tell me solemn: 'Long as yer mistis keep dis 'bout her, trouble'll neber stay so long dat joy won't conquer him in de end.' So, honey, I done put dat charm in Missee Hagar draw 'long wid her tickler fixins an' I wants yer, Marthy, to take keer ob it," she concluded, with a grave shake of her turbanned head. Marthy was duly impressed, and stood looking at her mother with awe in every feature of her little brown face.

" 'Deed an' I will, mammy."

"My young Miss will be all right ef dat St. Clair Enson keeps 'way from hyar," continued the woman reflectively.

"Who's St. Clar Enson?" asked Marthy.

"Nemmin' 'bout him. Sometime I'll tell you when you gits older. All you got ter do now is ter take mighty good keer o' your mistis and de baby," replied her mother, with a knowing wag of her head. "Fling anudder chunk on dat fire!" she called to one of the boys playing on the floor. "Gittin' mighty cole fer dis time ob year, de a'r smell pow'rful lack mo' snow."

A shadow fell across the doorsill shutting out the light for a moment, that came through the half-open doorway. Marthy gave a shriek that ended in a giggle as a young Negro, tall, black, smiling, sauntered into the kitchen; it was Isaac. Aunt Henny threw her arms high above her head in unbounded astonishment.

"En de name ob de Lawd! Isaac! What's gwine ter happen ter dis fambly now, Ike, dat you's come sneakin' home?"

Isaac grinned. "Isn't you pow'rful glad ter see me, Aunt Henny? I is ter see you an' Marthy. Marfy's a mighty likely lookin' gal, I 'low." He gave a sly roll of his eye in the direction where the girl stood regarding the athletic young Negro with undisguised admiration.

"None o' dat," sputtered Aunt Henny. "Don' you go tryin' ter fool wid dat gal, you lim' ob de debbil. Take yo'se'f right off! What yer doin' hyar, enyhow? Dis ain't no place fer you."

"My marse tell'd me ter come," replied Isaac, not at all ruffled by his reception. "I ain't gwine ter go right off; ain't tell'd none o' de folks howdy yit."

"Your marse tell'd you ter come! What fer he tell'd yer to come?" stormed Aunt Henny, with a derisive snort. "Dat's what I want ter know. *My* marse'll have somethin' ter say I reckon, ef *yer* marse *did* tell'd yer ter come. An' I b'lieve you's a liar, 'deed I do. I don' b'lieve yer marser knows whar you is at, dis blessid minnit."

Isaac chuckled. "I'se come home ter see de new mistis an' de leetle baby; I cert'n'y hopes dey is well. Marse St. Clar'll be hyar hisself bimeby."

Aunt Henny stood a moment silently regarding the boy. Fear, amazement and curiosity were blended in her honest face. Plainly, she was puzzled. "De debbil turn' sain'," she muttered to herself, with a long look at the unconscious Isaac, who sat toasting his cold bare toes before the roaring fire. "Dis house got mo' peace in it, an' Marse Ellis happier den he been sence his mar, ol' Missee Enson, died; but," and she shook her turbanned head ominously, " 'tain't fer long. I ain't fergit nuffin'; I isn't lived nex' dis Enson Hall so many years fer nuffin.'"

"I'se walk'd a long way slippin' officers"—began Isaac.

"Um!" grunted Aunt Henny, with the look of alarm still in her eyes, "officers! dat's what's de matter."

"Dey'll hab ter see Marse St. Clar, tain't me. He sol' me. I runned 'way. I come home, dat's all. Kain't I hab suthin' to eat?"

"Ef 'tain't one it's t'odder. Befo' God, I 'lieve you an' yo' marse bof onhuman. Been sol'! runned 'way! hump!" again grunted Aunt Henny.

Meanwhile Marthy had made coffee and baked a corncake in the hot ashes. Isaac sniffed the aroma of the fragrant coffee hungrily. There was chicken and rice, too, he noticed as she placed food on the end of a table and motioned him to help himself. Isaac needed no pressing, and in a moment was eating ravenously.

"Tell you de troof, Aunt Henny," he said at last, as he waited for a fourth help, "Marse St. Clar git hard up de oder night in a little play comin' up de bay, an' he sell me to a gempleman fer sixteen hundred dollars. But, Lor', dat don' hol' Isaac, chile, while he's got legs."

"Dat's jes' what I thought. No use yer lyin' ter me, Isaac, yer Aunt Henny *was born wif a veil.* I knows a heap o' things by seein' 'em fo' dey happens. I don' tell all I sees, but I keeps up a steddyin' 'bout it."

"Dar's no mon can keep me, I don't keer how much Marse St. Clar sells me; he's my onlies' marser," continued Isaac, as he kept on devouring food a little more slowly than at first.

"Lawd sakes, honey; you's de mos' pow'rfulles' eater I'se seed fer many a day. Don' reckon you's had a good meal sence yer was home five years ago. Dog my cats ef I don' hope Marse Ellis will jes' make yer trot."

"He kin sen' me back, but I isn't gwine stay wid 'em," replied Isaac, with his mouth full of food.

"You cain't he'p yo'se'f."

"I kin walk," persisted Isaac doggedly.

"Put you in de caboose an' give yer hundred lashes," Aunt Henny called back, as she waddled out of the kitchen to find her master.

"Don' keer fer dat, nudder."

Isaac improved the time between the going and coming of Aunt Henny by making fierce love to Marthy, who was willing to meet him more than half way.

The breakfast-room was redolent with the scent of flowers, freshly cut from the greenhouses; the waxed floor gleamed like polished glass beneath the fur rugs scattered over it, and the table, with its service for two, was drawn in front of the cheerful fire that crackled and sparkled in the open fireplace. All the luxuries that wealth could give were gathered about the young matron. It was a happy household; the hurry and rush of warlike preparations had not reached its members, and the sting of slavery, with its demoralizing brutality, was unknown on these plantations so recently joined. Happiness was everywhere, from the master in his carriage to the slave singing in the fields at his humble task. Breakfast was over, and as Ellis glanced over the top of his morning paper at his wife and baby, he felt a thrill of intense pride and love.

As compared with her girlhood, Hagar's married life had been one round of excitement. Washington and many other large cities had been visited on their brief honeymoon. They were royally entertained by all the friends and relatives of both families, and the beautiful bride had been the belle of every assembly. Ellis was wrapped up in her; intimate acquaintance but deepened his love. Her nature was pure, spiritual, and open as the day. Gowned in spotless white, her slender form lost in a large armchair, she sat opposite him, dandling the baby in her arms. She looked across at him and smiled.

"Well, pet," he smiled back at her, "going to ride?"

She shook her head and set every little curl in motion.

"I won't go out today, it is so cold; we are so comfortable here before the fire, baby and I."

"What a lazy little woman it is," he laughed, rising from his seat and going over to stand behind her chair, stroke the bright hair, and clasp mother and child in his arms. Hagar rested her head against him, and held the infant at arm's length for his admiration.

"Isn't she a darling? See, Ellis, she knows you," as the child cooed and laughed and gurgled at them both, in a vain effort to clinch something in her little red fists.

"This little beggar has spoiled our honeymoon with a vengeance," he replied with a laugh. "I cannot realize that it is indeed over, and we have settled down to the humdrum life of old married folk."

"Can anything ever spoil that and its memories?" she asked, with a sweet upward look into his face. "Indeed, I often wonder if I am too happy; is it right for any human being to be so favored in life as I have been."

"Gather your roses while you may, there will be dark clouds enough in life, heaven knows. No gloomy thoughts, Mignon; let us be happy in the present." He kissed the lips raised so temptingly for his caress, and then one for the child. He thought humbly of his own career beside the spotless creature he had won for life. While not given to excesses, yet there were things in the past that he regretted. Since the birth of their child, the days had been full of emotion for these two people, who were, perhaps, endowed with over-sensitive natures given to making too much of the commonplace happenings of life. Now, as he watched the head of the child resting against the mother's breast, he ran the gamut of human feelings in his sensations. Love and thanksgiving for these unspeakable gifts of God—his wife and child—swept the inmost recesses of his heart.

"Please, Marse Ellis!" cried Aunt Henny's voice from the doorway, "please, sah, Marse St. Clar's Isaac done jes' dis minnit come home. What's I gwine ter do wid him?"

"What, Henny!" Ellis cried in astonishment; "St. Clair's Isaac? Where's his master?"

"Dunno, Marse Ellis, but dar's allers truble, sho, when dat lim' o' Satan turns up; 'deed dar is."

Ellis left the room hurriedly, followed by Aunt Henny. Hagar sat there, fondling the child, a perfect picture of sweet womanhood. She had matured wonderfully in the few months of married life; her girlish manner had dropped from her like a garment. Eve's perfect daughter, she accomplished her destiny in sweet content. Presently the door opened, and her husband stood beside her chair again; his face wore a troubled look.

"What is it?" she asked, with a sweeping upward glance that noted every change of his countenance.

"St. Clair's Isaac."

"Well, and is he so serious a matter that you must look so grave?"

"My dear, the slaves all look upon him as a bird of evil omen; for myself, I look upon it as mere ignorant superstition, but still I have a feeling of uneasiness. They have neither of them been at the Hall for five years. Isaac says his master is coming—that he expected to find him here. What brings them is the puzzler."

"News of your marriage, Ellis; a natural desire to see his new relative. I see nothing strange in that, dear."

"He can't feel very happy about it, according to the terms of the will; probably he has been counting on my not marrying, and now, being disappointed, comes for me to pay his debts, or perform some impossible favor."

"Why impossible?"

"St. Clair is an unsavory fellow, and his desires are not likely to appeal to a man of honor," replied Ellis, with a short, bitter laugh.

"So bad as that?" said his wife regretfully; it was the first shadow since the beginning of their honeymoon. She continued: "Promise me, Ellis, to bear with him kindly and grant him anything in reason, in memory of our happiness."

In the kitchen Aunt Henny, with little braids of hair sticking out from under turban, talked to Marthy.

"Ef Marse Ellis listen to me, he gwine ter make dat Isaac quit dese diggin's."

"Law, mammy," laughed Marthy, showing her tiny white teeth and tossing her head, "you don' want ter drive de po' boy 'way from whar he was born, does yer?" Marthy was a born coquette, and Isaac was very gallant to her.

"Dat all I gwine ter say. Nobody knows dat Marse St. Clar an' his Isaac better'n I does. I done part raise 'em bof. I reckon my ha'r'd all turn plum' white ef dem two hadn't don lef' dese parts."

"How you come to raise 'em, mammy, an' what made 'em try ter turn yo' ha'r plum' white?"

"Dev'ment, honey, pur' dev'ment! It 'pears lack 'twas only yesterday dat I was a gal wurkin' right yere in dis same ol' kitchen. Marse Sargeant he lose heap money, an' all ob dem move ter St. Louis ter 'trench an' git rich ergin; Marse Enson

he want me fer ol' Miss, an' so Marse Sargeant done leave
me hyar at Enson Hall. While I was hyar bof ob dem imps
was born, but Marse St. Clar he good bit older dan Isaac.
Many's de time he run me all ober dis plantation when he
no bigger'n dat Thomus Jefferson, 'cause I wouldn't give dat
Isaac fus' help from de chickuns jes' roasted fer dinner befo'
de fambly done seed nary leg ob 'em. Chase me, chile, wid
a pissle pinted plum' at me."

"Lordy! wha' you reckon he do ef he come back hyar
now?"

"I don' reckon on nuffin but dev'ment, jes' same as he
done time an' time agin when he were a boy—jes' dev'ment."

"Mammy, you say oder day when Missee Hagar git mer-
ried to Marse Ellis: 'Now dat St. Clar'll stan' no chance ob
gittin' de property'; what you mean by dat?"

"Didn't mean nuffin," snapped her mother, with a suspicious look at her. "G' 'long 'bout yo' bisness; you's gittin'
mighty pert sence you git to be Miss Hagar's maid; you's
axin' too many questions."

In a day or so the family settled down to Isaac's presence
as a matter of course. Aunt Henny's predictions about the
weather were verified, and the week was unpleasant. The
wind blew the bare branches of the trees against the veranda
posts and roared down the wide fireplaces; snowflakes were
in the air. Hagar and Ellis had just come in from a canter
over the country roads; she went immediately to her room to
dress for dinner, but Ellis tarried a moment in the inviting
room which seemed to command his admiration. The luxuries
addressed themselves to his physical sense, and he was conscious of complete satisfaction in the knowledge that his wealth
could procure a fitting setting for the gem he had won. Other
thoughts, too, crept in, aroused by the talk of a friend where
they had called on the way home. He had not thought of

war, and was not interested in politics; still, if it were true that complications were arising that demanded a settlement by a trial of arms, he was ready. "Perhaps we are too happy for it to last," he muttered; "but, come what will, I have been blessed." His gaze followed Marthy's movements mechanically, as she lighted the wax candles and let fall the heavy curtains, shutting the gloom outside in the gathering darkness. He was aroused from the deep revery into which he had fallen by the sound of wheels on the carriage drive. In a moment, before he could cross the room, the door opened and St. Clair Enson entered, followed by the slave-trader, Walker.

"St. Clair! Is it possible!" he cried, striding forward to grasp his brother's hand. "Is it really you? Welcome home!" They shook hands warmly, and then Ellis threw his arm about St. Clair's shoulders, and for a moment the two men gazed in the depths of each other's eyes with emotion too deep for words. The younger man *did* feel for an instant a wave of fraternal love for this elder brother against whom he meditated [an evil] deed.

"Why, Ellis, I do believe you're glad to see me. You're ready to kill the fatted calf to feast the prodigal," St. Clair said, as they fell apart. "My friend, Mr. Walker—Walker, my brother."

"Glad to see you and welcome you to Enson Hall," said Ellis in cordial greeting, his hospitable nature overcoming his repugnance for this man of unsavory reputation.

"Thanky, thanky," said Walker, as he awkwardly accepted the armchair Ellis offered him, and drew near the blazing fire.

"Just in time for dinner; you will dine with us, Mr. Walker." Walker nodded assent.

"Well, Ellis, how's the world using you? You're married,

lucky dog. Got your letter while I was at the nominating convention; it must have followed me about for more than a month. Thought I'd come up and make the acquaintance of my new sister and niece," remarked St. Clair, with careless ease.

"Yes," replied Ellis. Somehow his brother's nonchalant air and careless words jarred upon his ear. "You are always welcome to come when you like and stay as long as you please. This is your home."

"Home with a difference," replied St. Clair, as an evil smile for an instant marred his perfect features.

"He won't stand much show of gittin' eny of this prop'ty now you's got a missus, Mr. Enson," ventured Walker, with a grin. "He's been mighty anxious to meet your missus. Most fellers isn't so oneasy about a sister-in-law, but I reckon this one is different, being report says she's a high-stepper," said Walker, as he grinned at Ellis and cleared his mouth by spitting foul tobacco juice on the polished hearth. Ellis bowed coldly in acknowledgment of his words.

"Mrs. Enson will be down presently. This certainly is a joyful surprise," he said, turning to St. Clair. "Why didn't you send word, and the carriage would have met you at the station?"

"Oh, we came out all right in Walker's trap."

"I'll have it put up." Ellis rose as he spoke.

"No, no; my man will drive me back to the city shortly," Walker broke in.

"I hope you are doing well, St. Clair; where are you from now?"

"Just from Charleston, where I have made a place for myself at last. Politics," he added significantly.

"Ah!"

"Great doin's down in Charleston; great doin's," Walker broke in again.

"No doubt of it; how do you think this matter will end?"

"It's goin' to be the greatest time the world ever saw, Mr. Enson. When we git a-goin' thar'll be no holdin' us. The whole South, sah, is full of sodjers, er-gittin' ready to whup the Yanks t'uther side of nex' week. That's how it's goin' to end."

"Then it will really be war?"

"The greatest one the worl' ever seen, sah, unless the Yanks git on their knees and asks our pardon, and gives up this govinment to their natral rulers. Why, man, ain't yer heard? You's a patriot, ain't you? Yer a son of the sunny South, ain't yer?"

Ellis smiled at his enthusiasm, although filled with disgust for the man.

"When one has his family to think of, there are times when he forgets the world and thinks of nothing but his home. Be that as it may, I am no recreant son of the South. I stand by her with all I possess. I can imagine nothing that would turn me a traitor to my section."

"Spoken like a man. That's the talk, eh, Enson?" he said, appealing to St. Clair, who nodded in approval.

"Do all you can, I say, for the Confederate States of America, from givin' 'em yer money down to helpin' 'em cuss."

"When the time comes I shall not be found wanting. By the way, St. Clair, your boy Isaac is here. Came on us suddenly the other day."

"Ha, ha, ha! the little black rascal. Didn't I tell you he'd do Johnson out of that money? He's the very devil, that boy."

"Like master, like man," replied St. Clair, with a shrug of his handsome shoulders.

"What is it?" asked Ellis sternly; "no cheating or swindling, is there?"

"He's a runaway. I sold him to a gentleman about a week ago," was St. Clair's careless answer.

"What is the man's name, and where is he to be found? he must be reimbursed or Isaac returned to him," said Ellis, looking sternly at his brother. "Enson Hall is no party to fraudulent dealings."

"I'm glad to hear you say that, Mr. Enson; I'm up here lookin' for a piece of property belonging to me, and said to be stopping on this very plantation."

"Impossible, sir; all our slaves have been here from childhood, or have grown old with us. You have been misinformed."

"I reckon not. As I was tellin' your brother here, it's a mighty onpleasant job I've got before me, but I must do my dooty." Walker put on a sardonic smile, and continued:

"I see, sah, that you don' understan' me. Let me explain further: Fourteen years ago I bought a slave child from a man in St. Louis, and not being able to find a ready sale for her on account of her white complexion, I lent her to a Mr. Sargeant. I understand that you have her in your employ. I've come to get her." Here the slave-trader took out his large sheepskin pocketbook, and took from it a paper which he handed to Ellis.

Ellis gazed at Walker in bewilderment; he took the paper in his hand and mechanically glanced at it. "Still your meaning is not clear to me, Mr. Walker. I tell you we have no slave of yours on this plantation," but his face had grown white, and large drops of perspiration stood on his forehead.

"Well, sah, I'll explain a leetle more. Mr. and Mrs. Sargeant lived a number of years in St. Louis; they took a female child from me to bring up—*a nigger*—and they passed her off on the commoonity here as their own, and you have *married* her. Is my meaning clear now, sah?"

"Good God!" exclaimed Ellis, as he fell back against the wainscotting, "then this paper, if it means anything, must mean my wife."

"I can't help who it means or what it means," replied Walker, "this yer's the bill of sale, an' there's an officer outside there in the cart to git me my nigger."

"This paper proves nothing. You'll take no property from this house without proper authority," replied Ellis with ominous calm. Walker lost his temper, apparently.

"I hold you in my hand, sah!" he stormed; "you are a brave man to try to face me down with stolen property."

Ellis rose slowly to his feet. Pale, teeth set, lips half parted, eyes flashing lightning—furious, terrible, superb in his wrath. His eyes were fixed on Walker, who, frightened at his desperate look, rose to his feet also, with his hand on his pistol. "You would murder me," he gasped.

Ellis laughed a strange, discordant laugh.

"There is, there must be some mistake here. My wife was the daughter of Mr. Sargeant. There is not a drop of Negro blood in her veins; I doubt, sir, if you have ever seen her. And, Mr. Walker, if you do not prove the charges you have this day insulted me by making, your life shall pay the penalty."

"Well, sah, fetch her in the room here; I reckon she'll know me. She warn't so leetle as to fergit me altogether."

Just at this moment Hagar opened the door, pausing on the threshold, a fair vision in purest white; seeing her husband's visitors, she hesitated. Ellis stepped quickly to her side and took her hand.

"My dear, are you acquainted with this gentleman? Do you remember ever seeing him before?"

She looked a moment, hesitated, and then said: "I think not."

Walker stepped to the mantel where the wax-light would fall full upon his face, and said:

"Why, Hagar, have you forgotten me? It's only about fourteen years ago that I bought you, a leetle shaver, from Rose Valley, and lent you to Mrs. Sargeant, ha, ha, ha!"

Hagar put her hand to her head in a dazed way as she heard the coarse laugh of the rough, brutal slave-trader. She looked at Ellis, put out her hand to him in a blind way, and with a heartrending shriek fell fainting to the floor.

(To be continued.)

CHAPTER V.—(Concluded)

"I thought she'd remember," exclaimed Walker.

Ellis raised his wife in his arms and placed her upon a sofa. St. Clair stood watching the scene with a countenance in which curiosity and satisfaction struggled for the mastery.

"Throw a leetle water in her face, and that'll bring her to. I've seen 'em faint befo', but they allers come to."

Ellis was deathly white; he turned his flaming eyes upon the trader:

"The less you say, the better. By God! I have a mind to put a ball in you now, you infernal hound!"

"Yes, but she's mine; I want to see that she's all right," and Walker shrank away from the infuriated man.

Ellis took his wife in his arms and bore her from the room. Shortly, Aunt Henny brought them word to dine without him, their rooms were ready, and he would see Mr. Walker in the morning after he had communicated with his lawyer. The officer was dismissed, and drove back to the town. As they sat at the table enjoying the sumptuous fare and perfect appointments, St. Clair said to Walker:

"Is this thing true?"

"True as gospel. The only man who could prove the girl's birth is the one I took her from, and he's dead."

"Well, you've done me a mighty good turn, blame me if you have'nt. I shan't forget it. Here's to our future prosperity," and he touched his wineglass to his friend's.

"I don't mean you shall forget," was Walker's reply as he sat his glass down empty. "Now, siree, you hang about here for a spell and watch the movements. He'll pay me all right, but you mustn't let him snake her off or anything. Ef things look queer, jes' touch the wires and I'll be with you instanter."

On the following morning Ellis Enson's lawyer, one of the ablest men of the Maryland Bar, pronounced the bill of sale genuine, for it had been drawn up by a justice, and witnessed by men who sent their affadavits under oath.

"There is but one thing to be done, Mr. Walker," Ellis said, after listening to his lawyer's words. "What do you want? How much money will it take to satisfy you to say no more about the matter?"

"I don't bear you any malice for nothing you've said ter me; perhaps I'd do about the same as you have ef it was my case. Five thou, cash, will git her, though ef I toted her to New Orleans market, a handsome polished wench like her would bring me any gentleman's seven or eight thou, without a remark. As for the pickaninny—"

"What!" thundered Ellis, "the child, too?"

"In course," replied Walker, drawing his fingers in and out his scraggy whiskers, "the child follows the condition of the mother, so I scoop the pile."

Ellis groaned aloud.

"As I was sayin'," continued Walker, "the pickaninny will cost you another thou, and cheap at that."

"I would willingly give the money twice over, even my whole fortune, if it did not prove my wife to be of Negro blood," replied Ellis, with such despair in his tones that even these men, inured to such scenes from infancy, were touched with awe.

The money was paid, and within the hour the house had resumed its wonted quiet and all was apparently as before; but the happiness of Enson Hall had fled forever.

CHAPTER VI

Marthy was horrified to see how her mistress arose from the couch where her husband placed her, fall on her knees beside it, and burst into wild tempestuous sobbing.

"Lor', Missee Hagar! Lor', honey! Don' cry so, don', honey!"

Hagar suddenly arose, caught her by the shoulders and turned her toward the light, minutely examining the black skin, crinkled hair, flat nose and protruding lips. So might her grandmother have looked.

"Fo' mercy sake, is you sick, Miss Hagar?" cried the girl, frightened at the strange glare in the large dark eyes. But Hagar turned away without replying. Marthy hurried down stairs.

"My soul, Mammy," she cried as she burst into the kitchen, "Miss Hagar done gone clean destructed."

Once more Hagar crouched upon the floor. She felt like writhing and screaming, only her tongue seemed paralyzed. She thought and thought with agonizing intensity. Vaguely, as in a dream, she recalled her stay in Rose Valley and the terror of her childish heart caused by the rough slave-trader. Could it be true, or was it but a hideous nightmare from which she would soon awake? Her mother a slave! She wondered that the very thought did not strike her dead. With shrinking horror she contemplated the black abyss into which the day's events had hurled her, leaving her there to grovel and suffer the tortures of the damned. Her name gone, her pride of birth shattered at one blow! Was she, indeed, a descendant of naked black savages of the horrible African jungles? Could it be that the blood of generations of these unfortunate ones flowed through her veins? Her education, beauty, refinement, what did they profit her now if—horrible thought—Ellis, her husband, repudiated her? Her heart almost ceased beating with the thought, and she crouched still lower in the dust of utter humiliation.

Then she rose and walked about the room; it was crowded with her wedding finery. She touched an article here and there with the solemnity that we give to the dead—they were relics of a time that would never return to her. She examined her features in the mirror, but even to her prejudiced eyes there was not a trace of the despised chattel. One blow with her open hand shattered its shining surface and the pieces flew about in a thousand tiny particles; she did not notice in her frenzy that the hand was torn and bleeding. Then she laughed a dreadful laugh: first, silently; then in a whisper; then a peal that clashed through the quiet house and reached the sorrow-stricken man in the silent library. He shuddered, but did not move; he could not face her yet. Aunt Henny and Marthy stood outside the locked door and whispered to each other: "Missee Hagar done gone mad!"

She paused an instant, in her ceaseless promenade about the room, beside the dressing table where her husband's picture reposed in its nest of silk and lace; she paled and shuddered. Could she expect him to forget all his prejudices, which were also her own? Slavery—its degradation, the pining and fretting of the Negro race in bondage—had always seemed right to her. Although innocent of cruelty to them, yet their wrongs were coming home to her in a two-fold harvest. Yes, Ellis would give her up; he must; it was his duty. Only this morning she was his wife, the honored mistress of his home; tonight what? His slave, his concubine! Horrible fatality that had named her Hagar. Somewhere she had read lines that came back to her vividly now:

> "Farewell! I go, but Egypt's mighty gods
> Will go with me, and my avengers be.
> And in whatever distant land your god,
> Your cruel god of Israel, is known,
> There, too, the wrongs that you have done this day
> To Hagar and your first-born,
> Shall waken and uncoil themselves, and hiss
> Like adders at the name of Abraham."

Then she gazed once more upon the pictured face with the strained look we place upon the face of the dead before they are hidden from us forever. They brought the child to the door and begged her to open to it. She heeded it not. Let it die; it, too, was now a slave.

The night passed; it was dawn again. There were sounds

of life from the house below. Some one came slowly up the stairs and paused at her door. Then Ellis's voice, sounding harsh and discordant, said:

"It is I, Hagar."

She opened the door. She nerved herself to hear what he might say. The sense of her bitter shame overpowered her, and she shrank before him, cowering as he closed the door, and stood within the room.

Twice he essayed to speak, and twice a groan issued from his white lips. How could he bear it! She stood before him with clasped hands and hanging head as became a slave before her master. How changed, too, he thought, a blight had even fallen upon her glorious beauty. He who had always upheld the institution as a God-given principle of humanity and Christianity, suddenly beheld his idol, stripped of its gilded trappings, in all its filthiness. Then in his heart he cursed slavery.

"Hagar, I have bought you of that man—Walker—he will not annoy you again."

She did not speak or raise her eyes. Ellis bit his lips until the blood ran in the effort to restrain himself for her sake.

"I have thought the matter over and much as I wish it might be otherwise, much as I would sacrifice for you, I feel it my duty as a Southern gentleman, the representative of a proud old family, to think of others beside myself and not allow my own inclinations to darken the escutcheon of a good old name. I cannot, I dare not, and the law forbids me to acknowledge as my wife a woman in whose veins courses a drop of the accursed blood of the Negro slave."

Still she stood there motionless.

Ellis was in torture. Why did she stand there like a forlorn outcast, in stony despair?

"Speak!" he cried at last, "for God sake say something or I shall die!"

Then she raised her eyes to his for one fleeting moment.

"I do not blame you. You can do nothing else."

He moved a step toward her with a smothered groan, "Dearest, dearest," he whispered, and the tone of his voice carried in it his unshaken love.

"Do not,—do not,—" broke from her white lips and with a smothered cry of agony her reserve broke down and she flung herself upon the couch face down.

Ellis went to her and knelt beside her with his arms about her. Five minutes must have passed while they communed in spirit. There was no sound but the girl's hysterical sobbing.

"I am going away," he said at length: "I cannot stay here and live. I may never return, but I shall leave you amply provided for." Then he rose to his feet and rushed from the room. She heard his footsteps echoing down the empty corridor and pause before the door of the nursery.

Ellis loved his wife devotedly, but the shame of public ostracism and condemnation seemed too much for inherited principles. An hour passed. Once more Ellis resumed his measured pacing in the library. The clock ticked slowly on the mantel, but the beating of his heart outstripped it. He could not follow the plans he had laid out as the path of duty. His visit to the nursery had upset them; parental love, love for his innocent wife, was too strong to be easily cast aside. The ticking of the clock maddened him. It seemed the voice of doom pursuing him—condemning him as a coward— coward—coward. He could stand it no longer. Once more he mounted the stairs to his wife's room.

"Hagar, I cannot do it. We cannot alter the fact that we

are bound by all the laws of God and man for better or worse. I have thought it all out, and I have planned a way."

"It is impossible," she said in quiet despair. "You cannot overcome this fearful thing that has fallen upon us. I myself think and feel as you do. It is enough; I accept my fate."

"Oh, no, no; do not say that!"

"Yes, Ellis," she repeated, her face like snow in its pallor. "Hagar, you do not know what you are saying. You love me, and I love you as my very soul. How were we to know? How could we tell? Therefore, having committed a sin in innocence—if sin it be, and I do not so believe it, for things appear in a different light to me now—we will together live it down. Surely heaven cannot fix the seal of this crime on us forever." The supplication of his voice, his speaking eyes, shook Hagar's heart, so tired and worn with emotion. Her eyes were full of compassion as they rested on him, her lips firm and cold. "I love you, Ellis; you know that, and by that love, although I am your slave and chattel, I know that your love demands naught for your wife but honor. The force of circumstances cannot degrade you—cannot change your chivalrous nature."

"Great heavens! You misunderstand me. I have no hope, no life, apart from you, and I hold you as I cling to salvation, my love, my soul! Listen, Hagar, I have a plan." Bending over her he rapidly outlined a plan of life abroad. They would be remarried, and sail from a Northern port for Europe; there, where the shadow of this crime could not come, they would begin life anew. He had mapped it all out carefully and as she listened she was convinced—it was feasible; it could be done.

Neither of them noticed that the door was ajar; neither did

they hear the light footfall that paused beside it. It was St. Clair.

"Walker was right. We must stop that game," he muttered to himself.

CHAPTER VII

Two weeks had passed since Ellis left his home on the pretext of urgent business, but in reality to make necessary arrangements for an indefinite stay abroad. Ill news travels fast and it was well known all over the plantations and in the neighborhood that the terrible discovery of Hagar's origin had broken up the home life at Enson Hall. Save for St. Clair's presence, the Hall had settled back into its old bachelor state with one difference—in the mistress's suite a beautiful despairing woman sat day after day, with her infant across her knees, eating her heart out in an agony of hope and fear waiting the reprieve from a living death that Ellis's return would bring her.

Here was a woman raised as one of a superior race, refined, cultured, possessed of all the Christian virtues, who would have remained in this social sphere all her life, beloved and respected by her descendants, her blood mingling with the best blood of the country if untoward circumstances had not exposed her ancestry. But the one drop of black blood neutralized all her virtues, and she became, from the moment of exposure, an unclean thing. Can anything more unjust be imagined in a republican form of government whose excuse for existence is the upbuilding of mankind!

These were sorrowful days for the Negroes who could not

bring themselves to look upon their beloved mistress as one
of their race, a share in their sad destiny.

Aunt Henny spent most of her spare time praying and
coaxing Hagar out of the apathy into which she had fallen.

"Bless de Lawd! I know'd dev'ment was on han' when
Marse St. Cla'r done comed home," she said one morning to
Marthy. "Las' time he was here ol' Marse he bus' a blud
vessel in his head an' never know'd a blessed thing fer a
munf, den he die. 'Fore dat he shoot a mon to de college an'
beat de prefesser 'mos' to def. Dais a cuss on dat boy, sho."

"How you tink it come so, Mammy?"

"I hern tell from Aunt Di, who nussed Missee Enson. See
hyar, chile, I don' no 'bout tellin' a disrespons'ble gal like
you fambly secrets,—an' ef you goes to 'peatin' my words all
'roun' de plantation, I hope Marse Ellis whop yer back."
Marthy rolled her eyes in terror and promised to keep her
mammy's revelations as sacred as Scripture.

"You know's dat no one neber goes nigh de old summer
house down dar close to de wharf at de foot ob de garden,
don' you?"

Marthy nodded, and her eyes grew larger as she listened
with bated breath for the ghostly story she was sure would
follow.

"Jes' 'fore Marse St. Cla'r was born, ole Missee Enson
was settin' in there an' a turrible thunder storm came up an'
jes' raised Jeemes Henry with houses an' trees, an' tored up
eberythin'. Ol' Miss so dar 'feared to move even one teeny
bit her li'l' finger. While she sot dar all white an' trimbly de
debbil jes' showed he face to her an' grinned."

"Sure nuff debbil, mammy?" whispered Marthy in awed
accents. Her mammy nodded solemnly in reply.

"Ol' Miss jes' went into conwulshuns an' when dey fin'

her she in dead faint. Dat night Marse St. Clair was born, an' ef de debbil ain't de daddy den dat ol' rapscalion neber had a borned servant in dis sinful wurl'."

"Mammy what you tink de reason de debbil show hisse'f to old Missee Enson?"

"De trubble wid you is, Marthy, dat you is de mos' 'quis'tive gal on dis plantation; you want to know too much, but de ol' fo'ks been hyar long time say dat ol' Marse git mad one day wid Unc' Ned, an' tell oberseer 'whop him.' Unc' Ned conjure man; neber been whopped in all he life. He jes' rub hisse'f all ober wid goopher, put a snake skin 'roun' he neck, a frog in one pocket an' a dry lizard in de oder, an' den he pray to de debbil: 'Dear debbil, I ax you to stan' by me in dis' my trial hour, an' I'll neber 'sert you as long as I live. I's had de power, continer de power; make me strong in your cause, make me faithful to you, an' help me to conquer my enemies, an' I will try to deserve a seat at your right han'!"

As Marthy listened an ashy hue overspread her face and she asked breathlessly:

"Did dey whop him?"

"Bless yer soul, gal, dat was de afternoon 'fore dey was 'gwine ter whop him in de mornin', an' dat bery night de debbil 'pear to ole Miss, an' Unc' Ned neber was whopped tell de day he died, neber."

"He must a been a power, mammy, he cert'nly must."

"But de strangest part was dis: At de bery time ole Miss seen de debbil in de summer house, de oberseer was in de barn an' he 'clar' dat ober in de east corner he saw de lightnin' play, an' while he looked he see hell wid all its torments an' de debbil dar, too, wid his cloven foot, an' a struttin' 'bout like he know'd he was boss; de oberseer was so skeered dat

he run, an' he run, an' he run an' he neber stop runnin' tell
he git plum inter Baltymo'."

" 'Spec'·he know'd he 'long'd to be debbil."

"Course! An' den he sen' ol' Marse word to sen' him his
clo's: 'neber lib on dat plantation agin fer twice yer money;
money no 'ducemen'."

"Mammy, mammy," this in a whisper, "do you b'lieve
Miss Hagar got nigger blud in her?"

"Course not, honey. Somebody roun' hyar done conjured
her. Dat debbil, St. Cla'r, I spec. Now, Marthy, take dat
big silver tray of things up dar to dat po' chile, an' you keep
a poundin' 'tell she ope de do,' po' li'le chile."

Marthy obediently disappeared to execute orders and Aunt
Henny with a dubious shake of her head lifted up her voice
in song:

> I'm a gwine to keep a climbin' high,
>> See de hebbenly lan';
> Till I meet dem er angels in a de sky,
>> See de hebbenly lan'.
>
> Dem pooty angels I shall see,
>> See de hebbenly lan';
> Why don' de debbil let-a-me be,
>> See de hebbenly lan'.

* * * * *

Day succeeded day. There was little communication between
the town and Enson Hall. Inclement weather prevailed for it
was now the latter part of January. The fire of curiosity still
burned fiercely among the rich planters over the "Enson
horror," as it was called, but up at the Hall all seemed quiet.
One bitter morning St. Clair sat at breakfast the picture of
luxurious ease. He felt himself master of the situation already,

and had assumed all the airs of ownership. Aunt Henny felt drawn, sometimes, to "shy a plate at him," as she expressed it to herself.

The odor of roses and lilies mingled pleasantly with that of muffins and chocolate. A man came striding up the avenue. It was Dr. Gaines, the family physician, who owned a neighboring plantation.

"Where is Mr. Enson?" he asked of Isaac, who answered his clamorous call on the resounding brass knocker.

"At breakfas', massa."

"I must see him at once. I have news for him."

As the doctor entered the room, St. Clair Enson was leaning back in his chair snapping his fingers at a hound stretched on a rug at his side. The doctor was unceremonious:—

"I regret to say, that I come as the bearer of evil tidings."

"Shall I bid Isaac set another plate, doctor? No? You have taken breakfast? At this hour? You are a primitive people in this rural district, truly. You should mingle with the world as I have and become capable of enjoying the delights and privileges of civilized life. May I ask the nature of the news you bring?" The doctor was a kind old man though somewhat brusque. He averted his eyes, and answered in a low voice.

"It relates to your brother. Mr. Enson, when did Ellis leave home, and when was he expected back?"

"My brother Ellis? He left home about two weeks ago, for what reason he did not state. I do not know when to look for his return; he may drop in, unexpectedly, at any moment."

The doctor was preternaturally grave.

"And you have heard nothing from him since?"

"No, I have not."

The doctor grew graver yet.

"My dear sir, early this morning my boy Sam had occasion

to cross the foot of your land, where the remains of the old wharf enter the stream, and there he stumbled upon a frightful thing—the dead body of a man!"

"Not a pleasant sight," said St. Clair as he helped himself to another hot cake.

"Evidently, the body has been there two or three days. There is an ugly wound in the head that completely disfigures the face, and an empty pistol by the side of the body tells its own pitiful tale. St. Clair Enson that dead man was—"

St. Clair shifted uneasily in his chair as he looked the speaker in the eye, then started to his feet.

"My brother?"

"Your brother!"

To Dr. Gaines's eyes the cold, pale face into which he gazed did not change, only the gaze sought the floor.

"That is strange. Was he robbed also?"

"No. A large sum of money is on the body; papers and his watch. Sam ran home to me, and I summoned help, and was among the first to reach the spot."

The hound leaped suddenly to his feet and began to howl.

"Was it murder or suicide?" asked St. Clair in a calm voice.

"That cannot be decided yet. Finding his valuables untouched, and his hand frozen to his pistol, seems to point to suicide; that will be determined at the inquest." Dr. Gaines turned from the window by which he was standing, and said: "The remains of your brother are being brought home."

A little procession of Negroes, with heads uncovered, advanced up the avenue, slowly, between the grand old beeches, their tread-echoing in a solemn thud upon the frozen ground. A cloth was spread decently over the mangled face. In the silence and majesty of death the master returned to his home. His unlucky life had come to a sudden close. In midnight solitude and shadowed by mystery the curtain fell on the tragedy.

St. Clair advanced with a firm step to meet the bearers; there was no sign of grief in his face. The servants crowded the hall, standing in terrified silence broken only by Aunt Henny's sobs and lamentations. St. Clair lifted the cloth that covered the dead face with a hand that did not tremble, under the curious gaze of Dr. Gaines.

"Mr. Enson," said the doctor at length, "your brother had a wife or one whom we believed his wife," he corrected at St. Clair's negative gesture. "Will you not notify her of his death? She must be suffering anxiety concerning him."

"True; I had forgotten her," muttered St. Clair with a shrug of his handsome shoulders. "Yes, doctor, you break the news to her." The doctor left the room. Presently there was a scream in a woman's voice as of one in mortal agony, an opening and closing of doors and a hurrying of feet; then silence broken only by the pitiful wail of a young child.

There was an inquest at which Walker, the speculator, corroborated the evidence of St. Clair Enson—that the deceased was laboring under great depression at the time of his leaving home, and of his avowed purpose to shoot himself as the shortest way out of his family difficulties. This testimony so clearly given produced a profound impression upon the listeners. It was hoped by many that Hagar would testify, but they were doomed to disappointment. The pistol was well-known to many friends as well as to his servants, as the one Ellis Enson always carried. The watch was the old-fashioned timepiece that his father had carried before him. The papers were legal documents made by the family lawyer and having no bearing on the case.

The jury rendered a verdict of suicide. Plainly, Ellis Enson had died by his own hand.

There was a stately funeral: St. Clair Enson buried his brother with every outward mark of wealth and pomp. The servants moved about the house with red eyes and stealthy steps while from the quarters the wind bore the sound of mournful wailing.

It was a bleak night. The new master of the Hall and the slave-trader, now his inseparable companion, sat before the fire consulting about the disposal of the slaves.

"I'm going to let them all go, Walker, and only keep a small working gang to till the ground and look after the Hall."

"Jes' so," replied Walker, as he folded a fat bundle of bills into his pocket-book and carefully replaced the same in his hip pocket.

"That's a sensible thing to do. It won't be six months from now before we'll all be fighting Yankees like mad, and then where'd your niggers be so nigh as this plantation is to Washington. Best be on the safe side is my idee. And there's the missis—" At this moment the door opened unceremoniously and Hagar came straight up to the two men, seated before the blazing fire. Her dark eyes shone like stars, her face was white as the snow that covered the fields outside, her long hair hung in a straggling mass, rough and unkept, about her shoulders and over her sombre dress. A more startled apparition could not well be imagined. An exclamation broke from the lips of both men.

"I have come without your bidding, sir, for I have something to say to you," she said, addressing St. Clair without bestowing a glance on the man Walker. She cast a wild look around the sumptuous room.

"So you take your ease while he sleeps in his coffin. You need not frown. I do not fear you. Life has no terrors to offer me now." She towered above him as he sat crouched in his chair, and she looked down upon him with a wicked glare in her eyes.

"The question I came to ask is this—St. Clair Enson, do you believe that your brother died by his own hand?"

"Most certainly," Enson constrained his white lips to answer.

"Ellis was killed, murdered—shot down like a dog! What did the pistol prove? Nothing. His pockets had not been rifled. That proves nothing. Neither his great trouble brought to him by his marriage with me—a Negro—would have driven him to self-destruction. He was murdered!"

A chill crept over her listeners. No one had ever seen the gentle Hagar Sargeant in her present character.

"Murdered?" gasped St. Clair.

"Yes," she shouted. "You are his murderer!"

He recoiled as if she had struck him a blow.

"Mad woman! You are mad I say, trouble has turned your brain!"

"It was you who drove him forth from a happy home. You who found your twin demon and brought home the story that broke his heart, ruined his life and gained for you the wealth you have always coveted. I repeat, you are his murderer!"

St. Clair cringed; then he sprang to his feet and seized her by the arm.

"This is too much for any man to stand from a nigger-wench. You have sealed your own fate. Off you go, my fine madam, to the Washington market in short meter. I would have kept you near me, and made your life as easy as it has been in the past, but this settles it. Walker," he said as he turned to the speculator, "you have my permission to take this nigger and her brat whenever it pleases you." Then he released her.

Hagar eyed the man critically from head to foot.

"Selfish, devilish, cruel," she said slowly; "think not that your taunts or cruelties can harm me; I care not for them. No heart in your bosom; no blood in your veins! You are his slayer, and his blood is crying from the ground against you this very hour."

It was more than he could bear. Again he sprang from his seat and seized her arm. Walker took her by the other one and between them they dragged her toward the entrance.

"Easy, easy!" exclaimed Walker in a warning voice to St. Clair. "Don't injure the sale of your property, Enson." St. Clair dropped his hold and again returned to his seat by the fire.

"There, there, my dear, you're a leetle bit excited an' no wonder. Go to your room and rest yourself, my dear, I recommend gin. Gin with a leetle hot water, sugar and spice is very nice, very nice for hysterics, and soothing, very soothing to a gal's nerves." Walker punctuated his remarks with many a little thump and pat in her back.

With a defiant smile, Hagar paused on the threshold and said:

"It's the truth! you're his murderer, and in spite of the wealth and position you have played for and won, you have seen the last on this earth of peace or happiness." Then striking her breast, she added:

"As I have parted with the same friends! Pleasant dreams to you, St. Clair Enson, master of Enson Hall!"

CHAPTER VIII

It will be remembered that on February 4, 1861, a provisional government was formed for the "Confederate States of America." This provisional government was soon superseded by a "permanent" one, under whose constitution Jefferson Davis, Alexander H. Stevens and other officials were to serve six years, from February 22, 1862. A Peace Congress composed of delegates from twenty states, held a session for three weeks at Washington, in February, 1862. In March, same year, a Commission also went to the Capital City to negotiate for a settlement of difficulties; but all these overtures failed. Being called to Washington as a leading delegate, with power to help settle all these great questions that were then agitating the country, St. Clair Enson and Walker decided that it would be best to close the Hall, leaving Isaac, Aunt Henny and Marthy in charge of the house, and take the rest of the hands to Washington, where so many rich and influential men would congregate from the most southern parts of the country, that they would be assured of quick sales and large profits.

On the morning of departure, the small colony of black men and women sat and stood about the familiar grounds stunned and hopeless. Here most of them were born, and here they had hoped to die and be buried. The unknown future was a gulf of despair. Ellis was a good master, kind and considerate; their sincere mourning for him was mingled with grief at their own fate.

In the midst of a motley group Hagar stood with her child clasped in her arms,—hopeless, despairing. She had felt her degradation before, but not until now had she drained the bitter cup of misery.

Ellis Enson's lawyer had questioned her about her husband's business.

"Did he give you free papers?" with a pitying glance at the fair, crushed woman.

"When he returned, he intended to take me and the child abroad after making ample settlements."

The legal gentleman sighed.

"It was a great oversight—a great mistake."

So no papers, bearing upon the case, being found, all the Sargeant fortune reverted by law to the master. Nothing could be done.

Then began the humiliating journey to Washington, herding with slaves, confined in pens like cattle, the delicately nurtured lady tasted of the torments of those accursed. Her brain grew wild; she folded her infant closer to her breast— sang, whispered, laughed and wept.

Upon reaching the private slave-pen, a number of which then disgraced the national capital, she fell into a state of melancholy from which nothing aroused her but the needs of the child.

A purchaser was soon found for the handsome slave, in a New Orleans merchant who agreed to take the child, too, for the sake of getting the mother out of the city without trouble.

At the dusk of the evening, previous to the day she was to be sent off, as the prison was being closed for the night, Hagar, with her child closely clasped in her arms, darted past the keeper and ran for her life. It was not far from the prison to the long bridge which passes from the lower part of the city, across the Potomac, to the forests of Arlington

Heights. Thither the fugitive directed her flight. The keeper by this time had recovered from the confusion incident to such a daring and unexpected attempt, he rallied his assistants and started in pursuit. On and on she flew, seeming tireless in her desperate resolve. It was an hour when horses could not be easily obtained; no bloodhounds were at hand to run her down. It was a trial of speed and endurance.

The pursuers raised the hue-and-cry as they followed, gaining steadily upon the fugitive. Astonished citizens poured forth from their dwellings to learn the cause of the alarm, and learning the nature of the case fell in with the motley throng in pursuit. With the speed of a bird, having passed the avenue, she began to gain, and presently she was upon the Long Bridge. Panting, gasping, she hushed her babe, appealed to God in broken sentences, and gathered all her courage to dash across the bridge and lose herself in the friendly shelter of the woods. Oh, will she,—can she, make it! Already her heart began to beat high with hope. Courage! She had only to pass three-quarters of a mile more and all would be well, the woods would shelter her, night would cover her and save her.

Just as the pursuers passed the draw they beheld three men slowly approaching from the Virginia shore. They called to them to help arrest the runaway slave. As she drew near they formed a line across the bridge to intercept her. Now the panting woman, hard-pressed on every side, suddenly stopped.

She looked wildly and anxiously around to see if all hope were indeed gone; far below the ridge rolled the dark waters, sullen, angry, threatening. Before and behind were the voices of the profane, inhuman monsters into whose hands she must inevitably fall. Her resolution was taken. She kissed her babe, clasped it convulsively in her arms, saying:

"Alas, poor innocent, there is one gift for thee yet left for your unfortunate mother to bestow,—it is death. Better so than the fate reserved for us both."

Then she raised her tearful, imploring eyes to heaven as if seeking for mercy and compassion, and with one bound sprang over the railing of the bridge, and sank beneath the waters of the Potomac river.

(To be continued.)

CHAPTER IX

TWENTY YEARS LATER

It was a fine afternoon in early winter in the year 1882, in the city of Washington, the beautiful capital of our great Republic. Pennsylvania Avenue was literally crammed with foot-passengers and many merry sleighing parties, intent on getting as much enjoyment as possible out of the day.

Freezing weather had been followed by a generous fall of frozen, down-like flakes. Quick to take advantage of a short-lived pleasure, vehicles of every description were flying along the avenue filled with the elite of the gay city. The stream of well-dressed pedestrians moved swiftly over the snowy pavements, for the air was too cold for prolonged lingering, watching with interest, in which envy mingled to some extent, the occupants of the handsome carriages gliding along so rapidly on polished runners. Every notable of the capital was there from the President in his double-runner to the humble clerk in a single-seated modest rig.

A sumptuous Russian sleigh drawn by two splendid black horses, with a statuesque driver in ebony handling the ribbons, attracted the attention of the crowd as it dashed down the avenue and paused near the capitol steps. Two ladies were its occupants. The elder was handsome enough to demand more than a passing glance from the most indifferent, but her young companion was a picture as she nestled in luxurious ease among the costly robes, wrapped in rich furs, from which her delicate face shone out like a star upon the curious throng. That she was a stranger to the crowd could be easily told from the questioning glances which followed the turn-out.

As they passed the Treasury Department two men, both past their first youth, though one was at least twenty years older than the other, came down the steps, and paused a moment, to follow with their eyes the Russian sleigh with the beautiful girl, before mingling with the living stream that flowed from between the great stone columns and spread itself through the magnificent streets of the national capital.

"Really, Benson," remarked the elder man as they resumed their walk, "the most beautiful girl I have seen for many a day. You know everyone worth knowing; who is she?"

At this moment an elderly man of dark complexion, in stylish street costume, but with a decidedly Western air, came down the capitol steps followed by a young man. Both were warmly greeted by the occupants of the sleigh. The dark man spoke a few words to the driver, then both men entered the carriage and it dashed off rapidly.

"That is Senator Bowen, his wife and daughter. He is the new millionaire senator from California. I am not acquainted with the ladies, but after their ball I intend to become assiduous in my attentions."

"Oh! then they are the Bowens! How I wish I knew them. I predict a sensation over the young beauty. Who's the young man?"

"Cuthbert Sumner, my private secretary. Deuced fine fellow, too."

The conversation drifted away from the Bowens, and they were apparently forgotten.

"How was it at the Clarks' last night, Benson, as bad as you expected?"

"Worse if possible. It was dev'lish slow! Nothing stronger than bouillon, not a chance to buck the tiger even for one moment, not a decent looking woman in the rooms. All the women fit for pleasant company give that woman's house a wide berth. Dashed if I blame 'em. The only thing that gives the Clarks a standing is his position. I can't see how he puts up with her. If I had a sanctimonious woman like her for a wife I'd cut and run for it, dashed if I wouldn't."

His companion laughed long and loud.

"No fun for you there, eh, Benson? My boy, you'll never fit into the dignified position of a father of this country, I fear. Oh, well; it's hard to teach an old dog new tricks."

"Yes, but think of not being able to give your friends a decent time, because your wife has a fad on temperance and thinks it a sin to smell a claret cup or a brandy-and-soda. A man with a wife of that sort ought to leave her at home, where she could rule the roost to her heart's content. The seat of government is no place for a missionary." "Well, there's always a way to remedy such things when you know your hostess."

"Of course, of course," General Benson hastened to reply. "Our bouillon was washed down with Russian tea a la Russe. We doctored it in the coatroom."

The two men indulged in a hearty laugh.

"Well, Benson, you'll do," remarked the elder when their mirth had somewhat subsided. "For a dignified chief of a division you're a rare bird."

After a moment's silence, General Benson asked:

"Is Amelia come?"

"Yes, got here last night?"

"Good. It's a relief to be with a woman who can join a man in a social glass, have a cigar with him, or hold her own in winning or losing a game with no Sunday-school nonsense about her. It's hard work keeping up to it, Major; one needs a friend to help one out."

"When's the session end?"

"Next week, thank heaven."

"Sick of politics, too, old man?"

"No; but it's been nothing but wind. Words—words—words—"

"And mutual abuse," broke in the Major, laughing. "Exactly; with nothing accomplished. Can't seem to throw much dust in the eyes of these old fossils."

"The truth is, Benson, the South has a hard, rough road before her to even things up with the North; we've got to go slow until some of the old fire-eaters die out and a new generation comes in."

"It'll be slow enough, never you fear. At present we are in a Slough of Despond; heaven knows when we'll get out of it. My position in the Treasury brings the secret workings under my eye. I know."

"Slough!" retorted the Major; "call it a bog at once. And to think of the money we have lost for the Cause."

"And my exile abroad that my mix-up in the Lincoln assassination caused me. Do you know, Major, if it were known that I am my father's son, they'd hang me even now with little ceremony."

"Thank God they don't know it, my boy, and take courage."

"I'll get mine out of it by hook or by crook," replied Benson with a savage look. "The country owes me a fortune, and I'm bound to have it."

The two had reached the corner made historical by the time-honored political headquarters, Willard's Hotel. They paused before separating.

"By the by, Major, I'll get you cards for the Bowens' ball if you like. It would be a great chance for Amelia."

"If I like! Why, man, I'll be your everlasting debtor."

"Very well; consider it done."

"A thousand thanks." The friends parted.

General Benson entered the hotel, where he had apartments, and the Major wended his way to his home, a handsome house in a quiet side street.

' CHAPTER X

THE FAMILY OF A MILLIONAIRE

Senator Zenas Bowen, newly elected senator from California, and many times a millionaire, occupied a mansion on 16th Street, N. W., in close proximity to the homes of many politicians who have made the city of Washington famous at home and abroad.

There were three persons in the Bowen family—the Honorable Zenas Bowen, his wife Estelle and his daughter Jewel. This was his second season in Washington. The first year he was in the House and his work there was so satisfactory to his constituents that the next season he was elected with a great flourish of trumpets to fill the seat in the Senate, made vacant by a retiring senator.

The Honorable Zenas was an example of the possibilities of individual expansion under the rule of popular government. Every characteristic of his was of the self-made pattern. In familiar conversation with intimate friends, it was his habit to fall into the use of ungrammatical phrases, and, in this, one might easily trace the rugged windings of a life of hardship among the great unwashed before success had crowned his labors and steered his bark into its present smooth harbor. He possessed a rare nature: one of those genial men whom the West is constantly sending out to enrich society. He had begun life as a mate on a Mississippi steamboat. When the Civil War broke out, he joined the Federal forces and at its close was mustered out as "Major Bowen." His wife dying about this time, he took his child, Jewel, and journeyed to California, invested his small savings in mining property in the Black Hills. His profits were fabulous; he counted his pile way up in the millions.

His appearance was peculiar. Middle height, lank and graceless. He had the hair and skin of an Indian, but his eyes were a shrewd and steely gray, wherein one saw the spirit of the man of the world, experienced in business and having that courage, when aroused, which is common to genial men of deadly disposition. Firm lips that suggested sternness gave greater character to his face, but his temper was known to be most mild. He dressed with scrupulous neatness, generally in black broadcloth. There was no denying his awkwardness; no amount of polish could make him otherwise. His relation to his family was most tender, his wife and daughter literally worshipping the noble soul that dwelt within its ungainly casket.

After Fortune had smiled on him, one day while stopping at the Bohemian, a favorite resort in 'Frisco, he was waited on by a young woman of great beauty. The Senator fell in love with her immediately and at the end of a week proposed marriage. Fortunate it was for him that Estelle Marks, as she was called, was an honorable woman who would not betray his confidence. She accepted his offer, vowing he should never have cause to regret his act. One might have thought from her eager acceptance that in it she found escape, liberty, hope.

"Yes," she said, "I will marry you."

He was dazed. He could not speak for one moment so choked was he with ecstasy at his own good fortune. He covered his eyes with his hand, and then he said in a hoarse voice: "I swear to make you happy. My own happiness seems more than I can believe."

Then she stooped suddenly and kissed his hand. He asked her where she would like to live.

"Anywhere you think best," was her reply.

He assured her that the North Pole, Egypt, Africa—all were one to him, with her and his little daughter. And so they were married.

He had never regretted the step. Estelle was a mother to the motherless child, and being a well-educated woman, versed in the usages of polite society, despite her recent position as a waitress in a hotel, soon had Jewel at a first-class school, where she could be fitted for the position that her father's wealth would give her. Nor did Estelle's good work end there. She recognized her husband's sterling worth in business and morals, and insisted upon his entering the arena of politics. Thanks to her cleverness, he made no mistakes and many hits which no one thought of tracing to his wife's rare talents. Not that Bowen was a fool; far from it. Mrs. Bowen simply fulfilled woman's mission in making her husband's career successful by the exercise of her own intuitive powers. His public speeches were marked by rugged good sense. His advice was sagacious. He soon had enthusiastic partisans and became at last a powerful leader in the politics of the Pacific Slope. All in all, Mrs. Bowen was a grand woman and Senator Bowen took great delight in trying to further her plans for a high social position for himself and the child.

Jewel Bowen's beauty was of the Saxon type, dazzling fair, with creamy roseate skin. Her hair was fair, with streaks of copper in it; her eyes, gray with thick short lashes, at times iridescent. Her nose superbly Grecian. Her lips beautifully firm, but rather serious than smiling.

Jewell was not unconscious of her attractions. She had been loved, flattered, worshipped for twenty years. She was proud with the pride of conscious worth that demanded homage as a tribute to her beauty—to herself.

Her tastes were luxuriously simple; she reveled in the dainty accessories of the toilet. To the outside world her dress was severely plain, but her dressmaker's bill attested to the cost of her elegant simplicity.

It was but a short time since Jewel had been transported from her quiet Canadian convent into the whirl of Washington life, a splendid house, more pretty dresses than she could number, a beautiful mother, albeit a step-mother, more indulgent than most mothers, fairly adoring the sweet and graceful girl so full of youth's alluring charm, and a father who was the noblest, tenderest and wisest of men. But she was a happy-hearted girl, full of the joy of youth and perfect health. She presented a bright image to the eye all through the fall, as she galloped over the surrounding country on her thoroughbred mare, followed by her groom and two or three dogs yapping at her heels.

There was perfect accord between her and her step-mother. Mrs. Bowen shared the Senator's worship of Jewel. From the moment the two had met and the child had held her little arms toward her, blinking her great gray eyes in the light that had awakened her from her slumbers, and had nestled her downy head in the new mother's neck with a sigh of content, almost instantly falling asleep again, with the words: "Oh, pitty, pitty lady!"

Estelle Bowen had kissed her passionately again and again, and from that time Jewel had been like her very own. The young step-mother trained the child carefully for five years, then very reluctantly sent her to the convent of the Sacred Heart at Montreal, where she had remained until she was eighteen. Then followed a year abroad, and her meeting with Cuthbert Sumner.

About this time events crowded upon each other in her young life. Her father's rise was rapid in the money world and, together with his political record, gave his family access to the wealthiest and most influential society of the country.

Cuthbert Sumner, her acknowledged lover, was an only child of New England ancestry favored by fortune like herself. His father, a wealthy manufacturer, was the owner of a business that had been in the Sumner family for many generations. His mother had died while he was yet a lad. It was a dull home. The son just leaving Harvard, had been expected to assume the responsibilities of his father's establishment, but having no taste for a commercial life, and being fitted by nature as well as education for a career in politics, his father reluctantly gave his consent that Cuthbert should have his wish after a few years spent in travel had acquainted him with the great world.

Mr. Sumner, senior, finding his son's desires still unchanged upon his return from abroad, used his influence and obtained for him a position in the Treasury as private secretary in General Benson's department. So young Sumner was duly launched upon the sea of politics. The world of fashion surged about him and he soon found himself a welcome guest in certain homes. He had little leisure for society, but sought it more after he attended Jewel Bowen's "coming-out" reception, a year previous to this chronicle. There he had seen a maiden in white, her arms laden with fragrant flowers, with beautiful fearless eyes which looked directly into the secret depths of his heart.

Sumner was twenty-six and this was not his first experience with women. He had been in love with the sex, more or less, since the day he left off knee-breeches. As he looked into Jewel's eyes he remembered some of his experiences with a pang of regret. He was no better, no worse than most young fellows. He had played some, flirted some, had even been gloriously hilarious once, for all of which his conscience now whipped him soundly. Jewel looked upon him with mingled feelings, in which curiosity was uppermost. In her world money was the potent factor; but in this man she saw the result of generations of culture and wealth combined.

One afternoon when they were calling, about the time of her "coming-out" party, a friend of Mrs. Bowen had mentioned him: "Such a fascinating man! and so handsome! Will you let me bring him? He's a man you must know, of course, and the sooner the better."

"We shall be very pleased," Mrs Bowen replied; "any friend of yours is welcome."

"Thanks. That's settled then."

"He looks very different from the most of the men one meets in Washington," remarked Jewel, who was examining the pictured face that smiled at her from its ornate frame on the mantel.

"How?"

"Oh, I don't know. More manly, I suppose would explain it."

"Wait till you know him," returned the matron with a meaning smile.

"Cuthbert Sumner," Jewel repeated to herself. Yes, they talk so much of him, all the women seem to have lost their hearts to him. I wonder if he will, after all, be worth the knowing."

That was the beginning. The end was in sight from the time they first met. It was a desperate case on both sides. None was surprised at the announcement of the engagement the previous winter. It was understood that the wedding would take place at Easter.

*   *   *   *   *

"The Bowens are in town." That meant a vast deal to the important section of Washington's world which constitutes "society," for the splendid mansion, closed since the daughter's brief introduction to society, it was rumored, would be added to the list of places where one could dance, dine and flirt. Festivities were to open with a ball—a marvel of splendor, for which five hundred invitations had been issued.

Senator Bowen was walking down the avenue the next afternoon, on his way home, when he was joined by General Benson, who had developed lately a passion for his society.

The two men frequented the same clubs and transacted much official business together, but there had been nothing approaching intimacy between them. If the shrewd Westerner had given expression to his secret thoughts they would have run somewhat in the following vein:

"Got a hang-dog look about that off eye which tells me he's a tarnation mean cuss on occasion. He's all good looks and soft sawder. However, that don't worry me any; it's none o' my funeral."

After the two men had exchanged the usual civilities, the latest political question looming up on the horizon was discussed; finally, the conversation turned upon the coming ball.

"By the by, Senator, I wish I dared ask for cards for a friend of mine and his daughter. They have just arrived in town for the season, and know no one. He, the father, is the newly-appointed president of the Arrow-Head mines; the daughter is lovely; a fine foil for Miss Jewel. Unexceptional people, and all that."

"Certainly, General," the Senator hastened to reply. "What address?"

With profuse thanks, General Benson handed him a card, on which appeared the name:

HENRY C. MADISON.
Corcoran Building.   Washington, D. C.

"I will speak to Mrs. Bowen right away."

* * * * *

Mrs. Bowen and Jewel were enjoying a leisure hour before dinner, in lounging chairs before the blazing grate-fire in the former's sitting-room. There was a little purr of gratification from both women as they heard a well-known step in the hall.

"Well, here you both are," was Senator Bowen's greeting as he kissed his wife and daughter and flung himself wearily into a chair.

"Tired?" asked his wife.

"Yes, some of these dumb-headed aristocrats are worse to steer into a good paying bit of business for the benefit of the government treasury, than a bucking bronco."

"How late you are, papa," here broke in Jewel from her perch on her father's knee, where she was diligently searching his pockets. It had been her custom from babyhood, and never yet had her search been unrewarded.

"I'd have been here earlier only I met General Benson and he always has so many questions to ask, especially about my little lass, that he kept me no end of time."

"Don't be wicked, papa," smiled Jewel, "because you spoil me; you think everyone must see with your eyes."

"Ah! pet; it's just wonderful how well all the old and young single fellows know me since you have grown up. But we won't listen to 'em just yet, Blossom; not even Sumner shall part us for a good bit; your pa just can't lose you for a good spell, I reckon."

"No man shall part us, dad; if he takes me, he must take the whole family," replied Jewel with a loving pat on the sallow cheek.

"We'll see, we'll see. There's another bid for an invite to your shin-dig," he continued, with a laugh, as he tossed the card given him by General Benson into his wife's lap. "It's mighty pleasant to be made much of; it's worth while getting rich just to see how money can change the complexion of things, and how cordial the whole world can be to one man if he's got the spondulix."

"My dear Zenas," said Mrs. Bowen, with a shake of her

head and a comical smile on her face, "don't talk the vernacular of the gold mines here in Washington. You'll be eternally disgraced."

"Well, Mrs. Senator, I've fit the enemy, tackled grizzlies, starved, been locked up in the pens of Libby Prison, and I've come out first best every time, but this thing you call society beats me. The women make me dizzy, the men make me sick, and a mighty little of it makes me ready to quit, fairly squashed. Them's my sentiments."

A cry of delight broke from Jewel,—"O dad!" as she brought to view a package in a white paper. Mrs. Bowen left her seat to join in the frolic that ensued to gain possession of it. At last the mysterious bundle was unwrapped, the box opened and a pearl necklace brought to view of wonderful beauty and value. The senator's eyes were full of the glint and glister of love and pride as he watched the faces of his wife and daughter. After a moment he brought out another package, which he gave to his wife.

"There, Mrs. Senator, there's your diamond star you've been pining after for a month. I ordered them quite a while ago; happened to be passing Smith's and stopped in, found 'em ready and here they be. What women see in such gewgaws is a puzzler to me. I can tolerate such hankering in a young 'un, but being you're not a chicken, Mrs. Senator, and not in the market, and still good looking enough to make any man restless with no ornaments but a clean calico frock, your fancies are a conundrum to yours truly. But these women folks must be humored, I suppose."

With this the Senator plunged into his dressing-room, which adjoined his wife's sitting-room, and began the work of dressing for dinner and the theatre.

"Cuthbert coming?" he called to his daughter, who still lingered.

"Yes, papa."

"Jewel, dear, have Venus be particular with your toilet tonight; I will overlook you when she has finished."

"That the name of your new maid, Blossom?" the Senator's voice demanded. There were many grunts, groans and growls issuing from the privacy where his evening toilet was progressing because of refractory collar buttons and other unruly accessories.

"Yes, papa."

"Hump! Name enough to hang her: Venus, the goddess of love and beauty! Can she earn her salt?"

He appeared at the door now struggling into an evening vest. He employed no man, declaring no valley de chamber should boss him around. He'd always been free and didn't propose to end his days in slavery to any slick-pated fashion-plate who didn't know the color of gold from the inside of a brass kettle.

"I don't know what I would do without her. I have been intending to speak to you for some time concerning her brother. He is a genius, and Venus has given up her hopes of becoming a school teacher among her people to earn money to help develop his talents. Can't we do something for them, papa? I have said nothing to her yet."

"Hump! You're always picking up lame animals, Blossom; from a little shaver it's been the same. If you keep it up in Washington, you'll have all the black beggars in the city ringing the area bell. However, I'll look the matter up. If the girl ain't too proud to go out as a servant to help herself along, there may be something in her."

CHAPTER XI

WHO IS SHE?

At eight that evening——Theatre was filled to overflowing, for Modjeska was to interpret the heart-breaking story of "Camille." Senator Bowen and his handsome wife; Jewel and Cuthbert Sumner occupied a box, and were watching intently the mimic portrayal of life. Jewel was listening earnestly to Modjeska's words; the grand rendering of the life story of a passionate, loving, erring, noble woman's heart touched her deeply. The high-bred grace, the dainty foreign accent, the naturalness of the actress, held her in thrall and she did not take her eyes from the stage. As the curtain went down on the second act she lifted her glass and slowly scanned the house. Suddenly she paused with a heart that throbbed strangely. Directly across from her sat a woman—young in years, but with a mature air of a woman of the world. "Surely," thought Jewel, "I know that face." The girl had a woman's voluptuous beauty with great dusky eyes and wonderful red-gold hair. Her dress of moss-green satin and gold fell away from snowy neck and arms on which diamonds gleamed. Just then Sumner uttered an exclamation of surprise. He had turned, almost at the same moment with Jewel, and swept a careless glance over the house, bowing to several, mostly well-known people either by profession or social standing, but had declined to see more than one fair one's invitation. Passing, as it were, a box on the left, his glance had rested on a face that instantly arrested it and caused him to exclaim. An elderly man sat with the vision of loveliness. In repose the girl's face lost some of its beauty and seemed care-worn; one felt impressed that girlhood's innocence had not remained untouched.

The lady was watching their box intently, and seeing herself discovered smiled a brilliant smile of recognition as she inclined her head in Sumner's direction holding his glance for one instant in a way that seemed to call him to her side. He bowed, then turned his head away with a feeling of confusion that annoyed him. He did not offer to go to her, however.

"Do you know her? Who is she, Cuthbert?" asked Jewel, intercepting both smile and bow.

"It is Miss Madison," he replied, lifting his glass non-chalantly. "I did not know she was in Washington. I have not seen her for three years. Looking remarkably well, is she not?"

"She is glorious! Her face somehow seems familiar to me. I must have met her. Have you seen much of her?"

"Can't say that I have. Met her at a ball at Cape May. But I found the place so dull I packed up and went home. After that I went abroad. Then I met a sweet little woman who has led me captive at her chariot wheels ever since."

Then followed some talk dear to the souls of lovers and the beauty opposite was forgotten. But throughout the next act Jewel felt her heart contract as the dusky eyes followed her movements with a restless, smouldering fire in their depths that pained her to see.

Amelia Madison watched the box opposite with hungry intensity. She was studying Jewel's face mentally saying: "There is not another woman in the house like her. She is like a strain of Mozart, a spray of lilies. My God! how he looks at her—he never looked at me like that! He respects her; he worships her—"

She sank back in breathless misery.

Aurelia Madison and Cuthbert Sumner had met one summer at Cape May. They had loved and been betrothed; had quarreled fiercely over a flirtation on her part and had separated in bitterness and pain; and yet the man was relieved way down in a corner of his heart for he had felt dimly, after the first rapture was over, that he was making a mistake, that she was not the woman to command the respect of his friends nor to bring him complete happiness. Yet after a fashion she fascinated him. Her grace, her beauty, thrilled his blood with rapture that he thought then was Love. Love came to him a later guest, and the purity and tenderness of Jewel's sweet face blotted out forever the summer splendor of Aurelia Madison's presence. Now it was all over; he knew he had never loved her, and that he was fortunate to have found it out in time.

No one knew of this episode in Aurelia Madison's life. Her father had been away on one of his periodical tours, and the girl was accountable to none but an old governess who acted as chaperone.

Since that time she had led a reckless life. Had lived at Monte Carlo two seasons, aiding her father in his games of chance, luring the gilded youth to lose their money without murmuring. Hers had been a precarious life and a dangerous one. Sometimes they were reduced to expedients. But through it all the girl held her peace, set her teeth hard, and waited for the day when she should again meet Cuthbert Sumner, trusting to the effect of her great beauty, and the fact that he had once loved her passionately, to re-establish her power over the man she worshipped. Once his wife, she told herself, she would shake off all her hideous past and become an honest matron. Honesty she viewed as a luxury for the wealthy to enjoy. Thank heaven, Cuthbert Sumner's wife could afford to be honest. They had met again, but how? All her hopes were dust.

Now she saw Jewel lifted her eyes to his with devotion, love and faith in them; she saw him look down eagerly, with truest, tenderest love. The last act was on. She could bear it no longer, but rose impatiently, with rage and hatred in her heart, and attended by her father, left the house. When next Jewel stole a glance in the direction of the stranger her place was empty.

CHAPTER XII

A PLOT FOR TEN MILLIONS

It was near nine o'clock the next morning and General Benson was still invisible. His colored valet was moving about noiselessly, making ready for his master. Breakfast was on the table in its silver covers. A bell rang; Isaac disappeared.

General Benson's renown as a great social leader rested, not only on his lavish expenditure and luxurious style of living at Willard's Hotel, where he monopolized one of the most expensive suites, but upon his mental and physical attributes as well. The ladies all voted him a charming fellow. He had a remarkably sweet and caressing voice, which added to his attractions. The many women to whom he had vowed eternal fidelity at one moment, only to abandon heartlessly the next at the rise of a new star in the firmament of beauty, sighed and wept at his defection and voted him the most perfect lover imaginable. It was hinted that one girl had committed suicide solely on his account. But still the ladies believed in his professions.

The members of the various clubs that he affected acknowledged him to be an admirable card-player, a good horseman, an expert with sword or revolver, as well as an unusually agreeable companion in a search after pleasure; generous, too, with his money. But with all his popularity and increase of fame, his fortune declined, and he found himself at the present time embarrassed for money, his capital growing smaller each month in spite of a large salary. Debts of honor must be met, and to keep a good name one's opponent must sometimes win. Then, too, he was growing old; he carried his years well, but fifty was looming perilously near.

He and his friend Major Henry Clay Madison, President of the Arrow-Head Mining Company of Colorado, newly established in the city, had a mutual interest in the great scheme that was to make the fortunes of the different shareholders, but even the generous payments he received as his share of the profits made out of verdant men of means who became easy prey because of General Benson's sweet persuasive voice and exalted position in the political world, failed to assist him out of his financial dilemma. Within a month a new scheme had entered his mind,—one that dazzled him the possibilities were so great, a scheme which if successfully handled would put millions in the pockets of a trio of unscrupulous adventurers,—Major Madison and his daughter and himself.

As the clock chimed nine, General Benson entered the room and seated himself at the breakfast table. A moment later his valet informed him that Major and Miss Madison wished to see him.

"Very well; show them in, at once."

Presently the valet ushered them in. The major we have

mentioned before; he was short, stout, more than fifty, with gray hair and ferret-like eyes, close-set, and a greenish-gray of peculiar ugliness; a close observer would take exception to them immediately. He was scrupulously attired in the height of fashion. He was accompanied by the strange beauty who had attended the theatre the night before.

"Well, General, you sent for us and here we are. How are you?" was the major's greeting as he shook hands with General Benson and then flung himself into an arm-chair.

"Very well, indeed, thanks, Madison. What, is it indeed you, Aurelia?" he exclaimed on beholding the girl. "How delightful to have you with us once again!"

The lady inclined her head slightly in answer to her host's warm greeting, ignored his offered hand, and subsided onto a chair with a preoccupied air, a slight frown puckering her forehead.

"Don't mind Aurelia, General; she's mooning as usual," laughed her father.

"You are looking very fit, Major," remarked Benson, recovering from the confusion caused by Aurelia's coolness. "Have a B. and S.?"

"Don't care if I do."

Benson poured a brandy-and-soda for his guest and another for himself; passed the cigars to him and the cigarettes to Miss Madison. She took one, lit it, and drew away in a manner that showed her keen enjoyment. A smile passed over Benson's face as he covertly watched her.

"Well, Madison," the General said, after a few moments' enjoyment of the weed, "I sent for you to come here this morning on a matter of business, because I shall not be able to call on you at any time today, for I may have to go out of town at any moment on some confounded office business. It's a nuisance, I say. The office interferes too much with a man's pleasure. If my plans succeed I'll cut the whole thing."

"Indeed! I imagine we are mutually interested when you speak of 'business.' You're not ruined I take it. Do you want to borrow money of me?" said the Major with a laugh as he drew his chair a trifle closer to his friend. The lady evinced no interest in the conversation.

"On the contrary, I wish to offer you a chance to make some."

"You are extremely kind, Benson; you could not have chosen a more opportune time for your offer. Will you believe it—I was compelled to part with a diamond pin this morning," replied Madison, touching his polished shirt-front. "But what can I do for you?"

"Since we joined forces, Madison, on the strictly respectable basis, we have gained fame and influence, and but little money. It takes money to maintain our position, and plenty of it. This you know. I have studied the situation and am convinced that our only surety for providing for the future lies in a coup that shall net us millions, on which we may retire."

"Yes, but how to get it," replied Madison with a mournful shake of the head. "Work is not in our line, unsafe expedients are dangerous and not to be thought of. I do not fancy running my head into a noose. One can't do much but go straight here, and money's a scarce article."

"Be patient. You need have no apprehension that I shall suggest anything dangerous, Madison; though the time was when you were the risky one and I the one to hesitate," with a significant uplifting of the eyebrows.

"True; but time has changed my ideas. I have a hankering for respectability that amounts to a passion."

"Remain as respectable as you wish, my friend; I have a legitimate scheme that will make us masters of ten millions! No risk; nothing necessary but judicious diplomacy."

Miss Madison had evinced no interest until now, but at the words "ten millions" uttered by this man whom she knew to be practical, astute in business and no dreamer, she seemed to awaken from her lethargy. She retained her self-possession, however, and maintained her unruffled calm, remarking carelessly, even sarcastically: "May I ask the nature of the plan, General, and where my usefulness comes in?"

"I was about to explain that point, my dear; but first permit me to ask a question,—has the idea of acquiring a fortune by a wealthy marriage ever occurred to you?"

"Yes, I admit it has. But you know too well my reasons for hesitating in such a course."

Benson moved uneasily in his seat, and for a moment his eyes dropped under the steady gaze that the girl bent upon him—eyes large, dreamy, melting, dazzling the senses, but at this moment baleful. A dull flush mounted to his brow.

"See here, Aurelia, have you tried to find an opportunity?"

"Possibly," she answered coldly.

"And you met with no success?"

"Evidently not, as I am single."

"Then your efforts were misdirected."

"Do you think so?" mockingly.

"Most assuredly I do. Your attention was bestowed upon men for whom you had conceived a real liking. That is not the way to bring success in such a venture."

"It is the wrong lead for a woman like me,—an adventuress, to forget her position for one instant and allow her heart to guide her head. What fool wrote 'Poverty is no crime?' I know of none greater. It is responsible for every crime committed under the sun. It is a foul curse!"

"Why, Aurelia, girl, what has come to you this morning? You talk like a man with the blue devils after losing all night at poker," said her father.

Her answer was a shrug of her handsome shoulders as she resumed her listless attitude.

"Listen to me; I will unfold a scheme that shall remove the curse of poverty, and give you for a husband a man who will fill the bill, heart and all."

He rose, approached the mantel, and turning his back upon it, rested both elbows on the marble—a position which brought him face to face with his guests, and asked: "Are you acquainted with Cuthbert Sumner?"

"Know him by sight and reputation. Clerk in your department," replied Madison. Aurelia did not speak, but a flush came into her face, a light to her eyes. One might have felt the thrill that passed over her form.

"What do you think of him?"

"He's all right; a genial fellow, but careful not to go too far; handsome, too, by Jove. No money, though?"

"O yes," nodded Benson. "Only in the department for experience in political life. His father's very wealthy. New England manufacturer."

"Indeed!"

"He's the one I've picked out for our lady here."

"But he's engaged," broke in Aurelia.

"Exactly. And that brings me to the rest of the scheme. Sumner is about to marry Bowen's daughter. By the way,

Aurelia, you got the cards for the ball, did you not?" Aurelia bowed in assent.

"Jewel Bowen is the Senator's only child, and his heiress. She will receive ten millions upon her wedding day. What I propose is that Aurelia fascinate the gentleman, thus leaving the field clear for me. I have taken a decided fancy to Miss Bowen and her fortune. If I succeed there is a million for you, Madison, and another for Aurelia. Sumner, too, has pots of money, and we shall all be able to settle down into quiet respectability. What do you think of my plan?"

"By Jove, Benson," blurted out Major Madison, fairly thunder-struck at the magnificence of the vista opened before him, "what a splendid idea! How admirably you have planned things!" Benson nodded and smiled:

"All remains with Aurelia, and certainly with her magnificent beauty to help us, we need fear no failure."

"Spare me your compliments. This is probably your last chance, General. So you think I can win this Mr. Sumner from his betrothed?" she said.

"Precisely."

"That is a droll idea. Do you think—"

"I think, I repeat, that you can easily make the person referred to sufficiently in love with you to do anything you ask."

Suppose he proves obdurate? What then? You cannot judge all men alike."

"Break the engagement, if you can do nothing more. During a fit of insanity, if it lasts but a week, an hour even, you will have ample time to accomplish my desires."

"And then?"

"I will look after mademoiselle. It will make no difference

to you. Your compensation will be my affair. It is only his money that you would want."

"Oh, I see!" There was a world of sarcasm in the three words uttered by a smiling mouth. "My dear General, you are indeed a marvel! No one knows better than you how to make love to a young girl."

"You are the cleverest woman I know, Aurelia. I knew you would comprehend the situation perfectly." After a moment's reflection the girl replied: "Yes, I think I'll try it. It will probably be announced before long that the marriage is broken off. I will earn my million, never fear. I shall, doubtless, find it an agreeable task."

"And a husband, too, my girl," added her father.

"Perhaps."

"Are we to be intimate friends or simply business acquaintances?" asked the Major of General Benson.

"Business friends will be best. Let us have no appearance of collusion."

"When shall we see you again?" asked the Major as they rose to go.

"Just as soon as you have something to tell me. How fortunate that Aurelia has never been introduced to Washington society. She will take the place by storm."

Then the friends separated.

(To be continued.)

CHAPTER XIII

PLAYING WITH FIRE

About lunch time that same morning, as Sumner was leaving the office, a note was brought to him by a servant in plain livery:

> "May we not be friends for the sake of the old days, when no other woman was dearer than I? Come to me just once."
>
> Aurelia.

New York Avenue.

Sumner's brow was knit as he scanned the sheet of ivory paper in his hand, with its emblazoned monogram. He muttered an imprecation. Elise Bradford, the stenographer, glanced up from her work in surprise. Sumner was a gentleman in the office and a great favorite with all the employees; it was rare to hear an uncouth expression from the lips of this man, who honored all womanhood.

"I thought that was all over and done with," he muttered to himself. "What is the use of going through with it all again? Well, I suppose I must go once for decency's sake, but I'll take care to make short work of it. There shall be no misunderstanding."

Then softer thoughts came to him as he took from a pile of commonplace, business letters on his desk, a slim satiny envelope. It was from Jewel. He opened it and read the few lines it contained, reminding him of an appointment that he had with her for the evening.

"My little Blossom!" he said gently.

But his little Blossom did not keep him from going to see Aurelia Madison. She was less than nothing to him. He had never met her from the day he left Cape May until the night before. He never even thought of her. Yet he went to call upon her. Reluctantly and distastefully—but he went.

He was ushered into the drawing-room scented and flower-filled. A moment later Aurelia came into the room from the library. Ah, she stirred even his cold heart.

A white negligé clothed her from throat to foot, and her wonderful hair was caught in a mass low down on her neck. A deep light was in the dusky eyes that bewildered a man and weakened his energies. In an instant she came swiftly to him—the white arms were about his throat, the warm lips against his.

"My love! my love!" she murmured softly, and Cuthbert Sumner (blind and foolish) was not the kind of man to let the memory of little Blossom prevent him from holding a beautiful, yielding form closely clasped in his arms, and returning clinging kisses with interest when such a rare opportunity offered.

I question if there are many men that would.

She was playing a part in a desperate game that meant everything to her. This was her first move toward the end she had vowed to accomplish. She would be victorious; she swore it. Her rôle was not a hard one for she worshipped this man so cold and unyielding to her arts. She would have preferred the lilies of virtuous winning; debarred from that she would take the torments of a love to which she had no right. By-and-by, she said:

"Bert, do you love her very much?"

He bowed with a long look in her face.

"And NOT as you loved ME!" she said passionately. "Tell me about her."

"My dear Aurelia, can a man sing the praises of one beautiful woman to another?"

"Tell me about her," she said again with the imperious gesture that Sumner remembered so well in that summer at the Cape. "I have not loved you for two long years, Bert Sumner, without learning every phase of your mind. When do you marry her?"

"At Easter," he replied proudly, disdaining further subterfuge.

"And you can sit there calmly and tell it to me—to me —," she bit her lip a moment; there was less time than she had thought.

"She is very wealthy?"

"Yes, as the world counts it, but I care not for that; if she had nothing it would be the same to me."

"I believe you. And I could see her beauty for myself; and she is good, not like me."

"She is an angel, my white angel of purity," he replied with a look of reverence on his face.

Aurelia was a gorgeous tropical flower; Jewel, a fair fragrant lily. Men have such an unfortunate weakness for tropical blooms, they cannot pass them by carelessly, even though a lily lies above their hearts. Cuthbert could not ignore this splendid tropical flower; it caused his blood to flow faster, it gave new zest to living—for an hour. Jewel was his saint, his good angel; and he loved her truly with all the high love a man of the world can ever know. He trusted her for her womanly goodness and truth. And Jewel returned his love with an intensity that was her very life.

Aurelia looked at him and sighed heavily.

"May I know her?"

"I am sure, I cannot say. You may possibly meet her at some party."

"Then you do not object absolutely. I am glad, for we have invitations to Mrs. Bowen's ball. I want to go."

She looked at him keenly. "I think I have met Miss Bowen before. If I mistake not, we were at the Montreal convent at the same time. I am older than she, and left just after she entered. I remember her as a sweet cherub who resembled a pictured saint."

"Quite a coincidence," he replied with all his usual courtliness for womankind; but for all that he mentally anathematized the idiot who had sent the cards and the convent where the girls had met. He was vexed, and she felt it.

"Yes, I shall go—"

She caught her breath sharply and then fell at his feet in all her exquisite beauty.

"Can you never, NEVER love me again, Bert? My life, my soul is yours! Can you not give me a little love in return?"

He lifted her up gently.

"It is too late to ask that now, Aurelia. Try and forget that you have ever loved me. Believe me, you will be happier. No one can more bitterly regret than I the misery of our past. Let us begin anew."

She thrust him from her wildly, and bade him go if he did not wish to see her fall dead at his feet.

Cuthbert went away sadly.

He knew the full power of Aurelia Madison's siren charms. Nor was her emotion all feigned. She really felt all she had expressed. What was pride compared to the desolation that swept over her when she realized that his heart was hers no longer? Her great love obliterated even the thought of his wealth. She felt she should triumph, in spite of the coldness with which he had received her professions of love. Yes, she would be his wife, even thought it were a barren honor, since his heart was not hers.

"If his love is not for me, it shall be for no one else," she told herself, as she thought over her afternoon's work and prepared for the next move in the drama.

And so Cuthbert Sumner went back to his little Blossom, whose calm, pure face was continually before him.

CHAPTER XIV

RENEWING OLD ACQUAINTANCE

The following afternoon Major Madison's carriage rolled up to the Bowen mansion on Sixteenth Street, and stopped. From it Aurelia stepped, clad richly and daintily in a becoming calling costume. She had determined to storm the citadel, as it were, and carry it by assault.

She rang the bell and asked the footman if Miss Bowen was at home.

"Yes, Miss—. What name please?"

She gave the man a card on which she had written, "Known to you as Aurelia Walker," and was shown into a morning-room to wait, Would Jewel recognize her, she wondered. Would she be pleased to meet her again?

Presently she heard the gentle frou-frou of silken skirts down the broad stairway and the next instant Jewel Bowen stood before her, holding out her hand in frankly-glad recognition—Jewel in a tea-gown that was a poem, a combination of palest rose-satin and cream lace. Surprise and pleasure mingled in her speaking face.

"The card said, 'Aurelia Walker.' Can it be possible that you are the same Aurelia whom I knew in Montreal? How delightful to meet you again."

Her greeting was most cordial, and put Aurelia instantly at her ease. After a time spent in recalling reminiscences of school life, and pleasant girlish chatter, Aurelia said:

"I must explain the change in name,—papa was embarrassed financially, and he placed me at school, calling himself Walker while he earned the money to satisfy his creditors; that saved him much annoyance, and as soon as he could satisfy their demands, we resumed our rightful name."

"Pray do not speak of it, Aurelia; such things are annoying, but cannot always be helped," replied Jewel with a smile. "Won't you come to the drawing-room and meet mamma?"

How beautiful everything was, thought the girl, as she passed up the broad marble stairs with velvet carpet in the centre, on which the foot fell noiselessly, and statues and flowers in niches and on landings, while the walls were hung with lovely frescoes that impelled one to pause and admire.

The drawing-room door was flung open, and they were in a spacious apartment with painted ceiling, and all things rich and harmonious in tone. In a moment she was standing before Mrs. Bowen, who greeted her warmly, as if truly glad to meet her daughter's school friend. No lovelier vision was ever seen than these two girls as they entered the Bowen drawing-room. Mrs. Bowen was a cultured lady and their grace and beauty gratified her taste.

She conversed freely and pleasantly with the unexpected guest, although after the first feeling of wonder and satisfaction at so much loveliness, she was surprised and puzzled at the vague feeling of distrust and dislike that personal contact with her young guest brought to her. It was intangible. She shook it off, however, the beautiful face and voice were so enchanting that she could not resist them, and felt ashamed of her distrust.

"Come and sit down by the fire and let us have a long chat before anyone else comes in. We never know how long we may be alone," said Jewel, indicating a seat near her own.

"This is very cosy and homelike," remarked Aurelia as she took the seat offered. "I have been so lonely since I came to the city."

"Poor child," remarked Mrs. Bowen in a sympathetic voice, "are you very much alone? How long since you lost your mother?"

"I cannot recall her at all, dear Mrs. Bowen," the girl answered, lifting a pair of dusky eyes, swimming in tears, for a moment to her face. "Papa is so intent on the fortunes of the mine, just at present, that he gives me very little attention. Indeed, I believe he forgets at times that he has a daughter," this last with a little sigh of martyrdom.

Mrs. Bowen melted more and more to her guest.

"Then stay and dine with us. Let me send away your carriage." She rang the bell and gave the order to the servant. "We have a few jolly people coming—not a dinner-party, you know, but just a few friends."

"I shall be delighted. How kind you are," replied Aurelia, feeling dizzy over her good luck.

"Thanks," said Jewel, pressing her hand. "Here comes tea, and with it papa."

Senator Bowen welcomed his guest with his usual Western heartiness.

"By Jove," he thought to himself, "she's a stunner! But

my little girl doesn't lose a thing by contrast. What a sight for sore eyes the pair of them makes!"

Then he remarked aloud to the guest: "I know your father, my dear; I shall try and see more of him after this. My daughter's friends are my friends."

There were, beside Aurelia, four people to whom Mrs. Bowen introduced her. Two of them, the Secretary of the Treasury and his wife—she knew by sight, but Mr. Carroll West and a pretty widow, Mrs. Brewer, were total strangers. Lord Browning, the English Ambassador, and Lady Browning were shortly announced, and quickly following them came Cuthbert Sumner, completing the party.

"This is my dear friend, Aurelia Madison, Cuthbert; we were at school together. You remember that I told you at the theatre her face seemed very familiar to me."

"Delighted to meet you again, Miss Madison," he said as he bowed over her hand, suppressing a start of amazement at the sight of her. To himself he added:

"Confound the woman; what does she mean? Is she following me up? That won't help her any."

Aurelia thoroughly ingratiated herself with Lady Browning, paying her the greatest deference. Finding her ladyship much interested in religious topics and charitable projects, she affected an enthusiastic interest in them, and was rewarded by overhearing Lady Browning express herself as delighted with Miss Madison.

"Such a beautiful girl, and so intelligent to talk with."

She went down to dinner with Mr. West, who seemed much impressed with his lovely partner.

Cuthbert's attention would wander to the couple opposite him at table. West was talking to her with animation, while Aurelia smiled and sparkled, and looked irresistibly bewitching. West had but a small income for a wealthy man, and had always been incorrigible until now, but he seemed to have surrendered at last. Cuthbert watched her covertly, not at all deceived by the gaiety of her manner.

"So, the moth is still fluttering about the flame. Let her beware; I would sacrifice her without a moment's hesitation if I thought she meant Jewel harm."

He showed nothing of this outwardly, being as calm, smiling and well-bred as ever. But he was seriously annoyed by the inscrutable conduct of the woman opposite him. It was a vague feeling that he could not grasp—a shadow no larger than a man's hand.

Dinner over, the gentlemen did not linger long behind the ladies. Back in the drawing-room once more, Mrs. Bowen whispered to her husband:

"Do ask Miss Madison to play, Zenas."

"I will when I get a chance. West seems to have such a lot to say to her that it would be cruel to spoil sport."

Mrs. Bowen looked and laughed:

"I'll ask her myself then. Miss Madison, I am sure you are musical," she said to the girl, with a smile. "Will you not favor us?"

Aurelia signified her willingness and Mr. West, a minute later, had installed her at the piano, and stood by listening with delight to her playing. And she was worth listening to for she was a cultured amateur of no mean ability, and gave genuine pleasure by her performance. Mr. West was more and more infatuated each moment he spent in her society. Mrs. Bowen thanked her warmly as she rose from the instrument, followed by the plaudits of the company.

"Miss Madison," said the pretty widow, "you play beautifully."

"Do I?" queried Aurelia, laughing, "but then I cannot sing, Jewel can, though—divinely, I hear."

"Flatterer!" said Jewel as she passed Aurelia's seat on her way to the piano, attended by Sumner.

"What is it to be?" he asked her as he turned over the contents of a folio.

"Will you choose, Cuthbert?"

A jealous pang shot through Aurelia's heart, as her ear caught the words, but she set her teeth hard.

Sumner took from the folio "Some Day," by Wellington.

"Always a favorite of mine, you know," he said.

She gave him a quick, trustful look, and smiled as she began the accompaniment.

Conversation was hushed; everyone listened while the rich, pure voice filled the room, giving the old song with the dramatic fire of a professional. There was a buzz of admiration when Jewel had finished. Cuthbert bent over with pride and delight shining in his face, and his softly-spoken "Thanks sweetheart," was heard distinctly by the woman sorely tried by jealous pain.

"Don't leave the piano; sing something else," came from all parts of the room.

"Very well," she said, and then gave with delicious pathos that sweet old song, "Dreaming Eyes."

The listeners were charmed. The singer rose, crossed the room and seated herself beside Aurelia. Their renewed acquaintance seemed destined to ripen into a close intimacy.

"Aurelia," the girl said as they sat there somewhat apart from the others, "Will you come with us to the—Theatre tomorrow night—we have a box?"

Surnames were dropped from that night. How did it

happen? CIRCE alone knew. But after that these two were much together.

"Such a lovely morning, Jewel! You must come for a turn with me." or, "I shall be alone all day; do come and make the hours bright for me."

Sumner's first undefined fears gradually subsided. Time, rolling on springs of pleasure, passed swiftly bringing the night of the ball.

CHAPTER XV

THE BALL

The Bowen mansion was ablaze with light. Servants in livery hurried about attending the arrival of guests. Outside the house a continuous stream of carriages deposited the fortunate ones bidden to the feast.

The ball-room was a vast apartment arched, with a gallery of carved oak, in which the orchestra was seated. The rooms were filling fast, yet at no time, even when the crowd was densest, was there a pressure for room. Flowers wreathed the gallery, the national colors hung in the angles, banks of roses were everywhere. Mrs. Bowen, in white velvet, old lace and diamonds, stood near the entrance, supported by her husband, her daughter and Cuthbert Sumner. The house party was enforced by several gentlemen of political importance and their wives.

> "Inglass of satin,
> And shimmer of pearls."

Jewel Bowen stood, a flush on her cheeks, her hair falling in waving masses, pearls clasping her white throat and arms, her large gray eyes like wells of light. An only child and heiress of many millions, she would have been the bright star of fortune to the gilded youth of Washington had not Cuthbert Sumner stood first in the field; albeit, a man might be pardoned for losing his head had she possessed only her youth and beauty.

A band hidden away in the great mansion discoursed Rossini's dreamy music in a concert during the arrival of guests. Fashionable Washington greeted its world and congratulated itself on being there, discussed the host and hostess, admired the arrangements for dancing just as the dear five hundred always have done and always will do. It was evident that the Bowen ball was to be the hit of the season. The Senator was voted charmingly original, and his wife attracted as much comment and attention as the debutantes who graced the occasion.

"I hear that we are to have a new beauty introduced tonight. A girl who is fairly startling, remarked one man to another. The rumor was started by Mrs. Bowen saying to a number of dancing men, with a roguish smile:

"Don't fill up all your dances, for there is another beauty coming. Nobody you know, either. A stranger in the city."

"We have heard something of her charms through West, I think, Madam Bowen. You mean Miss Madison. West is fairly a drivelling idiot over her at present. I'm worried over the poor chappie."

"Tiresome man, why couldn't he allow me the pleasure of trapping society. Have either of you met her?"

"Alas, for your intended surprise, dear Mrs. Bowen, I have seen her on the boulevard once or twice," replied the one who had not yet spoken. "What a perfect pair Miss Jewel and she will make, and puzzle anyone to award the palm."

"Mrs. Bowen is certainly a charming hostess," remarked one to the other as they walked away, displaced by fresh relays of guests.

"She is really a beautiful woman, but too cold to please me," was the reply.

"She has a throat and shoulders of alabaster, a superb head and a flower-like face."

"Hear, hear! Wasting compliments on a passé elderly matron—it isn't like you, Rollins."

"A pretty woman is never passé; you fellows who are new in society have something to learn, let me tell you."

"Granted. But we don't waste ammunition on elderly females who have had their day."

"Has a woman, once a beauty, ever had her day?"

"What a queer fellow you are tonight, making flowery speeches about old folks."

"There is no denying the truth of what I said, though. It is human nature. With a woman it is her good looks—with a man his strength, which at no age will he ever admit to be materially lessened any more than a woman will allow her good looks quite gone into the past, or if they do admit a decay of their charms or strength there is still a feeling of pride in what they were once."

"Here endeth the first lesson," laughed his companion as they separated to find partners for the opening number.

Other men, older than the two recorded, remarked the nobleness and charm of the hostess.

"There is a story written on her face, if I mistake not; I would give much for the power to read it," said a famous student of psychology to a celebrated physician, as they stood together surveying the brilliant scene.

"Granted she is beautiful, but she looks a creature of snow and ice. The daughter is more to my liking."

"Yes, but you must confess that they are alike."

"Alike, yet unlike; in the daughter there is fire and life, and a little diablerie, if I mistake not."

Ah! but the beautiful Mrs. Bowen is only step-mother to the lovely Jewel."

"Is it possible? I should have thought them of one blood. Who was madam before her marriage?"

"No one knows," was the reply, accompanied by a suggestive shrug of the shoulders. "We do not inquire too closely into one's antecedents in Washington, you know; be beautiful and rich and you will be happy here."

Meantime the room was filling fast. Directly the butler announced "General Benson," Senator Bowen moved forward a pace and shook him warmly by the hand and then presented him to his wife and daughter. A puzzled look swept over his face as he bent for an instant above Mrs. Bowen's hand. Then he stole a furtive glance at her white impassive countenance, started slightly—looked again with a quick indrawn breath. There was now a questioning look in her eyes of seeming surprise at the evident interest—a quick contraction of the straight brows, the next second the dark eyes drooped, but he felt conscious that under those long lashes they still watched him. It passed in a second of time, there was no change in the beautiful cold face of the elegant woman of the world save that one might have imagined that she grew whiter, if possible. Then he recovered himself and turned with easy self-complacency to Jewel:

"Am I too late for the first dance?" he asked in his most courtly style.

"The first is gone certainly," smiled Jewel.

"Well, never mind; the first waltz, then."

"So sorry, General, but it is promised," with an arch glance at Sumner, who was standing back of her.

"Oh! I see. You unprincipled fellow, to steal the march on the world of us who are in darkness. We must all give first place to your claim, Sumner, lucky boy," he said with a genial laugh. "The fourth then? I shan't get another chance, so I must secure my luck while I can."

"With pleasure."

"And the one right after supper, dare I ask?"

"Very well," she replied again, smiling at his persistency.

The General took her card and inscribed his name against two members, and as the opening bars of the first dance sounded, and her partner came to claim her, bowed and moved away.

There was a movement near the door, and "Major Madison and Miss Madison" were announced. There was a moment's hush as they entered the ball-room, and every man present mentally uttered an exclamation of surprise and admiration. For once rumor had not lied. This woman was quite the loveliest thing they had ever seen, startling and somewhat bizzarre, perhaps, but still marvellously, undeniably lovely. Her gown was a splendid creation of scarlet and gold. It was a magnificent and daring combination. Her hair was piled high and crowned with diamonds. A single row of the same precious stones encircled her slim white throat. She looked superbly, wondrously beautiful.

Truly this girl was an exquisite picture, but it bewildered

one so that the eye rested on Jewel's slender, white-robed figure with pleasure, and intense relief.

Sumner was talking with Mrs. Vanderpool, the wife of a New York millionaire, as the Madisons entered, and turned at her exclamation:

"What a lovely girl! Who is she, Mr. Sumner?"

"She is the daughter of Major Madison, President of the Arrow-Head gold mines, so much talked about at present. You admire that vivid style?"

"Do introduce me, Mr. Sumner, I adore pretty girls." He was greeted by a flash from Aurelia's dark eyes, and a brilliant smile as he came up to give the desired introduction. Already she was surrounded and her ball card besieged.

"Miss Madison, Mrs. Vanderpool."

Both ladies bowed and immediately opened an animated conversation that ended in Aurelia's promising to grace Mrs. Vanderpool's german with her presence. Then Sumner gave the elder lady his arm across the room to join Mrs. Bowen. He passed Aurelia again on his way to the card-tables, in an adjoining room.

"You are going to ask me to dance, Mr. Sumner, of course?" she said to him as he paused an instant beside her chair. Her manner gave the bystanders the idea that they were old and intimate acquaintances. Her words and way jarred on Cuthbert. He took her card, and after consulting her, scribbled his name down for the after-supper dance, bowed and passed on.

He drew a deep breath of relief as he saw Jewel talking to the Russian ambassador, an old man in gorgeous dress and orders blazing on his breast.

"You are lucky, Excellency, to have a moment of Miss Bowen's time bestowed on you."

His Excellency bowed his head.

"I was just telling this lovely little lady that I must not be selfish, that I must give way for others who have a better right to her company than an old man like me."

"I have enjoyed talking with you so much," Jewel said simply.

"Thank you, my child. I see a friend of mine over in the corner. I can leave you in safe hand, now Sumner has come. By-and-by, perhaps, you will let me return and have a few more pleasant moments."

Sumner felt his vague sense of repulsion, which his encounter with Aurelia had aroused, fade, as he came in contact with the pure fascination of his betrothed. He smiled down at her tenderly. How inexpressibly sweet and lovely she was!

The band was playing a delicious waltz. Aurelia, flashing in her jewels, was flying round in the arms of West, who was her shadow. Sumner's brows met in a frown.

"How lovely Aurelia is!" cried Jewel with eager enthusiasm. "She is the most beautiful woman in the rooms."

"Bar one," said Cuthbert, smiling.

"Oh, you; you don't count. You are prejudiced," replied Jewel, laughing. "She seems to get on very will with Mr. West. I wonder—"

"Little matchmaker! I imagine West stands no chance in that quarter. He has nothing but his salary."

"Would that make a difference with her?" in a surprised, regretful tone.

"I imagine that they are not wealthy. Miss Madison, if I read her correctly, will marry for money."

The next instant his arm encircled Jewel's waist, he held her form pressed closely to his throbbing heart, and they glided away from earth to a short period of heaven.

As an intimate friend of the family, and soon to be a son of the house, Cuthbert Sumner had shared the dispensing of hospitality with Senator Bowen.

"My boy," said the older man, "just fix the thing up when you see 'em lagging. I'm going into the card-room and have a game with Madison. He's an old duffer like myself. You understand all this sort of thing, but I'll be hanged if I ain't sick of it before I begin."

So Sumner had found himself pretty busy. After that waltz, however, which came just before supper, he and Jewel had a few precious moments together in the conservatory, sitting out the remainder of their dance. Then came supper, at which Sumner insisted upon being her escort. "I will not waive every enjoyment for the pleasure of others," he declared firmly.

CHAPTER XVI

THE SPIDER'S WEB

The first dance after supper Jewel had given to General Benson.

"A short Elysium at last for me," whispered the gallant General as he passed his arm about her slight form. Jewel was a Western girl with all the independence that the term implies. She glanced up at her partner, as they whirled away, with a little amused smile slightly sarcastic; "I expected something different from you. Something at least original."

"Well, it is Elysium to find one's step perfectly duplicated."

"Oh, that is easy where one's partner is master of the art

as you are. I imagine that you are one of the best dancers here."

"You are fond of dancing?" asked the General, after a silence.

"Yes; that weakness was born with me."

"In the tremendous crowd, I could not judge. But I can speak from this waltz—you dance like a fairy. Are you pleased with Washington?"

"Oh, yes; but I miss the freedom of the ranch, the wild flight at dawn over the prairie in the saddle, and many other things."

He looked at her with glowing eyes: "There we have congenial tastes. I am never so happy as when in the saddle."

The ball-room was a whirl of fair faces and dazzling toilets—the light, the heat, the perfume almost oppressive.

Knowing himself to be a fascinating conversationalist, he took advantage of a pause in the music to speak of the heat and suggest a turn in the conservatory where he knew that he could exert this power of enchantment. Jewel was nothing loth.

They stood a moment, before taking seats, at an open glass door gazing out on the gardens sered and withered and covered in places with patches of snow, but bathed in moonlight. There was something solemn in the scene, merriment seemed out of place; even soft laughter jarred on the nerves. See looked up to the heavens, where the Southern cross shone in all its brilliancy surrounded by myriads of other stars. The glorious Southern moon rode high in the sky. The flutes and viols were pouring out their maddest music.

"How glorious," Jewel said softly.

"Ay glorious indeed!"

"I mean the moon," she said.

"I mean your eyes, fair lady."

"You will persist in saying pretty things, General," she replied, turning away indifferently.

The General bit his lip in vexation. It was not to be easy work, that was plain.

There was a subdued murmur of voices and sometimes a ripple of laughter, for many couples stood, or strolled about the extensive greenhouses. They were lighted softly, from the arched dome, by silvery lamps; fountains flashed scented waters into marble basins where aquatic plants of strange beauty had found a home. Leading from the main conservatory were many arbors and grottoes, transformed for the time being by draperies of asparagus vines and roses into a charming solitude for two. The cool stillness was refreshing after the head of the ball-room.

"Really, this is well done," remarked the General, stopping to admire the effect. "None of the balls I have attended in Washington was so beautiful."

"Another compliment, General?"

"It is not flattery to speak the truth."

They seated themselves on a rustic chair for two, and the General entertained her with tales of his travels in Italy and India, and cyclone and typhoon, all very fascinating to the girl before whom life was just opening.

"Were you long out of the United States, General?"

"About ten years," he replied, looking down. "It was this way, Miss Jewel, I was a hot-blooded young fellow who could see no wrong in the decision of his section to secede from the union of states; and so, when it all ended disastrously, I gathered together what remained of my shattered fortunes, and went abroad until the pain of recollection should be somewhat dimmed. I returned almost a foreigner."

"Ah!" she said, with a gentle sigh of pity, "how dreadful that time must have been. Thank heaven, ours is a united country once more. And you are mistaken, too, in your judgment: we have no foreigners here. We have effaced the word by assimilation; so, too, we have no Southerners—we are Americans."

The General accented her remark by a courtly bow, and then he drifted into an animated description of a sail down the Mediterranean Sea. Jewel could imagine that she inhaled the odor from boatloads of violets, brought to her senses by his wonderful descriptive powers.

At this moment their enjoyable tête-à-tête was interrupted by the sound of a woman's voice in passionate pleading.

*   *   *   *   *

Early in the evening Aurelia Madison had whispered to General Benson:

"If you can, take Jewel into the conservatory after supper. I shall have something interesting for her to hear."

"How are you getting on? Any progress?"

"Wait," was her answer.

After supper Sumner went to her to claim his dance. It was a duty-dance and a painful one he found it. As they floated down the long room, Aurelia gazed up at him with flushed cheeks and glittering eyes.

She had taken a great fancy to Jewel Bowen, not only because the latter was very kind to her—kinder than anyone had ever been to her in her lonely, reckless life, but because she really carried in her heart a spark of what passed for love and which would have developed but for Sumner. She could even admire Jewel's beauty without jealousy; she did not envy her her wealth although so pinched herself in money matters, and yet—strange nature of women, or of some women—for that reason she was the more determined to triumph over her as a woman, and, if she could, stab her. She had forced the friendship with that intention.

She felt instinctively that Cuthbert shrank from allowing a continuance of the intimacy between them, and she resented it. Yes, she would have her fling, her triumph; Jewel should know, beyond a doubt, that Cuthbert Sumner and his fortune was hers, belonged to her—Aurelia Madison.

Now she watched his face and resented his cold, preoccupied air.

"How quiet you are; aren't you well?"

"Never better," he replied, with an apology for his seeming indifference. After all she was a woman, and a beautiful one. Why should he try to mar her favorable reception among the élite.

"Only, I am not Jewel; is that it?"

"Pardon. Let us speak of something else. Shall I take you to have some refreshment?" he said coldly.

"Oh, let us go to the conservatory. I want air and rest," she said, slipping her hand through his arm. "I have seen nothing of you all the evening. Now you must devote a short time to me." Her air was bolder that Sumner had ever noticed before. He bowed low in acquiescence, though he would willingly have left her there.

She bit her lip and a dogged look came into her face that was not pleasant to see, and in her heart she felt that she could take the strong, handsome man and dash him senseless at her feet. She hid her feelings well, and glanced up at him with a pretty pleading look.

"Oh! Bert, I keep forgetting—of course—," then she broke suddenly, "I wish you loved her less!"

"A useless wish," said Sumner coldly. "Happen what may, Jewel must always be my first thought."

"Aye, your best and truest love," she said through her teeth.

They were in the deserted conservatory where all was coolness and shadow; Sumner walked by her side until they reached one of the grottoes, where from between the folds of the rose-curtain drapery a rustic seat held its inviting arms toward them. Aurelia dropped upon it:

"I am afraid I can't give you many minutes," he said with a cool smile. "Senator Bowen naturally expects me to assist him in looking after the guests."

The band was playing divinely and the notes came to them in waves of undulating melody. Sumner never forgot that night, and the music of the band haunted him ever after.

She sat there in sad languor that would have touched any heart but his. They talked a moment of indifferent subjects, then he arose and offered his arm with a motion that indicated a return to the ball-room. But with a low and exceedingly bitter cry she stood up.

"Must we part like this? My God! I cannot bear it! Have you no mercy, no pity?"

The tears were streaming down her cheeks, she held out her hands imploringly.

With deepest sympathy and pity he took them in his.

"Aurelia, you will forget. Believe me, dear, you will forget all this in a very little while. What good would my love do you now. It could bring you nothing but sorrow. We must forget each other. I hope—I know you will be happy yet. God be with you, dear girl." He bent down and pressed his lips to her trembling hands, feeling himself a wretch for bringing sorrow to this beautiful woman who loved him so.

But she flung her arms about him, and clung to him in desperation and the abandonment of grief, sobbing hysterically, with low, quivering moans, that cut him to the heart.

"Aurelia, do not weep so. It is torture for me to hear you."

"I hope I may die! Oh, if I only could!" she sobbed faltering and shivering, and clinging to him, and he put his arms about her and kissed twice on the brow. Her lovely wet face was pressed close against his cheek.

A deep sigh startled him. He lifted his head. Standing in the doorway of the curtained recess, pallid as a ghost, all the graceful beauty gone from her wan face, with frightened woful eyes and despair in every feature, stood Jewel. With a loud exclamation, with rage and impatience and disgust, he shook the exquisite form from his bosom.

(To be continued.)

CHAPTER XVII

It was long after midnight and the guests were leaving, when Sumner, with white, set face, sought Mrs. Bowen and asked for Jewel. She was much concerned over her daughter.

"I do not understand it," was her reply to his eager questions; "Jewel sent word by General Benson that she was not well, and had gone to her rooms. She was all right, and as gay as possible all day. I though you would know."

Finding that he could not explain matters that night, and would accomplish nothing by waiting, Sumner left the scene of revelry, desiring to be alone. How it had all happened he could not tell. But what a sentimental fool he felt himself to be, for allowing himself to be betrayed into acting such a scene in so public a place. Still, he felt that he could blame no one but himself. Aurelia was free from any intention of scheming for how could she know of Jewel's presence at just that moment? So he argued, lulling his suspicions to rest.

At eight o'clock, while breakfasting, there came a letter from Jewel with his ring enclosed. Then, indeed, it seemed to him that life was over. With mad and bitter wrath, he cursed Aurelia Madison; then he started for Jewel's home. The servant who answered the summons was one wont to have a welcoming smile for the familiar visitor. There was no expression in his well-trained face when he informed Sumner that the ladies were not at home. Night found him again at the Bowen mansion. Mrs. Bowen was coldness itself; Jewel begged to be excused.

Despair seized him. Everything, every one, was repulsive to him. Days of insane recklessness followed. A month went by in this manner—working furiously days, spending his nights in search of the excitement that is supposed to drown care. Then he grew calmer. He would seek Jewel again; he would force her trust; she should believe in him. Life was not worth living without her. For one touch of her cool hand, one glance from her calm eyes, one smile on the sweet, earnest lips, he would barter wealth and fame, and all the world had to offer—aye life itself!

They had met frequently in society during this memorable month, but Jewel passed her lover without a sign of recognition or with a slight bend of the head in acknowledgment of his reverential uncovering. General Benson was always in close attendance, and Aurelia Madison also, was often her companion.

After the usual nine days of wonderment and surmises as to the cause of the estrangement between lovers, public curiosity turned to speculating on the middle-aged general's chances with the fair heiress

* * * * *

At seven o'clock one evening, Cuthbert sat at his desk in his rooms lost in sombre thoughts. He had determined to devote himself to the hardest of tasks, heavy brain work, when his heart and soul were racked with agony. He was busy on a political treatise. He was considered a brilliant writer. If he could make a stir in the literary world, it would please his father, and he had no one else to think of now.

Work! Could he work? He flung out his arms over the papers on the desk before him, and bowed his head upon them.

"If I knew that the suffering was for myself alone, my Blossom, I could bear it better."

He lifted himself at last haggard and weary as with weeks of sleepless toil, resolved to devote himself to his chosen work.

"What I am I will live on to the end—Ambition my only bride." He was striving with all his young courageous heart to kill the memory of the girl he loved. It was a bitter task, and an impossible one.

Modern pessimist are fond of crying that love, as well as chivalry, has died out of our practical world. If this were true, then Sumner lived after his century, for his belief in higher and better things was intense. He had a desire to worship purity in any shape, to champion the weak, and carve a pathway to honor that was characteristic of the chivalrous days of old.

The minutes passed, half-past seven ticked away, and then

eight, and he never moved. He sat with his face on his two hands, his elbows planted on the table.

"I will not think more about her," he said to himself, doggedly. "I will not—I will not."

John, his servant, a New England colored man who had known him from his youth, had put his evening clothes out in the dressing-room, and now entered the room to remind his master of an engagement to dine.

"It's time you was dressed, Mr. Cuthbert," he said in his quiet way. John was eager for his master to leave Washington and return to Massachusetts and the family home.

" 'Deed," he argued to himself, "this Washington's no city for me. Give me old New England every time; it's God's own country. They's nuthin' human about the South for chocolate complected gents like me, no matter how you fix it. The pint of the argument is in the scorpion's tail. Jes' so; and this here Southern idea of colored Americans ain't good fer black nor white when you's done had a New England raisin'."

"Mr. Cuthbert's an altered man sense the night of that there Bowen ball," he told himself again and again, "if he ain't twenty years older in his looks then I'm blind in one eye and can't see out of the 'tother. He'll be best off if he gets back home to the old gentleman. Dog my cats but there's something strange in this whole kickup or my name ain't John Robinson."

Sumner roused himself at last: "What's the time, John?" he was asking as the bell of the suite rang shrilly.

If that's Mr. Badger, show him in," he said as John went out of the room.

Cuthbert stood gazing down into the fire. He heard voices

outside, but he gave them no heed; there was always a good-natured controversy between his friend and his servant.

A slap on the back, and "Holloa, Sumner, old man!" made him start round and put his gloomy thoughts behind him, and greet his friends, Will Badger and Carroll West.

"Ah! How are you, Will? How are you, West? How goes it?" he said, holding out his hand in greeting to his guests.

"Thought I'd bring West with me, and after we dine at the club, take a look in at the Madisons, this is their at home night. West's agreeable," with a laugh and a meaning look in the latter's direction.

Sumner hesitated. Aurelia had written him again and again, but he had not answered her impassioned letters. She had begged him to call and let her help set matters right, but as yet, he had not been able to bring himself to comply with her request.

"Well," he replied to Will Badger after a moment, "I don't mind. Have a glass of wine while I change."

"Thanks—we don't mind," said West.

West never did mind. He was fond of a social glass, and Sumner was noted for his fine wine and excellent brand of cigars.

"Yes, we'll have a little game with the Major," he remarked, as he helped himself from the side-board. "Great fun, the Major knows a thing or two about life does the old man."

"He knows enough to win your money, I suppose, you foolish boy," replied Sumner.

"It's very little I've lost there. He always insists on returning me my money."

"Have others been as fortunate?"

"That's there own fault; the Major wins fair every time," replied West hotly.

"Oh, West, you're prejudiced in his favor," broke in Badger.

"A pretty daughter is a trump card."

"She can't help being charming and attracting men to the house," stoutly maintained West.

"Charming, but dangerous, my dear fellow."

"She's my friend. I would be more to her if it were not for my poverty. Don't malign her, Badger, I won't stand it."

"My dear boy," broke in Sumner, soothingly, "Badger and I are your friends. Don't be angry with us; we mean it for your good. Aurelia Madison is one of those women with whom mere friendship is impossible. Men must always be half her lovers and therein lies the secret of her power—of any woman's power over our sex, if she is inclined to use that power to our detriment. Oh! she's circumspect," he continued as West attempted a vehement interruption. "I believe that it is not in her to care enough for any one to kick over the advantages of respectability for his sake, but she'll sail close to the wind."

West laughed bitterly: "You speak from experience I suppose; the city is ringing with your broken engagement and its cause."

Sumner stood silent. The blow was a keen one because the wound was so recent.

"Oh, come, fellows; drop it," hastily exclaimed Badger. "What do we care for Miss Madison except as any man admires a handsome woman. She'll bowl you over, Carrie, my son; she's using you just now to suit her own purposes. You're young yet," he continued affectionately, "but when you've had two or three seasons of this sort of thing, you'll hold your own with the deepest of them."

"Yes, West," rejoined Sumner who had regained his self-possession, "there are scores of just such women in the world: I will own that once I thought Aurelia Madison divine, but," shrugging his shoulders, "I have changed my opinion, and I am not sorry to have escaped from her toils. If you enjoy her society, continue to do so, but be careful; don't let her snare you."

"You ought to do some of your preaching to old Bowen. Dogged if he ain't gone on her worse than I am; any way, it looks so; he's there every night."

"What!" exclaimed Sumner.

"Let up, West, why don't you?" said Will Badger giving him a meaning look. "It's my idea, Cuthbert, that Senator Bowen is putting money into the mine. That's what I think is the attraction. I intended to speak to you about it some days ago."

Sumner made no reply, and in a few moments the trio left the house.

Washington society, with its proneness to overlook small trespasses, was beginning to talk about the Madisons. Some declared the beautiful daughter but a bait to snare the unwary, and openly voted the Major "shady." A good deal of money changed hands in the salon of the unpretentious house on New York Avenue: it was whispered also that the mine was a gigantic swindle. As yet these reports were but floating rumors; no one had made open complaint.

Meanwhile, the evenings were gay in the drawing-room where Aurelia smiled and flirted with the greatest intellects of the great Republic. There was an excellent buffet, obsequious servants, the soft shuffle of cards, and in the billiard room at the rear of the house, a chosen few rattled dice or gave themselves up to the fascinations of rouge-et-noir.

It was past eleven when the servant opened the door of Major Madison's salon and the three friends entered. Sumner found himself in a fair-sized and well-furnished room, containing a semi-grand piano; it was the one he had entered on his formal visit. Aurelia was the only woman present. The Major came forward from a group near the fire-place to receive them.

"So pleased to see you," he said, shaking hands in his cordial fashion. "Aurelia, my dear, here is Mr. Sumner." West was already standing by the beauty's chair, and Badger had passed on to a group of men in another part of the room.

Aurelia was exquisitely dressed in her favorite colors, cream and terra-cotta, combined in a wonderful gown.

"Well, Mr. Sumner, have you honored us at last?" she queried as she laid her hand lightly in his. Then as her father moved away she said with a bitter smile:

"The fault was not mine. I would have died rather than Jewel should have heard my foolish words."

Her manner more than her words, broke down all Sumner's lingering suspicions, and he warmed perceptibly toward her. She was but a girl, impassioned, impressionable. What right had he to accuse her of perfidy. Some one came up to them and interrupted her.

Yes, she would give them music. She went to the piano and Sumner followed her. She played popular selections from the latest opera bouffe, and then a morcean in a style that satisfied the most critical taste.

Senator Bowen had just entered the house and paused for the music to cease before speaking to Miss Madison, then he went up to her passing Sumner with a cold nod. Presently

Major Madison and he disappeared, and Sumner felt they had gone to the card room. He wandered about for a while seeing enough to alarm him at the ascendency Major Madison had evidently gained over the Senator. As he stood at the door of the room watching the party where Senator Bowen sat staking large sums of rouge-et-noir and losing at every turn of the wheel, he felt dejected at his own helplessness. Gaming was Senator Bowen's only vice, a legacy from the old days when as mate he played every night for weeks as the cotton steamer made her trips up and down the river highways in the ante-bellum days. Sumner determined to rescue the honest old man from the toils of these sharpers. Just then Aurelia came up to him and touched his arm.

"I wish to speak with you, Bert, come with me."

He gave her his arm and they went to the vacant library. As they passed from view one man standing back of Senator Bowen's chair watching the game said to another:

"Sumner rich?"

"Very."

"It would be a fine thing for Miss Madison to catch him in the rebound. He seems fascinated."

"Indeed it would. And why not? She is of good blood, and he does not need money."

"Ah, no! only beauty and love. She is worthy of a coronet."

The soft light of tender sympathy was on Aurelia's face. Sumner clasped both her hands in his and begged her to tell him all she knew of Jewel.

"That is why I brought you here," was her serious reply. "I mean to undo this tangled web which I have unwittingly woven."

"Is she well? does she hate me? Dare I go to her?" he asked with passionate earnestness.

Disengaging one of her hands, Aurelia laid it on his shoulder, while she answered in soothing tones:

"Jewel is quite well, Bert dear, but she is allowing General Benson to monopolize her attention; in fact, I sometimes fear that the mischief is beyond repair and that she is pledged to him. But I am sure she loves you still. Trust a woman's intuitive powers. She cannot deceive me. Whatever she has done has been in a spirit of pique which needs but your presence to overcome. We will save her if it is not too late."

"Bless you for those words," he said, "your sympathy is very sweet to me."

"Be patient, and leave it all to me; I will bring you together again."

"You have filled my mind with forbodings," he said dejectedly, "I fear it is too late."

"Not too late, Bert; leave me the hope, at least, of redeeming myself in the eyes of Jewel. I have arranged for a meeting between you on Tuesday. On that day the Senator and Mrs. Bowen go to the President's reception. Jewel has a cold and will not be able to accompany them. She expects me to spend the evening with her. I waive my engagement in your favor, Bert; see that you improve your opportunity."

Tears filled her eyes, her voice broke, she was pale with emotion. She was proud of the intense feeling she displayed, and felt that she was acting her part splendidly. For a moment Sumner was speechless, then he kissed her hand and said in a broken voice, as he turned to go:

"God bless you, Aurelia."

* * * * *

At four A.M., General Benson, Major Madison and Aurelia stood alone in the deserted drawing-room.

The Major waved in triumph two checks for large amounts, bearing Senator Bowen's signature.

"That's all right, Madison, but it is slow work—too slow for me. How are you getting on, Aurelia?"

She looked at him with an evil smile on her face that destroyed all its marvelous beauty: "I have told Cuthbert Sumner to call on Jewel, Tuesday evening. The Senator and his wife will be out, the girl alone. I think, General, you can do the rest, and settle the matter once for all."

"By jove, Aurelia, I will convince him of my triumph against all odds. You've earned your husband and your million."

CHAPTER XVIII

The burst of gaiety which the ball brought into Jewel's life, made the succeeding days of gloom more depressing. Her high spirits had received a severe shock in her supposed discovery of Cuthbert's treachery, from which they rallied with difficulty.

"Don't stand there, my darling, those large windows are always draughty."

"I feel nothing of the sort, mama; don't libel this beautiful house, if you please."

"Beautiful house indeed; I shall be glad when June is come. I long for the breeze of the ranch."

"There will be more snow by tomorrow, mama."

"Of course! It seems to me that everything is out of joint. Think of snow in Washington in March!"

Jewel left the window where the light was darkening. She

smiled at Mrs. Bowen and one could see how wan and delicate she looked.

"Mama, you are pessimistic to-day," she said kneeling beside the fire and stretching out her hands to the blaze.

Mrs. Bowen made to reply. In truth, her heart was bitter within her breast. She made an effort to appear cheerful before Jewel, not altogether successful.

The two ladies were in the favorite lounging room of the family—the small reception room. Jewel's great mass of bright hair rolled at the back of her small head, seemed too heavy a weight for it, while the hand that held the fleecy shawl about her was so shadowy as to fill one with apprehension. Yet she did not complain, only her parents noted the change in her since the night of the great ball, with feelings of uneasiness.

"My dear," said the Senator to his wife in one of their conversations about the best course in the matter, "My dear, if it were left to me, I'd shoot Sumner on sight. Out in 'Frisco his life wouldn't be worth a cuss. I've as much as I can do to keep decent and not put a ball into his miserable carcass. Think of a feller philandering after two women to once, either of them handsome enough to satisfy any reasonable man even if he is dead sot on looks in a female. Blast my eyes, Mrs. Senator, it's lucky we start for 'Frisco as soon as the session closes. I'd not answer for holding in much longer.

"Who'd have believed it possible! Sumner seems such a decent feller. Talk about deceit in women! Women ain't in it compared with these Eastern raised gents they call men!"

Then Senator Bowen retired to his club to vent his rage in pushing billiard balls about. It was during one of his fits of impotent wrath that he fell into Major Madison's toils and became an easy victim.

"Oh! my dove," murmured Mrs. Bowen to herself, as she had murmured many a time during the past few weeks; "my gentle, proud, suffering flower, how I wish I could take the pain out of your young heart and bear it for you; it is so hard to see that look on your child face, and feel that the sunshine is gone for you, and then realize that with all my love I can do nothing—nothing, nothing. A woman's life is hard, hard, from the cradle to the grave. O, God! why were we made to bear all the punishment for Adam's fall! Why are men so cruel? Why did he win her heart to throw it one side as a worthless bauble?"

Mrs. Bowen was crocheting an afghan and the needle dropped from her long white fingers and a settled look of pain crept like a veil over the beautiful proud face as she gazed into the fire.

Aurelia had been to see Jewel, had told her with many tears and sobs, of the broken engagement between herself and Cuthbert, that they still loved each other, that Sumner blamed himself for believing that he had forgotten her (Aurelia) and had engaged himself to Jewel without realizing the true state of his feelings, and now he would never marry—neither of them felt that they could know happiness without the thought of Jewel's wrongs before them. Could they not be friends still, she and Jewel? She was so lonely and miserable feeling that she had brought so much suffering on her dear friend. Mrs. Bowen heard it all but deep in her heart was a doubt of the specious pleader.

"I wish we had not been so hasty, and had given Cuthbert a chance to explain," she remarked to Jewel one day.

"There is nothing to explain," replied Jewel lifting her

head proudly. "I saw and heard it all for myself. He told me he had only met Aurelia casually at the Cape, leaving almost immediately; now I find beyond a doubt, that they were actually engaged. Nothing can alter the fact that he had something to conceal and for that reason deceived me. Then, too, papa has met him at the Major's, and has heard the gossip of the clubs. It proves itself, mama; there is nothing more to be said. I—I have learnt my lesson—I shall never be so foolish again. I have to thank Mr. Sumner for teaching me worldly wisdom."

"I had thought better things of Cuthbert. I would never have believed him to be the cruel, selfish man he has proved. Well, may he have some peace before he marries Aurelia, for I suppose it will end that way. He will be punished if he marries her or I greatly mistake her nature."

Jewel knelt on, gazing into the fire. She was silent for a time, and then she said gently:

"You dislike Aurelia, mama, simply for my sake. It is not like you to be unjust."

Mrs. Bowen glanced at her sharply.

"It is not that alone, Jewel, but I believe her false. I have a presentiment that there is something wrong. O, my darling, do be careful. I think it would kill your father if anything happened to you," exclaimed Mrs. Bowen as she folded her daughter in her loving arms.

Jewel answered her tender embrace with warm kisses.

"Dear mama, the sting is taken out of all the pain when I remember that no matter what comes my own darling father and mother see no fault in their dear girl."

Ah! children who have not needed it yet, believe that the wound must be mortal that cannot be soothed by parental balm and oil. Those dear ones have the power to restore self-respect though they may be powerless to restore happiness. Mrs. Bowen put the girl from her and left the room.

"Yes, I, too, shall be glad to return to the ranch. It will be quiet and peaceful there. I shall forget."

She shivered. "Forget," she repeated, pressing her hands to her breast, and moving to and fro in agitation, "no, no! I shall never forget—I shall remember as long as I live."

She rose to her feet and began walking the length of the room. The opening of the door aroused her, and turning with a slight frown, she saw General Benson.

The frown deepened as she saw him place a basket of lovely flowers on a table. She did not desire him to bring her gifts; but this did not cause her pain. It was the vision of a by-gone-day, when some one else was wont to come softly into the room with beautiful flowers.

Her face flushed for a moment, then became paler than ever. She gave General Benson her hand silently, he bit his lip when he saw how quickly she withdrew it.

"Sam told me I should find Mrs. Bowen here," he said courteously.

"Mama is in her room. I will ring and let her know you are here."

"Wait one moment," he pleaded. "I have brought you some flowers, Miss Jewel."

"They are very beautiful," she answered coldly; "and you are very kind, General Benson."

"Flowers suit you," he said in his soft caressing voice, that had never failed him with other women, but which was wasted on Jewel. "You should always be surrounded with them, Miss Jewel."

She did not smile. This man's admiration jarred on her.

Her father liked his pleasant ways and found him a good companion to wile away the hours, but somehow she could not assume the easy familiarity of friendship with him.

She took herself to talk for her growing dislike of him. Why should she be so ungenerous to one so kind? Why should she shrink from him with a loathing she could not repress? She had never voiced her feelings but she knew that her mother felt with her toward this sauve, diplomatic gentleman. She had once seem him kick the dog that followed him, cowed and faithful only through fear, and she disliked him for the cowardly act. She spoke to him about it.

"Oh, one must be in the fashion!" he replied, never dreaming of the anger and disgust beneath the girl's cold exterior. "And dogs were made to kick. People talk a lot of rubbish about the faithfulness of dogs. It's all bosh! Their devotion means dread of the whip, or a strong boot, Miss Jewel."

Jewel's disgust was so great that for the moment she lost all other feeling, every remnant of respect and liking fled. He had forgotten the incident; and though resenting the girl's coldness, he did not associate his own cruelty with it. In fact, he put it down to coquetry, and it only inflamed his admiration and strengthened his determination to make this girl his wife. He wondered if Senator and Mrs. Bowen would oppose him?

Jewel's stepmother was a woman of the world, and between General Benson and herself there was no great liking. He felt uneasy in her presence, that under her rather haughty manner a keen sight was hidden that read his motives. Senator Bowen was more to his liking. In reply to Mrs. Bowen's cautious questioning concerning General Benson, the Senator's answer was:

"The government, my dear, gives him its confidence by

placing him in a responsible position. That is enough for me. Uncle Sam never employs rascals to transact his business."

Opposition or not, General Benson meant to win in the end. Aurelia might fail with Cuthbert, but he would win with Jewel. He was irritated by the delay; apart from his vanity which was injured by Jewel's indifference, it was time the engagement was announced. His creditors were unpleasantly pressing. His property in Baltimore was mortgaged up to its full value. There was nothing for it but this marriage with the California millionaire's heiress.

Heiresses were not easily found. It was only a question of time and management, and Jewel must be his wife.

"Yes, you are one of those beings for whom it seems flowers were especially created. I always think of you as a delicate lily or a white rose."

The girl's face flushed, but not with pleasure.

"Mama must see them. She will admire them," she said as she rang the bell, and sent a message to Mrs. Bowen.

General Benson bit his lip. He had intended speaking to her today, but it was not an easy thing to do. She kept him at bay.

"Have you seen Miss Madison lately?" he asked sauntering up to the fire. Jewel shook her head.

"Not this week," and the troubled look returned to her eyes.

"She is a great girl," said Benson with a laugh—he leaned against the over-mantel and stroked his moustache: "She and Sumner are going the pace. I suppose we cannot expect lovebirds to remember anything outside their paradise." Jewel shivered.

"She loves him still," he said to himself between his teeth.

"Well, it is no matter; she may love him now, but I shall alter that when she is my wife."

Then with the innate cruelty of his nature he continued:

"Sumner is to be congratulated, if what I hear is true; the Madisons are a fine old Southern family, and Miss Aurelia is worthy of her race." He hid a smile behind his hand.

"It is quite refreshing in these matter-of-fact days to come upon a real genuine romance. Love, they say, is out of fashion, if so, I am afraid Sumner is a long way behind the times, for I am told he is madly in love. That I guessed the first time I saw them together. One could read his infatuation in his eyes. Miss Madison's magnificent beauty easily accounts for it. Her face is her fortune, most assuredly." Jewel drew herself away a few steps. The pain he hoped to give her was not there. She had schooled herself to bear hearing the news of the engagement at any time. He could arouse her indignation—pride; this he did successfully.

"Then it is settled. Aurelia is very beautiful," she said quietly. "She is my friend, and I think her one of the most beautiful women I have ever seen."

He smiled.

"Ah, pardon, Miss Jewel; I had forgotten while speaking that you were more than ordinarily interested. Always sweet and generous, Miss Jewel, most rarely so, for one beautiful woman seldom acknowledges another."

"Here is mama." Jewel turned to the door with a faint sigh of relief. "Will you excuse me, General Benson, I want to catch the next mail?"

General Benson did not stay much longer. He was not at his ease with Mrs. Bowen. He was furious with Jewel for retiring and leaving him with her mother. He set it down against her in his book of reckoning to be settled in a future not far-distant.

Mrs. Bowen went to Jewel after he was gone. "You have not looked at your flowers, Blossom," she said gently. Her daughter colored.

"They are very beautiful, but—"

"They give you no pleasure?"

"I do not like presents from General Benson."

"You do not like him?" queried her mother, stroking the wonderful coils of shining hair.

The girl shivered.

"No—no. I do not like him at all; he is very kind, but I cannot bring myself to like him, mama, dear."

Mrs. Bowen kissed her brow.

"Nor do I; he is a bad man and I shall find a way to stop his calling here." She paused a moment lost in deep thought. "Perhaps it is well that we do not return to Washington next fall. I am glad your father has so decided."

The small hours of the morning found Jewel still sitting before her bedroom fire. She had returned from a reception, and had dismissed her maid, telling Venus that she would manage without her.

She was thinking of words she had heard that confirmed the report that Sumner and Aurelia were engaged. She had not seen the latter for a number of days, but she felt that she might expect her at any moment to confirm the report. What is first love? Some say first love is "calf love," a silly infatuation for an insipid hero or heroine.

Others will tell you first love is the only true passion; that it comes but once to every human being; that the intense yearning for the sound of a beloved voice, the sight of an adored face, the clasp of a hand, only fills the heart once in a lifetime. The question as to whether it is the deepest love must be answered by each individual.

"The heart knoweth its own bitterness," says Holy writ. So also it knoweth its own joy. Jewel was a firm believer in the strength of first love. And now she found herself suffering the pangs of love despised, the anguish of disappointment, the humiliation of neglect. Ever before her inner sight was the merry dancing, daring, the glancing fun in those dark eyes so recently her sun. How little she had been to him that he could so soon forget.

Oh, they were beautiful eyes, she thought, with a stirring of the old rapture at her heart. What a noble face he has! high-bred, refined, and manly, too! There was not another man to compare with him; and—he belonged to another. A bitter pang smote upon her, a keen memory of the events of the past weeks. She wept over her baseless dreams, and prayed for strength to solve the problem of her life.

"How shall I meet him?" she asked herself. "How shall I be calm, conventional to Mr. and Mrs. Cuthbert Sumner?" Long she sat there pondering many things.

CHAPTER XIX

The last of March came, but winter still lingered in the lap of spring. Jewel's couch was drawn up before the blazing fire; the parlor was snug and comfortable, just cosey enough for a semi-invalid. The room was half-panelled with oak, and the furniture was of the same material covered with bright silk and embroidered cushions.

Jewel was not well and had excused herself from attendance at the President's reception. Her mother had ensconced her in the small reception parlor promising to return early, and bidding her doze away the time until then. She was not asleep. Her eyes were open, and fixed upon the fire; they were filled with intense pain, and her hands were clenched, while now and then a shiver ran through her frame, as she turned restlessly from side to side.

She sought solitude that evening, and yet the sound of Sam's voice in the hall admitting a visitor whose tones betrayed Gen. Benson, was not distasteful to her.

He was very much at home now, and drew a low chair round between her and the fire, after bidding her good evening, took his place there, and gazed steadfastly into her face a few moments without speaking.

"Of what are you thinking?" he asked gently.

"I am thinking what a horrible thing it is that we women are always loving the wrong men—worthless, heartless men, who cannot appreciate in even a small degree the love we waste upon them."

He took one of her hands in his.

"Look at me," he said. "You are very young—you will get over this happening—this episode in the life of every young girl. Don't start. How can anyone who cares for you, help knowing that you have suffered through loving the wrong man? But time is a great healer. Now don't try to free your hand. It must belong to me some day, so why not let it rest in mine now?"

She shivered as she turned from him.

"You don't understand," she said speaking very low. "My heart is dead, or only so much alive that I can feel it ache. I can never love—never marry. I must go on living—expiating my wilful blindness in being so reckless as to love a—a villain with all my heart and soul."

The tears rolled slowly down her face.

"Won't you let me try to comfort you?" he asked.

She shook her head. "You cannot give me back the man I believed in," she replied.

Benson rose, frowning heavily.

"Can't I horsewhip him or do something to punish the scoundrel?"

"No, no!"

"You don't love him still?"

"No," she answered. "But I can never hate him. Don't let's talk about it any more," she continued wearily. "Dead loves are like dead people—talking will not bring them back."

"I will make you forget him some day," he said, kissing her hand.

"I wish you could," she replied with a sigh.

Benson felt encouraged, and determined to follow up his advantage.

"What has put you in this state?" he asked tenderly.

"Why are you not at the reception?" she laughed evasively.

"That is not answering my question?" he retorted. "Either you need a doctor or your distress of mind calls for an adviser. Shall I hold your hand, and see if I can mesmerize you into telling me all your thoughts?" he continued half-laughing. Jewel drew back in alarm. She raised herself on her arm and looked away from him into the fire.

"You have no right to question me as you know."

"Why won't you give me the right?" he asked earnestly. "Look, Jewel, I love you and trust you so much, I am ready to take you on any terms. I should be glad and proud to marry you tomorrow, and wait for time to bring me love."

"Why will you tease me?" she asked desperately. "Be my friend without asking reward, but never hope to be anything else."

The girl was sitting now on the couch that had served her

for a resting place. She bowed her head; the long silken lashes lay on her cheeks.

He still held her hand; and as he gazed down upon her face, so pale and sorrowing, his pulses throbbed with greater passion.

"Jewel you are an angel! Be one to me. You have many years to live; you could not, would not pass them alone. Be merciful then to one who worships the ground you tread! I know my heart. It is yours. None other can, shall ever share it. Accept my love and me, my darling!"

He was bending over her, his breath ruffled the soft rings of her hair. His feverish earnestness moved her. She felt a great pity for him. For the time she forgot her repugnance.

"He feels as I feel," she thought.

What would she not have done for him in her compassion! Anything but what his lips pleaded for; that was impossible.

"I am so sorry—so very sorry!" she said, and the light of her eyes, even the touch of her fingers confirmed her words. "But you see I have no love to give."

"Jewel," lightly he placed his arm about her, "I give you my love; I ask but, in return, you. Let me have the right of loving you through life. I will be content; for I shall live in hope that my affection shall one day win yours. If you must think your whole first love given, let me hold the second place in your heart."

"Is second love possible?" she asked.

"Most surely. Give me that; I will be satisfied." Her lips moved; assent seemed to quiver on them, when looking up, she gazed directly into Cuthbert Sumner's eyes. He had been waited upon to the room by Sam, and had stood there looking at them without being noticed so absorbed had they been in their conversation.

With a cry Jewel staggered to her feet.

"Jewel, Jewel, hear me," cried Sumner in desperation, "I pray you, before you part us forever. Do not be rash; for God's sake, let me speak, hear me!" She waved him back as he stepped toward her.

General Benson was bewildered; his active mind comprehended instantly the peril of the moment—the frustration of his plans if he hesitated an instant—and his ready wit saved him. It was the time for decisive action. With a swift movement he placed himself at Jewel's side, took her hand in his, and thus faced Sumner.

"Mr. Sumner, this intrusion is unwarrantable. Miss Bowen is my promised wife."

Cuthbert bowed his head, and turning, rushed from the room and from the house.

(To be continued.)

❧ ❧ ❧

CHAPTER XX

Cuthbert Sumner tendered his resignation to General Benson to take effect at the close of the official year, and it was accepted. "I have no feeling but friendship for you, Mr. Sumner," said the General after he had folded the document away. "I hope and trust that whatever happens we shall remember each other without enmity," he continued in his sweet voice so effective with most people. "Still, feeling that it must be unpleasant for you to serve under me, when we consider existing circumstances, without doubt what you propose is the best course."

It was ten o'clock the next day and Sumner sat at his desk looking out occasionally at the gathering storm that threatened to send March out with tumultuous blustering winds and heavy rain. The secretary and the stenographer occupied the same apartment with the chief. The ceiling of the apartment was lofty, there were elegant paintings on the walls, and the furniture was luxurious. There were rich hangings at the windows, carpets and rugs on the floor, lounges were grouped about the spacious room giving it more the appearance of a boudoir than a public office. The style of the wardrobes ranged about the walls would lead one to infer that all the conveniences for dining or longing could be easily found within its four walls. Nor would one have been mistaken in inferring such to be the case; indeed, the chief's lunch was generally served in this room in sumptuous style by his valet. It was rumored, too, that here gay spreads and bachelor parties were not unknown; happenings at which grave questions of state were sometimes decided.

A warm fire burned in the grate for there was a chill in the air that furnace heat did not entirely remove, and the large pile of blazing coals shed a glowing radiance of cheerfulness on all around.

General Benson, it was evident, though a servant of the people, was using their resources freely to gratify an extravagant taste. His was the life of a popular official floating at the ease of his own sweet will.

The only other occupant beside Cuthbert and Benson was Elise Bradford the stenographer. This woman was elegantly attired, and here again one noticed how utterly out of keeping her dress was with the work supposed to be performed by a simple government clerk. She was tall, fair and pale, with a countenance that impressed one with it resigned expression and sad dignity.

General Benson sat before his splendidly covered table where cut-glass bottles of eau de cologne gleamed, vases of fragrant flowers charmed the eye, and ornamental easels of costly style held pictures of fashionable ladies. He was looking over some papers which had just been submitted by Cuthbert. This morning he was abstracted and silent. Finally he called Sumner to him in a recess of a curtained window and said:

"Sumner, I have a favor to ask of you."

"I shall be happy to grant it if it is in my power, General."

"Thanks, I felt sure such would be your answer. I shall have to ask you and Miss Bradford to work overtime tomorrow and Sunday. This work must have our special attention. It is of such a nature that I can not confide it to an ordinary clerk. I cannot superintend to work myself because a party is to leave here on Saturday, myself among the number, for New York, on official business—two or three Senators and a Cabinet official to represent the President. We shall not return for ten days and I shall depend upon you to keep the office business in hand."

"I will do all that I can willingly," replied Sumner.

"And I think I'll go off now. The time is short until five tomorrow. I have some preparations to make. You may as well take charge at once."

Leaving Sumner he stepped to the side of Miss Bradford and engaged in a whispered conversation. Cuthbert was a discreet person and gave no heed to the couple. He was used to the manners of many high officials with their female clerks, and paid no attention to what did not concern him. He had observed that an apparent intimacy existed between his chief and Miss Bradford. If they knew that he had noticed them they gave no sign that his knowledge was an annoyance. His presence was treated with the utmost decorum.

The whispered talk kept on for some time. Finally, whatever subject had been under discussion seemed to have been satisfactorially arranged, and the chief arose from the seat he had occupied beside the lady and shook her hand warmly, with the words:

"At Easter then without fail."

"Poor Jewel," thought Cuthbert, "what will be her fate when she is the wife of this man who is but a reformed rake seeking to re-instate himself in society by a high political position and a rich marriage."

As the thought lingered in his mind, General Benson paused beside his desk. Sumner could not refrain from giving him an admiring glance nor could he wonder at the infatuation of most women for the handsome chief who stood there drawing on his gloves, his costly fur-lined coat unbuttoned and nearly sweeping the carpet giving an added charm to this handsome face, elegant figure and gracious manner.

"I have intrusted you with a delicate piece of business, Mr. Sumner." His voice was impressive. "The official relations between us have always been coordinate in character. I am confiding in you now as I would in a personal friend. You will find some additional papers to be collated in my desk," he continued drawing him behind the rich folds of the curtains back of the official desk. He gaze was fixed full in Sumner's face with such earnestness and anxiety that at once appealed to the secretary's sympathy. Sumner's face was like an open book in its candor and innocence of guile, as he replied quietly:

"You may trust me, General Benson, to respect your

confidence. Personal matters have no entrance where they would interfere with obedience to my superiors."

"And, see here, Sumner, you may be detained later to-morrow night than tonight. Your work will probably keep you until sharp midnight, perhaps past. I have given the watchman notice of your being here by my orders. Here is my private entrance key and you can let yourself and Miss Bradford out without trouble. See that everything is safely closed up. You shall be handsomely compensated for your extra labor, although I know that you have no thought of the money," he added in answer to Sumner's deprecating wave of the hand. "Good-bye," and giving him his hand, the chief shook his warmly, and left the room."

They heard him descending the stairs, talking and laughing with messengers and others employed about the building, in the genial way for which he was noted among government employees.

CHAPTER XXI

Time and tide wait for no man; brains may throb, and hearts may ache or break, but the world rolls on just the same, for weal and woe, whether the grim skeleton that comes an unbidden guest on so many a man's hearth is shrouded in elegance or bare in all its appalling hideousness.

It was not until two P.M. of Sunday that the secretary and stenographer had time to rest as they neared the close of their labors. Sumner felt a weariness of spirit and a dull aching of the heart that was not due to overwork. Worriment had removed the fresh heartful bloom from his face, but the paleness and thinness added to its refinement and intellectuality; while the restless feverish dilation of his dark eyes rendered them singularly striking and brilliant. More than once during this wretched time he had been possessed with a longing to be back with his father in their quiet New England home.

"Yes, this shall be my last year in politics. I'll go home and take up the business for which I was born; it will please my father."

As he turned to resume his work with a sigh, he became conscious that Miss Bradford was watching him. There had been a time when he had felt a passing admiration for the good-looking stenographer, and had paid her some attention, but after he met Jewel he had never pretended to give her a second thought.

She, on her side, had not resented his dessertion but always seemed to retain a genuine regard for him which had shown itself in many neighborly acts of kindness which the close intimacy of office life often brings about between women and men. She had been rattling the keys of her typewriter at a furious rate of speed all day, and now, with a final pull of the carriage, finished her work. Then she rose with a sigh, crossed the room and flung herself down on one of the couches opposite Sumner's desk, evidently bent on conversation.

"Mr. Sumner, you look—oh, I don't know how you look, but I should say a rest would do you good."

"I shall have one when the vacation comes. I am going home and I shall not return to Washington."

"Are you going for good?" she asked in a surprised tone.

"Yes," he answered as he adjusted a pile of manuscript, and began folding up the papers scattered over his desk. "Washington holds no charm for me."

She was silent for a time and as she sat buried in deep thought she tapped the floor with one foot in restless fashion. At length she said:

"Don't think me intrusive, or that I seek to harrow your feelings, but isn't this sudden resolve the result of the misunderstanding between you and Miss Bowen?"

"I will answer you as frankly as you have asked, Miss Bradford; it is so."

There followed another pause, a silence so long that the young man thought that she had forgotten his presence. Suddenly she spoke again.

"Mr. Sumner, I like you; I trust you; why I know not, for my experience in life has not been of so pleasant a nature as to cause me to trust anyone; not a man, surely. But today I feel a desire to talk on forbidden subjects, to take someone into my confidence."

Sumner looked at her keenly as he said significantly:

"It is a safe rule, Miss Bradford, to keep one's own counsel."

"I feel impelled to tell you what I am about to disclose, by an unseen power. Do you not believe in unseen forces influencing our acts?" she asked wistfully.

"I cannot deny that I have sometimes felt the same influence of supernatural powers that you speak of, and I do firmly trust that the world of shadows and mystery to which we are all bound may be one of infinite love, infinite calm and rest."

"For those who have been upright here," while a look of pain crossed her face. "But what of those among us who have been guilty of many sins? That is the thought that haunts me tonight." She pushed her hair from her face with one hand as she looked up at him.

"Why trouble ourselves with such questions, Miss Bradford? Why not simply trust the judgment that sees not as man sees?"

She felt calmed as she looked into the true, earnest face opposite her. "Thank you," she said at last, simply. Then—

"May I tell you?"

"Whatever confidence you honor me by giving shall be sacredly respected."

"I know that. Did I not tell you that I trusted you? But you have my permission to tell Jewel Bowen as much as you think fit, for it is her due."

Sumner colored as he said:

"I am not on terms of intimacy with Miss Bowen."

"I know that, too," she replied impatiently, "but you probably will be after you hear what I have to tell you. I, too, am about to leave Washington. When I leave the office tonight I shall never return. Easter is two weeks off, and at Easter I am to be married to General Benson."

"Married—General Benson! Impossible! You jest!" exclaimed the startled man.

"To General Benson," she repeated emphatically.

"But—Miss Bowen—"

"Will have a welcome release," she broke in. "It is a long-delayed ceremony that should have been performed five years ago. I have a son four years old, Mr. Sumner!"

Sumner could not answer her. He stared at the woman before him with unseeing eyes. He could not believe that he had heard aright.

"A son four years of age!" he repeated mechanically in shocked surprise. "This is most extraordinary! How can it be possible?" No wonder you are incredulous.

"Wait, wait!" she went on, "give me time. I will tell you

all; it is your right to know. It has all been arranged so suddenly that my brain is in a whirl—I cannot think!"

She flung herself down against the cushions of the couch, and endeavored to grow calm. Sumner waited, disturbed, unhappy, heartsick, over this scene, fearing he knew not what. He watched her labored breathing, her clenched hands, and there was a long pause.

Sumner cast anxious glances over at the bowed head opposite him supported on its owner's hand. The fire blazed cheerily, and outside the wind rose, whirling the rain in great sheets against the window panes. It was a wild night.

Finally Elsie Bradford sat up pushing her hair back restlessly from her temples, and faced him white and agitated.

"All this misery that you have endured for the past month," she began slowly,—"all the sorrow, you owe to one man. He has tortured you, fooled you, deceived you—Yes, it is true; but I—God help me—I love him."

"I do not comprehend your meaning, Miss Bradford, to whom do you refer?" he asked soothingly, for there was the glitter of fever in her eyes.

"Silence!" she interrupted sternly. "I must tell you certain things for your own welfare and the welfare of the girl you love. I dare not hide them. Perhaps—who knows—it may be put down to my credit in that great future life toward which we are all journeying. In the years that are coming, when you are both happy and forgetful of this present miserable time, remember me and my misery with pity."

Sumner could only wait in pained surprise for her to continue. She pressed her hands convulsively to her heart, as she sat there white as death, and trembling all over.

"Did it ever occur to you, Cuthbert Sumner, that you are the victim of a plot?"

"You will speak in riddles, Miss Bradford. I must confess that I do not understand you."

"And yet you are a man of remarkable intelligence, and not a child in the world's ways. I cannot swear to it, but I believe that you have fallen into the net of two adventurers and a daring adventuress. Have you noticed any intimacy between General Benson and the Madisons?"

"No; they seem to be merely chance acquaintances."

"And yet, they are partners in crime, and I believe that General Benson introduced the Bowens to the Madisons."

"Great heavens! No!" cried Sumner a great light breaking in upon him at the bare possibility of such a thing being true. "Miss Bradford, are you sure?" he asked hurriedly.

"I am almost certain of the truth of what I say; you can easily ascertain if I am correct in my suspicions. I believe the intention was, your fortune for Aurelia Madison, Miss Bowen's for the General."

"But where do you get you information? Upon what are your suspicions based? Surely you have something to go upon," cried Sumner recovering from his first bewilderment.

"How can I tell you? Oh! the shame of it all will kill me," she said as she drew a long shuddering breath.

"Your distress pains me, Miss Bradford," said Cuthbert gently as he watched the wretched girl; he was moved more than he cared to show—indignant—furious over the conduct of this scoundrel in a high place. He went to one of the wardrobes and opened the door disclosing a compartment used as a wine closet. He quickly filled a glass from a costly cut-glass decanter, and carried it to the half-fainting woman urging her to drink it.

She took it eagerly from his hand and drained the glass.

"Yes, yes, I must go on. It is part of my punishment—

my atonement! It is such misery, shame!" she sobbed bro-
kenly. "I heard he was about to marry Miss Bowen. I accused
him of treachery toward you in the matter. I threatened him
with exposure. I told him that he must make atonement to
me and the child at once. He must do it or I would speak; I
would go to Miss Bowen with the whole miserable story."

"And he?" questioned Sumner gently, yet sternly, stifling
his own feelings for the sake of the heart-broken woman
before him, giving out strength and protection with womanly
tenderness to soothe. "Tell me all, and be sure that I will
speak of nothing that you desire kept secret."

"To have you understand the man known as General
Benson, I must tell you a portion of my history."

"Excuse me," broke in Sumner, "you say 'known as General Benson,' is not that his true name?"

"No, it is not. And I cannot give you the true one. I have
my own thoughts about it, however, When I was eighteen
years of age, I came from Kentucky, where I was born, to
Washington seeking employment.

I was left an orphan while an infant, and brought up by
my aunt who was too poor to support me after I entered
womanhood. She did the best for me that she could, however,
and I started out with high hopes, telling her that I should
soon be able to repay her for her kindness and care. I had
heard much of the large salaries paid to government clerks,
and determined to seek employment here.

Arriving in the city, I went to call upon the congressman
from our district to whom I brought letters of introduction.
He received me kindly, and said that he would do his best
to have me appointed. After a week he sent me word to call
at the Treasury Building. There he introduced me to General
Benson who wanted a clerk. The General immediately en-

gaged me, and it is needless for me to say that I was overjoyed at my good fortune. I was able to send my aunt money, and for a time I was perfectly happy. It is useless to dwell on the details—I wish to hurry over this part of my life—suffice it that in six months time I had become the chief's victim.

I am abhorrent to you, no doubt. You who have been rich all your life may despise me; but I had tasted poverty, I appreciated its effect on my future welfare, and I sickened at the thought."

She paused a moment to take breath, for she had spoken rapidly, as if eager to have done with the shameful and painful details. "Official wealth, power and opportunity were my ruin. I was led to confide in the chief by his high position; and he, like others in such places, deceived me and betrayed that confidence. He was my first lover, for I was but eighteen, and I loved him as we always love the first man who teaches us what love is. I admired his genial ways, his distinguished air, and even his success in his vices was a source of pride to me. He took advantage of my youth to mold me to his fancy, and make me like himself. Oh, I can never make you realize the depravity of our elegant chief.

For a long time he was content with my love. I was young enough and pretty enough to satisfy even him. But after a while he met Aurelia Madison, and then my agony began,"

"What!" exclaimed Sumner, "do you know what you say? Aurelia Madison one of General Benson's mistresses?"

"That is not the worst thing about her," replied the woman with a bitter smile. Will you believe me when I tell you that she is a quadroon?"

"Impossible! you rave!" almost shouted the young man.

"I would it were not true. Yes, she is a quadroon, the child of Major Madison's slave, born about the time the war broke out. That is why the two men find in her a willing tool."

"My God!" exclaimed Sumner as he wiped the perspiration from his face, "a negress! this is too horrible." Repeated shocks had unnerved him, and he felt weak and bewildered.

"Do not blame her. Fate is against her. She is helpless. The education of generations of her foreparents has entered into her blood. I should feel sorry for her if I could, but I feel only my own misery and degredation. I am selfish in my despair. Happy, prosperous people sympathize with the woes of others, but sometimes I feel like laughing at their mimic woes, my own are so much greater in comparison.

Yet Aurelia in a measure deserves our pity. The loveliness of Negro women of mixed blood is very often marvellous, and their condition deplorable. Beautiful almost beyond description, many of them educated and refined, with the best white blood of the South in their veins, they refuse to mate themselves with the ignorant of their own race. Socially, they are not recognized by the whites; they are often without money enough to but the barest necessities of life; honorably, they cannot procure sufficient means to gratify their luxurious tastes; their mothers were like themselves; their fathers they never knew; debauched whitemen are ever ready to take advantage of their destitution, and after living a short life of shame, they sink into early graves. Living, they were despised by whites and blacks alike; dead, they are mourned by none. You know yourself Mr. Sumner, that caste as found at the North is a terrible thing. It is killing the black man's hope there in every avenue; it is centered against his advancement. We in the South are flagrant in our abuse of the Negro but we do not descend to the pettiness that your section practices. We shut our eyes to many things in the South because of our near relationship to many of these despised people. But black blood is everywhere—in society and out, and in our families even; we cannot feel assured that it has not filtered into the most exclusive families. We try to stem the tide but I believe it is a hopeless task."

Sumner listened to her bound by the horrible fascination of her words. At last he said:

"But a white man may be betrayed into marrying her. I certainly came near to it myself."

"Very true; and if she had been a different woman, she would have succeeded, you would have been proud of your handsome wife because of your ignorance of her origin. As life, real life, has unfolded to my view, I have come to think that there is nothing in this prejudice but a relic of barbarism."

"Perhaps your reasoning is true; I will not attempt a denial. But I am thankful for my deliverance."

"Your feeling is natural; certainly, I do not blame you," she said, and after a slight pause resumed her narrative.

"One day the General came to me and told me that we must part. 'I owe you many obligations for your kindness. You have made the past few months very pleasant; of course you knew it was only for awhile, and that it must end some day. It is past now, and we will each go our way just as if we had never met. You must know that with men of the world these things are very natural and very pleasant. Here is some money; and he thrust a well-filled purse in my hands.

My heart was filled with terror and agony. 'But you said that you loved me.' I managed to falter in a dazed way. 'Well, perhaps, for the moment. But—can't you understand these things? I will spare you as much as I can; if I am harsh you press me to it.' He spoke lightly, carelessly, to me as I stood before him crushed for all eternity—to me, who had fallen, without a thought of resistance, under the charm of his manner and beauty, that have ruined more than one woman among those who are above me in wealth and position. It is left for men to change quickly. He seemed dumb, frozen, dead to all feeling. His heart and mind were filled with the dazzling beauty of his new love—the Negress Aurelia Madison. He had nothing left for me—not even pity. Then he continued,—

'Elise, it is particularly necessary for my future plans that this affair of ours be kept secret. If you bury it in your heart, and seal your lips upon it, you shall be recompensed finally, I will never lose sight of you and the boy, but direct that a large sum shall be paid to you yearly. If not—people have died for a less offense than that.'

While he was talking I was thinking deeply and rapidly. I felt that my only chance lay in matching his cunning with diplomacy. I made up my mind to compromise the matter. He was stronger than I; I could do nothing at present. Finally I told him that I would agree to all he asked if he would allow me to retain my position in the office with him, and would provide for the boy and educate him.

This he agreed to do, and there has been a sort of armed neutrality between us ever since. I have learned much by being here. I know enough to ruin him. I planned for it and I have succeeded. He dares not go against me now, and so he has promised marriage, and I shall once more hold my head up among honest women."

Sumner felt a great wave of pity sweep over him at the thought of this delicate woman hoping to cope with the cunning deviltry of the man she had unmasked; but he could not find it in his heart to speak one discouraging word. His eyes filled with tears which were no shame to his manhood.

"Where is the child?" he asked when he could collect his scattered thoughts enough to speak.

"In Kentucky with my aunt," she replied naming a town.

"If what you tell me is true, and knowing what I do, I cannot doubt your story, General Benson is a consummate villain, a dangerous man," said Sumner as he paced the floor in excitement and wrath. "It is not possible that such things can be and go unpunished."

"You know now why I think it all a plot against you. Cannot you see for yourself?"

"Yes; I can never repay you for what you have done."

"Do not mention it. I shall be repaid if only you circumvent that woman, and all is made right between you and Miss Bowen."

It had grown very dark and Sumner lighted the gas.

"I will call a herdic and see you home," he said, "if you will come now. It is long past the dinner hour. We have been here long enough. I feel it impossible to stop here longer, the place stifles me."

"I cannot go yet," she replied, "I have papers to sort and many articles to destroy as well as to gather up. I never wish to see the place again."

"I will stay then until you are ready to go."

"No; that is not necessary, thank you. Give me the key. I will lock up and leave it with the watchman."

"Well, then, if you are not afraid," he said reluctantly. He was dazed by all he had heard and wished to be alone. When he was ready to leave, he took her hand in his and shook it warmly.

"Good-bye, my friend; you have given me renewed hope."

In after years, Cuthbert remembered her face with its varying, changing tints—hope and despair—each struggling for the mastery.

"Yes," she said softly, "I am your friend, but friendships are short—made to be severed. Still, I am sure we shall meet again. How strange it is that lives are touching thus all the time—strangers yesterday, today helping each other—let us hope so at least—touching—parting—but not forgotten—not utterly forgotten."

There was a new dignity in her manner that he had never noticed in the silent stenographer. But there was still a weary, listless tone in her voice.

He pressed her white fingers with his strong eager hand, feeling his heart throb with suppressed excitement—the joy of living once more. He lifted her cold hand and touched it with his lips.

"Good-bye, then, once more; someone said once that meant 'God bless you'; I could say no more if I knew that our parting would be eternal which it is not. I want you to know Jewel."

She looked at him steadily a moment, then her face fell; a slight tremor passed over her face; she was unaccustomed to the chivalrous treatment that men give to women whom they respect. The hand he had kissed fell to her side. As he turned to close the door of the apartment, she was still standing where he had left her, with listless hands and bent head.

CHAPTER XXII

Cuthbert's mind was in a tumult as he walked down the stairs and through the corridors of the great building. His strained nerves relaxed; he felt the intense relief of a man who throws a heavy load from his shoulders.

He accepted without question the story told him by Miss Bradford and her suggestion of a vile plot by these arch-conspirators to gain possession of a fortune. The story was feasible whichever way he viewed it. "Yes, it must be so." The more the thought of it, the more he wondered at his own blindness in not solving the problem before. His eyes flashed, and he clenched his hands in anger. His mood boded ill for his enemies. Already his mind was filled with plans to disconcert the plotters.

He hailed a passing herdic and was driven to his rooms. He felt sick, giddy, his hands trembled. This unexpected revelation, while it caused him intense happiness, nearly overcame him. He longed to be alone in his rooms where he could think over what he had heard. But in the midst of his joy and his plans to see Jewel and explain this great wrong and mystery to her, came thoughts—sorrowful thoughts of the woman who had befriended him. What would be her fate? he asked himself. Surely it was but a question of time before the chief, with his method of living, would disappear beneath the maelstrom of his own unprincipled acts.

It was nine o'clock when he arrived at home thoroughly worn out. A splendid fire in the grate bade him a cordial welcome. John served him a good dinner. After making a pretense of eating, Sumner sat with his wine untasted on the table before him, smoking and staring into the fire. He sat there for hours smoking and thinking. Troubled thoughts disturbed him, shadows lingered on his face which the pleasant surroundings had not the power to dispel. He was deeply impressed by the insignificant trifles that had solved the secret of this wicked plot, in a skillful woman's hands, and more than thankful to know that through her he held the threads of the labyrinth in his own strong hands. He retired to rest worn out in mind and body. Physical and mental exhaustion brought some degree of calm, and he slept, but his slumber was fitful and broken, and he could still hear the moaning of the wind and the beating of the rain against the window panes. Mingled with these sounds were distorted dreams—bearing a shadowy relation to the scenes through which he had just passed.

In those uneasy slumbers he dreamed that he was in a deep, dark pit. Darkness blacker than the blackest night was all about him; but as he lay there, for he dreamed that he was reclining on the floor of the pit, suddenly beneath his body he felt a movement as of a monstrous body—a regular undulating movement. Then it seemed borne in upon his mind that the pit was a snake's den; the monsters—three in number—pythons of immense size to whom human victims were offered as sacrifices. He had been thrown to these sacred reptiles as their next victim. In his dream, horror and terror paralyzed both thought and action for a time. Then he realized that he must act quickly. As he looked into the dense darkness a tremulous ray of light pierced the gloom of the pit and for an instant Jewel's face smiled upon him, then disappeared. In that instant of light he discerned a ladder leading to an opening at the top of the pit, through which he must have been thrown into the horrible dungeon. As he calculated his chances of escape, he heard the dragging and sweeping of a long ponderous body in motion moving toward him. With a determined wrench he broke the spell that bound him, sprang up the ladder and reached the blessed light of day.

He awoke bathed in perspiration, shivering with horror, his heart beating with fear. He lay there a while trying to shake off the effects of his dream, but for a time it seemed impossible; it would not slip away as dreams do; it was too vivid not to leave unpleasant thoughts behind.

Finally he sprang up. It was very early but he rang for John, and took time to make a careful and refreshing toilet. By half-past eight he was ready for the excellent breakfast brought by the delighted John who had not seen his master so cheerful for many weeks.

He wrote a note and despatched it by messenger to the department saying he would be late, and to refer all matters to the assistant secretary until he came.

He wandered aimlessly about the rooms wondering how he could possibly content himself while he waited for a conventional hour to come for a call on Jewel. At length he resolved to go for a walk, and was just getting into his street garments when there was a loud ring at the outer door of the suite. John answered it. He herd a question in a man's voice:

"Is Mr. Sumner at home?"

Then as he turned from the window to answer John's call, he saw his servant's frightened face, and close behind him an officer. Sumner stood still in amazement.

"Mr. Cuthbert Sumner?" asked the officer.

"I am Mr. Sumner. What is your business with me?"

"Well, sir," said the man laboriously, "there's been a murder up at the Treasury building there. Young woman found this morning. You're wanted to be at the inquest."

"But I know nothing of this affair. Who's the woman?"

The officer pulled a paper from his pocket and held it out awkwardly toward him:

"Sorry, sir, to disturb you. Miss Bradford is the victim; you are held on suspicion being the last gent, or person, seen in her company. Charge of murder!"

"Murder!" cried the horrified man.

The officer nodded as he replied:

"Ay, sir; and bad enough it is. Prussic acid was the means, sir, given in a glass of wine. Miss Elise Bradford, clerk at the Treasury Building. Body discovered by watchman early this morning."

"Great heavens!" said Sumner reeling back, "it can't be possible that the girl is dead—murdered!"

The officer's look said plainly enough,—"you know all about it." The police are quick to make victims.

"I know nothing about it. She was all right when I left her at eight yesterday after we had finished our work. I—"

"Stop, sir," said the man. "I am bound to warn you that whatever you say will be used as evidence against you."

"Let it be so," returned Sumner haughtily. "I have nothing to hide. I am absolutely guiltless of the crime as you will find."

"Maybe so, sir," replied the man civilly. "But meanwhile you must come with me."

Sumner was calm and self-possessed.

"You are free to examine my effects," he said. "I shall be ready to go with you in five minutes."

"I cannot lose sight of you, sir."

"Certainly not."

The faithful John stood by loudly protesting against the indignities put upon his master. Sumner gave him a few directions about the rooms. A herdic was called, and in five minutes the policeman and his prisoner were driven to the Police Court. The police evidence was given, and the prisoner having been remanded until after the inquest, was removed to the cells.

(To be continued.)

CHAPTER XXIII

Marthy Johnson knelt on the kitchen floor surrounded by heaps of fine white clothing sorting them into orderly piles. It was six o'clock on Monday morning. The gaudy little clock on the mantel, flanked by red vases elaborately gilded and filled with paper sunflowers, had just finished striking. The coffee pot was giving out jets of fragrant steam, and the pan of hot corn pone was smiling in an inviting manner from the back of the range. The square deal table between the windows held plates, mugs, knives and forks for three. The woman sang as she sorted:

"Oh, the milk-white hosses, milk-white hosses,
Milk-white hosses over in Jerden,
Milk-white hosses, milk-white hosses,
I long to see that day.
"Oh, hitch 'em to the chariot, hitch 'em to the chariot,
Hitch 'em to the chariot over in Jerden,
Hitch 'em to the chariot, hitch 'em to the chariot,
I long to see that day."

We last saw Marthy on the Enson plantation. Years have added to her weight, but other than that, hers is the same

frank, fun-loving countenance, with its soft brown tint, its
dazzling eyes and teeth.

Her tidy calico gown was hidden by an immense blue-and-
white-checked apron, and a snowy towel tied turban-fashion
hid her soft crinkly hair.

"Reckon I'd better fry that ham; it's gittin' on toward seven
right smart," said Marthy with a glance at the clock. "My
word, but where is mammy! I's clean worried out of my wits
'bout the child. Oliver-oh—Oliver!" she cried, opening a
door which led from the kitchen to the regions above.

"What's wanting, mummy?" was wafted back in a male
voice just turning into manhood.

"Your granny, Oliver; you must go hunt her child. I
never knowed her to stay away all night but once befo'. You
mus' git your breakfas' an' hunt her."

"Granny's all right, ma. I'm busy. Got a thesis for first
recitation this morning. 'Deed I can't spare the time to go
way over to the treasury from Meridian hill."

"You, Oliver, you; move yourse'f now, hyar me? Your
pa's never 'roun' when he's wanted, an' your sister's slavin'
herse'f like a nigger to help ejekate yer. My Lord, how
worthless men folks is! You've got a *teaseus*, have you?" she
continued, waxing more wroth each moment. "An' your
granny that's made of you like you was a baby may be daid
up thar in the treasury or moulderin' in some alley an' you
hollerin' down these stairs to me that you can't go an' holp
her 'cause you's got a *teaseus*. I 'spec's we's all made a fool of
you a-gettin' you into college. You's jes' like yer daddy; you's
the born spit of him. My word, if you don't stir them long
legs o' yourn out o' this lively, I'll take you down sure's I'm
yer mammy; I'll take yer down if you was as big as a house."
The flood of angry words ended in a flood of tears. Her face

was buried in the ample folds of her gingham apron when Oliver entered the kitchen.

He was a good-looking lad, tall and slender, a shade lighter brown than his mother, but with her pleasant, kindly face, laughing eyes and fun-loving countenance. He had a gay and fearless bearing that was the pride of Marthy's heart. She often told her mother in confidence, when Oliver was out of hearing:

"Mammy, yer gran'son's a born gin'ral; I never seen any man to 'pare with the swing dat's on him outside o' ol' Gin'ral Burnsis."

And in this opinion Aunt Henny joined.

"Now, ma, don't cry," said the boy putting his arm about his mother's neck and kissing her cheek. "I'm going right off. I'm as fond of granny as can be. Don't now go and work yourself all up. I'm going this blessed moment." Marthy cried comfortably on the shoulder of her big son and allowed him to coax her into a better frame of mind. "You are a good boy, Ollie, and I didn't mean all them hard things I jes' said, honey. Don' you go an' lay 'em up agin me, son; your ol' mammy's jes' worrited to death."

"Well, I ain't like dad, am I, ma?"

"No, bless yer heart, honey; yer ain't. You an' Venus is my comfits. Lawd, what a mis'able ol' 'ooman I'd be without you chilluns."

Marthy made Oliver sit down to his breakfast, waiting on him with a mother's fondness, piling his plate with the delicious fried ham and the smoking corn pone, and pouring his coffee with care.

"Do you know, ma," said Oliver between generous mouthfuls of bread and great gulps of coffee, as he ate with the hearty enjoyment of youth, "when I get through college, you shan't do a thing but wear a black silk dress every day and fold your hands and rock. I'm sick of seeing you in the washtub and Venus running to wait on the laides fit to break her neck. I'm going to take care of you both."

"When you 'spec' that time goin' ter come, silly chile? yer mammy 'spec' to wurk 'tell she draps inter the grave. Colored women wasn't made to take their comfit lak white ladies. They wasn't born fer nuthin' but ter wurk lak hosses or mules. Jes' seems lak we mus' wurk 'tell we draps into the grave."

"It won't be so always, ma. You'll see."

"Does you think money's jes' a growin' on bushes ready to shuck into your hand when you gits through college? Pears lak to me, Oliver, you'd better make up yer min' to hussle aroun' fer awhile. I don't want ter feel that a chile o' min's too biggotty to do anything hones' fer a livin'. Don' you turn up yer nose at washin', an' yer may jes' thank God ef you gits a 'ooman when you git jined that'll help you out in that business when college learnin' ain't payin'. An' don' spend yer extra money on silk dresses fer no 'ooman to lay roun' in. Caliker's done me all my life an' I ain't the worst 'ooman in the wurl' neither."

"Well, I'll wark fer you my own self, and I'll make money enough to keep you like a lady, college or no college."

"I wish it mote be so; but I jes' trimbles to have you talk that a-way, honey; jes' keep a still tongue and saw wood. Don't speak about your plans beforehan'. Never let anybody know what you reckon on doin' in the future 'cause the devil is always standin' 'roun' listenin' to you, an' that gen'man jes' nachally likes to put his cloven foot into a good basket of aigs an' smash 'em. 'Member what yer ma tells yer, honey."

"Now, ma, you don't believe all them old signs about

hoodooing and such stuff. There isn't a thing in it, it's nothing but superstition."

"Don't talk to me 'bout yer suferstition; there is some things in this wurl that college edication won't 'splain, an' you can't argify an' condispute with 'em, neither. I've had my trials, Oliver, but tryin' to bring you an' yer sister to a realisin' sense of the sin in the wurl is hard on me, an' it lays on my mind. Now las' night I had a dream that a ghos' stood right up side 'o the bed lookin' at me. That's turrible bad luck; an' its bein' a female ghos' means that trouble is comin' to this family thro' a 'ooman. Now, this mornin' I gits up an' fin' yer granny ain't been her all night. It's borne in on me that sumthin' is wrong. Where 'bouts did you drap her, honey, when you picked the clos' up las' evenin'?"

"The last place we went, ma, was to Senator Bowens. Granny went 'roun' to the kitchen to talk to Mis' Johnson while I went up to Venus. Granny said she was short off for breath and Mis' Johnson gave her a cup of coffee and a cutlet. Granny's fond of chicken cutlets."

"Um," replied his mother, "Mis' Johnson's a born lady cook or no cook. Chicken cutlets," she mused. "Some new Yankee fashion cookin' chicken, I reckon, bein' Mis' Johnson's from out Bos'n way. Wha's it taste like, Oliver, didn't they ask yer to have a bite with 'em"?

"Chicken cutlets are common, ma," replied Oliver, with the indifference of familiarity. "Just slap your chicken in egg and bread crumbs, drop it into hot fat and there you are."

"Do you like 'em, son?" inquired his mother, while one could see in the watery look that lurked about the corners of her mouth a determination to try chicken cutlets at the first opportunity.

"I like 'em *fine* ma."

Marthy sighed, and then returned to the original subject. "What did granny say when you lef' her?"

"She said that she'd a right smart turn of washing up and dusting that she'd left over from Saturday afternoon because the clerks were working overtime in one of the departments. I left her at the foot of the steps on the north side."

"Well, honey, I don' kno'," and Marthy shook her head dubiously. Run along to yer pa now, an' then up to the 'partment to fin' yer granny. 'Deed, God knows I hope the ol' lady's safe, but I mistrus' mighty much, I do."

"I think you're worrying for nothing, ma; I'm not a bit anxious. Sometimes has to stop late, and she might have stayed all night because she was afraid to walk home alone."

Marthy shook her head solemnly. "Wha'd she be 'fraid of a po' black 'ooman with nuthin' to steal? 'Tain't a soul gwine tech her. She ain't young an' purty makin' a 'ticemen' fer people; men isn't chasin 'roun' street corners in Wash'nt'n after ugly ol' 'oomen's. No Oliver; fifteen year ago this blessid winter when you and your sister was twenty tots, jes' like this yer granny stayed away, an' sot all night on top o' ninety thousan' dollars wurth o' greenbacks. The night befo' it happened I dreamt I was carried up to glory'settin' on a cloud an' playin' on a golden harp, which means suddint honors an' el'vations; nex' thing I knowed the Presidunt 'pinted mammy prominen'ly to a firmamen' persition in the 'partment at forty dollars a munf. Then I was able to sen' yer sister to school an' keep her nice in spite 'o yer daddy's racketty ways. Yer granny's holped me powful. Yer pa's money don' 'mount to a hill o' beans in my pocket, but mammy's kep' him straigh, an' ennythin'd happen the ol' lady I'd be nachally obleeged to giv' up the ghos'."

"Ef you don' fin' your granny, stop at yer pa's an' bein' as

the Gin'ral's away yer pester him to try an' hunt her up. An'
don' fergit to stop inter Senator Bowen's an' see yer sister.
Jes' ask her ef Miss Jewel's summer wrappers is to be clar-
starched or biled-starched. 'Deed, my head's clean gone
runnin' after mammy this mornin'. An' ef you see the madam
or Miss Jewel, make yer manners. Them white ladies is a-
payin' fer yer schoolin'. Git down ter bus'ness, now, hyar
me, son? money talks."

As Oliver disappeared from view around the corner of the
street, Marthy closed the outer door an re-entered the kitchen.
Her naturally hopeful nature re-asserted itself and she took a
brighter view of the situation. "I reckon I'll laugh if mammy
comes in now all right. I wonder which way Ollie 'll go?
Like as not he'll walk down G street an' mammy'll come on
the keers. Now, I'll jes' hussle roun' an' git them clo's out o'
the tub agin' they git here."

Life had been checkered for Marthy since emancipation
when she had joined her lot with St.Clair Enson's Isaac, in
the "holy bonds of matrimony." "Like master like man," was
a true prophecy in Isaac's case, and had caused the little brown
woman a world of worry.

Isaac had obtained the billet of valet to General Benson,
no one knew how, for up to that time he had been a ne'er-
do-well, working when the notion pleased him or when actual
starvation compelled him to exert himself, at other times
swearing, drinking and fighting.

It was a time of rejoicing when, upon arriving home one
night, after his daily lounge about the Bay or Buzzard's Nest,
looking for something to stimulate his weary system, he
announced to his family that he had been "hired" by General
Benson. Marthy rejoiced exceedingly although, as she told
Aunt Henny,—

"What in the wurld the Gin'ral 'spects to git out o' Ike in the way o' wurk passes me."

Her mother shook her head ominously.

"De Gin'ral mus' be plum crazy. 'Twon' las'."

After three months had rolled by, the poor little brown wife began to take courage. Ike was working "stiddy" although she had not yet seen the color of his money and she was still dependent upon the washing with which a number of families supplied her, and the substantial help given by her old mother's labor at the treasury.

"Pears lak, mammy, I can see some way to raise the mor'gage."

"Fu' w'y, Marthy?"

"Ike's so stiddy."

Aunt Henny shook her head.

"Wha' you reckin de bill is, chile?" asked the old woman, removing her pipe from her mouth. Work was over and her chair and pipe in the warmest corner near the kitchen range, were comforting to the wornout frame. Aunt Henny was seventy, but save for rheumatism she had not changed since she left the Enson plantation. Sometimes she would bend her limbs, shake her head and sigh, "Dey neber be easy goin' 'gin, fuh sho', but I got a heap o' hope outen dem whilst dey ben limber, my soul; de bes' laigs I'll eber hab in dis wurl."

"We does owe on the mor'gage five hundred dollars," said Marthy in reply to her mother's question.

"My wurd, but de money grow slow; I got one hunder' dollars up stairs 'tween the feather bed an' de mattress. You make Ike fotch out de res'. Cayn't rightly feel de place is ourn till we's paid up. When I sees you an' de chillun under your own roof, I gwine ter gib up de ghos' in peace. An' Marthy, don't neber be a plum fool an let Ike wurrit you into raisin' money on de place, ef he gits inter scrapes let him git out as he gits in, widout any holp but de debbil. Ef you eber let dat mon take de bread outer yer mouf dat way, an' I'm daid, I gwine ter riz up outer de grave an' hit yer; yas, I'll rawhide yer jes' as I user down on de plantation."

Marthy gasped but heaved a sigh of satisfaction over the thought of the hundred dollars.

"Well, I'se glad as glad 'bout the money, mammy. An' Ike's jes' got to pony up to the pint of that other fo' hundred dollars."

"Hump!" grunted Aunt Henny. "I don' trus' him. Dat niggah no leanin' pos' fer me. I'se gwine call on Gen'ral Benson myse'f, an' ef he de right kin' o' white gen'man, he gwine holp me in a 'spiracy ter make Ike raise dat money. Wha' you say to dat, Marthy?"

"I likes it *fine*," Marthy cried, overjoyed at what she considered a brilliant plan to subjugate the irresponsible Isaac.

Shortly after this conversation, Marthy applied to her husband for money.

"I ain't got no money fer ye, Marthy," he said in answer to her request.

"Ain't got no money, an' you been wurkin' stiddy fer munfs! What's gone come of it I'd like ter know." Isaac scratched his head in perplexity.

"I 'low to do better by yer, Marthy; you's ben a good gal to me, an' I 'low I ain't done the right thing by you in every way sence we was jined, but I'se turned over a new leaf; I ain't drawed a red cent o' my wages sence I went to wait on the Gin'ral. I jes' lef' it in his han's fer 'ves'men'. Major Madison an' Gin'ral's spec'latin' in mines. Dey owns de Arrow-Head, an' all my wages an' all de money, Gin'ral kin raise has ben put in dat gol' mine up in de Col'rady hills."

"The Lawd save us, Ike! Then we'll done lose this place,'
she cried. "The mor'gage money done come due in June, an'
Mis' Jenkins been mighty kind, but he's boun' to fo'close
'cause I hear he want money pow'ful bad to meet his need-
cessities. O, Lawd! what is we gwine do?" she moaned rocking
herself to and fro while the tears streamed down her cheeks.

"Don' you take on, Marthy," her husband said soothingly.
"I'll git de money from de Gin-ral all right. I know I ain't
been a 'sponsible man fer yer, but I'se got human feelin',
ain't I? Ain't I proud o' my gal an' my boy what's in de
college? Wha' you tink I'se turned over a new leaf fo' ef it
warn't to see them chilluns holdin' up dar heads 'long wif de
bes' ob de high-biggotty Wash'nt'n 'stockracy? Thar daddy's
gwine ter make 'em rich an' when you an' me is moulderin'
ter clay dem chillun's gwine ter be eatin' chickun an' a-settin'
on thar own front do' steps jes' like de Presidun'."

"I don' trus' no' white man. 'Member all the money went
up in the Freedman's bank, don' yer? I don' guess he'd be
slow makin' a profit outen yer by keepin' yer wages. Plenty
gentmen'd do it 'fore yer could bat yer eye."

"You tew ha'sh, Marthy. De Gen'ral an' de major been
mighty fine ter your husban', gal. Don' you worry, dat
money's safe."

"I 'spicion him jes' the same," replied his wife sullenly.

"De major do be under some repetition as a bad character,
but de Gin'ral's all right. Dar's heap o' his paw in 'im," he
continued in a musing voice. "Dar neber was a better man
den ol' massa, an' I orter know. Law*se*, de times me an'
young massa had t'gedder, bar hunts, an' gamblin' 'bouts,
an' shootin' and ridin'. He goin' so fas' I skacely cud keep
up tuh him. We bin like brudders. All his clo's fits me
puffick! Our size is jes' de same as ever. En jurin' de wah I

jes' picked him twice outen de inimy's han's; my sakes dem was spurious times."

"You, Isaac, wha' in the lan' you talkin' 'bout? Is you gone crazy? Them remarks o' yourn is suttingly cur'ous." Isaac started to his feet, and there was a guilty look on his face.

"What was I sayin', Marthy? 'Clar fo' it, my thoughts was miles 'way from hyar."

"Do hish! Ef I didn't kno' yer age, Isaac Johnson, I'd think you gone dotty. I 'clar fo' it, I hope you ain't goin' ter have sof'n o' the brain from drinkin' all Sam Smith's bad rum over to Buzzard's Nes'. I hern tell o' sech happenin's, but I pray the Lawd not to pile that trib'lation on top o' me."

After this occurrence, Aunt Henny sought General Benson's presence as the only hope of getting money out of Isaac. From this interview the old woman returned with a look of terror and consternation on her face. When questioned by Marthy as to the outcome of the interview she would say nothing of her success, only repeating the words: "I'se seed a ghos'! Lawd, my days is done."

Marthy went heavily about her work as spring approached. But for her children she would have given up the unequal struggle. Just at the darkest hour the Bowens had become interested in Venus and Oliver, and soon the little brown mother had felt a revival of hope in her breast, as she planned to make bold and go herself to Miss Jewel and ask the dear young lady to intercede with the Senator and get him to take up the hateful mortgage.

After Oliver left the house, his mother rubbed away industriously, and under her skilful fingers the delicate clothing was soon floating like snow-capped billows in tubs and boilers. When noon was signalled from the observatory upon the hill, spotless garments waved in the keen air from every line in the large drying yard at the rear of the cottage.

" 'Clar fo' it, Oliver's missed his school, an' mammy ain't come yet."

Half distracted with terror and fearing the worst, Marthy sat down in the midst of her disordered kitchen and sobbed aloud.

Suddenly she heard the click of the little gate. The next moment she saw Oliver's face at the door. It needed but a glance to tell that something extraordinary had happened. He was breathless from running, his face ashen, his large eyes were distended to twice their usual size.

"O, ma, there's been a murder up to the treasury—"

"Don' tell me it's yer granny!" shrieked his mother.

"No'm; 'taint granny; it's a young lady; and Mr. Sumner that was Miss Jewel's beau is arrested, an' granny ain't been seen *nowhere* since she went into the building last night. Pa'll be home after he's been to the station to notify the police about granny, an' Venus can't leave Miss Jewel; she's taking on so."

"O, yer po' granny, Oliver! I jes' cayn't bar up under this. O, where's my mammy! Good Lawd, where's she at?"

CHAPTER XXIV

"Terrible discovery this morning in Treasury building! Arrest, on suspicion, of Mr. Cuthbert Sumner!"

That was the startling head-line that met Jewel Bowen's eyes on that eventful Monday morning, and sent the blood back to her heart.

She had opened the paper lazily, glanced at the leaders, and with, "There's never anything interesting in the paper," turned to another sheet, and suddenly sat transfixed, her wide eyes seeing nothing but that one startling head-line that danced before her straining gaze, then stood still,—that at first appeared to be printed in great black type and then turned into blood-red letters!

In an instant the reserve and coldness of weeks was swept aside. He was again her lover. His deadly peril gripped her very heart-strings, and filled her whole being anew with all the strength and passion of woman's noblest love, that, at once, without a second's pause, throws aside all but honor itself for the being who is her world.

She had not read the account of the tragedy, but not for one instant did a thought of guilt associate itself in her mind with Cuthbert Sumner. *Guilty of a heinous crime!* She laughed aloud at the bare idea. In that moment she forgot the new duties lately assumed toward another. Promises had been forced upon her she had told herself often of late, with regret, and none could blame her if she swerved in the moment of trial from the exact path of duty. Now, she thanked God it was not yet a crime to think of the man she loved.

She calmed herself presently, and read the brief account given in the morning edition of the "Washington News." With the sheet closely clutched in her hand she sought her mother. Mrs. Bowen's maid was just serving her lady with breakfast as Jewel knocked and then entered the room. Mrs. Bowen was seated comfortably before the fire, opening her morning mail.

"Jewel, what on earth is the matter? What is wrong?" exclaimed her mother, startled at the strange look on her face.

"Cuthbert is arrested, charged with murder!"

Mrs. Bowen turned very white.

"Great heaven! Jewel! No, no, it is too horrible!"

"Read that," said the girl, laying the paper in her mother's lap.

The elder woman read the printed sheet and gazed up at her daughter with incredulous eyes.

"You do not believe him guilty?"

"Guilty!" the one word spoke volumes.

"What can we do to help him? It is unfortunate that your father is away."

"I have not thought yet." The determined woman spoke in the next sentence, "I shall visit him first of all."

"Jewel!" exclaimed her mother in a shocked tone. "What will the General think?"

"What he pleases," was the defiant answer.

Before Mrs. Bowen could protest, there was a hurried knock at the door, which, opening, admitted Venus. There were traces of tears on her face.

"Please, Miss, Mr. Sumner's man is in the hall asking if you will see him for a minute."

"Show him right up here, Venus."

John entered the presence of the two ladies with deep distress and alarm in his honest face. He looked years older than he did the day before. There was a strong affection between master and man. He came forward eagerly, his hands holding his cap and twitching nervously.

"Oh, Mrs. Bowen an' young Miss, I beg your pardon, but—but—I don't know what to do. I've telegraphed the ol' gent'man—

"Yes, John—when will he be here?" The ladies spoke together.

"The ol' gent'man's had shock, an' the doctor dassent to

tell him, but the family lawyer will be here tomorrow to take charge; but I can't keep still, miss,—ma'am—I had to come an' see you. I've been in the Sumner family, boy an' man, for twenty years, an' they're used me white, ma-am—miss, right straight through. 'Clare, I'd do anyting on yearth for Mr. Cuthbert."

"How does your master bear it, John?"

"Like a lamb, miss—ma'am—I've been there now, jes' cam from there, been taking his orders an' things. All he says is 'John, there's a mistake; it'll be all right in a day or two. But I don't believe it. I feel oneasy. I thought maybe you all would tell what more I can do."

"That's right, John. We will help you all we can. These are evil days that have come to us lately." But in spite of her brave words, Mrs. Bowen looked about her in a helpless, bewildered way. Then she appealed to her daughter, "Jewel, what do you advise, dear?"

"The first thing to do is to see Cuthbert; I'm going to drive down to the jail and have a long talk with him."

"Jewel!"

"Well, mamma, if we intend to benefit him, there is but one way. Venus, order me a herdic; I won't wait for the carriage," she said, turning to her maid. "Why, what are you crying about, silly child; they can't hang Mr. Sumner without a trial."

"Yes'm; I know that. But it's my granny, too, miss. We can't find her," said the girl with a burst of tears. Again John spoke, trying to explain the matter to the bewildered ladies.

"It's ol' Mis' Sargean'—"

"What did you say?" interrupted Mrs. Bowen sharply, leaning forward in her chair.

"Sergeant, ma'am, Ol' Aunt Henny Sargeant, she's Venus's

gran'mother. She's a cleaner up at the department, an' she's disappeared; ain't been seen sense last night, when she went into the building to clean up. Taking that an' putting it with the murder an' other funny things that's been happening about Mr. Sumner lately, it 'pears to me that something underhand is going on," he said with a deferential bow.

"Venus, come with me. John, be good enough to order the herdic. I will look into this matter and see what can be done," and Jewel turned to leave the room.

"Please, miss, do you mind if I take a seat on the box?" asked John.

"Certainly not."

And the trio quitted the room leaving Mrs. Bowen alone.

CHAPTER XXV

As the day grew older the excitement increased in the city over the murder of Elise Bradford. The circumstances surrounding the victim, as given out in the second editions of the press, the mysterious disappearance of the old scrubwoman and the high social and official position of the accused, gave rise to all sorts of sensational rumors.

"Very queer affair," said one man to another, nodding significantly. "A good deal behind it all, of course. Young men will be young men; you can't put an old head on young shoulders," he added, repeating the trite sayings as if they were original with himself.

"H'm, yes. Ugly facts, though, the wine-glasses especially. I take it the old Negress would be an important witness in the case."

"Yes. What about the wine-glasses? I haven't read the paper very carefully; just sketched it."

"Why, it seems they must have had wine together and he put prussic acid in her glass. But he denies it; says he gave her a glass of wine because she seemed faint, but he took none himself. In short, he cannot explain the presence of the *second* glass. The odd thing about it is his walking out and leaving the body there, if he did it, with no attempt at concealment."

"You don't say so! By Jove, what did he expect? And he claims to be innocent?"

"Yes; but of course, he'd do that. I suppose his lawyers will claim that it was suicide. Fact is, he must have found himself in a mess and took this method of getting clear. These young bloods are as bad as the worst when you corner them."

"It must have been that way. And then, again, what he says may be true, somehow. From what one hears of him, he is incapable of a crime like this. He is called a man of spotless honor."

"Well, perhaps, except where there's a woman in the case. We are men ourselves, and we know."

The other nodded in acquiescence.

Will Badger and Carroll West met in the corridor of the jail, one just coming from a conference with the prisoner, the other seeking an interview.

Kind-hearted Badger was feeling very much cast down over his friend's predicament.

"Think he did it, Badger?" asked West after they had exchanged greetings.

"No more than you or I," was the decisive answer. "I

would not believe the blackest evidence against his bare word. I know the man."

"I'm with you, but—well—confound the jade, I say, to get Sumner in this fix. Of course, there's another man. Who is he? Have you an idea?

Badger shook his head and sighed. "The examination is tomorrow at ten. Try and be there, West."

"I will, sure. The Madisons awfully cut up over this affair; she was almost in hysterics when I stopped in to talk it over. The Major isn't himself either."

"No wonder. Well, we shan't know anything positive until after the hearing. So long."

The friends separated.

Shortly after noon, Jewel arrived at the jail. The interview between her and Cuthbert was long and painful, but both were happier than they had been for many weeks. Sumner told Jewel the facts of his intimacy with Amelia, blaming himself greatly for all the trouble that had followed his first deception. "I should have been frank with you, Jewel, and all would have been well."

Jewel's gentle heart was at last at rest; perfect confidence was established between the re-united lovers. As she rose to go, he said:

"It may go hard with me tomorrow at the examination; indeed, I know it will. There will be difficult work ahead for my attorneys. So many things have happened to separate us, Jewel, that I dread the future."

The tears stood in her eyes. She turned her head to hide them.

"Dare I express my selfish hopes—my wishes?"

For answer she threw herself into his arms again, and as

he held her thus he whispered his request with an eager look upon his face.

She blushed violently, hesitated, then drawing herself up proudly said:

"I will do as you wish."

"Tomorrow morning then, at eight, I shall be waiting."

"I will not fail you," was her low reply, as snatching her hand hastily from his detaining clasp, she turned to accompany the officer from the cell.

As she passed through the office she asked the captain for the address of the chief of the secret service.

"You mean Mr. Henson, I take it, Miss?"

"If he is the celebrated detective, he is the very one."

"Well, Miss, its No.—Pennsylvania Avenue; but he takes no outside cases. His government duties are all that he finds time for."

"Still, I will call on him."

The man bowed, and she passed on. Months ago she remembered hearing her father speak of the great powers of this detective. Why it had lingered in her mind she knew not, but now a hidden force impelled her to seek his aid.

She shrank from nothing that might benefit her lover. Shrink! was that like it, the proud flush on the soft cheek, the warm light in her eyes? Her heart throbbed fast in the excess of happiness it was to know that he was true, that all misunderstandings were buried spectres, and that she—she alone held his heart. Let the world do its worst, she could repay by showing every trust in him. After tomorrow she would have the right to stand beside him, though all the world should frown. Her thoughts did not go beyond the present. He would be proved innocent, she was sure. Money could do anything and there would be no sparing of any moment to clear him.

The herdic seemed to creep over the space between the station and the detective's chambers. Her very heart seemed on fire under intense, suppressed excitement and the emotion that surged beneath her calm, conventional exterior.

No.—Pennsylvania Avenue was a large brick building where lawyers congregated. Jewel alighted from the herdic, leaving Venus in it. Mr. Henson's office was on the second floor. She paused before a door upon the glass panels of which appeared the letters: "J. Henson, Detective." She opened the door and entered. There were a number of clerks in the room busily writing. One elderly man near the door was in charge.

Yes, Mr. Henson was in and would no doubt see the lady if she could wait awhile, he said in reply to Jewel's inquiry. Placing a chair for her he took her card and disappeared behind a door marked "Private." Presently he returned saying that if she would come with him, Mr. Henson would receive her.

The great detective was seated at his desk writing. He did not look up as she entered, but said:

"Be seated, madam; I will give you my attention in one moment."

Jewel saw a well-preserved man of sixty odd years, middle height, and rather broad, but not fleshy. His thick iron-gray hair covered his head fully and curled in masses over a broad forehead. He was well and carefully dressed. Presently he looked up from his work and glanced in her direction; then she saw that he had expressive dark eyes and a pleasant face which might have been handsome in youth, but for a long livid scar that crossed his face diagonally. A sabre might have made that deep, dangerous cut.

The light in the room was faint, and Jewel did not perceive the pallor that spread over the man's face as he gazed at her; the words he was about to utter died away unsaid, his chest heaved an instant in a convulsive movement which he controlled by a violent effort. There was silence as the man and girl gazed at each other, mutually attracted by a hidden affinity. It was but a second that the pause endured.

"You wish to speak with me, Miss?"

Then Jewel aroused herself from the spell which had held her since she encountered the piercing gaze of the quiet elderly man before her. The sound of his voice generated a feeling of relief in her breast, of trust and confidence. She could not analyze the sensation of complete rest that came to her with the few words just spoken.

"I wish to speak with you," she replied tremulously; then, recovering herself: "When I say that I am deeply interested in the murder that has just been committed, and that Mr. Sumner is my dearest friend, you will know what I want."

"I understand, Miss Bowen," he said, glancing at the card in his hand. "I seldom take cases outside of the government; still, I will hear what you have to tell me. I think this may be an exception to my rule."

He motioned her to the chair beside him and then placed a note-book on the desk before him.

"Mr. Sumner is innocent," said the girl in a trembling voice. "He will have able counsel, I know; but I shall feel better if you will take charge. I have heard so much of your skill and wonderful powers of discernment that no one else could satisfy me."

The man looked at the beautiful girl before him with

something akin to worship in his eyes. When he spoke again his voice had taken on an added softness, his words seemed to carry a caress hidden beneath their commonplace utterance.

"Thank you; I am greatly interested. Even the newspaper accounts bear evidence that this is a remarkable case, and there is generally a good deal hidden behind what they give out. Now tell me all you know of the matter."

Calmed by his gentle tones, Jewel gave a brief account of the affair as told her by Sumner. When she ceased speaking Mr. Henson, who had listened with down-cast eyes and unmoved countenance, said:

"It is a curious case, very. There seems no clue; but, if I mistake not, you have suspicions of someone." His eyes rested on her face in a peculiarly impressive manner.

"Why do you think so?"

"I trace it in the tones of your voice. Now tell me the name of the person you suspect and why."

The girl hesitated, then said in a low tone:

"General Benson!"

"Ah!" It was but a breath, but it spoke volumes. "And have you mentioned this to anyone?"

"Only to Mr. Sumner, but he will not entertain the thought. He thinks the idea absurd because the General is in New York, and can hardly know more than the bare outlines of the case as yet."

"Just so. But upon what do you base your thought?

"Oh, Mr. Henson," and she clasped her hands and raised her wonderful, beseeching gray eyes to his face, "I can not tell. There is a feeling of conviction that he knows all about the crime if he is not the assassin. There has been an adverse fate at work since General Benson crossed my path. There has been a train of unfortunate circumstances attending our whole acquaintance. It is absurd to suspect him I know, but I cannot help it." The detective looked at her again with the immovable expression peculiar to him.

"Your woman's intuition warns you; is that it?"

She bowed her head in acquiescence.

"And I have confidence in intuitive deductions," he muttered; then, aloud, "My dear child, gentlemen like General Benson sometimes do queer things under pressure of circumstances. You may be right. I will see Mr. Sumner; he will probably be more explicit with me than he could be with you. I will do my best for you. In fact, I shall put all my powers into my work, for it is an uncommon riddle you have set me to solve."

As she rose to go she asked his terms. He named a fair price. "But if you succeed in clearing him, and I know that you will, Mr. Henson, you shall receive a princely reward." Jewel laid her check for a goodly retainer, upon the desk before him. Henson looked and tapped the desk with his pencil, but did not notice the check. Then he rose, touched a bell, and accompanied his fair client to the door.

*   *   *   *   *

Before nine o'clock on Tuesday morning, attended by her maid, with the jail officials for witnesses, Jewel Bowen became the wife of the suspected murderer, Cuthbert Sumner.

(To be continued.)

CHAPTER XXVI

The evening of the eventful day that made Jewel, Cuthbert Sumner's wife, closed in heavy and sombre. The hearing had the expected ending, and Sumner was held for trial in the following September, before the grand jury for wilful murder. The evidence was circumstantial, but damaging in the extreme. It showed exclusive opportunity for reasons unknown, but it was whispered about town that the girl had been an unwedded mother. Added to this was the knowledge of the broken engagement between the prisoner and Miss Bowen, and the fact that Miss Madison had at one time been affianced to him, and it was expected that she would be called by the prosecution to show the fickle nature of his relations with women.

At seven o'clock in the evening of that same day, robed in black velvet, Jewel paced restlessly up and down the floor of the library, sometimes pausing to listen to sounds from without, sometimes approaching the window and trying to pierce the gloom. The dinner bell rang; for no matter what our griefs, or how dark the tragedies which are enacted about us, meals are still served and eaten, just as if the hearts assembled about the board were never wrenched nor broken.

The points brought out in the evidence were soon making their way about the city, and excitement and interest grew momentarily. Sumner smiled in bitterness of heart. He hardly knew himself in the picture drawn. Jewel sat in an obscure corner of the audience room of the court, heavily veiled, and listened to the testimony with a heart bursting with indignation. Each moment the load at her heart grew heavier. They both realized at last that this was no child's play but a struggle to the death. Sumner clenched his hands and registered a vow to spend his fortune, if necessary, to clear his name, for the sake of the dear incentive, the thought of whom warmed his heart and made him bold to meet impending disaster.

The two ladies took their accustomed places at table, each secretly regretting the absence of the Senator. With him at home, dinner was wont to be a festive meal, where laughter and wit cheered the household or chance visitor. A dismal air hung over the room now; the servants moved to and fro with unaccustomed solemnity. The mother and daughter addressed each other seldom: each was buried in her own thoughts. Presently both rose from the table and passed into the library, where coffee was served.

After the servants had retired and they were safe from intrusion Mrs. Bowen broke the silence that brooded over them. She had watched Jewel closely all through the meal, studying her looks, thinking over her words and striving to arrive at satisfactory conclusions. At length she said quietly:

"Now, my dear, you have told me next to nothing, nor have I asked seeing how pale and tired you are, but I must talk with you about this marriage. I fear you have been very rash. My dear, I positively dread your father's return; dearly as he loves you, he will be very angry." After a pause she continued, clasping and unclasping her fingers nervously. "Oh, the talk there will be when this affair is known! Why didn't you consult me, child? I could have devised some way of helping the poor fellow without requiring you to sacrifice yourself. I am disappointed in Cuthbert Sumner."

"Do not use the word 'sacrifice,' mamma; I am glad to have the right to stand by Cuthbert in this dark hour. And why say anything to you of our intention? No one can blame you now. Beside, we have agreed to say nothing at present, about the marriage."

"But your whole life will be spoilt if he is found guilty."

"Mother," said the girl, sinking on her knees by Mrs. Bowen's side, "don't despair; it will all come right in a little while, I am sure it will. And you have always called yourself his friend, even when I was against him. You *cannot* believe him guilty; you are too just in your judgment, mamma."

Jewel was kneeling in the full light of the glowing fire, the ruddy glare fell on her white face, and the plaits of bright hair wound closely around her small head. Mrs. Bowen sighed as she gazed in admiration at her daughter. The great gray eyes glowed like diamonds, but there was a world of passionate anguish in their depths. The flower-like mouth was compressed with the intensity of the pain which filled her breast.

Again Mrs. Bowen sighed and moved uneasily in her seat.

"Yes; but this is so different—a man accused of murder."

"How so, mamma? Is friendship in sunshine so different from friendship in shade?" There was sarcasm on the delicately chiseled features.

"What a champion you are, Jewel; once, perhaps, I should have acted and felt as you do."

"But now, mamma—?"

"Now, my child, I am of the world—wordly."

"Do you think papa will be very angry?" asked the girl with trembling lips after a short silence.

"We can expect nothing less. He is too fond of you to hold his anger long, however. I shall stand with you, Jewel, if it is any comfort for you to know it. I am glad, glad, glad, that you cannot marry General Benson." Jewel marvelled much at the strange look on her mother's face as she uttered these words.

"My dear mamma!" and the two women embraced each other. Then followed another silence broken by the elder woman.

"What impression did you receive from the evidence—I mean apart from the conclusions drawn by the jury?" A quiver went through the girl as she replied:

"I was confirmed in my belief in his innocence, although everything seemed to point the other way. Aurelia Madison's evidence was against him. She gave the impression that he came and went at her beck and call."

"She is false to the core—a dangerous woman."

"I agree with you, mamma. But her beauty blinds men. I dread her influence on the jury."

"There is no soul there—nothing but sensuality."

"Soul! there is no need for soul in a woman's beauty for it to dazzle most men," was the bitter answer.

"I marvel much over the matter. It seems to me there is something incomplete in the case—something to be explained. That poor girl! I can see no reason for murdering her. She may have been killed by mistake.

"That is scarcely likely."

"Cases of mistaken identity are common enough. It's a mysterious affair; I hope it may be cleared up without any delay."

"I hope so," added Jewel. "Murder will out; there lies my hope for our success in tracing the murderer."

"What does Mr. Henson say?"

"Not much; we have had no time to talk. He has hardly got to work yet; but he told me to keep my courage up, and that he thought he should be able to throw some light on the dark points of the story. He has talked with Cuthbert."

Before Mrs. Bowen had time to reply the lace and satin portière was pushed aside and Venus advanced toward them with a solemn and awe-stricken face.

"What is it, Venus?" asked Mrs. Bowen, regarding her with surprise.

"Please, Mrs. Bowen," she said hesitatingly, "Senator Bowen——"

"Oh, papa is come," cried Jewel in delight.

"No. Miss——"

At this point General Benson's well-known figure appeared in the entrance.

"Mrs. Bowen—Jewel—" he exclaimed as he hurried toward them. "I am the bearer of evil tidings. Senator Bowen was taken ill in New York, and we have hastened to bring him home as soon as it was possible to move him. Have a room prepared instantly, the ambulance will arrive almost immediately."

Before another hour had elapsed, the great hush—which is the shadow of the grim visitant, whom no earthly power may shut out—had fallen on the Bowen mansion. The servants walked with noiseless tread and spoke in whispers.

Senator Bowen was ill until death. He had been suddenly striken down by a shock. The Washington delegation had been tendered a banquet at a famous New York club, and a hilarious time had been enjoyed. The New Yorkers had outdone themselves in catering for the amusement of their guests.

Senator Bowen had enjoyed himself hugely. Along in the early morning hours a servant passing the door of his room had caught the sound of some one struggling for breath within. Entering, he beheld the Senator lying on the bed, one hand pressed to his heart, the other hanging inert. His eyes were wild, his pale countenance lined with purple marks.

The man went for help and soon medical aid had rendered all the relief possible. As soon as he could make himself understood the stricken man urged them to take him home.

After the first burst of grief, Mrs. Bowen and Jewel took up their places in the sick room along with the trained nurses. Each looked at the other in awe and consternation over the awful suddenness of this event. Surprising events had followed one another rapidly the past few days. They dared not think of the next cruel blow that Fate might deal them.

The doctors and nurses came and went softly. The hours drew out their long, anxious length. At the close of the third day the sick man fell into a heavy stupor, from which the doctors said he might rally—probably would—and he might linger two or three days longer; but the end was inevitable. Should he rally he must be kept quiet, and on no account excited; his heart was weak.

Mrs. Bowen undertook to see these instructions carried out. Jewel, pale and distressed, shared her mother's watch. She was in agony; her love for her father was strong, deep and tender. She was his idol, and he was hers, and until she met Cuthbert Sumner she had always felt that if he died she should not care to live another hour. She could never remember his having been cross to her in her whole life. In her eyes his very faults were virtues.

At midnight Mrs. Bowen persuaded her daughter to go and lie down.

"Keep your strength, my child, there is much to go through. If your father wakes I will surely call you."

When alone she drew her chair to the fire and sat there in shadow, watching the face of the silent figure on the bed that looked so ghastly in the light of the shaded light. It was very still; the tired nurses in the next room, dozed. Events long passed, returned in full force and pictured themselves vividly before her inner senses. How kind this man had been to her; how much she owed to his love and care. And now the hour had come for her to lose a protector who had never failed her. Wealth she might have, but it would not supply the tender deference and loving solicitude of wedded life that had been hers.

She shuddered at her thoughts. Why did the past haunt her so persistently? Presently she found herself weeping softly.

There are brave natures—women's perhaps, more often than men's—which bear up in a sea of adversity, and present a bold front to the buffeting winds of life's uncertainties. And sometimes these brave natures fine a safe haven for their frail barks. Mrs. Bowen was one of these. She had never known trouble, save by name, since she met Zenas Bowen some twenty years before; and now behold, she is confronted by a very tempest of sorrow. In the midst of her reveries she was startled to hear her own name pronounced:

"Estelle."

It was Senator Bowen who spoke. In an instant his wife was at his side.

"Dear Zenas, you are better?" she said cheerfully.

"Yes, my brain is clear. I have been watching you, Estelle. Where is Jewel?"

"In her room; I made her lie down. Do you want her?"

"Poor child; let her sleep."

His eyes roved restlessly about the familiar room.

"It is good to be at home—so good."

"Yes—but you must not talk. Drink this and sleep." She held a soothing draught to his lips, lifting the powerless head in her arms with all a mother's tenderness. He drank it obediently and then lay back on his pillow and a satisfied look of peaceful rest overspread his pale features. He held his wife's hand in a nerveless grasp.

"We have been happy, Estelle. You have been a perfect wife. I have left you well provided for. Them rascals got some of it, but not the whole of it by a durned sight; Zenas ain't such a fool as he seems," a gleam of his old fun-loving spirit was on the pain-worn face.

"If Jewel marries the General—"

"No, Zenas," she interrupted; then she stopped remembering the doctor's caution. But the sick man did not grasp the significance of her words. His mind wandered.

"No you don't, General; my little girl shan't be forced. I, her father, say it. When, where and who she likes; that's my idea. I tell you, no!"

Then he looked at his wife with fast-glazing eyes, and said:

"The little hair trunk—tell her—no difference—just the same."

Feebly he raised his arm. His wife knew his desire. She placed it about her neck. Then he drew her head nearer. A soft light radiated his features.

"My faithful wife!" he whispered. The cold lips touched her cheek.

"Zenas, Zenas!" exclaimed Estelle with a burst of emotion as she kissed the chill brow.

There was one long-drawn breath. The distracted wife sprang to the bell and rang a peal that brought the nurses hurrying in.

"Senator Bowen is worse!" she cried, wringing her hands helplessly.

The head nurse bent over the bed, then rising, said:

"Senator Bowen is dead, madam."

Again Washington society was stirred by an unexpected calamity among its leading people. Interest was heightened because of the close association which existed between the Bowens and the chief actor in the Bradford tragedy. The ill-starred trip of the delegation that had started so gaily on its Canadian mission was the talk of the capital.

CHAPTER XXVII

The funeral was over. Senator Bowen was at rest in the handsomest cemetery of the capital after many honors had been paid to the sterling worth of the rugged Westerner. Condolences flooded the widow and orphan. The contents of the will were not yet known, but it was supposed that both ladies were left fabulously rich.

One event had crowded so closely upon another that General Benson was given no opportunity for confidential conversation with the woman he desired to make his wife.

The loss of her father was a terrible shock to Jewel, and she kept to her rooms, weeping passionate tears and refusing to be comforted. A sense of horrible loneliness, of grief, apprehension, and the weight of some unknown calamity weighed her young heart down. Young, beautiful, well-born, and wealthy, surrounded by every luxury money could purchase or a cultivated taste long for. Jewel was supremely wretched. Her father dead, her husband a prisoner, accused of the deadliest of crimes, the girl was a prey to a thousand vague fears and haunting suspicions. She dreaded, too, the coming of the day set apart for reading the will, for General Benson could no longer be avoided. She had written him a letter asking a release from promises made, but as yet had received no reply.

Senator Bowen had been buried two weeks when, at an early hour, the family lawyer appeared at the house and was ushered into the breakfast room where, attired in deep mourning, Mrs. Bowen sat in solitary state making a pretense of eating.

Mr. Cameron was a pale, small, dark-haired man, with

sharp eyes and thin lips; a hard, but honest face, and a short temper.

Somewhat alarmed by the troubled look on the solicitor's face, Mrs. Bowen asked anxiously—

"Is anything wrong, Mr. Cameron?"

"Well, madam, I hope not; but I thought I would ask you for a cup of coffee, lay the case before you and talk it over. I heard some surprising news last night," he continued, as he seated himself and swallowed the steaming beverage that Mrs. Bowen poured for him, the discreet servant having left the room at a glance from his mistress. "Did you know that your husband made a will while in New York?" he questioned abruptly, watching her with keen, bright eyes.

"A will in New York? No—surely not!"

"There is such a will in existence; it is held by General Benson, who came to me last night with the astonishing information. He will be here by eleven to have the instrument read. Of course, this later document leaves the one in my possession null and void."

Mrs. Bowen had grown very white as she listened to the lawyer, and a fixed look of intense thought was in her eyes.

"What are the terms of this new will? do you remember?"

"Not all of them; but Major Madison is left sole trustee, and General Benson executor and guardian of Miss Bowen until she is of age. Think of it!" cried the excitable man, "all the immense business of the estate, ready money, etc., *absolutely* in the control of these men!"

A wonderful change came over Mrs. Bowen at these words. She was stung to the quick. She sprung from her chair as if moved by a spring; her lips quivered, her eyes dilated with what seemed like terror.

"General Benson and Major Madison!" she exclaimed in a hoarse voice, "surely you jest."

"Would it were a jest, my dear madam. Think of it! This magnificent estate and fortune to be left in the hands of two such villains as General Benson and his pal, Major Madison. Yes, villains, madam; and I will undertake to prove my position should they bring action against me for slander. What could my old friend, Bowen, have been thinking about! He must have lost his head completely," continued Mr. Cameron, looking with accusing eyes at the black-robed figure across his second cup of coffee. "Madison had done him out of a million in his bogus company already. A child could see that it was a cheat and a sham."

For one instant, at these words, Mrs. Bowen's face wore the look of a lioness bereft of her young; but her alarm seemed to subside as quickly as it arose. The lawyer was too excited himself to notice the expressions of consternation and alarm that flitted across the pale face of the silent woman before him. After a silence, she asked: "Have you examined this will, Mr. Cameron? Are you sure it is genuine?"

The old attorney put his cup down with emphasis and said with a bow: "Madam, it is a pleasure to talk with you. You have expressed my own thoughts in your question. The Bowen millions would be a great temptation to a set of sharpers. I have not examined the document, but I will; and you may trust me to find any flaw that exists."

"Let us be calm. If it is as we suspect, we shall gain nothing by allowing these men to see that we suspect them. Do not oppose them, but use every legal means to retain control of the estate until we prove our suspicions groundless."

The expression of her face was intense, even fierce; her

mouth was tightly closed, her eyes strained as though striving to pierce the veil which hides from us the unseen.

Mr. Cameron looked his admiration of the fearless woman before him, and after a few more words they settled themselves to calmly wait developments.

At this same hour General Benson and his honored associate, Major Madison, sat in the former's room talking earnestly of the business in hand.

"Now, Madison, we have started on the last part of our enterprise and it is full of peril: one flaw will destroy the whole structure which we have labored so hard to raise. We must preserve all our trumps. Aurelia has failed in her part: we must not fail."

"Pshaw!" said the Major, "we shall succeed. What is there to fear? the man is dead."

"There will be many questions asked, and, doubtless, that old fox of a lawyer is even now hunting for evidences of fraud. Don't underrate the danger, Madison. Our projects are dangerous, and the slightest mistake will prove fatal. But while there are one hundred chances against us, there are the same number in our favor. We know this, too, Madison,— necessity knows no law; we must go ahead!"

"There's the old woman: she'll kick on the will, and kick hard. What'll you do with her?"

There was a peculiar smile on the General's face as he said:

"She'll struggle a little: the scene today will be a stormy one, so be prepared; but I hold a trump ahead of her."

"The deuce you do!"

"She can't escape from us any more than the girl can."

The Major whistled softly as he murmured "Amen," and then said: "I have faith in your judgment, Benson."

Benson took several turns up and down the long room and finally assumed his favorite attitude before the mantel.

"You do well to feel so, Major. I anticipate no difficulty in assuming full control of the Bowen millions, and how sorely we need them, you and I know, Major."

"But the girl—how will you manage her?"

Benson's face darkened, but he only waved his hand significantly. "Be calm. I wish the whole business was as easily disposed of as the girl."

"She's the only link in the chain that appears weak to my thinking, and she is the key of the old man's cash-box. Who would ever have thought of her kicking over the traces so completely and marrying Sumner?" and the Major relighted his cigar, which had gone out while he was talking.

"Keep quiet about that, Madison; let them think us surprised by their news today. Pray observe my caution; I will explain later.

"I am glad it is all right. That old attorney worries me, too. Women are deceitful hussies; a man never knows what they are at." General Benson laughed softly at the Major's suggestion.

"What!" he said, "shall the foolishness of a mere girl stop us now, when we are so near the goal? By no means. If she attempts to thwart me, so much the worse for her. Wait for me, Major," and General Benson left the room to speak with Isaac.

Left alone, Major Madison went to the window and stood looking out at the passing throng.

"It is impossible not to admire Benson's nerve and his infernal penetration," he thought half-aloud. "He reasons out a position and plans from the most trivial circumstances. He always falls on his feet. How many close calls we have had since we joined forces: yet, thanks to his luck, we have come out first best every time. Yes, he has wonderful ability and his extraordinary audacity and nerve may be trusted to carry us safely through a difficult undertaking like the present one. What a profession we have adopted and practised for twenty years. Justice never sleeps, the old fogies tell us, but I'll be dog-goned if the old woman ain't in a dead swoon when Benson's on the rampage."

Shortly after this the two friends stepped from their carriage before the Bowen mansion. The Major, in his black clothes, white cravat and spectacles might readily have passed for an eminent divine about to administer consolation to the bereaved widow and orphan.

Jewel stood in the great library waiting for General Benson, who had requested an interview. The reading of the will had shown her how dependent she would be upon this man. The thought of him as a guardian made her sick at heart. What could her father have been thinking about? She was bewildered by the difficulties which had suddenly beset her path. She who had been petted and shielded all her life saw an existence of strife and danger opening dimly in the future.

"How will it all end," she asked herself drearily, "if Cuthbert should be condemned? He shall not be; he must not be," she told herself, shutting her teeth hard and drawing a long breath.

Presently General Benson entered the room closely followed by Mrs. Bowen, who crossed the room to Jewel's side and took her hand tenderly in hers. Together they faced General Benson, and this silent defiance filled the man with rage. He came to a halt immediately in front of the pale girl, who had risen to her feet on his entrance.

"I want to tell you, Jewel, in answer to your letter, that I shall not give you up," he began abruptly. "Nothing is changed since you gave me your promise and I shall hold you to it. Your father expected it, too, when he made me your guardian."

"Sir," said Jewel, in a voice almost unintelligible from agitation, "I know that my conduct is extraordinary, but so are the circumstances surrounding my acts; I do not propose to justify myself. It is a great favor that I ask at your hands, but I entreat you to relinquish a project so fraught with unhappiness for both of us. Your generosity will spare me many sad and sorrowful hours, and surely you could not desire an unwilling bride."

"All is fair in love, Jewel," replied the General, who had listened apparently cold and unmoved, but inwardly a passion of rage and jealousy was gnawing at his heart. Then he continued with a malicious smile, "Why not yield gracefully to the inevitable?"

At these words the girl's every instinct arose in arms. She contrasted this scene with her father's fond indulgence and in hot anger longed to show this usurper how she despised his brief authority. There was a look of utter disgust on her face.

"I would have spared you, General Benson, but you need no leniency from me. There is no hope that I shall ever become your wife. I am already married to—Cuthbert Sumner!"

In a moment the man's manner changed.

"Ah!" he said, and the exclamation burst from his lips in a hiss; the elegant society man disappeared—hideous passion gave glimpses of depths of infamy—one beheld the countenance of a devil. "I have heard something of this before; but it does not concern me; it does not alter my plans. I should be foolish to allow a dead man to mar my future; and a dead man Sumner will be, for the law will remove him from my path. Nothing can save him." Jewel measured the man before her with flaming eyes; she turned from him toward the door with a gesture expressive of loathing; she halted on the threshold.

"Hear me, General Benson, I will never become your wife; never, I swear it. Now do your worst."

As the door closed behind the angry girl the man turned to Mrs. Bowen, who stood watching the scene. "And you, madam, are you in league with the misguided girl who undertakes to defy my authority and rights?" The cool sarcasm of his tones was a combination of insolence and impudence.

"You are speaking to Senator Zenas Bowen's widow. You will kindly alter your words and tone when we are conversing, General Benson." Mrs. Bowen spoke in her usual calm, dignified tone. The General's face became purple, then pale; his white teeth gleamed savagely. His elaborate bow was full of mockery as he replied:

"I await your answer, madam, to my question."

"You shall have it," Mrs. Bowen exclaimed in exasperation. "I shall support Jewel in her desires. I am convinced her father would never force her to act against her inclinations."

There ensued a moment of intense silence when she had finished speaking. General Benson was utterly transfigured. There was not the slightest vestige remaining of the elegant chief of a high official bureau; the sweet voice was changed— it was hard and rasping and had a ring in it that reminded one of the slums. He advanced toward Mrs. Bowen and seized her roughly by the arm.

"So you will assist that headstrong girl to defy me, will you? Well, do it at your peril! Do it, and I will tell your story to the world. I know you; I knew you instantly the first night I saw you in this house. This girl is not your child; why should you care. I have no desire to harm you. Just let things take their course and I will never disturb you in any way."

Uncontrollable terror had spread over Mrs. Bowen's features at these words. Her lips moved but gave forth no sound.

"You do not answer, madam!" exclaimed her tormentor. Then with a diabolical smile of evil triumph he added, "I am correct then in my surmise; you do not deny it?"

The white lips moved: this time her words were distinguishable,—"No! I do not understand what you mean." "I mean—," and he bent toward her and whispered in her ear. That whisper seemed to arouse her benumbered faculties. She moved toward him with disheveled hair, foaming lips and one arm outstretched in menace. He sprang back from her with a smothered oath: "It is true: you cannot deny it."

"I admit nothing; I deny nothing. Prove it if you can," she muttered in a strained tone.

"Then it is war, is it? Very well, I give you until May to think it over. If you do not come to your senses by that time, I shall proceed to act. Think of it, madam; think well," and the General turned and abruptly left the room.

Mrs. Bowen stood there panting, crushed; her eyes alone gave signs of animation; they glared horribly. As the door closed behind her enemy she sighed; she sunk on the carpet. She had fainted.

CHAPTER XXVIII

Time passed on, bringing in the early summer. It was the close of a beautiful June day and the sunset was still glowing and burning as it reluctantly bade the world good-night. Venus stood by an open window gazing anxiously into the twilight. Jewel had gone to the jail early in the day, leaving her maid at home. Mrs. Bowen had been in the room a number of times asking for her daughter. She was always uneasy now when Jewel was away from her, and her face wore a strained look of expectancy pitiful to see.

General Benson's anger seemed to have spent itself in the dire threats he had made on the day the will was read; he had left the women in peace, being scrupulously polite when they met to transact business.

Mrs. Bowen was anxious to leave the hot city, and it was agreed between her and Jewel to go to Arlington Heights, where the latter could still be in close proximity to the prisoner and continue her visits with ease. She had gone that day to tell him not to be depressed if the time between her calls was longer than usual.

The glow of sunset faded from the sky, and the summer twilight deepened into night, still Jewel did not appear. It was a warm night; the upper windows were all open; the diamond-studded sky was like a sea of glass. Another hour went by. Mrs. Bowen was pacing the floor restlessly. Venus came up from the servants' quarters with soup and wine for her mistress.

"Now do be persuaded to eat something, madam," said the maid. "You're just as white as death, and you've sat here waiting for Miss Jewel, without your dinner and you must be quite faint. Here it's nine o'clock, and you always dine at half-past seven. I reckon my young lady's all right. She'll turn up presently as bright as a dollar, sure's you're born."

So Mrs. Bowen smiled and allowed herself to be cheered by the devoted girl, and took some soup and a little of the wine; but she could not rest, and listened to every sound that came faintly to the great mansion from the outside.

Hour succeeded hour and it was eleven o'clock; nobody thought of going to bed. As she sat listening there came a sharp quick ring at the outer bell. Venus herself, anxious for tidings from her loved mistress, rushed to the door ahead of the butler. It was a note which was handed her by a man well muffled up, who instantly disappeared in the thick shrubbery about the lawn. Venus hastened to Mrs. Bowen. With a smile she opened the envelope. The next moment she uttered a cry and gasped for breath.

"Whatever is the matter?" cried the frightened maid.

"This letter—this letter! Help me—help me! Your lady has been abducted!" Mrs. Bowen fell back unconscious in her chair.

The terror-stricken maid opened the letter with shaking hands and read the following lines:

"I always keep my word. If you value your reputation and your step-daughter's *welfare*, you will not seek to find her. In due time she will reappear."

* * * * *

Meanwhile what had become of Jewel? She had elected to walk to the jail and back because of the beauty of the day. At the jail she found Mr. Henson, and they had stayed talking over the difficulties of the case until twilight was falling. But that did not disturb her for Mr. Henson would walk back with her, and the Washington streets, famous for their loneliness and seclusion, stretching like immense parks in all directions, would be robbed of their usual terrors for lone female pedestrians.

Mr. Henson accompanied her to the great entrance gates; there he left her, and she started up the carriage path at a rapid gait. Along the edges of the drive the underwood was so thick, and the foliage of the trees arching overhead so full and dense that towards the centre of the drive it was in semi-twilight, and thick shades of darkness enveloped all things. In the half-light Jewel thought she discerned a vehicle—a close carriage, she fancied—standing at one side of the drive.

Surprised, but not startled, because of the close proximity of the house, the girl advanced. The next moment she was startled enough; a chill of fear went through her woman's heart and it stood still for one instant with a thrill of sickening terror, for suddenly out from the gloomy shade of the trees, into the drive, stepped two men, rough-looking ruffians wearing black half-masks.

The one who was evidently the leader said in a hoarse voice, probably disguised:

"Now, Jim."

Instantly both moved toward her.

Jewel was a Western girl. She did not scream. She had been brought up on a ranch; one of her early habits remained fixed, and even in Washington she was never unarmed when without male escort. The jewelled toy she carried was a present from her father, and he had taught her to use it with deadly effect. Many a day they had hunted together, the young girl bringing down her game in true sportsmanlike style.

Instantly now her hand sought her pocket, in the very instinct of self-defense and desperation; she drew her revolver with intent to fire, but quick as a flash the leader flung himself upon her and wrenched the weapon from her hand. He then threw his arm about her slender form, drawing her towards the carriage.

The passion of terror and desperation lent the girl unnatural strength in her frantic struggle for freedom. The man was forced to place his other hand to stifle her screams.

"You come along quietly, missee, an' you'll be all right; but ef yer screams it won't be pleasant."

"You coward!" she gasped, as he bore her to the carriage. "You coward! Name your price, and let me go."

"Thar you are, now, slick as grease." She was in the carriage then. "Yer money won't help you with me, missee. You're a brave gal, but what's your strength to a man's? Drive on like h—, Jim."

The cold drops of agony stood on the girl's brow as the horror of her position grew upon her each moment.

"Where are you taking me?"

"I'm goin' ter take yer jes' a little journey outside o' Washington fer a few days. Don't you be feared; thar's nuthin' goin' hurt ye."

Who was this man holding her, refusing bribe, yet vowing to protect her from harm. She looked into the masked face in an agony of appeal and doubt and fear in the great gray eyes. The man was touched.

"Don't now, *don't*, missee, look that skeered. Nothin' ain't goin' hurt you, I tell you. Ise got a little gal o' my own."

The girl did not answer. Like a light it flashed across her who was the author of this outrage.

"I know your employer!" she said fiercely. "But he shall learn that I fear him not. I defy him still."

(To be continued.)

❧ ❧ ❧

CHAPTER XXVIII.—(Concluded.)

When Jewel came to herself she was lying on an old-fashioned canopied bed with a coverlet thrown over her. The room was evidently, originally designed for a studio, and was lighted by a skylight; even now a flood of sunlight streamed from above, making more dingy and faded by comparison the appearance of the dusty canvases and once luxurious furniture scattered about the apartment. Evidences of decay were everywhere; a broken easel leant against the wall, and on a table odds and ends of tubes, brushes and other artistic paraphernalia were heaped in a disorderly mass. There were also a couch and easy chairs in faded brocade.

The girl looked about her with lanquid interest scarcely realizing what had happened to disturb the serenity of her daily life. Presently, however, the power of thought returned and with it a flood of memories concerning the outrage of the night before. She was a prisoner, but where?

What a terrible sensation it was to wake to the consciousness of being a prisoner! A prisoner! she, Jewel Bowen, who until recently had never known a care in her short existence of twenty years. Now all the waves and billows of life were passing over her threatening to engulf her. Could it be that all her bright hopes for the future were to end here in this lonely chamber?

With the thought she arose hastily from the bed and began walking despairingly about, examining the room. After a tour of the apartment she gave it up. Her prison was well-chosen. The doors were bolted, and no window gave a possibility of escape. There was no chance of attracting attention, by her cries, from passers-by, even if scores of persons traversed the streets about this house; no one would know that within its walls a desolate girl suffered the keenest of mental torture.

She paced the room frantically, and shook the doors of her prison violently until she was obliged to sink exhausted upon the couch. "They will hardly let me die of hunger," she told herself, resolving to save her strength for questioning whoever should bring her food.

Crouching upon the couch, she listened. Not a sound broke upon her ear. It seemed to her that desolation engulfed her. Presently, as she sat there, the sound of a football came to her strained ears, then a key grated in the lock, the door swung open, and a tall, pleasant-featured black man entered the room, bearing a tray. He carefully locked the door behind him, removing the key from the lock. He wheeled forward a small table and deftly arranged the contents of the tray upon it.

Jewel launched an avalanche of questions at him, but he returned no answer. He went and returned a number of times, bringing her clothing, books and luxuries of the toilet, all indicating that a long captivity was in prospect. At lunch time an aged Negress brought her food, but all efforts to engage her in conversation were unavailing; a more morose and repulsive specimen of the race Jewel had never met.

After this there was a monotonous interval of time passed in the agony of silence. Her meals were furnished regularly and all other needs lavishly supplied. One day was the record of another.

Four weeks must have passed since she was brought to this place, still she had no knowledge of her captors, nor where her prison was located. One change, however, was made— they gave her the freedom of an adjoining room as the summer heat increased, but the windows were barred and looked out upon extensive gardens filled with the ruins of what must once have been buildings and offices of a large plantation. The once well-kept walks were overgrown with weeds, and a heavy growth of trees obstructed the view in all directions.

One night she sat by the window gazing at the stars and eating her heart out in agony and tears. She could not sleep; insomnia had added its horrors to her other troubles. Suddenly the sky became overcast and the stars disappeared. A storm threatened. Low mutterings of thunder and gusts of rising wind foretold a summer shower. At intervals a lightning flash lit up the inky blackness of the scene. Finally the flashes became so vivid that the girl moved her seat from the window to a less exposed position with a scornful laugh at her own fear of death. "Truly," she thought bitterly, "self-preservation has been called the first law of nature. How we strive to preserve that which is of so little value."

Up and down the sides of the room her eyes wandered aimlessly; sometimes she felt that she was losing her mind. Presently a painting fixed into the wall arrested her attention. It was the portrait of an impossible wood nymph, but so faded that its beauty—if it had once possessed any—was entirely gone.

As she gazed at it indifferently the centre bulged outward,

and a small strip of canvas swung to and fro as if from a draught of air.

Jewel sprang to her feet and ran to the picture. She trembled with sudden hope. Where did the draught come from? Carefully she raised the torn strip of canvas and inserted her hand beneath it, feeling along the wall back of the picture. There was a narrow recess behind it. Greatly excited by this discovery, she flew to the table where her dinner-service still remained, seized a knife and cut the canvas close to the frame for a good distance up. The she tremblingly raised the cloth.

Oh! joy! it revealed a passage usually closed by a door which had become unfastened and now swung idly in the breeze made by the rising wind.

Thank heaven, it was an hour when she was free from interruption. No one would disturb her until morning. She took the lamp in her hand. Escape seemed very near. Scarcely waiting to widen the aperture, she crept through, and soon stood, covered with dust, trembling shaken with emotion, in the dark passage which the canvas had hidden.

She paused and strained her ears to listen for sounds in the silent house. None came. Then she crept on very, very cautiously.

The passage was dark. It had evidently led to the servants' quarters at the back of the house when mirth and gaiety held high revel in the glorious old mansion. She went swiftly on, till she came to a black baize door. She pushed it open with difficulty. Here she paused irresolute, for this door gave admission to the front of the house; there was a passage at right angles with the one just quitted, with stairs leading above and below. She glided toward the latter, seized hold of the banisters, descended into another passage with many doors opening into it. The doors were all closed.

What a rambling old place it was. In the excitement of the instant she had felt no terror, but now an icy chill seized her and her heart throbbed heavily.

She noticed now that one of the doors in the passage was ajar! Dare she pass it? To advance was appalling, but the case was a desperate one. With her heart throbbing wildly she stood motionless one instant, then she ventured past the unclosed door.

She shaded her lamp with one hand and with fascinated gaze took in, in one brief instant, the contents of the room. Her eyes wandered from the bare floor and walls to the table, the two chairs, and then to a bed in one corner. There her gaze lingered, for on the bed lay a woman of dark brown complexion and wrinkled visage; about her head was wound a many-hued bandanna handkerchief. The woman's eyes were open and fixed in terror and amazement upon the girl who had just entered the room. They gazed at each other for one moment, these two so strangely met, then the old woman threw her arms above her head, exclaiming:

"Bless Gawd! I'se ready! Praise de Lor'! He done sen' his Angel Gabriel to tote me home to glory."

The sound of her voice broke the spell that bound Jewel.

"Who are you, Auntie, and what makes you think me an angel?"

"Lor', honey, is you human sho' nuff? Why when I seen yo' face er'shinin' on me dar, an' hearn yer sof' step comin' en de lonely night, I made sho' it was de Lor' come to carry dis' po' sinner to er home in glory. I 'spec' I been shut up her so long I'se gittin' doaty. I'se a po' ol'black 'ooman, been dragged 'way from my home an' chillun an' locked up here by a limb o' de debbil 'cause he's 'fraid I tell his wicked actions. But 'deed chile, whar'd you come from? Does you live in dis place?"

Jewel shook her head sadly.

"I'm a prisoner, too, Auntie. I've been shut up here for four weeks now. I happened to find a way out of my room tonight, and I thought I might possibly escape. Can you tell me where I am?"

"Yes, honey, I can. You's down on de ol' Enson plantation in Ma'lan'. I was born on de nex' joinin' place myself. But who brung you here? What's your name, chile?"

"I haven't seen my captor yet, but I believe it to be General Benson. My name is Jewel Bowen."

"Mercy, King! My lovely Lor'd, but ain't dis curus?" exclaimed the old woman, greatly excited. "My gran'darter is yo' waiter, Venus Johnson!"

It was not Jewel's turn to become excited.

"Then you are—?"

"Aunt Hennie Sargent; dat's me."

CHAPTER XXIX

Meanwhile there was mourning at the Bowen mansion, for the joy of the house had fled with Jewel. Mrs. Bowen sent for the family lawyer and then went to bed; trouble was wearing her out, and there was danger of her becoming a confirmed invalid.

Mr. Cameron put the machinery of the law in motion to find the missing girl, but there progress seemed to end.

Now the sorely tried mistress discovered what a treasure she had in the maid Venus. The girl was everywhere attending

to the business of the house and waiting on the invalid
mistress. She visited the jail with news for the restless unhappy
man confined there, never seeming to weary in well-doing.
Venus preserved a discreet silence concerning the letter received on the night of the abduction, but the brain of the
little brown maid was busy. She had her own ideas about
certain things, and was planning for the deliverance of her
loved young mistress.

When Jewel had been absent about two weeks, Venus asked
leave to pay her mother a visit one evening. Marthy had
heard nothing from the police in relation to Aunt Hennie,
and she was overjoyed to see her daughter; it gave her an
opportunity to pour her sorrows and griefs into sympathetic
ears.

She bustled about the neat kitchen setting out the best that
her home afforded for supper, and Oliver dropped his books
in honor of his sister's visit, making it a festival.

When the meal was on the table, smoking hot,—corn
pone, gumbo soup, chicken and rice and coffee of an amber
hue,—the children ate with gusto. The mother's eyes shone
with happiness as she watched their enjoyment, pressing upon
them, at intervals, extra helps.

"Have some mo' this gumbo soup, my baby. I reckon you
don' git nothin' like it up yonder with all the fixin's you has
there."

"Well, my Lord, ma, I won't be able to walk to the cars
if I keep on stuffing myself," replied Venus as her mother
filled her plate again with the delicious soup.

"Say, Venus," broke in Oliver, with a grin on his mis-
chievous face, "who's the good-looking buck that came to the
end of the street with you the last time you were home?"

"What's that?" cried Marthy, sharply.

Oliver laughed and clapped his hands, "Ma's like a hen with chickens; she's afraid of the fellows, Vennie."

Venus laughed, too, a little shame-facedly. "Oh, now, Ollie, ain't you got no cover to your mouth? That was Mr. Sumner's man, John. I had to see him about a message from Mrs. Bowen to Mr. Sumner, and so he was polite enough to come with me to our street, it being pretty dark."

"That's all right," said Marthy in a relieved tone. "Mr. Williams is a perfec' gent'man. You're only a leetle gal, Venus, if you is out to work, an' there's time 'nuff for you to git into trubble. You don' wan' to fill yo' head up with 'viggotty notions 'bout fellars yet. I got married young when I'd doughter been playin' with baby rags; I don' want my gal to take on eny mo' trubble en her haid than she can kick off at her heels. You Venus, mark my wurds, an' 'member what I tell's you ef I'm moulderin' in the clay to dus' an' ashes tomorrer,—gittin' jined to a man's a turrible 'spons'bility, 'specially the man. You want to think well an' cal'ate the consequences of the prevus ac'. Mymy, mymy!" she continued musingly, "how that carries me back to the las' time ol' Mis' Sargeant whopped me. She says to me, 'Marthy, did you take the money off my dresser table? tell me the troof,' and I dussan' lie, an' so I said 'Ys'm; Ike Johnson tol' me to do it an' he'd buy me a red ribbin fer my hair.' Ol' miss says 'Marthy, you's 'mitted the *prevus* ac',' an' I'm gwine whop you,' an' the ol' lady laid it onto me right smart with her slipper. Ike Johnson's been gittin' me inter trubble ever sense that time.

Oliver, when you was born an' I foun' you was a man chile I said to myself, 'Lord, how come you let me bring one of them mule critters into the wurl to make trubble for some po' 'ooman? An' ef ever you git jined, an' treat yo' wife as yo' pa's treated me, I hope you'll git yo' match, an' she'll wallop the yearth with you, 'deed I does."

"Daddy been home lately?" asked Venus carelessly after the meal was cleared away.

"No, chile, he ain't," replied her mother. "He was home— le' me see—jes' befo' the fus' of the munf. He brought me the mor'gage money."

"How much was it?"

"Four hundred dollars Venus, chile, you could have knocked me down with a feather, I was so outdone from 'stonishmen' when he throwed it into my lap and said 'dar's you' mo-'gage.' "

"Now, ma, where'd he get *all* that money I'd like to know? He never got it honest, that's my belief."

"Yes, I reckon he did, honey, this time. Gin'ral Benson give it to him. Yo' granny asked the Gin'ral about it 'way in the winter."

"Hump!" exclaimed Venus.

"He ain't been home sense. Gin'ral's bo't a plantation out o' Baltimo' a bit, an' yo' pa's holpin' to fix it up. I reckon he'll be thare 'bout all summer. He took a few clo's an' things with him when he was home." Venus looked at her mother intently, but remained silent.

"Dear, dear, Venus," Marthy continued beginning to cry, "ef I only knew where was yo' granny or what had come to her, I'd be a happy 'ooman this night. An' to think of Miss Jewel, too, that dear beautiful girl with a face like an angel out of glory. The ways of the Lord is pas' follerin', an' that's a fac'."

"What's dad say about granny?" asked Venus suddenly. "*He* ain't worried none, bless yo' soul. He ain't studyin' 'bout the dear ol' so'l. He ain't got no mo' blood in him than a lizard. He's the onerist man! Says to me, 'quit frettin'; the ol' 'ooman 'll turn up safe quicker'n scat', he says. 'She's tuf; nothin' ain't gwine kill the ol' hornet.' Them's yo' pa's words to me."

"What do you expect from dad, ma? you know him. You ought to if anybody does. Granny makes him toe the mark, that's why he dislikes her."

"That's so, sho' 'nuff, baby; an' what we know 'bout Ike Johnson's mean capers would fill a book. It's twenty years come nix Chris'mus sense we jumped the broomstick together. We was the very las' couple jined befo' the s'render, an' ef it hadn't been for yo' granny, we'd all been in the po' house long ago an' fergit."

When it was time to start for home Oliver escorted his sister to the car. On the way she questioned him closely and learned many things concerning her father that her mother had failed to mention.

"It's as sure as preaching," she told herself late that night as she was preparing for bed, "it's as sure as preaching that somebody who knows something must take hold of Miss Jewel's case or that son of Sodom will carry his point. The police are slower 'n death. Dad's up to his capers. He can fool ma, but he can't pull the wool over my eyes; I'm his daughter. Hump! well, we'll see about it. It's a burning shame for dad to go on this way after all Miss Jewel's kindness to us. But I'll balk him. I'll see him out on this case or my name ain't Venus Johnson."

"I'll see if this one little black girl can't get the best of as mean a set of villains as ever was born," was her last thought as her eyes closed in slumber.

Mr. Henson sat in his office the next morning thinking deeply. He had just returned from New York, where he had carefully examined the ground, trying to find a flaw in the Bowen will, drawn and signed in that city, but not a particle of encouragement had rewarded his efforts. He was much depressed over his failure to obtain a clue to what he was convinced was a clever forgery committed by two dangerous men. His vast experience did not aid him; he was forced to declare that the criminals had covered their tracks well.

Mr. Cameron had just left him after acknowledging *his* inability to fix a point that would legally stay the enforcement of the will.

All was dark; but the man felt that if he could obtain the slightest clue, he could unravel the whole plot without difficulty. But how to gain a clue was the question. He had determined to start the next day for Kentucky in the hope of finding Elise Bradford's aunt and the child of the dead woman, hoping that this might furnish the key to the mystery.

The morning sunshine streamed into the room. The intense heat was enervating. He drew his chair before the large open window on the side where the sun had not reached and directly in the wake of an electric fan. He leaned his head upon his hand and thought over the situation.

All his efforts had been to ascertain if there were any real grounds for the suspicions, which had been aroused in Miss Bowen's mind, and which his interviews with Sumner had confirmed. The news of her abduction had come as a distinct shock to him when it was given him upon his return from New York. The beautiful girl had aroused all the man's innate chivalry; springs of tenderness long dead to any influence had welled up in his soul, and he felt a mad desire, uncontrollable and irresistible, to rescue her, and take dire vengeance on her captors.

Her haunting influence was wrapped about him; he could

see her, feel her presence and almost catch the tones of her low voice in the silent room. Ever and anon he glanced about him as if seeking the actual form of the fair spirit that had so suddenly absorbed his heart and soul.

He was satisfied in his own mind that General Benson was the criminal, but to this man who had become a legal machine, tangible evidence was the only convincing argument that he knew.

Presently a clerk entered the room and announced that a woman wished to speak with him.

"Show her in," he replied to the man's query.

A few seconds passed, and then the opening door admitted a young colored girl who had an extremely intelligent, wide-awake expression.

Venus was not at all embarrassed by the novelty of her surroundings, but advanced toward the chief with a businesslike air, after making sure that the retiring clerk had actually vanished.

"I'm Miss Jewel Bowen's maid," she declared abruptly. The detective whirled around in his chair at her words, and in an instant was all attention. His keen eyes ran over the neat little brown figure standing demurely before him, with a rapid mental calculation of her qualities.

"What is your name?"

"Venus Camilla Johnson."

"How long have you been in Miss Bowen's employ?"

"All the winter."

"Who sent you here?"

"Nobody. I keep my business to myself. Things are too curious around Wash'nton these days to be talking too much."

The shadow of a smile lurked about the corners of Mr. Henson's mouth.

"Well, what do you want? Time is precious with me."

"Yes, sir; I won't keep you long, but you see Miss Jewel's been my good angel and I jus' had to come here and unburden my mind to you or burst. You see, sir, it's this way,—the Bowen family is *white* right through; mos' *too* good for this world. They've got piles of money, but mymy, mymy! since the Senator's gone, and Mr. Cuthbert's done got into trouble from being in tow with Miss Madison, they be the mos' miserablest two lone women you ever saw."

Venus forgot her education in her earnestness, and fell into the Negro vernacular, talking and crying at the same time.

Mr. Henson waited patiently. He knew that she would grow calmer if he did not notice her agitation.

"It's hard for me to go back on my own daddy," continued the girl, "but it's got to be done. I suspicion him more and more every minute I'm alive, I do. Miss Jewel's stolen away, and the old lady's taken down to her bed, an' my daddy is waltzing through the country looking after General Benson's business down on a plantation in Maryland. I'm no fool, Mr. Henson; he's my daddy, but Isaac Johnson's a bad pill. He's jus' like a bad white man, sir,—he'll do anything for money when he gets hard up."

Mr. Henson sat with pale face regarding the woman before him. His eyes gleamed and were fixed searchingly upon her.

Finally he asked:

"Who are your parents? I take it they were once slaves. Where were they born?"

"Ma's Aunt Henny Sargeant's daughter Marthy, and daddy's Isaac Johnson. They lived on adjoining plantations in Maryland. Dad belonged to Mr. Enson, and Ma to Mrs. Sargeant. Ma says it was a terrible misfortune that she did live next door to the Ensons, leastwise Oliver and me'd never had Ike Johnson for our daddy."

"Any relation to the Aunt Henny who was employed by the government and who has disappeared?" the detective asked.

"Yes, sir; that's her," replied the girl, nodding her head.

"Poor granny; I reckon she's dead all right. Ma takes it terrible hard. Does nothing but cry after granny all day while she's working. I tell her I *cain't* cry till I find Miss Jewel. Ma says I'm unfeeling; but, Lord, you cain't help being just as you're built. Say, Mr. Henson, I've made bold to bring you something. I took it away from the madam the night Miss Jewel was stolen."

Mr. Henson took the envelope that the girl extended to him, and read the note contained therein.

"Who do you think sent this, Venus?"

"No one but old Benson."

Again the chief smiled at the quaint answer. But he looked at her still more searchingly, as he asked:

"Did anything of a particularly suspicious nature occur to make you hold that opinion?"

"Well, yes, sir; there did. Something I overhead General Benson say to the old lady."

"Oh, then, you were listening."

"I reckon I was, and a good job, too, or I wouldn't have this to tell you. It was the day the will was read. Mr. Cameron was gone, and the three of 'em—Mrs. Bowen, Miss Jewel and General Benson were in the library. Miss Jewel went out and left the other two together.

He hollered at the madam like he was crazy, and I was standing there outside the door with the old Senator's boot-jack in my hand, expecting that I'd have to go in and hit the General over the head with it to protect the madam. He says to her, 'So, you will assist that headstrong girl to defy me, will you? well, do it at your peril!' then he went close up to her—so close that their noses almost touched, and I thought it was about time for the boot-jack, sure,—but all he did was to whisper to her, and the old madan gave a screech and keeled over on the floor like she was dead.

I 'clare to you, Mr. Henson, I was skeered enough to drop, but I didn't say a word, no sir; I just went in as soon as the General went out, and I picked the old lady up and got her to her room, and when she came to her self there was nobody to ask her what was the matter because they didn't know what I could have told them. But Madam hasn't been herself since. I believe my soul that he skeered the life out of her. When Miss Jewel didn't come home, and that note came instead, I just made up my mind it was Venus for General Benson, and that I'd got to cook his goose or he'd cook mine."

"You do not like General Benson, I see."

"Like him! who could, the sly old villain. He's mighty shrewd, and—" she paused.

"Well, what?"

"Foxy," she finished. "He tries to be mighty sweet to me, but I like a gentleman to stay where he belongs and not be loving servant girls on the sly. I owe Miss Jewel what money cain't pay, and I'm not ungrateful.

"*I* believe the old rapscallion has got her shut up somewhere down in Maryland, and dad's helping him. Oh, I didn't tell you, did I, that dad's his private waiter?"

"Ah!" exclaimed the chief, for the first time exhibiting a sign of excitement.

"Now we're getting down to business, my girl. I understand your drift now. You have done well to come to me."

Venus smiled in proud satisfaction at his words of praise. The man sat buried in deep thought for a time before he spoke again. Finally he said:

"I need help, Venus; are you brave enough to risk something for the sake of your mistress?"

"Try me and see," was her proud reply.

"It comes to just this: someone must go down to this plantation in Maryland, and hang around to find out if there is truth in our suspicions. Can you wear boys' clothing?" he asked abruptly.

Venus showed her dazzling teeth in a giggle. She ducked her head and writhed her shoulders in suppressed merriment as she replied:

"*Cain't* I? well, I reckon."

"Then you'll do. There's no time to be lost. Disguise yourself as a boy. Be as secret about it as possible. Tell no one what you are about to do, or where you are going, and meet me at the station tonight in time for the ten o'clock train for Baltimore. My agent will be waiting for you on the Avenue, just by the entrance, disguised as your grandfather Uncle Henry, a crippled old Negro, fond of drink. You are to be Billy, and both of you are going home to Baltimore. We will fix the rest of the business after you reach the village.

God grant that this plan may hasten the discovery I have been seeking."

CHAPTER XXX

Enson Hall reminded one of an ancient ruin. The main body of the stately dwelling was standing, but scarcely a vestige of the once beautiful outbuildings remained; the cabins in the slave quarters stood like skeletons beneath the nodding leaves and beckoning arms of the grand old beeches. War and desolation had done their best to reduce the stately pile to a wreck. It bore, too, an uncanny reputation. The Negroes declared that the beautiful woods and the lonely avenues were haunted after nightfall. It had grown into a tradition that the ghost of Ellis Enson "walked," accompanied by a lady who bore an infant in her arms.

The Hall was in charge of an old Negress, known all over the country as "Auntie Griffin." She was regarded with awe by both whites and blacks, being a reputed "witch woman" used to dealing and trafficking with evil spirits.

Tall and raw-boned, she was a nightmare of horror. Her body was bent and twisted by disease from its original height. Her protruding chin was sharp like a razor, and the sunken jaws told of toothless gums within.

Her ebony skin was seamed by wrinkles; her eyes, yellow with age, like Hamlet's description of old men's eyes, purged "thick amber and plum-tree gum." The deformed hands were horny and toilworn. Her dress was a garment which had the virtue of being clean, although its original texture had long since disappeared beneath a multitude of many-hued patches.

Auntie Griffin only visited the village for supplies; she was uncongenial and taciturn. She made no visits and received none. Lately, however, it was noticed that the old woman had a male companion at the Hall, an elderly, dudish colored man whom she announced, on her weekly visit to the store, as her brother Ike, come to spend a short time with her.

It was well along in August when an old Negro calling himself Uncle William Henry Jackson, accompanied by his grandson Billy, a spritely lad, scarcely more than a boy, wandered into the village and took possession of one of the dilapitated antebellum huts, formerly the homes of slaves, many of which still adorned the outskirts of the little hamlet.

Uncle William Henry claimed to be a former inhabitant who had belonged to a good old Southern family of wealth, made extinct by the civil strife. The oldest resident—a Negress of advanced age who was an authority on the genealogy of the settlement—claimed to remember him distinctly, whereupon he was adopted into their warm hearts as a son of the soil and received the most hospitable treatment; in two weeks he had settled down as a fixture of the place. The old man claimed to be a veteran of the late Civil War, and that he was in receipt of a small pension which provided food for himself and grandchild. Uncle William spent most of his time sitting on a half-barrel at the door of the general store, chewing tobacco, making fishing rods from branches which Billy brought him from the woods and telling stories, of which he had a wonderful stock. The rods he turned out were really pieces of artistic work when they left his hands, and the owner of the store agreed to find a market for the goods.

Thus the old man was happily established, to quote his own words, "fer de res' ob my days," sitting in the sun with a few old cronies of his own cut—white and black harmoniously blended—spinning yarns of life in camp, and, for the truth must be told, drinking bad moonshine rum.

He never tired of describing the battle scenes through which he had passed.

"Do I know anythin' 'bout Wagner? I should say so, bein' I was in it," was his favorite prelude to a description of the famous charge.

"No, honey, I didn' lef' dat missin' leg dar. I lef' dat leg ober to For' Piller. But fer all dat, Wagner was a corker, yes, sah, a corker. From eleven o'clock Friday 'tel four o'clock Saturday we was gittin' on the transpo'ts, we war rained on, had no tents an' nothin' to eat. Thar was no time fo' we war to lead de charge. We came up at quick time an' when we got wifin 'bout one hunde'd yards, de rebs open a rakin' fire. Why, mon, they jes' vomited the shot inter us from de fo't, an' we a-walkin' up thar in dress parade order; they mowed us down lak sheep. De fus' shot camed down rip-zip, an' ploughed a hole inter us big 'nuff to let in a squadron, an' all we did was ter close up, servin' our fire; but I tell you, gent'men, we looked at each other an' felt kin' o' lonesome fer a sight o' home an' fren's.

Colonel Shaw walked ahead as cool as ef he war up to Boston Common, singing out, 'steady, boys, steady!' Byme-by de order come in a clar ringin' voice, 'charge! Foreard, my brave boys!' We started on a double-quick, an' wif a cheer an' a shout we went pell-mell; wif a rush into an' over de ditch them devils had made an' fenced wif wire. But we kep' right on an' up de hill 'tel we war han' to han' wif de inimy. Colonel Shaw was fus' to scale de walls. He stood up thar straight an' tall lak de angel Gabrul, urgin' de boys to press on. I tell you, sah, 'twas a hot time.

Fus' thing I 'member clearly after I got het up, was I seed a officer standin' wavin' his sword, an' I heard him holler, 'Now, give 'em h——, boys, give 'em h——!' an then thar come a shot; it hit him—zee-rip—an' off went his head; but, gent'men, ef you'll b'lieve me, dat head rolled by me, down de hill sayin' as it went, 'Give 'em h——, hoys, give 'em h——!' until it landed in de ditch; an' all de time de mon's arms was a wavin' of his sword."

"Come off, Uncle," exclaimed one of the circle of listeners. "Who ever heard of a man's talkin' after his head was cut off?"

"Gent'men," replied Uncle William solemnly, "dat ar am a fac'; I see it wif my own two eyes, an' hyard it wif my own two ears. *It am a fac'*."

"I've heard lies on lies," drawled another on-looker, "from all kinds of liars—white liars and niggers—but that is the mos' *infernal* one I ever listened to."

"I'll leave it to Colonel Morris thar ef sech things ain't possibul. Ain't you seen cur'us capers cut when you was in battle, sah?"

"Don't bring me into it, Uncle William Henry, I'm listening to you," laughed the Colonel, who had just driven up and was about entering the store to make a purchase.

"It am a fac'; I 'clar it am a fac'," insisted the old man. "Thar was the officer talkin', and' then the shot hit him so suddint dat he hadn't time to stop talkin'. Why de water in de ditch mus' have got in his mouf fer *I seen* him *when he spit it out!*" At this there was a roar of laughter from the crowd, and the first speaker slapped Uncle William Henry on the back with a resounding blow.

"That's a tough one for a professor, Uncle. I know you're dry. Come, have a drink."

When they had all returned to their places, the old man resumed his narrative.

"When I looked agin, Colon Shaw was gone. The Johnnies had pulled him over the parapet down onter de stockades, an' dat was de las' seen of as gallan' a gent'man as ever lived. I tell you, mon, when I seen dat, I fel' lak a she wil' cat, an' I jes' outfit a blin' mule. I tore an' I bit lak a dog. I got clinched wif a reb, an' dog my cats, fus' thing I know'd I was chawin' him in de throat an' I never lef' go 'tel he give a groan an I seed he was gone. Jes' then I seen three or fo' Johnnies running 'long de parapet toward me shoutin', 'S'render, you d— nigger.' I looked an' seen dat all 'bout me they was clubbin', stabbin' an' shootin' our boys to death, an' our men was fightin' lak devils themselves.

"Well, sah, when I seen them Mr. Whitemen makin' fer me, I jes' rolled down de hill to de ditch, an' plantin' my gun ba'net down in de water, I lepped acrost to de other side. I was flyin' fer sho, you may b'lieve, an' fus' thing I heard was, 'Halt! who goes thar?' It was de provy guard, a black North Carolina regiment stationed thar to return stragglers to their posts. I sung out, clar an' loud, thinkin' I was suttinly all right then: 'Fifty-fourth Massachusetts!' But I felt de col' chills creep down my back when I heard de order: 'Git-a-back-a-dar, Fifty-fourth!' an' every mon's gun said 'click, clack.' You may b'lieve, gent'men, dat I got back.

"I wandered aroun' fer a spell lak a los' kitten; finally, I stumbled into de lines, an' I crep' unner a gun-carriage an' slep' thar 'tel mornin'."

Now it happened that Isaac Johnson was lonely in his enforced solitude, and being of social disposition, soon made it a habit to wend his way to the corner store and listen to Uncle William Henry's stories. Having plenty of money, he treated freely and was soon counted a "good fellow" by all the frequenters of the place.

At first Isaac drank moderately, mindful of his responsibilities, but soon his old habits re-asserted themselves. Moreover, Uncle William liked the social glass also; and finally the two became so intimate that they would wend their way to the hut in the woods, where the latter had taken up his residence, and there enjoy to the full the contents of a gallon-jug which was concealed under a loose board in the floor. In short, Isaac got drunk, and losing all sense of caution, remained away from the Hall two days and nights, hidden in the hut from prying eyes. The first time this happened, old William Henry recovered control of himself as soon as Isaac was locked in drunken slumber upon Billy's bed, behind the curtains, which divided the one room into sleeping apartments.

He went to the door then and waved a handkerchief three times, nailed it to the side of the hut and retired.

Ten minutes after this act the lad Billy entered the woods which led to Enson Hall.

The path, though often ill-defined, was never quite obliterated, and he came at last to where the trees grew thinner, and the Hall was visible. Then he emerged upon the broad stretch of meadow and crossing it was soon on the grounds. There he paused and looked cautiously about. Twilight was falling. The scene was wild and romantic. There was no sight nor sound of human beings.

He passed the rusty gates and sped swiftly across the law to the shelter of bushes near the wide piazzas. He sank down in their shadow and waited.

Nothing occurred to break the heavy silence. Not a human creature crossed the unkept grounds. The soft summer wind lazily stirred the grass growing in rank luxuriance. The scene was desolate and depressing enough. So it continued for over an hour. Darkness finally succeeded the soft twilight. Then the lad re-appeared and skirted the sides and front of the building carefully.

Presently he espied a wild honeysuckle that had climbed to the third story of the house and blended its tendrils gracefully with the branches of a giant sycamore that stretched its arms so near to the house that they tapped gently against the irons that barred a window high above its head.

With the agility of a cat, the boy was quickly finding his way up, up to the window of the room where Jewel was allowed to exercise and breathe the sweet summer air from the woods and fields. A subdued light gleamed in the window behind the iron bars.

Hush! what noise was that? It was the sound of voices in conversation. The lad ceased his climbing and rested, listening intently for a repetition of the sound. Again it came—first a sweet young voice that had a weary, despondent note; then, in answer the tones of an aged Negro voice in the endeavor to comfort and encourage.

The listener waited no longer, but rapidly mounted to the window just above his head, reached the lower end of the rusty iron bar which divided the broken casement into two, and drew himself up to the ledge, and peered in.

*   *   *   *   *

Mr. Henson was aroused from slumber at midnight that night to receive an important telegram, which read: "All O.K. Just as we thought. Come on and bag the game."

(To be continued.)

CHAPTER XXXI

By the middle of September Washington awoke from the stagnation incident to the summer vacation, and was ready to begin the business of another working year. The departments were re-opened and hundreds of stragglers returned to work in the great government hives, all eager for the excitement of the great murder trial.

Sunday, the day before the opening of the trial, Cuthbert Sumner sat in his cell looking pale and careworn but still preserving his outward composure though racked by inward torture. Jewel's abduction had been a worse blow to him than his own arrest, and uncertainty as to her fate had nearly driven him wild; but today Hope had smiled her April smile from amid the clouds that threatened and he was at peace. His lawyer had just left him, bidding him to be of good cheer for all things pointed to a happy ending of his troubles.

Absorbed in thought he sat dreaming of the future and planning for a period of felicity that should atone for the suffering of the present time. Suddenly the key grated in the lock and the door swung open to admit a visitor. He recoiled as from a blow when he met the gaze of Aurelia Madison who stood staring at him with a glance in which curiosity, fear and love were mingled. She stood in the center of the gloomy, cell like a statue, her dazzling beauty as marvelous as ever, the red-gold hair still shining in sunny radiance, the velvet eyes resting upon the man before her with a hidden caress in their liquid depths. Sumner shuddered as he gazed and remembered the dead girl's story. When alone with this woman, she had always possessed an irresistible attraction for him, and in spite of the past the old sensation returned in full force at this unexpected encounter, mingled with fear and repulsion. She broke the spell which held them silent.

"Bert! my Bert!" She stretched out her hand to him, but he made no move to take it. The blood flushed her cheek.

"Why will you not take my hand?" She moved a step nearer to him; but he rose to his feet and drew back.

With a passionate cry she fell on her knees before him, seized his hand and covered it with kisses.

"Do not repulse me. See me at your feet. Bert! let me save you. Do not spurn me, I beseech you."

"Save me? Miss Madison, you jest," replied Sumner in a voice made quiet by a strong effort.

"I do not jest. I can and *will* save you." Her eyes were fixed upon his face in eager intensity. With a shock of surprise Sumner was convinced that she spoke the truth; but he stood there looking down upon her with all the coolness and sternness of a judge.

"You tell me news," he said at length.

"Great God! do not doubt me now. I can save you. All I ask in return is that you take me to your heart again as your affianced wife, and I shall be content."

"Ah! I thought so. There is a price attached to your generosity."

"Do not be so merciless. If you only knew—"

"I *do* know!" broke from Sumner's lips as he flung her off. She reeled back, gasping for breath. Still upon her knees, she gazed up into his immovable countenance. For a full minute there was dead silence. Then Sumner spoke.

"Do not let us have any more mistakes. If my acquittal depends upon the plan you have mentioned, Miss Madison, I shall never be free."

"Why do you speak thus?" she asked as she rose to her feet.

"For many reasons," he replied, significantly.

The woman looked utterly despondent. There was a pause— an exciting pause.

"Surely," she said at length, "you can have no hope that Jewel will return to you. Even if you were free, General Benson will hold her to her promise."

"Do not speak her name," cried Sumner, fiercely. "It is sacrilege for your perjured lips to name her whom you have so tricked, deceived and abused. A bad promise is better broken than kept, and *my wife*, formerly Miss Jewel Bowen, felt the truth of the old adage when she consented to *marry me in this very cell*." He could not repress the note of triumph in his voice as he uttered the words, but he was not prepared for what followed.

"No!" she cried out, with a passion terrible to see. "You have not dared—you could not dare—"

"Stop!" said Sumner sternly. "I warn you; do not try me too far. You will act wisely if you drop this whole matter and leave Washington and the society where you have queened it so long under false pretenses, for solitude and seclusion where you may escape the scorn of the world."

"What do you mean?" she demanded, her features pale to the very lips. She stood at bay, but in her face it could be seen that she measured his strength struggling with a new and horrible dread.

"God forbid that I should make you a social outcast!" he replied. "Need I speak plainer?"

Aurelia listened to him with the watchfulness of a tiger, who sees the hunter approaching, her strong, active brain was on the alert, but now her savage nature broke forth; she laughed aloud ferociously and then began a tirade of abuse that would have honored the slums.

Weary of the whole proceeding, disgusted with himself and the infatuation that had once enthralled him, he said at last, in desperation:

"Let us end this scene and all relations that have ever existed,—if you were as pure as snow, and I loved you as my other self, *I would never wed with one of colored blood, an octaroon!*"

Wordless, with corpse-like face and gleaming eyes she faced him unflinchingly.

"If I had a knife in my hand, and could stab you to the heart, I would do it!"

"I know you would!"

"But such weapons as I possess I will use. I will not fly— I will brave you to the last! If the world is to condemn me as the descendant of a race that I abhor, it shall never condemn me as a coward!"

Terrible though her sins might be—terrible her nature, she was but another type of the products of the accursed system of slavery—a victim of "man's inhumanity to man" that has made "countless millions mourn." There was something, too, that compelled admiration in this resolute standing to her guns with the determination to face the worst that fate might have in store for her. Something of all this Sumner felt, but beyond a certain point his New England philanthropy could not reach.

He bowed his head at her words and said,—"As you will, I have warned you!"

She stood at the full of her splendid stature, her eyes gleaming, her ashen lips firmly set, then she turned from him and gave the signal that brought the warden to let her out. Silently, without a backward look, she passed from the cell, and the prisoner was once more left in solitude.

At nine o'clock that same night, Chief Henson stood near a gas-lamp on the platform of the Baltimore & Ohio railroad station, glancing through a few lines from his colored agent, placed in his hands by plucky little Venus Johnson that very morning. The latter had gone on to the Bowen mansion to prepare the mistress for an unexpected arrival.

Chief Henson was particularly pleased with the ability shown by his colored detectives. Smith, the male agent, was a civil war veteran who had left a leg at Honey Hill, and on that account a grateful government had detailed him for duty on Chief Henson's staff of the secret service, and he had helped his chief out of many a difficult position, for which Mr. Henson was not slow nor meagre in his acknowledgments.

Five minutes after the train was in, Chief Henson saw Smith advancing toward him, accompanied by two females, closely veiled.

From out the swarming crowd the great detective stepped and motioned the man to follow with one of the females while he himself led the way with the other to the Bowen carriage outside the depot on the Avenue. Having placed the women in the carriage, and given the coachman his directions he and Smith entered a herdic and were driven rapidly to his office where they remained talking until the first hours of the morning.

Meanwhile Venus had resumed her duties as suddenly as she dropped them. The servants wondered among themselves, but not a comment was made. The news that the faithful girl brought seemed to restore Mrs. Bowen's lost vitality; she insisted on rising and being dressed, and received Jewel in her arms at the great entrance doors.

Supper was served in Mrs. Bowen's private parlor. Anyone who had entered the room would have been surprised at the kind solicitude and graciousness shown old Aunt Henny who was an honored guest. Mrs. Bowen's attention was evenly divided between her step-daughter and the old Negress. Venus waited on the company and for the time all thoughts of caste were forgotten while the representatives of two races met on the ground of mutual interest and regard.

Again and again Venus was called upon to repeat the story of her adventures.

"Yes, Mis' Bowen," she said for the twentieth time, "when I peeked in through that window and saw Miss Jewel an' gran sitting there talkin', I was plum crazy for a minute. Then I climb down as fas' as any squirrel an' I made tracks fer Mr. Smith, an' I told him what I'd seen. He says to me, says he, 'now, Venus, how in time 'm I goin' to get you into that house? We can't break the windows an' git in because they're ironed. 'Clar,' says he, "I don't know where I'm at.' Well, you know Mis' Bowen, I ain't a bit slow, no'm, if I do say it, an' I jus' thought hard for a minute, an' then *it struck me!* Says I to him, 'git a move on dad there. You and me together mus' tote him to the house. When we git there you knock up the ol' woman an' make her let you put dad in; keep up all the fuss you can,' says I, 'an' in the kick-up why I'll sneak in and hide. You be waitin' by the front door, an' I'll have 'm out in a jiffy.' 'Good!' says he, 'two heads is better'n one if t'other is a sheep's head.' 'Much 'bliged for callin' me a fool,' says I. 'Welcome,' says he, 'but I take off my hat to you, young lady, I does, an' I'm goin' to give the chief a pointer to git you on the staff,' says he. 'Here's something to help the cause along,' an' he gave me a big bunch of keys an' a dark lantern. 'Try the keys on the big front door,' he says.

"Well, everything worked preticularly fine, Mis' Bowen. Dad was so drunk he couldn't stand, an' he didn't know whether he was afoot or ridin'. I slipped in all right, got my lady an' gran, an' got away as slick as grease.

"Dad ain't shown his head since; Mr. Henson's lookin' fer him, but I know he'll keep shy. I reckon he don't want to see ol' Ginral Benson fer one right smart spell. He's skeered all right—skeered to pieces."

Aunt Henny said nothing, but once in a while she would nod her turbaned head in seeming perplexity, as she furtively watched every movement made by Mrs. Bowen. For her part, Mrs. Bowen seemed uneasy under the old woman's persistent regard.

CHAPTER XXXII

At last the eagerly looked for day of the Bradford murder trial came. Society had been on the qui vive ever since Sumner's arrest, and in twenty-four hours preceding the opening of the trial, public interest had gone up to almost unparralled intensity of excitement, which the facts already known of the case increased as the time for the crisis approached. Among these facts was the one of the disappearance of the principal witness for the defense. Extraordinary disclosures were anticipated, and the wildest rumors were afloat, some of which contained a few grains of truth.

The police told off for duty at the court had their work cut out for them, for crowds began to gather long before the opening hour, some to get in—some to see the notables in society, and the government swells arrive in quick succession. Before ten the room was crowded in every available place, and further admission was refused except to those engaged in the case.

Will Badger and Carroll West made their way slowly to their places among a nest of their set, including Mrs. Brewer and Mrs. Vanderpool and other friends of Sumner. Badger and West expected to be called by the defense.

The entrance of General Benson and Major Madison caused a flutter as they took their places in the space reserved for witnesses by the prosecution. Aurelia's tall, graceful form in a handsome dark gown followed the men. She received the various salutes which came to her from all parts of the crowded room with her usual polished elegance, but the fashionable world was puzzled; there was that in her appearance which suggested tragedy.

"Good heaven!" thought Carroll West, "I wonder if there can be any truth in the rumor I have just heard! How exquisite she looks, and pale—yes, and anxious too. I wonder if she cares for Sumner. I wonder what it all means anyhow. Heaven help her safely through this ordeal."

And she had need of all the sympathy that his kind heart could bestow, for the close of the trial would see her homeless, friendless, moneyless, under the ban of a terrible caste prejudice, doubly galling to one who, like herself, had no moral training with which to stem the current of adverse circumstances that had effectually wrecked her young life.

But all society missed its queen, Jewel Bowen, about whom the wildest reports were circulated, but no one knew the truth concerning her trip out of town. Jewel had an interview with her husband early in the morning, and it was decided that

Mrs. Bowen and she would not enter the court room until the day when Aunt Henny was to give her testimony. Sure now of Cuthbert's acquittal the ladies were content to wait patiently the law's course.

General Benson was ignorant, as yet, of his prisoner's escape. Isaac had disappeared and Ma'am Griffin did not dare send him word. So in ignorance of the true state of affairs, he was his own imperious self.

Presently counsel were in their places. The Attorney General and a distinguished advocate for the government; and for the defence, ex-Governor Lowe, of Massachusetts, brilliant in criminal cases, had associated with him the Bowen family lawyer, Mr. Cameron, and—mightiest of all in interest of the accused, was the guidance and keen incisive intelligence of the sleuth hound E. Henson, Chief of the Secret Service Division.

Just after ten the buzz of talk suddenly ceased, hushed by the indescribable settling of a crowd long in expectancy, as the officials took their seats. The hush became breathless as the spectators waited the appearance of the one man for whom they had all gathered here that day—the prisoner. A buzz of admiration passed through the crowd as the accused passed to his seat. Erect, easy, dignified, Sumner took his place with the same grace that had marked his entrance into the crowded halls of pleasure. He met the steady stare of those thousand eyes cooly, steadily.

"How splendidly he bears himself!" whispered one to another. He had made a distinctly good impression.

Now came the necessary formalities. The jury to be called a mysterious algebraic proceeding to the uninitiated, where the value of the x is evolved to the amazement of the onlooker. The twelve men good and true were selected in this instance with very little trouble for a case so widely known and discussed. They were unchallenged and so, presently, were duly sworn; then the official question was put:

"How say you, prisoner at the bar—guilty or not guilty?"

The answer came in clear tones, low and steadily:

"Not guilty!"

The Attorney-General arose and began the trial with a recapitulation of the circumstances attending the murder of Elise Bradford, and the evidence adduced at the inquest. "And," said the learned counsel, "there can be little doubt that the secret of the crime lies in the victim's past. Clever detectives are of that opinion, and they argue logically enough that the fear of exposure of a guilty secret has been once more the motive of a terrible tragedy. The prisoner admits that he had been particularly attracted by the murdered girl at one time. It is known that they were alone together all that fatal Sunday afternoon in the deserted Treasury Building. He alone had exclusive opportunity to commit the crime. He admits that he gave her a glass of wine from the store kept for the chief's private use, but tells us that he left the victim in her usual health at eight that night, she refusing his escort home on a plea of wanting to pack up her belongings as she did not intend to return to work the next week having resigned her position. All this story will be proved a tissue of falsehoods unless the prisoner has the power to prove who *did* administer poison to the dead woman—if he did not do it himself—after he left the office on that fatal night.

The learned counsel weighed strongly all these stubborn facts, in an eloquent speech, which told with the audience. The case looked black for the accused. But the brilliant ex-governor smiled serenely as he glanced over the sea of faces.

The trial dragged itself along with varying interest through two days. On the third day Aurelia Madison was called to prove the prisoner's gallantry and fickleness.

She did not glance at the prisoner as she passed to the witness box, impassive and lovely, but gave her evidence in a clear, concise manner that carried conviction with it. When she had finished, the tide of public opinion was strengthened against the prisoner. Like a whited sepulchre, full of hatred, she attempted to swear away the life of an innocent man to gratify her wish for revenge. By her testimony society learned for the first time the secret of the broken engagement between the accused and Jewel Bowen. Her story caused a sensation.

"Heavens! It looks strange!" whispered Mrs. Vanderpool to her neighbor Mrs. Brewer. But the end was not yet. As the witness turned to leave the stand, Governor Lowe said blandly:

"One moment, Miss Madison; I wish to ask you a few questions."

The girl paused; a white shade passed over the classic features.

"You are Major Madison's daughter?"

"Yes."

"He is your father?"

"Yes; so I am told," this last haughtily.

"Describe your mother as you remember her."

"I do not remember my mother—I never saw her. I know nothing of her."

"Where were you born?"

"In Jackson, Mississippi, I am told."

"How much money were you to receive the day Mr. Sumner married you and General Benson married Miss Jewel Bowen?"

"I don't understand your meaning."

"Weren't you to have a million given you the day you married Mr. Sumner? Yes or no."

"My dowry was a million dollars, if that is what you mean."

"Call it what you like, young lady; that was your share of the boodle with the man thrown in. That is all."

A buzz of excitement went over the crowded room. The prosecution looked at each other in blank amazement. Major Madison moved about uneasily in his seat. He was the next one called.

He knew very little of the prisoner. He was abroad at the time the engagement was made between the accused and Miss Madison, and could add little to the testimony already given. Knew Mr. Sumner as a visitor at houses where they were mutually acquainted, and had invited him to card parties in his own home.

Again the brilliant advocate asked but few questions.

"Miss Aurelia Madison is your daughter?"

"Yes."

"Born in Mississippi?" The Major nodded.

"Who was her mother?"

"My wife."

"The servant—slave or what might you call her—that stood to you in that relation? Is it not so?" blandly insinuated the questioner.

"We object," interposed the Attorney-General hurriedly to the evident relief of the enraged witness.

"Your objection is sustained," returned the judge.

Not at all disconcerted, Governor Lowe bowed pleasantly to judge, jury, lawyers and witnesses, in token of submission.

"Well, Major, did you ever know a man by the name of Walker? Or, weren't you known by that name once yourself?"

"Yes, I took that name when I was in money difficulties and hiding from my creditors."

"The man I mean was a slave-trader, notorious all over the South, who was one of the band of conspirators that murdered President Lincoln. Did you ever meet him?"

"I never have," replied the witness visibly disturbed.

"Business good, Major? How are the Arrow-Head gold mine securities turning out?"

"As well as I can expect."

"But not so well as you could wish; meantime you run a faro bank with your daughter as the snare and incidentally black mail and bunco a rich family to repair your shattered fortunes. That is all, major."

The excitement increased momentarily among the spectators. It was easy to perceive that Governor Lowe was but reserving his forces. The last witness called by the prosecution was General Benson, and nothing was elicited from him but the fact that the murdered woman had worked in his department for five years, was competent and faithful. He had no knowledge of her family nor connections outside the office. He had noticed that Mr. Sumner was somewhat partial to the good-looking stenographer, but he attached no importance to that fact, he had been young once himself. The audience was captivated by his winning manners and genial smiles. Governor Lowe took all his rights in the cross-examination.

"You gave your name as Charles Benson, General? Ever known to the public by any other name?"

For a moment the General was nonplussed.

"Sir!" with freezing haughtiness, "I do not understand you."

"My question was a plain one; but I will put it in another form—Weren't you originally known as St. Clair Enson? Isn't that the only name you have a right to wear?"

Sensation in the court room.

"We object," from the Attorney-General.

"Your objection is sustained," from the judge.

Governor Lowe was in no wise disconcerted. Again he bowed to the judge, then faced the witness still bland and smiling.

"How old was Miss Bradford when she entered your employ?"

"Eighteen, I believe."

"Awhile back you said you thought nothing of Mr. Sumner's attentions to the good-looking stenographer because you were young once yourself. I hear you are still very partial to the ladies, age has not deadened your sensibilities to their infinite charms. Did you not also offer attention to your good-looking stenographer? Did not your attentions become so warm that for various *pressing* reasons you promised Miss Bradford marriage?"

"Your questions are an outrage sir!"

"Plain yes or no, that is all I want."

"Most emphatically *No!*" thundered the witness, livid with rage. Again Governor Lowe bowed.

"Just one question more. Where were you on the night of the murder, in New York or Washington?"

"I was in New York."

The silence in the room was intense. One sensational question had followed another so rapidly that the vast throng of people found no expression for their wonderment save in silence. What was this man showing?

"Thank you, General, that is all."

That closed the prosecution.

"By Jove! more lies under this than we can see," whispered West to Badger.

Still the testimony of the state was clear on all essential points strengthened by numberless details pointing toward the guilt of the prisoner. So the third day ended, and the public felt repaid for their interest; it bade fair to go down in history as an extraordinary criminal incident.

CHAPTER XXXIII

Thursday there was a settling down for a fresh start, an intense expectancy throughout the court. All felt that they were nearing a crisis. There were many new faces seen amid the throng and among them were the well-known features of Mrs. Bowen and Jewel, both closely shrouded in their sombre mourning robes.

Speculation was rife as to the line of the defense. What were they to hear now? What was, what could be the defense that could overpower the weight of evidence already given which seemed to make a fatal verdict a foregone conclusion? And yet, somehow, from the highest to the lowest of that hushed, excited throng, there was a curious, subtle feeling that some such resistless power lay in that reserved defence now about to be launched.

Perhaps the wish was "father to the thought." The calm confidence and lack of anxiety on the part of the defense hinted of powerful resources.

One lawyer remarked to another, "It looks as if he had a reserve force that will absolutely reverse the battle."

The prisoner sat with folded arms, cool, motionless as a statue, outwardly, but within, the man's blood was on fire.

Now Governor Lowe, with courtly manner and in sonorous tones, took up his part in the drama, beginning with the prisoner's alleged reckless youth as brought out in Miss Madison's testimony, mainly. He admitted that his client had been wild but not to the point of profligacy. He spoke tenderly of the absent, aged father—a helpless invalid—and his indulgence of an only child—motherless, too, from birth—proud, passionate, high-spirited, indulged, uncontrolled personally and in the expenditure of money, and that at this most dangerous period of a lad's life, the young man had met Miss Madison and succumbed to her fascinations, whom he intended to show was but a beautiful adventuress.

"The court," he said, "has been prejudiced against my client more by this woman's evidence than by any other testimony introduced for the government, added to that the sympathy of the whole audience has been aroused by the spectacle of a helpless woman's trust betrayed. Bah! Let me briefly unfold to you, gentlemen of the jury, the truth of the garbled tale so skilfully woven by a designing woman."

Governor Lowe then related the story of the past winter and the broken engagement, as known to our readers, with added facts to show that his client had in no way wronged the woman, who knew perfectly well what she was about, having previously become a party in a conspiracy designed to force Cuthbert Sumner into marriage, and at the same time, give the control of the wealth of a well-known family into the hands of 'the gang' through the daughter of the house, the bethrothed of the accused.

Counsel then told of Aurelia's proposition of the day before the opening of the trial, and that the warden was a listener to the conversation between the prisoner and the witness; of her offer to give testimony at the trial which should free him, as she *knew the guilty party;* of the prisoner's scornful rejection of the offer, and his final retort when he told her that if she were as pure as snow, he would *never wed with one of colored blood!*"

Here the astute counsel paused for his telling point to take effect. Nor was he disappointed in his calculations, for its action was as an electric shock upon the aristocratic gathering. "And now, your honor, and gentlemen of the jury," he resumed with solemn impressiveness, "I am going to prove that my client's version of his connection with this affair is absolutely true; that he was not the perpetrator of the deed, but by the irony of Fate he has been placed in a position where it was next to impossible for him to prove his innocence. After Mr. Sumner left Miss Bradford in the office on that fatal Sunday night, a person who shall be nameless still, for a time, a man high in official life, a leader in society, did enter said office and talk with the murdered woman whom he had promised to marry in a short time. While there they took wine together, he himself pouring it out and placing in her portion the arsenic, grains of which were found in the empty glass, and in the woman's stomach after death, as testified to before you by the coroner, et al."

Again he paused, for he could feel the horror that thrilled the crowd.

"This man, gentlemen of the jury, was aware of the relation formerly existing between Miss Madison and the accused, and scoundrel that he is, used the woman as a tool for the base purpose of blackmail which fortunately a higher power has frustrated; and for other reasons as well, planned to leave Mr. Sumner so surrounded and connected with Miss Bradford as to render it impossible for him to extricate himself from the charge of murder."

The counsel's manner was most effective as he made his charges; the whole scene so dramatic that only a sensational melo-drama could have rivalled its power. A subdued "whew-w!" went from mouth to mouth as a faint glimmer of the truth began to show something of the possibilities of the line taken by the defence.

"Finally, thanks to the astuteness, experience and daring of the very clever detective, who has really had active charge of the whole case, and to whom the highest praise is due, a *witness of the crime will be produced!*"

The audience was astounded; they had hoped for a sensation; their desire was more than realized.

Governor Lowe wound up his brilliant effort with a slight peroration—knowing well its good effect upon a jury—and amidst murmurs of applause, was ready to call his witness.

The first was John Williams, Sumner's valet, who testified to the regularity of his master's habits and his abstemious living. During the cross-examination, John got angry and told the Attorney-General that the Sumners were top-crust, sure; and never one of them had been known to show up as underdone dough no half-and-half's, if it wasn't so he'd eat his own head; he didn't object to meeting any man who disputed the "pint," in a slugging match, the hardest to "fend" off. The judge called him to order and the witness took his seat in a towering rage over the "imperdunce" of Southern white folks, anyhow.

Then West and Badger took the stand to refute the charge of inveterate gambling that had been made against the prisoner by Miss Madison. West was questioned only about Sumner and not of his own connection with the Madisons for which he was devoutly thankful. The fact was brought out that the Madison house was a gambling palace where men were fleeced of money for the sake of the smiles of the beautiful Aurelia, by the young fellow's tale of Sumner's warning to him against allowing himself to be ensnared by the Madison clique.

The watchmen and one or two cleaners were also placed upon the stand to prove that Mr. Sumner *did* leave the Treasury Building at the hour sworn to by him.

After that the motherless and worse than fatherless child— a beautiful fair-haired boy, was led forward and stood upon a chair in the witness-box, to give emphasis to the point made by counsel that the dead woman had a pressing claim upon some man who wished to rid himself of her as encumbrance. Some of the women spectators wept, and many men felt uncomfortable about the eyes. Then Gov. Lowe said: "I call Aunt Henny Sargeant." Two officers led the tottering old Negress from the ante-room to the witness chair. Aunt Henny had aged preceptibly since her imprisonment, but her faculties were as keen as ever. As she entered the crowded court-room, there was a cry, quickly suppressed, from the back seats of the room:

"Oliver, that's yer granny! My God, she's livin' yit!"

"Aunt Henny, I believe you have been in the employ of the government at the Treasury Building?"

"Yes, honey, I has."

"Tell the court how you came to be employed."

"Well, honey, I foun' a big pile o' greenbacks—mus' a bin 'bout a million dollars, I reckon,—one night when I was sweepin', an' I jes' froze to 'em all night. I neber turned 'em loose 'til de officers come in de mornin'; money's a mighty onsartin' article, chillun. People won' steal if they don' get a chance, dat's my b'lief. Then de Presidun' an' lots of other gemman made a big furze over me, an' dey done gib me my job fer life."

"Now, Aunt Henny, do you remember where you were on Sunday evening, March 20, between six and ten o'clock?"

"Yas, honey, I does, fer I warn't in bed, nuther was I to home. I was at the Building doin' some dustin' in Gin'ral Benson's 'partmen', that I'd lef over from the afternoon befo'."

"Yes; well tell us what happened that evening at the Building."

"Well, honey, I wen' in pas' the watchman, who arst me wha' I was after, an' I tol' him. Den I wen' up to Gin'ral Benson's 'partmen', which was whar I'd lef' off. I has a skilton key dat let's me git in whar I wants to go. After I'd been in 'bout an hour, I hearn people talkin' in one ob de rooms—the private office—an' I goes 'cross de entry an' peeks roun' de corner ob de po'ter—"

"The what?" interrupted the judge.

"Po'ter, massa jedge; don' yer kno' what a po'ter am?"

"She means, portière, your honor," explained Gov. Lowe, with a smile. "Go on, aunty."

"I peeked 'roun' de corner ob de po'ter, an' I seed Miss Bradford an' de Gin'ral settin' talkin' as budge as two buzzards. He jes was makin' time sparkin' her like eny young fellar, an' fer a mon as ol' as I kno' *he* is, I tell you, gemmen, he was jes' makin' dat po' gal b'lieve de moon was made o' green cheese an' he'd got the fus' slice."

A suppressed laugh rippled through the room.

"What happened then?"

"Honey, my cur'osity was bilin' hot to see what was gwine on, an' I keep peekin' an' peekin'; byme-by I hearn de glasses clickin', an' I took another look, 'cause tho' I'm a temprunce 'ooman, an' I b'long to de High Co't o' Gethsemne, an' de Daughters ob de Bridal Veil, I neber b'lieve dat good wine is gwine ter harm on' ol' rheumatiz 'ooman like me; no, sah; dar ain't none o' yer stiff-necked temprunce 'bout yer Aunt Henny; I ain't no better than quality. I know'd dat was good stuff dat de chief had in thar 'cause I'd done taste some ob it befo', an' I'd promis' myself to taste it agin dat very night as soon as dat couple was gone. While I was thinkin' 'bout it, de Gin'ral turned his back to Miss Bradford as he poured de wine from de 'canter, an' dat brung him full facin' me what I was a peekin' at him, an' bless my soul, gemman, I seed dat villyun drap somethin' white inter de glass an' then turn 'roun' an' han' it to Miss Bradford. I was dat skeered I thought I'd drap, an' while I was a makin' up my min' what do so, suddintly she threwed up both arms an' screeched out *"My God, Charles, you've pizened!"*

Great sensation in the court, and the crier restored order.

"What happened then, Aunty?"

"Bless my soul, honey, I don't know what did happen, somethin' dat neber come across me in all my life befo'. I tell you, gemmen, it takes somethin' to make a colored woman faint, but dat's jes' wha' I did, massa jedge; when I seed dat po gal fro up her arms an' hern her screech I los' all purchase ob myself, an' I ain't got over it yet."

The old negress rocked herself to and fro in her chair. She made a weird picture, her large eyes peering out from behind the silver-bowed glasses, her turbaned head and large, gold-hoop earrings, and a spotless white handkerchief crossed on her breast over the neat gingham dress.

"And then, Aunty?" gently prompted Gov. Lowe.

"When I come to myself agin, I was in prison, an' my own son-in-law was a keepin' me locked up."

"Was that the reason you did not inform the authorities of what you had seen?" asked the judge.

"Yas, sah; yas, massa jedge."

"Now, Aunt Henny, I want you to tell the court when and where you knew General Benson before you saw him in the employ of the government," said Gov. Lowe.

"We object, your honor," promptly interrupted the Attorney-General.

"The objection is not well taken, Mr. Attorney-General. I think Gov. Lowe has a right to put the answer in evidence. We are not here to defeat the ends of justice. Proceed, Aunt Henny."

"He ain't Gin'ral Benson no more'n I'm a white 'ooman. His name's St. Clair Enson; he was born nex' do' to de Sargeant place on the Enson plantation. Ise one ob de fus' ones what held him when he was born. Ise got a scar on me, jedge, where dat imp ob de debbil hit me wid a block ob wood when he warn't but seven years ol'. Fus' time I seed him in dat 'partmen' I know'd him time I sot my eye on him, an' den I know'd thar'd be rucktions kicked up, fer ef eber der was a born lim' o' de debbil it's dat same St. Clair Enson."

"That will do, aunty. Perhaps my legal brother may wish to cross-examine."

The Attorney-General then took the witness in hand and conducted a skilful cross-examination without shaking the old woman's testimony. Finally he said:

"One last question and I am through; you spoke of your son-in-law—what has he to do with General Benson?"

"He!" snorted Aunt Henny indignantly, "thar ain't no kind ob devilmen' St. Clair Enson was ever mixed up in dat Ike Johnson warn't dar to help him. Ike's my gal's husban';

he's Gin'ral Benson's valley; he was gave to St. Clair Enson when dat debbil was a baby in de cradle."

During the testimony of this last witness, Gen. Benson and Maj. Madison were busily talking to each other, with an occasional word to the Attorney-General.

As Aunt Henny retired to her seat in the ante-room. Gov. Lowe arose, and in an impassioned speech moved the prisoner's release, and the taking into custody of the man really guilty—General Benson.

Scarcely waiting for him to finish, the Attorney-General sprang to his feet and attacked the defense fiercely. Then ensued a scene unparalleled in the history of courts of justice.

"On what would you base such an unheard of precedent? on the evidence of a Negress? Would you impugn the honor of a brilliant soldier, a brave gentlemen—courteous, genial, standing flawless before the eyes of the entire country? Such a man as General Benson cannot be condemned and suspicioned by the idiotic ramblings of an ignorant *nigger* brought here by the defense to divert attention from the real criminal, who attempts to shield himself under the influence of the Bowen millions. In the same spirit that has actuated my legal brother, while deprecating violence of any kind as beneath the dignity of our calling, I would feel myself justified in sounding the slogan of the South—lynch-law! if I thought this honorable body could be influenced to so unjust a course as is suggested by Gov. Lowe."

Instantly a chorus of voices took up the refrain—"That's the talk! No nigger's word against a white man! This is a white man's country yet!"

For a brief space, judge, jury and advocates were nonplussed; women shrieked and men flinched, not knowing what the end might be. But above the uproar, which was answered by the crowd outside, rang the voice of the police-sargeant as he formed his men in line at the door ready to charge the would-be violators of the peace. Before the determined front of the police, the crowd quieted down and order was restored.

Then Gov. Lowe arose once more:

"May it please your honor, and gentlemen of the jury, I have still another witness to present, and the last one, I call the chief of the Secret Service Division."

Once again there was silence in the room. Curiosity was on tiptoe. Many men in high places knew the chief well by reputation but had never met him. He had successfully coped with many important cases and had saved the government millions of dollars. He entered the witness-box calmly as if oblivious of the curiosity of the crowd.

"Mr. Henson, I believe that for any years you have been in the secret service."

"Yes, for fifteen years I have served the government in the capacity of a detective. Previous to that time I was a soldier and served three years, on the Federal side, at the front."

"Now, Mr. Henson, we will ask you to tell the court what you know of this case, in your own way."

At the first sound of his voice, Mrs. Bowen, who up till this time had been sitting with lowered veil, suddenly swept it one side and stared at the man in the witness-box with a strained, startled gaze. His eyes, wandering over the audience, rested on her white face. For one instant he wavered and seemed to hesitate, then by an effort he regained his composure and began his story.

"I was first called into this case by Miss Jewel Bowen. I took hold of it because of the interest she aroused in my mind, and out of pity for her distress. After I met and conversed with Mr. Sumner, I was satisfied in my own mind of his innocence, and that he was the victim of a conspiracy."

In a brief, incisive way, which carried weight to many doubting minds, he detailed the substance of the information he had obtained.

"Being brought into the issues growing out of the intimacy between General Benson and the Bowen family because of his engagement to Miss Bowen, I, very naturally, was placed in charge of the business of accumulating the facts in regard to Senator Bowen's death in New York. I have found out that he made no will while there, and that the one offered here for probate by Gen. Benson *is a forgery*.

"After Senator Bowen's death his daughter was abducted, and in the search which I caused to be made for her, we found, concealed in the same house, the Negress, Aunt Henny. So, step by step, we have been able to fix the murder of Miss Bradford, the forged will of Senator Bowen, the abduction of Miss Bowen and of Aunt Henny—the most important witness in this case—upon a band of conspirators numbering three people, all well known in society and having the entrée to the best houses."

"Do we quite understand you, Mr. Henson," asked the judge, "that in your opinion the prisoner at the bar has been the victim?"

"Yes, your honor, but only because he stood in the way of their obtaining the Bowen millions. That was the intention in the start—to obtain that immense fortune. Other than the strong attachment existing between Miss Bowen and Mr. Sumner, he would never have been molested.

"It now becomes my duty to make a statement in regard to the testimony of the last witness."

His face was set and stern. It was evident that he struggled to maintain his composure.

"What she has said concerning Gen. Benson is absolutely true. It is a long story, gentlemen, but I will be as brief as possible."

Then in graphic words that held the vast crowd spellbound, he told the story of Ellis and St. Clair Enson, as our readers already know it up to the discovery of Hagar's African descent. The judge forgot his dignity, a shock waved over the court-room. People seemed not to breathe, the interest was so intense, as they listened to the burning words of the speaker.

"When Ellis Enson returned home after completing his arrangements for taking his wife abroad, he was set upon in Enson woods by his brother and the unprincipled slave driver, Walker, and beaten into unconsciousness. When he came to himself he was in South Carolina enrolled as a member of the Confederate army. Here he remained until a good opportunity offered, when he deserted and returned home to find that his wife, child and slaves (of whom Aunt Henny was a valued house servant), had been driven to the Washington market, where his wife in desperation had thrown herself and infant into the Potomac river.

"Stripped of his fortune, home and family, cursing God and man, he entered the army on the Federal side, seeking death, but determined to carry destruction first to those who had so cruelly wronged him. But death comes not for the asking, and the ways of God are inscrutable."

He paused and passed his hand over his beaded forehead. Gen. Benson sat like a marble statue, and his nails reddened where he gripped the arms of his chair. The sound of voices came in from the street through the open window. Inside there was silence like the grave.

"Ellis Enson always supposed that his brother St. Clair stayed abroad where he had hidden after he was found guilty as one of the conspirators against the life of President Lincoln, but when I was called into this case, I found that he was in this country, serving the government he had basely betrayed, and still steeped in crime, along with his pal, Walker. Gentlemen, General Benson is St. Clair Enson, and his friend, Major Madison, is the notorious trader, Walker.

"As for me, I no longer need to conceal my identity. Gentlemen—" he gasped and faltered, and put his hand to his throat as though the words choked him.

"General Benson is my brother—I am Ellis Enson!"

As he finished speaking Mrs. Bowen sprang to her feet with a scream; she made a step towards him—then stopped— while these words thrilled the hearts of the listeners:

"Ellis! Ellis! I am Hagar!"

(To be continued.)

૨ ૨ ૨

CHAPTER XXXIV

At Mrs. Bowen's impassioned cry, Chief Henson turned an appealing look upon the judge, who bowed his head as if understanding the mute question; he reached the fainting woman's side with one stride, and lifted her tenderly in his strong arms, then he bore her from the crowded room, followed by the maid and weeping step-daughter. The spectators fell back respectfully before the stern man over whose white face great tears, that did not shame his manhood, coursed unheeded.

When the excitement incident to Chief Henson's story (or Ellis Enson, as we must now call him) had somewhat subsided, the trial was resumed.

Governor Lowe called no other witnesses, but at once rose to address the jury for the prisoner, and never, perhaps, had the great politician and leader been more eloquently brilliant than on that occasion. He ranged up the whole mass of evidence with a bold and masterly grasp that could not be outrivalled.

In burning words he laid bare the details of the plot for millions, explaining that when General Benson found himself defeated in all directions, and threatened with exposure by the woman he had ruined, if he persisted in marrying Miss Bowen, he had conceived the idea of a diabolical deed—to murder Miss Bradford and allow the guilt to rest upon Cuthbert Sumner, thus ridding himself of two obstacles at one stroke.

He painted vividly the stealthy return of General Benson from New York to Washington, his arrival at the Treasury Building, his concealment in the great wardrobes, with which his department was supplied, his long wait for the departure of Mr. Sumner, during which he heard the dead woman's confession to the secretary; his meeting with Miss Bradford, down to the last awful move in the tragedy witnessed by the old Negress, Aunt Henny, who fainted with horror at the tragedy of the night. "He returned to New York as secretly as he left the city," continued the Governor, "because his flight had occurred on the Sabbath, when all the members of the committee were bent on individual pleasure, and as he was in his place on Monday morning no one noticed his absence. Then, in his devotion to his employer's interests, the faithful servant and ex-slave, Isaac Johnson, knowing no law save the will of his former owner, faithful to the traditions of slavery still, concealed the only witness of the crime, failing only in one point—that he did not murder the old woman (his mother-in-law) as commanded by General Benson, but kept her in confinement. In attempting to force Miss Bowen to marry him by abducting her and concealing her in an old country house, detectives searching for her found the missing witness, whom we have heard here today.

"The romance of the situation is enhanced by the fact that in just retribution the brother so inhumanly betrayed and abandoned, even as was Joseph of old, by his brethren, was the Nemesis placed upon the criminal's track to put him in the power of outraged justice."

With a splendid peroration, and a tender reference to the unexpected meeting of the cruelly-separated husband and wife, the Governor sat down and the Attorney-General followed him in a speech of great ability; but he knew the verdict was a foregone one, that his own remarks were but a form, that the weight of evidence in "this most extraordinary case" left him but one course. He felt, too, a savage bitterness towards Benson or Enson, that made him pant for the trial which he knew must come. In fact, officers were already stationed near the precious trio ready to take them in charge the moment all preliminary proceedings were over.

The Attorney-General concluded his speech with the words, "Justice is all that we are seeking, gentlemen of the jury, and in your hands I leave the prisoner's interests, knowing that you will return a verdict in accordance with the evidence given, that will give us all the right to welcome Mr. Sumner among us again fully reinstated in the confidence and esteem of the whole country."

The judge's charge followed, with a finely-balanced summing up which displayed all the power and glory of English jurisprudence; even the prisoner followed him with admiring forgetfulness of self. Finally the case was given to the jury; they consulted together a few minutes for the sake of appearances, without leaving their seats, then the foreman rose and announced: "We find the prisoner not guilty."

"Is this your verdict, Mr. Foreman?" asked the clerk.

"It is," he answered.

"So say you all, gentlemen of the jury?"

"We do," in chorus from the box.

If there had been much doubt which way public opinion and sympathy had set during the trial, there was absolutely none when the verdict "not guilty" was given, for the long-repressed excitement found vent in an outburst of applause that for a time defied official control. Like wildfire the news spread to the people outside, and cheer after cheer rent the air, the crowd swaying and pushing in a vain attempt to get a glimpse of the late prisoner; but as soon as he could, Sumner left in a carriage with Badger and West, faithful John Williams on the box, for his apartments, and later the Bowen mansion.

Sumner could never have told very precisely what passed after the verdict had been given, save that as in a dizzy dream he heard applause within and cheers without; then he saw the fetters on the wrists of General Benson and saw him hurried from the room between two officers, followed by Major Madison and Aurelia. The two villains had sat nonplussed and dumbfounded during the stirring events just chronicled, making no effort to escape. Governor Lowe rushed the business of their arrest, and this was ably seconded by the judge and the Attorney-General.

Presently Sumner found himself in a mass of humanity in a room with Governor Lowe and Mr. Cameron, receiving congratulations and invitations. He thanked all in his pleasant way and declined; he could not bear society just yet.

That verdict gave back life to Jewel and to him, but he was unhappy and anxious over her situation with her step-mother; the wonderful revelation of Mrs. Bowen's identity with the slave Hagar was a shock to him. It was a delicate situation, but, of course, he told himself, "Mrs. Bowen could see that with all sympathy for her and her sad story, it was impossible for Jewel to be longer associated with her in so close a relationship as that of mother and daughter. He comforted himself with the thought that the unfortunate woman was the second wife of Senator Bowen, and that was a fortunate fact. He would do all that he could for Mrs. Bowen, but the social position of Mrs. Sumner demanded a prompt separation.

Cuthbert Sumner was born with a noble nature; his faults were those caused by environment and tradition. Chivalrous, generous-hearted—a manly man in the fullest meaning of the term—yet born and bred in an atmosphere which approved of freedom and qualified equality for the Negro, he had never considered for one moment the remote contingency of actual social contact with this unfortunate people.

He had heard the Negro question discussed in all its phases during his student life at "Fair Harvard," and had even contributed a paper to a local weekly in which he had warmly championed their cause; but so had he championed the cause of the dumb and helpless creatures in the animal world about him. He gave large sums to Negro colleges and on the same princpal gave liberally to the Society for the Prevention of Cruelty to Animals, and endowed a refuge for homeless cats. Horses, dogs, cats, and Negroes were classed together in his mind as of the brute creation whose sufferings it was his duty to help alleviate.

And Jewel? She, too, felt that straining of the heart's chords as she waited in her private sitting room for her lover-husband. She was alone. Ellis Enson was with her step-mother. After Mrs. Bowen returned to consciousness, Jewel had stolen away unnoticed by the strangely reunited pair, leaving them in sacred seclusion.

She held the evening paper in her hand. It contained a column headed, "Sensational Ending of the Famous Bradford Tragedy."

After detailing the day's events, the editor gave the story of the white slave Hagar (Mrs. Bowen), and her extraordinary recognition of her former husband and master in the person of Chief Henson of the Secret Service Division. The editor went on to say:

"No trace of woman or child was found after her leap over the bridge into the river. She was supposed to have been drowned. The woman, however, was picked up by a Negro oyster-digger and concealed in his hut for days. At the breaking out of the war she drifted to California and in a few years married the wealthy miner, Zenas Bowen. This story, showing, as it does, the ease with which beautiful half-breeds may enter our best society without detection, is a source of anxiety to the white citizens of our country. At this rate the effects of slavery can never be eradicated, and our most distinguished families are not immune from contact with this mongrel race. Mrs. Bowen has our sympathy, but we cannot, even for such a leader as she has been, unlock the

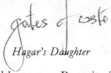

gates of caste and bid her enter. Posterity forbids it. We wait the action of Mr. Ellis Enson (Chief Henson) with impatience, praying that sentiment may not overcome the dictates of duty."

Jewel's tender heart was full of pity and love for her stepmother. Now she knew for the first time whence came the fountain of love so freely lavished upon her by this heartbroken mother.

"How she must have suffered," murmured the girl to herself. Then, as she mentally counted up the years that had passed since the events chronicled by the paper, she said aloud in some surprise, "Why, I must be about the age of the poor baby girl. How wonderful!" She was glad to be alone after all these weeks of tempest and today's climax, with its reaction. Mingled with her own joy at Cuthbert's release was a silent, wordless awe of Chief Henson's declaration in the court room and her stepmother's avowal. But, strange to say, the girl felt none of the repugnance that the announcement of Mrs. Bowen's origin had brought to Sumner. Her own happiness was so great that all worldly selfishness was swept away.

Hush! She suddenly rose from the couch where she was sitting, with wide eyes and quivering form, hearing the soft musical voice outside, so yearned for all these dreadful weeks, now fast disappearing like a horrible nightmare before the rosy glow of Hope's enchanting rays. She saw the door open and shut—saw Cuthbert's tall form enter—she sank upon the couch, putting out her hands to him in a trustful, childlike way.

Without a word he flung himself beside her and folded her in his arms with a passion and strength that were resistless.

"Mine at last! My darling! My one love—my wife!" For a second there was a blank—life itself seemed to stand still, and time and space were obliterated. "Husband!" she said at length with smothered passion. He stopped and kissed her in a strange, awed way—silently, solemnly, as a man might who had been so near the grave—heart to heart, soul to soul, conscious only in that supreme moment paradise was touched! So for some minutes they sat in soul communion. Sumner broke the silence after a time. "Heaven only can reward Chief Henson and Venus Johnson for their rescue of you, my treasure. May heaven forget me if I ever forget their devotion to my dear wife. I tell you, Jewel, I was maddened when the news was brought to me of your abduction. I would have been a murderer in truth could I have been free for one moment to meet Benson!"

The wife's lips touched his softly, lovingly—true woman to the core—as a "ministering angel."

"But, dearest, God protected me."

There was another eloquent pause. Then Sumner said abruptly:

"Tomorrow our marriage must be properly advertised. It is Thursday now; on Monday you must come with me to my father. After you have seen him, you shall plan our future."

Jewel laid her head against him. "Your wishes are mine, Cuthbert."

Then they talked a while of the strange revelations made at the trial, of the discovery of Negro blood in Aurelia Madison and Mrs. Bowen.

"With the knowledge that we now possess of her origin, we can no longer wonder at her wicked duplicity," said Sumner.

"That is true in her case," replied Jewel, "but a truer, sweeter, more perfect woman than mamma does not live on the earth; how do you account for it?"

"Depend upon it, those characteristics are but an accident of environment, not the true nature of her parent stock. I have always heard that the Negro race excelled in low cunning."

"True," repeated Jewel, dreamily, "but then there are Venus and Aunt Henny."

"Yes, and my faithful John. I suppose these exceptions prove the rule. Still I am thankful that Mrs. Bowen is only your step-mother."

Then they drifted back into their lovers' talk once more.

> "Look thro' mine eyes with thine, true wife,
> Round my true heart thine arms entwine;
> My other dearer life in life,
> Look thro' my very soul with thine!"

It was midnight when the wedded lovers separated. In the hall they met Ellis Enson, as we shall hereafter call him.

The man's face wore a look of solemn joy. He shook Jewel's hand silently. He urged Sumner to go to his room with him and spend the night, for he had much to say to him in regard to the late trial. Sumner felt obliged to accept the invitation, and the two men went away together.

The early morning hours found them still talking over the trial, but their greatest interest was in the story of the elder man—the strange trials in two lives.

"How do you intend to fix it?" questioned Sumner.

"Of course Mrs. Bowen is very much shaken, but we shall be quietly remarried on Sunday, and then I shall take my wife away. When we return I hope to have possession of Enson Hall, where we shall take up our permanent abode. I hand in my resignation today, to take immediate effect."

"I honor you for your resolution, Enson, but indeed I have not your strength of character. I could never solve the social problem in that high-handed manner. Have you no fear of public opinion?"

"My dear boy, I know just where you are. I went all through the old arguments from your point of view twenty years ago. I wavered and wavered, but nature was stronger than prejudice. I have suffered the torments of hell since I lost my wife and child."

He rose from his seat and strode once down the room, then back again, pausing before the young man.

"Sumner," he said, with impressive solemnity, "race prejudice is all right in theory, but when a man tries to practice it against the laws which govern human life and action, there's a weary journey ahead of him, and he's not got to die to realize the tortures of the damned. This idea of race separation is carried to an extreme point and will, in time, kill itself. Amalgamation has taken place; it will continue, and no finite power can stop it."

"But, my dear Enson, you do not countenance such a— such a—well—terrible action as a wholesale union between whites and blacks? Think of it, my dear man! Think of our refinement and intelligence linked to such black bestiality as we find in the slums of this or any other great city where Negroes predominate!"

Enson smiled at the other's vehemence.

"Certainly not, Sumner; but, on the other hand, take the case of Aurelia Madison. Did you ever behold a more gorgeously beautiful woman, or one more fastidiously refined? Had her moral development been equal to her other attainments, and you had loved her, how could you endure to have a narrow, beastly prejudice alone separate you from the woman pre-destined for your life-companion? It is in such cases that the law of caste is most cruel in its results."

"I think that the knowledge of her origin would kill all desire in me," replied Sumner. "The mere thought of the grinning, toothless black hag that was her foreparent would forever rise between us. I am willing to allow the Negroes education, to see them acquire business, money, and social status within a certain environment. I am not averse even to their attaining political power. Farther than this, I am not prepared to go."

"And this is the sum total of what Puritan New England philanthropy will allow—every privilege but the vital one of deciding a question of the commonest personal liberty which is the fundamental principle of the holy family tie."

"When one considers the ignorance, poverty and recent degradation of this people, I feel that my position is well taken," persisted Sumner. "Ought we not, as Anglo-Saxons, keep the fountain head of of our racial stream as unpoluted as possible?"

Enson smiled sadly; a holy light for one instant illumined the scarred face of the veteran:

" 'A boy's will is the wind's will, And the thoughts of youth are long, long thoughts,' " he quoted softly. "You will learn one day that there is a higher law than that enacted by any earthly tribunal, and I believe that you will then find your nature nobler than you know."

"You make me feel uncanny, Enson, with your visionary ideas. Thank God, I have my wife; there I am safely anchored."

"Amen!" supplemented Enson softly, as they clasped hands in a warm goodnight.

CHAPTER XXXV

On Friday the court room was again crowded to the doors by spectators eager to view the closing scenes in the celebrated case.

The soi-disant General Benson was arraigned on a charge of wilfully murdering Elise Bradford, and was committed for trial in October. Major Madison, or Walker, the ex-slave driver, and his daughter Aurelia were also in court, Madison for forgery in connection with Senator Bowen's will.

Nothing criminal was charged against Aurelia; in fact, no one desired to inflict more punishment on the unfortunate woman, and when she left the court room that day she vanished forever from public view.

Deadly pale, but proudly self-possessed, Ellis Enson gave his testimony at the hearing, fixing a steadfast, unflinching gaze on the livid, haggard face that glared back with sullen hate and fear in every line. So for a moment of dead silence, of untold pain to one, those two men, sons of one father, but with a bridgeless gulf between them, stood face to face after many years.

The story had to be told again, however deeply it racked one soul to be forced to give deadly testimony against the murderer, who, outcast by his own evil deeds, was still his father's son. The ghastly facts stood out too clearly for hesitation, and St. Clair Enson, alias Gen. Charles Benson, was remanded for trial.

Owing to the unsavory character of the prisoner extra precautions were taken by the warden to prevent a rescue or an escape.

At one o'clock Saturday morning the guard upon the outer

wall that surrounded the jail saw a shadow that seemed to move. At first he thought it a stray cat or dog, then as he wached he saw that it stole along the wall suspiciously; obedient to orders, he fired; the shadow fell to earth.

The men who came running at the sound of the shots bore the wounded man back into the jail, where they found that their burden was the body of St. Clair Enson, and that he was dead. The guard's bullet had taken a fatal effect.

In the prisoner's bed crouched Isaac Johnson in a vain endeavor to cover up his former owner's flight. A gaping hole at one side of the cell told where an entrance had been effected. How Isaac had managed to cut his way through the solid masonry always remained a mystery to the authorities.

Thus ended St. Clair Enson's career of vice and crime. Walker, alias Major Madison, died in the state prison.

CHAPTER XXXVI

Late Saturday afternoon, Hagar, so long known to us as Mrs. Bowen, reclined in semi-invalid fashion on the couch in her boudoir. She had exchanged her deep mourning for a house dress of white cashmere, profusely touched with costly lace. Her dark hair, showing scarcely a touch of silver, was closely coiled at the back of her shapely head. In spite of a shade of sadness her countenance was serene.

She was happy—happier than she had ever hoped to be in this life. True, no callers begged admittance into the grand mansion, no cards overflowed the receivers in the spacious entrance hall, since the sensational items disclosing her identity had appeared in the columns of the daily press; that fact did not disconcert her in the least. One thing alone troubled her,—Sumner's determination to separate her from Jewel.

The tender-hearted woman who had been his champion and friend throughout dark days of suspicion and despair, could not understand his antipathy to her. The two ladies did not worry themselves unduly, however, trusting that time and their united persuasions would win him to a better frame of mind.

The ceremony of the morrow would see her united to the husband of her youth. She thought only of that.

Ellis wished to settle the whole of Senator Bowen's immense fortune upon Jewel, but the latter would not hear of so unjust a proceeding. So the mansion was to be left in the care of Marthy Johnson, Aunt Henny and Oliver, while Mr. and Mrs. Enson were abroad. Venus was to go to Massachusetts with her young mistress, and the plan was that she and John Williams should be married about Christmas. The travellers were to start on their journeys early Monday morning. Suddenly Senator Bowen's last words, "The little hair trunk!" flashed across the lady's mind. It had been his in his first wife's time. He had clung to it through poverty and prosperity. It was in the late Senator's dressing-room which opened into the room where she was lying. Secretly blaming herself for neglecting the shabby object of his love and care, Hagar rose hastily and passed into the adjoining room.

Everything was as he had left it. How lonely it seemed without the jovial, genial presence of the man who had saved her from despair. Tears came to her eyes as she stood gazing upon familiar objects, each bearing the personality of the man who had gathered them about him. Over in a corner stood the little hair trunk. She moved slowly toward it, and presently was on her knees before it with the lid thrown back.

She sat there, prone upon the floor, for a time, gazing in mute sadness upon the contents—shabby, peculiarly made garments of the fashion in vogue before the war, mementoes of that other wife of his young manhood, and, strange mixture, a number of clay pipes, burned black by use, and fishing tackle, all mingled in a motley heap.

She took up the first wife's picture, opened the case and gazed into the eyes of the blowzy girlish face in its hideous cape bonnet, the long spiral curls falling outside the ruche that faced the head covering. Not a pretty face; no, but honesty and kindliness of heart were written there, silently claiming their tribute, turning the contemptuous smile to gentle reverence.

Hagar closed the case softly and placed it beside her on the floor with the other articles which her sense of neatness and order had caused her to fold carefully in regular piles, ready to replace in the shabby receptacle.

She had often wondered who Jewel resembled and where she had obtained the dainty, high-bred elegance of face and figure; surely not from father nor mother. Today her curiosity was again aroused; the desire to know pursued her so persistently that she was amazed.

The small velvet case containing Senator Bowen's daguerrotype, taken in early youth, had a peculiar fascination for her. His face smiled up at her, round, jolly, rubicund, a dimple in his chin and a laugh in his eyes, which the straight hair, combed flatly to the sides of his head, could not render sedate. Hagar felt a film gather to her eyes. What a god he had been to her! How devoted! How gentle! And he was a man of strong intellect and staunch integrity. She had no cause to be ashamed of him. He had saved her from despair. Next to her God she placed this man, whom she knew instinctively would never have forsaken her, never for one instant would he have wavered from his constancy to her, no matter what the cause, were she but true to him.

Ellis had come back to her; yes, but although love forgave, love worshipped at his shrine, love could not blot out the bitter memory of the time when he had failed her.

She closed the case with a nervous click, and went on with her sorting and folding. The very last thing that she found was a brown paper parcel, tied with coarse string. She undid the knot with the feeling of pride which attends the operation of succeeding in untying a string without cutting it. She smoothed out the kinks and curls and laid it carefully at her side ready for use again; then she removed the paper, expecting to see a man's wearing apparel; to her surprise a roll of white cashmere, yellow with age, met her eyes; it was wrapped about other articles. The kneeling woman felt the room spinning round her as she held the packet in her hand. There was something vaguely familiar in that ordinary piece of yellow cashmere; one side being visible showed a deep embroidered design tracing the edge of the deep hem. She could not move. Every muscle was paralyzed, and a flood of memories rushed in turmoil through her brain.

Trembling, breathless with excitement, she began to unroll the bundle. The last fold, as it fell apart, revealed the outer covering to be an infant's cloak of richest material and beautifully embroidered. With quivering fingers the agitated woman continued to shake out the garments that the cloak enfolded—a tiny dress, dainty skirts, a lace cap—in short, all the articles necessary to make up the attire of a child of love and wealth.

"Oh, merciful heaven! How came these here?" she whispered with white lips, as she pressed each tiny garment to her lips, and rained tremulous kisses on the exquisite lace cap. "My baby, my baby!"

She threw herself upon the floor and lay there weeping scalding tears. Before her lay the garments that her own hands had fashioned twenty years before, for the little daughter who had come to bless the union of Ellis Enson and herself. Half in terror she gazed upon them as upon the ghost of one long since departed. She made a movement and a metallic sound drew her attention to an object that slipped from among the clothing to the floor. It was a gold chain, from which depended a locket.

"My mother's locket!" she gasped. "Ah! Until this hour I had forgotten it; it was about my darling's neck when last I dressed her. My God! How comes it here? Why do I find it in Zenas Bowen's trunk?"

She touched a spring and the outer lid sprang back, showing a piece of paper pressed in the space usually devoted to pictures. The paper fell upon the floor unheeded. The writing was in Senator Bowen's hand, but she did not notice it; she was pressing her fingers along the margin of filagree work which decorated the edge of the locket; presently the back fell apart; then she pressed again and a third compartment opened and from it the face of Ellis Enson in his first youth smiled up into her own.

How well she remembered all the minute details of the history of the locket in the shadowy past, brought so vividly to her memory by the dramatic events of the last few days. Her mother had given her the locket at the time of her father's death, and had told her that it was a valued heirloom, and had explained to her the intricate working of the triple case. Probably no one had ever discovered the secret spring, and the case was supposed to be empty. After Mrs. Sargeant's death, she had in turn explained to Ellis, and placed his pictured face there, and when, tortured and tormented by persecution, she was driven from her home to the slave market, she had placed the locket about the baby's neck; why, she knew not.

Gazing at it now with sick and whirling brain, there came a step outside in her sitting room. She dragged her leaden limbs to the door and beheld Ellis. The bright smile on his face at sight of her seemed to chase away the years and renew his lost youth.

"My darling," he began, "you see I have managed to return earlier than I expected. I could not support the purgatory of absence from you longer. But what is the matter?"

Hagar could not answer him. Leaning against the door-frame, she looked him in the eyes, then extended her hand, the open locket lying on her palm.

"Ellis," she said, in a husky whisper, "I have just found this—here—in this room—in Senator Bowen's old trunk of relics. What can it mean? For God's sake, try and explain it to me. I cannot grasp the meaning of it at all."

Ellis's face was as white as her own, but he spoke soothingly to the distracted woman. Then his trained eye travelled beyond her to where the folded paper lay forgotten.

Taking her in his arms, he placed her upon the couch in the sitting-room, and then picked up the paper, first tenderly straightening each tiny garment and placing them all together in a pile upon a chair. Closing the door carefully behind him, he drew a chair to the side of the couch where Hagar lay weeping.

"Now, Hagar, my dear," he said, coaxingly, "you will try and be good and command yourself. God grant by these

tokens that we may trace our darling's last resting place—a
message from heaven!"

"Oh, how selfish I am, Ellis! You need comfort as much
as I do," she cried, her love on fire at sight of the tears in
his eyes, which he tried in vain to suppress. And then for a
little while the childless parents held each other's hands and
wept. Presently Ellis opened the paper from the locket. It
seemed but a leaf from a memorandum book, but what a
change it wrought in the lives of four people!

> March, 1862.—Went up the Potomac on the "Zenas
> Bowen" for oysters. Brought off 100 guns, 300 pounds of
> ammunition, Charleston, S. C. Picked up log floating outside
> the bay with a girl baby less than one year old attached to it
> by clothing. Must have floated many hours, but the sleeping
> child was unhurt. Clothing rich; no clue to parents or rela-
> tives.

> November, 1862.—Have adopted child and shall call her
> "Jewel." Have placed this mem. inside locket found on child
> for future reference.

> > Zenas Bowen.
> > Mary Jane Bowen.

There was a sound of weeping in the quiet room. "The
Divine Father hears all prayers, sees all suffering. In His
own good time the All-Merciful has had mercy." The solemn
words broke from Ellis.

"And I have said in my anguish, there is no God. He does
not heed my woes. Blasphemer that I am!" cried Hagar.

"And she is here in this very house! My God, I thank
Thee! Ellis, do not fear, I am strong; go, I beseech you, lose
not a moment, bring her to me—bring my Jewel, my
daughter, to my arms. Ah, did not my heart yearn over her

from the first, when, as a tender baby girl, I held her to my aching heart, and soothed my deep despair? Go, go—at once—Ellis! This suspense is more trying than all that has gone before. You do not know a mother's feelings. Shall I live till your return?"

Ellis, alarmed at her state, choked down his own feelings, and left the room in search of Jewel.

*　*　*　*　*

Who can paint the most sacred of human emotions? Clasped in her mother's arms, and shown the proofs preserved by her adopted father of her rescue from the death designed by her distracted mother, Jewel doubted not that she was Hagar's daughter.

CHAPTER XXXVII

All night the new-found daughter and husband watched beside Hagar's couch. They feared for her reason. But joy never kills, and at length she slept, and Jewel stole away to take her needed rest.

When alone again in her room, after the startling revelation that had come to her, she sat a long time, trying to realize the complete change in her future which this discovery would bring. She did not deceive herself; the cup of happiness was about to be snatched from her lips. Cuthbert, who was the one object of her passionate hero worship, would turn from her with loathing. There were dark circles about her eyes and her cheeks were ghastly. She loved her mother, she was proud of her father but feelings engendered for twenty years were not to be overcome instantly. It was horrible—a living nightmare, that she, the petted darling of society, should be banned because of her origin. She shrank as from a blow as she pictured herself the astonishment, disgust and contempt of her former associates when they learned her story. The present was terrible, the future more awful still. Overcome by her thoughts, moans burst from her overcharged heart; she stretched out her arms in an abandonment of grief and dropped senseless in the middle of her room, and so Venus found her in the early morning hours. Heaven help her, for it must also be written for her as for her ill-fated mother:

> "Better the heart strings had never known
> The chord that sounded its doom."

Venus knew the whole story. Mr. Enson had called Marthy, Aunt Henny and Venus into the room and told them very solemnly the facts in the case. There was much weeping and rejoicing.

"My soul," cried Venus to her mother when they were alone, "what about Mr. Sumner? If he goes back on Miss Jewel it'll kill her; it will break her heart."

"It's my 'pinion dat it's already broke, honey; a gal brung up like her has been's gwine break her heart to fin' herself nuthin' but common nigger trash. I jes' hope de debbil's give St. Clair Enson a good hot place down thar to pay him for his devilmen' here on yearth, 'deed I does," said Aunt Henny.

Jewel sent for her father and they talked the matter over. Mr. Enson could give her little hope. He was forced to acknowledge that Sumner was strongly prejudiced. He promised to see him, however, and tell him the story and hear his reply to Jewel, who sent also a pathetic note bidding him farewell:

> "I know your prejudice against amalgamation: I have
> believed with you. My sin, for it is a sin to hold one set of

God's creatures so much inferior to the rest of creation simply because of the color of the skin, has found me out. Like Miriam of old, I have scorned the Ethiopian and the curse has fallen upon me, and I must dwell outside the tents of happiness forever. I know you pity my poor mother; she has been so unhappy. I am proud of my father; he is a noble man. I will write again tomorrow and perhaps see you; but, oh, pray not today!"

Twenty-four hours passed and left Sumner as they found him, in mental torture. Then his good angel triumphed. He swore he would not give her up, and then he learned the power of prayer. He was ready to overlook and forgive all if only Jewel were left him. As his entreaties went up to a compassionate God the words rose ever before him.

"Many waters cannot quench love, neither can the floods drown it. All Thy waves and Thy billows have gone over me, but the heart is not easily closed. Love is strong as death."

Evening found him hastening toward the Bowen mansion. The house looked desolate. He rang the bell at the great entrance doors. Marthy Johnson answered the imperative summons.

"Lor', Mr. Sumner, Lor', sir!"

"Where are they all, Marthy?" he asked abruptly.

"Gone to de continen', Mr. Sumner. Massa Ellis say, you young folks'll git better lef' by your lonesomes; dat's what he tol' me tell you, sir."

Sumner left her in deep despair. He went home to his father for a brief time and then started for the Continent himself.

At the end of a year, mindful of poor John's devotion, for he vowed not to marry Venus till his master settled down,

Sumner returned to America and again sought the Bowen mansion. Again Marthy answered his summons, and told him that the family were at Enson Hall. He did not notice the pity on the woman's face.

He never paused until he reached the pretty little rustic town in Maryland that held his heart, his dove of peace. And then a great fear fell upon him, undefined and foreboding. He sent John on with his luggage to the Hall, and wandered up the country road with beating heart and feverish pulses. In a few minutes he would see her, she would be beside him, loving, forgiving. The tears came into his eyes, and he whispered a prayer. He drew his hat over his face and wandered off across a daisied field until he had overcome his emotion. A little graveyard nestled close beside the road. He was on the broad Enson acres, and in that enclosure dead and gone Ensons had slumbered for centuries. It was cool and shady and restful, and unconsciously he stepped into it.

Suddenly with a great cry he stood still before a fair, slender shaft of polished cream-white marble,

Jewel, aged 21.

"Not my will, but Thine be done!"

He fell down with his face upon her grave. She had died abroad of Roman fever.

* * * * *

Cuthbert Sumner questioned wherein he had sinned and why he was so severely punished.

Then it was borne in upon him: the sin is the nation's. It must be washed out. The plans of the Father are not changed in the nineteenth century; they are shown us in different forms. The idolatry of the Moloch of Slavery must be purged

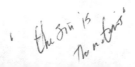

from the land and his actual sinlessness was but a meet offering to appease the wrath of a righteous God.

Across the lawn of Enson Hall a child—a boy—ran screaming and laughing, chasing a gorgeous butterfly. It was the child of St. Clair Enson and Elise Bradford, the last representative of the Enson family.

Cuthbert watched him with knitted brows. In him was embodied, a different form, a lesson of the degradation of slavery. Cursed be the practices which pollute the soul, and deaden all our moral senses to the reception of the true doctrines of Divinity.

The holy institution of marriage ignored the life of the slave, breed indifference in the masters to the enormity of illicit connections, with the result that the sacred family relation is weakened and finally ignored in many cases. In the light of his recent experiences Cuthbert Sumner views life and eternity with different eyes and thoughts from what he did before he knew that he had wedded Hagar's daughter. Truly had Ellis Enson spoken when he judged him nobler than he knew.

> "A boy's will is the wind's will,
> And the thoughts of youth are long, long thoughts."

THE END

WINONA

*A Tale of Negro Life in
the South and Southwest*

❧ ❧ ❧

CHAPTER I

Crossing the Niagara river in a direct line, the Canadian shore lies not more than eight miles from Buffalo, New York, and in the early 50's small bands of Indians were still familiar figures on both the American and Canadian borders. Many strange tales of romantic happenings in this mixed community of Anglo-Saxons, Indians and Negroes might be told similar to the one I am about to relate, and the world stand aghast and try in vain to find the dividing line supposed to be a natural barrier between the whites and the dark-skinned race. No; social intercourse may be long in coming, but its advent is sure; the mischief is already done.

From 1842, the aborigines began to scatter. They gave up the last of their great reservations then before the on-sweeping Anglo-Saxon, moving toward the setting sun in the pasture lands surrounding the Black Hills.

Of those who remained many embraced Christianity; their children were sent to the pale-face schools; they themselves became tillers of the soil, adopting with their agricultural pursuits all the arts of civilized life, and cultivating the friendship of the white population about them. They, however, still clung to their tribal dress of buckskin, beads,

[*Winona* originally appeared in serial from in the *Colored American Magazine* in the following issues: vol. 5, nos. 1–6 (May–October 1902). In the original publication, each episode was preceded by a synopsis, which I have deleted. "(To be continued)" lines, however, have been retained in the body of the text to indicate for the reader the serialized structure of the novel.— H.V.C.]

feathers, blankets and moccasins, thereby adding picturesqueness of detail to the moving crowds that thronged the busy
streets of the lively American city. Nor were all who wore
the tribal dress Indians. Here and there a blue eye gleamed
or a glint of gold in the long hair falling about the shoulders
told of other nationalities who had linked their fortunes with
the aborigines. Many white men had been adopted into the
various tribes because of their superior knowledge, and who,
for reasons best known to themselves, sought to conceal their
identity in the safe shelter of the wigwam. Thus it was with
White Eagle, who had linked his fortunes with the Senaca
Indians. He had come among them when cholera was deci-
mating their numbers at a fearful rate. He knew much of
medicine. Finally, he saved the life of the powerful chief Red
Eagle, was adopted by the tribe, and ever after reverenced as
a mighty medicine man.

Yet, through Erie County urged the Indians farther West,
and took up their reservations for white settlers, their thirst
for power stopped short of the curtailment of human liberty.
The free air of the land of the prairies was not polluted by
the foul breath of slavery. We find but one account of slaves
brought into the country, and they were soon freed. But the
free Negro was seen mingling with other settlers upon the
streets, by their presence adding still more to the cosmopolitan
character of the shifting panorama, for Buffalo was an anti-
slavery stronghold,—the last most convenient station of the
underground railroad.

It was late in the afternoon of a June day. It was uncom-
monly hot, the heat spoke of mid-summer, and was unusual
in this country bordering upon the lakes.

On the sandy beach Indian squaws sat in the sun with their
gaudy blankets wrapped about them in spite of the heat,

watching the steamers upon the lakes, the constant traffic of the canal boats, their beaded wares spread temptingly upon the firm white sand to catch the fancy of the free-handed sailor or visitor. Upon the bosom of Lake Erie floated a canoe. It had been stationary at different points along the shore for more than an hour. The occupants were fishing; presently the canoe headed for an island lying close in the shadow of Grand Island, about a mile from it. The lad who handled the paddle so skilfully might have been mistaken for an Indian at first glance, for his lithe brown body lacked nothing of the suppleness and grace which constant exercise in the open air alone imparts. He wore moccasins and his dress otherwise was that of a young brave, save for feathers and paint. His flashing black eyes were fixed upon the island toward which the canoe was headed; as the sunlight gleamed upon his bare head it revealed the curly, crispy hair of a Negro.

The sunlight played, too, upon the other occupant of the canoe, as she leaned idly over the side trailing a slim brown hand through the blue water. Over her dress of gaily-embroidered dark blue broadcloth hung two long plaits of sunny hair.

Presently the canoe tossed like a chip at the base of wooded heights as it grated on the pebbly beach. The two children leaped ashore, and Judah pulled the canoe in and piled it and the paddles in the usual place, high in a thicket of balsam fir. Winona had removed her moccasins and carried them in her hand while they made the landing; Judah balanced his gun, the fishing-rods and the morning's catch of fish on a rod.

They took their way along the beach, wading pools and walking around rocks, gradually ascending the wooded heights above them round and round, until they stood upon the crest that overlooked the bay and mainland.

The island was the home of White Eagle. When the Indians gave up Buffalo Creek reservation to Ogeten in 1842, and departed from Buffalo, he had taken up his abode on this small island in the lake, with an old woman, a half-breed, for his housekeeper. Hunting, fishing, trapping and trading with the Indians at Green Bay gave him ample means of support. But it was lonely with only a half-deaf woman for a companion, and one day White Eagle brought to the four-room cottage he had erected a handsome well-educated mu-lattress who had escaped from slavery via the underground railroad. With her was a mite of humanity whose mother had died during the hard struggle to reach the land of Freedom. In the end White Eagle crossed the Canadian shore and married the handsome mulattress according to English law and with the sanction of the Church; the mite of black humanity he adopted and called "Judah."

In a short time after the birth of Winona, the wife sickened and died, and once more the recluse was alone. Yet not alone, for he had something to love and cling to. Winona was queen of the little island, and her faithful subjects were her father, Judah and old Nokomis.

So transparent was the air on this day in June, that one could distinguish strips of meadow and the roofs of the white Canadian houses and the sand on the edges of the water of the mainland. The white clouds chased each other over the deep blue sky. The dazzling sunshine wearied the eye with its gorgeousness, while under its languorous kiss the lake became a sapphire sea breaking into iridescent spray along the shore.

The children were on a high ridge where lay the sun-flecked woods. They were bound for the other side, where lurked the wild turkeys; and partridges and pigeons abounded, and gulls built their nests upon rocky crests.

Singing and whistling, Judah climbed the slopes, closely followed by Winona, who had resumed her moccasins. The squirrel's shrill, clear chirp was heard, the blackbirds winged the air in flight, and from the boughs above their heads the "robin's mellow music gushed." Great blossoms of pink and yellow fungus spotted the ground. Winona stopped to select from among them the luscious mushroom dear to her father's palate. Daisies and bell-shaped flowers of blue lay thick in the grasses, the maples were still unfolding their leaves; the oak was there and the hemlock with its dark-green, cone-like folliage; the graceful birch brushed the rough walnut and the stately towering pine.

The transparent shadows, the sifted light that glimmered through the trees, the deer-paths winding through the woods, the green world still in its primal existence in this forgotten spot brought back the golden period unknown to the world living now in anxiety and toil.

A distant gleam among the grasses caught the girl's quick eye. She ran swiftly over the open and threaded her sinuous way among the bushes to drop upon her knees in silent ecstacy. In an instant Judah was beside her. They pushed the leaves aside together, revealing the faint pink stems of the delicate, gauzy Indian-pipes.

"Look at them," cried Winona. "Oh, Judah, are they not beautiful?"

The Negro had felt a strange sense of pleasure stir his young heart as he involuntarily glanced from the flowers to the childish face before him, aglow with enthusiasm; her wide brow, about which the hair clustered in rich dark rings, the beautifully chiselled features, the olive complexion with a hint of pink like that which suffused the fragile flowers before them, all gave his physical senses pleasure to contemplate. From afar came ever the regular booming of Niagara's stupendous flood.

"But they turn black as soon as you touch them."

"Yes, I know; but we will leave them here where they may go away like spirits; Old Nokomis told me."

"Old Nokomis! She's only a silly old Indian squaw. You mustn't mind her stories."

"But old Nokomis knows; she speaks truly," persisted the girl, while a stubborn look of determination grew about her rounded chin.

"When you go to school at the convent next winter the nuns will teach you better. Then you will learn what you don't know now. You're only a little girl."

There was silence for a time; Judah sank in the tall grass and aimed for a tempting pigeon roosting low in the branches of a tree. Nearer he stole—his aim was perfect—he was sure of his prey, when a girlish voice piped,—

"Did they tell you that at school?"

"There now! You've spoilt it! why did you speak?"

"Well, I wanted to know," this in a grieved tone.

"Wanted to know what?"

"Did they tell you that at school?"

"Tell me what?"

"That Nokomis is silly?"

"Of course not! They didn't know old Nokomis. But in school you learn not to believe all the silly stories that we are told by the Indians."

The boy spoke with the careless freedom of pompous youth.

They moved on through the woods over the delicate tracery

of shadowy foliage, and climbed down the steep sides of the hilly ridge that rose above a quiet cove on the other side where they had made what they called a kitchen. Winona led the way in her eagerness to reach the shore. She had been silent for some time, absorbed in thought.

"I tell you, Judah, I will not go to the convent school. I hate nuns."

"Ho, ho!" laughed Judah. "But you must; the father has said it."

"Papa cannot make me. I will not."

"Ah, but you will when the time comes, and you will like it. I doubt not you will want to leave us altogether when you meet girls your own age, and learn their tricks."

"Stop it, Judah!" she cried, stamping her small foot like a little whirlwind, "you shall not torment me. I do not want to leave papa and you for a lot of nuns and strange girls who do not care for me."

"What, again!" said Judah, solemnly. "That makes three times since morning that you've been off like a little fury."

"I know it, Judah," replied the girl, with tears in her eyes, "but you are so tantalizing; you'd make a saint lose her temper, you know you would."

"Oh, well; we shall see—Look, Winona!" he broke off abruptly, pointing excitedly out over the bosom of the lake. Three birds floated in the deep blue ether toward the island. "Gulls!"

"No! No! They're eagles, Judah!" cried the girl, as excited as he.

"Sure enough!" exclaimed the boy.

The birds swerved, and two flew away toward the mainland. The third dropped into the branches of a maple. "It's a young eagle, Winona, and I'm going to drop him!" catching up his weapon he leaned forward, preparing to take careful aim. Suddenly there was a puff of smoke that came from behind a bend in the shore just below where they were standing. A dull report followed and the eagle leaped one stroke in the air and dropped like a shot into the waters of the lake. A boat shot out from the beach with two men in it. They picked up the dead bird and then pulled towards the spot where the children stood intently watching them. They came on rapidly, and in a moment the occupants stood on the beach before the surprised children.

They were white men, garbed in hunter's dress. They seemed surprised to see the girl and boy on an apparently uninhabited island, and one said something in a low tone to the other, and motioned toward the crisp head of the boy. They spoke pleasantly, asking the name of the island.

Winona shrank behind Judah's back, glancing shyly at them from beneath the clustering curls that hung about her face.

"This island has no name," said Judah.

"Oh, then it is not a part of the Canadian shore?"

The questioner eyes the boy curiously. Judah moved his feet uneasily in the pebbles and sand.

"Not that I ever heard. It's just an island."

"Do you live here?"

"Yes, over there," pointing toward the other side.

"We're mighty hungry," joined in the other man, who had pulled the boat to a safe resting place out of the reach of the incoming tide.

"We'll pay you well for your fish," he added.

"You are welcome to as much as you wish," replied Judah politely, at once passing over a number of trout and a huge salmon.

"Show them our fireplace, Judah," said Winona, at length

finding her tongue. Judah led the way silently toward the sheltered cove where they had constructed a rude fireplace of rocks, and where the things necessary for their comfort during long tramps over their wooded domain, were securely hidden.

The children busied themselves with hospitable preparations for a meal, and the men flung themselves down on a bed of dry leaves and moss, lighted their pipes, and furtively watched them.

"Likely nigger," commented one.

"Worth five hundred, sure. But the girl puzzles me. What is she?" replied the one who seemed to be the leader.

"She's no puzzle to me. I'll tell you what she is—she's a nigger, too, or I'll eat my hat!" this with a resounding slap upon the thigh to emphasize his speech.

"Possible!" replied the leader, lazily watching Winona through rings of smoke. "By George! Thomson, you don't suppose we've struck it at last!"

"Mum's the word," said Thomson with an expressive wink. Judah brought some wood and Winona piled it on until a good bed of coals lay within the stone fireplace. Then she hung the fish on pieces of leather string, turning them round and round. Soon they lay in platters of birch, a savory incense filling the air, and in no time the hunters were satisfying their hunger with the delicious salmon and trout, washed down by copious draughts of pure spring water from a nearby rill whose gentle gurgle one could distinguish as it mingled with the noise of the dashing surf and the roar of the falls.

The children stood and watched them. Judah fingering lovingly the feathers of the dead eagle which he had taken from the boat.

"You haven't told us who you are," suggested the leader with a smile.

"She's White Eagle's daughter; I'm adopted."

"I see. Then you're Indians?"

Judah nodded. Somehow he felt uneasy with these men. He did not trust them.

"Not by a long sight," muttered Thomson. "Nothin' but nigger blood ever planted the wool on top of that boy's head."

Suddenly, faint and clear came a blast on a horn, winding in and out the secret recesses of the woods. Again and yet again, then all was still.

The men were startled, but the children hastily gathered up their belongings and without a word to the strangers bounded away, and were soon lost in the dark shadows of the woods.

"Well, cap't, this is a rum 'un. Now what do you reckon that means?"

"I have an idea that we've struck it rich, Thomson. Come, unless we want to stay here all night, suppose we push out for civilization?"

CHAPTER II

One sultry evening in July, about a month later than the opening of our story, a young man was travelling through the woods on the outskirts of the city of Buffalo.

The intense electric heat during the day had foretold a storm, and now it was evident that it would be upon him before he could reach shelter. The clouds sweeping over the sky had brought darkness early. The heavens looked of one uniform blackness, until the lightning, quivering behind them, showed through the magnificent masses of storm-wreck, while the artillery of the Almighty rolled threateningly in the distance.

For the sake of his horse, Maxwell would have turned

back, but it was many hours since he had left the railroad, travelling by the stage route toward the city. In vain he tried to pierce the gloom; no friendly light betrayed a refuge for weary man and beast. So they went on.

Suddenly the horse swerved to one side, in affright as the electric fluid darted in a quivering, yellow line from the black clouds, lighting up the landscape, and showing the anxious rider that he was near the turnpike road which led to the main street. He spurred his horse onward to reach the road while the lightning showed the way. Scarcely was he there when the thunder crashed down in a prolonged, awful peal. The storm had commenced indeed. The startled horse reared and plunged in a way to unseat an unskilled rider, but Maxwell sat firmly in the saddle; he drew rein a moment, patted the frightened animal and spoke a few kind words to soothe his terror. On every side now the lightning darted incessantly; the thunder never ceased to roll, while the rain descended in a flood. As the lightning blazed he caught glimpses of the turbulent water of the lake, and the thunder of Niagara's falls rivalled the artillery of heaven. It is no pleasant thing to be caught by such a storm in a strange city, without a shelter.

As he rode slowly on, the road developed a smooth hardness beneath the horse's feet, the vivid flashes showed board sidewalks; they showed, too, deep puddles and sluices of water pouring at a tremendous rate through the steep, canal-like gutters which bordered the way. A disk of landscape was photographed out of the night, etching the foliage of huge, dripping trees on either side, and the wide-spreading meadows and farm lands mingled with thickets and woodland. Only a few farm houses broke the monotony of the road between the stage route and the city.

"Heavens, what a country!" muttered the rider.

It was a pleasant voice, nicely modulated, and the fitful gleams of light showed a slender, well-knit figure, a bright, handsome face, blue eyes and a mobile mouth slightly touched with down on the upper lip. A dimple in the chin told of a light and merry heart within his breast.

"What a figure I must be," he laughed gaily, thinking of his mud-bespattered garments.

With the idea of suiting his dress to the country he was about to visit, Warren Maxwell had fitted himself out in Regent street with a suit of duck and corduroy with wide, soft felt hat, the English idea, at that period, of the "proper caper" for society in America.

As he rode along the lonely way his thoughts turned with sick longing toward his English home. What would they say to see him tonight, weary, hungry and disgusted? But he had come with a purpose; he was determined to succeed. There were three others at home older than himself; his own share in the family estate would amount to an annuity scarcely enough to defray his tailor's bill. Sir John Maxwell, baronet, his father, had reluctantly consented that Warren should study law when he found that neither the church nor medicine were congenial to his youngest, favorite son. Anything was better than trade. The old aristocrat metaphorically held up his hands in horror at the bare thought. In family council, therefore, it was decided that law, with money and old family influence might lead to Parliament in the future; and so Warren took up the work determined to do his best.

One day Mr. Pendleton, head of the firm, called him into his private office and told him that some one in their confidence must go to America. It was on a delicate mission relating to the heir of Carlingford of Carlingford. The other members of the firm were too old to undertake so arduous a journey; here was a chance for a young, enterprising man. If he were successful, they would be generous—in fact, he would become a full partner, sharing all the emoluments of the position at once. Of course Maxwell was interested, and asked to be given the details.

"You see," said the lawyer, "We've had the management of the estates for more than fifty years—all the old lord's time. It was a bad business when young Lord George and his brother fell in love with the same woman. It seems that Captain Henry and Miss Venton—that was the lady's name—had settled the matter to their own liking; but the lady's father favored Lord George because he was the heir and so Captain Henry was forced to see himself supplanted by his brother. Soon after a terrible quarrel that took place between the young men, Lord George was found dead, shot in the back through the heart. The Captain was arrested, tried and convicted of the crime. I remember the trial well, and that my sympathy was all with the accused. He was a bonny and gallant gentleman—the captain. Let me see—" and the old man paused a moment to collect his scattered thoughts.

"Let me see—Wait—Yes, he escaped from prison and fled to America. The lady? Why come to think of it she married a nephew of the old lord."

"And was the guilty party never found?"

"No—I think—In fact, a lot of money was spent on detectives by the old lord trying to clear his favorite and lift the stain from the family name; but to no purpose. Lord George cannot live many months longer, he is eighty-five now, but he thinks that Captain Henry may have married in America, and if so, he wants his children to inherit. For some reason he has taken a strong dislike to his nephew, who, by the way, is living in the southern part of the United

States. If you go, your mission must remain a profound secret, for if he lives, Captain Henry is yet amenable to the law which condemned him. Here—read these papers; they will throw more light on the subject, and while doing that make up your mind whether or not you will go to America and institute a search for the missing man." So Maxwell started for America.

"Heavens, what a flash!" exclaimed the young man, aroused from the reverie into which he had fallen. "Ah, what is that yonder?" Before him was a large wooden house with outlying buildings standing back from the road.

"Whoever dwells there will not refuse me shelter on such a night. I will try my luck."

Urging his tired horse forward, in a moment he stood before the large rambling piazza which embraced the entire front of the establishment. From the back of the house came the barking of dogs, and as he sprang to the ground the outer door swung open, shedding forth a stream of light and disclosing a large, gray-bearded man with a good-natured face. Around the corner of the house from the direction of the outbuildings, came quickly a powerful negro.

"Well, stranger, you've took a wet night fer a hossback ride," said the man on the piazza.

"I find it so," replied Warren with a smile. "May I have shelter here until the morning?"

"Shelter!" exclaimed the man with brusque frankness, "that's what the Grand Island Hotel hangs out a shingle fer. Western or furrin's welcome here. I take it from your voice you don't belong to these parts. Come in, and 'Tavius will take yer hoss. 'Tavius! Oh, 'Tavius! Hyar! Take the gentleman's hoss. Unstrap them saddle-bags and hand 'em hyar fus'."

'Tavius did as he was bidden, and Warren stepped into a room which served for office, smoking-room and bar. He followed his host through the room into a long corridor and up a flight of stairs into a spacious apartment neatly though primitively furnished. Having deposited the saddle-bags, the host turned to leave the room, pausing a moment to say:

"Well, mister, my name's Ebenezer Maybee, an' I'm proprieter of this hyar hotel. What may yer name be?"

Warren handed him a visiting card which he scanned closely by the light of the tallow candle.

" 'Warren Maxwell, England.' Um, um, I s'pose you're an 'ristocrat. Where bound? Canidy?"

"No," replied Warren, "just travelling for pleasure."

"Oh, I see. Rich. Well, Mr. Maxwell, yer supper'll be 'bilin on the table inside a half-hour: Fried chicken, johnny cake and coffee."

In less than an hour the smoking repast was served in the hotel parlor, and having discussed this, wearied by the day's travel, Maxwell retired and speedily fell asleep.

It must have been near midnight when he was awakened by a loud rapping. What was it? Mingled with the knocking was a sound of weeping.

Jumping on to the floor, and throwing on some clothing, Maxwell went into the corridor. All was darkness; the rain still beat against the window panes now and again illuminated by sheet-lightning. Listening, he heard voices in the office or bar-room, and in that direction he started. As he drew nearer he recognized the tones of his host.

"What is it? What is the trouble?" he asked as he entered the room.

A strange group met his eye under the flickering light of the tallow candle—a lad in Indian garb and a girl not more than fourteen, but appearing younger, who was weeping bitterly. She had the sweetest and most innocent of faces, Warren thought, that he had ever seen. A pair of large, soft brown eyes gazed up at him piteously.

"It's White Eagle's son and daughter. Something has happened to him and they want me to go with them to the island. You see I'm a sort of justice of the peace and town constable an' I've done the Injuns in these parts some few favors and they think now I can do anything. But no man can be expected to turn out of a dry bed and brave the lake on sech a night as this. I ain't chicken-hearted myself, but I draw the line thar."

In spite of his hard words and apparent reluctance to leave home, Mr. Maybee had lighted two lanterns and was pulling on his boots preparatory for a struggle with the elements.

"Who is White Eagle?" asked Warren.

"He's a white man; a sort of chief of the few Injuns 'roun' hyar, and he lives out on a small island in the lake with a half-breed squaw and these two children. They're poor—very poor."

"What seems to be the trouble with your father?" asked Warren, turning to the stoical lad and weeping girl.

"I believe he's shot himself, sir," returned the boy respectfully, in good English. "O, come, Mr. Maybee. My father—oh, my father!" exclaimed the girl between her sobs, clinging to the landlord's hand.

The anguish of the tone, the sweet girlish presence, as well as the lad's evident anxiety under his calmness, aroused Warren's compassion.

"If you will wait a moment I will go with you. I know something of medicine, and delay may be dangerous."

Uttering a pleased cry the girl turned to him. "Oh, sir! Will you? Will you come? Do not let us lose time then— poor papa!"

"If you go I suppose I must," broke in Mr. Maybee.

"But you don't know what you're about," he continued as they left the room together: "You must remember, mister, that these people are only niggers and Injuns."

"Niggers! Mr. Maybe, what do you mean?"

"It's a fac'. The boy is a fugitive slave picked up by White Eagle in some of his tramps and adopted. The girl is a quadroon. Her mother, the chief's wife, was a fugitive too, whom he befriended and then married out of pity."

"Still they're human beings, and entitled to some consideration," replied Warren, while he muttered to himself, thinking of the tales he had heard of American slavery,— "What a country!"

"That's so, mister, that's so; but it's precious little consideration niggers and Injuns git around' hyar, an' that's a fac'."

For all his hard words, Ebenezer Maybee was a humane man and had done much for the very class he assumed to despise. He did not hesitate to use methods of the Underground railroad when he deemed it necessary.

When Warren returned to the room, the two children stood where he had left them, and as soon as Mr. Maybee joined them they started out.

Through mud and rain they made their way, the rays from the lanterns but serving to intensify the darkness. Very soon a vivid flash threw into bold relief the whiteness of the hissing lake.

"What did you come over in, Judah, canoe or boat?" shouted Mr. Maybee, who headed the party.

"The boat," called back Judah. "I thought you might come back with us."

"Good!" shouted Mr. Maybee.

When they were all seated in the boat, after some difficulty, Judah stood upright in the bow and shoved off. Each of the two men had an oar.

Not even an Indian would ordinarily trust himself to the mercy of the water on such a night, but Judah steered out boldly for the little isle without a sign of fear.

"Judah knows his business," shouted Mr. Maybee to Maxwell. "He'll take us over all right if anybody can."

At first Warren noticed nothing but the safety of the craft, and the small figure crouched in the bottom of the boat. Every swell of angry waters threatened to engulf them. The boat shivered; foam hissed like steam and spent its wrath upon them. The lightning flashed and the thunder rolled. There was no sky—nothing but inky blackness.

Rain streamed over their faces. Warren's hair hung in strings about his neck. The dangers gathered as they lessened the five miles between the mainland and the island. The young Englishman loved aquatic sports and his blood tingled with the excitement of the battle with the storm. The day had brought him adventures, but he did not shrink from death by drowning were it in good cause.

Presently the shore loomed up before them, and after much skilful paddling, they entered the sheltered cove that answered for a bay. The boat grounded and Judah sprang out, holding it fast while the others landed. It was a relief to them to feel the hard, sandy beach beneath their feet and to know that the danger was over for the present.

"Let us go faster," said Winona. "We are close now, sir—close," turning to Warren.

She ran on in front, threw open the door to the little cottage, and entered. The pictured remained with Warren always,—the bare room with unplastered floor and walls of rough boards; the rude fireplace filled with logs spouting flames; the feeble glow of the "grease lamp"; the rude chairs and tables. At one side, on a bed of skins, was extended the figure of a man. The old squaw was rocking to and fro and moaning.

"Ah! my bird!" said old Nokomis, raising her withered hands. "It is no use—it is too late."

"What do you mean. Nokomis?" demanded Winona.

"White Eagle has answered the call of the Great Spirit," replied the old woman, with a sob.

"Dead! My father!"

The girl gave one quick, heart-breaking cry, and would have fallen had not Warren caught her in his arms. Gently he raised her, and followed Judah into another room, and laid her on a bed.

"Ah," said the lad, "how will she bear it if it is true, when she gets back her senses? How shall we both bear it?"

"Come, let us see if nothing can be done for your father. Nokomis may be mistaken."

"Yes, true;" replied the boy in a hopeless tone.

Back in the kitchen where Mr. Maybee was already applying restoratives, Warren began an examination of the inanimate form before them. It was the figure of a fine, handsome man of sixty years, and well-preserved. They stripped back the hunting shirt and Warren deftly felt for the wound. As he leaned over him, he gave a startled exclamation, and rising erect ejaculated:

"This is no accident. *It is murder!*"

CHAPTER III

"Murder!"

The gruesome word seemed to ring through the silent room.

"Murder!" ejaculated old Nokomis, aghast. "It is a mistake. Who would kill White Eagle? There lives not an Indian in the whole country round who does not love him. No, No."

There was horror on the face of the young man regarding her so steadfastly. Her withered, wrinkled face was honest enough, her tones genuine.

"No!" exclaimed Mr. Maybee, recovering from the stupor into which Warren's words had thrown him. "Blame my skin! where's the blud?"

Warren regarded him steadily a moment, then said, "Look! Internal hemorrhage."

He half raised the body and pointed to a bullet hole in the back.

"By the Etarn'l!" was Maybee's horrified exclamation. "Must 'a bled to death whilst we was comin'."

Warren nodded.

"God in heaven!" cried Judah, sinking on his knees beside the bed of skins. "It is true! But who has done it? Who could be so cruel? No one lives here but ourselves. Murdered! My father! My master!"

"Hush!" said Mr. Maybee, sternly. "Hush. 'Tain't no time fer cryin' nor makin' a fuss. Tell us all you know about this business."

"He went out after supper to look after the canoes. In a short time we heard a shout and then a cry, 'Help! help!' and we ran to him, Winona and I. He was leaning against a tree, and said nothing but. 'Get me to the house; get a doctor, I am hurt.' We flew to do his bidding. The rest you know."

Maxwell's brain was in a tumult of confusion. Thoughts flew rapidly through it. Suddenly he had been aroused from his solitary life in a strange land to become an actor in a local tragedy. The man lying on the bed of skins had certainly been murdered. Who then was the assassin?"

Again he looked at Nokomis, who was intently watching him. She shook her head mournfully in answer to his unasked question. Mr. Maybee was nonplussed. "What's to be done? Terrible! Murder! Why, it will kill the girl."

Warren Maxwell started. For a moment he had forgotten the delicate child in the next room rendered so suddenly an orphan, and in so fearful a fashion.

"A doctor must be summoned to certify the cause of death, and the police authorities must be notified," Warren said at length. "Right you are, pard," returned Maybee. "I'm hanged ef this business hain't knocked the spots out of yours truly. I'll take the boat and Judah here, and be back by sunrise."

He turned away, but Judah lingered, giving a wistful look into Maxwell's face.

"Yes," said Warren, laying his hand on the lad's shoulder, "I will tell her."

With a gesture of thanks Judah followed Mr. Maybee out into the night.

Pulling himself together, Warren, followed by Nokomis, entered the room where he had left Winona. She lay on the bed where he had placed her, still unconscious, her long hair lank with the rain, streamed about her face; her lips were lightly parted, even younger and more beautiful than he had at first thought; and as he remembered her story and the position that the death of her father placed her in, his soul went out to her in infinite pity.

"Poor child! Poor little thing!" he mused. "Heaven must have sent me here at this awful moment. You shall not be friendless if I can help you."

He questioned Nokomis closely. The old woman shook her head.

"Alone except for old Nokomis and Judah. White Eagle loved her very much. Old Nokomis will take care of her."

Between them the girl was restored to consciousness, and learned the truth of her father's death told by Warren as gently as possible. She heard him with a stunned expression, pale lips and strained eyes; suddenly, as she realized the meaning of his words, she uttered a piercing cry, and sprang up exclaiming:

"My father! Oh, my father! Murdered!"

She would have rushed from the room. She struggled with Warren, trying with her small fingers to unclasp his, which with tenderness held her; she turned almost fiercely upon him for staying her. The paroxysm died as quickly as it came, leaving her weak and exhausted.

Ebenezer Maybee returned at sunrise, bringing men with him. The great storm had cleared the air of the electric heat, and the morning was gloriously beautiful. The dark forest trees were rich in the sunshine, the streams and waters of the lakes laughed and rippled as happily as if no terrible storm had just passed, carrying in its trail the mystery of a foul and deadly crime. Search revealed no trace of the assassin; no clue. There were but two strangers in the city who had visited the island, and they immediately joined the searchers when they learned of the tragedy. The storm had obliterated all traces of the murderer. There was nothing missing in the humble home that held so little to tempt the cupidity of a thief. There was not even a scrap of paper found to tell who White Eagle might have been in earlier, happier days.

Everyone seemed to regard Warren Maxwell as the person in authority. The police consulted him, referred to him; Mr. Maybee confided in him, and Winona clung to him with slender brown fingers like bands of steel. As far as Warren could learn, she had no friend in the world but the hotel keeper. What a different life this poor child's must have been from any he had ever known.

Old Nokomis repeated many times a day: "Surely it was the Great Father must have sent you to us."

Judah walked about all day with a dazed expression on his face, crying silently but bitterly, and a growing look of sullen fury on his dark face that told of bitter thoughts within. Over and over again his lips unconsciously formed the words:

"I'll find him when I'm older if he's on top of the earth, and then it'll be him or me who will lie as my poor master lies in there today."

Then came the funeral. The Indians gathered from all the adjoining cities and towns and from the Canada short, to see the body of the man they had loved and respected committed to the ground. They buried him beneath the giant pine against which he was found leaning, wounded to death. Curiosity attracted many of the white inhabitants, among whom were the two strangers referred to in the first part of this narrative.

Two days after the funeral, Mr. Maybee and Warren sat in the latter's room talking of Winona and Judah.

"It was a fortunit thing for us all, Mr. Maxwell, that you happened to be aroun' during this hyar tryin' time. You've been a friend in need, sir, durn me ef you ain't."

"Yes;" replied Warren, smiling at the other's quaint speech, "it was a time that would have made any one a friend to those two helpless children."

"Maybe, maybe," returned the hotel keeper, dubiously. "But you must remember that every man warn't built with a soul in his carcass; some of 'em's only got a piece of liver whar the heart orter be." Warren smiled again.

"Mr. Maybee, I want to ask you a question—"

"Go ahead, steamboat; what's the question?"

"What is to become of Winona after I leave this place? It is different with the boy—he can manage somehow—but the girl; that is what troubles me."

"Look hyar, young feller;" said Maybee, stretching out a big, brown hand. "I don' guess she'll ever have to say she's got no friend while Ebenezer Maybee's proprietor of the grand Island Ho-tel. My wife's plum crazy to git that young kidabid. We's only awaitin' till the news of this unfortunit recurrence has blowed over, and she gits a little used to bein' without her pa. As fer Judah, thar's plenty to do roun' the stables ef he likes. But, Lor,' that Injun-nigger! You can't tame him down to be just an' onery galoot like the most of 'em you see out hyar. White Eagle taught him to speak like a senator, ride bareback like a hull circus; he can shoot a bird on the wing and hunt and fish like all natur. Fac'." he added noting Warren's look of amusement. "Truth is,—neither of them two forlorn critters realizes what 'bein' a nigger' means; they have no idee of thar true position in this unfrien'ly world. God knows I pity 'em." But to Warren Maxwell it seemed almost sacrilege—the thought of that beautiful child maturing into womanhood among such uncouth surroundings. His mind revolted at the bare idea. At length he said with a sigh:

"What a pity it is that we know nothing of White Eagle's

antecedents. There may be those living who would be glad to take the child."

"He was a gentleman, as your class counts 'em, Mr. Maxwell. But he never breathed a word what he was, an' he kept away from his equals—meanin' white men."

"And few men do that without a reason," replied Maxwell. "Do you know whether he was English or German?"

Mr. Maybee shook his head. "He warn't Dutch, that's certain; he was a white man all right. I cal'late he mote 'a been English."

"Mr. Maybee, I've been thinking over the matter seriously, and I have determined to write home and see if something can't be done to educate these children and make them useful members of society. In England, neither their color nor race will be against them. They will be happier there than here. Now, if I can satisfy you that my standing and character are all right, would you object to their going with me when I sail in about three months from now?"

Mr. Maybee gazed at him in open-mouthed wonder. "Yer jokin'?" he said at length, incredulously.

"No, I mean it."

Still Mr. Maybee gazed in amazement. Could it be possible that the heard aright?

"Je-rusalem! but I don't know what to say. We don' need no satisfyin' 'bout you; that's all right. But the idea of your thinkin' about edjicatin' them two Injin-niggers. You've plum got me. An' too. I cal'lated some on gittin' the gal fer my wife. Still it would be good fer the gal—durn me, but it would."

Then he turned and grasped Warren's hand hard.

"Mr. Maxwell, you're a white man. I jes' froze to you, I did the fus' night you poked yer head in the door."

"And I to you," replied Warren, as he returned the warm hand-pressure.

"Don' you ever be skeery whilst yer in Amerika an' Ebenezer Maybee's on top o' the earth. By the Etarn'l, I'll stick to you like a burr to a cotton bush, durn me ef I don't."

Again the men clasped hands to seal the bond of brother-hood.

"Meantime, Mr. Maybee, I wish you to take charge of them. I am called to Virginia on important business. I will leave a sum of money in your hands to be used for their needs while I am gone. When I return, I shall be able to tell just what I can do, and the day I shall leave for England."

Mr. Maybee promised all he asked, and then retired to the bar-room to astonish his cronies there by a recital of what the English gent proposed to do for two "friendless niggers." Maxwell rowed over to the island to tell Winona of his departure and the arrangements made for her welfare. He laughed softly to himself as he thought of his own twenty-eight years and his cool assumption of the role of Winona's guardian. Yet he was not sorry. Upon the whole, he was glad she had been surrendered to his care, that there would be no one to intrude between them; and he felt that the girl would also be glad; she appeared to rely upon him with childlike innocence and faith. How could he fail to see that the brown eyes clouded when he went away, and brightened when he approached?

He secured the boat and directed his steps to the tall pine where she usually sat now. She was sitting there by the new-made grave, her hands folded listlessly in her lap. Her eyes were fixed upon the sunlit waves and were the very home of sorrow. At that moment, turning she beheld him. A sudden radiance swept over the girl's features. Sorrow had matured her wonderfully.

"Ah! it is you. I have been waiting for you."

"You were sure I would come," he smiled, taking her hand and seating himself beside her.

"Yes. And I know you never break your word—never. You said you wished to speak to me of my future."

"Exactly. I could not go to England and leave you here alone and friendless, Winona," he replied. "I could not bear it."

The girl shivered. A month ago, she was a happy, careless child; today she had a woman's heart and endurance. Of course he must go sometime, this kind friend; what should she do then?"

"Yet I must stay. I have nowhere else to go."

"Surely you know of some friends—relatives?"

She shook her head.

"Papa never spoke of any. He used to say that we two had only each other to love, poor papa. Oh!" with a piteous burst of grief, "I wanted no one else but papa, and now he is gone."

"As He gave, so He has a right to take, Winona," said Warren, gravely. He saw that she was indeed "cast upon his care;" surely there must have been some dark shadow in White Eagle's past life to cause him to bury himself here in a wilderness among savages. Well, it must be as he had planned. He explained to Winona all that he had told Mr. Maybee.

"And you will take Judah with you?"

"Certainly," replied Warren, "You shall not be separated." The girl heaved a deep sigh of content. "I will go with you to your home gladly."

Judah was as pleased as Winona when told of the plans for the future. Each looked upon Warren Maxwell as a god. Judah went with him to the mainland. Winona saw him depart bravely. She watched the boat until they effected a landing. Once he turned and waved his hat toward the spot where she was standing. When he was no longer visible she threw herself down upon the new-made grave in an abandonment of grief, weeping passionately.

*   *   *   *   *

One month from that day Warren Maxwell, bright, smiling and filled with pleasurable anticipations drew rein again before the Grand Island Hotel. As before, 'Tavius was there to take his horse; Mr. Maybee met him at the door; but about them both was an air of restraint.

"Well, Mr. Maybee," he said gaily, "How are you, and how are my island protégés? I'll row over after dinner and surprise them."

"Come with me, Mr. Maxwell, I have something to tell you," replies his host gravely.

Surprised at his solemn manner, Warren followed him to the chamber he had occupied on the occasion of his first visit. "It's a sorry tale sir, I must tell you; and in all my life I never befo' felt ashamed of bein' an American citizen. But I can be bought cheap, sir; less than half price'll git me."

"The day after you lef' thar was a claim put in by two men who had been stoppin' roun' hyar fer a month or more lo-catin thar game, the durned skunks. They was the owners of White Eagle's wife an' Judah's mother, sir—nigger traders from Missouri, sir. They puts in a claim fer the two children under the new act for the rendition of fugitive slaves jes' passed by Congress, an' they swep' the deck before we knowed it or had time to say 'scat.' Ef we'd had the least warnin', Mr. Maxwell, we'd a slipped the boy an' gal over to Canidy in no time, but you never know where a sneakin' nigger thief is goin' to hit ye, 'tain't like fightin' a man. Before we knowed it they had 'em as slick as grease an' was gone."

"But how could they take the children? They were both born free. It was an illegal proceeding," cried Warren in amazement.

"The child follows the condition of the mother. That's the law."

"My God, Mr. Maybee," exclaimed Warren as a light broke in upon his mind. "Where is she now—the poor, pretty child?"

"Down on a Missouri plantation, held as a slave!"

"My God!" Warren gazed at him for a time bereft of speech, dazed by a calamity too great for his mind to grasp. "My God! can such things be?"

(To be continued.)

CHAPTER IV

A few miles out from Kansas City, Missouri State, on a pleasant plain sloping off toward a murmuring stream, a branch of the mighty river, early in the spring of 1856, stood a rambling frame house two stories high, surrounded with piazzas, over which trailed grape-vines, clematis and Virginia creepers. The air was redolent with the scent of flowers nor needed the eye to seek far for them, for the whole front of the dwelling, and even the adjoining range of wooden stables, were rendered picturesque by rich masses of roses and honeysuckle that covered them, and the high, strong fence that enclosed four acres of cleared ground, at the end of which the buildings stood. Mingled with the scent of the roses was the fragrance of the majestic magnolia whose buds and blossoms nodded at one from every nook and unexpected quarter.

This was "Magnolia Farm," the home of Colonel Titus. He was an Englishman by birth and education who had invested his small fortune in a plantation and many slaves in the great Southwest; he had also traded in horses, selling, training, doctoring, taking care of horses, or, indeed, making money by any means that came in his way (or out of it, for the matter of that); all was grist that came to his mill. In time his enterprising spirit met with its reward and he became a leading man in all affairs pertaining to the interest of the section. The death of his wife, whom he tenderly loved, soon after the birth of their only child, had left him solitary. This affliction tendered, therefore, to deepen his interest in politics, and he eventually became one of the most bitter partisans on the side of slavery, contrary to the principles of most of his nationality. In his pro-slavery utterances he outdid the most rabid native-born Southerners. In 1854 his famous speech at St. Joseph, Missouri, at the beginning of the trouble in Kansas, had occasioned the wildest enthusiasm at the South, and the greatest consternation at the North.

"I tell you to mark every scoundrel among you who is the least tainted with abolitionism, or pro-slavery, and exterminate them. Neither giving nor taking quarter from the d——d rascals. To those who have qualms of conscience as to violating laws, state or national, I say, the time has come when such impositions must be disregarded, as your rights and property are in danger. I advise you, one and all, to enter every election district in Kansas, in defiance of Reeder and his myrmidons, and vote at the point of the bowie-knife and revolver. Neither take or give quarter as the cause demands it. It is enough that the slave-holding interests wills it, from which there is no appeal."

With the memory of recent happenings in the beautiful Southland, against the Negro voter, engraved upon our hearts, these words have a too familiar sound. No, there is very little advancement in that section since 1854, viewed in the light of Gov. Davis' recent action. The South would be as great as were her fathers "if like a crab she could go backward." Reversion is the only god worshiped by the South.

Bill Thomson, whose reputation for pure, unadulterated "cussedness" was notorious in this semi-barbarous section, was his overseer and most intimate friend. Thomson's wife was the Colonel's housekeeper, and, with the owner's invalid daughter, these four persons made up the "family" of the "big house."

The summer sun hung evenly over the great fields of cotton; the rambling house cast no shadow, but the broad piazza at the back afforded ample shade from the mid-day rays, sheltered as it was by great pines; within their reach, too, lay the quarters. The porch overlooked the blooming fields where a thousand acres stretched to the very edge of the muddy Missouri. This porch, with its deep, cool shadows, commanded a view of the working force, and made it a favorite resting place for the Colonel and his daughter Lillian. The crippled girl found complete happiness seated in her rolling chair gazing out upon the dusky toilers who tilled the broad acres of foaming cotton.

His daughter's affliction was a great cross to the Colonel. His thoughts were bitter when he saw other young girls swinging along the highway reveling in youthful strength that seemed to mock the helplessness of his own sweet girl.

"Why had this affliction been sent upon her?" he asked himself. If he had sinned why should punishment be sent upon the innocent and helpless? He rebelled against the text wherein it is taught that evil deeds shall be visited upon the progeny of the doer unto the third and fourth generations.

Far off in lovely England, ancestral halls might yet await her coming, if, perchance, Destiny should leave him in Fortune's lap. There was a letter lying snugly in his pocket, from a firm in London, that promised much, if—

It was near the noon siesta, and the Colonel sat on the piazza smoking his pipe and waiting the time to blow the horn for dinner. His daughter sat there, too, with an open book on her lap, and a dreamy look in her deep blue eyes that would wander from the printed page to the beautiful scene before her.

The sound of sharp words in a high-pitched voice and answering sobs broke in upon the quiet scene.

"There's Mrs. Thomson scolding Tennie again," observed Lillian. The words of that lady came to them distinctly from the hallway:

"What's the matter with you today? You leave your work for the other girls. What are you moping about? Is it Luke?"

"Luke been conjured," came in a stifled voice.

"By whom?"

Mrs. Thomson was a woman of considerable education and undoubted piety, but her patience was as short as piecrust. At her question all Tennie's wrath broke forth.

"Dat yaller huzzy, Clorinder; she conjured Luke till he gone plum wil' over her. Ef eber I gits my han's on her, she goin' 'member me de longes' day she lib."

"Hush, I tell you! This stuff must end right here."

"But, Mistis, dat nigger—"

"Hush your mouth! Don't you 'but' me! Do you get the cowhide and follow me to the cellar, and I'll whip you well for aggravating me as you have today. It seems as if I can never sit down to take a little comfort with the Lord, without your crossing me. The devil always puts you up to disturbing me, just when I'm trying to serve the Lord. I've no doubt I'll miss going to heaven on your account. But I'll whip you well before I leave this world, that I will. Get the cowhide and come with me. You ought to be ashamed of yourself to put me in such a passion. It's a deal harder for me than it is for you. I have to exert myself and it puts me all in a fever; while you have only to stand and take it."

The sounds died away, and once more quiet reigned. The Colonel resumed his train of thought, his brow contracted into a frown as he watched the rings of smoke curling up from the bowl of his pipe. He sighed. His daughter, watching him, echoed his sigh, because she thought her father was changing. He was a tall, powerful man with dark hair and beard fast whitening. He had deep-set eyes that carried a shifting light; they had the trick, too, of not looking one squarely in the face.

"His hair is right gray," she said to herself, sadly, "and he is beginning to stoop; he never stooped before. He's studying, always studying about the mortgages and politics. Oh, dear, if I'd only been a boy! Maybe I could have helped him. But I'm only a girl and a cripple at that." She changed the sigh into a smile, as women learn to do, and said aloud, "Here's Winona with your julep."

The girl bore a goblet on a waiter filled with the ruby liquid and a small forest of mint. The Colonel smiled, his annoyances forgotten for a moment; he lifted the glass gallantly, saying: "Your health, my daughter!"

As he sipped and drank, the girl laughed gleefully and proceeded to refill his pipe, he watching her the while with fond eyes. Winona watched the scene with bent brows. So, happy had she been with her dead father, not so long ago.

She had passed from childhood to womanhood in two years

of captivity—a womanhood blessed with glorious beauty that lent a melancholy charm to her fairness when one remembered the future before such as she. She had been allowed at lessons with her young mistress and had wonderfully improved her privileges. The Colonel and Thomson encouraged her desire for music, too; "It'll pay ten dollars for every one invested," remarked the latter. It was now two years since the two friends had returned from a mysterious absence, bringing Winona and Judah with them. The time seemed centuries long to the helpless captives, reared in the perfect freedom of Nature's woods and streams.

Winona was given to Lillian for a maid, and under her gentle rule the horrible nightmare of captivity dragged itself away peacefully if not happily.

With Judah it was different; he was made assistant overseer, because of his intelligence and his enormous strength. As graceful as vigorous, he had developed into a lion of a man. But his nature seemed changed; he had lost his sunny disposition and buoyant spirits. He was a stern, silent man, who apparently, had never known boyhood. He was invaluable as a trainer of horses, and scrupulously attentive to his other work, but in performing these duties he had witnessed scenes that rivalled in cruelty the ferocity of the savage tribes among whom he had passed his boyhood, and had experienced such personal abuse that it had driven smiles forever from his face.

Thomson wore the physique of a typical Southerner. People learning of his English ancestry were surprised and somewhat doubtful as they noted his sharp profile, thin lips, curved nose and hollow cheeks. His moustache and hair, coal black in color, increased the doubt.

As we have said, there was no greater scoundrel in Missouri than Bill Thomson. Men declared there was "a heap in him.

Other bad ones were jes' onery scamps; but Bill had a head on him."

He it was who was organizing and drilling numbers of companies of men, in case the d——d Yankees proved unruly, to burn and loot the infant territory and carry it into the slave-holding lines by fire and fraud.

Into this man's hands Judah was given body and soul.

CHAPTER V

Judah's first experience of slave discipline happened in this wise: A man in Kansas City had foolishly paid five hundred dollars for a showy horse, not worth half the amount, a perfect demon whom nobody dared venture near. The purchaser was about to shoot the vicious beast, when Bill Thomson happened along, and offered five hundred even odds that he would take the animal to Magnolia Farm and break him to saddle and bridle in ten days, Thomson being of the opinion that no one knew as much about a horse or a mule as he did, and priding himself on his success with animals.

He soon found that the horse was more than he had bargained for. The beast couldn't be cajoled or coaxed—not a man daring to go near him or within reach of his head. In order to get him to the farm he was starved and drugged.

"Well, boys, I reckon it aint' no use; the ugly beast's beat me, and I lose the bet," said Thomson to the little group of men gathered at a gate of the enclosure, the next morning after the animal arrived at the farm. It was a rough group made up of gamblers and sporting men, who had heard of the bet and came to Magnolia Farm to witness the battle between the horse-dealer and horse.

"Yes, I'm licked. He's a reg'lar fiend that hoss is. I'm a done coon this day, an' the hoss will have to be shot. I invite you all to stop to the shootin' party."

"Never know'd you to git beat befo', Bill," remarked one, striking the haft of his bowie knife; "an' to lose five hundred dollars slick off, too; sho!"

"My mettles up, boys. If I can't break the hoss in, no one can; that's true, ain't it?"

"For startin' sure!" came from the crowd.

"What's the good of lettin' a vicious brute like that live?" and Thomson ended with a volley of oaths.

"Bill's plum wil'," said one of the crowd.

" 'Nough to make him, I reckon," returned the first speaker. "Bill allers did swear worse'n a steamboat cap'n. The Foul Fiend himself would be swearin' to be beat by that tearin' four-legged [beast.]

The group waited breathlessly for Thomson's next move as he stood gazing toward the refractory beast. Just at this moment Judah came up and touched his hat respectfully to the group of men.

"Don't shoot him yet, sir; I can tame that horse and win your bet for you," he said to Thomson.

It would be difficult to describe the effect produced on the group by those few cool, daring words—a breathless pause, each looking at the other in incredulous amazement; then a murmer of admiration for the speaker went from man to man, Thomson himself, who had recoiled from the boy, staring in open-eyed wonder at his cool assertion.

"You go near the beast! What do you know about breaking hosses? He'd throw you and kill you or trample you to death, an' I'd be just fifteen hundred dollars more out of pocket by the onery brute."

It was a picture for an artist,—the Negro passively waiting the verdict of his master, his massive head uncovered in humility. There was not among them all so noble a figure of a man, as he stood in a somewhat theatrical attitude—a living statue of a mighty Vulcan. Into the group Colonel Titus walked with a commanding gesture.

"Let him try, Thomson, for the honor of the farm. I believe he can do it. I'll stand the loss if there is any."

A murmur of approval broke from the crowd. At the Colonel's words, Judah stepped forward and began giving his orders without a shade of servility, seeming to forget in the excitement of the moment his position as a slave. Once more he moved as a free man amidst his fellows and for the time being forgot all else. Thomson watched him with an evil smile upon his wicked face.

"Get me a saddle and bridle ready, Sam," he called to a stable boy, "and a strong curb, too." He walked toward the stable at the end of the range which had been given up to the horse, followed by the men of the group.

"Take car', Jude," cautioned Sam. "He'll put his head out an' bite. He tried to kick de do' out yes'day!"

Heedless of the warning, Judah kept on, with the remark, "I think he's feeding."

"Take car', thar!" yelled Sam; "He's comin' at yer," as a savage snort came from within. The crowd fell back respectfully, all save Judah.

The horse rushed forwards, butting his chest against the iron bar, as he thrust his head over the top of the half-door. His ears were laid back, his eyes rolling, and his mouth open to bite, showing rows of terrible teeth. Judah did not move or tremble.

"Got grit," observed one to the other.

"Wish I owned a gang o' niggers jes' like him."

"I don't," replied his neighbor. "Them big, knowin' niggers is dang'rous."

Judah stretched out his hand and gave a half-pat to the animal's nose, withdrawing it as he attempted to seize his arm, snapping viciously.

"Stand back, all of you," commanded the boy, as he moved around, facing the animal. Then began an exhibition of mind over instinct. The power of the hypnotic eye was known and practised among all the Indian tribes of the West. It accounted for their wonderfull success in subduing animals. Judah concentrated all the strength of his will in the gaze that he fixed upon the horse. Not a muscle of his powerful face moved for one instant, his glowing eyes never wavered, his eyelids did not quiver, but immovable as a statue he stood pouring the latent force on which he relied upon the vicious brute. And its effect was curious; he stared back at the boy for a few seconds with rolling eyes and grinning teeth, then his eyes wavered, he pawed the ground uneasily, flung up his head with an angry snort, half of fear, and running backwards, reared erect. Still Judah's gaze did not falter; his eyes were immovably fixed upon the uneasy animal; he dropped again, butted his muzzle on the ground, shook his mane and ran about the shed for five or ten minutes, all to no purpose; when he halted opposite the opening, Judah's unflinching gaze was still fixed upon him. A half hour must have passed in this way. At the end of that time the horse came to the opening again, trembling, and his coat foam-flecked. The men watched in breathless silence the battle-royal.

"Sugar, Sam," called Judah, still keeping his eye on the horse, and stroking his muzzle gently. The horse was much subdued, and took the lumps of sugar from his hand without an attempt at biting.

"Wal, I'm blessed!" came from the crowd.

"Hand me the bit and bridle, Sam."

"You ain't going inside, Jude?" said the Colonel.

"In a minute, yes."

With a sleight-of-hand movement a bit of sugar was in the creature's mouth, together with the bit, and the strap slipped over his head. The animal was bitted, the bridle in his conqueror's hand.

"Unbolt the door, Sam; open it wide enough for me to get in," and Judah entered the stable. "Steady, boy, steady. Sh— ho!" talking to, coaxing the half-cowed beast, the boy got the saddle on his back, and tightened the girths. "Now, gentlemen," called Judah, "Sam will fling open the door the minute I seize the bridle. Stand clear for your lives."

He gathered curb and snaffle at the loop into his bridle-hand, slid his right down and gripped it close at the bit. Before the animal could bite, rare or kick, the door was flung wide and man and steed dashed out together, Judah letting go his right hand and flinging himself into the saddle instantly, tightening the curb with both hands, and driving his feet into the stirrups.

A buzz of excitement and admiration broke from the crowd of men now too deeply stirred for words. The battle-royal had begun. The horse plunged forward, reared wildly, pawed the air, and whirled around. Judah struck him a hard blow between the ears with the whip, only to have him kick out behind in a furious attempt to throw the rider over his head. In rapid succession the animal plunged, reared, kicked, ran to and fro, and suddenly made a buckleap into the air. There was an exclamation, followed by a ringing cheer, as the men saw the boy still keeping his seat. The moment the creature's hoofs touched the ground, Judah drove the spurs into his flanks and they dashed away at a mad gallop. Then followed an exhibition of the most daring horsemanship ever witnessed in Kansas City. Rising in his stirrups, Judah, while keeping perfect control of the animal, converted the four acres of enclosure into a circus-arena, round which the horse was forced at a gallop under the sting of the whip, and in the true style of reckless Indian riding on the Western plains.

"Well done!' "Hurrah for the nigger! he's beat the hoss into the middle o' nex' week!" These and similar exclamations broke from the delighted spectators. Beaten completely, trembling in every limb and flecked with foam, the horse followed his conqueror quietly to the stables.

Colonel Titus was throwing his hat wildly up in the air in the enthusiasm of the moment, but Bill Thomson stood quietly by with an evil look distorting his face into a grin of malice and fury.

"Say, Colonel," whispered a man in the crowd, "I wudn't be in that ar nigger's shoes, not fer no money. Bill's mad 'cause he'd beat the hoss."

"Oh, that's all right. Bill's square. Come, all hands, let's go up to the house and liquor. What'll you have?" The Colonel bore the reputation of being the freest gentleman in Kansas City.

For a number of days after this affair, Thomson went about the farm in a brown study. As the men had said, he was "bilin' mad 'cause the nigger had got the dead wood on him." He's got to be broken in; he knows too much," he might have been heard muttering between his clinched teeth.

Judah had received an ovation from the sporting fraternity

and bade fair to become a popular idol. Thomson was offered
large sums of money for him from several men, but refused
them all with the words, "Money won't buy him till I'm
through with him."

Because of his daughter's feelings slaves were never whipped
on the plantation, but were sent to the slave prison in the
city.

About a week later Judah was ordered to take a note to the
prison in Kansas city. Being a new comer on the plantation,
he was not yet familiar with its ways, and taking the note,
suspecting no evil, delivered it at the "bell gate." The man
who received the note after reading it called to a burly Negro:
"Pete take this nigger, and strap him down upon the stretcher;
get him ready for business."

"What are you going to do to me?" cried the horrified lad,
at the man's words.

"You'll know d——d quick! Strip yourself; I don't wan to
tear your clothes with my whip. I'm going to tear your black
skin."

Finding that pleading would be in vain, the lad fought
madly, until overcome by three sturdy blacks who were called
in to assist. They felled him to the ground and bound him
with cords.

"Take him to the shed," commanded the whipper. "String
him up to a cross-beam. He's to have twenty lashes to
begin with, then he's to be whipped until we have orders to
stop."

Strung up by his thumbs to the cross-beams, gashed,
bleeding, every blow of the whip was torturing agony. The
boy uttered not a groan. He had learned his lesson of
endurance in the schools of the Indian stoic, and he bore his
punishment without a murmur. But every stroke of the

merciless lash was engraved on his heart in bleeding stripes that called for vengeance. In the midst of the scene Thomson strolled in.

"Very good," he said, after viewing the work a moment. "Let him breathe a minute, boys, then ten more. Now, Judah, this is a taste of wholesome discipline you're getting. You've got to be brung down. I'm going to do it if I have to have you whipped every month for a year. I'm goin' to break your spirit and teach you a nigger's place; an' if your life's wurth anything to you the quicker you learn your lesson the better. No more high-head carryin', gentlemanly airs, and dictionary talk; breaking hosses in ain't wuth a cent to a nigger," he added with a malicious leer. "All right, boys, give him ten more," and while they were being administered the monster stood by calmly smoking his cigar.

"Got grit," said the whipper. "Ain't whimpered."

"Now, boys, ease up again while I finish my little speech to the gentleman."

"You've got to learn to say 'massa.' It don' matter what you can do nor how much you know, nor how handsome you think yourself, you ain't one grain better than any other nigger on the plantation. If you forget this lesson, it'll be the worse for you. Now, once more, boys," he continued, turning to the whippers, "make it a dozen and smart ones to wind up with!"

* * * * *

All this had happened in the first year of captivity, and since that time Judah had apparently learned his place.

CHAPTER VI

It was still the pleasant month of May when, as the Colonel sat in his favorite seat on the back piazza, just before noon Bill Thomson rode up to the back of the house followed by a strange horseman.

"I've brought you a visitor, Colonel, a stranger and yet not a stranger, bein' as we've met before. He brings you news," Thomson called out as they prepared to mount the piazza steps. "Mr. Maxwell, Colonel Titus. Mr. Maxwell has come all the way from London to bring you news from the Hall. Now I know he's welcome. Mr. Maxwell, sir, in the Colonel you see a Southron of the Southrons, but old England will always hold first place in his hospitable heart. So, Colonel?"

"That's the right sound, William. Mr. Maxwell, do you stop with us over night sir?"

"I fear that I must tax your hospitality to that extent. Your uncle died six months ago. The estate will be yours in one year if the direct heir is not found. Your signature will be needed to certain papers that will prove your identity and residence here, and we shall also want affidavits made out for filing. All this is a mere formality required by law. Of course, Mr. Pendleton has charge of the estates, being the family lawyer, and is only anxious that the rightful heir inherit. You remember Mr. Pendleton, do you not, Colonel Titus?"

"Oh, yes! Old Pen, we boys used to call him. I hope he'll continue to look after my affairs, if the estate comes to me. I remember him as a very reliable man."

Warren bowed in acknowledgement of the compliment

paid his chief. "I have no doubt he will be pleased to serve you. There is very little doubt of your succeeding to the baronetcy—practically we have demonstrated that fact, and I think your claims pass unquestioned."

"Be seated, Mr. Maxwell; make yourself comfortable. Jude!" he called, "Jude, I say!"

Maxwell started involuntarily, as Judah came out from the hallway. At last he had found a clew to the lost ones! His pulses beat fast, but his facial muscles told no tale. But his almost imperceptible start was noticed by the two men, who exchanged glances.

"Take the gentleman's horse, and tell Mrs. Thomson we have a guest over night," said the Colonel to the waiting servant. Judah's impassive face gave forth not a gleam of intelligence as he departed to obey his master's orders.

"Now, Mr. Maxwell," said the Colonel as they sat sipping the fragrant mixture sent out to them by Mrs. Thomson by the unfortunate Tennie, "you said something about no dispute over my being next of kin. Kindly explain that remark."

"Certainly," replied Warren, smiling. "This is my second trip to America in two years, hunting up the Carlingford heirs. I thought I had found Lord George's younger son, Henry, on my first trip, but after a fruitless chase, I was forced to give it up. We are convinced that he is dead and without issue."

"Just so! Poor Henry! His was a sad fate. But it was his destiny. Do you believe in destiny, my young friend?"

"I believe that many things we call destiny may be over-come by resolving to conquer difficulties, not allowing them to conquer us."

"True, very true," replied the Colonel, meditatively.

"Mr. Maxwell, you have expressed the position of our

people to a dot concerning the little difficulty we are having with Kansas. Now the North thinks they're going to beat in the fight, and the fools are going to try to fight us, but it's the destiny of the South to rule in this glorious country, an' if it ain't our destiny we'll make it so, d——d if we don't when I get the boys fixed. Got a cool two hundred and fifty coming down here from Virginia nex' week; boys who don' care a cuss what they do so long as they beat the Free States out."

"Thomson," broke in the Colonel, "it appears to me that I have seen Mr. Maxwell before. What do you say?"

"I reckon you have. Don' you remember our hunting trip at Erie two years ago? and the murder of White Eagle?"

"Sure enough! Mr. Maxwell was the young Englishman who took such a prominent part in the affair."

Warren bowed gravely.

"Most unfortunate affair! Strange, too, that the man should have been killed just when the children needed him most. If he had lived, Thomson, in all probability, would not have recovered his property." He paused with a keen glance in Warren's quiet face, but it told nothing. His voice, too, was calm and even as he inquired:

"Then Mr. Thomson was the owner of the unfortunate children?"

"Yes," returned Thomson, "I'd been hunting them gals and their mother for nigh fifteen years, an' it was just luck and chance my meeting up with them young ones."

Warren puffed away at his cigar as though it were his only object in life.

"Fine cigar," he observed, at length.

"Particularly fine. The tobacco was raised by my own hands right over there for my private use," said the Colonel.

"What do you think of our institutions, Mr. Maxwell?" asked Thomson, nonchalently. "They've made this country. 'Spose you have some compunctions of conscience over us, eh? Most Englishmen do at first. But, man, look at the advantage it gives, the prosperity it brings, the prestige it gives our fine gentry all over the world. You must confess that we are a grand people."

"Yet you complained of a tea tax, and fought a 'liberty fight' on that pretext," observed Warren drily.

"Jes' so, jes' so! But see what we've done for the Africans, given them the advantages of Christian training, and a chance to mingle, although but servants, in the best circles of the country. The niggers have decidedly the best of it. The masters suffer from their ignorance and incompetency."

"How do you think the excitement over the Kansas-Nebraska matter will end?" questioned Maxwell, avoiding a statement of his own opinions.

"There are warm times ahead. The Yankees have got to be forced to leave the States. We'll make ourselves a living terror to them. The trouble is bein' stirred up by a lot of psalm singing abolitionists and an old lunatic named Brown. Yankees won't fight; they'll scatter like chaff before my Rangers. Now, there's fighting blood for you; every man owns a nigger and loves the South and her institutions, an' they ain't goin' to be beat out o' Kansas for an extension to the institution."

"Well, gentlemen, my opinion is that you are wrong. A government cannot prosper founded on crushed and helpless humanity," replied Maxwell firmly.

"Well, well," interrupted the Colonel, "There are two sides to every question. Some day—soon, perhaps, you will realize that we are a chivalrous, gallant people, worthy of the admiration of the world."

"While the Free Staters think themselves in the right, you also feel that your side is right."

"Precisely. They have inherited their ideas as we have ours. We do not agree. It is our duty to convince them of their error, and with God's help we will do it."

"But surely, you do not defend the atrocities committed against helpless women and children that are perpetrated by your side in Kansas every day?"

"Defend them? No! But I sympathize with the feelings of the perpetrators. You condemn them wholly without comprehending them or their motives, thus injuring them and doing mischief to yourself. Each group of men in this country has its own standard of right and wrong, and we won't give our ideas up for no d——d greasy, Northern mechanic."

"That's the right sort, Colonel," nodded Thomson, in sypmathetic approval.

The announcement that dinner was served cut short further discussion, much to Warren's relief. The Colonel's words impressed the young man greatly. But ever in opposition to specious argument arose thoughts of Winona and Judah and the terrible work done at the sacking of Oswatamie.

The remainder of the day was spent in riding over the plantation, and studying the beauties of the "institution" as propounded by the philosophical Colonel. Once only, Warren's anxious gaze descried Winona wheeling the chair of her crippled mistress up and down the lawn, but when the men returned to the house both were invisible.

He and the Colonel were seated upon the piazza in the soft Southern night talking over the points of law in claiming the

Carlingford estate, when Mrs. Thomson called the latter for a moment into the house. Something blacker than the black night passed him as he sat there alone. Warren was startled, and it was some moments after the figure passed, before he realized that a man had spoken to him in passing: "Leave your window unlatched."

Pleading fatigue, the young man retired early, but not to sleep. His pulse beat at fever heat; his excited fancy could detect the sound of drums and the hurrying of marching feet. He sunk into a feverish slumber, from which he was awakened by the weeping of distressed females. He listened—all was still; it was the imagination again. He could not sleep, so he arose and looked carefully after his pistols. Danger seemed all about him, but he unlatched the window and drew it back softly, then stretched himself again upon the bed.

About one o'clock he was awakened from a light slumber by some one shaking him, and sitting up, found Judah beside him,—his dark face distinctly visible by the moon's dim light. Sitting in the darkness, the sweet scent of the magnolia enveloping them in its fragrance, the faint sounds of insect life mingling with the murmur of rustling leaves. Warren Maxwell listened to whispered words that harrowed up his very soul. To emphasize his story, Judah stripped up his shirt and seizing the young white man's hand pressed it gently over the scars and seams stamped upon his back.

"I could bear it all, Mr. Maxwell," he concluded, "but Winona—" here his voice broke. "They've educated her to increase her value in the slave market, and next week Mr. Thomson takes her and me up the river to sell us to the highest bidder. If help does not come I have sworn to kill her before she shall become slavery's victim. It is impossible for me to put in words the fate of a beautiful female slave on these plantations; the torture of hell cannot surpass it."

A great wave of admiration swept over Warren at Judah's words. It was the involuntary tribute of Nature to nobility of would wherever found. The boy had become a man, and his demeanor was well calculated to inspire admiration and trust. Something truly majestic—beyond his years—had developed in his character. Warren thought him a superb man, and watched him, fascinated by his voice, his language, and his expressive gestures. Slavery had not contaminated him. His life with White Eagle had planted refinement inbred. In him was the true expression of the innate nature of the Negro when given an opportunity equal with the white man.

Impulsively, Maxwell laid his arm affectionately about the neck and shoulders of the youth.

"No extremes, Judah, until all else fails. I can buy you both if it comes to that, and my promise to take you to England with me still holds good."

"I doubt that you will be allowed to buy us. There is a stronger reason for our destruction underlying all this than is apparent. Don't let it be known that we have held any communication with you, or that you are at all interested in our fate. Be cautious."

"I will remember. But I shall have to study this matter over. I hardly know how to meet this issue if the use of money is denied us. When do you leave?"

"Monday, on the 'Crescent.' "

"Then I'll plead pressing business and leave tomorrow to meet you on board the steamer when she sails. Trust me, Judah, I will not fail you."

The tears were in Judah's throat as he tried to thank him.

"I do trust you Mr. Maxwell, next to God. I knew you would be here soon; I dreamt a year ago that I saw you coming toward me out of a cloud of intense blackness. I have watched for you ever since. I was not at all surprised when I saw you riding up the avenue today; only for my hope in you as our deliverer, I'd have shot myself months ago."

"There is a God, Judah," replied Warren solemnly.

"But He seems far off from my unfortunate race," replied the man bitterly.

"Never doubt Him; His promises are aye and amen. With God's aid, I will save you or sacrifice myself."

They parted as silently as they had met.

CHAPTER VII

The steamer "Crescent" tugged and pulled at her moorings as if impatient of delay. It wanted two hours of sailing time. Down the gang-plank a strange figure sauntered, clad in buckskin breeches suspended by one strap over a flannel shirt open at the throat; high-topped boots confined the breeches at the knee; a battered hat was pushed back from a rubicand face, and about his waist a belt bristled with pistols and bowie knives. Warren smiled at the odd figure, then, with an exclamation of surprise, threw away his cigar and walked up to the newcomer.

"Mr. Maybee, of Erie?" he queried, holding out his hand.

The party addressed turned his round, smiling face in Maxwell's direction, and after one searching glance that swept his countenance in every lineament, grasped the proffered hand in a mighty clasp.

"Dog my cats, ef it ain't Mr. Maxwell! I'm pow'ful glad

to meet you ag'in. How long you been here? Whar you bound?"

"I landed in New York just four weeks ago. Still on business for my firm."

"I 'spose it's in order to look out fer adventures when you an' me gits together. Remember the fus' night we met? What a swingin' ol' time we had. Poor old White Eagle! Nary sound have I heard, Mr. Maxwell, since, of them unfortoonit children neither. Might a been swallered like Jonah by the whale for all I know. I'm right chicken-hearted when I wake up at night, an' think about the leetle gal, po' pretty critter!"

"Mr. Maybee, I feel like a miserable cur whenever I think how supinely I have rested while such a horror was perpetrated—and yet I call myself a man! Your government cannot long survive under a system that thrusts free-born people into slavery as were those helpless children. May I have a word with you in private?"

"Hu—sh!" said Mr. Maybee, looking cautiously around, "them are sentimen's breathes pizen in this loorid atmosphere. Ef one of the galoots walkin' about this deck was to hear you, you'd dance on air at the yard arm in about two minutes. Them's dang'rous opinions to hold onto in free Ameriky," replied Mr. Maybee with a sly twinkle in his eye. "See that pile o' lumber out on the wharf? Well, that's the best place I know on to have a leetle private conversation with a friend. The boat won't start fer some time yet, an' I can straddle one end o' the pile an' keep a sharp lookout for listeners."

"There'll be a war in this country in less than two years, I predict," continued Maxwell, as they walked ashore. "No need o' waitin' two years, mister; jes' make it two months. The prelude to the war that's comin' was struck last fall when all Western Missouri poured into Kansas an' took the ballot

out of the hands of our citizens, sir. Eli Thayer's teachin' all
the North to emigrate into bleedin' Kansas an' fight it out.
That's me, mister; I says to Ma' Jane, my wife, 'good-bye,
Ma' Jane, ef I don't come back you'll know I've gone in a
good cause, but John Brown's calling for volunteers an' I'm
boun' to be in the fight.' So, I've left her power of attorney,
an' the business all in her name, an' here I am. It beats all
natur how fightin' jes' grows on a man once he's had a taste.
Mr. Maxwell, do you know anythin' about the transfiguration
of souls that some college fellars advocates? Dad gum it, I
believe mos' of us must have been brutes once. Yes, sir, dogs
an' vicious hosses, an' contrary mulses an' venomous reper-
tiles. Yes, sir, there's goin' to be a fight, an' I'm spilin' to
git in it."

"Is it possible that matters are as critical as you say?"

"Critical! You may call 'em so, my boy. Six months ago I
took up a claim outside o' Lawrence. One mornin', a fortnit
later, twenty-eight men tied their hosses to the fence and one
asked me: "Whar you from? East?' 'Yes," says I. 'Then you're
a d——d abolitionist,' another says politely. 'Of course,' says
I, an' in less than a half-hour the place was cleaned out, my
shack burnt to the ground an' my cattle driven off. Me an'
two or three of the boys put up a decent fight or I wouldn't
be sittin' here talkin' to you today. 'Taint their fault."

"You amaze me, Mr. Maybee."

"Do I?" queried the other with a grim smile. "Well here's
another nice leetle caper o' theirs: Bud Wilson's wife writ
home to her folks in Massachusetts detailin' some o' the facts
concernin' the sackin' o' Oswatamie, an' addin' a few words
in her own language in comments, etc., on certain actions o'
the Territory militit (Missouri roughs), an' her folks let the
newspapers have the whole story. My soul! The Rangers came

over from this side under that devil, Bill Thomson, an' one mornin' when Bud was gone they went to the house an' took his ol' woman inter the woods an' pulled her tongue out as far as possible an' tied it to a sapling. Well, I won't pain yer feelin's by recountering the rest o' the po' critter's sufferin's, but they was the mos' dreadfulles' that you can imagine, until she mercifully gave up the ghos' and ex-pired. How's that strike you?"

"My God!" exclaimed Warren, shuddering with horror.

"Here's another: These same Kickapoo Rangers, Bill Thomson captaing, marched to Leavenworth an' took Capt. R. P. Brown (no relation to Capt. John Brown) prisoner, he surrenderin' himself and men on certain conditions. Imme-juntly the terms of that surrender was violated. One young feller was knocked down, an' a Ranger was goin' to cut him with his hatchet (Thomson has 'em all carry hatchets so as to skulp the foe like Injuns do), and Capt. Brown prevented him. After that they removed the Captaing up to Easton an' put him in a separate buildin' away from his men. Then the devils rushed on him an' beat him to the floor an' cut him in the head with their hatchets, one wound bein' many inches long an' enterin' the brain. The gallant Captaing was at the mercy of his enemies then, an' they jumped on him an' kicked him. Desparately wounded, he still lived; an' as they kicked him, he said, 'Don't abuse me; it is useless; I am dying.' Then one of the wretches—Bill himself—leaned over the posterate man an' squirted tobacco juice in his eyes. Them's our leetle ways o' doin' things in free Ameriky, Mr. Britisher, when other folks talks too free or dares to have opinions o' thar own without askin' our permission to so think contrairy agin us. Yes, sir, I'm a John Brown man. I go with Brown because I can do as I please—more in-dependent-like—than as if I was with Jim Lane, 'though I'll 'low Lane's gittin' in some fine work, an' we'll swing Kansas inter line as a free State quicker'n scat when we git down to bisiness. It's these things brings me on this side noysterin' roun' lookin' for employment."

"I'm a pretty good shot, Mr. Maybee, and after I finish this matter for the firm, I should like nothing better than to put myself and my pistols at the disposal of Mr. Brown," said Warren sternly, with flashing eyes.

Mr. Maybee ejected a small stream of tobacco juice from his mouth and smoothed the end of the board he was whittling, to his entire satisfaction, before replying.

"Volunteers is ac-ceptable, certainly, ef they brings weapons and ammunition. This is goin' to be no child's play. The oppersite party is strong in cussedness; on our side, we know we're right, an' we've made up our minds to die right on the spot, but never to yield. Still, we're not advertisin' our idees on the housetops, my friend; di-plomacy, says I an' all of us, is an ef-fectooal weapin' in many cases, therefore I advocate that we perceed to di-plomate—kin' o' play 'roun' a spell, an' feel the t'other side. I'll consider it an honor to nesheate you any time you feel too sot, into the ranks of the Free Soilers, John Brown, captaing. Now, what's the business you wanted to lay befo' me?"

Thoroughly aroused by Maybee's words and trembling with excitement, Warren briefly related his unexpected meeting with Judah, and the peril of the captives. Mr. Maybee listened in amazement, chewing and spitting tobacco juice like an automaton in his excitement, with many ejaculations of surprise: "Sho now! "Want ter know!" "That ar Thomson, too! Dad gum 'im fer an onery skunk! I've jes' got to kill 'im; can't help it! He hung three of our best men down to

Oscaloosa two weeks ago, tortured 'em fus' tho'." "Cu'rous how things does happen in this sinful wurl!"

"They mus' be rescued right off! right off!" he said, when Warren had finished. "We must git 'em on the Underground railroad this night. You go with the boat an' I'll cut across country an' com—moonicate with Parson Steward. We've got a good hour's start of the vessel, an' there'll be sand-bars to cross,—an',—O Lord, ef we'd only git such a thunder storm as we had the night White Eagle was murdered, it'd be the makin' of this expe—dition. It's been threat'ning all afternoon. Lord, let her come."

Briefly they arranged their plans.

"Tell Judah to git Thomson drunk; put somethin' in the liquor, if necess'ry, then git ashore somehow at Weston. I'll meet you there with hosses an' we'll put fer Steward's shack. Ef once he gits the gal in his clutches, even Bill Thomson won't git her agin."

With hurried good-byes the men separated, Mr. Maybee going up the wharf at a swift gait. Warren went aboard the steamer and seated himself in a secluded corner to watch for Judah and mature his plans.

Just before the last bell rang Thomson came aboard with his slaves. Even the rude passengers were moved by the beauty of the slave girl. Every soft curve of her waist and supple body was followed by the close-fitting cotton gown; her hair, worn short since captivity, clustered in a rich, ravelled plume about her brows and neck; the soft, gazelle-like eyes were large with anxiety, but her step was firm, and she bore herself like a young princess as she crossed the deck to go below. The girlish figure appealed to Warren's tender heart. He was used to the society of famous beauties in the proudest court of the Old World; he had flirted and danced with them in the abandonment of happy youthful hours, and more than one lovely girl had been smitten with his frank, good-looking boyish face and honest, manly bearing, but never before had his heart contracted and thrilled as it did now under the one appealing glance thrown hurriedly and timidly in his direction by the young slave girl.

Scarcely were they under way when the threatening storm was upon them. It began in a dreary drizzle with occasional mutterings of thunder.

Warren noticed that Judah was seated on the deck in the slave-pen next to an airshaft, and he concluded to find the cabin communication with the shaft and reach Judah by it.

The night fell fast. Maxwell hid himself in his stateroom before supper, having made the pleasing discovery that a port-hole in his stateroom opened directly beside Judah's seat on the deck. A note was easily slipped to the slave telling him of Mr. Maybee's plan, and asking what was the best course to pursue, then he sat there in darkness waiting a movement on Judah's part, assured that his fertile brain would find a plan of escape.

In the cabin Thomson was the center of a congenial set of kindred spirits, young Virginians, going back to St. Louis after a campaign against the Free Soilers. They were reciting the glories of the expedition,—singing, shouting and making night hideous. Their favorite song ended in an uproarious chorus:

> You Yankees tremble, and
> Abolitionists fall:
> Our motto is, Southern Rights
> For all!

One of their number had been fatally shot in a quarrel at a hotel in Kansas City; they were carrying the body home, and had ordered the coffin brought in and placed in the center of the cabin, where, as they said, the poor fellow might have the comfort of witnessing one more good time even though beyond the possibility of joining in it.

In the gambling and drinking bout that followed, Thomson was the most reckless, and soon he, and the rest of the party, was stretched upon the floor, on tables, and lounges in a drunken stupor from which nothing could arouse them. The few women passengers were fastened in their staterooms.

Warren took his saddle-bags in his hand, and stole out upon the deck, picking his way in disgust among the bestial party blocking his path. Half-way to Weston they had struck upon a sand-bar and there they hung, shuddering and groaning in the teeth of the storm.

He seated himself near the railing. The rolling thunder mingled with the hoarse shouting of the officers and the answering cries of the crew. There were flashes of lightning at intervals. Presently a soft touch fell on his arm. He turned and saw Judah crouching in the shadow of a mast.

"They won't be off this bar before morning. I'm going to drop a boat over the side the next heavy crash that comes. Winona is waiting just back of you. It'll take nerve, but it is the only way. We must be silent and careful."

The soft murmur ended, and once more Maxwell was alone. He had noticed the small boats standing along the sides of the vessel as he came aboard in the afternoon, but had not thought of utilizing them for the purpose of rescue. His heart beat to suffocation, his nerves were strung to their utmost tension. A soft hand stole into his; he pressed it convulsively, instinctively knowing that it was Winona, but they exchanged no words.

There came a deafening crash. The bolt struck a capstan, knocking down the first mate and glancing off into the sea.

Surely God was with them. Simultaneously with the crash there was a faint plash in the water, but the vivid lightning flash that followed revealed nothing. There came a lull in the storm but confusion reigned on the vessel; no one thought of the slaves. "Now!" came a warning whisper. In an instant Warren grasped the girl about the waist, swung her clear of the railing and held her suspended by the wrists over the black, boiling flood. "All right, let her drop!" came in another whisper. Warren let go his hold and listened with bated breath for the result. There came another faint plash, a grating sound as the foaming waves carried the little craft against the wooden ribs of the steamer. Then silence.

Judah, standing upright in the boat, caught Winona in his arms as deftly as a ball is caught and tossed from one player to another. His Indian training in managing canoes made him fearless now, and his giant strength served him well.

"All right; come ahead," came to Warren's listening ears. He dropped his saddle-bags, instantly following them; he let himself down hand over hand, then swung clear and landed lightly in the center of the frail craft, steadied by the giant black. Silently the little party rested in the shadow of the great hull until another lightning flash had passed, then each man settled an oar in the row-locks, and Judah pushed off into the night.

(To be continued.)

CHAPTER VIII

There came a knock at Preacher Sampson Steward's cabin door that same night about midnight. Instantly his mind was on the alert. He had been stretched on the bed at full length for an hour listening intently to sounds outside. The thunder and lightning had ceased, and the rain and the wind beat a monotonous tattoo against the window panes. There was a world of possibilities in that knock. He could not from the sound tell whether it heralded peace or war, and these were troublous times in Kansas. It was in Preacher Steward's nature to speak his convictions fearlessly, and this made him a special object of hatred to many pro-slavery men who would have gladly rid the country of his presence, did not his well known courage and marksmanship afford him some protection against open attack.

A tallow candle sputtered in its place on the stand. Near the stand was the window, protected by a wooden shutter. Beside him on the bed where he lay half-dressed, his wife and two children lay wrapped in slumber. The knock was repeated; Steward sprang to the floor, reached out his hand and grasped his pistols, laying them handy for use on the stand by the sputtering candle, seized his rifle, cocked it, slipped the heavy iron bolt of the door with his free hand, stepped back a pace and drew a bead on the door, then with set face and tightly drawn lips, he said firmly:

"Come in!"

The door swung open, admitting a gust of rain and wind. The tall, stout figure of Ebenezer Maybee was outlined against the blackness of the night, his attire plentifully sprinkled with the mud and rain. One hand held a driving whip, the other grasped the door-latch, while his keen eyes watched the white face behind the rifle whose muzzle almost touched his breast, yet giving no sign of fear.

"What!" The parson turned fighter with a vengeance," he said at length, in quiet tones. "This ain't at all 'bligatory on you, Steward. You ought to know my knock by this time. Put up your gun."

Steward instantly complied.

"Is it you, Maybee?" he queried, standing the weapon with its muzzle against the wall. "Come in!"

"Somethin' inter-estin' you've picked up by the way of makin' your friends welcome, Steward?" Maybee replied, with a grim smile, as he closed the door and advanced to grasp the minister's extended hand.

"God forgive me, Maybee, but it is more than human nature can stand. Sunday week it was only by a special act of Providence that my congregation escaped massacre. Since then I'm a marked man. I am on special guard duty tonight."

"What's up?"

"Had a message from the Rangers."

An exchange of significant glances followed this speech.

"Oh, I see. Perhaps then we'd better bring in our fugitives at once."

"What have you this time?"

"A young man and woman and a young Englishman, who is helping them away. It's a long story. All of 'em's good shots; the gal ain't slow on a pinch."

"Good!" replied the parson, evidently relieved. "We can put her in the loft. The Lord sent you, Maybee; it's inspiration to have some one to help out in an emergency."

"You're really expectin' trouble, then?"

"Yes; but let's get them in as quickly as possible. After that I'll tell you all about it."

The storm had chilled the air, and the parson kindled a fire in the stove, throwing on a plentiful supply of wood.

"I'm ready. Come to the door."

Maybee obeyed; the parson blew out the candle, leaving the room in darkness.

"Now bring them in. I'll stay here till you return. Be careful, and lose no time."

Maybee opened the door and the darkness instantly swallowed him. When he returned with the fugitives, Steward saw dimly, by the firelight shining among the shadows, the beautiful girl and the stalwart black. He regarded Winona with a look of vague wonder and admiration. In all his life he had seen no women to compare with her.

He noted, too, the golden hair and fair complexion of the young Englishman. It was no common party that sought the shelter of his rude cabin on this stormy night. His familiar eye noted the signs of strength, too, in the youthful figures.

"Good!" he told himself. "If we do have a call from the Rangers, we'll die with our boots on; that's some satisfaction."

He beckoned to Maybee, and speaking a few words to his wife who was awake, thrust his pistols into an inner pocket, and directing Warren to bolt the door after them and not to open save at a given signal, the two men went out into the storm to feed and stable the horses. This accomplished, they returned to the house, and after carefully fastening the door, Steward lighted the candle and began preparing supper for his unexpected guests.

"Now, Maybee, where from and where bound? Tell me all about it."

In a few graphic sentences, in his peculiar mixed dialect, Mr. Maybee rehearsed the story with which we are so well acquainted.

The parson listened intently with an occasional shake of the head or a sympathetic glance in the direction of Winona. "I caught up with 'em at the ferry, an' I took the ol' road so's to lessen the chances of pur-suit or of meetin' any on-welcome company on the way. I've sent word to Captaing Brown to look out for us. It was a bluff game with odds, but we've won," he concluded.

Steward laughed.

"We have generally proved winners even with the odds against us."

Warren leaned back against the wall of the rude cabin wearied from the long nervous strain, but listening intently to all that passed.

"Judah's a lion, and Winona has the pluck of a man," Maybee went on. "She doesn't whimper, but jes' saws wood an' keeps to her in-structions."

Warren spoke now.

"You have as many manoeuvres to gain admittance to your house as some of the Indian fighters I used to read about when a boy. What are you expecting tonight, Mr. Steward?"

"Some of the gang," replied the parson, stopping in his occupation of cutting strips of bacon for the frying pan. "They have threatened me with vengeance because I sheltered John Brown and his men on their way north a month or two back. Reynolds brought me word this morning that they had concluded to visit me tonight. Reynolds hasn't the nerve to come out as I do, and avow his principles, but maybe it's better so that the gang don't know it; through him I keep informed of all their movements."

"Don't know thar leetle program, do you?" carelessly questioned Maybee, as he threw back the lid of the coffee-pot to keep its contents from boiling over.

"No; Reynolds didn't learn that," replied Steward, as he adjusted the meat in the pan and placed it over the fire, "He thinks their intention is to decorate my anatomy with tar and feathers."

"Mos' cert'n'ly," nodded Maybee, as he took his turn at tending the frying meat while Steward sliced potatoes to brown in the bacon fat after the meat was cooked.

"Mr. Steward, if we had been of their number when we came to the door just now, what would you have done?" asked Warren.

The parson held his knife over a half-peeled potato, and looked the young man in the face, while his eyes glowed with excitement.

"Well, had you been one of Bill Thomson's riders, I would have sent a bullet through you without a word. It is written: 'This day will the Lord deliver thee into my hand; and I will smite thee, and take thy head from thee.' "

"Pardon me for what I am about to say," continued Warren, "but I cannot understand how you can reconcile such a proposed course with your profession. I make no pretention to piety myself, but I have a profound respect for those who conscientiously do."

The preacher faltered.

"Don't misunderstand me," Warren hastened to say, seeing the man of God hesitate. "I am not charging you with anything. I simply cannot reconcile the two ideas, that's all. I don't quite understand your position."

"That's jest what I've wanted to say to Steward here, many a time, but not being gifted with gab, which mos' people calls eddi-kation, I haven't been able to perceed like the prefesser," meaning our English friend, Mr. Maxwell. "Thar was that secret citizens' meetin' down in the timber, and Steward was fer shootin' down at sight without a trial all onery cusses that was even suspected of bein' onfriendly to the principles of the Free-Staters. Dad gum 'em, that's my methods to a T, but it's kin' o' rough jestice fer a parson," chuckled Maybee.

"Well, gentlemen, what would you do in my place? What show have I against a gang of ten or more men unless I meet them promptly with the initiative? What better course could I have pursued with the mob that came to our church during service? When I beheld them round about us and heard their savage cries, when I saw the terror of the women and children and bethought me of their fate if perchance, the men were all slain, I girded up my loins and taking a pistol in each hand, I led forth my elders and members against the Philistines; and I said to them: 'This day I will give the carcasses of your hosts unto the fowls of the air, and the wild beasts of the earth; that all the earth may know that there is a God in Israel." Verily, not one was spared.

"Tonight I was here single-handed. I have a wife and two children dependent on me for support. Must I be denied the right of defense gainst superior numbers because I hate slavery and have the courage of my convictions?"

The speaker's eyes—his whole face, in fact—glowed and scintillated with holy wrath and conviction in the justice of his case.

"No, let me explain further!" Warren hastened to exclaim, "It is not your defense that I question, but your aggressive spirit. Now, as I understand it, these men are a part of the territorial militia; if so, do not your acts smack somewhat of treason?"

"Treason! the word by which traitors seek to hang those who resist them. I hate the laws that make this country a nursery for slavery, and I resist them by rescuing all who come to me for refuge. Three hundred will not excuse the number that have passed this station on the underground railroad since I have been here. Oppression is oppression, whether it enslaves men and women and makes them beasts of burden, or shuts your mouth and mine if we utter humane protests against cruelty. If this is treason, make the most of it; there's one thing certain, unless I am caught napping, they are going to pay dearly for whatever advantage they secure over me."

"I concur with you," Warren replied, rising from his seat, and pacing back and forth thoughtfully. "You have a perfect right to defend your home from brutal attack, and so long as I am here I am subject to your orders. But let us hope the storm will soon blow over; the South well see its error and the Negroes will be granted freedom by peaceful means."

Steward and Maybee laughed silently and heartily at the young man's earnest words.

"Ef you stayed 'roun' here long nuff and warn't a British subjec', my fren', you might git a taste of this scrimmage that'd con-vince you that the South is a horned hornet on the nigger question. Time 'n tide nor God A'mighty won't change the onery skunks. Them's my sentimen's."

"The storm," said Judah with wild exultation in his voice, "the storm is but gathering force. These bloody happenings which are convulsing Missouri and Kansas are but the pre-liminary happenings to a glorious struggle which will end in the breaking of every chain that binds human beings to servitude in this country."

Warren regarded him in astonishment.

"Why do you think so, Judah?"

"I cannot tell. But I feel that the sin will be punished in a great outpouring of blood and treasure until God says it is enough. The day of deliverance of the Negro is at hand."

"Amen! The boy is a true prophet. 'Behold, the Lord's hand is not shortened, that it cannot save; neither his ear heavy, that it cannot hear.' Bring your chairs up to the table and have some hot coffee and a bit to eat."

The meal over, from which all rose refreshed and strengthened, Steward placed a ladder against the wall and mounting it, threw back a trap door in the ceiling closely concealed by festoons of strings of dried apples and bunches of onions and herbs. He then returned to the room and lit an extra candle, beckoning Winona to follow him up the steep ascent. Speaking a few words of caution to her, he descended the ladder, which he removed and put out of sight. Warren watched his movements with great curiosity. How fast he was gaining a true knowledge of life and living here in these American wilds among a rough but kindly people. These friends of the fugitive slaves lived by but one principle, "Greater love than this hath no man."

His refined sensibilities were satisfied by the melodramatic coloring of his surroundings. The atmosphere of art had affected him enough for him to perceive the beauties of the picture made by the stalwart men, the gigantic black's refined prowess and the noble lines and graceful pose of Winona's neck and shoulders.

Preacher Steward moved out a number of wooden sea chests from beneath the tall, four-posted bed where his wife and children lay wrapped in slumber. He spread at the extreme back of the open space a pair of blankets and then signed Judah to creep under the bed; when he had done so, the parson pushed back the trunks as nearly as possible to their old positions, thus completely concealing the fugitive from view.

"We can't start before five o'clock, and we may as well get all the rest we can," said Maybee.

It was after midnight when Warren, Maybee and their host lay down upon the floor which was spread with a buffalo robe and blankets.

"It's the best the railroad can offer under the circumstances. The railroad isn't wealthy and we have to put up with some discomforts."

"This beats sleeping on the ground without blankets, as we sometimes bivouac out to Captaing Brown's camp, all holler," replied Maybee, sleepily. "Declar', I'm dead beat."

"As I understand it, this isn't a railroad; it is only hiding fugitives as they pass to Canada."

"Exactly. But many people believe in an underground railroad, with regular trains running on time, stopping points, and everything in railroad style?"

"Really?"

"You bet," grunted Maybee, half-asleep.

"Yes, sir; some men of fair intelligence, too, have faith in it. They can account for the results we accomplish in no other way. A fugitive is passed along by us, night after night, until he secures his freedom. Our methods are a profound mystery."

"Let 'm stop right thar," returned Maybee. "You fellers'd better git to sleep."

Steward extinguished the light, placed his weapons where

they could be reached instantly, and laid down by Warren. The rain still fell gently down in a patter on the roof, the little clock ticked in its place over the wooden stand. Warren could not sleep. An hour passed. There was a footstep. Warren's ear alone caught the sound. He raised himself on his elbow and grasped his pistol. There were more steps. They came nearer. A hand was passed cautiously over the door. Warren touched the form of Steward.

"What is it?" he asked in a whisper.

"Listen!"

The movement at the door continued as softly as before.

"Who's there?" called out Steward.

"Travellers; we want to find the road."

"Where from?"

"Missouri."

"Where yer boun?" shouted Maybee, jumping to his feet. There was a sound of parleying in subdued voices at Maybee's question. Then came the answer, "Nebraska."

"You're right for that. This is the Jim Lane route. Keep the main road and you'll not miss it," again answered Steward. A moment passed. Then came the inquiry: "Can you put us up till mornin,?"

"Cayn't do it," spoke up Maybee again. "Our beds are full. How many of you?"

"Two"

"Sorry, but you'll have to keep on. Can't do anything for you."

"Say, have you seen anything of a nigger man an' gal an' a white man a-pilotin' 'em?"

"Nary one, mister," again spoke up Maybee.

"Reckon we'll push on then."

The sound of horses' feet died in the distance.

After that there was no more sleep in the cabin, though the remainder of the night passed in quiet.

Steward and his guests were early astir. The storm had cleared. The men left the house to prepare for an early start at the first streaks of dawn; when they returned, Mrs. Steward had breakfast ready.

Silence pervaded the little band. Each was pre-occupied with thoughts he did not care to discuss.

CHAPTER IX

In the early morning light they rode away through the quiet beauty of the woods. The sweetness of the cool air was grateful to them after the feverish anxiety of the night. The dew of the morning sparkled on bud and leaf, and the sunlight sifted dimly through the trees.

Parson Steward rode at the head of the small cavalcade, and Mr. Maybee at the rear; Winona was between Warren and Judah. It was Warren, however, who had helped her to mount and who did the countless trivial things which add to one's comfort, and are so dear to a woman, coming from one man.

Winona was only sixteen, and she was dreaming the first enchanted dream of youth. She did not attempt to analyze the dazzling happiness it was to once more meet and be remembered by the one object of the pure-hearted and passionate hero-worship of her childish soul; but in which, alas! for her lay the very seed of the woman's love, that must now too surely spring up into full life, forcing her presently to know it by its right name.

For two years he had been a cherished, never forgotten

memory; but whom in bodily form she was never to see again. Yet so small is the world, within a week he had suddenly walked into her life again, he had offered his frankest, loyalest friendship, and opened his prisondoors with that strong right hand of his which had both power and will.

She rode along the forest lanes in a waking dream; she was too young to look far into the future, the present was enough for her. One thing was certain, she would never, never marry, because, of course, it was quite impossible she should ever marry Warren Maxwell, and a union with another would be horrible to her.

In the life she had led as a slave, this poor child had learned things from which the doting mother guards the tender maidenhood of her treasure with rigid care; so the girl thought of marriage or its form, with the utmost freedom. No, she would try to serve this man in some way, in the course of her life, she knew not how, but sometime she would be his guardian angel—she would save his life at the sacrifice of her own—nothing was too great to render him in service for his noble generosity.

It was a child's dream in which there mingled unconsciously much of the passionate fervor of the woman, the desire to devote herself and to suffer for her hero, to die for him even, if it would serve him.

As for Warren—no man could look quite unmoved on the living picture the girl made as she sat on her horse with ease and held the reins with no uncertain hand. She was so little changed, yet so much; some taller, but the same graceful form, now so rounded, the same exquisite contour of feature, and soft, dark face so full of character, so vivid with the light of the passionate soul within.

He could not dream the wild leap and throb of the young heart as she turned and caught his blue eyes bent earnestly upon her. She had early learned control in a hard school, but the light in her eyes, the joy in her face, was beyond hiding.

That chemistry of the spirit which draws two irresistibly together, through space and against time and obstacles, kept them conscious only of each other. Winona resisted the intimation of happiness so like what had come to her in her beloved Erie's isle while with her father, yet so unlike. This joy was a beam from heaven; blessedness seemed so near.

Judah watched them, himself forgotten, and his features hardened. Was it for this he had suffered and toiled to escape from his bonds? If they had remained together in slavery, she would have been not one whit above him, but the freedom for which he had sighed had already brought its cares, its duties, its self-abnegation. He had hoped to work for her and a home in Canada; it had been the dream that had buoyed his heart with hope for weary days; the dream was shattered now. He saw that the girl would not be satisfied with his humble love.

"So it is," he told himself bitterly. The white man has the advantage in all things. Is it worth while struggling against such forces?"

A while he mused in this strain as they swept on in silence, save for the subdued tones of the couple beside him. Then came softer thoughts, and his face lost the hard, revengeful look. He would not despair; the end was not yet. Many men had admired pretty faces. Let Maxwell beware and let it end in admiration only; he knew the worth of a white man's love for a woman of mixed blood; how it swept its scorching heat over a white young life, leaving it nothing but charred embers and burnt-out ashes. God! had he not seen. He—Judah—was her natural protector; he would be faithful to White Eagle's trust.

Towards twilight, they swerved from the direct road and entered a wooded slope. For some hours the hills surrounding Lawrence had been the point they were making. The naked woods showed the cup-like shape of the hills there—a basin from which radiated upward wooded ravines edged with ribs of rock where a few men could hold the entrance against great odds. In this basin on the edges of a creek John Brown was encamped. The smoke of a fire was visible in the dim light. As they advanced, a picket's gun echoed a warning from rock to rock. They halted then and dismounted, tying their horses to the branches of trees and stood ready to answer questions. Two men with guns came out from the bushes, with the words: "Stop thar. Free or pro-slavery? Whar you from?" Warren learned afterwards that these were two of Brown's sons.

Receiving satisfactory answers from Maybee and the Parson, our party passed on until they reached the creek where a group of horses stood saddled for a ride for life, or to hunt for Southern invaders. In an open space was a blazing fire, from which the smoke they had seen came; a pot was hung over it; a woman with an honest, sunburned face was superintending the preparations for supper. Three or four armed men were lying on red and blue blankets on the ground, and two fine-looking youths—grandsons of John Brown—stood near, leaning on their arms.

Old John Brown himself stood near the fire with his shirt sleeves rolled up, a large piece of pork in his hands which he had cut from a pig, barely cold, lying near.

In the woods' dark shadows nestled rude shelter-huts made from the branches of trees.

The travellers received a hearty welcome, and a number of women immediately surrounded Winona and hurried her to the largest hut.

Warren saw her once before leaving the next morning. "Good-bye, Winona; I shall return in a few weeks at longest. You are safe now until we can reach Canada."

"Good-bye, Mr. Maxwell. Do not speak so confidently. How can we tell that you will ever return or that I shall ever see Canada? I hate these good-byes," she said, with trembling lips.

Warren took the childish hand in his and kissed it. "Let us add 'God willing.' "

"No more time," called Parson Steward. "We've a good twenty miles and a bit before night," the next moment they had shaken hands with Maybee and Judah, and were riding out of camp.

The condition of Warren's mind was one of bewilderment. He had never in his life imagined anything like his experiences of the past few days. Now and again across the confusion of his mind, images floated vaguely—a white throat tinted by the firelight, a supple figure, a rapt young face, a head held with all a princess' grace, and dark, flashing eyes. The sound of a sweet voice, soft but not monotonous, fascinated his senses, as he recalled the tones repeating commonplace answers to commonplace questions. Somehow, the poor gown accented the girl's beauty.

Toward the close of the next day, the two men rode along in silence, save when Steward broke forth in song. He was singing now in a good baritone voice.

"A charge to keep I have,
 A god to glorify;
A never-dying soul to save,
 And fit it for the skies."

Warren listened to him dreamily. The voice chimed in harmoniously with the surroundings. The evening shadows were falling rapidly and the soft twilight folded them in its embrace. Maxwell was to stop another night at the cabin, and then riding on some fifteen miles, connect with the next boat on its regular trip to St. Louis.

Presently the singer changed his song to grand old "Coronation," his powerful voice swelling on the air-waves, mingling with the rustling of the leaves stirred by the balmy air, echoing and re-echoing through the wooded glen: "Praise God from whom all blessings flow." The young man wondered that he had never before realized the beauties of the noble hymn.

All the while their horses covered the ground in gallant form. Wonderful to relate, they had met with no marauding parties; but here and there, Steward pointed out to him the signs of desolation in the dreary woods where once prosperous farms had smiled; now the winds sighed over barren fields and broken fences, and the ghostly ruins of charred houses lifted their scarred skeletons against the sky in a mute appeal for vengeance.

The horsemen came to the high-road; soon they would be out in the open, clear of the woods. Warren's mind, by one of those sudden transitions which come to us at times, seemed to carry him bodily into his peaceful English home. He could see the beautiful avenues of noble trees, and the rambling, moss-covered manse; he could see the kindly patrician face of his father, and his brothers and sisters smiled at him from every bush. The Parson was ahead.

Suddenly he saw the horse stop.

"Ssh!"

Steward threw the word of caution over his shoulder at Maxwell. They halted, standing motionless in their tracks. A moment of breathless silence passed; then came the second sound of the soft clink of metal against stone, though no one was visible in the ghostly shadows of the twilight. Warren sat motionless as Steward peered about with the stealthy caution of a fox.

Why should the horse tremble? It was a second before he realized. He lurched forward in the saddle; there was a sharp pain in his shoulder; his arm dropped useless. He heard another shot, followed by a wild shout in the "fighting parson's" voice—"Blow ye the trumpet blow!" "Slay and spare not!"

Then another shot came to his benumbed faculties; then silence; he was galloping on in the darkness. On and on his frightened horse whirled him. By this time he was so faint from his wound that he could only dimly discern objects as he was whirled past the trees. Half a mile farther, the animal stumbled as he leaped over an obstacle in the path. Riderless, he sped over the highway; Warren lay motionless under the blossoming stars.

Out from the shadows of the trees came figures and voices.

"Hold the light. He ain't dead, is he?" queried the familiar voice of Bill Thomson.

"Looks like it, but reckon he's only wounded," replied Gideon Holmes, Bill's lieutenant.

Thomson bent over the insensible man, deftly feeling his

heart's motion. Then he raised himself and stood looking down thoughtfully on the youth.

It was a motley crowd of Southern desperadoes, men who stopped at nothing in the line of murder and rapine.

"Say, Jim," whispered a slight, thin man to his neighbor, "I wouldn't be in that young feller's shoes fer money——"

"What's he studyin', do ye reckon, Dan?"

"Hell!" was the expressive answer.

"What's agin the boy?" asked Jim.

"Stole two o' his niggers, so he says."

"Well, sir! Nasty mess. He won't git off easy."

"No. Say, what's Bill doin' neow? Looks interestin'."

Thomson had taken the gold from Warren's money-belt and the contents of his saddle-bags and was parcelling money and clothing impartially among his followers. Warren's revolvers were stowed in Thomson's own belt; then his garments followed suit, one man getting his boots, another his coat, still another his hat and so on.

While this was going on the unfortunate man revived and stared up into the devilish face of Bill Thomson. He groaned and closed his eyes.

"Howd'y, Mr. Maxwell? Didn't think I'd meet up with you so soon again, did you? Well, I've got you. Been after you ever since you left the 'Crescent,' and a mighty pretty chase it's been. Now, I want my niggers. I ain't foolin'. Where's they at?"

"I can't tell you," gasped Warren painfully.

"Look here, my friend, you've got to tell me. It's worth your life to you. You answer me true an' straight an' I'll make it all right for you. If you don't——" He paused ominously. "I'll let a Missouri crowd kill you! It won't be nice, easy killin', neither."

"I can't tell you,' again Warren answered, looking up resolutely into the sinister face bending above him.

"Got grit," muttered Sam to Dave.

Warren was trembling, and the cold drops in the roots of his hair ran down his forehead. He was not afraid, he was a man who did not know the name of fear or cowardice, but Thomson's evil looks sent a chill to his heart. Ebenezer Maybee's words of a few nights back rang in his ears monotonously: "You might git a taste of this scrimmage that'd con-vince you that the South is a horned hornet on the nigger question."

"Well," said Bill, "made up yer mind? Spit it out!"

Warren looked him in the eye without flinching; he did not answer.

Bill Thomson was what is called "foxy." He eyed his prisoner a spell and then said in quite another tone:

"Look a-here. I ain't goin' back on old England. You're my countryman, and I'm goin' to give you a square deal. You're what we call to home a high-tined gentleman. If you'll give us all the points possible an' lead the gang by the rout you've jes' come, you needn't say one word. I don't want no man to give his pals away. Will you?"

Their eyes met. The glitter of steel crossed under the lantern's light. Maxwell compressed his lips. Winona stared at him across the shadows of the dim old woods. "Be true," she whispered to the secret ear of his soul. With rapture he read aright the hopeless passion in her eyes when he left her. He knew now that he loved her. With sudden boldness he answered his tormentor.

"You have no right to claim either Winona or Judah as your slave. They are as free as you or I. I will never aid and abet your barbarous system, understanding it as I do now."

There was a cry and a general movement on the part of the crowd.

"Let him free his mind!" said Bill, waving the men back. "What do you mean by 'barbarous system'?"

"I mean a system that makes it right to force a free man or woman into slavery. A system which makes it a crime to utter one's honest convictions."

"Wal, I reckon that'll do fer now," broke in Gideon Holmes.

"I have committed no crime against your laws; if so, why, leave me in the hands of the law.'

"We take the law into our own hands these times," replied Gideon.

"Let me labor with him a spell, Gid." Gideon subsided, muttering.

"In the fus' place you are foun' guilty of associatin' with Northern abolitionists; besides that, they have so far corrupted your better judgment as to cause you to become a party to runnin' off slaves.

"Now, Mr. Maxwell, bein' a british subjec', you may not know that in the South sech actions is accountable with murder and becomes a hangin' affair. Because of your ignorance of our laws, and, whereas, you have fallen into evil company, we will give you a show for your life if you will own up and tell all you know, and help us to recover our property; otherwise, sorry as I should be to deal harshly with a gentleman of your cloth, the law mus' take its course."

"I am aware that I can expect no mercy at your hands. I have spoken freely and stated my honest convictions."

"An' free enough you've been, by gosh!" said Gideon, again breaking in.

Just at this point two men rode out of the woods leading a horse that Warren recognized. It was the parson's.

"Where's he at?" queried Bill.

"Dead's a hammer," answered the one in charge, at whose side dangled the pistols of the "fighting parson."

"Sure?"

"Sure."

"Git anything out of him about my niggers?"

"No use, Bill; they're up to Brown's camp. Nex' week they'll be in Canidy."

"Well, this one won't escape," said Bill, with a great oath, and a black, lowering look at the prisoner.

Without more talk, Warren was lifted to the back of the parson's horse and firmly bound. Then began a long, wild ride through the night in darkness and silence, bound, help-less, stabbed by every stumble.

Sometimes they trotted on high ground, sometimes the horses were up to their knees in the bog; and once Warren felt a heave of his horse's flanks, and heard the wash of water as if the animals were swimming. He tried to collect his thoughts; he tried to pray, but his mind would wander, and with the pain from his wound and the loss of blood, he was half-delirious. His thoughts were a jumble of hideous pic-tures.

Meanwhile, Sam and Dan talked together in whispers.

"Fifteen hundred dollars for the slaves or the slave-stealer, dead or alive, that's what the Colonel had advertised."

"A right smart o' money," replied Dan, "an' only eight o' us to git it."

"Kin' o' sorry 'bout the parson. It'll make again us up North," continued Sam.

"Ya-as, that's so, fur a fac'," acquiesced Dave.

"An' what a hunter he was, shoot the wink off yer eye!" O, Lord, warn't he chock full o' grit. Min' the time he says to Bill, 'you ride fas', but Death'll cotch you, an' after death the judgmen'!" queried Sam.

Dan chuckled at the recollection. "Got the dead wood on Bill then, I reckon."

"You bet!" replied Sam, with emphasis.

"Dear, dear, ain't it turrible fur't have't do a man like that mean!" continued Dan.

"But 'twould be terrible to lost the money. I can't tell which would be turriblest!"

"That's a fac'."

"Who's that fool gabin'?" came in a fierce whisper from the front. Then followed silence.

They had emerged from the swamp and were riding through a high, fertile region of farming lands. The moon was rolling high in the heavens, while far toward the east was a faint lightning, the promise of dawn.

Once after crossing a bridge they pulled up and listened, and then rode off into the bushes and stood quietly in hiding. They were evidently anxious to avoid pursuit. Once pistol shots followed them as they fled through the night.

At Weston a crowd of men awaited them, and crossed over to the other side in company with Bill's party. Warren was thrown into a wagon. Presently they stepped from the boat to Missouri's shore.

CHAPTER X

Warren looked about him in the light of the flaming torches. Men poured down to the water's edge as fast as they could come. The crowds which surged through the streets day and night were rushing toward the wagon where lay the prisoner, their faces distorted like demons with evil passions.

Bill Thomson mounted the wagonseat and with an oratorical flourish recounted the prisoner's against the "principles of the institootion."

"Gentlemen, take notice!" said Gid Holmes as Bill finished. "This yere man is a abolitionist an' a nigger thief, two crimes we never overlooks, bein' dangerous to our peace and principles. What's your will, gentlemen? Speak out."

"Give him a thrashing first!" "Hang him!" "Burn him!"

And the ruffians dragged the wounded man from the wagon and threw themselves upon him—kicking him in the body— in the face and head—spitting upon him and maltreating him in every way. He defended himself well for a while; his bright head would rise from their buffeting.

"To the cross-roads!" came the hoarse cry from a thousand throats.

Tramp, tramp, on they rushed like a dark river, with cries whose horror was indescribable. It was not the voices of human beings, but more like the cries of wild animals, the screaming of enraged hyenas, the snarling of tigers, the angry, inarticulate cries of thousands of wild beasts in infuriated pursuit of their prey, yet with a something in it more sinister and blood curdling, for they were men, and added a human ferocity.

On they rushed from north, south, east and west, eyes

aflame, faces distorted, the brute latent in every human being coming out from his lair to blot out the man, the awful cries, waning, waxing.

Maxwell was in the midst, half-running, half-dragged by a rope knotted about his neck. He fell; the thirsty executioners lifted him up, loosened the rope and gave him time to breath.

The tall young figure looked at the crowd with scorn. The British idea of fair play was in his mind.

"Thousands against one," he seemed to say, "Cowards!"

The crowd moved on a little more slowly, and Warren was able to keep his feet without a tremor.

Some ran on before, and began gathering wood, for it was determined to burn the prisoner as a more fearful example of the death that awaited the men who dared interfere with the "institution." Warren was dragged to the foot of the cross-roads sign and securely bound; the wood was piled about him. The circle was not built as high as his knees, for a slow fire steadily increased, would prolong the enjoyment. Thomson himself carried the brand to light the pile. His eyes met Warren's as he knelt with the blazing pine. Not a word passed between them. A horrible and engrossing interest kept every eye on the glowing light. Presently the barrier of flame began to rise. A thousand voiced cry of brutal triumph arose—not to the skies, so vile a thing could never find the heavenly blue; it must have fallen to the regions of the lost.

They who speak or think lightly of a mob have never heard its voice nor seen its horrible work.

(To be continued.)

CHAPTER X.—(Concluded.)

From the town came the ringing of bells set in motion when the party landed, still startling the night with their brazen clamor. The wildest excitement prevailed—armed riders dashed recklessly up and down in front of the place of execution, yelling, cursing, threatening.

The most trivial incidents accompany the progress of death. Warren noticed the faint light of the morning chasing away the stars. His keen sight lost not one change in the landscape. Children were in the crowd worming their way among the promiscuous legs and arms in the endeavor to gain a peep at the proceedings; one wee tot had fallen over backwards felled by the unexpected movement of the particular legs that obstructed his view. Warren was conscious of a deep sense of pity for the infants whom ignorance tortured from childhood's simple holiness as cruelly as the mob was about to torture him. There came to him then a realizing sense of all the Immortal Son must have suffered on His way to Golgotha to die a shameful death through the ignorance and cruelty of a heartless world. If the story of the crucifixion had at times presented difficulties to an inquiring, analytical mind, this experience cleared away the shadows and the application of the story of the Redeemer came to him as a live coal from the altar of Infinite Truth.

The crew of the ferry-boat was hurrying forward with the wood stored aboard for the fires under the boilers; sounds of chopping came to his ears above the yells and shouts of the mob, and reverberated along the edges of the sky. Men were chopping fuel, others ran with arm-loads of it to build around the stake which had the festive air of a May-pole. Another group thought that the spectacle needed illumination at its beginning and were heaping fuel on a camp-fire, and its crackle could be heard almost as far as its light reached.

Men swaggered about the vast bluster and deep curses, howling for the sacrifice, quenching their thirst and fanning their fury anew at a temporary bar in the wagon where an enterprising individual was dispensing drinks to the crowd at a nominal price.

The sky overhead began to assume a roseate tinge. Swarming figures became more and more distinct. The fragrant wind encroaching from the woods, bringing its sweet odors, swept the smoke sidewise like an inverted curtain.

All was ready. There came a deafening cheer when Thomson moved pompously forward and with a theatrical gesture applied the torch; then followed silence deep and breathless as they waited to gloat over the victim's first awful shriek of agony.

The flames rose. Warren ground his teeth, determined to die and make no moan to please and gratify the crowd. The sweat of physical anguish and faintness moved in drops on his forehead. His face was distinctly visible in the fierce glare. His arms were bound down against his sides, the wounded one causing him frightful torture. His shirt was open at the throat, showing the ivory firmness of his chest and the beating pulse in the white brawn. As the flames gathered headway the sky grew brighter and the shadows melted away; the crowing of cocks came faintly, above the horrid din, borne on the young morning air.

Suddenly off to the right came the sound of galloping

hoofs. So imperative was the clatter that the attention of the crowd was forced for a moment from the victim at the stake.

On, on swept the riders in mad haste to the scene of torture, now distinctly visible through the cloud of dust that had at first partially concealed them from view; and now they rose in their stirrups shouting and waving their hats as if in warning. The fiends about the funeral pile made way for the cavalcade which was headed by Colonel Titus. All the party wore the uniform of State constables. "Halt!" cried the Colonel as he sprang from his horse at the edge of the crowd and cleared the open space immediately in front of the sign-post at one bound, followed by his companions. The crowd fell back respectfully. He and his men kicked the blazing wood from the stake, and scattered it with hands and feet as far as they could throw it. His own clothing smoked, and his face flamed with the exertion. The colonel cut Warren's bonds, while his men continued to stamp out the fire. The crowd watched them in sullen silence.

"Fools!" he shouted, when at length the fire's headway was subdued, "what are you doing?"

"Burning a nigger-thief," shouted Gideon Holmes in reply.

"None of your monkeyin', Bill Thomson; speak up. You had charge of this affair," said Titus, not deigning to notice Holmes. Bill answered with a vile oath.

The crowd stood about in curious clusters. As the fire died down, the dawn became more pronounced. The brutal carnival seemed about to die out with the darkness as quickly as it had arisen.

"And you have been allowing your men to do that which will put us in the power of every Northern mudsill of an abolitionist, and eventually turn the tide which is now in our favor, against us!" The Colonel wheeled about and faced Thomson. "Was this the understanding when you started on the expedition?"

Bill still stood sullen-faced and silent before his accuser.

"Have we not jails strong enough to hold prisoners?" Titus asked, significantly.

"Dead men tell no tales," declared Thomson, with a long look into his questioner's eyes.

"True," returned the Colonel with an answering glance. "But let all things be done in decency and order and according to the process of law. This man ain't no army. There warn't no need of your raisin' and chasin' and burnin' him like a parcel of idiots."

" 'Pears to me you're d——— finicky 'bout law an' all that jes' this particular time," sneered Bill, with an evil leer on his face.

The Colonel eyed him keenly while a look of disgust spread slowly over his speaking face.

"Thomson, I gave you credit for having more sense. This man is a British subject. How are we to impress the world with our fair and impartial dealing with all mankind, and the slavery question in particular, if you and a lot more hot-headed galoots go to work and call us liars by breaking the slate?"

There were murmurs of approval from the crowd.

"Fac' is thar's nothin' fer us to do but to light out, ain't that the idee, Colonel?" asked Jim Murphy.

"That's the idea, Murphy; burn the wind the whole ca-boodle of you!" The crowd began to disperse slowly.

"All very good," broke in Thomson with a swagger. "I'll take mine without the law. I'd ruther stay right here and carry out the programme, it'd be more satisfactory to the boys in the long run. Law is a delusion, as the poet says, an' a snare. We git plenty o' law an' no jestice. S'pose the law lets the prisoner go free? You'll be a real pop'lar candidate fer Missouri's next gov'ner."

"No fear of that in this State," replied the Colonel with an ugly, brutal look that caused a shudder to creep over Warren who was surrounded by the constables. So full of malice were the tone and look that all signs of the polished elderly gentleman and doting father were lost, and one felt that this man could perpetrate any crime, however foul. In spite of the quiet tones the Colonel's blood was at boiling point because of Thomson's stubborness. Titus turned to the constables: "Gentlemen, secure the prisoner. Thomson, fall in there and lend a hand; be quick about it. We've had too much of your fool talk a'ready. When I give my men an order, I 'low for them to obey me right up to the chalk mark."

Bill gave him a long look and without a word mounted his horse, and rode away—not with the troop.

The constables instantly obeyed the Colonel's order, and in a second Warren was lifted to the floor of the wagon and driven rapidly toward the jail.

CHAPTER XI

In the Brown camp the great family of fugitives dwelt together in guileless and trusting brotherhood under the patriarchal care of Captain Brown, who daily praised the Eternal Sire, and one soul of harmony and love was infused into each individual dweller.

John Brown was a man of deep religious convictions; but

mingled with austerity were perfect gentleness and self-renunciation which inspired love in every breast. But amid the self-denying calmness of his deportment, those who looked deeply into his eyes might discern some cast of that quiet and determined courage which faced his enemies in later years before the Virginia tribunal where, threatened with an ignominious death, he made the unmoved reply—"I am about God's work; He will take care of me."

The fugitive slaves who came in fear and trembling were strengthened and improved by contact with the free, strong spirit of their rescuer and his associate helpers of proscribed Free Staters.

Weeks must elapse, perhaps, before a force of sufficient strength could be organized to protect the fugitives on their perilous trip to Canada. In the interval Captain Brown was pastor, guide and counsellor. The instruction of youth he considered one of the most sacred departments of his office, so it happened that in the camp the ex-slave received his first lessons in the true principles of home-building and the responsibility of freedom. There he first heard God's commands in the words of Holy Writ:

"He hath made of one blood all the nations of the earth."

"There is no respect of persons with God."

"Do to another as you would that another should do to you."

"Remember those in bonds as bound with them."

In the field the negro learned for the first time in his life the sweetness of requited toil together with the manliness of self-defence, for the musket was companion of the implements of rural toil, as in the days of Nehemiah the restorers of Jerusalem wrought "every man with one hand upon the wall and with the other held his spear, having his sword girded by his side;" and also that it was better to die than to live a coward and a slave.

Winona was quartered at the Brown domicile. With her story and her beauty she was an object of uncommon interest to all in the camp. She became Captain Brown's special care and the rugged Puritan unbent to spoil and pet the "pretty squaw," as he delighted to call her.

And to Winona all the land had changed. The red-golden light that rested upon it near the evening hour was now as the light of heaven. The soft breezes that murmured through the trees and touched her cheek so gently, seemed to whisper, "Peace and rest. Peace and rest once again. Be not cast down."

There was the touch of sympathy and comfort in the rugged Captain's hand pressed upon her short-cropped curls. It gave her courage and robbed her heart of its cold desolation. She felt she was no longer alone; heaven, in her dire need, had sent her this good man, upon whom she might rely, in whom she could trust. Though much older, Captain Brown reminded her of her father, and her quiet childhood dependent upon him for constant companionship had given her a liking for elderly people, and she treated Captain Brown with a reverential respect that at once won his confidence and affection.

But there was not a day nor an hour that she did not think of Maxwell. She craved for news of his safety. When the daily routine of work was ended, the girl would steal into the woods which skirted the camp and climb to a seat on the high rocks watching eastward and westward for some sign of the young Englishman's return.

Some impulse of the wild things among whom she had lived drove her to a hole in under the bluff. It was necessary to descend to find it. Presently she was in a tunnel which led into a cavern. She made herself a divan of dried moss and flung herself down at full length to think. Time's divisions were lost on those days when the girl felt that she neglected no duty by hiding herself in her nook. She had come upon the eternal now as she lay in a sweet stupor until forced to arouse herself. She stared across the space that divided Maxwell from her with all the strength of her inner consciousness. That light which falls on the spot where one's loved one stands, leaving the rest of the landscape in twilight, now rested about him. With rapture she saw again the hopeless passion in Warren's eyes when he left her. Her hands and feet were cold, her muscles knotted, her face white with the force of the cry that she projected through space, "Come back to me!"

And this young creature just escaped from cruel bondage gave not a thought to the difficulties of her position. In the primal life she had led there had entered not a thought of racial or social barriers. The woods calmed her, their grays and greens and interlacing density of stems, and their whisper of a secret that has lasted from the foundation of the world, replacing her fever with the calmness of hope. In the midst of her sweet perplexity came another trouble.

Judah's capabilities were discovered very soon by Captain Brown and his sons, and he was appointed special aid and scout to the camp. Nothing could have suited him better. All day he scoured the woods, following the trail of parties of desperadoes or bringing in the fruits of the line or rifle to supply the needs in fish or meat. Twice he saved them from surprise by bands of marauders, and soon his name was heralded with that of Brown as a brave and fearless man bold to recklessness.

Sometimes Winona accompanied him on his trips when

not fraught with much danger; once he tried to broach the subject nearest his heart, but a movement on her part—the carriage of the head, a queenly gesture—served to intimidate him and forced back the words.

The next night he passed in the woods, with his rifle, on a bed of leaves, studying over the problem of his life. "Why should I hesitate? We are of the same condition in life in the eyes of the world." But even while the thought was in his mind he knew that what he desired could never be. Unconsciously he was groping for the solution of the great question of social equality.

But is there such a thing as social equality? There is such a thing as the affinity of souls, congenial spirits, and good fellowship; but social equality does not exist because it is an artificial barrier which nature is constantly putting at naught by the most incongruous happenings. Who is my social equal? He whose society affords the greatest pleasure, whose tastes are congenial, and who is my brother in the spirit of the scriptural text, be he white or black, bond or free, rich or poor.

The next morning Judah built a fire in a deep ravine to cook his breakfast, and then scattered the embers that the smoke should give no sign.

All the morning he waited near her favorite haunts determined to speak out the thoughts that filled his mind. He began to fear at last that she was not coming. A little noise down the path reached his ear. In a moment he could hear slow foot-falls, and the figure of the girl parted the bushes, which closed behind her as she passed through them. She passed quite near him, walking slowly; she was very pale; her face bore traces of mental suffering. For a moment she stood there, listless, and Judah watched her with hungry eyes at a loss what to do. The sun lighted her hair, and in the upturned eyes he saw the shimmer of tears. "Winona!" He couldn't help it. The low cry broke from his lips like a groan; the next instant the girl faced him. She looked with quick wonder at the dark face with its mute appeal. Then a sudden spasm caught her throat, and left her body rigid, her hands shut, and her eyes dry and hard—she knew, instinctively, what he suffered.

"Oh, Judah! Hav'n't we been through enough without this?"

The girl trembling at the knees sank to a seat on the rocks, and folding her arms across her knees, laid her forehead against them.

"I'm going away, Winona, as soon as you are safe in Canada," he went on after a little pause. "It'll be pretty hard to leave you, but I want you to know how I've been thinking about you and sorrowing over your sorrow and hoping that you might get over your liking for Maxwell, seeing that you're only a slip of a girl, and think of me as the one who would die for you and ought naturally to care for your wants —" He spoke hesitatingly; there was a question in his last words, but the girl shook her head sadly, her tears falling to the ground. Her sorrow gave way in a great sob now, and he turned in sharp remorse and stood quite near her.

"Don't cry, Winona," he said. "I'm sorry for you and myself and Maxwell. It's this cursed slavery that's to blame. If your father had lived all this would never have happened."

"I am sorry—so very sorry! But you see, Judah, it cannot be; I have no love to give."

Judah stood beside her, his heart bursting with suppressed emotion. The bitter words would break from his lips.

"The white man gets it all—all!"

"Do you forget all that Mr. Maxwell has done for us,

Judah, that you condemn him so bitterly? It is not like you—
you who are generally so generous and true-hearted. He
knows not of my love and will never know. Is he to
blame?"

"You are right—you are right! But how is a man to
distinguish between right and wrong? What moral responsibility rests upon him from whom all good things are taken?
Answer me that."

They were walking now toward the camp; the shadowy
trees tossed their arms in the twilight and the stars came out
one by one in the sky. Only the silent tears of the girl at his
side gave answer to his question.

A month had passed since the fugitives had reached the
camp. Captain Brown eagerly awaited the return of Warren
with Parson Steward to help them on the trip to Canada.

The wild flowers swayed above their counterfeits in every
gurgling stream; the scent of wild grapes was in the air; the
cliffs and rocks blossomed with purple and white and pink
blooms. The birds sang and the bees droned in the woods on
the morning when, wild and dishevelled, Parson Steward's
wife and two children found their way into the Brown camp.

"My heavenly marster!" shrieked the widow in incoherent
wailing. "The Rangers done caught my husband and shot
him; they've carried the young Englishman to jail. What will
become of me and my poor children?"

No one slept that night when the fate of the two gallant
men was known, and the oaths uttered were not loud but
deep.

Captain Brown, like a prophet of old, drew his spare form
erect. Lightning flashed from his mild eyes and sword-thrusts
fell from his tongue.

Then and there a rescue party was planned to take Warren
out of the hands of the Philistines. The only trouble was to

spy out the jail where he was confined; but there seemed little hope of success, for it appeared that since his trial Warren had disappeared from public view, and the Pro-Slavery men were very reticent. Ebenezer Maybee volunteered to secure the desired information.

As was the fashion in those days, the women listened but did not intrude their opinions upon the men, being engaged in performing the part of Good Samaritan to the widow and orphans. But long after the meeting had broken up Winona crept into the woods not to weep, but to think. She leaned against a tree and her hopeless eyes gazed down the darkening aisles; she prayed: "Help me to help save him!"

In the morning she sought an interview with Captain Brown.

CHAPTER XII

Meanwhile the wagon containing Maxwell and surrounded by constables stopped at the door of a frame building in the heart of the city, and with blows and threats Warren was pushed and dragged into a bare room and told that it was his quarters until business hours. The passageway and room were filled with a motley crowd and the vilest epithets were hurled after him. Presently a man came in with a lighted candle, seized his sound arm and looked him over from head to foot . in the most insulting manner. Warren shook him off and asked him if he called himself a man to so insult a wounded stranger.

"Don't you dare speak to a white man except to answer questions, you d——d nigger-thief!"

"I shall appeal to the British consul for protection from

your vile insults," said Warren in desperation. "It will cost your government dear for tonight's business."

"If you get the chance to complain," laughed the ruffian. "By G—d! you've got to die today, and by this revolver," he continued, drawing his weapon and brandishing it fiercely. He was applauded by the crowd, and it looked as if Warren were doomed when constables arriving saved further trouble. Maxwell felt that he would almost rather have been burned, than to endure the insults of such brutes.

After much entreaty, he succeeded in getting some water, but nothing more, though almost famished. Burning with fever from his wound and his contact with the funeral pile, and fainting for want of nourishment, not having tasted food since the morning before, the young man felt unable to sustain many more shocks to his system.

At length, without medical attendance, the crowd left him to get such sleep as he might upon the bare floor, without bed or covering of any kind. Retreating to a corner of the room, seated upon the floor with his back to the wall, Warren passed the hours silent and motionless.

He meditated upon his position in the heart of a hostile country although supposed to advocate and champion the most advanced ideas of liberty and human rights. What a travesty the American government was on the noblest principles! Bah! it made him heartsick. He had listened to the tales of Maybee and Steward as exaggerations; he had not believed such scenes as he had just passed through, possible in a civilized land. The words of the man who had just taunted him: "If you get the chance to complain," haunted him.

If he were not allowed to communicate with his consul, then, indeed, hope was dead. What would be his fate? The misery in store for him appalled him. And Winona—! He dared not allow his thoughts to dwell upon her. That way madness lay. So the long hours dragged out their weary length.

At eight o'clock breakfast was brought to him, and when he had begun to despair of receiving medical aid, a doctor came in and dressed his wounded arm. After this, he was marched through the streets to a room in the hotel where he was placed before the glass doors—much as is a wild beast caged in a menagerie. His reception was demoniacal. Everybody was out. Again, while en route to the seat of Justice, he endured the ignominy of oaths, yells and missiles; again the air resounded with cries of "Give him hemp!" "The rope is ready!" And so they arrived at the Court House.

The large unfinished room was filled to overflowing with the unwashed Democracy of Missouri—a roof with bare brick walls and open rafters overhead, from which hung down directly above the prisoner three new ropes with the hangman's knot at the end of each. Fierce faces, rough and dirty, with the inevitable pipe, or tobacco saliva marking the corners of the mouth, filled in the picture, while a running accompaniment of the strongest and vilest oaths ears ever heard suggested all the horrors of mob violence. The court proceeded with its farcical mockery of justice. Warren undertook to act as his own counsel, and drew up the following protest:

"I, the undersigned, a British subject, do hereby protest against every step taken thus far by the State of Missouri in this case; declaring that my rights as a British subject have been infamously violated and trampled upon.
                                                    "Warren Maxwell."

This he handed to the magistrate, who, without giving it any attention, threw it one side.

Colonel Titus and Bill Thomson were the principal witnesses against him. The Colonel told how basely the young man had betrayed his hospitality by aiding his slaves, Winona and Judah, to escape.

Thomson testified to the fact that the prisoner consorted with abolitionists of the John Brown stripe, being, when captured, in company with "fighting Steward," a red-handed criminal.

The case was given to the jury who returned a verdict of "guilty," without leaving their seats. Then followed the judge's charge and sentence:

"Warren Maxwell—It is my duty to announce to you the decision of this court as a penalty for the crime you have committed. You have been guilty of aiding slaves to run away and depart from their master's service; and now, for it you are to die!

" 'Remember now thy Creator in the days of my youth,' is the language of inspired wisdom. This comes home appropriately to you in this trying moment. You are young; quite too young to be where you are. If you had remembered your Creator in your past days, you would not now be in a felon's place, to receive a felon's judgment. Still, it is not too late to remember your Creator.

"The sentence of the law is that you be taken to the State prison for one year; and that there you be closely and securely confined until Friday, the 26th day of May next; on which day, between the hours of ten in the forenoon and two in the afternoon, you will be taken to the place of public execution, and there be hanged by the neck till your body be dead. And may God have mercy on your soul!"

Overwhelmed by the mockery of a trial, Warren heard the words of the judge but they carried no meaning to his overwrought senses. He sat in a stupor until hurried by the constables to the carriage that was to convey him to prison.

Days of pain and unconsciousness followed, and when at last consciousness returned, he founded himself in a room sixteen feet square, with a small grated window at each end, through which he could catch a glimpse of the street.

Under the room in which he was confined was another of the same size, used as a lock-up for slaves who were usually put there for safe-keeping while waiting to be sent South. The room had a hole for the stove-pipe of the under room to pass through, but the stove had been removed to accommodate a larger number of prisoners. This left a hole in the floor through which one might communicate with those below. This hole in the floor afforded diversion for the invalid who could observe the full operation of the slave system. Sometimes, too, he could communicate with the slaves or some white prisoner by means of the stove-hole. When all was quiet a note was sent down through the hole, the signal being to punch with the broom-handle.

Many heart-rending scenes were enacted before his sight in the lower room. Infamous outrages were committed upon free men of color whose employment as cooks and stewards on steamers and sailing vessels had brought them within the jurisdiction of the State. Such men were usually taken ashore and sold to the highest bidder. One man who had his free papers on his person, produced them to prove the truth of his story; the official took the papers from him, burned them, and sold him the next week at public auction. Two Negroes were whipped to death rather than acknowledge the men who claimed them as their owners. One horror followed another in the crowded cage where a frightful number of human beings were herded together. They could not sleep; that is to say, forget their misery for one moment. And how hot it was already! The rays of the fierce summer sun of the South seemed to burn and sear Warren's suffering brain and dry up the healthful juices into consuming fever and ultimate madness.

One day he was aroused to greater indignation than usual by hearing heart-rending cries come from the lower room. Hurrying to the stove-hole he gazed one moment and then fell fainting with terror and nausea upon the floor. He had seen a Negro undergoing the shameful outrage, so denounced in the Scriptures, and which must not be described in the interests of decency and humanity.

That night Maxwell was again ill—delirious—requiring the care of two physicians and a slave who was detailed to nurse him.

Unhappily we tell no tale of fiction. We have long felt that the mere arm of restraint is but a temporary expedient for the remedy, but not the prevention, of cruelty and crime. If Christianity, Mohammedanism, or even Buddhism, did exercise the gentle and humanizing influence that is claimed for them, these horrors would cease now that actual slavery has been banished from our land; because, as religion is the most universal and potent source of influence upon a nation's action, so it must mould to some extent its general characteristics and individual opinions. Until we can find a religion that will give the people individually and practically an impetus to humane and unselfish dealing with each other, look to see outward forms change, but never look to see the spirit which hates and persecutes that which it no longer dare enslave, changed by any other influence than a change of heart and spirit.

The liberties of a people are not to be violated but with

the wrath of God. Indeed, we tremble for our country when we reflect that God is just; that His justice cannot sleep forever; that considering natural means only, a revolution of the wheel of Fortune, an exchange of situation is among the possibilities.

All through the long delirium of pain and weariness Warren was conscious of the tender care of his nurse. To the sick man the wearing, jarring sound of voices rising out of a black pit was ever present and unbearable. At times they were to him the cries of the ruffians who pursued him to the stake; the vengeance of the mob seemed to fill the little room and charge the atmosphere with horror. Again it was the sound of the pistol shot that killed Parson Steward, and the patient would shudder at the blood everywhere—on shirts, hands and faces, and splashing the sides of the bare walls; or it was the flames mounting higher and higher, licking his body with hungry tongues, or it was the rushing of whirling waters against the vessel's side as he swung Winona over the side of "Crescent."

Finally, as he lay tossing and tormented with these phantom terrors in his eyes and ears, the sound died away into the soft hush of a tender voice stilling the tumult.

The nurse was a young mulatto known as Allen Pinks. The boy had been cook and head-waiter on board a steamboat on the Missouri river. He had been paid off, according to his story, at St. Joseph. From there he had started for Leavenworth, walking down the Missouri bank of the river with a white man. At the ferry he was stopped on suspicion of being a fugitive slave and lodged in the calaboose; from there he was removed to the State prison until the time of sale. He had made himself very useful about the jail doing chores and nursing the sick, for which he seemed to have a particular vocation. Very soon Allen Pinks was a great favorite and allowed many privileges; hearing of Maxwell's illness he asked to be allowed to nurse him, and the jailer was more than glad to have him do it.

At last there came a day when the prisoner's wild wide eyes were closed, and the boy rose from his long watch by the side of the rude cot bed with hope in his heart. He stood, for a second, looking down upon the calm face of the sleeper with a sorrowful smile on his dark brown face. "Fast asleep at last," he whispered. "I must go see to his broth."

Just then a hideous yell arose from the room below. With a light bound the lad reached the stove-hole.

"Hush your noise!" he called in a low tone of authority. "Haven't I told you he must sleep?"

"Got a black boss dis time," came up from the hole in a gruff voice, followed by a low laugh.

"He's asleep now, and everything depends on his waking up right. But you set up a howl that would wake the dead!"

"Howl? dat's singing," came again from the hole in the floor.

"Well, keep your singing to yourself."

The noise subsided, and the young nurse turned again to his patient.

He stood for some moments gazing down on the Saxon face so pitifully thin and delicate. The brow did not frown nor the lips quiver; no movement of the muscles betrayed the hopeless despair of the sleeper's heart. The cot gave a creak and a rustle. The nurse was leaning one hand on the edge of the miserable pallet bed bending over the sick man. There was a light touch on his hair; a tear fell on his cheek; the nurse had kissed the patient!

When the door had closed behind the lad, Warren opened

his eyes in full consciousness; and as he brushed the tear from his face, there came a puzzled look into his eyes.

Presently Allen returned with the soup and found him awake. His features lighted up with intelligence and sympathy on making the discovery, and finding him free from fever.

"Well, how are you getting on, sir?" he asked in the softest of musical voices, and feeling Warren's pulse, as he seated himself on a stool at the bedside.

"Who are you? Haven't I met you somewhere? Your voice has a familiar sound."

"I fancy you don't know me," replied Allen with a smile.

"You've saved my life."

"That's a subject we won't speak of just now, sir; you must be very quiet."

"Oh, to be well and free once more!' broke in a plaintive tone from the invalid.

"If you will only remain quiet and easy in your mind, there's no doubt all may yet be well," replied the boy with significant emphasis as he held Warren's eye a second with a meaning gaze.

Many questions came crowding to Warren's lips; but Allen silenced him firmly and gently.

"Bye and bye, sir, I will tell you all I can, but you must drink this broth now and sleep."

Warren drank the soup and with a feeling of peace new to him, turned his face to the wall and slept.

One week longer Warren lay on his rude bed. Allen refused to talk but told him that he had no cause for anxiety.

Maxwell was fascinated by his nurse; he thought him the prettiest specimen of boyhood he had ever met. The delicate brown features were faultless in outline; the closely cropped black hair was like velvet in its smoothness. He could not shake off the idea that somewhere he had known the lad before in his life. At times this familiarity manifested itself in the tones of the voice soft and low as a woman's, then again it was in the carriage of the head or the flash of the beautiful large dark eyes. It was an evasive but haunting memory.

One day Allen said: "Mr. Maxwell, I'm not to tend you any longer after this week. I'm to be sold."

"Sold!" ejaculated Warren in dismay.

Allen nodded. "It's getting too hot for me, and I'm going to run for it."

"What shall I do without you?" said Warren with a sick feeling of despair at his heart.

"Have you no hope of escape? Have you never thought of being rescued?" asked the lad in a whisper with a cautious motion of the hand toward the door.

"Oh, Allen!" faltered Warren in speechless joy.

The lad gave him time to recover himself a bit; then, after glancing around the corridor to see that no one was listening, returned to his patient.

"I am here in the interest of your friends! I leave tonight. Tomorrow you will receive a communication from your friends. We must hasten our plans for Thomson is expected on a visit here any day."

"Go on; go on; tell me what to do."

"There is nothing for you to do but to be ready at a moment's notice. The plans are all well laid, and will be successful, unless Thomson should upset us."

"I fear that man," replied Warren with a shudder.

"You certainly have good reason," said Allen. "But he does not reside in this vicinity and we may be able to avoid him."

"He would be only too happy to wreak his vengeance upon me. Yes, I fear him."

Allen did his best to reassure Warren, and discussed with

him the plan of escape as far as he knew it, and concluded
by saying:

"I shall not see you again. Keep up your heart. Barring
accident, you will soon be free."

At night Allen went as usual to the well to draw the water
for supper, and did not return. The alarm was given, but no
trace of the boy was found.

CHAPTER XIII

The next morning dawned hot and sultry; all day there were
signs of a thunder storm.

Towards dark the door of Warren's cell opened and a
young man with a carpet bag, apparently in a great hurry to
catch a train, and accompanied by the jailer, came to the
grated door and informed Warren that he had been requested
by the British consul at New York, who had heard of his
case, to see him and to say to him that his case would be
investigated and all done that could be done, and that he
would hear from the consul in person in a few days.

The visitor was quite curious about the hall, looking around
a great deal, and as he stood with his back to the grated door
talking to the jailer, whose attention he directed to some
means of ventilation outside, Warren saw a small slip of
paper in the hand which he held behind him, and took it.

When he was alone again, he unfolded it with trembling
fingers. It contained the words: "Be ready at midnight."
Scarcely had he recovered from the excitement which the note
caused him, when he heard footsteps and voices again approaching his cell and in a few seconds the sallow, uncanny
face of Bill Thomson was framed in the doorway.

"It seems to me, you fellows ain't as careful as you might be. Had a visitor sent by the British consul, did he? Well that won't save his neck. I tell you, Bub," he said, directly addressing the prisoner, "saltpetre won't save you. You've got to go, by G—d. D——n these newspaper men I say; a set of ornery skunks; meddling with business that don't consarn 'em. But they don't euchre me this deal."

Warren made no answer, and in a short time the visitor passed on. With senses strained to their utmost tension, he watched the shades of night envelope the landscape. He listened to the striking of the clock in the corridor outside his cell, tolling the lagging hours, with beating heart. Gradually all sound died away and the hush of night fell upon the earth, broken only by the fury of the storm which now broke scattering destruction in its wake. Far off the river sounded a mimic Niagara as it swelled beyond its boundaries. In the midst of his anxiety the young man noted the strange coincidence of the storms which had attended three critical periods in his history while in America. With this thought in his mind he heard the clock toll off twelve strokes. As the last one died slowly away there came a thundering knock at the outer prison door. It came again, and yet again. He heard a door slam and then the voice of the jailer, "What do you want?"

"We are from Andrew County, with a prisoner we want put in jail for safe keeping."

"Who is he?"

"A notorious horse thief."

"Have you a warrant?"

"No; but it's all right."

"I can't take a man without authority."

"If you don't it will be too bad; he's a desperate character, and we've had hard work to catch him. We'll satisfy you in the morning that it's all right."

The jailer went down and let them in. When they were inside where the light fell upon their faces he started back with the cry:

"It's Allen Pinks!"

The men with him were Maybee and old John Brown.

"Yes, Mr. Owens," said Captain Brown grimly, "it's the boy, and it's too late to make a noise. If you resist or give an alarm, you are a dead man. The lower door is guarded, and the jail surrounded by an armed force."

Warren beheld the scene from between the bars of his cell door with anxious heart; even as he looked he saw a dark object pass behind the group and advance along the corridor wall, but his attention was drawn from the shadow as a door opened far down the row and Bill Thomson, fully dressed, faced the group, pistol in hand.

He advanced step by step with his eyes fixed upon the negro lad. The boy involuntarily uttered a cry and covered his face with his hands.

"Well, sir! if it ain't Winona! Looks interestin', Owens, that you couldn't tell a gal dressed up in boys clo's! This strikes me heavy."

Warren standing helpless in his cell saw and heard all, and understood many things that had puzzled him. There are loves and loves; but Warren told himself that the love of the poor forsaken child before him was of the quality which we name celestial. All the beauty and strength of the man, and every endowment of tenderness came upon him there as the power came upon Samson; and he registered a promise before heaven that night.

"Halt!" cried Captain Brown, as Thomson moved a step nearer. "Halt, or you're a dead man!"

"So it is murder you propose to commit?"

"No; we have come in peace, if let alone, to rescue our friend Maxwell. If you interfere with us the worst is your own. Disarm him, Mr. Maybee."

But Thomson aimed his pistol straight at Winona's breast, and cried: "I fire if you come a step nearer."

Warren groaned. "Oh, for a moment's freedom and a good weapon in my hand!"

Suddenly a lurid glare lighted up the hall, and Warren saw a dark shadow creeping in Thomson's rear. Something of an extraordinary nature was about to happen.

"It is Judah! It is Judah!"

It was indeed Judah. He had crept along gradually advancing nearer and nearer, bending almost double in observation; then like a wild beast preparing to pounce upon his prey, he stiffened his powerful muscles, and with a bound sprang upon Thomson, seizing him in an iron grasp, and dragging him backward to the ground with such violence that his pistol flew from his hand. Placing one foot upon the breast of the prostrate man to prevent him from rising, he picked up the pistol, crying:

"It is between you and me, now. Our roles are reversed. It is you who must die."

He was about to fire, when Captain Brown hastily interfered:

"No, no; it won't do. Spare him!"

"Spare him! For what? To afford him an opportunity to do more mischief? No, No!"

"Let us release Maxwell first and get outside the building then, if you insist upon this thing," said Maybee.

"Quick, then! I will not answer for myself. Your safety is not the only thing to be considered; I must think of myself as well. If I do not kill this man, he will murder me by inches if I fall into his hands, as he has already tried to do. I hate him, I hate him! It is my enemy I would slay, not yours."

(To be continued.)

❧ ❧ ❧

CHAPTER XIII.—(Concluded.)

With a rapid movement he stooped, placed the barrel of his pistol at Thomson's forehead and—would have pulled the trigger but for the interference of John Brown, who threw himself upon the enraged black and stayed his hand.

"Don't do it; not this time, Judah. I know your feelings, but you'll have another chance, for these fellows will be after us again. There's too much at stake now; we owe Mr. Maxwell something for all he has suffered. Don't do it."

"Yes," chimed in Maybee; "if you let up now, Judah, I'll be tee-totally smashed if I don't lend you a hand and stand by for fair play."

"Why stay my hand? Vengeance is sweet," replied Judah, his dark, glowing eyes fixed in a threatening gaze upon his foe bound and helpless at his feet.

"There is a time for everything, my son. Stay thy hand and fear not; vengeance is mine," said John Brown.

Judah was silent for a moment, but stood as if gathering strength to resist temptation. Finally he said:

"I am the Lord's instrument to kill this man. Promise me that when this villain's life shall lie in the gift of any man in the camp, he shall be given to me as my right, to deal with him as I see fit."

"We promise," broke from Captain Brown and Ebenezer Maybee simultaneously.

Sternly the determined trio, aided by Winona in her boy's attire, secured the officials of the jail and quieted the prisoners. It was hard to resist the entreaties of the slaves confined there, but, after a hurried consultation, it was deemed advisable not to burden themselves with fugitive slaves.

With few words the business of releasing Maxwell was carried forward. When Maybee unlocked the door of Warren's cell with the warden's key, there were tears in his eyes as he beheld the wreck that two months of imprisonment and brutal treatment had made of the stalwart athlete. The burns were not yet healed, and great red scars disfigured his face in spots; he still wore his arm in a sling; starvation, physical weakness and lack of cleanliness had done their worst.

Maybee's heart was too full for words as he folded the emaciated form in his arms, and openly wiped the tears from his eyes; his were the feelings of a father: "This, my son, was dead and is alive again."

"Oh, never m-min' my cryin'! 'Taint nothin'. Some fellers cries easier than others," he muttered as the tears rolled unchecked down his cheeks. Winona was sobbing in company and Judah was feeling strange about the eyes also.

"I never thought to see you again, boys" said Warren solemnly, as he held their warm, friendly hands and felt the clasp of honest friendship. "I understand the slavery question through and through. Experience is a stern teacher."

"Min' my words to you, Maxwell? But God knows I didn't reckon they'd come home to you so awful an' suddint-like. I have never feared for you, my boy, even when things l-looked blackes'; but if you don' fin' Bill Thomson somewhere, some time, an' choke him an' tear his win'pipe to fiddlestrings, you ain't got a drop of British blood in yer whole carcass!"

"Amen!" ejaculated Captain Brown. "Come, boys, time's up."

Judah lifted Maxwell in his strong arms preparatory to carrying him out to the waiting vehicle. He felt all his passionate jealousy die a sudden death as pity and compassion stirred his heart for the sufferings of his rival. "Here is another white man who does not deserve death at a Negro's hands," he told himself.

Winona was silent and constrained in manner. For the first time since she had adopted her strange dress she felt a wave of self-consciousness that rendered her ashamed. She turned mechanically and walked by Judah's side as he bore his almost helpless burden to the wagon, and seated herself beside the driver, still silent.

Warren, reclining on fresh straw in the bottom of the cart, wondered in semi-consciousness at the sweetness of the air dashed in his face with the great gusts of rain, and at his own stupidity in not recognizing Winona; beneath the stain with which she had darkened her own exquisite complexion, he could now plainly trace the linaments that had so charmed him. Then, lulled by the motion of the vehicle and weakened by excitement, he slept the sleep of exhaustion.

Captain Brown had ordered the prisoners placed in Warren's abandoned cell, and, locking the door, took the key with them to clog the movements of pursuers as much as possible; then they passed out, closing and fastening the great outer door and also taking that key with them.

Meanwhile, outside the building, in the most advantageous positions, hidden by the blackness of the night, ten stalwart Free-State men had waited with impatience the return of Captain Brown and his companions.

The storm favored the rescuing party; not a sound disturbed

their watch but the awful peals of thunder reverberating over the land in solemn majesty. Torrents of rain drenched them to the skin, but inured to hardships they rejoiced in the favor which the storm bestowed.

As the rescuers issued from beneath the jail's shadow, Judah bearing Warren in his arms, the guard gathered silently about the wagon in silent congratulation that thus far they had been successful; then mounting their waiting horses, the whole party rode as fast as possible toward the river.

As dawn approached the storm cleared, and the first faint streaks of light that appeared in the east were tinged with the sun-god's brilliant hues. By this time our party had reached the riverbanks, and Warren was removed to the boat, the horses and wagon being returned to the friendly settlers who had loaned them, and in the sweet freshness of the dawn, strong arms propelled the boat toward the Kansas shore.

On the Kansas side fresh horses awaited them and another wagon. Friends met them at short intervals along the route, the people turning out en masse in an ovation to the rescuers and rescued, for Maxwell's story was known in every village and town throughout the country. They stopped at a comfortable farmhouse for breakfast, and Warren was allowed the luxury of a bath and given clean though coarse clothing.

They travelled all day and night, seeming not to feel fatigue but bent upon distancing a pursuing party, finding fresh horses at intervals, and food in abundance. Thus the settlers exemplified in kind acts the sympathy that upheld the common cause of human rights for all mankind.

The journey to the Brown camp was not a short one, and burdened with an invalid, it added to the length of time necessary to make the trip. Every step, too, was fraught with danger, but not a murmur came from the men who with stern faces and senses alert cautiously picked their way to safety. It was still twenty miles across country as the crow flies, after three days of swift travelling; the meandering of the road added five more. Then there was a barrier of foothills, and finally the mountains which lifted themselves abruptly out of the flat rolling surface surrounding them.

There might be marauding parties hiding in the brush and thickets, and for aught the horsemen knew, the stacks of hay and fodder that rose like huge monuments on every side, out of the twilight gloom surrounding the lonely farms, might conceal dozens of their foes. The nights were wearing for they never knew quite how the situation was going to develop.

Most of the time Warren was in a semi-conscious state exciting fears of a return of fever and delirium. The sight of guns and the constant talk of the battle yet to come had a depressing effect upon the invalid; they gave a sinister effect to his freedom. Soon the smiling sunlit valley they were entering became to his disordered fancy a return into the dangers and sufferings of a Missouri prison.

Much to Captain Brown's relief, the late afternoon found them in the pleasant hollow two miles distant from the camp, and night gave them safety within the shadow of the great hills.

CHAPTER XIV

The physical shock to Maxwell's system had worked no lasting harm to his constitution. Freedom, cleanliness and nourishing food were magical in their effects, and a week after his rescue found him up and about gradually joining in the duties of the camp.

And what an experience it was to this young, tenderly nurtured aristocrat! It was his function to watch the shifting panorama of defiance to despotism as outlined in the daily lives of the patriotic abolitionists with whom his lot was now cast. He lived in an atmosphere of suspicion, for to be identified with John Brown was a forfeit of one's life; a price was on the head of every individual associated with him. Yet with all the discouraging aspects of the cause these men had espoused, scarcely a day went by that did not bring news of the movement of the enemy, sent by some friendly well-wisher, or a token of good feeling in the form of much needed supplies, and even delicacies for the sick.

The menace of impending danger, however, hung over them constantly. The very ground was honey-combed with intrigue set on foot by resolute and determined Southerners who vowed to crush out all opposition and make the institution of slavery national, and with this determination conspiracies of every kind were abroad to circumvent the North and its agents, of whom the Kansas pro-slavery men were the most belligerent, in the growing desire of that section to make freedom universal within the borders of the United States. He saw plainly that the nation was fast approaching an alarming crisis in its affairs, and, by contrast with the arguments and attitude of the South, that the weight of principle was with the North where the people had been alarmingly docile and conservative. The efforts, in Congress, and in pro-slavery political conventions, were but an aggravation, and not satisfactory to either side, adding fuel to the flame that was making terrible inroads upon the public peace.

The Brown men were restless because of enforced inactivity, for all felt a blow was impending, marvelling that it was so long delayed, and anxious to force an issue—anything was better than uncertainty—for the lengthened time of waiting was a terrible strain upon the nerves.

Captain Brown sought the company of Maxwell frequently, conversing freely of his hopes and fears. The young man was greatly impressed with the clearness and value of his knowledge of military tactics. He was familiar with all the great battles of ancient and modern times; had visited every noted battlefield of old Europe and carefully sketched plans of the operations and positions of the opposing forces. These maps were a source of delight to the old man who went over them with Warren, explaining with great enthusiasm the intricacies of the manœuvres. During this intimacy, Captain Brown revealed to his guest his own great scheme for an insurrection among the slaves—an uprising of such magnitude that it should once and for all time settle the question of slavery.

Maxwell promised money and ammunition and arms, but his heart was heavy as he listened to plans and purposes that had been long in maturing, brooded over silently and secretly, with much earnest thought, and under a solemn sense of religious duty. What would be the fate of the band of hero-martyrs who would dash themselves to bloody death under the inspired influence of their intrepid leader? The prison walls would shake from summit to foundation, and wild alarm would fill every tyrant heart in all the South, of this he had no doubt, but would the effort be crowned with success? It was hardly possible.

Summer was advancing ever deeper in dust. The sky was tarnishing with haze. The sunsets longer in burning out in the west, in tragic colors. Scouts were continually posting back and forth. Warren had promised himself while in prison never to complain of the dispensations of Providence should he live to enjoy freedom again; but at the end of the second

week of convalescence he was imploring to be allowed to join
the scouting parties of skirmishers. The stir of the camp fired
his blood; he was devoured by anxiety to be among the busy
people of the world once more, to know what events had
transpired in his absence and how the world had wagged
along without his help, forgetting that a vacuum is quickly
filled and we are soon forgotten.

"The sooner I get out of this the better, Maybee;" he
exclaimed one day, rousing himself from painful memories
of home and his failure to accomplish the mission he had set
out so confidently to perform. "I want to get home!"

"Jest so," replied Maybee, with ready sarcasm. "We'll start
tomorrow morning on foot."

"No—you know what I mean. I want to—"

"Oh, yes, cert'nly; jest so. We might, ef you're in a great
hurry, start this evenin'. The Rangers are all over the place
between here an' civilization, but we won't stop for that, for
with a strong fightin' man like you fer a companion there'd
be nothin' to fear—about gittin' a through ticket to glory this
week."

"Cease jesting, Maybee! What I want is to make every
hour tell upon the work of getting well—not only on my own
account, but—we owe that poor girl something."

"Hem!" grunted Maybee, shooting the young man a keen
look under which he colored slightly. "That's right; always
keep the weaker vessel in yer mem'ry; trust in the Lord and
keep yer powder dry, as our friend Brown'd say. And that
remin's me of 'Tarius up home. 'Tarius got religion and
when the day came roun' fer the baptism' it was a January
blizzard, although well along in the month of April. 'Tarius
ain't fond of cold weather no how, and he didn't show up
along with the other candidates. Next day the minister came

up to look after 'Tarius. 'Don' ye trus' in de Lawd, brother?'
says the minister. 'Yes, brother,' says Tarius, 'I trust pintedly
in de Lawd; but I ain't gwine fool wif God!' That's my advice
to you, Maxwell; don't you fool with Providence; jest let
well-enough alone."

The next afternoon Mr. Maybee came rushing back to the
cabin which was their mutual home.

"Well, young feller, we're in fer it, an' no mistake. You'll
git fightin' a-plenty before forty-eight hours."

"What's it?" queried Maxwell languidly, "another false
alarm?"

"No, by gosh; it's the real thing this time. The Rangers
are at Carlton's. You remember hearin' Parson Steward speak
of Reynolds, don' you?" Maxwell nodded.

"He's come up to camp an' brought Brown the news."

"How soon will they get here?"

"Cayn't tell; maybe tomorrow an' perhaps not before nex'
week; but it's boun' to come. Dog my cats, if I'm sorry. I
fairly itch to git my hands on the onery cusses that killed the
parson."

"Anything is better than waiting; it takes the life out of a
man. I shall not feel safe until I get my feet on British soil
once more. God being my helper, Maybee, I'll never set foot
on the soil of the 'greatest (?) Republic on earth' again," he
finished earnestly.

Mr. Maybee chuckled.

"Con-vinced are you? They used ter tell me when I was a
little shaver that the proof of the puddin' was in swallerin'
the bag—that is, pervidin' it was a biled puddin'. I'll 'low
them varmints heat you pretty hot, but there's nothin' so
convincin' as ex-perience. I might a talked to you fer forty

days an' nights, wastin' my breath fer nothin', an' you'd a said to yourself 'Maybee's stretchin' it; 'taint quarter so bad as he makes out;' but jest as soon as they git to work on your anatermy yer fin' out that Maybee was mild by comparison. The South's a horned hornet on the 'nigger' question. Time n'r tide, n'r God A'mighty aint goin' to change 'em this week."

"Well, I'm ready for them; I'm feeling decidedly fit," replied Maxwell.

"Good. Reynolds left you a message, a sort of warning. Thomson says the nex' time he gits you he'll fix you, law or no law; he's goin' to flog you first like a nigger, an' then burn you an' send your ashes to your folks in England in a chiny vase. How's that strike you?"

"He will if he's lucky; but I have my doubts."

Maybee gazed at him in silent admiration a moment before he said: "British grit a plenty in you, by thunder; that's the talk."

Preparations immediately went forward in the camp for meeting the enemy. Winona's cave on the mountainside was to be stored with provision, ammunition and all other necessaries. The men worked all night in detachments, watch and watch.

Warren had seen very little of Winona; she kept with the women.

Thinking of the coming conflict, Warren climbed the slope leading to the top of the highest peak, and established himself there as a lookout. It was near the cave in which supplies were being stored, and where the women and children would find a refuge. Presently he saw Winona loitering up the hillside with downcast eyes. As she drew near, the magnetism of his gaze compelled her glance to seek his face. She started, and would have turned back but Warren called out in a kindly voice not in the least alarming:

"Come, see this fine sweep of country. We cannot be surprised."

The sudden blush that had suffused her cheek at sight of him died out, leaving her serious and calm. The last few days she had thawed somewhat out of her coldness, for care could not live with youth and gaiety and the high-tide of summer weather, and the propinquity, morning, noon and night, of the society of the well-beloved one.

More and more Warren felt toward her as to a darling, irresistible child, and sometimes as to a young goddess far beyond him, as he realized how pure and sweet the inner life of this childwoman. The noisome things that creep and crawl about the life of the bond chattel had fallen away from her. She was unique: a surprise every day in that she was innocence personified and yet so deliciously womanly,

> "Standing, with reluctant feet,
> Where the brook and river meet,
> Womanhood and childhood fleet!"

In this last week of returning strength, Winona imagined, when she saw Maxwell sitting among the men of the camp moody and silent, that he was remembering his home with longing and awaiting the moment for safe departure with impatience.

During her weeks of unselfish devotion when she had played the role of the boy nurse so successfully, she had been purely and proudly glad. Now, little by little, a gulf had opened between them which to her unsophisticated mind could not be bridged. There lay the misery of the present time—

she was nothing to him. Does any love resign its self-imposed tasks of delightful cares and happy anxieties without a pang? Like any other young untrained creature, she tormented herself with fears that were but shadows and railed at barriers which she herself had raised, even while she argued that Fate had fixed impassable chasms of race and caste between them.

"How a man glories in war," she said, after a silence, from her seat on a jagged rock overhanging the cliff.

"You, with your Indian training, ought to feel with us and not think of fear," said Warren.

"But then, I am not of the blood."

"True."

His reply fell upon her ear like a reproach—a reflection upon her Negro origin. Her suspicion sounded in her voice as she replied:

"Better an Indian than a Negro? I do not blame you for your preference."

"Why speak with that tone—so scornfully? Is it possible that you can think so meanly of me?"

She could not meet his eye, but her answer was humbly given—her answer couched in the language of the tribes.

"Are you not a white brave? Do not all of them hate the black blood?"

"No; not all white men, thank God. In my country we think not of the color of the skin but of the man—the woman—the heart."

"Oh, your country! Do you know, I believe my dear papa was of the same?"

Her head rested against the tree back of her; the lace-work of the pine ashes formed upon her knees and enveloped her as a cloud.

He nodded in reply, and continued, musingly, as his eyes wandered off over the plain at his feet:

"England is a country to die for—rich, grand, humane! You shall see it for yourself."

"Which is my country, I wonder? Judah says that he will not fight for the Stars and Stripes if war comes—the flag that makes the Negro a slave. This country mine? No, no! The fearful things that I have seen——" she broke off abruptly. "My father's country shall be mine."

"Better reserve your decision until you marry."

"I shall never marry."

"But why?" asked Warren, opening his eyes in surprise. "Nonsense; all girls expect to marry, and do—most of them."

"I cannot marry out of the class of my father," she replied, with head proudly erect. "It follows, then, that I shall never marry."

"Nonsense," again returned Warren. "You will not live and grow old alone. Mere birth does not count for more than one's whole training afterward, and you have been bred among another race altogether."

"But the degradation of the two years just passed can never leave me; life will never seem quite the same," she said in a stifled voice full of pain. "I shall be a nun." She ended with a little laugh, but the voice quivered beneath it.

Warren scarcely knew how to answer her; he felt awkward and mere words sounded hollow.

"See here," he began abruptly; "it is no use to dwell on a painful subject; just strive to forget all about it and take the happiness that comes your way. As for the last alternative—you will not be happy."

"That cannot be helped. Perhaps I should not be happy if I married," she went on with a smile upon her lips, but deep gravity in her eyes. "It would depend upon the man who must know all my past. Nokomis used to say 'they are all the same—the men. When you are beautiful they kill each other for you; when you are plain they sneer at you.' "

"Old Nokomis! She spoke of red men, not white men."

"Yes; all the same Nokomis said: men are men. People will never forget that my mother was an American Negress even if I forget. No," concluded the girl with a wise little shake of her cropped head, "I shall go to the convent."

Warren dissembled his intense amusement, but beneath his smile was a tear for the tender, helpless creature trying so bravely to crush out of sight the tender flowers of her maiden heart. At length he said:

"Who can foresee the future? There are men with red blood in their veins; not all are empty caskets. How can you talk of convents—you who will go to England with me; and perhaps, who can tell, you may marry a duke. But believe me, Winona, you think too seriously of your position," he concluded, dropping his jesting air.

" 'You have too much respect upon the world:
They lose it that do buy it with much care.' "

Silence fell between them for a time, and the evening shadows gradually shut the eye of day. Clear and shrill upon the air fell the notes of a bugle, once—twice—thrice—it rose in warning cadence. Winona sprang to her feet with the words, " 'Tis Judah! There is danger! Let us go at once!"

So violent was her start that she came perilously near falling to the plain below, which on this side the hill was a sheer descent of many feet, to where the Possawatomie rilled along its peaceful course.

"God!" broke from Warren's white lips as he caught her

just in time. For a second he held her in a close embrace, she clinging to him in affright. There was extraordinary gravity in both look and tone as he leaned his cheek against the cropped curly head that nestled close to his throat like a frightened child, and said: "Winona, let me say it now before we go to meet we know not what—thank God I have known you—so noble, so patient, so sweet. Despite the dangers of our situation, the hours we have passed together have been the happiest of my life."

Forgetful of time and place, youth yielded to the sway of the love-god, and for one dazzling instant the glory of heaven shone upon them.

"What harm just once?" thought the girl as she rested in his embrace. "Tomorrow it may not matter about race or creed, one or both of us will belong to eternity; pray God that I may be the one to go."

CHAPTER XV

It was not Judah who had blown the warning blast, but it came from one of his party sent by him to warn them of the approach of the enemy. The messenger was pale as death, the veins standing out on his forehead, and his left arm hanging useless at his side. The horse, panting and covered with foam, stopped, and Maybee caught the rider in his arms.

"What is it, boy?" he asked.

"Rangers," the poor fellow gasped out. "Three hundred around the old farmhouse. Coming down on you. Judah says he can hold them off until daybreak. I got out, but they shot me."

Captain Brown seemed transformed; his eyes burned like coals. Maybee put his hand on his shoulder.

"What'll you do, Captain, start now or later?"

"Two hours after midnight. The boy knows his business," was the laconic reply as, drawing long, deep breaths, John Brown made for the horses.

The evening was spent in preparations for the start. The camp was abandoned, the women hastily fleeing to the refuge on the mountainside. Three men were to be left to guard the cave, but every woman carried a rifle in her hand and was prepared to use it. Winona was in command of the home-guard.

The last words of counsel and instruction were spoken. It was nearly daylight. Faint streaks of light were already visible in the eastern horizon. They left the camp two hours after midnight and the last look that Warren gave toward the mountain showed him the slight figure of Winona with rifle in hand waving him a farewell salute.

To Maxwell the one hundred intrepid riders, with whom he was associated, represented a hopeless cause. How could they hope to conquer a force of three hundred desperadoes? But Warren knew not the valor of his companions nor the terror which the Brown men inspired.

The attacking point was an hour's fast riding from camp. The dawn increased rapidly. Maybee fell back to Warren's side with an air of repressed excitement, and his eyes blazed. He touched the young man's arm as they rode and pointed to the left where they saw, in a cloud of dust, another party of horsemen coming toward them.

"Who are they, friends or enemies?"

"Reinforcements. They are the boys Reynolds has collected to help us. Nothing the matter with him or them, you bet.

Reynolds ain't been the same since Steward was killed. His heart's broke 'long with it an' he's wil' fer revenge. Every one of the boys with him is a fighter, too, from 'way back. I know 'em, Maxwell; an' now,—me, if we don't give them hell-hounds the biggest thrashing they've had since the campaign opened, you may call me a squaw. But who's that riding beside Reynolds?" he broke off abruptly. "Dog my cats, may I be teetotally smashed ef it don't look like Parson Steward!"

"No!" cried Warren in a fever of excitement at the words. "Impossible!"

"We'll soon know," replied Maybee.

On they sped over the space that separated the two parties. Then the order came to halt, and Parson Steward rode into the midst of the column while the men broke into wild cheering at sight of him. There was not much time to spend in greeting, but the vice-like grip of friendly hands spoke louder than words. Warren could not speak for a moment as before his mind the picture of the last night spent in Steward's company passed vividly. The parson, too, was visibly affected.

"Praise God from whom all blessings flow," he said solemnly.

"Amen," supplemented Maxwell, then they rode cautiously forward, the Captain keeping his men at the steady pace at which they had started out. Now and then a stray shot from the farmhouse showed them that Judah was holding his own. The firing increased as they neared the house, coming mainly from the shelter of trees and bushes at the side. Finally it became incessant, and the Captain beckoned to Maybee, after he had halted the column, and they rode cautiously ahead.

Soon they returned, and coming to Warren drew him to the flank of the company.

"My boy, you are going under fire. Are you prepared for any happening? Are you all right?"

"All right," replied Warren.

"Well," said Captain Brown with a sigh, "shake hands; fire low; look well to the hinder side of your rifle. God bless you!" and he passed forward to the head of the column. The parson went with him.

Maybee was beside himself with excitement over the parson's rescue.

"Now you'll see some fun," said he; and then, all of a sudden the fire of battle caught him and he flew into a sort of frenzy. He rode quickly behind the men, saying in low, concentrated tones: "Give 'em—boys! Remember our friends they've butchered, and our women and little children. Give 'em—, I say!" Then growing calmer he turned to Warren once more, saying: "Maxwell, I reckon you've got as big a score to settle as anyone of us." Then he, too, wrung Warren's hand and rode away to the head of the column.

A man fell dead in the Brown ranks. The Rangers now advanced in solid column to meet them. Then came the order to charge, and with a wild yell the pent-up excitement of the men broke forth and pell-mell they hurled themselves upon the foe.

Then ensued a wild scene; a turmoil of shots, cries, groans and shrieks—pandemonium on earth. Maxwell very soon found himself in the thickest of it, off his horse and doing his part in a fierce hand-to-hand encounter with one who had fired a pistol straight at him. The bullet flew wide of the mark and in an instant he had flung the snarling demon down and had hurled himself upon him. They struggled fiercely back and forth tearing at each other with all their might. Gideon Holmes' long, lithe fingers were sunk deep in his throat in an endeavor to force him to release his hold. With a mighty effort, Maxwell brought the butt of his pistol down on his enemy's face in a smashing blow. At last he had caught the full spirit of the fiercest; the blood mounted to his brain, and with ungovernable rage, thinking only of the sufferings he had endured in the dreadful time of imprisonment, he continued his rain of blows upon his prostrate foe until the very limpness of the inert body beneath him stayed his hand.

Through the smoke he saw Captain Brown and Parson Steward and Ebenezer Maybee fighting like mad, with blazing rifles, and deep curses from Maybee mingling with the hoarse shouting of passages of Scripture by the parson.

"Behold, the uncircumcised Philistine, how he defies the armies of the living God." And again—"Let no man's heart fail because of him; thy servant will go and fight with this Philistine;" "Fear not, neither be thou dismayed."

It was a terrible struggle between the two great forces—Right and Wrong. Drunken with vile passions, the Rangers fought madly but in vain against the almost supernatural prowess of their oponents; like the old Spartans who braided their hair and advanced with songs and dancing to meet the enemy, the anti-slavery men advanced singing hymns and praising God.

The last stand was made. The desperadoes fled in all directions. Some went toward the hills; among them was Thomson. He spurred his horse across the plain, abandoning him at the edge of the rising ground. For hours he skulked among the trees or crawled or crept over stones and through bushes, gradually rising higher and higher above the plain.

Brown's forces swarmed over the ground, slaying as they met the flying foe. He saw Col. Titus pursued by Judah, speeding over the plain; he saw them meet and the Colonel fall. A moment—a moment—a convulsive uplifting of arms, and then Judah turned and slowly began climbing the ascent.

Thomson, regardless of consequences, sprang clear of the underbrush and darted up the mountainside. Once he thought he heard a rifle crack—on—on he sped. He climbed upon a ledge and lay there, peeping through a crevice made by the meeting of gigantic rocks, and gaining his breath. He saw no one. Evidently Judah had missed him, and he began to plan a descent from the opposite side. Searching the cliff for a landing place, he saw the Possawatamie gurgling along sixty feet below over pebbles, a torrent in winter but now only a silver thread that trickled lightly along.

He saw a jutting ledge ten feet below which promised an easy footing to the valley; once there he could soon evade pursuit. He bound his rifle securely to him by his belt and crawled out on the shelving rock; then swinging clear by the aid of a tough sapling, he cautiously dropped. He paused to regain his breath, gazing speculatively about him the while. Yes, it was as he had thought. On this side the cliffs broke into a series of giant steps which led easily to the river. "Lucky once more," he chuckled, speaking his thoughts aloud. "That black demon had missed again. Nex' turn is mine, an' I sha'n't miss him."

Thus musing he turned to begin the descent—and faced Judah where he stood in the shadow of a great boulder, with a smile on his face, watching the movements of his enemy the overseer. Thomson turned as if to run down the mountainside.

"Stop where you are!" thundered the giant black.

The man obeyed, but his hand sought his rifle.

"Hands up!" again came the pealing voice. The order was given along the barrel of a gleaming rifle. Thomson's hands went up obediently.

"You are surprised to see me," said Judah grimly. A period of silence ensued. It was a dramatic scene, far from the scene of recent strife. The morning sun had broke in dazzling splendor over the earth; the birds were feeding their young families and flew from tree to tree in neighborly fashion; the murmur of bees humming and of the stream far below mingled harmoniously. All was peace. But within two human hearts surged the wild passions of fierce animals at bay.

Judah looked at his foe with the air of one about entering upon a momentous task. Thomson stood with the narrow ledge for a foothold and the clouds of heaven at his back, facing he knew not what. His head throbbed and in his ears were the drum-beats of an army; his heart was sick with terror for this human torturer, this man-mangler and woman-beater was an arrant coward. When he could bear the silence no longer he spoke:

"I suppose I am your prisoner?"

Judah smiled. It was a terrible smile, and carried in it all the pent-up suffering of two years of bodily torture and a century of lacerated manhood. Thomson feared him, and well he might. Again he spoke. The sound of his own voice gave him courage; anything to break the horrible silence and the chill of that icy smile.

"I am to be treated as a prisoner of war?"

This time Judah answered him.

"Would you have treated me as a prisoner of war if you had captured me?"

"No," broke involuntarily from Thomson's lips.

"Very well!"

"I demand to be taken before Captain Brown. Surely he is human; he will not give me into the hands of a savage to be tortured!" exclaimed the wretch in frantic desperation.

Again Judah smiled his calm, dispassionate smile as he examined his rifle, and then slowly brought it to his shoulder. "You who torture the slave without a thought of mercy, and who could treat a young white man—one of your own race— as you did Mr. Maxwell, fear to be tortured? Why, where is your boasted Southern bravery that has promised so much?"

Bill's teeth glittered in a grin of hate and fear.

"God! It's murder to kill a man with his hands up!" he shrieked.

"It rests with you whether or not I shoot you," replied Judah calmly. "I am going to give you one chance for life. It is a slim one, but more than you would give me."

Bill eyed him with a venomous look of terror and distrust; but his manner had changed to fawning smoothness.

"Judah," he began, "look a-here, I own I done you dirt mean, I do. I ask yer pardon—I couldn't do more'n that ef you was a white man, could I? Well, sir, I know you're a brave nigger, an' I know, too, it's nat'ral for you to lay it up agin me, fer I done yer dirt an' no mistake. But I had to; ef I'd showed you quarter, every nigger on the plantation 'd been hard to handle. It was necessary discipline, boy; nothin' particular agin you."

Bill's beady black eyes never left the Negro's face as he watched for a sign of wavering in the calm smile.

"Look a-here, I can tell you a heap of things 'd be worth more'n my life to the gal, an' Titus couldn't blame me for givin' the scheme away; what's money to life? It's worth a fortune to you to know what I can tell you this minute; only let me out of this, Jude."

But Judah knew his man. Not for one instant did Thomson deceive him. He judged it a righteous duty to condemn him to death.

"You stole Winona's liberty and mine. I know what your promises are worth. Do you think I would listen to a proposition coming from you, you infernal scoundrel? Get ready. I've sworn to kill you and I intend to keep my oath. When I count three jump backwards or I put a bullet into your miserable carcass. If you are alive when you strike the river, you can swim ashore; it's one chance in ten. Choose."

Bill grew white; his eyes gleamed like those of a trapped rat, but he seemed to realize that it was useless to plead for mercy at the hands of the calm, smiling Negro before him.

"One!" counted Judah, moving toward Thomson a step as he counted. There he paused, desiring that the wretch should suffer all, in anticipation, that he had caused others to suffer.

"Two!" Thomson moved backward involuntarily, but still he did not lose his footing. Again Judah paused.

"Three!"

With a wild curse, Thomson sprang off the ledge. A fearfully quiet moment followed. Judah did not move. There came a crashing of underbrush, a sound of rolling rocks and gravel, a plash of water—silence.

(To be continued.)

CHAPTER XV.—(Concluded.)

A superb, masterful smile played over the ebon visage of the now solitary figure upon the mountainside. In his face shone a glitter of the untamable torrid ferocity of his tribe not pleasing to see. The first act in his bold and sagacious plans was successful; once free, it only remained for him to carry them out with the same inexorable energy.

The upraised hands and straining eyeballs, rigid and stone-like, the gapping, bloodless lips, the muttered curse—all had passed from sight like an unpleasant dream. Judah, intently listening to the ominous thud, thud, thud, of that falling body, the swish of displaced bushes, and the rattle of gravel and stones, was not moved from the stoicism of his manner, save in the fearful smile that still played over his features. Then, as he listened, there came a last awful cry, a scream that startled all nature and awoke echo after echo along the hillside—a scream like no sound in earth or heaven—unhuman and appalling. He made a step forward to the brink and looked over and then drew back.

A while he leaned upon his gun in meditation. He was a morbid soul preying upon its recollection, without the gift of varied experience; it was not strange that vengeance seemed to him earth's only blessing. To him his recent act was one of simple justice. Hate, impotent hate, had consumed his young heart for two years. An eye for an eye was a doctrine that commended itself more and more to him as he viewed the Negro's condition in life, and beheld the horrors of the system under which he lived.

Judged by the ordinary eye Judah's nature was horrible, but it was the natural outcome or growth of the "system" as practiced upon the black race. He felt neither remorse nor commiseration for the deed just committed. To him it was his only chance of redress for the personal wrongs inflicted upon Winona and himself by the strong, aggressive race holding them in unlawful bondage. Time and place were forgotten as he stood there like a statue. He was back in the past. His thoughts ran backwards in an unbroken train until the scene before him changed to the island and the day when the careless happiness of his free youth was broken by the advent of the strangers, Colonel Titus and Bill Thomson. Then had followed the murder of White Eagle.

Yes, once he had a friend, but he was dead—dead by a man's hand. And he—but a moment since went over the cliff. It was well!

As through a mist, queries and propositions and possibilities took shape, there on the cliffside, that had never before presented themselves to him. As he stood in the blazing sunlight, his brain throbbed intolerably and every pulsation was a shooting pain. Why had he been so dull of comprehension? What if a thought just born in his mind should prove true? O, to be free once more!

There was a rustle of leaves, and out from the shadow of the trees filed a number of anti-slavery men headed by Captain Brown and Parson Steward.

"Well, Judah," said Captain Brown, "we've been watching your little drama. You promised to kill him and you've done it."

"Boys," returned Judah, "and all of you, I leave it to you if I'm not right in ridding the world of such a beast as Thomson."

The men set up a cheer that echoed and re-echoed among the hills. The women in the cave heard with joyful hearts.

"I'd kill a snake wherever I f'und him," said one; "wudn't you, Parson?"

"Sure," replied the parson. "This is a holy war, and it's only just begun."

"This is a great day. Praise God from whom all blessings flow; we've put to flight the armies of the Philistines," said Captain Brown.

"It is justice! I am satisfied," said Judah, scanning each solemn face before him with his keen eyes.

Parson Steward wore the same calm, unruffled front touched with faint humor that had characterized him when first introduced to our readers. He was a trifle paler, but that was all that reminded one of the fact that only by a miracle, as it were, he had escaped death at the hands of cruel men. Judah grasped his hand in both of his.

"No wonder we have won, Parson; I heard them cry: 'Look at the Parson!' and then they fled in every direction."

"They reckoned he was dead, an' 'lowed he was a ghost. By gum, how they broke! It was easy work to pick them off," broke in one of the men.

"Perhaps you'll be good enough to tell me where you come from, Parson; you've been dead to us for weeks past."

"Yes; we all want to learn how the Parson got here," said Captain Brown.

"Oh, I been pretty near you right along," replied the Parson, not a whit hurried or excited by the interest of his audience. "That night on the road with young Maxwell was a terrible one. They caught me off my guard for the first time in my life. I was filled with shot and left for dead. Next morning Reynolds got wind of the proceedings and went out to find my remains and give me a decent burial. I was breathing when he got me. That settled it. He toted me on his back to his house and hid me in his loft, and there I lay eight long weeks and every one thinking me dead. Boys, it was a close shave, and when I thought of my wife and children it was tough, turrible tough on the old man, but I left them in the hands of that God who has never failed me yet, and here I am right side up with care, and the old woman and kids safe and hearty here in your camp." He ended solemnly, and the men doffed their ragged hats in humble homage.

"Amen!" said Captain Brown. "All's well that ends well," and they continued their tramp up the mountainside to the cave.

Impelled by a morbid fascination, Judah climbed down the mountain path seeking the bed of the stream below where lay the body of his foe.

CHAPTER XVI

All through the long morning Winona patrolled her beat listening with anxious heart to the sounds of distant firing which the breeze brought to her ears from time to time. At noon one of Captain Brown's daughters brought her coffee; it was the only break in her solitary vigil. She scanned the horizon with anxious eyes, but having no field-glass was unable to distinguish friend from foe among the figures scarcely discernible with the naked eye.

In the dim vistas of the woods it was cool and shady, but the sun beat down mercilessly upon the sides of the cliff, and as she watched the shifting rays she wondered how the battle went in sickening dread, and then rebuked her own impa-

tience for news. As the hours wore on, the shadows began to
lengthen; their long fingers crossed the hills pointing darkly
toward the river. The girl was unhappy and fearful in her
mind; yet she tried to comfort herself, but for a time her
firm head played her false enough to picture flames leaping
from the woods from the low roofs of the huts amid the corn-
stalks, and little children under merciless hoofs, and the awful
tumult of flight for life. That was no more than they must
expect if the Rangers won. "But they won't win!" she thought,
with a brave smile on her face and a heavy heart in her
bosom.

Overcome at length by the restless fever within, she determined to risk all in an endeavor to obtain news of her
friends—of Warren. She started toward the battle line about
the time Judah met Thomson on another spur of the mountain.
Reaching the stream Winona followed the bed for some
distance in the shadow of the cliff.

Suddenly, far above her head, she heard the gunshot, the
scream of agony tearing through space, at once an alarum
and rallying cry; it meant to the lonely girl all the savagery
of battle; it might mean havoc and despair. She covered her
face with her hands 'a moment, removing them the next
instant in time to see a falling body drop into the water almost
at her feet. Terror rendered her motionless. The soft waves
stole up and flung themselves over the quiet body huddled
there breast high in the stream. Then a new thought came to
her—"if it should be Warren!" Gathering herself up, she
stumbled through the grass to the edge of the river, fell on
her knees on the bank and surveyed the helpless shape lying
there. A groan broke from the white lips. She nerved herself
to move nearer. She took the unconscious head in both hands

and turned the face toward herself and—looked into the sightless eyes of Thomson.

Her relief was so great that she sobbed aloud; then after giving broken thanks that it was not Warren, she rose from her knees and began to look about her for means to succor the man before her. He was her enemy, but the mother instinct that dwells in all good women, which can look on death, gave her calmness and strength to do, and the heart to forgive.

She turned to seek help and faced Judah coming out from the trees. "Oh, Judah, he is alive!" she exclaimed, pointing to the inanimate figure in the water. Judah gazed at her in surprise, then said:

"What! Not dead yet? I thought I had settled his case for all time. How came you here?"

"I came out to look for the wounded. Help me to carry this man to camp; surely you are satisfied now. You cannot shoot a dying man," she said, sternly catching the ferocious light that still glimmered in his eyes as he lifted his gun to the hollow of his arm.

"I did it for you as much as for myself. Have you forgotten your father?" he added, reproachfully.

"I do not forget. God forbid! But you have done enough."

"Not enough," replied Judah. "He is the hater of my race. He is of those who enslave both body and soul and damn us with ignorance and vice and take our manhood. I made an oath; it was no idle threat."

He poised his gun. Quick as a flash the girl threw herself before the unconscious Thomson. "You shall not! You make yourself as vile as the vilest of them—our enemies. Let the man die in peace. See, he is almost gone."

"Yes, Judah, it is enough; she is right," said Warren Maxwell's voice as he joined the group by the stream. "Surely you must be sick of bloodshed. Have you not had enough?"

With a glad cry Winona was folded in her lover's arms.

"Let it be as you wish," said Judah after a short time, as he silently viewed the happiness of the lovers. Then he prepared to help Warren lift Thomson from the stream. They turned faint and sick at the sight of the man's wounds. "His back is broken," said Warren, in reply to Winona's questioning eyes.

"It were more merciful to shoot him on the spot," said Judah, but even he felt now the sheer human repulsion from such butchery master him, as they moved slowly and carefully up the steep ascent.

The Rangers were completely routed by the desperate valor of the Brown men. Incredible as it seemed, most of the enemy had been killed outright and a number of prisoners taken, who were to be tried by court-martial and shot, according to the rough justice of the times.

The anti-slavery men met with small loss, but among the wounded was Ebenezer Maybee. With the other wounded men he was carried back to camp; at sunrise the next morning he was aroused form his stupor by a volley of musketry. Steward was at his side. He asked what it meant.

"Well, partner, you know we won the fight," said he. "Captain Brown is a shootin" all the pris'ners; well, now, ain't that tough fer a prefesser?"

"No, not all the prisoners," replied the Parson. "The most of them have been begged off by young Maxwell. He's the most softest hearted young feller I ever met for such a good shot."

"This yer's a good cause to go in, Parson."

The Parson answered grufly, in a choked voice: "You ain't goin' nowhere, partner; we'll pull you through."

Maybee's face worked, and he planted a knowing wink in vacancy. "We've been partners fer a right smart spell, ain't we, Parson?"

The Parson frowned hard to keep back the tears. "You're a man to tie to, Maybee."

"No, now," sputtered Maybee, breaking down at last; "d— ye, Parson, don't make a baby er me." Then with a change of voice he asked, "What's come o' Thomson an' the colonel?"

"Devil's got the colonel and he's waiting fer Thomson; we've got him with a broken back next door to this house. Judah did it. My! but that boy's as ferocious as a tiger."

Maybee nodded. "Well, he's a good boy, is Jude; I've knowed him sense he was knee-high to a toad; been through a heap; don' blame him fer bein' ferocious. I ain't sorry I jined the boys, Parson, fer all I got my ticket. It's a good cause, Parson, a good cause, and you'll see a heap o' fun befo' you're through with it; wish't I could be here to see it, too. You found your ol' woman and the kids all safe, Parson?"

"I did," replied the Person, cordially.

"Jes' break it gently to Ma' Jane, partner, that I got my death in an hones' fight, an' tell her she's all right, havin' everything in her name an' power of attorney to boot."

"I will do so," promised the Parson, solemnly.

One of the men came in with a message for the Parson. Thomson was conscious and going fast; he wanted the Parson and Winona.

Thomson still lived; none knew why; his stupor had left him conscious. Paralyzed in every limb, he could talk in a strong voice and was perfectly sane, and recognized those about him, but he was going fast.

"How long do you give me, doc.?" he asked Warren, jokingly.

"Until it touches the heart," replied Warren solemnly.

"Then it will be soon?" Warren nodded.

Thomson appeared to be thinking. "No," he muttered finally with a sigh, "I got to own up. Colonel's dead, ain't he?" Warren bowed.

"Well, then, 'tain't no use holdin' out. Bring in the gal and Judah, an' take down every word I say if you want the gal to have her own. You're a lawyer, ain't you? Sent out here on the Carlingford case, warn't you? Never struck you that me and the Colonel knew where to find the man you was huntin', did it?" His voice was spent, and Warren, his mind in a tumult, held a glass of liquor to the dying man's lips, and then sent for Winona and Judah and Parson Steward. They came instantly, and with the transient vigor imparted by the liquor Thomson opened his eyes again and said, in a clear tone: "I'm here yet, Judah; I almost got the one chance you offered me, but it ain't for long I'll hender you; I'm goin' fast."

No one answered the wretch, baffled alike in base passion and violent deeds, but Parson Steward began a fervent prayer for the dying. Something of his awful need for such a petition must have filtered through the darkness of the sin-cursed heart and he presently comprehended dimly the great change before him. He whispered at the close:

"That's all right, Parson. I know I deviled you an' tried to kill you; I did the same to the nigger—an' to Maxwell— but I done the girl worse'n dirt. That's me you described in your prayer—a devilish wicked cuss, but I warn't always so, an' d—— me ef I ain't sorry! I'm goin' to try to make the damage I've done, good—to the girl, anyhow."

"Miserable sinners, miserable sinners, all of us. Madness is in our hearts while we live, and after that we go to the dead. God forgive us," muttered the Parson, not noting the dying man's profanity.

"Take down every word I say, Mr. Maxwell, an' let me kiss the Book that it's all true."

The scene was intensely dramatic. Winona sat with clasped hands folded on her breast; she knew not what new turn of Fortune's wheel awaited her. Judah's dark, handsome face and stalwart form were in the background where he stood in a group formed by Captain Brown and his sons, who had been called to witness the confession.

As for Warren Maxwell, he felt the most intense excitement he had ever experienced in his life. His hands shook; he could scarcely hold the pen. Most of us creatures of flesh and blood know what that terrible feeling of suspense, of dread, with which we approach a crisis in our fate. It is indefinable, but comes alike strong and weak, bold and timid. Such a crisis Maxwell felt was approaching in the fate of Winona and himself. There in we recognize the mesmeric force which holds mankind in an eternal brotherhood. Stronger than all in life, perhaps, is this mysterious force when a man feels that he has

> "Set his life upon a cast,
> And must abide the hazard of the die."

"Mr. Maxwell, you came to America to find the lost Captain Henry Carlingford, heir to the great Carlingford estates. You thought you were on a hopeless quest, did you not?" Warren nodded. It was noticeable that the man spoke in well-bred phrases, and had dropped his Southwestern accent. "You found the captain all right, but you never knew it. White Eagle was the man you wanted!"

There was a cry of astonishment from the listeners. Winona was in tears. Into Judah's eyes there crept the old ferocious glitter as he said:

"And so you murdered him! I have suspected as much for two years."

"No, no, Judah; I wasn't in that. Titus did the killing."

Now Warren lost sight of all personal interest in the case, seeing nothing but its legal aspect. He wrote rapidly questioning the man closely.

"Why did Col. Titus commit this murder? How came you to know this?"

With great effort Thomson replied:

"Titus hated him because he stood between him and a vast fortune, and he was also jealous of his wife's love for Henry Carlingford; he was her lover from childhood, and she loved him until death."

"Then if you know this, I want you to tell me who killed young Lord George. Miss Venton was affianced to him. You can tell if you will, for Miss Venton married Colonel Titus." Warren spoke sternly and solemnly.

Thomson muttered to himself and then was silent; all waited breathlessly in painful silence. Would he solve the riddle, and tell the story of the crime for which a guiltless man had been condemned by a jury of his peers years before?

"No, it won't neither," they heard him say, and then he spoke aloud: "Everything must be made clear?"

"Yes," said Warren, "if you wish to help this poor girl whom you have wronged so cruelly."

"It won't be against you when you get on the other side,

Thomson. Free your mind, my friend; it'll do you good. Terrible, verily, sir, is the Lord our God, but full of mercy," said Parson Steward.

"I'll take your word for it, Parson, but I never was much on religion; perhaps I'd fared better if I had been. Well, then, I killed Lord George. I swore to bring disgrace upon the entire Carlingford family. And I have done it; I have had a rich revenge. I was Lord George's valet; my sister, Miss Venton's maid. Lord George could never resist a pretty face, and my sister was more than that. Miss Venton loved Captain Henry, and Lord George found her an indifferent woman. She but obeyed her father's orders, and so Lord George made love to the maid, deceived her, and when he tired of his toy abandoned her to the usual fate of such women—the street. I found her when it was too late, and I swore revenge so long as one lived with a drop of the blood in his veins.

"One day the brothers quarrelled bitterly over Miss Venton; then was my chance. I shot Lord George in the back, and fled, knowing that suspicion would fall on Capt. Henry. It did; and two of my enemies were out of my way, for the Captain was tried and convicted and lived an outcast among savages for years; that was my little scheme for getting even. For the sake of his daughter Lillian, Colonel Titus killed White Eagle and held Winona as a slave, thus cutting off the last direct heir to Carlingford."

The faint voice ceased. The narrative was finished with great difficulty; the man failed rapidly. With a great effort he added: "Will you call it square, young fellow?—you and Winona—and Judah? I've done you bad, but I've told the truth at last. Mr. Maxwell—you know the rest—I reckon you'll marry the heiress—I'm glad.—Land in Canidy soon, boys; they'll be after you inside a week—big Government force——." Warren preserved his impassiveness by a struggle; the others followed the faint voice of the dying man with breathless attention; they felt that every word of this important confession was true.

Maxwell was filled with a hope that agitated him almost beyond control.

"Why, surely," he said, at length, in a voice that trembled in spite of himself, as he rose and joined Winona and Judah at the bedside, "I'm awfully grateful to you for telling me this; it makes my work easy."

"I sort o' hated to tell, fer a fac'," he said, falling back into his usual vernacular, "but I'm glad I done it." His voice failed; a gray shadow crept over the white face; all was still.

"Let us pray," and Parson Steward broke the silence. As they knelt about the bed, the crack of rifles broke in upon the fervent petition for mercy sent upwards by the man of God. It was the volley that carried death to the last of the captured Rangers. Guilty soul joined guilty soul in their flight to Eternity.

Ebenezer Maybee expressed no surprise when told of Thomson's confession.

"These happenings 'min' me o' the words o' the Psalmist that I've heard Parson quote so often: 'Thy right hand shall teach thee terrible things.' "

"Amen," said Steward. "But full of mercy, also, since they will deliver this poor girl from the hand of the spoiler."

Many tears were shed over Maybee's precarious condition, for he was dear to every soul in the camp. Winona and Judah established themselves as nurses at his bedside, bringing all their Indian knowledge of medicine to bear upon his case, and declaring that they would pull him through.

"My children," he said, after musing a while on the exciting tale just told him, "I believe I can match that story o' Thomson's. I have a surprisin' secret to unfol' to you. It will make the whole business clear. White Eagle must a perceived his end, an' he says to me, says he, jes' about a month before his disease, he says, 'Maybee, keep this here package if anything comes across me, 'tell my girl's a re-sponsible age.' After he was dead I said to myself—in the words of Scripter, 'a charge to keep I have' an't ain't safe to keep it; so I give the package to Ma' Jane an' she has it unto this day."

CHAPTER XVII

A week later our fugitives started for Canada via Buffalo, N. Y., by a circuitous path well known to Captain Brown. Mr. Maybee went along in an improvised ambulance, much improved in health and bearing well the fatigue of travel.

The Brown camp was deserted, and the Government troops, when they arrive, found only the blackened remains of the once busy settlement. Where the Rangers had paid the penalty of their crimes against the farmers of Kansas, the grass covered the sod as if it had never been disfigured or stained. The last gun had been fired in Kansas by Brown's forces, and he was next heard of in the Virginia insurrection which ended so fatally for the intrepid leader.

After many startling adventures and narrow escapes from capture, a group of bronzed and bearded men and one woman rode up one morning to the entrance of the Grand Island Hotel. It was our friends and the Brown family. The other refugees had passed in safety over the border into Canada, and the fugitive slaves were, at last, rejoicing on free soil.

The front of the hotel was deserted, the women being busy in the rear with their morning duties, and the usual hangers-on not being about.

Mr. Maybee, who was lying on a bed in the bottom of the wagon, sat up as the cavalcade paused, and cried:

"Ma' Jane! Ma'—Jane!"

"Ya'as," screamed a female voice from the rear, not "like a song from afar;" or, if so, it was set in four sharps. "What's up neow?"

To which Maybee, probably reckoning on the magnetic attraction of female curiosity, made no reply, which diplomatic course instantly drew his worthy better half—a big one, too—and far better than her vocal organ. She came followed by the cook, Aunt Vinnie, and 'Tavius. "Law sakes!" she cried, sticking her plump arms akimbo and staring in amazement at the company before her, "if it ain't Ebenezer—an' the Englishman—an' Jude!—an' 'Nona!!" Her astonishment could go no farther. The next instant she had folded the girlish form in her arms in an agony of joy.

"My precious child! Thank heaven we've got you back safe! It's been an awful time fer you."

"Wall, darn my skin!" cried Maybee, wiping his own eyes in sympathy with the weeping woman, "here's me, wounded an' dyin', been a stranger an' a pilgrim in hos-tile parts fer months, an' when I git home the wife of my bosom ain't no eyes fer me nor tears nuther—everybody else is fus'. I call all you boys to witness my treatment; I enter a suit for devorce at once. Ma' Jane, I'm goin' ter leave your bed an' board."

"You ain't no call to be jealous, Maybee, as you well know. Ef you're sick, I'll nuss you; ef you're hungry, I'll feed you."

Then these pilgrims of the dusty roads received a royal welcome from the bewildered woman. Their brown hands were shaken, their torn clothes embraced, their sunburnt faces kissed with a rapture that was amazing.

"Come in, everybody. 'Tavius, git a move on with them hosses and things! Vinnie, stop your grinnin' an' hustle with the dinner."

Mrs. Maybee expanded, metaphorically,—literal expansion would have jammed her in the doorway,—on hospitable cares intent.

'Tavius marched away grinning, while Mrs. Maybee ushered her guests into the house. How long seemed the time to Winona and Judah since they had been torn from that kindly shelter by the slave-hunters; terrible, indeed, had been the times that followed so swiftly.

After the travelers were somewhat rested and refreshed, the story of their adventures was rehearsed, and the stranger one of the wrongs and sorrows of White Eagle and his true name and position in the world was told to an interested crowd of listeners, for the news of Maybee's arrival with Winona and Judah had been industriously circulated by 'Tavius as soon as he could steal away from his duties, and a crowd of leading citizens filled the office, hall and piazza, anxious to see the wanderers and hear the miraculous story of their escape.

"Now, Ma' Jane, you remember the papers I gave you— White Eagle's paper's?"

"Of course,"

"I want you to fetch 'em out and give 'em to the child before us all. Then Mr. Lawyer Maxwell will see ef they is all correc'."

Mrs. Maybee brought a long tin box and placed it in her husband's hand. He opened it. "Let's see. Three legal dockymen's and a few pieces of jewelry. Them's 'em, I reckon. There you are, my girl," he said, tenderly, as he handed the package to Winona. Her attitude was at once tragic and pathetic as she drew back, for one instant, and stood in silent self-repression. A dizziness swept over her. What would the papers reveal? Their contents meant life or death to her hopes. She took the papers without speaking and passed them on to Warren almost mechanically.

"Read them—I cannot."

"Right, child," said Maybee.

There was breathless silence in the room as Warren unfolded the paper lying on top of the packet like a thick letter. All—honor for dead and living, ancient lands and name, home for the fondly loved child—lay sealed in the certificate of marriage and birth lying in Maxwell's right hand. The other papers related to his own story—a record of happenings after the fugitive from justice had arrived in America. The jewelry was jeweled family portraits, including one of Captain Henry when a young man; also a ring bearing the family crest. Nothing was missing—the chain of evidence was complete, even to the trained eye of the legal critic.

Then followed congratulations and good wishes from the friends who had done so much to make the present joy possible.

"I for one," said the representative to Congress, "from this day out condemn this cursed 'system' of ours. We're a laughing stock for the whole world, to say nothing of the wickedness of the thing."

"Right you are, Jameson; put them sentiments down for every man of us," cried a voice in the crowd.

Judah could say nothing, but he wrung Warren's hand hard.

"You go with us to England, Judah, and share prosperity as you have shared adversity. You shall choose your own path in life and be a man among men."

"I ain't any words to say, my girl!!" Maybee said huskily to Winona; "but you know what's in my ol' heart, I reckon, by what's in your own. I know you won't forget us when you're a great lady. Poor White Eagle, he had a rocky time of it, sure."

* * * * *

Many visits were made to the island by our three friends before the day when they embarked from Canada for old England. Oh, the rare delight they felt in the movement of the light canoe as they glided over the blue waters of the lake, and the thunders of Niagara sounded in their ears like a mighty orchestra rejoicing in their joy.

Again they stood on the high ridge where lay the sun-flecked woods, climbed the slopes and listened to the squirrel's shrill, clear chirp; watched the blackbirds winging the air in flight and heard the robin's mellow music gushing from the boughs above their heads. The Indian-pipes with their faint pink stems lay concealed among the bushes as of old.

Beneath the great pine that shaded White Eagle's grave they rested reverent, tempered sadness in their hearts. Winona buried her face in her lover's bosom with smothered, passionate sobs. Warren folded her close to him.

"My heart's dearest, you must not grieve; your time of

mourning is past. He is happy now as he sees your future assured. Through you he has conquered death and the grave; justice and honor are his after many years of shame." And she was comforted.

They made no plans for the future. What necessity was there of making plans for the future? They knew what the future would be. They loved each other; they would marry sooner or later, after they reached England, with the sanction of her grandfather, old Lord George; that was certain. American caste prejudice could not touch them in their home beyond the sea.

A long story full of deep interest might be written concerning the subsequent fortunes of John Brown and his sons and their trusty followers—a story of hardships, ruined homes and persecutions, and retribution to their persecutors, after all, through the happenings of the Civil War. But with these events we are all familiar. Judah never returned to America. After the news of John Brown's death had aroused the sympathies of all christendom for the slaves, he gave up all thoughts of returning to the land of his birth and entered the service of the Queen. His daring bravery and matchless courage brought its own reward; he was knighted; had honors and wealth heaped upon him, and finally married into one of the best families of the realm.

Winona celebrated in her letters to Mr. Maybee the wonders of her life in England, where all worshipped the last beautiful representative of an ancient family. The premature, crushing experiences of her young girlhood, its shocks and shameful surprises were not without good fruit. She is a noble woman. She is fortified against misfortune now by her deep knowledge of life and its inevitable sorrows, by love. Greater joy than hers, no woman, she believes, has ever known.

*   *   *   *   *

At intervals Aunt Vinnie found herself the center of groups of curious neighbors, white and black, who never tired of hearing her tell the story of Winona's strange fortunes. She invariably ended the tale with a short sermon on the fate of her race.

"Glory to God, we's boun' to be free. Dar's dat gal, she's got black blood nuff in her to put her on de block in this fersaken country, but over dar she's a lady with de top crus' of de crus'. Somethin's gwine happen."

An elderly white woman among the visitors drew a long breath, and declared that she had been lifted out of her bed three times the previous night.

"To be course," said Aunt Vinnie. "That's de angelic hos' hoverin' roun' you. Somethin's gwine drap. White folks been ridin' a turrible hoss in this country, an' dat hoss gwine to fro 'em you hyar me."

"De mule kicked me three times dis mornin' an' he never did dat afore in his life," said a colored brother; "dat means good luck."

"Jestice been settin' on de sprangles ob de sun a long time watchin' dese people how dey cuts der shines; um, um!" continued Vinnie.

"A rabbit run across my path twice comin' through de graveyard las' Sunday. I believe in my soul you're right, Aunt Vinnie," said 'Tavius.

" 'Course I'm right. Watch de sun an' see how he run; gwine to hear a mighty rumblin' 'mongst de dry bones 'cause jestice gwine plum' de line, an' set de chillun free," and as she retired to the kitchen her voice came back to them in song:

"Ole Satan's mad, an' I am glad,
  Send de angels down.
He missed the soul he thought he had,
  O, send dem angels down.
Dis is de year of Jubilee,
  Send dem angels down.
De Lord has come to set us free,
  O, send dem angels down."

THE END.

OF ONE BLOOD
Or, the Hidden Self

✌ ✌ ✌

CHAPTER I

The recitations were over for the day. It was the first week in November and it had rained about every day the entire week; now freezing temperature added to the discomforture of the dismal season. The lingering equinoctial whirled the last clinging yellow leaves from the trees on the campus and strewed them over the deserted paths, while from the leaden sky fluttering snow-white flakes gave an unexpected touch of winter to the scene.

The east wind for which Boston and vicinity is celebrated, drove the sleet against the window panes of the room in which Reuel Briggs sat among his books and the apparatus for experiments. The room served for both living and sleeping. Briggs could have told you that the bareness and desolateness of the apartment were like his life, but he was a reticent man who knew how to suffer in silence. The dreary wet afternoon, the cheerless walk over West Boston bridge through the soaking streets had but served to emphasize the loneliness of his position, and morbid thoughts had haunted him all day: To what use all this persistent hard work for a place in the world—clothes, food, a roof? Is suicide wrong? he asked himself with tormenting persistency. From out the

[*Of One Blood* originally appeared in serial form in the *Colored American Magazine* in the following issues: vol. 6, nos. 1–11 (November, December 1902; January–November 1903). In the original publication, each episode was preceded by a synopsis, which I have deleted. "(To be continued)" lines, however, have been retained in the body of the text to indicate for the reader the serialized structure of the novel—H.V.C.]

441

storm, voices and hands seemed beckoning him all day to cut the Gordian knot and solve the riddle of whence and whither for all time.

His place in the world would soon be filled; no vacuum remained empty; the eternal movement of all things onward closed up the gaps, and the wail of the newly-born augmented the great army of mortals pressing the vitals of mother Earth with hurrying tread. So he had tormented himself for months, but the courage was yet wanting for strength to rend the veil. It had grown dark early. Reuel had not stirred from his room since coming from the hospital—had not eaten nor drank, and was in full possession of the solitude he craved. It was now five o'clock. He sat sideways by the bare table, one leg crossed over the other. His fingers kept the book open at the page where he was reading, but his attention wandered beyond the leaden sky, the dripping panes, and the sounds of the driving storm outside.

He was thinking deeply of the words he had just read, and which the darkness had shut from his gaze. The book was called "The Unclassified Residuum," just published and eagerly sought by students of mysticism, and dealing with the great field of new discoveries in psychology. Briggs was a close student of what might be termed "absurdities" of supernatural phenomena or *mysticism,* best known to the every-day world as "effects of the imagination," a phrase of mere dismissal, and which it is impossible to make precise; the book suited the man's mood. These were the words of haunting significance:

"All the while, however, the phenomena are there, lying broadcast over the surface of history. No matter where you open its pages, you find things recorded under the name of divinations, inspirations, demoniacal possessions, apparitions, trances, ecstasies, miraculous healing and productions of disease, and occult powers possessed by peculiar individuals over persons and things in their neighborhood.

"The mind-curers and Christian scientists, who are beginning to lift up their heads in our communities, unquestionably get remarkable results in certain cases. The ordinary medical man dismisses them from his attention with the cut-and-dried remark that they are 'only the effects of the imagination.' But there is a meaning in this vaguest of phrases.

"We know a non-hysterical woman who in her trances knows facts which altogether transcend her *possible* normal consciousness, facts about the lives of people whom she never saw or heard of before. I am well aware of all the liabilities to which this statement exposes me, and I make it deliberately, having practically no doubt whatever of its truth."

Presently Briggs threw the book down, and, rising from his chair, began pacing up and down the bare room.

"That is it," at length he said aloud. "I have the power, I know the truth of every word—of all M. Binet asserts, and could I but complete the necessary experiments, I would astonish the world. O Poverty, Ostracism! have I not drained the bitter cup to the dregs!" he apostrophized, with a harsh, ironical laugh.

Mother Nature had blessed Reuel Briggs with superior physical endowments, but as yet he had had reason to count them blessings. No one could fail to notice the vast breadth of shoulder, the strong throat that upheld a plain face, the long limbs, the sinewy hands. His head was that of an athlete, with close-set ears, and covered with an abundance of black hair, straight and closely cut, thick and smooth; the nose was the aristocratic feature, although nearly spoiled by broad nostrils, of this remarkable young man; his skin was white, but of a tint suggesting olive, an almost sallow color which is a mark of strong, melancholic temperaments. His large mouth concealed powerful long white teeth which gleamed through lips even and narrow, parting generally in a smile at once grave, genial and singularly sweet; indeed Briggs' smile changed the plain face at once into one that interested and fascinated men and women. True there were lines about the mouth which betrayed a passionate, nervous temperament, but they accorded well with the rest of his strong personality. His eyes were a very bright and piercing gray, courageous, keen and shrewd. Briggs was not a man to be despised— physically or mentally.

None of the students associated together in the hive of men under the fostering care of the "benign mother" knew aught of Reuel Briggs's origin. It was rumored at first that he was of Italian birth, then they "guessed" he was a Japanese, but whatever land claimed him as a son, all voted him a genius in his scientific studies, and much was expected of him at graduation. He had no money, for he was unsocial and shabby to the point of seediness, and apparently no relatives, for his correspondence was limited to the letters of editors of well known local papers and magazines. Somehow he lived and paid his way in a third-rate lodging-house near Harvard square, at the expense of the dull intellects or the idle rich, with which a great university always teems, to whom Briggs acted as "coach," and by contributing scientific articles to magazines on the absorbing subject of spiritualistic phenomena. A few of his articles had produced a profound impression. The monotonous pacing continued for a time, finally ending at the mantel, from whence he abstracted a disreputable looking pipe and filled it.

"Well," he soliloquized, as he reseated himself in his chair,

"Fate had done her worst, but she mockingly beckons me on and I accept her challenge. I shall not yet attempt the bourne. If I conquer, it will be by strength of brain and will-power. I shall conquer; I must and will."

The storm had increased in violence; the early dusk came swiftly down, and at this point in his revery the rattling window panes, as well as the whistle and shriek of gusts of moaning wind, caught his attention. "Phew! a beastly night." With a shiver, he drew his chair closer to the cylinder stove, whose glowing body was the only cheerful object in the bare room.

As he sat with his back half-turned to catch the grateful warmth, he looked out into the dim twilight across the square and into the broad paths of the campus, watching the skeleton arms of giant trees tossing in the wind, and the dancing snow-flakes that fluttered to earth in their fairy gowns to be quickly transformed into running streams that fairly over-flowed the gutters. He fell into a dreamy state as he gazed, for which he could not account. As he sent his earnest, penetrating gaze into the night, gradually the darkness and storm faded into tints of cream and rose and soft moist lips. Silhouetted against he background of lowering sky and waving branches, he daw distinctly outlined a fair face framed in golden hair, with soft brown eyes, deep and earnest—terribly earnest they seemed just then—rose-tinged baby lips, and an expression of wistful entreaty. O how real, how very real did the passing shadow appear to the gazer!

He tried to move, uneasily conscious that this strange experience was but "the effect of the imagination," but he was powerless. The unknown countenance grew dimmer and farther off, floating gradually out of sight, while a sense of sadness and foreboding wrapped him about as with a pall.

A wilder gust of wind shook the window sashes. Reuel stared about him in a bewildered way like a man awakening from a heavy sleep. He listened to the wail of the blast and glanced at the fire and rubbed his eyes. The vision was gone; he was alone in the room; all was silence and darkness. The ticking of the cheap clock on the mantel kept time with his heart-beats. The light of his own life seemed suddenly eclipsed with the passing of the lovely vision of Venus. Conscious of an odd murmur in his head, which seemed to control his movements, he rose and went toward the window to open it; there came a loud knock at the door.

Briggs did not answer at once. He wanted no company. Perhaps the knocker would go away. But he was persistent. Again came the knock ending in a double rat-tat accompanied by the words:

"I know you are there; open, open, you son of Erebus! You inhospitable Turk!"

Thus admonished Briggs turned the key and threw wide open the door.

"It's you, is it? Confound you, you're always here when you're not wanted," he growled.

The visitor entered and closed the door behind him. With a laugh he stood his dripping umbrella back of the stove against the chimney-piece, and immediately a small stream began trickling over the uncarpeted floor; he then relieved himself of his damp outer garments.

"Son of Erebus, indeed, you ungrateful man. It's as black as Hades in this room; a light, a light! Why did you keep me waiting out there like a drowned rat?"

The voice was soft and musical. Briggs lighted the student lamp. The light revealed a tall man with the beautiful face of a Greek God; but the sculptured features did not inspire confidence. There was that in the countenance of Aubrey Livingston that engendered doubt. But he had been kind to Briggs, was, in fact, his only friend in the college, or, indeed, in the world for that matter.

By an act of generosity he had helped the forlorn youth, then in his freshman year, over obstacles which bade fair to end his college days. Although the pecuniary obligation was long since paid, the affection and worship Reuel had conceived for his deliverer was dog-like in its devotion.

"Beastly night," he continued, as he stretched his full length luxuriously in the only easy chair the room afforded. "What are you mooning about all alone in the darkness?"

"Same old thing," replied Briggs briefly.

"No wonder the men say that you have a twist, Reuel."

"Ah, man! but the problem of whence and whither! To solve it is my life; I live for that alone; let'm talk."

"You ought to be re-named the 'Science of Trance-States,' Reuel. How a man can grind day and night beats me." Livingston handed him a cigar and for a time they smoked in silence. At length Reuel said:

"Shake hands with Poverty once, Aubrey, and you will solve the secret of many a student's success in life."

"Doubtless it would do me good," replied Livingston with a laugh, "but just at present, it's the ladies, bless their sweet faces who disturb me, and not delving in books nor weeping over ways and means. Shades of my fathers, forbid that I should ever have to work!

"Lucky dog!" growled Reuel, enviously, as he gazed admiringly at the handsome face turned up to the ceiling and gazing with soft caressing eyes at the ugly whitewashed wall through rings of curling smoke. "Yet you have a greater gift of duality than I," he added dreamily. "Say what you will;

ridicule me, torment me, but you know as well as I that the wonders of a material world cannot approach those of the undiscovered country within ourselves—the hidden self lying quiescent in every human soul."

"True, Reuel, and I often wonder what becomes of the mind and morals, distinctive entities grouped in the republic known as man, when death comes. Good and evil in me contend; which will gain the mastery? Which will accompany me into the silent land?"

"Good and evil, God and the devil," suggested Reuel. "Yes, sinner or saint, body or soul, which wins in the life struggle? I am not sure that it matters which," he concluded with a shrug of his handsome shoulders. "I should know if I never saw you again until the struggle was over. Your face will tell its own tale in another five years. Now listen to this:" He caught up the book he had been reading and rapidly turning the leaves read over the various passages that had impressed him.

"A curious accumulation of data; the writer evidently takes himself seriously," Livingston commented.

"And why not?" demanded Reuel. "You and I know enough to credit the author with honest intentions.

"Yes; but are we prepared to go so far?"

"This man is himself a mystic. He gives his evidence clearly enough."

"And do you credit it?"

"Every word! Could I but get the necessary subject, I would convince you; I would go farther than M. Binet in unveiling the vast scheme of compensation and retribution carried about in the vast recesses of the human soul."

"Find the subject and I will find the money," laughed Aubrey.

"Do you mean it, Aubrey? Will you join me in carrying forward a search for more light on the mysteries of existence?"

"I mean it. And now, Reuel, come down from the clouds, and come with me to a concert."

"Tonight?"

"Yes, 'tonight,' " mimicked the other. "The blacker the night, the greater the need of amusement. You go out too little."

"Who gives the concert?"

"Well, it's a new departure in the musical world; something Northerners know nothing of; but I who am a Southerner, born and bred, or as the vulgar have it, 'dyed in the wool,' know and understand Negro music. It is a jubilee concert given by a party of Southern colored people at Tremont Temple. I have the tickets. Redpath has them in charge."

"Well, if you say so, I suppose I must." Briggs did not seem greatly impressed.

"Coming down to the practical, Reuel, what do you think of the Negro problem? Come to think of it, I have never heard you express an opinion about it. I believe it is the only burning question in the whole category of live issues and ologies about which you are silent."

"I have a horror of discussing the woes of unfortunates, tramps, stray dogs and cats and Negroes—probably because I am an unfortunate myself."

They smoked in silence.

CHAPTER II

The passing of slavery from the land marked a new era in the life of the nation. The war, too, had passed like a dream of horrors, and over the resumption of normal conditions in business and living, the whole country, as one man, rejoiced and heaved a deep sigh of absolute content.

Under the spur of the excitement occasioned by the Proclamation of Freedom, and the great need of schools for the blacks, thousands of dollars were contributed at the North, and agents were sent to Great Britain, where generosity towards the Negroes was boundless. Money came from all directions, pouring into the hands of philanthropists, who were anxious to prove that the country was able, not only to free the slave, but to pay the great debt it owed him,— protection as he embraced freedom, and a share in the great Government he had aided to found by sweat and toil and blood. It was soon discovered that the Negro possessed a phenomenal gift of music, and it was determined to utilize this gift in helping to support educational institutions of color in the Southland.

A band of students from Fisk University were touring the country, and those who had been fortunate enough to listen once to their matchless untrained voices singing their heart-breaking minor music with its grand and impossible intervals and sound combinations, were eager to listen again and yet again.

Wealthy and exclusive society women everywhere vied in showering benefits and patronage upon the new prodigies who had suddenly become the pets of the musical world. The Temple was a blaze of light, and crowded from pit to dome. It was the first appearance of the troupe in New England, therefore it was a gala night, and Boston culture was out in force.

The two friends easily found their seats in the first balcony, and from that position idly scanned the vast audience to beguile the tedious waiting. Reuel's thoughts were disturbed; he read over the program, but it carried no meaning to his pre-occupied mind; he was uneasy; the face he had seen outlined in the twilight haunted him. A great nervous dread of he knew not what possessed him, and he actually suffered as he sat there answering at random the running fire of comments made by Livingston on the audience, and replying none too cordially to the greetings of fellow-students, drawn to the affair, like himself, by curiosity.

"Great crowd for such a night," observed one. "The weather matches your face, Briggs; why didn't you leave it outside? Why do you look so down?"

Reuel shrugged his shoulders.

"They say there are some pretty girls in the troup; one or two as white as we," continued the speaker unabashed by Reuel's surliness.

"They range at home from alabaster to ebony," replied Livingston. "The results of amalgamation are worthy the careful attention of all medical experts."

"Don't talk shop, Livingston," said Briggs peevishly.

"You are really more disagreeable than usual," replied Livingston, pleasantly. "Do try to be like the other fellows, for once, Reuel."

Silence ensued for a time, and then the irrepressible one of the party remarked: "The soprano soloist is great; heard her in New York." At this there was a general laugh among the men. Good natured Charlie Vance was generally "stuck" once a month with the "loveliest girl, by jove, you know."

"That explains your presence here, Vance; what's her name?"

"Dianthe Lusk."

"Great name. I hope she comes up to it,—the flower of Jove."

"Flower of Jove, indeed! You'll say so when you see her," cried Charlie with his usual enthusiasm.

"What! again, my son? 'Like Dian's kiss, unmasked, unsought, Love gives itself' " quoted Livingston, with a smile on his handsome face.

"Oh, stow it! Aubrey, even your cold blood will be stirred at sight of her exquisite face; of her voice I will not speak; I cannot do it justice."

"If this is to be the result of emancipation, I for one vote that we ask Congress to annul the Proclamation," said Reuel, drily.

Now conversation ceased; a famous local organist began a concert on the organ to occupy the moments of waiting. The music soothed Reuel's restlessness. He noticed that the platform usually occupied by the speaker's desk, now held a number of chairs and a piano. Certainly, the assiduous advertising had brought large patronage for the new venture, he thought as he idly calculated the financial result from the number in the audience.

Soon the hot air, the glare of lights, the mingling of choice perfumes emanating from the dainty forms of elegantly attired women, acted upon him as an intoxicant. He began to feel the pervading excitement—the flutter of expectation, and presently the haunting face left him.

The prelude drew to a close; the last chord fell from the fingers of the artist; a line of figures—men and women—dark in hue, and neatly dressed in quiet evening clothes, filed noiselessly from the ante-rooms and filled the chairs upon the platform. The silence in the house was painful. These were representatives of the people for whom God had sent the terrible scourge of blood upon the land to free from bondage.

The old abolitionists in the vast audience felt the blood leave their faces beneath the stress of emotion.

The opening number was "The Lord's Prayer." Stealing, rising, swelling, gathering, as it thrilled the ear, all the delights of harmony in a grand minor cadence that told of deliverance from bondage and homage to God for his wonderful aid, sweeping the awed heart with an ecstasy that was almost pain; breathing, hovering, soaring, they held the vast multitude in speechless wonder.

Thunders of applause greeted the close of the hymn. Scarcely waiting for a silence, a female figure rose and came slowly to the edge of the platform and stood in the blaze of lights with hands modestly clasped before her. She was not in any way the preconceived idea of a Negro. Fair as the fairest woman in the hall, with wavy bands of chestnut hair, and great, melting eyes of brown, soft as those of childhood; a willowy figure of exquisite mould, clad in a sombre gown of black. There fell a voice upon the listening ear, in celestial showers of silver that passed all conceptions, all comparisons, all dreams; a voice beyond belief—a great soprano of unimaginable beauty, soaring heavenward in mighty intervals.

"Go down, Moses, way down in Egypt's land, Tell ol' Pharaoh, let my people go," sang the woman in tones that awakened ringing harmonies in the heart of every listener.

"By Jove!" Reuel heard Livingston exclaim. For himself he was dazed, thrilled; never save among the great artists of the earth, was such a voice heard alive with the divine fire.

Some of the women in the audience wept; there was the distinct echo of a sob in the deathly quiet which gave tribute to the power of genius. Spell-bound they sat beneath the outpoured anguish of a suffering soul. All the horror, the degredation from which a race had been delivered were in the pleading strains of the singer's voice. It strained the senses almost beyond endurance. It pictured to that self-possessed, highly-cultured New England assemblage as nothing else ever had, the awfulness of the hell from which a people had been happily plucked.

Reuel was carried out of himself; he leaned forward in eager contemplation of the artist; he grew cold with terror and fear. Surely it could not be—he must be dreaming! It was incredible! Even as he whispered the words to himself the hall seemed to grow dim and shadowy; the sea of faces melted away; there before him in the blaze of light—like a lovely phantom—stood a woman wearing the face of his vision of the afternoon!

CHAPTER III

It was Hallow-eve.

The north wind blew a cutting blast over the stately Charles, and broke the waves into a miniature flood; it swept the streets of the University city, and danced on into the outlying suburbs tossing the last leaves about in gay disorder, not even sparing the quiet precincts of Mount Auburn cemetery. A deep, clear, moonless sky stretched overhead, from which hung myriads of sparkling stars.

In Mount Auburn, where the residences of the rich lay far apart, darkness and quietness had early settled down. The main street seemed given over to the duskiness of the evening, and with one exception, there seemed no light on earth or in heaven save the cold gleam of the stars.

The one exception was in the home of Charlie Vance, or "Adonis," as he was called by his familiars. The Vance estate was a spacious house with rambling ells, tortuous chimney-stacks, and corners, eaves and ledges; the grounds were extensive and well kept telling silently of the opulence of its owner. Its windows sent forth a cheering light. Dinner was just over.

Within, on an old-fashioned hearth, blazed a glorious wood fire, which gave a rich coloring to the oak-panelled walls, and fell warmly on a group of young people seated and standing, chatting about the fire. At one side of it, in a chair of the Elizabethan period, sat the hostess, Molly Vance, only daughter of James Vance, Esq., and sister of "Adonis," a beautiful girl of eighteen.

At the oppostie side, leaning with folded arms against the high carved mantel, stood Aubrey Livingston; the beauty of his fair hair and blue eyes was never more marked as he stood there in the gleam of the fire and the soft candle light. He was talking vivaciously, his eyes turning from speaker to speaker, as he ran on, but resting chiefly with pride on his beautiful betrothed, Molly Vance.

The group was completed by two or three other men, among them Reuel Briggs, and three pretty girls. Suddenly a clock struck the hour.

"Only nine," exclaimed Molly. "good people, what shall we do to wile the tedium of waiting for the witching hour? Have any one of you enough wisdom to make a suggestion?"

"Music," said Livingston.

"We don't want anything so commonplace."

"Blind Man's Buff," suggested "Adonis."

"Oh! please not that, the men are so rough!"

"Let us," broke in Cora Scott, "tell ghost stories."

"Good, Cora! yes, yes, yes."

"No, no!" exclaimed a chorus of voices.

"Yes, yes," laughed Molly, gaily, clapping her hands. "It is the very thing. Cora, you are the wise woman of the party. It is the very time, tonight is the new moon, and we can try our projects in the Hyde house."

"The moon should be full to account for such madness," said Livingston.

"Don't be disagreeable, Aubrey," replied Molly. "The 'ayes' have it. You're with me, Mr. Briggs?"

"Of course, Miss Vance," answered Reuel, "to go to the North Pole or Hades—only please tell us where is Hyde house.'"

"Have you never heard? Why it's the adjoining estate. It is reputed to be haunted, and a lady in white haunts the avenue in the most approved ghostly style."

"Bosh!" said Livingston.

"Possibly," remarked the laughing Molly, "but it is the 'bosh' of a century."

"Go on, Miss Vance; don't mind Aubrey. Who has seen the lady?"

"She is not easily seen," proceeded Molly, "she only appears on Hallow-eve, when the moon is new, as it will be tonight. I had forgotten that fact when I invited you here. If anyone stands, tonight, in the avenue leading to the house, he will surely see the tall veiled figure gliding among the old hemlock trees."

One or two shivered.

"If, however, the watcher remain, the lady will pause, and utter some sentence of prophecy of his future."

"Has any one done this?" queried Reuel.

"My old nurse says she remembers that the lady was seen once."

"Then, we'll test it again tonight!" exclaimed Reuel, greatly excited over the chance to prove his pet theories.

"Well, Molly, you've started Reuel off on his greatest hobby; I wash my hands of both of you."

"Let us go any way!" chorused the venturesome party.

"But there are conditions," esclaimed Molly. "Only one person must go at a time."

Aubrey laughed as he noticed the consternation in one or two faces.

"So," continued Molly, "as we cannot go together, I propose that each shall stay a quarter of an hour, then whether successful or not, return and let another take his or her place. I will go first."

"No—" it was Charlie who spoke—"I put my veto on that, Molly, If you are mad enough to risk colds in this mad freak, it shall be done fairly. We will draw lots."

"And I add to that, not a girl leave the house; we men will try the charm for the sake of your curiosity, but not a girl goes. You can try the ordinary Hallow-eve projects while we are away."

With many protests, but concealed relief, this plan was reluctantly adopted by the female element. The lots were prepared and placed in a hat, and amid much merriment, drawn.

"You are third, Mr. Briggs," exclaimed Molly who held the hat and watched the checks.

"I'm first," said Livingston, "and Charlie second."

"While we wait for twelve, tell us the story of the house, Molly," cried Cora.

Thus adjured, Molly settled herself comfortably in her chair and began: "Hyde House is nearly opposite the cemetery, and its land joins that of this house; it is indebted for its ill-repute to one of its owners, John Hyde. It has been known for years as a haunted house, and avoided as such by the superstitious. It is low-roofed, rambling, and almost entirely concealed by hemlocks, having an air of desolation and decay in keeping with its ill-repute. In its dozen rooms were enacted the dark deeds which gave the place the name of the 'haunted house.'

"The story is told of an unfaithful husband, a wronged wife and a beautiful governess forming a combination which led to the murder of a guest for his money. The master of the house died from remorse, under peculiar circumstances. These materials give us the plot for a thrilling ghost story."

"Well, where does the lady come in?" interrupted "Adonis."

There was a general laugh.

"This world is all a blank without the ladies for Charlie," remarked Aubrey. "Molly, go on with your story, my child."

"You may all laugh as much as you please, but what I am telling you is believed in this section by every one. A local magazine speaks of it as follows, as near as I can remember:

" 'A most interesting story is told by a woman who occupied the house for a short time. She relates that she had no sooner crossed the threshold than she was met by a beautiful woman in flowing robes of black, who begged permission to speak through her to her friends. The friends were thereupon bidden to be present at a certain time. When all were assembled they were directed by invisible powers to kneel. Then the spirit told the tale of the tragedy through the woman. The spirit was the niece of the murderer, and she was in the house when the crime was committed. She discovered blood stains on the door of the woodshed, and told her uncle that she suspected him of murdering the guest, who had mysteriously disappeared. He secured her promise not to betray him. She had always kept the secret. Although both had been dead for many years, they were chained to the scene of the crime, as was the governess, who was the man's partner in guilt. The final release of the niece from the place was conditional on her making a public confession. This done she would never be heard from again. And she never was, except on Hallow-eve, when the moon is new.' "

"Bring your science and philosophy to bear on this, Reuel. Come, come, man, give us your opinion," exclaimed Aubrey.

"Reuel doesn't believe such stuff; he's too sensible," added Charlie.

"If these are facts, they are only for those who have a mental affinity with them. I believe that if we could but strengthen our mental sight, we could discover the broad highway between this and the other world on which both good and evil travel to earth," replied Reuel.

"And that first highway was beaten out of choas by Satan, as Milton has it, eh, Briggs?"

"Have it as you like, Smith. No matter. For my own part, I have never believed that the whole mental world is governed by the faculties we understand, and can reduce to reason or definite feelings. But I will keep my ideas to myself; one does not care to be laughed at."

The conversation was kept up for another hour about indifferent subjects, but all felt the excitement underlying the frivolous chatter. At quarter before twelve, Aubrey put on his ulster with the words: "Well, here goes for my lady." The great doors were thrown open, and the company grouped about him to see him depart.

"Mind, honor bright, you go," laughed Charlie.

"Honor bright," he called back.

Then he went on beyond the flood of light into the gloom of the night. Muffled in wraps and ulsters they lingered on the piazzas waiting his return.

"Would he see anything?"

"Of course not!" laughed Charlie and Bert Smith. "Still, we bet he'll be sharp to his time."

They were right. Aubrey returned at five minutes past twelve, a failure.

Charlie ran down the steps briskly, but in ten minutes came hastening back.

"Well," was the chorus, "did you see it?"

"I saw something—a figure in the trees!"

"And you did not wait?" said Molly, scornfully.

"No, I dared not; I own it."

"It's my turn; I'm third," said Reuel.

"Luck to you, old man," they called as he disappeared in the darkness.

Reuel Briggs was a brave man. He knew his own great physical strength and felt no fear as he traversed the patch of woods lying between the two estates. As he reached the avenue of hemlocks he was not thinking of his mission, but of the bright home scene he had just left—of love and home and rest—such a life as was unfolding before Aubrey Livingston and sweet Molly Vance.

"I suppose there are plenty of men in the world as lonely as I am," he mused; "but I suppose it is my own fault. A man though plain and poor can generally manage to marry; and I am both. But I don't regard a wife as one regards bread—better sour bread than starvation; better an uncongenial life-companion than none! What a frightful mistake! No!

The woman I marry must be to me a necessity, because I love her; because so loving her, 'all the current of my being flows to her,' and I feel she is my supreme need."

Just now he felt strangely happy as he moved in the gloom of the hemlocks, and he wondered many times after that whether the spirit is sometimes mysteriously conscious of the nearness of its kindred spirit; and feels, in anticipation, the "sweet unrest" of the master-passion that rules the world.

The mental restlessness of three weeks before seemed to have possession of him again. Suddenly the "restless, unsatisfied longing," rose again in his heart. He turned his head and saw a female figure just ahead of him in the path, coming toward him. He could not see her features distinctly, only the eyes—large, bright and dark. But their expression! Sorrowful, wistful—almost imploring—gazing straightforward, as if they saw nothing—like the eyes of a person entirely absorbed and not distinguishing one object from another.

She was close to him now, and there was a perceptible pause in her step. Suddenly she covered her face with her clasped hands, as if in uncontrollable grief. Moved by a mighty emotion, Briggs addressed the lonely figure:

"You are in trouble, madam; may I help you?"

Briggs never knew how he survived the next shock. Slowly the hands were removed from the face and the moon gave a distinct view of the lovely features of the jubilee singer— Dianthe Lusk.

She did not seem to look at Briggs, but straight before her, as she said in a low, clear, passionless voice:

"You can help me, but not now; tomorrow."

Reuel's most prominent feeling was one of delight. The way was open to become fully acquainted with the woman who had haunted him sleeping and waking for weeks past.

"Not now! Yet you are suffering. Shall I see you soon? Forgive me—but oh! tell me—"

He was interrupted. The lady moved or floated away from him, with her face toward him and gazing steadily at him.

He felt that his whole heart was in his eyes, yet hers did not drop, nor did her cheek color.

"The time is not yet," she said in the same, clear, calm, measured tones, in which she had spoken before. Reuel made a quick movement toward her, but she raised her hand, and the gesture forbade him to follow her. He paused involuntarily, and she turned away, and disappeared among the gloomy hemlock trees.

He parried the questions of the merry crowd when he returned to the house, with indifferent replies. How they would have laughed at him—slave of a passion as sudden and romantic as that of Romeo for Juliet; with no more foundation than the "presentments" in books which treat of the "occult." He dropped asleep at last, in the early morning hours, and lived over his experience in his dreams.

CHAPTER IV

Although not yet a practitioner, Reuel Briggs was a recognized power in the medical profession. In brain diseases he was an authority.

Early the next morning he was aroused from sleep by imperative knocking at his door. It was a messenger from the hospital. There had been a train accident on the Old Colony road, would he come immediately?

Scarcely giving himself time for a cup of coffee, he arrived at the hospital almost as soon as the messenger.

The usual silence of the hospital was broken; all was bustle and movement, without confusion. It was a great call upon the resources of the officials, but they were equal to it. The doctors passed from sufferer to sufferer, dressing their injuries; then they were borne to beds from which some would never rise again.

"Come with me to the women's ward, Doctor Briggs," said a nurse. "There is a woman there who was taken from the wreck. She shows no sign of injury, but the doctors cannot restore her to consciousness. Doctor Livingston pronounces her dead, but it doesn't seem possible. So young, so beautifully. Do something for her, Doctor."

The men about a cot made way for Reuel, as he entered the ward. "It's no use Briggs," said Livingston to him in reply to his question. "Your science won't save her. The poor girl is already cold and stiff."

He moved aside disclosing to Reuel's gaze the lovely face of Dianthe Lusk!

(To be continued.)

❧ ❧ ❧

CHAPTER IV.—(Concluded.)

The most marvellous thing to watch is the death of a person. At that moment the opposite takes place to that which took place when life entered the first unit, after nature had prepared it for the inception of life. How the vigorous life watches the passage of the liberated life out of its earthly environment! What a change is this! How important the knowledge of whither life tends! Here is shown the setting free of a

disciplined spirit giving up its mortality for immortality,—
the condition necessary to know God. Death! There is no
death. Life is everlasting, and from its reality can have no
end. Life is real and never changes, but preserves its identity
eternally as the angels, and the immortal spirit of man, which
are the only realities and continuities in the universe, God
being over all, Supreme Ruler and Divine Essence from
whom comes all life. Somewhat in this train ran Reuel's
thoughts as he stood beside the seeming dead girl, the cynosure
of all the medical faculty there assembled.

To the majority of those men, the case was an ordinary
death, and that was all there was to it. What did this young
upstart expect to make of it? Of his skill and wonderful
theories they had heard strange tales, but they viewed him
coldly as we are apt to view those who dare to leave the beaten
track of conventionality.

Outwardly cool and stolid, showing no sign of recognition,
he stood for some seconds gazing down on Dianthe; every
nerve quivered, every pulse of his body throbbed. Her face
held for him a wonderful charm, an extraordinary fascination.
As he gazed he knew that once more he beheld what he had
vaguely sought and yearned for all his forlorn life. His whole
heart went out to her; destiny, not chance, had brought him
to her. He saw, too, that no one knew her, none had a clue
to her identity; he determined to remain silent for the present,
and immediately he sought to impress Livingston to do
likewise.

His keen glance swept the faces of the surrounding physicians. "No, not one," he told himself, "holds the key to
unlock this seeming sleep of death." He alone could do it.
Advancing far afield in the mysterious regions of science, he
had stumbled upon the solution of one of life's problems: *the
reanimation of the body after seeming death.*

He had hesitated to tell of his discovery to any one; not even to Livingston had he hinted of the daring possibility, fearing ridicule in case of a miscarriage in his calculations. But for the sake of this girl he would make what he felt to be a premature disclosure of the results of his experiments. Meantime, Livingston, from his place at the foot of the cot, watched his friend with fascinated eyes. He, too, had resolved, contrary to his first intention, not to speak of his knowledge of the beautiful patient's identity. Curiosity was on tiptoe; expectancy was in the air. All felt that something unusual was about to happen.

Now Reuel, with gentle fingers, touched rapidly the clammy brow, the icy, livid hands, the region of the pulseless heart. No breath came from between the parted lips; the life-giving organ was motionless. As he concluded his examination, he turned to the assembled doctors:

"As I diagnose this case, it is one of suspended animation. This woman has been long and persistently subjected to mesmeric influences, and the nervous shock induced by the excitement of the accident has thrown her into a cataleptic sleep."

"But, man!" broke from the head physician in tones of exasperation, "rigor mortis in unmistakable form is here. The woman is dead!"

At these words there was a perceptible smile on the faces of some of the students—associates who resented his genius as a personal affront, and who considered these words as good as a reprimand for the daring student, and a settler of his pretensions. Malice and envy, from Adam's time until today, have loved a shining mark.

But the reproof was unheeded. Reuel was not listening. Absorbed in thoughts of the combat before him, he was oblivious to all else as he bent over the lifeless figure on the cot. He was full of an earnest purpose. He was strung up to a high tension of force and energy. As he looked down upon the unconscious girl whom none but he could save from the awful fate of a death by post-mortem, and who by some mysterious mesmeric affinity existing between them, had drawn him to her rescue, he felt no fear that he should fail.

Suddenly he bend down and took both cold hands into his left and passed his right hand firmly over her arms from shoulder to wrist. He repeated the movements several times; there was no response to the passes. He straightened up, and again stood silently gazing upon the patient. Then, like a man just aroused from sleep, he looked across the bed at Livingston and said abruptly:

"Dr. Livingston, will you go over to my room and bring me the case of vials in my medicine cabinet? I cannot leave the patient at this point."

Livingston started in surprise as he replied: "Certainly, Briggs, if it will help you any."

"The patient does not respond to any of the ordinary methods of awakening. She would probably lie in this sleep for months, and death ensue from exhaustion, if stronger remedies are not used to restore the vital force to a normal condition."

Livingston left the hospital; he could not return under an hour; Reuel took up his station by the bed whereon was stretched an apparently lifeless body, and the other doctors went the rounds of the wards attending to their regular routine of duty. The nurses gazed at him curiously; the head doctor, upon whom the young student's earnestness and sincerity had evidently made an impression, came a number of times to the bare little room to gaze upon its silent occupants, but there was nothing new. When Livingston returned, the group again gathered about the iron cot where lay the patient.

"Gentlemen," said Reuel, with quiet dignity, when they were once more assembled, "will you individually examine the patient once more and give your verdicts?"

Once more doctors and students carefully examined the inanimate figure in which the characteristics of death were still more pronounced. On the outskirts of the group hovered the house-surgeon's assistants ready to transport the body to the operating room for the post-mortem. Again the head physician spoke, this time impatiently.

"We are wasting our time, Dr. Briggs; I pronounce the woman dead. She was past medical aid when brought here."

"There is no physical damage, apparent or hidden, that you can see, Doctor?" questioned Reuel, respectfully.

"No; it is a perfectly healthful organism, though delicate. I agree entirely with your assertion that death was induced by the shock."

"Not *death*, Doctor," protested Briggs.

"Well, well, call it what you like—call it what you like, it amounts to the same in the end," replied the doctor testily.

"Do you all concur in Doctor Hamilton's diagnosis?" Briggs included all the physicians in his sweeping glance. There was a general assent.

"I am prepared to show you that in some cases of seeming death—or even death in reality—consciousness may be restored or the dead brought back to life. I have numberless times in the past six months restored consciousness to dogs and cats after rigor mortis had set in," he declared calmly.

"Bosh!" broke from a leading surgeon. In this manner the astounding statement, made in all seriousness, was received by the group of scientists mingled with an astonishment that resembled stupidity. But in spite of their scoffs, the young student's confident manner made a decided impression upon his listeners, unwilling as they were to be convinced.

Reuel went on rapidly; his eyes kindled; his whole person took on the majesty of conscious power, and pride in the knowledge he possessed. "I have found by research that life is not dependent upon organic function as a principle. It may be infused into organized bodies even after the organs have ceased to perform their legitimate offices. Where death has been due to causes which have not impaired or injured or destroyed tissue formation or torn down the structure of vital organs, life may be recalled when it has become entirely extinct, which is not so in the present case. This I have discovered by my experiments in animal magnetism."

The medical staff was fairly bewildered. Again Dr. Hamilton spoke:

"You make the assertion that the dead can be brought to life, if I understand your drift, Dr. Briggs, and you expect us to believe such utter nonsense." He added significantly, "My colleagues and I are here to be convinced."

"If you will be patient for a short time longer, Doctor, I will support my assertion by action. The secret of life lies in what we call volatile magnetism—it exists in the free atmosphere. You, Dr. Livingston, understand my meaning; do you see the possibility in my words?" he questioned, appealing to Aubrey for the first time.

"I have a faint conception of your meaning, certainly," replied his friend.

"This subtile magnetic agent is constantly drawn into the body through the lungs, absorbed and held in bounds until chemical combination has occurred through the medium of mineral agents always present in normal animal tissue. When respiration ceases this magnetism cannot be drawn into the lungs. It must be artificially supplied. This, gentlemen, is my discovery. I supply this magnetism. I have it here in the case Dr. Livingston has kindly brought me." He held up to their gaze a small phial wherein reposed a powder. Physicians and students, now eager listeners, gazed spell-bound upon him, straining their ears to catch every tone of the low voice and every change of the luminous eyes; they pressed forward to examine the contents of the bottle. It passed from eager hand to eager hand, then back to the owner.

"This compound, gentlemen, is an exact reproduction of the conditions existing in the human body. It has common salt for its basis. This salt is saturated with oleo resin and then exposed for several hours in an atmosphere of free ammonia. The product becomes a powder, and *that* brings back the seeming dead to life."

"Establish your theory by practical demonstration, Dr. Briggs, and the dreams of many eminent practitioners will be realized," said Dr. Hamilton, greatly agitated by his words.

"Your theory smacks of the supernatural, Dr. Briggs, charlatanism, or dreams of lunacy," said the surgeon. "We leave such assertions to quacks, generally, for the time of miracles is past."

"The supernatural presides over man's formation always," returned Reuel, quietly. "Life is that evidence of supernatural endowment which originally entered nature during the formation of the units for the evolution of man. Perhaps the superstitious masses came nearer to solving the mysteries of creation than the favored elect will ever come. Be that as it may, I will not contend. I will proceed with the demonstration."

There radiated from the speaker the potent presence of a truthful mind, a pure, unselfish nature, and that inborn dignity which repels the shafts of lower minds as ocean's waves absorb the drops of rain. Something like respect mingled with awe hushed the sneers, changing them into admiration as he calmly proceeded to administer the so-called life-giving powder. Each man's watch was in his hand; one minute passed—another—and still another. The body remained inanimate.

A cold smile of triumph began to dawn on the faces of the older members of the profession, but it vanished in its incipiency, for a tremor plainly passed over the rigid form before them. Another second—another convulsive movement of the chest!

"She moves!" cried Aubrey at last carried out of himself by the strain on his nerves. "Look, gentlemen, she breathes! *She is alive;* Briggs is right! Wonderful! Wonderful!"

"We said there could not be another miracle, and here it is!" exclaimed Dr. Hamilton with strong emotion.

Five minutes more and the startled doctors fell back from the bedside at a motion of Reuel's hand. A wondering nurse, with dilated eyes, unfolded a screen, placed it in position and came and stood beside the bed opposite Reuel. Holding Dianthe's hands, he said in a low voice: "Are you awake?" Her eyes unclosed in a cold, indifferent stare which gradually changed to one of recognition. She looked at him—she smiled, and said in a weak voice, "Oh, it is you; I dreamed of you while I slept."

She was like a child—so trusting that it went straight to the young man's heart and for an instant a great lump seemed to rise in his throat and choke him. He held her hands and chafed them, but spoke with his eyes only. The nurse said in a low voice: "Dr. Briggs, a few spoonfuls of broth will help her?"

"Yes, thank you, nurse; that will be just right." He drew

a chair close beside the bed, bathed her face with water and pushed back the tangle of bright hair. He felt a great relief and quiet joy that his experiment had been successful.

"Have I been ill? Where am I?" she asked after a pause, as her face grew troubled and puzzled.

"No, but you have been asleep a long time; we grew anxious about you. You must not talk until you are stronger."

The muse returned with the broth; Dianthe drank it eagerly and called for water, then with her hand still clasped in Reuel's she sank into a deep sleep, breathing softly like a tired child. It was plain to the man of science that hope for the complete restoration of her faculties would depend upon time, nature and constitution. Her effort to collect her thoughts was unmistakable. In her sleep, presently, from her lips fell incoherent words and phrases; but through it all she clung to Reuel's hand, seeming to recognize in him a friend.

A little later the doctors filed in noiselessly and stood about the bed gazing down upon the sleeper with awe, listening to her breathing, feeling lightly the fluttering pulse. Then they left the quiet house of suffering, marvelling at the miracle just accomplished in their presence. Livingston lingered with Briggs after the other physicians were gone.

"This is a great day for you, Reuel," he said, as he laid a light caressing hand upon the other's shoulder.

Reuel seized the hand in a quick convulsive clasp. "True and tried friend, do not credit me more than I deserve. No praise is due me. I am an instrument—how I know not—a child of circumstances. Do you not perceive something strange in this case? Can you not deduce conclusions from your own intimate knowledge of this science?"

"What can you mean, Reuel?"

"I mean—it is a *dual* mesmeric trance! The girl is only

partly normal now. Binet speaks at length of this possibility in his treatise. We have stumbled upon an extraordinary case. It will take a year to restore her to perfect health."

"In the meantime we ought to search out her friends."

"Is there any hurry, Aubrey?" pleaded Reuel, anxiously.

"Why not wait until her memory returns; it will not be long, I believe, although she may still be liable to the trances."

"We'll put off the evil day to any date you may name, Briggs; for my part, I would preserve her incognito indefinitely."

Reuel made no reply. Livingston was not sure that he heard him.

CHAPTER V

The world scarcely estimates the service rendered by those who have unlocked the gates of sensation by the revelations of science; and yet it is to the clear perception of things which we obtain by the study of nature's laws that we are enabled to appreciate her varied gifts. The scientific journals of the next month contained wonderful and *wondering* (?) accounts of the now celebrated case,—re-animation after seeming death. Reuel's lucky star was in the ascendant; fame and fortune awaited him; he had but to grasp them. Classmates who had once ignored him now sought familiar association, or else gazed upon him with awe and reverence. "How did he do it?" was the query in each man's mind, and then came a stampede for all scientific matter bearing upon animal magnetism.

How often do we look in wonder at the course of other men's lives, whose paths have diverged so widely from the beaten track of our own, that, unable to comprehend the one spring upon which, perhaps, the whole secret of the diversity hinged, we have been fain to content ourselves with summing up our judgment in the common phrase, "Well, it's very strange; what odd people there are in the world to be sure!"

Many times this trite sentence was uttered during the next few months, generally terminating every debate among medical students in various colleges.

Unmindful of his growing popularity, Reuel devoted every moment of his spare time to close study of his patient. Although but a youth, the scientist might have passed for any age under fifty, and life for him seemed to have taken on a purely mechanical aspect since he had become first in this great cause. Under pretended indifference to public criticism, throbbed a heart of gold, sensitive to a fault; desiring above all else the well-being of all humanity; his faithfulness to those who suffered amounted to complete self-sacrifice. Absolutely free from the vices which beset most young men of his age and profession, his daily life was a white, unsullied page to the friend admitted to unrestricted intercourse, and gave an irresistible impetus to that friendship, for Livingston could not but admire the newly developed depths of a nobility which he now saw unfolding day by day in Reuel's character. Nor was Livingston far behind the latter in his interest in all that affected Dianthe. Enthused by its scientific aspect, he vied with Reuel in close attention to the medical side of the case, and being more worldly did not neglect the material side.

He secretly sought out and obtained the address of the manager of the jubilee singers and to his surprise received the information that Miss Lusk had left the troupe to enter the service of a traveling magnetic physician—a woman—for a large salary. They (the troupe) were now in Europe and had heard nothing of Miss Lusk since.

After receiving this information by cable, Livingston sat a long time smoking and thinking: people often disappeared in a great city, and the police would undoubtedly find the magnetic physician if he applied to them. Of course that was the sensible thing to do, but then the publicity, and he hated that for the girl's sake. Finally he decided to compromise the matter by employing a detective. With him to decide that it was expedient to do a certain thing was the same as to act; before night the case was in the hands of an expert detective who received a goodly retainer. Two weeks from that day— it was December twenty-fourth—before he left his boarding place, the detective was announced. He had found the woman in a small town near Chicago. She said that she had no knowledge of Miss Lusk's whereabouts. Dianthe had remained with her three weeks, and at the end of that time had mysteriously disappeared; she had not heard of her since.

Livingston secured the woman's name and address, gave the man a second check together with an admonition to keep silence concerning Miss Lusk. That closed the episode. But of his observations and discoveries, Aubrey said nothing, noting every phase of this strange happening in silence.

Strangely enough, none of the men that had admired the colored artist who had enthralled their senses by her wonderful singing a few weeks before, recognized her in the hospital waif consecrated to the service of science. Her incognito was complete.

The patient was now allowed the freedom of the corridors for exercise, and was about her room during the day. The returns of the trance-state were growing less regular, although she frequently fell into convulsions, thereby enduring much suffering, sometimes lying for hours in a torpid state. Livingston had never happened to be present on these occasions, but he had heard of them from eye-witnesses. One day he entered the room while one was occurring. His entrance was unnoticed as he approached lightly over the uncarpeted floor, and stood transfixed by the scene before him.

Dianthe stood upright, with closed eyes, in the middle of the room. Only the movement of her bosom betrayed breath. The other occupants of the room preserved a solemn silence. She addressed Reuel, whose outstretched arms were extended as if in blessing over her head.

"Oh! Dearest friend! hasten to cure me of my sufferings. Did you not promise at that last meeting? You said to me, 'You are in trouble and I can help you.' And I answered, 'The time is not yet.' Is it not so?"

"Yes," replied Reuel. "Patience a while longer; all will be well with you."

"Give me the benefit of your powerful will," she continued. "I know much but as yet have not the power to express it: I see much clearly, much dimly, of the powers and influences behind the Veil, and yet I cannot name them. Some time the full power will be mine; and mine shall be thine. In seven months the sick will be restored—she will awake to worldly cares once more." Her voice ceased; she sank upon the cot in a recumbent position. Her face was pale; she appeared to sleep. Fifteen minutes passed in death-like stillness, then she extended her arms, stretched, yawned, rubbed her eyes— awoke.

Livingston listened and looked in a trance of delight, his keen artistic sense fully aroused and appreciative, feeling the glamour of her presence and ethereal beauty like a man poring over a poem that he has unexpectedly stumbled upon, losing himself in it, until it becomes, as it were, a part of himself. He felt as he watched her that he was doing a foolish thing in thus exposing himself to temptation while his honor and faith were pledged to another. But then, foolishness is so much better than wisdom, particularly to a man in certain stages of life. And then he fell to questioning if there could be temptation for him through this girl—he laughed at the thought and the next instant dismay covered him with confusion, for like a flash he realized that the mischief was already done.

As we have already hinted, Aubrey was no saint; he knew that fickleness was in his blood; he had never denied himself anything that he wanted very much in his whole life. Would he grow to want this beautiful woman very much? Time would tell.

*   *   *   *   *

It was Christmas-time—a good, sensible seasonable day before Christmas, with frost and ice in abundance, and a clear, bright, wintry sky above. Boston was very full of people—mostly suburban visitors—who were rushing here and there bent on emptying their purses on the least provocation. Good-nature prevailed among the pedestrians; one poor wretch stood shivering, with blue, wan face, on the edge of the sidewalk, his sightless eyes staring straight before him, trying to draw a tune from a consumptive violin—the embodiment of despair. He was, after all, in the minority, to judge by the hundreds of comfortably-clad forms that hurried past him, breathing an atmosphere of peace and prosperity.

Tomorrow the church bells would ring out tidings that another Christmas was born, bidding all rejoice.

This evening, at six o'clock, the two friends went to dine in a hotel in a fashionable quarter. They were due to spend the night and Christmas day at the Vance house. As they walked swiftly along with the elastic tread of youth, they simultaneously halted before the blind musician and pressed into his trembling hand a bountiful gift; then they hurried away to escape his thanks.

At the hotel Livingston called for a private dining room, and after the coffee was served, he said:

"Tell me, Briggs, what is the link between you and your patient. There is a link, I am sure. Her words while in the trance made a great impression upon me."

There was a pause before Reuel replied in a low tone, as he rested his arm on the opposite side of the table and propped his head up on his hand:

"Forgive me, Aubrey!"

"For what?"

"This playing with your confidence. I have not been entirely frank with you."

"Oh, well! you are not bound to tell me everything you know. You surely have the right to silence about your affairs, if you think best."

"Listen, Aubrey. I should like to tell you all about it. I would feel better. What you say is true; there is a link; but I never saw her in the flesh before that night at the Temple. With all our knowledge, Aubrey, we are but barbarians in our ideas of the beginning, interim and end of our creation. Why were we created? for whose benefit? can anyone answer that satisfactorily?

" 'Few things are hidden from the man who devotes himself earnestly and servicously to the solution of a mystery,' Haw-thorne tells us," replied Aubrey. "Have not you proved this, Reuel?"

"Well, yes—or, we prove rather, that our solution but

deepens the mystery of mysteries. I have surely proved the last. Aubrey, I look natural, don't I? There is nothing about me that seems wrong?"

"Wrong! No."

"Well, if I tell you the truth you will call me a lunatic. You have heard of people being haunted by hallucinations?" Aubrey nodded. "I am one of those persons. Seven weeks ago I saw Dianthe first, but not in the flesh. Hallow-eve I spoke to her in the garden of the haunted house, but not in the flesh. I thought it strange to be sure, that this face should lurk in my mind so much of the time; but I never dreamed what a crisis it was leading up to. The French and German schools of philosophy have taught us that going to places and familiar passages in books, of which we have had no previous knowledge, is but a proof of Plato's doctrine—the soul's transmigration, and reflections from the invisible world surrounding us.

"Finally a mad desire seized me to find that face a living reality that I might love and worship it. Then I saw her at the Temple—I found her at the hospital—*in the flesh!* My desire was realized."

"And having found her, what then?" He waited breathlessly for the reply.

"I am mightily pleased and satisfied. I will cure her. She is charming; and if it is insanity to be in love with her, I don't care to be sane."

Livingston did not reply at once. His face was like marble in its impassiveness. The other's soft tremulous tones, fearless yet moist eyes and broken sentences, appeared to awaken no response in his breast. Instead, a far-off gleam came into his blue eyes. At last he broke the silence with the words:

"You name it well; it is insanity indeed, for you to love this woman."

"Why?" asked his friend, constrainedly.

"Because it is not for the best."

"For her or me?"

"Oh, for *her*—!" he finished the sentence with an expressive gesture.

"I understand you, Aubrey. I should not have believed it of you. If it were one of the other fellows; but you are generally so charitable."

"You forget your own words: 'Tramps, stray dogs and Negroes—,' " he quoted significantly. "Then there is your professional career to be considered,—you mean honorable, do you not?—How can you succeed if it be hinted abroad that you are married to a Negress?"

"I have thought of all that. I am determined. I will marry her in spite of hell itself! Marry her before she awakens to consciousness of her identity. I'm not unselfish; I don't pretend to be. There is no sin in taking her out of the sphere where she was born. God and science helping me, I will give her life and love and wifehood and maternity and perfect health. God, Aubrey! you, with all you have had of life's sweetness, petted idol of a beautiful world, you who will soon feel the heart-beats of your wife against your breast when lovely Molly is eternally bound to you, what do you know of a lonely, darkened life like mine? I have not the manner nor the charm which wins women. Men like me get love from them which is half akin to pity, when they get anything at all. It is but the shadow. This is my opportunity for happiness; I seize it. Fate has linked us together and no man and no man's laws shall part us."

Livingston sipped his wine quietly, intently watching Reuel's face. Now he leaned across the table and stretched out his hand to Briggs; his eyes looked full into his. As their hands met in a close clasp, he whispered a sentence across the board. Reuel started, uttered an exclamation and flushed slowly a dark, dull red.

"How—where—how did you know it?" he stammered.

"I have known it since first we met; but the secret is safe with me."

CHAPTER VI

The scene which met the gaze when an hour later the young men were ushered into the long drawing-room of the Vance house was one well-calculated to remove all gloomy, pessimistic reasoning. Warmth, gaiety, pretty women, luxury,—all sent the blood leaping through the veins in delightful anticipation.

Their entrance was greeted by a shout of welcome.

"Oh, Aubrey! I am so glad you are come," cried Molly from the far end of the room. "Fancy tomorrow being Christmas! Shall we be ready for all that company tomorrow night and the ballroom, dining room and hall yet to be trimmed? Is it possible to be ready?"

"Not if we stand dwadling in idle talk." This from "Adonis," who was stretched full length on the sitting-room sofa, with a cigarette between his lips, his hands under his handsome head, surrounded by a bevy of pretty, chattering girls, prominent among whom was Cora Scott, who aided and abbetted Charlie in every piece of mischief.

Molly curled her lip but deigned no reply.

Bert Smith, from a corner of the room where he was about ascending a step-ladder, flung a book heavily at Adonis's lazy figure.

"Don't confuse your verbs," exclaimed Aubrey. "How can you stand when you are lying down, and were you ever known to do anything else but dwadle, Adonis—eh?"

"I give it up," said Charlie, sleepily, kicking the book off the sofa.

"Is this an amateur grocery shop, may I ask, Miss Vance?" continued Aubrey as he and Briggs made their way to their hostess through an avalanche of parcels and baskets strewn on the tables and the floor.

Molly laughed as she greeted them. "No wonder you are surprised. I am superintending the arrangement of my poor people's gifts," she explained. "They must all be sent out tonight. I don't know what I should have done without all these good people to help me. But there are *piles* to be done yet. There is the tree, the charades, etc., etc.," she continued, in a plaintive little voice.

"More particularly cetra, cetra," said Aubrey from Bert's corner where he had gone to help along the good works of placing holly wreaths.

"Oh, you, Aubrey—stop being a magpie." Aubrey and Molly were very matter of fact lovers.

"Molly," again broke in Charlie, "suppose the box from Pierson's has never come, won't you be up a tree?" and the speaker opened his handsome eyes wide, and shook off his cigarette-ash.

Molly maintained a dignified silence toward her brother. The firelight danced and dwelt upon her lovingly. She was so pretty, so fair, so slender, so graceful. Now in her gray plush tea-gown, with her hair piled picturesquely on the top of her small head, and fixed there with a big tortoise-shell pin, it would have been difficult to find a more delightful object for the gaze to rest upon.

"We shall have to fall back upon the wardrobes," she said at length. "You are a horrid wet-blanket, Charlie! I am sure I—"

Her remarks were cut short as the door opened, and with laughter and shouting a bevy of young people who had been at work in another part of the house rushed in. "It is come; it's all right; don't worry, Molly!" they sang in chorus.

"Do be quiet all of you; one can hardly hear oneself speak!"

The box from the costumer's had arrived; the great costume party was saved; in short, excitement and bustle were in full swing at Vance Hall as it had been at Christmas-time since the young people could remember.

Adonis lifted himself from the sofa and proposed to open the box of dresses at once, and try them on.

"Charlie, you are a brick!—the very thing!"

"Oh! yes, yes; let us try them on!"

Molly broke through the eager voices: "And we have not done the ball-room yet!" she said reproachfully.

"Oh! bother the ball-room!" declared Adonis, now thoroughly aroused. "We have all night. We can't do better than to don our finery."

Molly sat down with an air of resigned patience. "I promised Mr. Pierson," she observed quietly, "that the box should not be touched until he was here to superintend matters."

"Oh, Pierson be blowed!" elegantly observed her brother. But Reuel Briggs suddenly dropped his work, walked over, and sided with Molly.

"You are quite right, Miss Molly; and you Charlie and

Aubrey and the rest of you men, if you want to open the box tonight you must first decorate the ball-room. Business before pleasure."

"Saved!—saved! See my brave, true knight defends his lady fair." Molly danced, practising the step she was about to astonish the company with on Christmas-night. "I think I am what the Scotch call 'fev,' " she laughed. "I don't know why I feel so awfully jolly tonight. I could positively fly from sheer excitement and delight."

"Don't you know why?" observed Cora. "I will tell you. It is because this is your last Christmas as Molly Vance; next year—"

"Ah, do not!" interrupted Molly, quickly. "Who knows what a year may bring forth. Is it not so, Dr. Briggs?" she turned appealingly to Reuel.

"Grief follows joy as clouds the sunlight. 'Woe! woe! each heart must bleed, must break,' " was his secret thought as he bowed gravely. But on his face was a look of startled perplexity, for suddenly as she spoke to him it appeared that a dark veil settled like a pall over the laughing face at his side. He shivered.

"What's the matter, Briggs?" called out Adonis. They had reached the ball-room and were standing over the piles of holly and evergreen, ready for an onslaught on the walls.

"Don't be surprised if Briggs acts strangely," continued Charlie. "It is in order for him to whoop it up in the spirit line."

"Why, Charlie! What do you mean?" questioned Molly with an anxious glance at Reuel.

"Anything interesting, Charlie?" called out a jolly girl across the room.

"Briggs is our 'show' man. Haven't you heard, girls, what

a celebrity is with you tonight? Briggs is a philosopher—
mesmerism is his specialty. Say, old man, give the company
a specimen of your infernal art, can't you? He goes the whole
hog, girls; can even raise the dead."

"Let up, Charlie," said Aubrey in a low tone. It's no
joking matter."

There were screams and exclamations from the girls. With
reckless gaiety Adonis continued,

"What is to be the outcome of the great furore you have
created, Briggs?"

"Nothing of moment, I hope," smiled Reuel, good-na-
turedly. I have been simply an instrument; I leave results to
the good angels who direct events. What does Longfellow say
about the arrow and the song?

> 'Long, long afterwards, in an oak
> I found the arrow still unbroke;
> And the song, from beginning to end,
> I found in the heart of a friend.'

May it be so with my feeble efforts."

"But circumstances alter cases. In this case, the 'arrow' is
a girl and a devilish handsome one, too; and the 'air' is the
whole scientific world. Your philosphy and mysticism gave
way before Beauty. Argument is a stubborn man's castle, but
the heart is still unconvinced."

" 'I mixed those children up, and not a creature knew it,' "
hummed Bert Smith. "Your ideas are mixed, Don; stick to
the ladies, you understand girls and horseflesh: philosophy
isn't in your line."

"Oh, sure!" said Adonis unruffled by his friend's words.

"Charlie Vance," said Molly severely, "if we have any
more *swearing* from you tonight, you leave the room until

you learn to practice good manners. I'm surprised at your language!"

"Just the same, Briggs is a fraud. I shall keep my eye on him. It's a case of beauty and the beast. Oh," he continued in malicious glee, "wouldn't you girls turn green with envy, every man jack of you, if you could see the beauty!"

Thereupon the girls fell to pelting him with holly wreaths and evergreen festoons, much to the enjoyment of Mr. Vance, who had entered unperceived in the general melee.

"What is it all about, Dr. Briggs?" asked Molly in a low voice.

"It is the case of a patient who was in a mesmeric sleep and I was fortunate enough to awaken her. She is a waif; and it will be months before she will be well and strong, poor girl."

"Do you make a study of mesmerism, Doctor?" asked Mr. Vance from his armchair by the glowing fire.

"Yes sir; and a wonderful science it is." Before Mr. Vance could continue, Livingston said: "If you folks will be still for about ten minutes, I'll tell you what happened in my father's house when I was a very small boy; I can just remember it."

"If it's a ghost story, make it strong, Aubrey, so that not a girl will sleep tonight. Won't the dears look pretty blinking and yawning tomorrow night? We'll hear 'em, fellows, in the small hours of the morning, 'Molly, Molly! I'm so frightened. I do believe someone is in my room: may I come in with you, dear?' "

"Charlie, stop your nonsense," laughed his father, and Adonis obediently subsided.

"My father was Dr. Aubrey Livingston too," began Aubrey, "and he owned a large plantation of slaves. My father was deeply interested in the science of medicine, and I believe made some valuable discoveries along the line of mesmeric phenomena, for some two or three of his books are referred to even at this advanced stage of discovery, as marvellous in some of their data.

"Among the slaves was a girl who was my mother's waiting maid, and I have seen my father throw her into a trance-state many times when I was so small that I had no conception of what he was doing.

"Many a time I have known him to call her into the parlor to perform tricks of mind-reading for the amusement of visitors, and many wonderful things were done by her as the record given in his books shows.

"One day there was a great dinner party given at our place, and the élite of the county were bidden. It was about two years before the civil war, and our people were not expecting war; thinking that all unpleasantness must end in their favor, they gave little heed to the ominous rumble of public opinion that was arising at the North, but went on their way in all their pride of position and wealth without a care for the future.

"Child as I was I was impressed by the beauty and wit of the women and the chivalric bearing of the men gathered about my father's hospitable board on that memorable day. When the feasting and mirth began to lag, someone called for Mira—the maid—and my father sent for her to come and amuse the guests.

"My father made the necessary passes and from a serious, rather sad Negress, very mild with everyone, Mira changed to a gay, noisy, restless woman, full of irony and sharp jesting. In this case this peculiar metamorphosis always occurred. Nothing could be more curious than to see her and hear her. 'Tell the company what you see, Mira,' commanded my father.

"You will not like it, captain; but if I must, I must. All the women will be widows and the men shall sleep in early graves. They come from the north, from the east, from the west, they sweep to the gulf through a trail of blood. Your houses shall burn, your fields be laid waste, and a down-trodden race shall rule in your land. For you, captain, a prison cell and a pauper's grave."

The dinner-party broke up in a panic, and from that time my father could not abide the girl. He finally sold her just a few months before the secession of the Confederate States, and that was the last we ever knew of her."

"And did the prophecy come true about your father? asked Mr. Vance.

"Too true, sir; my father died while held as a prisoner of war, in Boston Harbor. And every woman at the table was left a widow. There is only too much truth in science of mesmeric phenomena. The world is a wonderful place."

"Wonderful!" declared his hearers.

"I am thinking of that poor, pretty creature living ill in that gloomy hospital without a friend. Men are selfish! I tell you what, folks, tomorrow after lunch we'll make a Christmas visit to the patients, and carry them fruit and flowers. As for your beautiful patient, Dr. Briggs, she shall not be friendless any longer, she shall come to us at Vance Hall."

"Molly!" broke simultaneously from Aubrey and Charlie.

"Oh, I mean it. There is plenty of room in this great house, and here she shall remain until she is restored to health."

Expostulation was in vain. The petted heiress was determined, and when Mr. Vance was appealed to he laughed and said, as he patted her hand:

"The queen must have her own."

At length the costumer's box was opened amidst jest, song and laughter. The characters were distributed by the wilful Molly. Thus attired, to the music of Tannhauser's march, played by one of the girls on the piano, the gay crowd marched and counter-marched about the spacious room.

In the early morning hours, Aubrey Livingston slept and dreamed of Dianthe Lusk, and these words haunted his sleep and lingered with him when he woke:

"She had the glory of heaven in her voice, and in her face the fatal beauty of man's terrible sins."

Aubrey Livingston knew that he was as hopelessly lost as was Adam when he sold his heavenly birthright for a woman's smile.

(To be continued.)

CHAPTER VII

Through days and days, and again through days and days, over and over again, Reuel Briggs fought to restore his patient to a normal condition of health. Physically, he succeeded; but mentally his treatment was a failure. Memory remained a blank to the unhappy girl. Her life virtually began with her awakening at the hospital. A look of wonder and a faint smile were the only replies that questions as to the past elicited from her. Old and tried specialists in brain diseases and hypnotic states came from every part of the Union on bootless errands. It was decided that nothing could be done; rest, freedom from every care and time might eventually restore the poor, violated mind to its original strength. Thus it was that Dianthe became the dear adopted daughter of the medical profession. Strange to say, Molly Vance secured her desire, and wearing the name of Felice Adams. Dianthe was domiciled under the roof of palatial Vance hall, and the small annuity provided by the generous contributions of the physicians of the country was placed in the hands of Mr. Vance, Sr., to be expended for their protege.

The astonishing nature of the startling problems he had unearthed, the agitation and indignation aroused in him by the heartless usage to which his patient must have been exposed, haunted Briggs day and night. He believed that he had been drawn into active service for Dianthe by a series of strange coincidences, and the subtle forces of immortality; what future acts this service might require he knew not, he cared not; he registered a solemn promise to perform all tasks allotted him by Infinity, to the fullest extent of his power.

The brilliant winter days merged themselves into spring. After one look into Dianthe's eyes, so deep, clear and true, Molly Vance had surrendered unconditionally to the charm of the beautiful stranger, drawn by an irresistible bond of sympathy. "Who would believe," she observed to Livingston, "that at this stage of the world's progress one's identity could be so easily lost and one still be living. It is like a page from an exciting novel."

With the impulsiveness of youth, a wonderful friendship sprang up between the two; they rode, walked and shopped together; in short, became inseparable companions. The stranger received every attention in the family that could be given an honored guest. Livingston and Briggs watched her with some anxiety; would she be able to sustain the position of intimate friendship to which Molly had elected her? But both breathed more freely when they noted her perfect manners, the ease and good-breeding displayed in all her intercourse with those socially above the level to which they knew this girl was born. She accepted the luxury of her new surroundings as one to the manner born.

"We need not have feared for her; by Jove, she's a thorough-bred!" exclaimed Aubrey one day to Reuel. The latter nodded as he looked up from his book.

"And why not? Probably the best blood of the country flows in the poor girl's veins. Who can tell? Why should she not be a thorough-bred."

"Ture," replied Aubrey, as a slight frown passed over his face.

"I am haunted by a possibility, Aubrey," continued Reuel. "What if memory suddenly returns? Is it safe to risk the unpleasantness of a public reawakening of her sleeping faculties? I have read of such tings."

Aubrey shrugged his handsome shoulders. "We must risk something for the sake of science; where no one is injured by deception there is no harm done."

"Now that question has presented itself to me repeatedly lately: Is deception justifiable for any reason? Somehow it haunts me that trouble may come from this. I wish we had told the exact truth about her identity."

" 'If 'twere done when 'tis done, then 'twere well it were done quickly" murmured Aubrey with a sarcastic smile on his face. "How you balk at nothing, Reuel," he drawled mockingly.

"Oh, call me a fool and done with it, Aubrey: I suppose I am; but one didn't make one's self."

Drives about the snow-clad suburbs of Cambridge with Briggs and Molly, at first helped to brighten the invalid; then came quiet social diversions at which Dianthe was the great attraction.

It was at an afternoon function that Reuel took courage to speak of his love. A dozen men buzzed about "Miss Adams" in the great bay window where Molly had placed Dianthe, her superb beauty set off by a simple toilet. People came and went constantly. Musical girls, generally with gold eyeglasses on aesthetic noses, played grim classical preparations, which have as cheerful an effect on a gay crowd as the perfect, irreproachable skeleton of a bygone beauty might have; or articulate, with cultivation and no voices to speak of, arias which would sap the life of a true child of song to render as the maestro intended.

The grand, majestic voice that had charmed the hearts from thousands of bosoms, was pinioned in the girl's throat like an imprisoned song-bird. Dianthe's voice was completely gone along with her memory. But music affected her strangely, and Reuel watched her anxiously.

Her face was a study in its delicate, quickly changing tints, its sparkle of smiles running from the sweet, pure tremor of the lovely mouth to the swift laughter of eyes and voice.

Mindful of her infirmity, Reuel led her to the conservatory to escape the music. She lifted her eyes to his with a curious and angelic light in them. She was conscious that he loved her with his whole most loving heart. She winced under the knowledge, for while she believed in him, depended upon him and gathered strength from his love, what she gave in return was but a slight, cold affection compared with his adoration.

He brought her refreshments in the conservatory, and then told his love and asked his fate. She did not answer at once, but looked at his plain face, at the stalwart elegance of his figure, and again gazed into the dark, true, clever eyes, and with the sigh of a tired child crept into his arms, and into his heart for all time and eternity. Thus Aubrey Livingston found them when the company had departed. So it was decided to have the wedding in June. What need for these two children of misfortune to wait?

Briggs, with his new interest in life, felt that it was good just to be alive. The winter passed rapidly, and as he threaded the streets coming and going to his hospital duties, his heart sang. No work was now too arduous; he delighted in the duty most exacting in its nature. As the spring came in it brought with it thoughts of the future. He was almost penniless, and he saw no way of obtaining the money he needed. He had not been improvident, but his lonely life had lived a reckless disregard of the future, and the value of money. He often lived a day on bread and water, at the same time sitting without a fire in the coldest weather because his pockets were empty and he was too proud to ask a loan, or solicit credit from storekeepers. He now found himself in great difficulty. His literary work and the extra cases which his recent triumph had brought him, barely sufficed for his own present needs. Alone in his bachelor existence he would call this luxury, but it was not enough to furnish a suitable establishment for Dianthe. As the weeks rolled by and nothing presented itself, he grew anxious, and finally resolved to consult Livingston.

All things had become new to him, and in the light of his

great happiness the very face of old Cambridge was changed. Fate had always been against him, and had played him the shabbiest of tricks, but now he felt that she might do her worst, he held a talisman against misfortune while his love remained to him. Thinking thus he walked along briskly, and the sharp wind brought a faint color into his sallow face. He tried to think and plan, but his ideas were whirled away before they had taken form, and he felt a giant's power to overcome with each inspiring breath of the crisp, cool March air. Aubrey should plan for him, but he would accomplish.

Livingston had apartments on Dana Hill, the most aris- tocratic portion of Cambridge. There he would remain till the autumn, when he would marry Molly Vance, and remove to Virginia and renew the ancient splendor of his ancestral home. He was just dressing for an evening at the theatre when Briggs entered his rooms. He greeted him with his usual genial warmth.

"What!" he said gaily, "the great scientist here, at this hour?"

Then noticing his visitor's anxious countenance he added: "What's the matter?"

"I am in difficulties and come to you for help," replied Reuel.

"How so? What is it? I am always anxious to serve you, Briggs."

"I certainly think so or I would not be here now," said Reuel. "But you are just going out, an engagement perhaps with Miss Molly. My business will take some time—"

Aubrey interrupted him, shaking his head negatively. "I was only going out to wile away the time at the theatre. Sit down and free your mind, old man."

Thus admonished, Reuel flung himself among the cushions of the divan, and began to state his reasons for desiring assistance: when he finished, Livingston asked:

"Has nothing presented itself?"

"O yes; two or three really desirable offers which I wrote to accept, but to my surprise, in each case I received polite regrets that circumstances had arisen to prevent the acceptance of my valuable services. That is what puzzles me. What the dickens did it mean?"

Aubrey said nothing but continued a drum solo on the arm of his chair. Finally he asked abruptly: "Briggs, do you think anyone knows or suspects your origin?"

Not a muscle of Reuel's face moved as he replied, calmly: "I have been wondering if such can be the case."

"This infernal prejudice is something horrible. It closes the door of hope and opportunity in many a good man's face. I am a Southerner, but I am ashamed of my section," he added warmly.

Briggs said nothing, but a dark, dull red spread slowly to the very roots of his hair. Presently Aubrey broke the painful silence.

"Briggs, I think I can help you."

"How?"

"There's an expedition just about starting from England for Africa; its final destination is, I believe, the site of ancient Ethiopian cities; its object to unearth buried cities and treasure which the shifting sands of Sahara have buried for centuries. This expedition lacks just such a medical man as you; the salary is large, but you must sign for two years; that is my reason for not mentioning it before. It bids fair to be a wonderful venture and there will be plenty of glory for those who return, beside the good it will do to the Negro race if it proves the success in discovery that scholars predict. I don't advise you to even consider this opportunity, but you asked for my help and this is all I can offer at present."

"But Dianthe!" exclaimed Reuel faintly.

"Yes," smiled Aubrey. "Don't I know how I would feel if it were Molly and I was in your place? You are like all other men, Reuel. Passion does not calculate, and therein lies its strength. As long as common sense lasts we are not in love. Now the answer to the question of ways and means is with you; it is in your hands. You will choose love and poverty I suppose; I should. There are people fools enough to tell a man in love to keep cool. Bah! It is an impossible thing."

"Does true love destroy our reasoning faculties?" Reuel asked himself as he sat there in silence after his friend ceased speaking. He felt then that he could not accept this offer. Finally he got upon his feet, still preserving his silence, and made ready to leave his friend. When he reached the door, he turned and said: "I will see you in the morning."

For a long time after Briggs had gone, Aubrey sat smoking and gazing into the glowing coals that filled the open grate.

All that night Reuel remained seated in his chair or pacing the cheerless room, conning ways and means to extricate himself from his dilemma without having recourse to the last extremity proposed by Aubrey. It was a brilliant opening; there was no doubt of that; a year—six months ago—he would have hailed it with delight, but if he accepted it, it would raise a barrier between his love and him which could not be overcome—the ocean and thousands of miles.

"Oh, no!" he cried, "a thousand times no! Rather give up my ambitions."

Then growing more rational he gazed mournfully around the poor room and asked himself if he could remain and see his wife amid such surroundings? That would be impossible. The question then, resolved itself into two parts: If he remained at home, they could not marry, therefore separation; if he went abroad, marriage and separation. He caught at the last thought eagerly. If then they were doomed to separate, of two evils why not choose the least? The African position would at least bind them irrevocably together. Instantly hope resumed its sway in Reuel's breast so fertile is the human mind in expedients to calm the ruffled spirit; he began to estimate the advantages he would gain by accepting the position: He could marry Dianthe, settle a large portion of his salary upon her thus rendering her independent of charity, leave her in the care of the Vance family, and return in two years a wealthy man no longer fearing poverty. He had never before builded golden castles, but now he speculated upon the possibility of unearthing gems and gold from the mines of ancient Meroe and the pyramids of Ethiopia. In the midst of his fancies he fell asleep. In the morning he felt a wonderful relief as he contemplated his decision. Peace had returned to his mind. He determined to see Aburey at once and learn all the particulars concerning the expedition. Providentially, Aubrey was just sitting down to breakfast and over a cup of steaming coffee Reuel told his decision, ending with these words: "Now, my dear Aubrey, it may be the last request I may ever ask of you, for who can tell what strange adventures may await me in that dark and unknown country to which Fate has doomed me?"

Livingston tried to remonstrate with him.

"I know what I am saying. The climate is murderous, to begin with, and there are many other dangers. It is better to be prepared. I have no friend but you."

"Between us, Reuel, oaths are useless; you may count upon

my loyalty to all your interests," said Aubrey with impressiveness.

"I shall ask you to watch over Dianthe. I intrust her to you as I would intrust her to my brother, had I one. This is all I ask of you when I am in that far country."

With open brow, clear eyes and grave face, Aubrey Livingston replied in solemn tones:

"Reuel, you may sail without a fear. Molly and I will have her with us always like a dear sister."

Hand clasped in hand they stood a moment as if imploring heaven's blessing on the solemn compact. Then they turned the conversation on the business of securing the position at once.

CHAPTER VIII

Reuel was greatly touched during the next three months by the devotion of his friend Livingston, whose unselfishness in his behalf he had before had cause to notice. Nor was this all; he seemed capable of any personal sacrifice that the welfare of Briggs demanded.

Before many days had passed he had placed the young man in direct communication with the English officials in charge of the African expedition. The salary was most generous; in fact, all the arrangements were highly satisfactory. Whatever difficulties really existed melted, as it were, before Aubrey's influence, and Reuel would have approached the time of departure over a bed of roses but for the pain of parting with Dianthe.

At length the bustle of graduation was over. The last article of the traveler's outfit was bought. The morning of the day of departure was to see the ceremony performed that would unite the young people for life. It was a great comfort to Reuel that Charlie Vance had decided to join the party as a tourist for the sake of the advantages of such a trip.

The night before their departure Aubrey Livingston entertained the young men at dinner in his rooms along with a number of college professors and other learned savans. The most complimentary things were said of Reuel in the after-dinner toasts, the best of wishes were uttered together with congratulations on the marriage of the morrow for they all admired the young enthusiast. His superiority was so evident that none disputed it; they envied him, but were not jealous. The object of their felicitations smiled seldom.

"Come, for heaven sake shake off your sadness; he the happy groom upon whom Fortune, fickle jade, has at last consented to smile," cried Adonis. So, amid laughter and jest, the night passed and the morrow came.

After his guests had departed, Aubrey Livingston went to the telegraph office and sent a message:

"To Jim Titus,

"Laurel Hill, Virginia:—
"Be on hand at the New York dock, Trans-Atlantic Steamship Co., on the first. I will be there to make things right for you. Ten thousand if you succeed the first six months.
                                                    A.L."

*   *   *   *   *

It was noon the next day and the newly wedded stood with clasped hands uttering their good-byes.

"You must not be unhappy, dear. The time will run by before you know it, and I shall be with you again. Meanwhile there is plenty to occupy you. You have Molly and Aubrey to take you about. But pray remember my advice,—don't attempt too much; you're not strong by any means."

"No, I am not strong!" she interrupted with a wild burst of tears. "Reuel, if you knew how weak I am you would not leave me."

Her husband drew the fair head to his bosom, pressing back the thick locks with a lingering lover's touch.

"I wish to God I could take you with me," he said tenderly after a silence. Dear girl, you know this grief of yours would break my heart, only that it shows how well you love me. I am proud of every tear." She looked at him with an expression he could not read; it was full of unutterable emotion—love, anguish, compassion.

"Oh," she said passionately, "nothing remains long with us but sorrow and regret. Every good thing may be gone tomorrow—lost! Do you know, I sometimes dream or have waking visions of a past time in my life? But when I try to grasp the fleeting memories they leave me groping in darkness. Can't you help me, Reuel?"

With a laugh he kissed away her anxieties, although he was dismayed to know that at most any time full memory might return. He must speak to Aubrey. Then he closed her lips with warm lingering kisses.

"Be a good girl and pray for your husband's safety, that God may let us meet again and be happy! Don't get excited. That you *must* guard against."

And Reuel Briggs, though his eyes were clouded with tears, was a happy man at heart that day. Just that once he tasted to the full all that there is of happiness in human life. Happy is he who is blessed with even *one* perfect day in a lifetime of sorrow. His last memory of her was a mute kiss and low "God bless you," broken by a sob. And so they parted.

In the hall below Molly Vance met him with a sisterly kiss for good-bye; outside in the carriage sat Mr. Vance, Sr., Charlie and Aubrey waiting to drive to the depot.

*   *   *   *   *

Reuel Briggs, Charlie Vance and their servant, Jim Titus, sailed from New York for Liverpool, England, on the first day of July.

*   *   *   *   *

The departure of the young men made a perceptible break in the social circle at Vance Hall. Mr. Vance buried himself in the details of business and the two girls wandered disconsolately about the house and grounds attended by Livingston, who was at the Hall constantly and pursued them with delicate attentions.

By common consent it was determined that no summer exodus could be thought of until after the travellers had reached August, all being well, they would seek the limit of civilized intercourse in Africa. While waiting, to raise the spirits of the family, it was decided to invite a house party for the remainder of July, and in the beauties of Bar Harbor. Soon gaiety and laughter filled the grand old rooms; the days went merrily by.

Two men were sitting in the billiard room lounging over iced punch. Light, perfumed and golden, poured from the rooms below upon the summer night, and the music of a waltz made its way into the darkness.

"What an odd fish Livingston has grown to be," said one, relighting a thin, delicate-looking cigar. "I watched him out of curiosity a while ago and was struck at the change in him."

"Ah!" drawled the other sipping the cooling beverage. "Quite a Priuli on the whole, eh?"

"Y-e-s! Precisely. And I have fancied that the beautiful Mrs. Briggs is his Clarisse. What do you think? She shudders every time he draws near, and sinks to the ground under the steady gaze of his eye. Odd, isn't it?"

"Deucedly odd! About to marry Miss Vance, isn't he?"

"That don't count. Love is not always legitimate. If there's anything in it, it is only a flirtation probably; that's the style."

"What you say is true, Skelton. Let's drink the rest of this stuff and go down again. I know we're missed already."

When they had swallowed the punch and descended, the first person they saw was Livingston leaning against the door of the salon. His face was abstracted and in dead repose, there lurked about the corners of his full lips implacable resolution. The waltz was ended.

Some interminable argument was going on, generally, about the room. Conversation progressed in sharp, brisk sentences, which fell from the lips like the dropping shots of sharpshooters. There was a call for music. Molly mentally calculated her available talent and was about to give up the idea and propose something else, when she was amazed to see Dianthe rise hurriedly from her seat on an ottoman, go to the piano unattended and sit down. Unable to move with astonishment she watched in fascination the slender white fingers flash over the keys. There was a strange rigid appearance about the girl that was unearthly. Never once did she raise her eyes. At the first sharp treble note the buzz in the room was hushed at stillness. Livingston moved forward and rested his arm upon the piano fastening his gaze upon the singer's quivering lips.

Slowly, tremulously at first, pealed forth the notes:

"Go down, Moses, way down in Egypt's land,
Tell ol' Pharaoh, let my people go."

Scarcely was the verse begun when every person in the room started suddenly and listened with eager interest. As the air proceeded, some grew visibly pale, and not daring to breathe a syllable, looked horrified into each other's faces. "Great heaven!" whispered Mr. Vance to his daughter, "do you not hear another voice beside Mrs. Briggs'?"

It was true, indeed. A weird contralto, veiled as it were, rising and falling upon every wave of the great soprano, and reaching the ear as from some strange distance. The singer sang on, her voice dropping sweet and low, the echo following it, and at the closing word, she fell back in a dead faint. Mr. Vance caught her in his arms.

"Mrs. Briggs has the soul of an artiste. She would make a perfect prima donna for the Grand Opera," remarked one man to Molly.

"We are as surprised as anyone," replied the young girl; "we never knew that Mrs. Briggs was musical until this evening. It is a delightful surprise."

They carried her to the quiet, cool library away from the glaring lights and the excitement, and at her request left her there alone. Her thoughts were painful. Memory had returned in full save as to her name. She knit her brow in painful thought, finally learning back among her cushions wearily, too puzzled for further thought. Presently a step paused beside her chair. She looked up into Livingston's face.

"Are you feeling better?" he asked, gently taking in his slender wrist and counting the pulse-beats.

Instead of answering his question, she began abruptly: "Mr. Livingston, Reuel told me to trust you implicitly. Can you and will you tell me what has happened to me since last

I sang the song I have sung here tonight? I try to recall the past, but all is confusion and mystery. It makes my head ache so to think."

Livingston suddenly drew closer to her.

"Yes, Felice, there *is* a story in your life! I can save you."

"Save me!" exclaimed the girl.

"Yes, and will! Listen to me." In gentle accents he recounted to her there in the stillness, with the pulsing music of the viols beating and throbbing in her ears like muffled drums, the story of Dianthe Lusk as we have told it here. At the close of the tale the white-faced girl turned to him in despair the more eloquent because of her quietness.

"Did Reuel know that I was a Negress?"

"No; no one recognized you but myself."

She hid her face in her hands.

"Who ever suffered such torture as mine?" she cried, bitterly. "And there is no rest out of the grave!" she continued.

"Yes, there is rest and security in my love! Felice, Dianthe, I have learned to love you!"

She sprang from his touch as if stung.

He continued: "I love you better than all in the world. To possess you I am prepared to save you from the fate that must be yours if ever Reuel learns your origin."

"You would have me give up all for you?" she asked with a shudder.

"Ay, from your husband—from the world! We will go where none can ever find us. If you refuse, I cannot aid you."

"Pity me!"

She sank upon her knees at his feet.

"I give you a week to think it over. I can love, but cannot pity."

In vain the girl sought to throw off the numbing influence of the man's presence. In desperation she tried to defy him, but she knew that she had lost her will-power and was but a puppet in the hands of this false friend.

CHAPTER IX

"The Doctor is so good to you about letters; so different from poor Charlie. I can't imagine what he finds to write about."

It was the first of August, and the last guest had left the mansion; tomorrow they started for Bar Harbor. Molly, Dianthe and Livingston sat together in the morning room.

"He tells me the incidents of the journey. This is the last letter for three months," said Dianthe, with a sigh.

"Of course, there is no love-making," said Aubrey, lazily letting fall his newspaper, and pushing his hands through his bright hair. He was a sight for gods and men. His handsome figure outlined against the sky, as he stood by the window in an attitude of listless grace, his finely-cut face, so rich in color and the charm of varying expression, turned indolently toward the two women to whom the morning mail had brought its offering.

"Have you ever read one of Reuel's letters?" Dianthe said, quietly. "You may see this if you like." A tap sounded on the door.

"Miss Molly, if you please, the dressmaker has sent the things."

"Oh, thank you, Jennie, I'll come at once!" and gathering up her letters, Molly ran off with a smile and a nod of apology.

Aubrey stood by the window reading Reuel's letter. His

face was deadly white, and his breath came quick and short. He read half the page; then crushed it in his hand and crossed the room to Dianthe. She, too, was pale and there was something akin to fear in the gaze that she lifted to his face.

"How dare you?" he asked breathlessly; "but you are a woman! Not one of you has any delicacy in her heart! Not one!"

He tore the letter across and flung it from him.

"I do not suffer enough," he said in a suffocated voice. "You taunt me with this view of conjugal happiness—with his *right* to love and care for you."

"I did not do it to hurt you," she answered. "Do you have no thought for Molly's sufferings if I succumb to your threats of exposure and weakly allow myself to be frightened into committing the great wrong you contemplate toward two true-hearted people? I thought you could realize if you could *know* how Reuel loves and trusts me, and how true and noble is his nature."

"Do you think I have room to pity Reuel—Molly—while my own pain is more than I can bear? Without you my ambition is destroyed, my hope for the future—my life is ruined."

He turned from her and going to a distant part of the room, threw himself into a chair and covered his face with his hands. Against her will, better promptings and desires, the unfortunate girl is drawn by invisible influences across the room to the man's side. Presently he holds her in his eager, strong embrace, his face and tears hidden against her shoulder. She does not struggle in his clasp, only looks into the future with the hopeless agony of dumb despair.

At length he broke the silence. "There is nothing you can feel, or say to me that I do not realize—the sin, the shame, the lasting disgrace. I know it all. I told you once I loved you; I tell you now that I cannot *live* without you!"

An hour later Dianthe sat alone in the pleasant room. She did not realize the beauty of the languid mid-summer day. She thought of nothing but the wickedness of betraying her friends. Her perfect features were like marble. The dark eyes had deep, black circles round them and gazed wistfully into the far, far distance, a land where spirit only could compass the wide space. As she sat there in full possession of all her waking faculties, suddenly there rose from out the very floor, as it were, a pale and lovely woman. She neither looked at Dianthe nor did she speak; but walked to the table and opened a book lying upon it and wrote; then coming back, stood for a moment fixed; then sank, just as she rose, and disappeared. Her dress was that of a servant. Her head was bare; her hair fell loosely around her in long black curls. Her complexion was the olive of mulattoes or foreigners. As the woman passed from her view, Dianthe rose and went to the table to examine the book. She did not feel at all frightened, recognizing instantly the hand of mysticism in this strange occurrence. There on the open page, she perceived heavy marks in ink, under-scoring the following quotation from the twelfth chapter of Luke: "For there is nothing covered that shall not be revealed." On the margin, at the end of this passage was written in a fine female hand, the single word, "Mira."

*   *   *   *   *

After luncheon Aubrey proposed that they go canoeing on the river. The idea was eagerly embraced and by five o'clock the large and luxurious canoe floated out from the boat-house upon the calm bosom of the lovely Charles rocking softly to the little waves that lapped her sides.

The day had been oppressive, but upon the river a refreshing breeze was blowing now that the sun had gone down.

For the time all Dianthe's cares left her and her tortured mind was at peace. Molly was full of life and jested and sang and laughed. She had brought her mandolin with her and gave them soft strains of delicious waltzes.

On, on they glided under the impetus of the paddle-strokes in Aubrey's skilful hands, now past the verdure-clad pine hills, now through beds of fragrant water-lilies getting gradually farther and farther from the companionship of other pleasure-seekers. On, into the uninhabited portion where silent woods and long green stretches of pasture-land added a wild loneliness to the scene.

How lovely was the evening sky with its white clouds dotting the azure and the pink tinting of the sunset casting over all its enlivening glow; how deep, and dark was the green of the water beneath the shadowing trees. From the land came the lowing of cows and the sweet scent of freshly spread hay.

Suddenly Aubrey's paddle was caught and held in the meshes of the water-lily stems that floated all about them. He leaned far over to extricate it and in a moment the frail craft was bottom up, its living freight struggling in the river. Once, twice, thrice a thrilling call for help echoed over the darkening land; then all was still.

(To be continued.)

CHAPTER X

The expedition with which Reuel Briggs found himself connected was made up of artists, savans and several men— capitalists—who represented the business interests of the venture. Before the white cliffs of the English coast were entirely lost to view, Reuel's natural propensities for leadership were being fully recognized by the students about him. There was an immediate demand for his professional services and he was kept busy for many days. And it was the best panacea for a nature like his—deep and silent and self-suppressing. He had abandoned happiness for duty; he had stifled all those ominous voices which rose from the depth of his heart, and said to him: "Will you ever return? and if you return will you find your dear one? and, if you find her, will she not have changed? will she have preserved your memory as faithfully as you will preserve hers?

A thousand times a day while he performed his duties mechanically, his fate haunted him—the renunciation which called on him to give up happiness, to open to mishap the fatal door absence. All the men of the party were more or less silent and distrait, even Charlie Vance was subdued and thoughtful. But Briggs suffered more than any of them, although he succeeded in affecting a certain air of indifference. As he gradually calmed down and peace returned to his mind, he was surprised to feel the resignation that possessed him. Some unseen presence spoke to his inner being words of consolation and hope. He was shown very clearly his own inability to control events, and that his fate was no longer in his own hands but ordered by a being of infinite pity and love. After hours spent in soul-communion with the spirit of Dianthe, he would sink into refreshing slumber and away in peace. Her letters were bright spots, very entertaining and describing minutely her life and daily occupation since his departure. He lived upon them during the voyage to Tripoli, sustained by the hope of finding one upon arriving at that city.

One fine evening when the sun was setting, they arrived

at Tripoli. Their course lay toward the southward, and standing on deck, Reuel watched the scene—a landscape strange in form, which would have delighted him and filled him with transports of joy; now he felt something akin to indifference.

The ripples that flit the burnished surface of the long undulating billows tinkled continually on the sides of the vessel. He was aware of a low-lying spectral-pale band of shore. That portion of Africa whose nudity is only covered by the fallow mantle of the desert gave a most sad impression to the gazer. The Moors call it "Bled el Ateusch," the Country of Thirst; and, as there is an intimate relation between the character of a country and that of its people, Reuel realized vividly that the race who dwelt here must be different from those of the rest of the world.

"Ah! that is our first glimpse of Africa, is it?" said Adonis's voice, full of delight, beside him.

He turned to see his friend offering him a telescope. "At last we are here. In the morning we shall set our feet on the enchanted ground."

In the distance one could indeed make out upon the deep blue of the sky the profile of Djema el Gomgi, the great mosque on the shores of the Mediterranean. At a few cable lengths away the city smiles at them with all the fascination of a modern Cleopatra, circled with an oasis of palms studded with hundreds of domes and minarets. Against a sky of amethyst the city stands forth with a penetrating charm. It is the eternal enchantment of the cities of the Orient seen at a distance; but, alas! set foot within them, the illusion vanishes and disgust seizes you. Like beautiful bodies they have the appearance of life, but within the worm of decay and death eats ceaselessly.

At twilight in this atmosphere the city outlines itself faintly, then disappears in dusky haze. One by one the stars came into the sky until the heavens were a twinkling blaze; the sea murmured even her soft refrain and slept with the transparency of a mirror, flecked here and there with fugitive traces of phosophorescence.

The two young men stood a long time on the deck gazing toward the shore.

"Great night!" exclaimed Adonis at length with a long-drawn sigh of satisfaction. "It promises to be better than anything Barnum has ever given us even at a dollar extra reserved seat."

Reuel smiled in spite of himself; after all, Charlie was a home-line warranted to ward off homesickness. On board there was the sound of hurrying feet and a murmur of suppressed excitement, but it had subsided shortly; an hour later "sleep and oblivion reigned over all."

In the morning, amid the bustle of departure the mail came on board. There were two letters for Reuel. He seated himself in the seclusion of the cabin safe from prying eyes. Travelling across the space that separated him from America, his thoughts were under the trees in the garden of Vance Hall. In the fresh morning light he thought he could discern the dress of his beloved as she came toward him between the trees.

Again he was interrupted by Charlie's jolly countenance. He held an open letter in his hand. "There, Doc., there's Molly's letter. Read it, read it; don't have any qualms of conscience about it. There's a good bit in it concerning the Madam, see? I thought you'd like to read it." Then he sauntered away to talk with Jim Titus about the supplies for the trip across the desert.

Jim was proving himself a necessary part of the expedition.

He was a Negro of the old régime who felt that the Anglo-Saxon was appointed by God to rule over the African. He showed his thoughts in his obsequious manner, his subservient "massa," and his daily conversation with those about him. Jim superintended the arrangement of the table of the exploring party, haggled over prices with the hucksters, quarreled with the galley cooks and ended by doing all the cooking for his party in addition to keeping his eye on "Massa Briggs." All of this was very pleasant, but sometimes Reuel caught a gleam in Jim's furtive black eye which set him thinking and wondering at the latter's great interest in himself; but he accounted for this because of Livingston's admonitions to Jim to "take care of Dr. Briggs."

Willing or not, the company of travellers were made to take part in the noisy scene on deck when a horde of dirty rascals waylaid them, and after many uses and combination of all sorts over a few cents, they and their luggage were transported to the Custom House. "Ye gods!" exclaimed Charlie in deep disgust, "what a jostling, and what a noise."

All the little world about them was in an uproar, everyone signalling, gesticulating, speaking at once. Such a fray bewilders a civilized man, but those familiar with Southern exuberance regard it tranquilly, well knowing the disorder is more apparent than real. Those of the party who were familiar with the scene, looked on highly amused at the bewilderment of the novices.

Most of them had acquired the necessary art of not hurrying, and under their direction the examination of the baggage proceeded rapidly. Presently, following a robust porter, they had traversed an open place filled with the benches and chairs of a "café," and soon the travellers were surprised and amused to find themselves objects of general curiosity.

Coffee and nargiles were there merely as a pretext, in reality the gathering was in their honor. The names of the members of the expedition were known, together with its object of visiting Meroe of ancient fame, the arrival of such respectable visitors is a great event. Then, too, Tripoli is the natural road by which Africa has been attacked by many illustrious explorers because of the facility of communication with the country of the Blacks. Nowhere in northern Africa does the Great Desert advance so near the sea. The Atlas range rises from the Atlantic coast, extending far eastward. This range loses itself in the gulf of Little Syrta, and the vast, long-pent-up element, knowing no more barrier, spreads its yellow, sandy waves as far as the Nile, enveloping the last half-submerged summits which form a rosary of oases.

Under the Sultan's rule Tripoli has remained the capital of a truly barbaric state, virgin of improvements, with just enough dilapitated abandon, dirt and picturesqueness to make the delight of the artist. Arabs were everywhere; veiled women looked at the Christians with melting eyes above their wrappings. Mohammedanism, already twelve centuries old, has, after a period of inactivity, awakened anew in Africa, and is rapidly spreading. Very unlike the Christians, the faithful of today are the same fervid Faithful of Omar and Mohammed. Incredulity, indifference, so widely spread among other sects are unknown to them.

Supper-time found the entire party seated on the floor around a well-spread tray, set on a small box. They had taken possession of the one living-room of a mud house. It was primitive but clean. A post or two supported the thatched ceiling. There were no windows. The furniture consisted of a few rugs and cushions. But the one idea of the party being sleep, they were soon sunk in a profound and dreamless slumber.

The next day and the next were spent in trying to gain an audience with the Sheik Mohammed Abdallah, and the days lengthened into weeks and a month finally rolled into oblivion. Meantime there were no letters for Dr. Briggs and Charlie Vance. Everyone else in the party had been blessed with many letters, even Jim was not forgotten.

Reuel had learned to be patient in the dolce far niente of the East, but not so Charlie. He fumed and fretted continually after the first weeks had passed. But promptly at two, one hot afternoon the Sheik knocked at the door of their hut. He was a handsome man of forty years—tall, straight, with clear brown eyes, good features, a well-shaped moustache and well-trimmed black beard. Authority surrounded him like an atmosphere. He greeted the party in French and Arabic and invited them to his house where a feast was spread for them. Presents were given and received and then they were introduced to Ababdis, an owner of camels who was used to leading parties into the wilderness. After much haggling over prices, it was decided to take fifteen camels and their drivers. Supplies were to consist of biscuit, rice, tea, sugar, coffee, wax candles, charcoal and a copious supply of water bags. It was decided not to start until Monday, after the coming of the mail, which was again due. After leaving Tripoli, it was doubtful when they would receive news from America again. The mail came. Again Jim was the only one who received a letter from the United States. Reuel handed it to him with a feeling of homesickness and a sinking of the heart.

Monday morning found them mounted and ready for the long journey across the desert to the first oasis. From the

back of a camel Charlie Vance kept the party in good humor
with his quaint remarks. "Say, Doc., it's worth the price.
How I wish the pater, your wife and Molly could see us
now. Livingston wouldn't do a thing to these chocolate colored
gentry of Arabia."

"And Miss Scott? where does she come in?" questioned
Reuel with an assumption of gaiety he was far from feeling.

"Oh," replied Charlie, not at all nonplussed. "Cora isn't
in the picture; I'm thinking of a houri."

"Same old thing, Charlie—the ladies?"

"No," said Charlie, solemnly. "It's business this time. Say,
Briggs, the sight of a camel always makes me a child again.
The long-necked beast is inevitably associated in my mind
with Barnum's circus and playing hookey. Pop wants me to
put out my sign and go in for business, but the show business
suits me better. For instance," he continued with a wave of
his hand including the entire caravan, "Arabs, camels, stray
lions, panthers, scorpions, serpents, explorers, etc., with a
few remarks by yours truly, to the accompaniment of the
band—always the band you know, would make an interesting
show—a sort of combination of Barnum and Kiralfy. The
houris would do Kiralfy's act, you know. There's money in
it."

"Were you ever serious in your life, Charlie?"

"What the deuce is the need of playing funeral all the time,
tell me that, Briggs, will you?"

The great desert had the sea's monotony. They rode on and
on hour after hour. The elements of the view were simple.
Narrow valleys and plains bounded by picturesque hills lay
all about them. The nearer hills to the right had shoulders
and hollows at almost regular intervals, and a sky-line of an
almost regular curve. Under foot the short grass always

seemed sparse, and the low sage-shrubs rather dingy, but as they looked over the plain stretching away in every direction, it had a distinctly green tint. They saw occasionally a red poppy and a purple iris. Not a tree was to be seen, nor a rock. Sometimes the land lay absolutely level and smooth, with hardly a stone larger than a bean. The soft blue sky was cloudless, the caravan seemed to be the only living creature larger than a gazelle in the great solitude. Even Reuel was aroused to enthusiasm by the sight of a herd of these graceful creatures skimming the plain. High in the air the larks soared and sang.

As they went southward the hot sun poured its level rays upon them, and the song of the drivers was a relief to their thoughts. The singing reminded travellers of Venetian gondoliers, possessing as it did the plaintive sweetness of the most exquisite European airs. There was generally a leading voice answered by a full chorus. Reuel thought he had never heard music more fascinating. Ababdis would assume the leading part. "Ah, when shall I see my family again; the rain has fallen and made a canal between me and my home. Oh, shall I never see it more?" Then would follow the chorus of drivers: "Oh, what pleasure, what delight, to see my family again; when I see my father, mother, brothers, sisters, I will hoist a flag on the head of my camel for joy!" About the middle of the week they were making their way over the Great Desert where it becomes an elevated plateau crossed by rocky ridges, with intervening sandy plains mostly barren, but with here and there a solitary tree, and sometimes a few clumps of grass. The caravan was skirting the base of one of these ridges, which culminated in a cliff looking, in the distance, like a half-ruined castle, which the Arabs believed to be enchanted. Reuel determined to visit this cliff, and saying nothing to any one, and accompanied only by Jim and followed by the warnings of the Arabs to beware of lions, they started for the piles of masonry, which they reached in a couple of hours. The moon rose in unclouded splendor, and Moore's lines came to his heart:

> "O, such a blessed night as this,
>   I often think if friends were near,
> How we should feel, and gaze with bliss
>   Upon the moonlight scenery here."

He strolled into the royal ruin, stumbling over broken carvings, and into hollows concealed by luminous plants, beneath whose shades dwelt noisome things that wriggled away in the marvelous white light. Climbing through what was once a door, he stepped out on a ledge of masonry, that hung sheer seven hundred feet over the plain. Reuel got out his pipe and it was soon in full blast, while the smoker set to building castles in the curls of blue smoke, that floated lightly into space. Jim with the guns waited for him at the foot of the hill.

Under the influence of the soothing narcotic and the spell of the silver moon, Reuel dreamed of fame and fortune he would carry home to lay at a little woman's feet. Presently his castle-building was interrupted by a low vail—not exactly the mew of a cat, nor yet the sound of a lute.

Again the sound.

What could it be?

"Ah, I have it!" muttered Reuel; "it's the Arabs singing in the camp."

Little did he imagine that within ten paces of him crouched an enormous leopard.

Little did he imagine that he was creeping, creeping toward him, as a cat squirms at a bird.

He sat on the ruined ledge of the parapet, within two feet of the edge; seven hundred feet below the desert sand glittered like molten silver in the gorgeous moonlight.

He was unarmed, having given Jim his revolver to hold.

Reuel sat there entirely unconscious of danger; presently a vague feeling struck him, not of fear, not of dread, but a feeling that if he turned his head he would see an enemy, and without knowing why, he slowly turned his head.

Great heavens! what did he see? A thrill of horror passed through him as his eyes rested upon those of an enormous brute, glaring like hot coals set in blood-red circles.

Its mouth was wide open, its whiskers moving like the antennal of a lobster. It lay on its belly, its hindquarters raised, its forepaws planted in the tawny sand ready to spring.

The moon played on the spots of its body. The dark spots became silvered, and relapsed into darkness as the animal breathed, while its tail lashed about, occasionally whipping the sand with a peculiar wish.

How was he to withstand its spring?

The weight of its body would send him over the precipice like a shot.

Strange to say a grim satisfaction came to him at the thought that the brute must go down with him. Where could he hold? Could he clutch at anything? he asked himself.

He dared not remove his eyes from those of the leopard. He could not in fact. But in a sort of introverted glance he saw that nothing stood between him and space but a bare, polished wall, that shone white beneath moonbeams.

"Was there a loose stone—a stone that would crush in the

skull of the blood-thirsty animal?" Not so much as a pebble to cast into the depths, for he had already searched for one to fling over, as people do when perched on imminences. He cried for help, "Jim! Jim! O-o-o-h, Jim!"

There came no reply; not the slightest sound broke the stillness as the sound of his cries died away.

Reuel was now cool—cool as a cucumber—so cool that he deliberately placed himself in position to receive the rush of the terrific brute. He felt himself moving gently back his right foot, shuffling it back until his heel came against an unevenness in the rock, which gave him a sort of purchase— something to back it.

He gathered himself together for a supreme effort, every nerve being at the highest condition of tension.

It is extraordinary all the thoughts that pass like lightning in a second of time, through the mind, while face to face with death. Volumes of ideas flashed through his brain as he stood on the stone ledge, with eternity awaiting him, knowing that this would be the end of all his hopes and fears and pleasant plans for future happiness, that he would go down to death in the embrace of the infuriated animal before him, its steel-like claws buried in his flesh, its fetid breath filling his nostrils. He thought of his darling love, and of how the light would go out of her existence with his death. He thought of Livingston, of the fellows who had gathered to bid him God speed, of the paragraphs in the papers. All these things came as harrowing pictures as he stood at bay in the liquid pearl of the silent moon.

The leopard began to move its hindquarters from side to side. A spring was at hand.

Reuel yelled then—yelled till the walls of the ruined castle echoed again—yelled as if he had 10,000 voices in his throat—yelled, as a man only yells when on his being heard depends his chance for dear life.

The beast turned its head sharply, and prepared to spring. For a second Briggs thought that a pantomime trick might give him a chance. What if he were to wait until the animal actually leaped, and then turn aside?

Carried forward by its own weight and momentum it would go over the ledge and be dashed to pieces on the rocks below.

It was worth trying. A drowning man catches at a straw. Instinctively Reuel measured his distance. He could step aside and let the brute pass, but that was all. The ledge was narrow. He was, unhappily, in very good condition The seavoyage had fattened him, and it was just a chance that he could escape being carried over by the brute.

He accepted the chance.

Then came the fearful moment.

The leopard swayed a little backward!

Then, to his intense delight, he heard a shout of encouragement in Vance's well-known voice, "Coming, Briggs, coming!"

The next moment a hand was laid on his shoulder from a window above; it was Charlie, who trembling with anxiety had crept through the ruin, and, oh, blessed sight! handed Reuel his revolver.

Briggs made short work of the leopard; he let him have three barrels—all in the head.

Vance had become alarmed for the safety of his friend, and had gone to the ruin to meet him. When very nearly there, he had heard the first cry for help, and had urged his camel forward. Arrived at the castle he had found Jim apparently dead with sleep, coiled up on the warm sand. How he could sleep within sound of the piercing cries uttered by Briggs was long a mystery to the two friends.

CHAPTER XI

The caravan had halted for the night. Professor Stone, the leader of the expedition, sat in Reuel's tent enjoying a pipe and a talk over the promising features of the enterprise. The nearer they approached the goal of their hopes—the ancient Ethiopian capital Meroe—the greater was the excitement among the leaders of the party. Charlie from his bed of rugs listened with ever-increasing curiosity to the conversation between the two men.

"It is undoubtedly true that from its position as the capital of Ethiopia and the enterpret of trade between the North and South, between the East and West, Meroe must have held vast treasures. African caravans poured ivory, frankincense and gold into the city. My theory is that somewhere under those pyramids we shall find invaluable records and immense treasure."

"Your theories may be true, Professor, but if so, your discoveries will establish the primal existence of the Negro as the most ancient source of all that you value in modern life, even antedating Egypt. How can the Anglo-Saxon world bear the establishment of such a theory?" There was a hidden note of sarcasm in his voice which the others did not notice.

The learned savan settled his glasses and threw back his head.

"You and I, Briggs, know that the theories of prejudice

are swept away by the great tide of facts. It is a *fact* that Egypt drew from Ethiopia all the arts, sciences and knowledge of which she was mistress. The very soil of Egypt was pilfered by the Nile from the foundations of Meroe. I have even thought," he continued meditatively, "that black was the original color of man in prehistoric times. You remember that Adam was made from the earth; what more natural than that he should have retained the color of the earth? What puzzles me is not the origin of the Blacks, but of the Whites. Miriam was made a leper outside the tents for punishment; Naaman was a leper until cleansed. It is a question fraught with big possibilities which God alone can solve. But of this we are sure—all records of history, sacred and profane,, unite in placing the Ethiopian as the primal race."

"Gee whiz!" exclaimed Charlie from his bed on the floor. "Count me out!"

"Don't touch upon the origin of the Negro; you will find yourself in a labyrinth, Professor. That question has provoked more discussion than any other concerning the different races of man on the globe. Speculation has exhausted itself, yet the mystery appears to remain unsolved."

"Nevertheless the Biblical facts are very explicit, and so simple as to force the very difficulties upon mankind that Divinity evidently designed to avoid."

"The relationship existing between the Negro and other people of the world is a question of absorbing interest. For my part, I shall be glad to add to my ethnological knowledge by anything we may learn at Meroe." Thus speaking Reuel seemed desirous of dismissing the subject. More conversation followed on indifferent subjects, and presently the Professor bade them good night and retired to his own tent.

Reuel employed himself in making entries in his journal, Charlie continued to smoke, at times evincing by a musical snore that he was in the land of dreams. Jim sat at some distance reading a letter that he held in his hand.

The night was sultry, the curtains of the tent undrawn; from out the silent solitude came the booming call of a lion to his mate.

Suddenly a rush of balmy air seemed to pass over the brow of the scribe, and a dim shadow fell across the tent door. It was the form of the handsome Negress who had appeared to Dianthe, and signed herself "Mira."

There was no fear in Reuel's gaze, no surprise; it was as if a familiar and welcome visitor had called upon him. For a moment an impulse to spring away into the wide, wide realms of air, seemed to possess him; the next, the still, dreamy ecstasy of a past time; and then he saw Jim—who sat directly behind him—placed like a picture on his very table. He saw him knit his brow, contract his lip, and then, with a face all seamed with discontent, draw from his vest a letter, seemingly hidden in a private pocket, reading thus:—

> "Use your discretion about the final act, but be sure the letters are destroyed. I have advised the letters sent in your care as you will probably be detailed for the mail. But to avoid mishap call for the mail for both parties. Address me at Laurel Hill—Thomas Johnson."
>
> "A. L."

Twice did the visionary scene, passing *behind* the seer, recross his entranced eyes; and twice did the shadowy finger of the shining apparition in the tent door point, letter by letter, to the pictured page of the billet, which Jim was at that very moment perusing with his natural, and Reuel Briggs with his spiritual eyes. When both had concluded the reading, Jim put up his letter. The curtains of the tent slightly waved; a low, long sigh, like the night's wind wail, passed over the cold, damp brow of the seer. A shudder, a blank. He looked out into the desert beyond. All was still. The stars were out for him, but the vision was gone.

Thus was explained to Reuel, by mesmeric forces, the fact that his letters had been withheld.

He had not once suspected Jim of perfidy. What did it mean? he asked himself. The letter was in Livingston's handwriting! His head swam; he could not think. Over and over again he turned the problem and then, wishing that something more definite had been given him, retired, but not to sleep.

Try as he would to throw it off, the most minute act of Jim since entering his service persisted in coming before his inner vision. The night when he was attacked by the leopard and Jim's tardiness in offering help, returned with great significance. What could he do but conclude that he was the victim of a conspiracy.

"There is no doubt about it," was his last thought as he dropped into a light doze. How long he slept he could not tell, but he woke with a wild, shrill cry in his ears: "Reuel, Reuel, save me!"

Three times it was repeated, clear, distinct, and close beside his ear, a pause between the repetitions.

He roused his sleeping friend. "Charlie, Charlie! wake up and listen!"

Charlie, still half asleep, looked with blinking eyes at the candle with dazzled sight.

"Charlie, for the love of God wake up!"

At this, so full of mortal fear were his words, Adonis

shook off his drowsiness and sat up in bed, wide awake and staring at him in wonder.

"What the deuce!" he began, and then stopped, gazing in surprise at the white face and trembling hands of his friend.

"Charlie," he cried, "some terrible event has befallen Dianthe, or like a sword hangs over our heads. Listen, listen!"

Charlie did listen but heard nothing but the lion's boom which now broke the stillness.

"I hear nothing, Reuel."

"O Charlie, are you sure?"

"Nothing but the lion. But that'll be enough if he should take it into his mind to come into camp for his supper."

"I suppose you are right, for you can hear nothing, and I can hear nothing now. But, oh Charlie! it was so terrible, and I heard it so plainly; though I daresay it was only my— Oh God! there it is again! listen! listen!"

This time Charlie heard—heard clearly and unmistakably, and hearing, felt the blood in his veins turn to ice.

Shrill and clear above the lion's call rose a prolonged wail, or rather shriek, as of a human voice rising to heaven in passionate appeal for mercy, and dying away in sobbing and shuddering despair. Then came the words:

"Charlie, brother, save me!"

Adonis sprang to his feet, threw back the curtain of the tent and looked out. All was calm and silent, not even a cloud flecked the sky where the moon's light cast a steady radiance.

Long he looked and listened; but nothing could be seen or heard. But the cry still rang in his ears and clamored at his heart; while his mind said it was the effect of imagination.

Reuel's agitation had swallowed up his usual foresight. He had forgotten his ability to resort to that far-seeing faculty which he had often employed for Charlie's and Aubrey's amusement when at home.

Charlie was very calm, however, and soothed his friend's fears, and after several ineffectual attempts to concentrate his powers for the exercise of the clairvoyant sight of the hypnotic trance, was finally able to exercise the power.

In low, murmuring cadence, sitting statuesque and rigid beneath the magnetic spell, Reuel rehearsed the terrible scene which had taken place two months before in the United States in the ears of his deeply-moved friend.

"Ah, there is Molly, poor Molly; and see your father weeps, and the friends are there and they too weep, but where is my own sweet girl, Dianthe, love, wife! No, I cannot see her, I do not find the poor maimed body of my love. And Aubrey! What! Traitor, false friend! I shall return for vengeance.

"Wake me, Charlie," was his concluding sentence.

A few upward passes of his friend's hands, and the released spirit became lord of its casket once more. Consciousness returned, and with it memory. In short whispered sentences Reuel told Vance of his suspicions, of the letter he read while it lay in Jim's hand, of his deliberate intention to leave him to his fate in the leopard's claws.

The friends laid their plans,—they would go on to Meroe, and then return instantly to civilization as fast as steam could carry them, if satisfactory letters were not waiting them from America.

(To be continued.)

☙ ☙ ☙

CHAPTER XII

Late one afternoon two weeks later, the caravan halted at the edge of the dirty Arab town which forms the outposts to the island of Meroe.

Charlie Vance stood in the door of his tent and let his eyes wander over the landscape in curiosity. Clouds of dust swept over the sandy plains; when they disappeared the heated air began its dance again, and he was glad to re-enter the tent and stretch himself at full length in his hammock. The mail was not yet in from Cairo, consequently there were no letters; his eyes ached from straining them for a glimpse of the Ethiopian ruins across the glassy waters of the tributaries of the Nile which encircled the island.

It was not a simple thing to come all these thousand of miles to look at a pile of old ruins that promised nothing of interest to him after all. This was what he had come for— the desolation of an African desert, and the companionship of human fossils and savage beasts of prey. The loneliness made him shiver. It was a desolation that doubled desolateness, because his healthy American organization missed the march of progress attested by the sound of hammers on unfinished buildings that told of a busy future and cosy modern homeliness. Here there was no future. No railroads, no churches, no saloons, no schoolhouses to echo the voices of merry children, no promise of the life that produces within the range of his vision. Nothing but the monotony of past centuries dead and forgotten save by a few learned savans.

As he rolled over in his hammock, Charlie told himself that next to seeing the pater and Molly, he'd give ten dollars to be able to thrust his nose into twelve inches of whiskey and soda, and remain there until there was no more. Then a flicker of memory made Charlie smile as he remembered the jollities of the past few months that he had shared with Cora Scott.

"Jolly little beggar," he mentally termed her. "I wonder what sort of a fool she'd call me if she could see me now whistling around the ragged edge of this solid block of loneliness called a desert."

Then he fell asleep and dreamed he was boating on the Charles, and that Molly was a mermaid sporting in a bed of water-lilies.

Ancient writers, among them Strabo, say that the Astabora unites its stream with the Nile, and forms the island of Meroe. The most famous historical city of Ethiopia is commonly called Carthage, but Meroe was the queenly city of this ancient people. Into it poured the traffic of the world in gold, frankincense and ivory. Diodorus states the island to be three hundred and seventy-five miles long and one hundred and twenty-five miles wide. The idea was borne in upon our travellers in crossing the Great Desert that formerly wells must have been established at different stations for the convenience of man and beast. Professor Stone and Reuel had discovered traces of a highway and the remains of cisterns which must have been marvellous in skill and prodigious in formation.

All was bustle and commotion in the camp that night. Permission had been obtained to visit and explore the ruins from the Arab governor of the Province. It had cost money, but Professor Stone counted nothing as lost that would aid in the solution of his pet theories.

The leaders of the enterprise sat together late that night, listening to the marvellous tales told by the Professor of the city's ancient splendor, and examining closely the chart which had remained hidden for years before it fell into his hands. For twenty-five years this apostle of learning had held the key to immense wealth, he believed, in his hands. For years he had tried in vain to interest the wealthy and powerful in his scheme for finding the city described in his chart, wherein he believed lay the gold mines from which had come the streams of precious metal which made the ancient Ethiopians famous.

The paper was in a large envelope sealed with a black seal formed to resemble a lotus flower. It was addressed:

> To the student who, having counted the cost, is resolute to once more reveal to the sceptical, the ancient glory of hoary Meroe.

Within the envelope was a faded parchment which the Professor drew forth with trembling hands. The little company drew more closely about the improvised table and its flickering candle which revealed the faded writing to be in Arabic. There was no comment, but each one listened intently to the reader, who translated very fully as he went along.

"Be it known to you, my brother, that the great and surpassing wealth mentioned in this parchment is not to be won without braving many dangers of a deadly nature. You who may read this message, then, I entreat to consider well the perils of your course. Within the mines of Meroe, four days' journey from the city toward Arabia, are to be found gold in bars and gold in flakes, and diamonds, and rubies whose beauty excels all the jewels of the earth. For some of them were hidden by the priests of Osiris that had adorned the crown of the great Semiramis, and royal line of Queen Candace, even from ancient Babylon's pillage these jewels came, a spectacle glorious beyond compare. There, too, is the black diamond of Senechus's crown (Senechus who suffered the captivity of Israel by the Assyrians), which exceeds all imagination for beauty and color.

"All these jewels with much treasure beside you will gain by following my plain directions.

"Four days' journey from Meroe toward Arabia is a city founded by men from the Upper Nile; the site is near one of its upper sources, which still has one uniform existence. This city is situated on a forked tributary, which takes its rise from a range of high, rocky mountains, almost perpendicular on their face, from which descend two streams like cataracts, about two miles apart, and form a triangle, which holds the inner city. The outer city occupies the opposite banks on either side of the streams, which after joining, form a river of considerable size, and running some five miles, loses itself in the surrounding swamps. The cities are enclosed within two great walls, running parallel with the streams. There are also two bridges with gates, connecting the inner and outer cities; two great gates also are near the mountain ranges, connecting the outer city with the agricultural lands outside the walls. The whole area is surrounded by extensive swamps, through which a passage known only to the initiated runs, and forms an impassible barrier to the ingress or egress of strangers.

"But there is another passage known to the priests and used by them, and this is the passage which the chart outlines beneath the third great pyramid, leading directly into the mines and giving access to the city.

"When Egypt rose in power and sent her hosts against the mother country, then did the priests close with skill and cunning this approach to the hidden city of refuge, where they finally retired, carrying with them the ancient records of Ethiopia's greatness, and closing forever, as they thought, the riches of her marvelous mines, to the world.

"Beneath the Sphinx' head lies the secret of the entrance, and yet not all, for the rest is graven on the sides of the cavern which will be seen when the mouth shall gape. But beware the tank to the right where dwells the sacred crocodile, still living, although centuries have rolled by and men have been gathered to the shades who once tended on his wants. And beware the fifth gallery to the right where abide the sacred serpents with jewelled crowns, for of a truth are they terrible.

"This the writer had from an aged priest whose bones lie embalmed in the third pyramid above the Sphinx."

With this extraordinary document a chart was attached, which, while an enigma to the others, seemed to be perfectly clear to Professor Stone.

The letter ended abruptly, and the chart was a hopeless puzzle to the various eyes that gazed curiously at the straggling outlines.

"What do you make of it, Professor?" asked Reuel, who with all his knowledge, was at sea with the chart. "We have been looking for mystery, and we seem to have found it."

"What do I make of it? Why, that we shall find the treasure and all return home rich," he replied the scholar testily.

"Rubbish!" snorted Charlie with fine scorn.

"How about the sacred crocodile and the serpents? My word, gentlemen, if you find the back door key of the Sphinx' head, there's a chance that a warm welcome is awaiting us."

Charlie's words met with approval from the others, but the Professor and Reuel said nothing. There was silence for a time, each man drawing at his pipe in silent meditation.

"Well, I'm only travelling for pleasure, so it matters not to me how the rest of you elect to shuffle off this mortal coil, I intend to get some fun out of this thing," continued Charlie.

There was a shout of laughter from his companions.

"Pleasure!" cried one. "O Lord! You've come to the wrong place. This is business, solid business. If we get out with our skins it will be something to be thankful for."

"Well, said Reuel, rousing himself from a fit of abstraction, "I come out to do business and I have determined to see the matter through if all is well at home. We'll prove whether there's a hidden city or not before we leave Africa."

The Professor grasped his hand in gratitude, and then silence fell upon the group. The curtains of the tent were thrown back. Bright fell the moonlight on the sandy plain, the Nile, the indistinct ruins of Meroe, hiding all imperfections by its magic fingers. It was wonderful sight to see the full moon looking down on the ruins of centuries. The weird light increased, the shadows lengthened and silence fell on the group, broken only by the low tones of Professor Stone as he told in broken sentences the story of ancient Ethiopia.

"For three thousand years the world has been mainly indebted for its advancement to the Romans, Greeks, Hebrews, Germans and Anglo-Saxons; but it was otherwise in the first years. Babylon and Egypt—Nimrod and Mizraim—both descendants of Ham—led the way, and acted as the pioneers of mankind in the untrodden fields of knowledge. The Ethiopians, therefore, manifested great superiority over all the nations among whom they dwelt, and their name became illustrious throughout Europe, Asia and Africa.

"The father of this distinguished race was Cush, the grandson of Noah, an Ethiopian.

"Old Chaldea, between the Euphrates and Tigris rivers,

was the first home of the Cushites. Nimrod, Ham's grandson, founded Babylon. The Babylonians early developed the energy of mind which made their country the first abode of civilization. Canals covered the land, serving the purposes of traffic, defense and irrigation. Lakes were dug and stored with water, dykes built along the banks of rivers to fertilize the land, and it is not surprising to learn that from the earliest times Babylonia was crowded with populous cities. This grandeur was brought about by Nimrod the Ethiopian."

"Great Scott!" cried Charlie, "you don't mean to tell me that all this was done by *niggers?*"

The Professor smiled. Being English, he could not appreciate Charlie's horror at its full value.

"Undoubtedly your Afro-Americans are a branch of the wonderful and mysterious Ethiopians who had a prehistoric existence of magnificence, the full record of which is lost in obscurity.

"We associate with the name 'Chaldea' the sciences of astronomy and philosophy and chronology. It was to the Wise Men of the East to whom the birth of Christ was revealed; they were Chaldeans—of the Ethiopians. Eighty-eight years before the birth of Abraham, these people, known in history as "Shepherd Kings,' subjugated the whole of Upper Egypt, which they held in bondage more than three hundred years."

"It is said that Egyptian civilization antedates that of Ethiopia," broke in Reuel. "How do you say, Professor?"

"Nothing of the sort, nothing of the sort. I know that in connecting Egypt with Ethiopia, one meets with most bitter denunciation from most modern scholars. Science has done its best to separate the race from Northern Africa, but the evidence is with the Ethiopians. If I mistake not, the ruins of Meroe will prove my words. Traditions with respect to

Memnon connect Egypt and Ethiopia with the country at the head of the Nile. Memnon personifies the ethnic identity of the two races. Ancient Greeks believed it. All the traditions of Armenia, where lies Mt. Ararat, are in accordance with this fact. The Armenian geography applies the name of Cush to four great regions—Media, Persia, Susiana, Asia, or the whole territory between the Indus and the Tigris. Moses of Chorene identifies Belus, king of Babylon with Nimrod.

"But the Biblical tradition is paramount to all. In it lies the greatest authority that we have for the affiliation of nations, and it is delivered to us very simply and plainly: 'The sons of Ham were Cush and Mizraim and Phut and Canaan . . . and Cush begot Nimrod . . . and the beginning of his kingdom was Babel and Erech and Accad and Calneh, in the land of Shinar.' It is the best interpretation of this passage to understand it as asserting that the four races—Egyptians, Ethiopians, Libyans and Canaanites—were ethnically connected, being all descended from Ham; and that the primitive people of Babylon were a subdivision of one of these races; namely, of the Cushite or Ethiopian.

"These conclusions have lately received important and unexpected confirmation from the results of linguistic research. After the most remarkable of Mesopotamian mounds had yielded their treasures, and supplied the historical student with numerous and copious documents, bearing upon the history of the great Assyrian and Babylonian empires, it was determined to explore Chaldea proper, where mounds of considerable height marked the site of several ancient cities. Among unexpected results was the discovery of a new form of speech, differing greatly from the later Babylonian language. In grammatical structure this ancient tongue resembles dialects of the Turanian family, but its vocabulary has been pronounced to be decidedly Cushite or Ethiopian; and the modern languages to which it approaches nearest are thought to be the Mahen of Southern Arabia and the Galla of Abyssinia. Thus comparative philology appears to confirm old traditions. An Eastern Ethiopia instead of being the invention of bewildered ignorance, is rather a reality which it will require a good deal of scepticism to doubt, and the primitive race that bore sway in Chaldea proper belongs to this ethnic type. Meroe was the queenly city of this great people."

"It is hard to believe your story. From what a height must this people have fallen to reach the abjectness of the American Negro," exclaimed a listener.

"True," replied the Professor. "But from what a depth does history show that the Anglo-Saxon has climbed to the position of the first people of the earth today."

Charlie Vance said noting. He had suffered so many shocks from the shattering of cherished idols since entering the country of mysteries that the power of expression had left him.

"Twenty-five years ago, when I was still a young man, the camel-driver who accompanied me to Thebes sustained a fatal accident. I helped him in his distress, and to show his gratitude he gave me the paper and chart I have shown you tonight. He was a singular man, black hair and eyes, middle height, dark-skinned, face and figure almost perfect, he was proficient in the dialects of the region, besides being master of the purest and most ancient Greek and Arabic. I believe he was a native of the city he described.

"He believed that Ethiopia antedated Egypt, and helped me materially in fixing certain data which time has proved to be correct. He added a fact which the manuscript withholds,—that from lands beyond unknown seas, to which many

descendants of Ethiopia had been borne as slaves, should a
king of ancient line—an offspring of that Ergamenes who
lived in the reign of the second Ptolemy—return and restore
the former glory of the race. The preservation of this hidden
city is for his reception. This Arab also declared that Cush
was his progenitor."

"That's bosh. How would they know their future king
after centuries of obscurity passed in strange lands, and
amalgamation with other races?" remarked the former speaker.

"I asked him that question; he told me that every descendant
of the royal line bore a lotus-lily in the form of a birthmark
upon his breast."

It might have been the unstable shadows of the moon that
threw a tremulous light upon the group, but Charlie Vance
was sure that Reuel Briggs started violently at the Professor's
words.

One by one the men retired to rest, each one under the
spell of the mysterious forces of a past life that brooded like
a mist over the sandy plain, the dark Nile rolling sluggishly
along within a short distance of their camp, and the ruined
city now a magnificent Necropolis. The long shadows grew
longer, painting the scene into beauty and grandeur. The
majesty of death surrounded the spot and its desolation spoke
in trumpet tones of the splendor which the grave must cover,
when even the memory of our times shall be forgotten.

CHAPTER XIII

Next morning the camp was early astir before the dawn; and
before the sun was up, breakfast was over and the first boat-
load of the explorers was standing on the site of the ruins

watching the unloading of the apparatus for opening solid masonry and excavating within the pyramids.

The feelings of every man in the party were ardently excited by the approach to the city once the light of the world's civilization. The great French writer, Volney, exclaimed when first his eyes beheld the sight, "How are we astonished when we reflect that to the race of Negroes, the object of our extreme contempt, we owe our arts, sciences and even the use of speech!"

From every point of view rose magnificent groups of pyramids rising above pyramids. About eighty of them remaining in a state of partial preservation. The principal one was situated on a hill two and a half miles from the river, commanding an extensive view of the plain. The explorers found by a hasty examination that most of them could be ascended although their surfaces were worn quite smooth. That the pyramids were places of sepulture they could not doubt. From every point of view the sepulchres were imposing; and they were lost in admiration and wonder with the first superficial view of the imposing scene.

One of the approaches or porticoes was most interesting, the roof being arched in regular masonic style, with what may be called a keystone. Belonging without doubt to the remotest ages, their ruined and defaced condition was attributed by the scientists to their great antiquity. The hieroglyphics which covered the monuments were greatly defaced. A knowledge of these characters in Egypt was confined to the priests, but in Ethiopia they were understood by all showing that even in that remote time and place learning and the arts had reached so high a state as to be diffused among the common people.

For a time the explorers wandered from ruin to ruin,

demoralized as to routine work, gazing in open astonishment at the wonders before them. Many had visited Thebes and Memphis and the Egyptian monuments, but none had hoped to find in this neglected corner, so much of wonder and grandeur. Within the pyramids that had been opened to the curious eye, they found the walls covered with the pictures of scenes from what must have been the daily life,—death, burial, marriage, birth, triumphal processions, including the spoils of war.

Reuel noticed particularly the figure of a queen attired in long robe, tight at neck and ankles, with closely fitted legs. The Professor called their attention to the fact that the entire figure was dissimilar to those represented in Egyptian sculpture. The figure was strongly marked by corpulency, a mark of beauty in Eastern women. This rotundity is the distinguishing feature of Ethiopian sculpture, more bulky and clumsy than Egypt, but pleasing to the eye.

The queen held in one hand the lash of Osiris, and in the other a lotus flower. She was seated on a lion, wearing sandals resembling those specimens seen in Theban figures. Other figures grouped about poured libations to the queen, or carried the standards graced and ornamented by the figures of the jackal, ibis and hawk. At the extremity of each portico was the representation of a monolithic temple, above which were the traces of a funeral boat filled with figures.

Professor Stone told them that Diodorus mentions that some of the Ethiopians preserved the bodies of their relatives in glass cases (probably alabaster), in order to have them always before their eyes. These porticoes, he thought, might have been used for that purpose. The hair of the women was dressed in curls above the forehead and in ringlets hanging on their shoulders.

One who had visited the chief galleries of Europe holding the treasures accumulated from every land, could not be unmoved at finding himself on the site of the very metropolis where science and art had their origin. If he had admired the architecture of Rome and the magnificent use they had made of the arch in their baths, palaces and temples, he would be, naturally, doubly interested at finding in desolate Meroe the origin of that discovery. The beautiful sepulchres of Meroe would give to him evidence of the correctness of the historical records. And then it was borne in upon him that where the taste for the arts had reached such perfection, one might rest assured that other intellectual pursuits were not neglected nor the sciences unknown. Now, however, her schools are closed forever; not a vestige remaining. Of the houses of her philosophers, not a stone rests upon another; and where civilization and learning once reigned, ignorance and barbarism have reassumed their sway.

This is the people whose posterity has been denied a rank among the human race, and has been degraded into a species of talking baboons!

> "Land of the mighty Dead!
> There science once display'd
> And art, their charms;
> There awful Pharaohs swayed
>
> Great nations who obeyed;
> There distant monarchs laid
> Their vanquished arms.
> "They hold us in survey—
>
> They cheer us on our way—
> They loud proclaim
> From pyramidal hall—

From Carnac's sculptured wall—
From Thebes they loudly call—
'Retake your fame!'

"Arise and now prevail
O'er all your foes;
In truth and righteousness—
In all the arts of peace—
Advance and still increase,
Though hosts oppose."

Under the inspiration of the moment, Charlie, the irrepressible, mounted to the top of the first pyramid, and from its peak proceeded to harangue his companions, lugging in the famous Napoleon's: "From the heights of yonder Pyramids forty centuries are contemplating you," etc. This was admirably done, and the glances and grimaces of the eloquent young American must have outvied in ugliness the once gracious-countenanced Egyptian Sphinx.

We may say here that before the excavations of the explorers were ended, they found in two of the pyramids, concealed treasures,—golden plates and tables that must have been used by the priests in their worship. Before one enormous image was a golden table, also of enormous proportions. The seats and steps were also of gold, confirming the ancient Chaldean records which tell of 800 talents of metal used in constructing this statue.

There was also a statue of Candace, seated in a golden chariot. On her knees crouched two enormous silver serpents, each weighing thirty talents. Another queen (Professor Stone said it must be Dido from certain peculiar figures) carried in her right hand a serpent by the head, in her left hand a sceptre garnished with precious stones.

All of this treasure was collected finally, after indemnifying the government, and carefully exported to England, where it rests today in the care of the Society of Geographical Research.

They never forgot that sunset over the ancient capital of Ethiopia at the close of the first day spent on the city's site, in the Desert. The awe-inspiring Pyramids throwing shadows that reminded one of the geometrical problems of his student days; the backsheesh-loving Arabs, in the most picturesque habiliments and attitudes; the patient camels, the tawny sands, and the burnished coppery sunlight! They had brought tents with them, leaving the most of the outfit on the opposite bank under the care of Jim Titus, whom Reuel had desired the professor to detail for that duty. Somehow since his adventure in the ruins with the leopard, and the mysterious letter-reading, he had felt a deep-seated mistrust of the docile servant. He concluded not to keep him any nearer his person than circumstances demanded. In this resolve Charlie Vance concurred; the two friends resolved to keep an eye on Titus, and Ababdis was sent for the mail.

Reuel Briggs had changed much. Harassed by anxieties which arose from his wife's silence, at the end of two months he was fast becoming a misanthrope. Charlie felt anxious as he looked at him walking restlessly up and down in the pale moonlight, with fiery eyes fixed on space. Charlie suppressed his own feelings over the silence of his father and sister to comfort Reuel.

"You ought not, my dear Briggs," he would say. "Come, for heaven's sake shake off that sadness which may make an end of you before you are aware." Then he would add, jestingly, "Decidedly, you regret the leopard's claws!"

On this night the excitement of new scenes had distracted the thoughts of both men from their homes, and they lay smoking in their hammocks before the parted curtains of the tent lazily watching Ababdis advancing with a bundle in his hand. It was the long expected mail!

CHAPTER XIV

It was some three weeks after this before Briggs was able to assume his duties. The sudden shock of the news of his wife's death over-weighted a brain already strained to the utmost. More than once they despaired of his life—Professor Stone and Vance, who had put aside his own grief to care for his friend. Slowly the strong man had returned to life once more. He did not rave or protest; Fate had no power to move him more; the point of anguish was passed, and in its place succeeded a dumb stupidity more terrible by far, though far more blessed.

His love was dead. He himself was dead for any sensibility of suffering that he possessed. So for many days longer he lay in his hammock seemingly without a thought of responsibility.

They had carried him back to the camp across the river, and there he spent the long days of convalescence. What did he think of all day as he moved like a shadow among the men or swung listlessly in the hammock? Many of the men asked themselves that question as they gazed at Briggs. One thought repeated itself over and over in his brain, "Many waters cannot quench love, neither can the floods drown it." "Many waters"—"many waters"—the words whispered and sung appealingly, invitingly, in his ears all day and all night. "Many waters, many waters."

One day he heard them tell of the removal of the door in

the pyramid two and one-half miles on the hill. They had found the Sphinx' head as described in the manuscript, but had been unable to move it with any instrument in their possession. Much to his regret, Professor Stone felt obliged to give the matter up and content himself with the valuable relics he had found. The gold mines, if such there were, were successfully hidden from searchers, and would remain a mystery.

The white orb of the moon was high in the heavens; the echoless sand gave back no sound; that night Reuel rose, took his revolver and ammunition, and leaving a note for Vance telling him he had gone to the third pyramid and not to worry, he rowed himself over to Meroe. He had no purpose, no sensation. Once he halted and tried to think. His love was dead:—that was the one fact that filled his thoughts at first. Then another took its place. Why should he live? Of course not; better rejoin her where parting was no more. He would lose himself in the pyramid. The manuscript had spoken of dangers—he would seek them.

As he went on the moon rose in full splendor behind him. Some beast of the night plunged through a thicket along the path.

The road ascended steadily for a mile or more, crossing what must have once been carriage drives. Under the light of the setting moon the gradually increasing fertility of the ground shone silver-white. Arrived at the top of the hill, he paused to rest and wipe the perspiration from his face. After a few minutes' halt, he plunged on and soon stood before the entrance of the gloomy chamber; as he stumbled along he heard a low, distinct hiss almost beneath his feet. Reuel jumped and stood still. He who had been desirous of death but an hour before obeyed the first law of nature. Who can wonder? It was but the re-awakening of life within him, and that care for what has been entrusted to us by Omnipotence, will remain until death has numbed our senses.

The dawn wind blew all about him. He would do no more until the dawn. Presently the loom of the night lifted and he could see the outlines of the building a few yards away. From his position he commanded the plain at his feet as level as a sea. The shadows grew more distinct, then without warning, the red dawn shot up behind him. The sepulchre before him flushed the color of blood, and the light revealed the horror of its emptiness.

Fragments of marble lay about him. It seemed to the lonely watcher that he could hear the sound of the centuries marching by in the moaning wind and purposeless dust.

The silence and sadness lay on him like a pall and seemed to answer to the desolation of his own life.

For a while he rambled aimlessly from wall to wall examining the gigantic resting place of the dead with scrupulous care. Here were ranged great numbers of the dead in glass cases; up and up they mounted to the vaulted ceiling. His taper flickered in the sombreness, giving but a feeble light. The air grew cold and damp as he went on. Once upon a time there had been steps cut in the granite and leading down to a well-like depression near the center of the great chamber. Down he went holding the candle high above his head as he carefully watched for the Sphinx' head. He reached a ledge which ran about what was evidently once a tank. The ledge ran only on one side. He looked about for the Sphinx; unless it was here he must retrace his steps, for the ledge ran only a little way about one side of the chamber.

He was cold and damp, and turned suddenly to retrace his steps, when just in front of him to the left the candle's light fell full on the devilish countenance of the Ethiopian Sphinx.

He moved quickly toward it; and then began an examination of the figure. As he stepped backward his foot crushed through a skull; he retreated with a shudder. He saw now that he stood in a space of unknown dimensions. He fancied he saw rows of pillars flickering drunkenly in the gloom. The American man is familiar with many things because of the range of his experience, and Reuel Briggs was devoid of fear, but in that moment he tasted the agony of pure, physical terror. For the first time since he received his letters from home, he was himself again filled with pure, human nature. He turned to retrace his steps; something came out of the darkness like a hand, passed before his face emitting a subtle odor as it moved; he sank upon the ground and consciousness left him.

(To be continued.)

CHAPTER XIV.—(Concluded.)

From profound unconsciousness, deep, merciful, oblivious to pain and the flight of time, from the gulf of the mysterious shadows wherein earth and heaven are alike forgotten, Reuel awoke at the close of the fourth day after his entrance into the Great Pyramid. That Lethean calm induced by narcotic odors, saved his reason. Great pain, whether physical or mental, cannot last long, and human anguish must find relief or take it.

A soft murmur of voices was in his ears as he languidly unclosed his eyes and gazed into the faces of a number of men grouped about the couch on which he lay, who surveyed him with looks of respectful admiration and curiosity mingled with awe. One of the group appeared to be in authority, for the others listened to him with profound respect as they conversed in low tones, and were careful not to obtrude their opinions.

Gradually his senses returned to him, and Reuel could distinguish his surroundings. He gazed about him in amazement. Gone were all evidences of ruin and decay, and in their place was bewildering beauty that filled him with dazzling awe. He reclined on a couch composed of silken cushions, in a room of vast dimensions, formed of fluted columns of pure white marble upholding a domed ceiling where the light poured in through rose-colored glass in soft prismatic shades which gave a touch of fairyland to the scene.

The men beside him were strangers, and more unreal than the vast chamber. Dark-visaged, he noticed that they ranged in complexion from a creamy tint to purest ebony; the long hair which fell upon their shoulders, varied in texture from soft, waving curls to the crispness of the most pronounced African type. But the faces into which he gazed were perfect in the cut and outline of every feature; the forms hidden by soft white drapery, Grecian in effect, were athletic and beautifully moulded. Sandals covered their feet.

The eyes of the leader followed Reuel's every movement.

"Where am I?" cried Briggs impetuously, after a hurried survey of the situation.

Immediately the leader spoke to his companions in a rich voice, commanding, but with all the benevolence of a father.

"Leave us," he said. "I would be alone with the stranger."

He spoke in ancient Arabic known only to the most profound students of philology. Instantly the room was cleared, each figure vanished behind the silken curtains hanging between the columns at one side of the room.

"How came I here?" cried Reuel again.

"Peace," replied the leader, extending his arms as if in benediction above the young man's head. "You have nothing to fear. You have been brought hither for a certain purpose which will shortly be made clear to you; you shall return to your friends if you desire so to do, after the council has investigated your case. But why, my son, did you wander at night about the dangerous passages of the pyramid? Are you, too, one of those who seek for hidden treasure?"

In years the speaker was still young, not being over forty despite his patriarchal bearing. The white robe was infinitely becoming, emphasizing breadth of shoulder and chest above the silver-clasped arm's-eye like nothing he had seen save in the sculptured figures of the ruined cities lately explored. But the most striking thing about the man was his kingly countenance, combining force, sweetness and dignity in every feature. The grace of a perfect life invested him like a royal robe. The musical language flowed from his lips in sonorous accents that charmed the scholar in his listener, who, to his own great surprise and delight, found that conversation between them could be carried on with ease. Reuel could not repress a smile as he thought of the astonishment of Professor Stone if he could hear them rolling out the ancient Arabic tongue as a common carrier of thought. It seemed sacrilegious.

"But where am I?" he persisted, determined to locate his whereabouts.

"You are in the hidden city Telassar. In my people you

will behold the direct descendants of the inhabitants of Meroe. We are but a remnant, and here we wait behind the protection of our mountains and swamps, secure from the intrusion of a world that has forgotten, for the coming of our king who shall restore to the Ethiopian race its ancient glory. I am Ai, his faithful prime minister."

Hopelessly perplexed by the words of the speaker, Reuel tried to convince himself that he was laboring under a wild hallucination; but his senses all gave evidence of the reality of his situation. Somewhere in Milton he had read lines that now came faintly across his memory:

> "Eden stretched her lines
> From Auran eastward to the royal tow'rs
> Of great Seleucia, built by Grecian kings,
> Or where the sons of Eden long before
> Dwelt in Telassar.

Something of his perplexity Ai must have read in his eyes, for he smiled as he said, "Not Telassar of Eden, but so like to Eden's beauties did our ancestors find the city that thus did they call it."

"Can it be that you are an Ethiopian of those early days, now lost in obscurity? Is it possible that a remnant of that once magnificent race yet dwells upon old mother Earth? You talk of having lived at Meroe; surely, you cannot mean it. Were it true, what you have just uttered, the modern world would stand aghast."

Ai bowed his head gravely. "It is even so, incredible though it may seem to you, stranger. Destroyed and abased because of her idolatries, Ethiopia's arrogance and pride have been humbled in the dust. Utter destruction has come upon Meroe the glorious, as was predicted. But there was a hope held out to the faithful worshippers of the true God that Ethiopia should stretch forth her hand unto Eternal Goodness, and that then her glory should again dazzle the world. I am of the priestly caste, and the office I hold descends from father to son, and has so done for more than six thousand years before the birth of Christ. But enough of this now; when you are fully rested and recovered from the effect of the narcotics we were forced to give you, I will talk with you, and I will also show you the wonders of our hidden city. Come with me."

Without more speech he lifted one of the curtains at the side of the room, revealing another apartment where running water in marble basins invited one to the refreshing bath. Attendants stood waiting, tall, handsome, dark-visaged, kindly, and into their hands he resigned Reuel.

Used as he was to the improvements and luxuries of life in the modern Athens, he could but acknowledge them as poor beside the combination of Oriental and ancient luxury that he now enjoyed. Was ever man more gorgeously housed than this? Overhead was the tinted glass through which the daylight fell in softened glow. In the air was the perfume and lustre of precious incense, the flash of azure and gold, the mingling of deep and delicate hues, the gorgeousness of waving plants in blossom and tall trees—palms, dates, orange, mingled with the gleaming statues that shone forth in brilliant contrast to the dark green foliage. The floor was paved with varied mosaic and dotted here and there with the skins of wild animals.

After the bath came a repast of fruit, game and wine, served him on curious golden dishes that resembled the specimens taken from ruined Pompeii. By the time he had eaten night had fallen, and he laid himself down on the silken cushions of his couch, with a feeling of delicious languor and a desire for repose. His nerves were in a quiver of excitement and he doubted his ability to sleep, but in a few moments, even while he doubted, he fell into a deep sleep of utter exhaustion.

CHAPTER XV

When he arose in the morning he found that his own clothing had been replaced by silken garments fashioned as were Ai's with the addition of golden clasps and belts. In place of his revolver was a jewelled dagger literally encrusted with gems.

After the bath and breakfast, Ai entered the room with his noiseless tread, and when the greetings had been said, invited him to go with him to visit the public buildings and works of Telassar. With a swift, phantom like movement, Ai escorted his guest to the farther end of the great hall. Throwing aside a curtain of rich topaz silk which draped the large entrance doors he ushered him into another apartment opening out on a terrace with a garden at its foot—a garden where a marvellous profusion of flowers and foliage ran riot amid sparkling fountains and gleaming statuary.

Through a broad alley, lined with majestic palms, they passed to the extreme end of the terrace, and turning faced the building from which they had just issued. A smile quivered for a moment on Ai's face as he noted Reuel's ill-concealed amazement. He stood for a moment stock-still, overcome with astonishment at the size and splendor of the palace that had sheltered him over night. The building was dome-shaped and of white marble, surrounded by fluted columns, and fronted by courts where fountains dashed their spray up to the blue sky, and flowers blushed in myriad colors and birds in gorgeous plumage flitted from bough to bough.

It appeared to Reuel that they were on the highest point of what might be best described as a horse-shoe curve whose rounded end rested on the side of a gigantic mountain. At their feet stretched a city beautiful, built with an outer and inner wall. They were in the outer city. Two streams descended like cataracts to the plain below, at some distance from each other, forming a triangle which held another city. Far in the distance like a silver thread, he could dimly discern where the rivers joined, losing themselves in union. As he gazed he recalled the description of the treasure city that Professor Stone had read to the explorers.

As far as the eye could reach stretched fertile fields; vineyards climbed the mountain side. Again Reuel quoted Milton in his thoughts, for here was the very embodiment of his words:

> "Flowers of all hue, and without thorn the rose,
> Another side, umbrageous grots and caves
> Of cool recess, o'er which the mantling vine
> Lays forth her purple grape, and gently creeps
> Luxuriant; meanwhile murmuring waters fall
> Down the slope hills, dispersed, or in a lake,
> That to the fringed bank with myrtle crown'd
> Her crystal mirror holds, unite their streams.
> The birds their choir apply; airs, vernal airs,
> Breathing the smell of field and grove, attune
> The trembling leaves, while universal Pan,
> Knit with the Graces and the Hours in dance,
> Led on th' eternal spring.

Far below he could dimly discern moving crowds; great buildings reared their stately heads towards a sky so blue and bewildering beneath the sun's bright rays that the gazer was rendered speechless with amazement. Shadowy images of past scenes and happenings flitted across his brain like transient reflection of a past perfectly familiar to him.

"Do you find the prospect fair?" asked Ai at length, breaking the settled silence.

"Fairer than I can find words to express; and yet I am surprised to find that it all seems familiar to me, as if somewhere in the past I had known just such a city as this." Ai smiled a smile of singular sweetness and content; Reuel could have sworn that there was a degree of satisfaction in his pleasure.

"Come, we will go down into the city. You who know the wonders of modern life at its zenith, tell me what lesson you learn from the wonders of a civilization which had its zenith six thousand years before Christ's birth."

"Six thousand years before Christ!" murmured Reuel in black stupidity.

""Aye: here in Telassar are preserved specimens of the highest attainments the world knew in ancient days. They tell me that in many things your modern world is yet in its infancy."

"How!" cried Reuel, "do you then hold communion with the world outside your city?"

"Certain members of our Council are permitted to visit outside the gates. Do you not remember Ababdis?"

"Our camel-driver?"

Ai bowed. "He is the member who brought us news of your arrival, and the intention of the expedition to find our city for the sake of its treasure."

More and more mystified by the words and manner of his guide, Reuel made no reply. Presently they entered a waiting palanquin and were borne swiftly toward the city. The silken curtains were drawn one side, and he could drink in the curious sights. They soon left the country behind them and entered a splendid square, where stately homes were outlined against the dense blue of the sky. A statue of an immense sphinx crouched in the center of the square, its giant head reaching far into the ethereal blue. Fountains played on either side, dashing their silvery spray beyond the extreme height of the head. Under umbrageous trees were resting-places, and on the sphinx was engraved the words: "That which hath been, is now; and that which is to be, hath already been; and God requireth that which is past."

Suddenly a crowd of men surged into the square, and a deep-toned bell sounded from a distance. Swiftly sped the bearers, urged forward by the general rush. The booming of the bell continued. They reached the end of the avenue and entered a side street, through a court composed of statues. They paused before a stately pile, towering in magnificence high in the heavens, a pile of marvellously delicate architecture worked in stone. The entrance was of incomparable magnificence. Reuel judged that the four colossal statues before it represented Rameses the Great. They were each sculptured of a single block of Syene granite of mingled red and black. They were seated on cubical stones. The four Colosses sitting there before that glittering pile produced a most imposing effect.

The steps of the temple were strewn with flowers; the doors stood open, and music from stringed instruments vibrated upon the air. The bearers stopped at a side entrance, and at a sign from Ai, Reuel followed him into the edifice.

All was silence, save for the distant hum of voices, and the faint sound of music. They halted before a curtain which parted silently for their entrance. It was a small room, but filled with a light of soft colors; when Reuel could command his gaze, he beheld about twenty men prostrated before him. Presently they arose and each filed past him, reverently touching the hem of his white robe. Among them was Ababdis, so transformed by his gorgeous robes of office as to be almost unrecognizable.

Ai now assumed an azure robe embroidered in silver stars and crescents that formed a sunburst in shape of a Grecian cross. He then advanced towards Reuel bearing on a silken cushion a magnificent crown, where the principal aigrette was shaped as a cross set with gems priceless in value. Astounded at the sight, the young man stood motionless while it was adjusted by golden chains about his head. The gems blazed with the red of the ruby, the green of the emerald, the blue of the sapphire, the yellow of the topaz, the cold white of priceless diamonds. But dulling all the glories of precious stones, peerless in their own class, lay the center ornament— the black diamond of Senechus's crown, spoken of in Professor Stone's record. A white robe of silken stuff was added to his costume, and again his companions filed past him in deepest reverence. Reuel was puzzled to understand why so great homage was paid to him. While he turned the thought in his mind, a bugle sounded somewhere in the distance, sweet and high. Instantly, he felt a gliding motion as if the solid earth were slipping from beneath his feet, the curtains before him parted silently, and he found himself alone on a raised platform in the center of a vast auditorium, crowded with humanity. Lights twinkled everywhere; there was the fragrance of flowers, there were columns of marble draped in amber, azure and green, and glitering lamps encrusted with gems and swung by golden chains from the sides of the building. A blazing arch formed of brilliant lamps raised like a gigantic bow in the heavens and having in its center the words

"HAIL! ERGAMENES!"

in letters of sparkling fire, met his startled gaze. Then came a ringing shout from the throats of the assembled multitude, "Ergamenes! Ergamenes!" Again and again the throng lifted up the joyous cry. Presently as Reuel stood there undecided what to do—not knowing what was expected of him, as silently as he had come, he felt the motion of the platform where he stood. The crowd faded from sight, the curtains fell; once more he stood within the little room, surrounded by his companions.

"Ababdis, Ai," he demanded, sternly, "What is the meaning of this strange happening, more like a scene from the Arabian Nights? Who is Ergamenes?"

"Thou art Ergamenes—the long-looked-for king of Ethiopia, for whose reception this city was built! But we will return to the palace, now that the people have satisfied somewhat their curiosity. At supper you shall know more."

Once more the bearers carried them swiftly beyond the confines of the city, and soon the palace walls rose before them. Reuel had hardly collected his scattered wits before he found himself seated at table and on either side of the board the Council reclined on silken cushions. His own seat was raised and placed at the head of the table. There was no talking done while what seemed to be a solemn feast was in progress. Servants passed noiselessly to and fro attending to their wants, while from an alcove the music of stringed instruments and sweetest vocal numbers was borne to their ears.

After supper, they still reclined on the couches. Then from the hidden recesses the musicians came forth, and kneeling before Reuel, one began a song in blank verse, telling the story of Ergamenes and his kingdom.

> "Hail! oh, hail Ergamenes!
> The dimmest sea-cave below thee,
>   The farthest sky-arch above,
> In their innermost stillness know thee,
>   And heave with the birth of Love.
> "All hail!
> We are thine, all thine, forevermore;
> Not a leaf on the laughing shore,
> Not a wave on the heaving sea,
>   Nor a single sigh
>   In the boundless sky,
> But is vowed evermore to thee!"

"Son of a fallen dynasty, outcast of a sunken people, upon your breast is a lotus lily, God's mark to prove your race and descent. You, Ergamenes, shall begin the restoration of Ethiopia. Blessed be the name of God for ever and ever, for wisdom and might are His, and He changeth the times and seasons; He removeth kings and countries, and setteth them up again; He giveth wisdom unto the wise, and knowledge to them that know understanding! He revealeth the deep and secret things; He knoweth what is in the darkness, and the light dwelleth with Him!

"Great were the sins of our fathers, and the white stranger was to Ethiopia but a scourge in the hands of an offended God. The beautiful temples of Babylon, filled with vessels of silver and gold, swelled the treasures of the false god Bel. Babylon, where our monarchs dwelt in splendor, once the grandest city to be found in the world. Sixty miles round were its walls, of prodigious height, and so broad that seven chariots could be driven abreast on the summit! One hundred gates of solid brass gave entrance into the city, guarded by lofty towers. Beautiful buildings rose within, richly adorned and surrounded by gardens. One magnificent royal palace was girdled by three walls, the outermost of which was seven miles and a half in compass. In its grounds rose the far-famed hanging gardens, terraces built one above one another to the height of three hundred and fifty feet, each terrace covered with thick mould, and planted with flowers and shrubs, so that the skill of man created a verdant hill on a plain. Nearly in the centre rose the lofty temple of Belus, the tower of Babel, whose builders had hoped to make its summit touch the very skies. Millions of dollars in gold were gathered in the chambers of the temple. The wealth, power and glory of the world were centered in the mighty city of Babylon.

"On the throne of this powerful city sat your forefathers, O Ergamenes!"

Part of the story had been given in recitative, one rich voice carrying grandly the monotonous notes to the accompaniment of the cornet, flute, sackbut, dulcimer and harp. Reuel had listened to the finest trained voices attempting the recitative in boasted musical circles, but never in so stately and impressive a manner as was now his privilege to hear. They continued the story.

"And Meroe, the greatest city of them all, pure-blooded Ethiopian. Once the light of the world's civilization, now a magnificent Necropolis.

"Standing at the edge of the Desert, fertile in soil, rich in the luxuries of foreign shores; into her lap caravans poured their treasures gathered from the North, South, East and West. All Africa poured into this queenly city ivory, frankincense and gold. Her colossal monuments were old before Egypt was; her wise men monopolized the learning of the ages, and in the persons of the Chaldeans have figured conspicuously the wisdom of ages since Meroe has fallen.

"Mother of ancient warfare, her horsemen and chariots were the wonder and terror of her age; from the bows of her warriors, the arrows sped like a flight of birds, carrying destruction to her foes,—a lamb in peace, a lion in time of war."

Once more the measure changed, and another voice took up the story in verse.

> "Who will assume the bays
>   That the hero wore?
> Wreaths on the Tomb of Days
>   Gone evermore!
> Who shall disturb the brave
> Or one leaf of their holy grave?
> The laurel is vow'd to them,
> Leave the bay on its sacred stem!
> But hope, the rose, the unfading rose,
> Alike for slave and freeman grows!

> "On the summit, worn and hoary,
> Of Lybia's solemn hills,
> The tramp of the brave is still!
> And still is the poisoned dart,
> In the pulse of the mighty hearts,
> Whose very blood was glory!

> Who will assume the bays
>   That the hero wore?
> Wreaths on the Tomb of Days
>   Gone evermore!"

Upon Reuel a strange force seemed working. If what he heard were true, how great a destiny was his! He had carefully hidden his Ethiopian extraction from the knowledge of the world. It was a tradition among those who had known him in childhood that he was descended from a race of African kings. He remembered his mother well. From her he had inherited his mysticism and his occult powers. The nature of the mystic within him was, then, but a dreamlike devotion to the spirit that had swayed his ancestors; it was the shadow of Ethiopia's power. The lotus upon his breast he knew to be a birthmark. Many a night he had been aroused from childhood's slumbers, to find his mother bending above him, candle in hand, muttering broken sentences of prayer to Almighty God as she examined his bosom by the candle's rays. He had wondered much; now he guessed the rest. Once more the clanging strings of the instruments chained his attention. The recitative was resumed.

"The Most High ruleth in the kingdom of men, and giveth it to whomsoever He will. He delivereth and rescueth, and He worketh signs and wonders in heaven and in earth. Pre-eminent in peace, invincible in war—once the masters of mankind, how have we fallen from our high estate!

"Stiff-necked, haughty, no conscience but that of intellect, awed not by God's laws, worshipping Mammon, sensual, unbelieving, God has punished us as he promised in the beginning. Gone are our ancient glories, our humbled pride cries aloud to God in the travail of our soul. Our sphinx, with passionless features, portrays the dumb suffering of our souls.

> Their look with the reach of past ages, was wise,
> And the soul of eternity thought in their eyes.

"By divine revelation David beheld the present time, when, after Christ's travail for the sins of humanity, the time of

Ethiopia's atonement being past, purged of idolatry, accepting the One Only God through His Son Jesus, suddenly should come a new birth to the descendants of Ham, and Ethiopia should return to her ancient glory! Ergamenes, all hail!

> "You come from afar
>   From the land of the stranger,
> The dreadful in war,
>   The daring in danger;
> Before him our plain
>   Like Eden is lying;
> Behind him remain
>   But the wasted and dying.
>
> "The weak finds not ruth,
>   Nor the patriot glory;
> No hope for the youth,
>   And no rest for the hoary;
> O'er Ethiop's lost plains
>   The victor's sword flashes,
> Her sons are in chains,
>   And her temples in ashes!
>
> "Who will assume the bays
>   That the hero wore?
> Wreaths on the Tomb of Days
>   Gone evermore!"

Upon his companions the song of the past of Ethiopia had a strange effect. Soothing at times, at times exciting, with the last notes from the instruments the company sprang to their feet; with flashing dark eyes, faces reflecting inward passions, they drew their short, sabrelike arms and circled about Reuel's throne with the shout "Ergamenes! Ergamenes!"

CHAPTER XVI

Once more Reuel found himself alone with Ai. It was far into the night, but he felt sleepless and restless. At last Ai broke a long silence:

"Tell me of the country from which you come, Ergamenes. Is it true that the Ethiopian there is counted less than other mortals?"

"It is true, Ai," replied Reuel. "There, the dark hue of your skin, your waving hair with its trace of crispness, would degrade you below the estate of any man of fair hue and straight locks, belonging to any race outside the Ethiopian, for it is a deep disgrace to have within the veins even one drop of the blood you seem so proud of possessing."

"That explains your isolation from our race, then?"

Reuel bowed his head in assent, while over his face passed a flush of shame. He felt keenly now the fact that he had played the coward's part in hiding his origin. What though obstacles were many, some way would have been shown him to surmount the difficulties of caste prejudice.

"And yet, from Ethiopia came all the arts and cunning inventions that make your modern glory. At our feet the mightiest nations have worshipped, paying homage to our kings, and all nations have sought the honor of alliance with our royal families because of our strength, grandeur, riches and wisdom. Tell me of all the degradation that has befallen the unfortunate sons of Ham."

Then in the deep, mysterious silence of the night, Reuel gave in minutest detail the story of the Negro, reciting with dramatic effect the history of the wrongs endured by the modern Ethiopian.

To his queries as to the history of these mountain-dwelling Ethiopians, Ai gave the following reply:

"We are a singular people, governed by a female monarch, all having the same name, Candace, and a Council of twenty-five Sages, who are educated for periodical visits to the outer world. Queen Candace is a virgin queen who waits the coming of Ergamenes to inaugurate a dynasty of kings. Our virgins live within the inner city, and from among them Candace chooses her successor at intervals of fifteen years.

"To become a Sage, a man must be married and have at least two children; a knowledge of two out-world languages, and to pass a severe examination by the court as to education, fitness and ability. After an arduous preparation they are initiated into the secrets of this kingdom. They are chosen for life. The inner city is the virgins' court, and it is adorned with beautiful gardens, baths, schools and hospitals. When a woman marries she leaves this city for the outer one.

"We have a great temple, the one you entered, dedicated to the Supreme or Trinity. It is a masterpiece of beauty and art. The population assembles there twice a year for especial service. It seats about 12,000 persons. The Sages have seen nothing equal to it in the outer world.

Octagonal in shape, with four wings or galleries, on opposite sides; the intervening spaces are filled with great prism columns, twenty-five feet high, made of a substance like glass, malleable, elastic and pure. The effect is gorgeous. The decorations of the hall are prepared natural flowers; that is, floral garlands are subjected to the fumes of the crystal material covering them like a film and preserving their natural appearance. This is a process handed down from the earliest days of Ethiopian greatness. I am told that the modern world has not yet solved this simple process," he said, with a gentle smile of ridicule.

"We preserve the bodies of our most beautiful women in this way. We suspend reflecting plates of the crystal material arranged in circles, pendant from the ceiling of the central hall, and thus the music of the instruments is repeated many times in sweetest harmony.

"We have serves at noon every seventh day, chiefly choral, in praise of the attributes of the Supreme. Our religion is a belief in One Supreme Being, the center of action in all nature. He distributed a portion of Himself at an early age to the care of man who has attained the highest development of any of His terrestrial creatures. We call this ever-living faculty or soul Ego.

"After its transition Ego has the power of expressing itself to other bodies, with like gift and form, its innate feeling; and by law of affinity, is ever striving to regain its original position near the great Unity; but the physical attractions of this beautiful world have such a fascination on the organism of man that there is ever a contention against the greater object being attained; and unless the Ego can wean the body from gross desires and raise it to the highest condition of human existence, it cannot be united to its Creator. The Ego preserves its individuality after the dissolution of the body. We believe in re-incarnation by natural laws regulating material on earth. The Ego can never be destroyed. For instance, when the body of a good man or woman dies, and the Ego is not sufficiently fitted for the higher condition of another world, it is re-associated with another body to complete the necessary fitness for heaven."

"What of the Son of man? Do you not know the necessity of belief in the Holy Trinity? Have not your Sages brought you the need of belief in God's Son?" Ai looked somewhat puzzled.

"We have heard of such a God, but have not paid much attention to it. How believe you, Ergamenes?"

"In Jesus Christ, the Son of God," replied Reuel solemnly.

"O Ergamenes, your belief shall be ours; we have no will but yours. Deign to teach your subjects."

When at last Reuel closed his eyes in slumber, it was with a feeling of greater responsibility and humility than he had ever experienced. Who was he that so high a destiny as lay before him should be thrust upon his shoulders?

(To be continued.)

CHAPTER XVI.—(Concluded.)

After these happenings, which we have just recorded, every day Reuel received callers in state. It seemed to him that the entire populace of that great hidden city turned out to do him homage. The Sages, clad in silver armor, attended him as a body-guard, while soldiers and officials high in the councils of the State, were ranged on both sides of the immense hall. The throne on which he sat was a massive one of silver, a bronze Sphinx couched on either side. The steps of the throne were banked with blossoms, offerings from the procession of children that filed slowly by, clad in white, wearing garlands of roses, and laying branches of palm, oleander flowers, lilies and olive sprays before their king.   .

Offering of gold, silver and gems, silken cloths, priceless articles moulded into unique and exquisite designs, swords of tempered steel, beside which a Damascus blade was coarse and unfinished, filled his artist soul with delight and wonder. Later, Ai escorted him to the underground workshops where brawny smiths plied their trades; and there the secrets of centuries dead and gone were laid bare to his curious gaze.

How was it possible, he asked himself again and again, that a nation so advanced in literature, science and the arts, in the customs of peace and war, could fall as low as had the Ethiopian? Even while he held the thought, the answer came: As Daniel interpreted Nebuchadnezzar's dream, so has it been and is with Ethiopia. "They shall drive thee from men, and thy dwelling shall be with the beast of the field, and they shall make thee to eat grass as oxen, and they shall wet thee with the dew of heaven, and seven times shall pass over thee, til thou knowest that the Most High ruleth in the kingdom of men, and giveth it to whomsoever He will. Thy kingdom shall be sure unto thee; after that thou shalt have known that the heavens do rule."

But the excitement and changes through which he had passed began to tell upon a constitution already weakened by mental troubles. Ai observed with much concern, the apathy which foretole a serious illness. Hoping to arouse him from painful thoughts which now engrossed his mind, Ai proposed that the visit to the inner city, postponed by the pressure of other duties, be made the next day.

That morning a company, of which the Sages formed a part, started for the inner city. They were to spend the night in travel, resting by day. The progress of the party was very slow, and in a direction Reuel had not yet explored. A deep yellow glow suffused the sky. This soon gave way to the powerful but mellow light of the African moon, casting long shadows over the silvery green of the herbage and foliage.

They encountered a perfect network of streams, pursuing their way through virgin forests, brilliant by daylight with beautiful flowers. The woods were inhabited by various kinds of birds of exquisite note and plumage. There were also a goodly number of baboons, who descended from the trees and ranged themselves on the ground to obtain a nearer view of the travellers. They grinned and chattered at the caravan, seeming to regard as trespassers in their domains.

The character of the country improved as they neared the interior. Reuel noticed that this was at variance with the European idea respecting Central Africa, which brands these regions as howling wildernesses or an uninhabitable country. He found the landscape most beautiful, the imaginary desert "blossomed like the rose," and the "waste sandy valleys" and "thirsty wilds," which had been assigned to this location became, on close inspection, a gorgeous scene, decorated with Nature's most cheering garniture, teeming with choice specimens of vegetable and animal life, and refreshed by innumerable streams, branches of the rivers, not a few of which were of sufficient magnitude for navigation and commerce. But Reuel remembered the loathsome desert that stood in grim determination guarding the entrance to this paradise against all intrusion, and with an American's practical common sense, bewailed this waste of material.

Proceeding along a mountain gorge, our travellers found the path straitened between the impending mountain on one side and a rapid and sparkling stream on the other. On the opposite side of the ravine the precipices rose abruptly from the very edge of the water. The whole appearance of this mountain pass was singularly grand, romantically wild and picturesquely beautiful. They were often obliged to clamber over huge masses of granite, fallen from the cliffs above;

and, on this account, progress was slow and toilsome. On turning an angle of the rock, about the centre of the gorge, the party were suddenly confronted by a huge, tawny lion, which stood directly in the path, with not a wall and scarce a space between. The path was so narrow in this place that it would have been impossible to pass the brute without touching him. Used to the king of the African jungle, the company did not shrink, but faced the animal boldly, although not without some natural physical fear. The lion, too, seemed to be taken by surprise. Thus the opponents stood at a distance of five yards, each staring at the other for several minutes. Had the travellers shown the least signs of fear, or had they attempted to escape, the fate of one, at least, would have been sealed. Now appeared an exhibition of the power of magnetism. Reuel stepped in advance of the foremost bearer, fixed his wonderful and powerful eyes upon the beast, literally transfixing him with a glance, poured the full force of his personal magnetism upon the animal, which almost instantly responded by low growls and an uneasy twisting of the head; finally, the terrible glance remaining inflexible and unwavering, the beast turned himself about and slowly withdrew with a stately and majestic tread, occasionally looking back and uttering a low growl, as if admonishing the travellers to keep their distance.

Murmurs of wonder and admiration broke from Reuel's companions, who were aware of the danger attending the meeting of a hungry lion at close quarters. His admirable intrepidity, and the remarkable powers which were his birthright, had preserved him and his companions.

"Truly, he is the King!' they murmured among themselves. And more than ever Ai watched him with increasing love and the fondness of a father.

Without further adventure they reached the portals of the

inner city. Their arrival was evidently anticipated, for they were received by a band of young females under the guardianship of a matron. By this escort they were shown to the palace and into the rooms set apart for their reception. Having rested for an hour, bathed and dined, they were ready for the ceremony of introduction. Another guard of women took them in charge, and the procession started down one passage, crossed a great, aisle-like hall, and came to a corresponding passage on the other side. On through seemingly endless colonnades they passed, till they came to a huge door formed of great winged creatures. Reuel had thought that nothing could surpass the palace in the outer city for beauty and luxury, but words failed him as his eyes drank in the glories of the lofty apartment into which they stepped, as an Amazon in silver mail threw wide the glittering doors, disclosing the splendor of the royal Presence-chamber. It was a lofty saloon lined with gilded columns, the sunlight falling from the open roof upon the mosaic floor beneath. The tapestries which lined the walls bore exquisite painting of love and warfare.

As the door opened, a voice called. The company halted before a curtained recess, guarded by a group of beautiful girls. Never had Reuel beheld such subtle grace of form and feature, such masses of coal-black hair, such melting eyes of midnight hue. Each girl might have posed for a statue of Venus.

The heavy curtains were lifted now, and discovered the Queen reclining upon a pile of silken cushions—a statue of Venus worked in bronze.

"The Queen is here!" exclaimed a voice. In an instant all present prostrated themselves upon the floor. Reuel alone stood erect, his piercing eyes fixed upon the woman before him.

Grave, tranquil and majestic, surrounded by her virgin

guard, she advanced gracefully, bending her haughty head; then, gradually her sinuous body bent and swayed down, down, until she, too, had prostrated herself, and half-knelt, half-lay, upon the marble floor at Reuel's feet.

"O Ergamenes, hast thou indeed returned to thine inheritance?" murmured a voice like unto silver chimes. Reuel started, for it seemed to him that Dianthe's own voice was breathing in his ears.

Knowing now what was expected of him, he raised the Queen with one hand, addressed her courteously in Arabic, led her to her silken couch, seated himself, and would have placed her beside him, but she, with a gesture of dissent, sank upon the cushions at his feet that had served her for footstools.

By this time the Sages had risen and now reclined on the silken couches with which the apartment was well supplied. Ai advanced and addressed the Queen; during this exchange of courtesies, Reuel gazed upon her curiously.

She reminded him strongly of his beautiful Dianthe; in face, the resemblance was so striking that it was painful, and tears, which were no disgrace to his manhood, struggled to his eyes. She was the same height as Dianthe, had the same well-developed shoulders and the same admirable bust. What suppleness in all her movements! What grace, and, at the same time, what strength! Yes; she was a Venus, a superb statue of bronze, moulded by a great sculptor; but an animated statue, in which one saw the blood circulate, and from which life flowed. And what an expressive face, full of character! Long, jet-black hair and totally free, covered her shoulders like a silken mantle; a broad, square forehead, a warm bronze complexion; thick black eyebrows, great black eyes, now soft and languishing—eyes which could weep in sorrow or shoot forth lightening in their anger; a delicate nose with quivering nostrils, teeth of dazzling whiteness behind lips as red as a rose; in her smile of grace and sweetness lurked a sense of power. He was astonished and lost in admiration in spite of himself. Her loveliness was absolutely and ideally perfect. Her attitude of unstudied grace accorded well with the seriousness of her face; she seemed the embodiment of all chastity.

The maidens of her household waited near her—some of them with baskets of flowers upheld in perfect arms. Some brought fruit in glittering dishes and wine in golden goblets of fairy-like fretword, which were served from stands of ivory and gold. One maiden knelt at her lyre, prepared to strike its chords at pauses in the conversation.

The attendants now retired modestly into the background, while Ai and the other Sages conversed with the Queen. She listened with downcast eyes, occasionally casting a curious, though deferential glance at the muscular figure beside her.

"And dost thou agree, and art thou willing to accept the destiny planned by the Almighty Trinity for thee and me from the beginning of all things, my lord?" she questioned at length in her flute-like voice.

"Queen Candace, thy beauty and graciousness dazzle me. I feel that I can love thee with all my heart; I will fulfill my destiny gladly, and I will cleave to thee until the end."

"Now," answered the Queen with sweet humility, "now, when thou, my lord, doth speak so royally, it doth not become me to lag in generosity." She paused.

Reuel, gazing into her beautiful face, was deeply moved by strong emotions. Again she spoke:

"Behold! in token of submission I bow to my lord, King Ergamenes." She bent herself slowly to the ground, and pressed her knees for one instant upon the mosaic floor.

"Behold," and she touched his forehead lightly with her lips, "in earnest of connubial bliss, I kiss thee, King Ergamenes. Behold," and she placed her hand upon his heart, "I swear to thee eternal fealty by the Spirit—the never-changing Trinity." This ceremony ended she seated herself once more beside him. Reuel felt himself yielding readily to her infinite attractiveness. In the azure light and regal splendor of the fragrant apartment, there was rest and satisfaction. All the dreams of wealth and ambition that had haunted the feverish existence by the winding Charles, that had haunted his days of obscure poverty in the halls of Harvard, were about to be realized. Only once had he known joy in his checkered life, and that was when he basked in the society of Dianthe, whom he now designated his spirit-bride. The delirium of that joy had ended in lamentation. Doubts and misgivings had assailed him in the silence of the night when Ai had left him and his influence was withdrawn. Then he had but a faint-hearted belief in the wonderful tale told to him, but here, under Queen Candace's magic influence, all doubts disappeared, and it seemed the most natural thing in the world to be sitting here among these descendants of the ancient Ethiopians, acknowledged as their King, planning a union with a lovely woman, that should give to the world a dynasty of dark-skinned rulers, whose destiny should be to restore the prestige of an ancient people.

Verily, if the wonders he had already seen and heard could be possible in the nineteenth century of progress and enlightenment, nothing was impossible. Dianthe was gone. The world outside held nothing dear to one who had always lived much within himself. The Queen was loving, beautiful— why not accept this pleasant destiny which held its alluring arms so seductively towards him? A sudden moisture filled his eyes; a curious vague softness and tenderness stole over him. Turning abruptly toward his hostess, he held out his own swimming goblet:

"Drink we a loving cup together, oh Queen Candace!" he said in a voice that trembled with earnestness. "I pledge my faith in return for thine!"

The Queen returned his ardent gaze with one of bright surprise and joyous happiness, and bending her head, drank a deep draught of the proffered wine.

"Almost thou lovest me, Ergamenes. May the Eternal Trinity hold fast our bonds!" With a graceful salute she returned the goblet. Reuel drank off in haste what remained within it.

"Behold! I have prepared against this happy hour," continued the Queen, and going to an inlaid cabinet at one side of the room, she took from it a curious ring of dull gold, bearing one priceless gem cut in the form of a lotus lily. "Hold forth thy hand," she said, and on his finger placed the ring.

"Thus do I claim thee for all eternity."

The Sages had watched the actors in this life-drama with jealous eyes that noted every detail with open satisfaction. At Queen Candace's last words, Ai extended his arms with the solemn words:

"And now it is done and never can be undone or altered. Let us hence, that the union may be speedily accomplished."

CHAPTER XVII

In a month the marriage was to be celebrated with great pomp and rejoicing. Preparations began as soon as the interview between the Queen and the prospective King was over.

After his return from his betrothal, the power of second sight which seemed to have left Reuel for a time, returned in full force. Restlessness was upon him; Dianthe's voice seemed ever calling to him through space. Finally, when his feelings became insupportable, he broached the subject to Ai.

The latter regarded his questioner gravely. "Of a truth thou art a legitimate son of Ethiopia. Thou growest the fruits of wisdom. Descendant of the wise Chaldeans, still powerful to a degree undreamed of by the pigmies of this puny age, you look incredulous, but what I tell you is the solemn truth."

"The Chaldeans disappeared from this world centuries ago," declared Reuel.

"Not all—in me you behold their present head; within this city and the outer world, we still number thousands."

Reuel uttered an exclamation of incredulous amazement. "Not possible!"

Silently Ai went to his cabinet and took down a small, square volume which he placed in Reuel's hand. "It is a record of the wisdom and science of your ancestors."

Reuel turned it over carefully,—the ivory pages were covered with characters sharply defined and finely engraved.

"What language is this? It is not Hebrew, Greek nor Sanskrit, nor any form of hieroglyphic writing."

"It is the language once commonly spoken by your ancestors long before Babylon was builded. It is known to us now as the language of prophecy."

Reuel glanced at the speaker's regal form with admiration and reverence.

"Teach me what thou knowest, Ai," he said humbly, "for, indeed, thou art a wonderful man."

"Gladly," replied Ai, placing his hand in loving tenderness upon the bowed head of the younger man. "Our destiny was foreordained from the beginning to work together for the upbuilding of humanity and the restoration of the race of our fathers. This little book shall teach your soul all that you long to know, and now grasp but vaguely. You believe in the Soul?"

"Most assuredly!"

"As a Personality that continues to live after the body perishes?"

"Certainly."

"And that Personality begins to exert its power over our lives as soon as we begin its cultivation. Death is not necessary to its manifestation upon our lives. There are always angels near! To us who are so blessed and singled out by the Trinity there is a sense of the supernatural always near us—others whom we cannot see, but whose influence is strong upon us in all the affairs of life. Man only proves his ignorance if he denies this fact. Some in the country from which you come contend that the foundations of Christianity are absurd and preposterous, but all the prophecies of the Trinity shall in time be fulfilled. They are working out today by the forces of air, light, wind,—the common things of daily life that pass unnoticed. Ethiopia, too, is stretching forth her hand unto God, and He will fulfill her destiny. The tide of immigration shall set in the early days of the twentieth century, toward Afric's shores, so long bound in the chains of barbarism and idolatry."

Reuel listened entranced, scarce breathing.

"I was warned of your coming long before the knowledge was yours. The day you left your home for New York, I sat within my secret chamber, and all was revealed to me."

"Ay, Ai," Reuel answered, feebly. "But how?"

"You believe that we can hold communion with the living

though seas divide and distance is infinite, and our friends who have passed to the future life of light are allowed to comfort us here?"

"I believe."

" 'Tis so," continued Ai. "Half by chance and half by learning, I long ago solved one of the great secrets of Nature. Life is wonderful, but eternity is more wonderful." He paused, regarding affectionately Reuel's troubled face.

"I will answer thy question presently. But can I do aught for thee? Dost memories of that world from which thou hast recently come disturb thee, Ergamenes? I have some feeble powers; if thou wilt, command them." Ai fell into the use of "thee" and "thou" always when greatly moved, and Reuel had become very dear to him.

"I would know some happenings in the world I have left; could my desire be granted, I might, perchance, lose this restlessness which now oppresses me."

Ai regarded him intently. "How far hast thou progressed in knowledge of Infinity?" he asked at length.

"You shall be the judge," replied Reuel. And then ensued a technical conversation on the abstract science of occultism and the future state.

"I see thou are well versed," said Ai finally, evidently well pleased with the young man's versatility. "Come with me. Truly we have not mistaken thee, Ergamenes. Wonderfully hast thou been preserved and fitted for the work before thee."

Reuel had the freedom of the palace, but he knew that there were rooms from which he was excluded. One room especially seemed to be the sanctum sanctorium of the Sages. It was to this room that Ai now conducted him.

Reuel was nearly overpowered with the anticipation of being initiated into the mysteries of this apartment. He found nothing terrifying, however, in the plain, underground room into which he was ushered. A rough table and wooden stools constituted the furniture. The only objects of mystery were a carved table at one end of the apartment, with a silken cloth thrown over its top, and a vessel like a baptismal font, cut in stone, full of water. Air and light came from an outside source, for there were no windows in the room. After closing the door securely, Ai advanced and removed the cloth from the table. "Sit," he commanded. "You ask me how I knew of your coming to my land. Lo, I have followed your career from babyhood. Behold, Ergamenes! What would you see upon the mirror's face? Friend or foe?"

Reuel advanced and looked upon the surface of a disk of which the top of the table was composed. The material of which the polished surface was composed was unknown to Reuel; it was not glass, though quite transparent; it was not metal, though bright as polished steel.

Reuel made no wish, but thought of the spot where the accident had occurred upon the River Charles weeks before. He was startled to observe a familiar scene where he had often rowed for pleasure on pleasant summer evenings. Every minute particular of the scenery was distinctly visible. Presently the water seemed to darken, and he saw distinctly the canoe containing Aubrey, Molly and Dianthe gliding over the water. He started back aghast, crying out, "It is magical!"

"No, no, Ergamenes, this is a secret of Nature. In this disk I can show thee what thou wilt of the past. In the water of the font we see the future. Think of a face, a scene—I will reflect it for thee on this disk. This is an old secret, known to Ethiopia, Egypt and Arabia centuries ago. I can reflect the past and the faces of those passed away, but the living and the future are cast by the water."

Reuel was awed into silence. He could say nothing, and listened to Ai's learned remarks with a reverence that approached almost to worship before this proof of his supernatural powers. What would the professors of Harvard have said to this, he asked himself. In the heart of Africa was a knowledge of science that all the wealth and learning of modern times could not emulate. For some time the images came and went upon the mirror, in obedience to his desires. He saw the scenes of his boyhood, the friends of his youth, and experienced anew the delights of life's morning. Then he idly desired to see the face of his loved Dianthe, as she last appeared on earth. The surface of the disk reflected nothing!

"You have not reached perfection then, in this reflector?"

"Why think you so?" asked Ai gravely.

"I have asked to see the face of a friend who is dead. The mirror did not reflect it."

"The disk cannot err," said Ai. "Let us try the water in the font."

"But that reflects the living, you say; she is dead."

"The disk cannot err," persisted Ai. He turned to the font, gazed in its surface, and then beckoned Reuel to approach. From the glassy surface Dianthe's face gazed back at him, worn and lined with grief.

" 'Tis she!" he cried, "her very self."

"Then your friend still lives," said Ai, calmly.

"Impossible!"

"Why do you doubt my word, Ergamenes?"

Then with great suppressed excitement and much agitation, Reuel repeated the story of Dianthe's death as brought to him by the last mail he had received from America.

"You say that 'Molly,' as you call her, was also drowned?"

"Yes."

"Let us try the disk."

They returned to the mirror and instantly the face of Molly Vance gazed at them from the river's bed, surrounded by seaweed and grasses.

"Can a man believe in his own sanity!" exclaimed Reuel in an agony of perplexity.

Ai made no reply, but returned to the font. "I think it best to call up the face of your enemy. I am sure you have one." Immediately the water reflected the debonair face of Aubrey Livingston, which was almost instantly blotted out by the face of Jim Titus.

"Two!" murmured Ai. "I thought so."

"If she then lives, as your science seems to insist, show me her present situation," cried Reuel, beside himself with fears.

"I must have a special preparation for the present," said Ai, calmly. He set about preparing a liquid mixture. When this was accomplished he washed the face of the disk with a small sponge dipped in the mixture. A film of sediment instantly formed upon it.

"When this has dried, I will scrape it off and polish the mirror, then we shall be ready for the demonstration. One picture only will come—this will remain for a number of days, after that the disk will return to its normal condition. But, see! the sediment is caked. Now to remove it and finish our test." At last it was done, and the disk repolished. Then standing before it, Ai cried, in an earnest voice:

"Let the present appear upon the disk, if it be for the benefit of Thy human subjects!"

Ai appeared perfectly calm, but his hands shook. Reuel remained a short remove from him, awaiting his summons.

"Come, Ergamenes."

For a few moments Reuel gazed upon the plate, his eyes

brilliant with expectation, his cheeks aglow with excitement. Then he involuntarily shuddered, a half suppressed groan escaped him, and he grew ashy pale. In a trice he became entirely unnerved, and staggered back and forth like a drunken man. Greatly alarmed, and seeing he was about to fall, Ai sprang to his side and caught him. Too late. He fell to the floor in a swoon. The picture reflected by the disk was that of the ancestral home of the Livingstons. It showed the parlor of a fine old mansion; two figures stood at an open window, their faces turned to the interior. About the woman's waist the man's arm was twined in a loving embrace. The faces were those of Aubrey and Dianthe.

Late that night Reuel tossed upon his silken couch in distress of mind. If the disk were true, then Dianthe and Aubrey both lived and were together. He was torn by doubts, haunted by dreadful fears of he knew not what. If the story of the disk were true, never was man so deceived and duped as he had been. Then in the midst of his anger and despair came an irresistible impulse to rise from his bed. He did so, and distinctly felt the pressure of a soft hand upon his brow, and a yielding body at his side. The next instant he could have sworn that he heard the well-known tones of Dianthe in his ears, saying:

"Reuel, it is I."

Unable to answer, but entirely conscious of a presence near him, he had presence of mind enough to reiterate a mental question. His voiceless question was fully understood, for again the familiar voice spoke:

"I am not dead, my husband; but I am lost to you. Not of my own seeking has this treachery been to thee, O beloved. The friend into whose care you gave me has acquired the power over me that you alone possessed, that power sacred to our first meeting and our happy love. Why did you leave me in the power of a fiend in human shape, to search for gold? There are worse things in life than poverty."

Calming the frenzy of his thoughts by a strong effort, Reuel continued his mental questions until the whole pitiful story was his. He knew not how long he continued in this communion. Over and over he turned the story he had learned in the past few hours. Ungovernable rage against his false friend possessed him. "Blind, fool, dupe, dotard!" he called himself, not to have seen the treachery beneath the mask of friendship. And then to leave her helpless in the hands of this monster, who had not even spared his own betrothed to compass his love for another.

But at least revenge was left him. He would return to America and confront Aubrey Livingston with his guilt. But how to get away from the hidden city. He knew that virtually he was a prisoner.

Still turning over ways and means, he fell into an uneasy slumber, from which he was aroused by a dreadful shriek.

CHAPTER XVIII

It was now two months since Reuel's strange disappearance from the camp of the explorers. Day after day they had searched every inch of the ground within and about the pyramids, with no success. Charlie Vance was inconsolable, and declared his intention of making his home at Meroe until Reuel was found. He scouted the idea of his death by falling a prey to wild beasts, and hung about the vicinity of the Great Pyramid with stubborn persistence. He was no longer the spoiled darling of wealth and fashion, but a serious-minded man of a taciturn disposition.

He spent money like water in his endeavor to find the secret passage, believing that it existed, and that in it Reuel was lost.

One morning he and Jim Titus laid bare a beautifully worked marble wall, built of fine masonry, with even blocks, each a meter and a half long, and below the exquisitely worked moulding two further layers of well-worked calcareous stone. The whole formed a foundation for a structure which had fallen into ruins about two and a half meters high. But this wall continued for thirteen meters only, and then returned at right angles at each end. On the inner side this marble structure was backed by large blocks of calcareous stone, and in the inner angles, they had with much labor to break up and remove two layers of block superimposed at right angles, one upon another. The entire party was much puzzled to learn what this structure could have been.

Sculptures and paintings lined the walls. As usual, there was a queen, attired in a long robe. The queen had in one hand the lash of Osiris and in the other a lotus flower.

At the extremity of each portico was the representation of a monolithic temple, above which were the traces of a funeral boat filled with figures.

After two days' work, the skilled diggers assured the explorers that they could do nothing with the debris but to leave it, as it was impossible to open the structure. But in the night, Charlie was kept awake by the thought that this curious structure might hold the expedition's secret; and remembering that perseverance was never beaten, set to work there the next morning, digging into the interior and breaking up the huge blocks which impeded his progress. The next day another impediment was reached, and it was decided to give it up. Again Charlie was awake all night, puzzling over the difficulties encountered, and again he made up his mind not to give it up. Charlie was learning many needed lessons in bitterness of spirit out in these African wilds. Sorrow had come to him here in the loss of his sister, and the disappearance of his friend. As Reuel had done in the night weeks before, so he did now, rising and dressing and securing his weapons, but taking the precaution to awaken Jim, and ask him to accompany him for a last visit to the Pyramid.

Jim Titus seemed strangely subdued and quiet since Reuel's disappearance. Charlie decided that their suspicions were wrong, and that Jim was a good fellow, after all.

As they trudged along over the sandy paths in the light of the great African moon, Charlie was glad of Jim's lively conversation. Anecdotes of Southern life flowed glibly from his tongue, illustrated by songs descriptive of life there. It really seemed to Vance that a portion of the United States had been transported to Africa.

They entered the great Pyramid, as Reuel had done before them, lit their torches, and began slowly and carefully to go over the work of excavation already done.

They passed down a side passage opening out of the outer passage, down a number of steps and along an underground shaft made by the workmen. Suddenly the passage ended. They halted, held up the lamps and saw such a scene as they were not likely to see again. They stood on the edge of an enormous pit, hedged in by a wall of rock. There was an opening in the wall, made by a hinged block of stone. This solid door had opened noiselessly, dark figures had stolen forth, and had surrounded the two men. As they discovered their strange companions, weapons of burnished steel flashed and seemed to fill the vault. Not a sound was heard but the deep breathing of men in grim determination and on serious business bent. Instantly the two travellers were bound and gagged.

(To be continued.)

CHAPTER XVIII.—(Concluded.)

Instantly, after the seizure, the eyes of the prisoners were blindfolded; then they were half led, half dragged along by their captors. As he felt the grip of steel which impelled a forward movement, Charlie bitterly cursed his own folly in undertaking so mad a venture. "Poor Reuel," he lamented, "was this the explanation of his disappearance?" Reuel had been the life of the party; next to Professor Stone, he was looked up to as leader and guide, and with his loss, all interest seemed to have dropped from the members of the expedition.

For half an hour they were hurried along what must have been deep underground passages. Charlie could feel the path drop beneath his feet on solid rock which seemed to curve over like the edges of a waterfall. He stumbled, and would have fallen if strong arms had not upheld him. He could feel the rock worn into deep gutters smoother than ice. For the first time he heard the sound of his captors' voices. One in command gave an order in an unknown tongue. Charlie wished then that he had spent more time in study and less in sport.

"Oh," he groaned in spirit, "what a predicament for a free-born American citizen, and one who has had on the gloves with many a famous ring champion!" He wondered how Jim was faring, for since the first frightened yell from his lips, all had been silence.

There came another brief command in the unknown tongue, and the party halted. Then Charlie felt himself lifted into what he finally determined was a litter. He settled himself comfortably, and the bearers started. Charlie was of a philosophical nature; if he had been born poor and forced to work for a living, he might have become a learned philosopher. So he lay and reflected, and wondered where this experience would end, until, lulled by the yielding motion and the gentle swaying, he fell asleep.

He must have slept many hours, for when he awoke he felt a strong sensation of hunger. They were still journeying at a leisurely pace. Charlie could feel the sweet, fresh air in his face, could hear the song of birds, and smell the scented air, heavy with the fragrance of flowers and fruits. Mentally thanking God that he still lived, he anxiously awaited the end of this strange journey. Presently he felt that they entered a building, for the current of air ceased, and the soft footsteps of the bearers gave forth a metallic sound. There came another command in the unknown tongue, and the bearers stopped; he was told to descend, in unmistakable English, by a familiar voice. He obeyed the voice, and instantly he was relieved of his bandage; before his sight became accustomed to the semi-darkness of the room, he heard the retreating steps of a number of men. As his sight returned in full, he saw before him Ai and Abdallah and Jim.

Abdallah regarded him with a gaze that was stolid and unrecognizing. The room in which he stood was large and circular. Floors and walls were of the whitest marble, and from the roof light and air were supplied. There were two couches in the room, and a divan ran about one of its sides. There was no door or entrance visible—nothing but the unvarying white walls and flooring.

"Stranger," said Ai, in his mellow voice, speaking English in fluent tones, "Why hast thou dared to uncover the mysteries of centuries? Art thou weary of life that thou hast dared to trifle with Nature's secrets? Scarce an alien foot has traversed this land since six thousand years have passed. Art weary of living?" As he asked the last question, Charlie felt a chill of apprehension. This man, with his strange garb, his dark complexion, his deep eyes and mystic smile, was to be feared and reverenced. Summoning up all his sang froid and determination not to give in to his fears, he replied,—

"We came to find old things, that we may impart our knowledge to the people of our land, who are eager to know the beginning of all things. I come of a race bold and venturesome, who know not fear if we can get a few more dollars and fresh information."

"I have heard of your people," replied Ai, with a mysterious sparkle in his eyes. "They are the people who count it a disgrace to bear my color; is it not so?"

"Great Scott!" thought Charlie, turning mental somersaults to find an answer that would placate the dignitary before him. "Is it possible that the ubiquitous race question has got ahead of the expedition! By mighty, it's time something was done to stop this business. Talk of Banquo's ghost! Banquo ain't in it if this is the race question I'm up against." Aloud he said, "My venerable and esteemed friend, you could get there all right with your complexion in my country. We would simply label you 'Arab, Turk, Malay or Filipino,' and in that costume you'd slide along all right; not the slightest trouble

when you showed your ticket at the door. Savee?" He finished
with a profound bow.

Ai eyed him sadly for a moment, and then said,—

"O, flippant-tongued offspring of an ungenerous people,
how is it with my brother?" and he took Jim's unresisting
hand and led him up to Charlie. "Crisp of hair," and he
passed his hand softly over Jim's curly pate. "Black of skin!
How do you treat such as this one in your country?"

Charlie felt embarrassed in spite of his assurance. "Well,
of course, it has been the custom to count Africans as our
servants, and they have fared as servants."

"And yet, ye are all of one blood; descended from one
common father. Is there ever a flock or herd without its black
member? What more beautiful than the satin gloss of the
raven's wing, the soft glitter of eyes of blackest tint or the
rich black fur of your own native animals? Fair-haired worshippers of Mammon, do you not know that you have been
weighed in the balance and found wanting? that your course
is done? that Ethiopia's bondage is about over, her travail
passed?"

Charlie smiled in inward mirth at what he called the
"fossilized piece of antiquity." "Touched in the forehead;
crank," was his mental comment. "I'd better put on the
brakes, and not aggravate this lunatic. He's probably some
kind of a king, and might make it hot for me." Aloud he
said, "Pardon, Mr. King, but what has this to do with
making me a prisoner? Why have I been brought here?"

"You will know soon enough," replied Ai, as he clapped
his hands. Abdallah moved to the side of the room, and
instantly a marble block slid from its position, through which
Ai and he departed, leaving the prisoners alone.

For a while the two men sat and looked at each other in helpless silence. Then Jim broke the silence with lamentations.

"Oh, Lord! Mr. Vance, there's a hoodoo on this business, and I'm the hoodoo!"

"Nonsense!" exclaimed Vance. "Be a man, Jim, and help me find a way out of this infernal business."

But Jim sat on the divan, lamenting and refusing to be comforted. Presently food was brought to them, and then after many and useless conjectures, they lay down and tried to sleep.

The night passed very comfortably on the whole, although the profound silence was suggestive of being buried alive. Another day and night passed without incident. Food was supplied them at regular intervals. Charlie's thoughts were varied. He—fastidious and refined—who had known no hardship and no sorrow,—why had he left his country to wander among untutored savages? None were there to comfort him of all his friends. These walls would open but to admit the savage executioner. He ground his teeth. He thought of Cora Scott; doubtless she thought him dead. Dead! No; nor would he die. He'd find a way out of this or perish; he'd go home and marry Cora. Now this was a most surprising conclusion, for Charlie had been heard to say many times that "he'd be drawn and quartered before he'd tie up to a girl of the period," which Cora undoubtedly was. As if aroused from a dream, he jumped up and going over to Jim, shook him. The Negro turned uneasily in his sleep and groaned. Again he shook him.

"Get up, Jim. Come, I'm going to try to get out of this."

"I'm afraid, Mr. Vance; it's no use."

"Come on, Jim; be a man."

"I'm ready for anything, only show me the way," replied

Jim in desperation. Their pistols had been taken from them, but their knives remained. They stored what food remained about their persons and began a thorough examination of the room.

"They certainly find an exit here somewhere, Jim, and we must find it too."

"Easier said than done, I fear, sir."

An hour—two hours, passed in fruitless search; the marble walls showed not a sign of exit or entrance. They rested then, sitting on the sides of the divans and gazing at each other in utter helplessness. The full moonlight showered the apartment with a soft radiance from the domed roof. Suddenly, Jim sprang forward and inserted his knife in a crevice in the floor. Instantly Charlie was beside him, working like mad on the other side. The slab began to waver to and fro, as though shaken by a strong force—the crack widened—they saw a round, flat metal button—Jim seized it with one hand and pried with the knife in the other—a strong breeze of subterranean air struck through the narrow opening—and with a dull reverberation half the flooring slid back, revealing what seemed to be a vast hole.

The men recoiled, and lay panting from their labors on the edges of the subway. Charlie blessed his lucky stars that hidden in his clothes was a bundle of tapers used by the explorers for just such emergencies. By great good fortune, his captors had not discovered them.

"What's to be done now, Jim?"

"Get down there and explore, but hanged if I want the job, Mr. Vance."

"We'll go together, Jim. Let's see," he mused, "What did Prof. Stone's parchment say? 'Beware the tank to the right where dwells the sacred crocodile, still living, although centuries have rolled by, and men have been gathered to the shades who once tended on his wants. And beware the fifth gallery to the right where abide the sacred serpents with jewelled crowns, for of a truth are they terrible," quoted Charlie, dreamily.

"You don't suppose this is the place you were hunting for, do you?" queried Jim, with eyes big with excitement.

"Jim, my boy, that's a question no man can answer at this distance from the object of our search. But if it is, as I suspect, the way to the treasure will lead us to liberty, for the other end must be within the pyramid. I'm for searching this passage. Come on if you are with me."

He lighted his taper and swung it into the abyss, disclosing steps of granite leading off in the darkness. As his head disappeared from view, Jim, with a shudder, followed. The steps led to a passage or passages, for the whole of the underground room was formed of vaulted passages, sliding off in every direction. The stairs ended in another passage; the men went down it; it was situated, as nearly as they could judge, directly beneath the room where they had been confined. Silently the two figures crept on, literally feeling their way. Shortly they came to another passage running at right angles; slowly they crept along the tunnel, for it was nothing more, narrowing until it suddenly ended in a sort of cave, running at right angles; they crossed this, halting at the further side to rest and think. Charlie looked anxiously about him for signs, but saw nothing alarming in the smooth sandy floor, and irregular contorted sides. The floor was strewn with bowlders like the bed of a torrent. As they went on, the cavern widened into an amphitheatre with huge supporting columns. To the right and left of the cave there were immense bare spaces stretching away into immense galleries. Here they paused to rest, eating sparingly of the food they had brought. "Let us rest here," said Charlie, "I am dead beat."

"Is it not safer to go on? We cannot be very far from the room where we were confined."

"I'll sit here a few moments, anyhow," replied Charlie. Jim wandered aimlessly about the great vault, turning over stones and peering into crevices.

"What do you expect to find, Jim, the buried treasure?" laughed Charlie, as he noted the earnestness of the other's search.

Jim was bending over something—wrenching off a great iron cover. Suddenly he cried out, "Mr. Vance, here it is!"

Charlie reached his side with a bound. There sat Jim, and in front of him lay, imbedded in the sand of the cavern's floor, a huge box, long and wide and deep, whose rusted hinges could not withstand the stalwart Negro's frantic efforts.

With a shuddering sigh the lid was thrust back, falling to one side with a great groan of almost mortal anguish as it gave up the trust committed to its care ages before. They both gazed, and as they gazed were well-nigh blinded. For this is what they saw:—

At first, a blaze of darting rays that sparkled out and shot out myriad scintillations of color—red, violet, orange, green, and deepest crimson. Then by degrees, they saw that these hues came from a jumbled heap of gems—some large, some small, but together in value beyond all dreams of wealth.

Diamonds, rubies, sapphires, amethysts, opals, emeralds, turquoises—lay roughly heaped together, some polished, some uncut, some as necklaces and chains, others gleaming in rings and bracelets—wealth beyond the dreams of princes.

Near to the first box lay another, and it lay gold in bars and gold in flakes, hidden by the priests of Osiris, that had adorned the crowns of queens Candace and Semiramis—a spectacle glorious beyond compare.

"The Professor's parchment told the truth," cried Charlie, after a few moments, when he had regained his breath. "But what shall we do with it, now we have it?" asked Jim in disconsolate tones. "We can't carry it with us."

"True for you, Jim," replied Vance, sadly. "This wealth is a mockery now we have it. Jim, we're left, badly left. Here we've been romping around for almost six months after this very treasure, and now we've got it we can't hold it. This whole expedition has been like monkeying with a saw mill, Jim, my boy, and I for one, give in beaten. Left, I should say so; badly left, when I counted Africa a played-out hole in the ground. And, Jim, when we get home, if we ever do, the drinks are on me. Now, old man, stow some of these glittering baubles in your clothing, as I am going to do, and then we'll renew our travels." He spoke in jest, but the tears were in his eyes, and as he clasped Jim's toil-hardened black hand, he told himself that Ai's words were true. Where was the color line now? Jim was a brother; the nearness of their desolation in this uncanny land, left nothing but a feeling of brotherhood. He felt then the truth of the words, "Of one blood have I made all races of men."

As they stooped to replace the cover, Jim's foot knocked against an iron ring set in the sandy flooring. "I believe it's another box, Mr. Vance," he called out, and dropping his work, he pulled with all his might.

"Careful, Jim," called Charlie's warning voice. Too late! The ring disappeared at the second tug, revealing a black pit from which came the odor of musk. From out the darkness came the sweeping sound of a great body moving in wavelets over a vast space. Fascinated into perfect stillness, Vance became aware of pale emerald eyes watching him, and the sound of deep breathing other than their own. There was a wild rattle and rush in the darkness, as Jim, moving forward, flung down his taper and turned to flee.

"The serpents! The serpents! Fly for your life, Jim!" shouted Charlie, as he dashed away from the opening. Too late! There came a terrible cry, repeated again and again. Charlie Vance sunk upon the ground, overcome with horror.

CHAPTER XIX

It must have been about one o'clock in the morning when Reuel started out of a fitful slumber by the sound of that terrible scream. He sprang to his feet and listened. He heard not a sound; all was silence within the palace. But his experience was so vivid that reason could not control his feelings; he threw wide the dividing curtains, and fled out upon the balcony. All was silence. The moonlight flooded the landscape with the strength of daylight. As he stood trying to calm himself, a shadow fell across his path, and raising his eyes, he beheld the form of Mira; she beckoned him on, and he, turning, followed the shadowy figure, full of confidence that she would show him the way to that fearful scream.

On they glided like two shadows, until the phantom paused before what seemed a solid wall, and with warning gaze and uplifted finger, bade him enter. It was a portion of the palace unfamiliar to him; the walls presented no hope of entrance. What could it mean? Mira faded from his gaze, and as he stood there puzzling over this happening, suddenly the solid wall began to glide away, leaving a yawning space, in which appeared Ai's startled and disturbed face.

"Back!" he cried, as he beheld his King. "Back, Ergamenes! how come you here?"

"What was the cry I heard, Ai? I cannot rest. I have been
led hither," he continued, significantly. Then, noticing the
other's disturbed vision, he continued, "Tell me. I command
you."

With a murmured protest, Ai stepped aside, saying, "Perhaps it is best."

Reuel advanced into the room. The hole in the floor was
securely closed, and on the divans lay Charlie Vance, white
and unconscious, and Jim Titus, crushed almost to a jelly but
still alive. Abdallah and a group of natives were working
over Vance, trying to restore consciousness. Reuel gave one
startled, terrified glance at the two figures, and staggered
backward to the wall.

Upon hearing that cry, Jim Titus stirred uneasily, and
muttered, "It's him!"

"He wishes to speak with you," said Ai, gravely.

"How came they here, and thus?" demanded Reuel in
threatening anger.

"They were searching for you, and we found them, too,
in the pyramid. We confined them here, debating what was
best to do, fearing you would become dissatisfied. They tried
to escape and found the treasure and the snakes. The black
man will die."

"Are you there, Mr. Reuel?" came in a muffled voice from
the dying man.

Reuel stood beside him and took his hand,—"Yes, Jim, it
is I; how came you thus?"

"The way of the transgressor is hard," groaned the man.
"I would not have been here had I not consented to take your

life. I am sure you must have suspected me; I was but a bungler, and often my heart failed me."

"Unhappy man! how could you plot to hurt one who has never harmed you?" exclaimed Reuel.

"Aubrey Livingston was my foster brother, and I could deny him nothing."

"Aubrey Livingston! Was he the instigator?"

"Yes," sighed the dying man. "Return home as soon as possible and rescue your wife—your wife, and yet not your wife—for a man may not marry his sister."

"What!" almost shrieked Reuel. "What!"

"I have said it. Dianthe Lusk is your own sister, the half-sister of Aubrey Livingston, who is your half-brother."

Reuel stood for a moment, apparently struggling for words to answer the dying man's assertion, then fell on his knees in a passion of sobs agonizing to witness. "You know then, Jim, that I am Mira's son?" he said at length.

"I do. Aubrey planned to have Miss Dianthe from the first night he saw her; he got you this chance with the expedition; he kept you from getting anything else to force you to a separation from the girl. He bribed me to accidentally put you out of the way. He killed Miss Molly to have a free road to Dianthe. Go home, Reuel Briggs, and at least rescue the girl from misery. Watch, watch, or he will outwit you yet." Reuel started in a frenzy of rage to seize the man, but Ai's hand was on his arm.

"Peace, Ergamenes; he belongs to the ages now."

One more convulsive grasp, and Jim Titus had gone to atone for the deeds done in the flesh.

With pallid lips and trembling frame, Reuel turned from the dead to the living. As he sat beside his friend, his mind was far away in America looking with brooding eyes into the past and gazing hopelessly into the future. Truly hath the poet said,—

"The evil that men do lives after them."

And Reuel cursed with a mighty curse the bond that bound him to the white race of his native land.

(To be continued.)

CHAPTER XIX.—(Concluded.)

One month after the events narrated in the previous chapter, a strange party stood on the deck of the out-going steamer at Alexandria, Egypt—Reuel and Charlie Vance, accompanied by Ai and Abdallah in the guise of servants. Ai had with great difficulty obtained permission of the Council to allow King Ergamenes to return to America. This was finally accomplished by Ai's being surety for Reuel's safe return, and so the journey was begun which was to end in the apprehension and punishment of Aubrey Livingston.

Through the long journey homeward two men thought only of vengeance, but with very different degrees of feeling. Charlie Vance held to the old Bible punishment for the pure crime of manslaughter, but in Reuel's wrongs lay something beyond the reach of punishment by the law's arm; in it was the accumulation of years of foulest wrongs heaped upon the innocent and defenceless women of a race, added to this last great outrage. At night he said, as he paced the narrow confines of the deck, "Thank God, it is night;" and when the faint streaks of dawn glowed in the distance, gradually creep-

ing across the expanse of waters, "Thank God, it is morning."
Another hour, and he would say, "Would God it were night!"
By day or night some phantom in his ears holloes in ocean's
roar or booms in thunder, howls in the winds or murmurs
in the breeze, chants in the voice of the sea-fowl—"Too late,
too late. 'Tis done, and worse than murder."

Westward the vessel sped—westward while the sun showed
only as a crimson ball in its Arabian setting, or gleamed
through a veil of smoke off the English coast, ending in the
grey, angry, white-capped waves of the Atlantic in winter.

CHAPTER XX

It was believed by the general public and Mr. Vance that
Molly and Dianthe had perished beneath the waters of the
Charles River, although only Molly's body was recovered.
Aubrey was picked up on the bank of the river in an
unconscious state, where he was supposed to have made his
way after vainly striving to rescue the two girls.

When he had somewhat recovered from the shock of the
accident, it was rumored that he had gone to Canada with a
hunting party, and so he disappeared from public view.

But Dianthe had not perished. As the three struggled in
the water, Molly, with all the confidence of requited love,
threw her arms about her lover. With a muttered oath,
Aubrey tried to shake her off, but her clinging arms refused
to release him. From the encircling arms he saw a sight that
maddened him—Dianthe's head was disappearing beneath the
waters where the lily-stems floated in their fatal beauty,
holding in their tenacious grasp the girl he loved. An appalling sound had broken through the air as she went down—

a heart-stirring cry of agony—the tone of a voice pleading with God for life! the precious boon of life! That cry drove away the man, and the brute instinct so rife within us all, ready always to leap to the front in times of excitement or danger, took full possession of the body. He forgot honor, humanity, God.

With a savage kick he freed himself and swam swiftly toward the spot where Dianthe's golden head had last appeared. He was just in time. Grasping the flowing locks with one hand and holding her head above the treacherous water, he swam with her to the bank.

Pretty, innocent, tender-hearted Molly sank never to rise again. Without a word, but with a look of anguished horror, her despairing face was covered by the glistening, greedy waters that lapped so hungrily about the water-lily beds.

As Aubrey bore Dianthe up the bank his fascinated gaze went backward to the spot where he had seen Molly sink. To his surprise and horror, as he gazed the body rose to the surface and floated as did poor Elaine:

> "In her right hand the lily,
> —All her bright hair streaming down—
> —And she herself in white,
> All but her face, and that clear-featured face
> Was lovely, for she did not seem as dead,
> But fast asleep, and lay as tho' she smiled."

Staggering like a drunken man, he made his way to a small cottage up the bank, where a woman, evidently expecting him, opened the door without waiting for his knock.

"Quick! here she is. Not a word. I will return tonight." With these words Livingston sped back to the river bank, where he was found by the rescuing party, in a seemingly exhausted condition.

For weeks after these happenings Dianthe lived in another world, unconscious of her own identity. It was early fall before her full faculties were once more with her. The influence which Livingston had acquired rendered her quiescent in his hands, and not too curious as to circumstances of time and place. One day he brought her a letter, stating that Reuel was dead.

Sick at heart, bending beneath the blight that thus unexpectedly fell upon her, the girl gave herself up to grief, and weary of the buffets of Fate, yielded to Aubrey's persuasions and became his wife. On the night which witnessed Jim Titus's awful death, they had just returned to Livingston's ancestral home in Maryland.

It would be desecration to call the passion which Aubrey entertained for Dianthe, love. Yet passion it was—the greatest he had ever known—with its shadow, jealousy. Indifference on the part of his idol could not touch him; she was his other self, and he hated all things that stood between him and his love.

It was a blustering night in the first part of November. It was twilight. Within the house profound stillness reigned. The heavens were shut out of sight by masses of sullen, inky clouds, and a piercing north wind was howling. Within the room where Dianthe lay, a glorious fire burnt in a wide, low grate. A table, a couch and some chairs were drawn near to it for warmth. Dianthe lay alone. Presently there came a knock at the door. "Enter," said the pale woman on the couch, never once removing her gaze from the whirling flakes and sombre sky.

Aubrey entered and stood for some moments gazing in silence at the beautiful picture presented to his view. She was gowned in spotless white, her bright hair flowed about her unconstrained by comb or pin. Her features were like marble, the deep grey eyes gazed wistfully into the far distance. The man looked at her with hungry, devouring eyes. Something, he knew not what, had come between them. His coveted happiness, sin-bought and crime-stained, had turned to ashes— Dead-Sea fruit indeed. The cold gaze she turned on him half froze him, and changed his feelings into a corresponding channel with her own.

"You are ill, Dianthe. What seems to be your trouble? I am told that you see spirits. May I ask if they wear the dress of African explorers?"

It had come to this unhappy state between them.

"Aubrey," replied the girl in a calm, dispassionate tone, "Aubrey, at this very hour in this room, as I lay here, not sleeping, nor disposed to sleep there where you stand, stood a lovely woman; I have seen her thus once before. She neither looked at me nor spoke, but walked to the table, opened the Bible, stooped over it a while, seeming to write, then seemed to sink, just as she rose, and disappeared. Examine the book, and tell me, is that fancy?"

Crossing the room, Aubrey gazed steadfastly at the open book. It was the old family Bible, and the heavy clasps had grown stiff and rusty. It was familiar to him, and intimately associated with his life-history. There on the open page were ink lines underscoring the twelfth chapter of Luke: "For there is nothing covered that shall not be revealed, neither hid that shall not be known." At the end of this passage was written the one word "Nina" ["Mira"?].

Without a comment, but with anxious brows, Aubrey returned to his wife's couch, stooped and impressed several kisses on her impassive face. Then he left the room.

Dianthe lay in long and silent meditation. Servants came

and went noiselessly. She would have no candles. The storm
ceased; the moon came forth and flooding the landscape, shone
through the windows upon the lonely watcher. Dianthe's
restlessness was soothed, and she began tracing the shadows
on the carpet and weaving them into fantastic images of
imagination. What breaks her reverie? The moonlight gleams
on something white and square; it is a letter. She left the
couch and picked it up. Just then a maid entered with a light,
and she glanced at the envelope. It bore the African postmark!
She paused. Then as the girl left the room, she slipped the
letter from the envelope and read:

> "Master Aubrey,—I write to inform you that I have not been
> able to comply with your wishes. Twice I have trapped Dr.
> Briggs, but he has escaped miraculously from my hands. I
> shall not fail the third time. The expedition will leave for
> Meroe next week, and then something will surely happen. I
> have suppressed all letters, according to your orders, and
> both men are feeling exceedingly blue. Kindly put that first
> payment on the five thousand dollars to my sister's credit in
> a Baltimore bank, and let her have the bank book. Next mail
> you may expect something definite.
>
> > "Yours faithfully,
> > "Jim Titus."

Aubrey Livingston had gone to an adjoining city on business, and would be absent three or four days.

That night Dianthe spent in his library behind locked
doors, and all about her lay open letters—letters addressed to
her, and full of love and tenderness, detailing Reuel's travels
and minutely describing every part of his work.

Still daylight found her at her work. Then she quitted it,
closed up the desk, tied up the letters, replaced them, left the
room, and returned to her boudoir to think. Her brain was

in a giddy whirl, and but one thought stood out clearly in her burning brain. Her thoughts took shape in the one word "Reuel," and by her side stood again the form of the pale, lovely mulattress, her long black curls enveloping her like a veil. One moment—the next the room was vacant save for herself.

Reuel was living, and she a bigamist—another's wife! made so by fraud and deceit. The poor overwrought brain was working like a machine now—throbbing, throbbing, throbbing. To see him, hear his voice—this would be enough. Then came the thought—lost to her, or rather she to him— and how? By the plans of this would-be murderer. O, horrible, inhuman wretch! He had stolen her by false tales, and then had polluted her existence by the breath of murder. Murder! What was murder? She paused and grasped for breath; then came the trembling thought, "Would he were dead!"

He would return and discover the opening of the letters. "O, that he were dead!"

She wandered about the grounds in the cold sunshine, burning with fever, and wild with a brain distraught. She wished the trees were living creatures and would fall and crush him. The winds in their fury, would they but kill him! O, would not something aid her? At last she sat down, out of breath with her wanderings and wearied by the tumult within her breast. So it went all day; the very heavens beckoned her to commit a deed of horror. She slept and dreamed of shapeless, nameless things that lurked and skulked in hidden chambers, waiting the signal to come forth. She woke and slept no more. She turned and turned the remainder of the night; her poor warped faculties recalled the stories she had read of Cenci, the Borgias, and even the Hebrew

Judith. And then she thought of Reuel, and the things he had told her on many an idle day, of the properties of medicine, and how in curiosity she had fingered his retorts used in experiments. And he had told her she was apt, and he would teach her many things of his mysterious profession. And as she thought and speculated, suddenly something whispered, as it were, a name—heard but once—in her ear. It was the name of a poison so subtle in its action as to defy detection save by one versed in its use. With a shudder she threw the thought from her, and rose from her couch.

We know we're tempted. The world is full of precedents, the air with impulses, society with men and spirit tempters. But what invites sin? Is it not a something within ourselves? Are we not placed here with a sinful nature which the plan of salvation commands us to overcome? If we offer the excuse that we were tempted, where is the merit of victory if we do not resist the tempter? God does not abandon us to evil prompters without a white-robed angel, stretching out a warning hand and pointing out the better way as strongly as the other. When we conquer sin, we say we are virtuous, triumphant, and when we fall, we excuse our sins by saying, "It is fate."

The days sped on. To the on-looker life jogged along as monotonously at Livingston Hall as in any other quiet home. The couple dined and rode, and received friends in the conventional way. Many festivities were planned in honor of the beautiful bride. But, alas! these days but goaded her to madness. The uncertainty of Reuel's fate, her own wrongs as a wife yet not a wife, her husband's agency in all this woe, the frailness of her health, weighed more and more upon a mind weakened by hypnotic experiments. Her better angel whispered still, and she listened until one day there was a happening that turned the scale, and she pronounced her own dreadful doom—"For me there's no retreat."

(To be continued.)

❧ ❧ ❧

CHAPTER XXI

It was past midday about two weeks later that Dianthe wandered about the silent woods, flitting through the mazes of unfamiliar forest paths. Buried in sad thoughts she was at length conscious that her surroundings were strange, and that she had lost her way. Every now and then the air was thick and misty with powdery flakes of snow which fell, or swept down, rather, upon the brown leaf-beds and withered grass. The buffeting winds which kissed her glowing hair into waving tendrils brought no color to her white cheeks and no light to her eyes. For days she had been like this, thinking only of getting away from the busy house with its trained servants and its loathsome luxury which stifled her. How to escape the chains which bound her to this man was now her only thought. If Reuel lived, each day that found her still beneath the roof of this man whose wife she was in the eyes of the world, was a crime. Away, away, looking forward to she knew not what, only to get away from the sight of his hated face.

Presently she paused and looked about her. Where was she? The spot was wild and unfamiliar. There was no sight or sound of human being to question as to the right direction to take, not that it mattered much, she told herself in bitterness of spirit. She walked on more slowly now, scanning the woods for signs of a human habitation. An opening in the trees gave a glimpse of cultivated ground in a small clearing, and a few steps farther revealed a typical Southern Negro cabin, from which a woman stepped out and faced her as if expecting her coming. She was very aged, but still erect and noble in form. The patched figure was neat to scrupulousness, the eye still keen and searching.

As the woman advanced slowly toward her, Dianthe was conscious of a thrill of fear, which quickly passed as she dimly remembered having heard the servants jesting over old Aunt Hannah, the most noted "voodoo" doctor or witch in the country.

"Come in honey, and res'," were her first words after her keen eyes had traveled over the woman before her. Dianthe obeyed without a murmur; in truth, she seemed again to have lost her own will in another's.

The one-roomed cabin was faultlessly neat, and the tired girl was grateful for the warmth of the glowing brands upon the wide hearth. Very soon a cup of stimulating coffee warmed her tired frame and brought more animation to her tired face.

"What may your name be, Auntie?" she asked at length, uneasy at the furtive glances cast by the eyes of the silent figure seated in the distant shadow of the chimney-corner. The eyes never wavered, but no answer was vouchsafed her by the woman in the corner. Somewhere she had read a description of an African princess which fitted the woman before her.

> "I knew a princess; she was old,
>   Crisp-haired, flat-featured, with a look
> Such as no dainty pen of gold
>   Would write of in a fairy book.

"Her face was like a Sphinx's face, to me,
        Touched with vast patience, desert grace,
    And lonesome, brooding mystery."

Suddenly a low sound, growing gradually louder, fell upon Dianthe's ear; it was the voice of the old woman crooning a mournful minor cadence, but for an instant it sent a chill about the girl's heart. It was a funeral chant commonly sung by the Negroes over the dead. It chimed in with her gloomy, despairing mood and startled her. She arose hastily to her feet to leave the place.

"How can I reach the road to Livingston Place?" she asked with a shudder of apprehension as she glanced at her entertainer.

"Don't be 'feared, child; Aunt Hannah won't hurt a ha'r of that purty head. Hain't it these arms done nussed ev'ry Livingston? I knowed your mother, child; for all you're married to Marse Aubrey, you isn't a white 'ooman."

"I do not deny what you say, Auntie; I have no desire so to do," replied Dianthe gently.

With a cry of anguish the floodgates of feeling were unloosed, and the old Negress flung her arms about the delicate form. "Gawd-a-mercy! My Mira's gal! My Mira's gal!" Then followed a harrowing scene.

Dianthe listened to the old story of sowing the wind and reaping the whirlwind. A horrible, paralyzing dread was upon her. Was she never to cease from suffering and be at rest? Rocking herself to and fro, and moaning as though in physical pain, the old woman told her story.

"I was born on de Livingston place, an' bein' a purty likely gal, was taken to de big house when I was a tot. I was trained by ol' Miss'. As soon as I was growed up, my mistress changed in her treatment of me, for she soon knowed of my relations with massa, an' she was hurt to de heart, po' 'ooman. Mira was de onlies' child of ten that my massa lef' me for my comfort; all de res' were sold away to raise de mor'gage off de prop'rty.

"Ol' marse had only one chil', a son; he was eddicated for a doctor, and of all the limb o' de devil, he was de worst. After ol' marse an' ol' miss' was dead he took a shine to Mira, and for years he stuck to her in great shape. Her fust child was Reuel——"

"What!" shrieked Dianthe. "Tell me—quick, for God's sake! Is he alive, and by what name is he known?" She was deathly white, and spread out her hands as if seeking support.

"Yes, he's living, or was a year ago. He's called Dr. Reuel Briggs, an' many a dollar he has sent his ol' granny, may the good Marster bless him!"

"Tell me all—tell me the rest," came from the lips of the trembling girl.

"Her second child was a girl,—a beautiful, delicate child, an' de Doctor fairly worshipped her. Dat leetle gal was yourself, an' I'm your granny."

"Then Reuel Briggs is my brother!"

"Certain; but let me tell you de res', honey. Dese things jes' got to happen in slavery, but I isn't gwine to wink at de debbil's wurk wif both eyes open. An' I doesn't want you to keep on livin' with Marse Aubrey Livingston. It's too wicked; it's flyin' in de face ob Almighty God. I'se wanted to tell you eber sense I knowed who he'd married. After a while de Doctor got to thinkin' 'bout keepin' up de family name, an' de fus' thing we knows he up an' marries a white lady down to Charleston, and' brings her home. Well! when she found out all de family secrets she made de house too hot to hol' Mira, and it was ordered that she mus' be sold away. I got on my knees to marse an' I prayed to him not to do it, but to give Mira a house on de place where she could be alone an' bring up de childrun, an' he would a done it but for his wife."

The old woman paused to moan and rock and weep over the sad memories of the past. Dianthe sat like a stone woman.

"Den I believe de debbil took possession of me body and soul. A week before my po' gal was to be sol', Misses' child was born, and died in about an hour; at about de same time Mira gave birth to a son, too. In de 'citemen' de idea come to me to change de babies, fer no one would know it, I being alone when de chil' died, an' de house wil' fer fear misses would die. So I changed de babies, an' tol' Marse Livingston dat Mira's boy was de dead one. So, honey, Aubrey is your own blood brother an' you got to quit dat house mejuntly."

"My brother!"

Dianthe stood over the old woman and shook her by the arm, with a look of utter horror that froze her blood. "My brothers! both those men!"

The old woman mumbled and groaned, then started up.

Aunt Hannah breathed hard once or twice. Minute after minute passed. From time to time she glanced at Dianthe, her hard, toil-worn hands strained at the arms of her chair as if to break them. Her mind seemed wavering as she crooned:

"My Mira's children; by de lotus-lily on each leetle breast I claim them for de great Osiris, mighty god. Honey, hain't you a flower on your breast?"

Dianthe bowed her head in assent, for speech had deserted her. Then old Aunt Hannah undid her snowy kerchief and her dress, and displayed to the terrified girl the perfect semblance of a lily cut, as it were, in shining ebony.

"Did each of Mira's children have this mark?"

"Yes, honey; all of one blood!"

Dianthe staggered as though buffeted in the face. Blindly, as if in some hideous trance, reeling and stumbling, she fell. Cold and white as marble, she lay in the old woman's arms, who thought her dead. "Better so," she cried, and then laughed aloud, then kissed the poor, drawn face. But she was not dead.

Time passed; the girl could not speak. The sacrilege of what had been done was too horrible. Such havoc is wrought by evil deeds. The first downward step of an individual or a nation, who can tell where it will end, through what dark and doleful shades of hell the soul must pass in travail?

> "The laws of changeless justice bind
> Oppressor and oppressed;
> And close as sin and suffering joined,
> We march to Fate abreast."

The slogan of the hour is "Keep the Negro down!" but who is clear enough in vision to decide who hath black blood and who hath it not? Can any one tell? No, not one; for in His own mysterious way He has united the white race and the black race in this new continent. By the transgression of the law He proves His own infallibility: "Of one blood have I made all nations of men to dwell upon the whole face of the earth," is as true today as when given to the inspired writers to be recorded. No man can draw the dividing line between the two races, for they are both of one blood!

Bending a little, as though very weak, and leaning heavily upon her old grandmother's arm, Dianthe at length set out for the Hall. Her face was lined and old with suffering. All hope was gone; despair was heavy on her young shoulders whose life was blasted in its bloom by the passions of others.

As she looked upward at the grey, leaden sky, tears slowly trickled down her cheeks. "God have mercy!" she whispered.

CHAPTER XXII

For two days Mrs. Livingston brooded in her chamber. Fifty times a day Aubrey asked for her. The maid told him she was ill, but not alarmingly so; no physician was called. She was simply indisposed, could not be seen.

Gazing in Dianthe's face, the maid whispered, "She sleeps. I will not disturb her."

Alone, she springs from her couch with all the energy of life and health. She paced the room. For two long hours she never ceased her dreary walk. Memories crowded around her, wreathing themselves in shapes which floated mistily through her brain. Her humble school days at Fisk; her little heart leaping at the well-won prize; the merry play with her joyous mates; in later years, the first triumphant throb when wondering critics praised the melting voice, and world-admiring crowds applauded. And, O, the glorious days of travel in Rome and Florence! the classic scenes of study; intimate companionship with Beethoven, Mozart and Hayden; the floods of inspiration poured in strains of self-made melody upon her soul. Then had followed the reaction, the fall into unscrupulous hands, and the ruin that had come upon her innocent head.

The third day Mrs. Livingston arose, dressed, and declaring herself quite well, went to walk. She returned late in the afternoon, dined with her husband, conversed and even laughed. After dinner they walked a while upon the broad piazzas, beneath the silent stars and gracious moon, inhaling the cold, bracing air. Then Aubrey begged her for a song. Once again she sang "Go down, Moses," and all the house was hushed to drink in the melody of that exquisite voice.

To mortal eyes, this young pair and their surroundings marked them as darlings of the gods enjoying the world's heaped-up felicity. Could these same eyes have looked deeper into their hearts, not the loathsome cell of the wretch condemned to death could have shown a sight more hideous. 'Twas late. Pausing at her chamber door, Aubrey raised her hand to his lips with courtly grace, and bade her good-night.

* * * * *

It was the first hours of the morning. From the deepest and most dreamless slumber that had ever sealed his eyes, Aubrey awoke just as the clock was striking two. 'Twas quite dark, and at first he felt that the striking clock had awakened him; yet sleep on the instant was as effectually banished from his eyes as if it were broad daylight. He could not distinguish the actual contact of any substance, and yet he could not rid himself of the feeling that a strong arm was holding him forcibly down, and a heavy hand was on his lips. He saw nothing, though the moon's rays shone full into the room. He felt nothing sensuously, but everything sensationally; and thus it was that with eyes half-closed, and seemingly fixed as by an iron vice, he beheld the door of his dressing-room— the private means of communication with Dianthe's rooms— very cautiously opened, and Dianthe herself, in a loose robe, crept into the room, and stealthily as a spirit glide to the side of his bed.

Arrested by the same trance-like yet conscious power that bound his form but left perception free, Aubrey neither spoke nor moved. And yet he felt, and partially beheld her stoop over him, listen to his breathing, pass her hand before his eyes to try if they would open; then he, with sidelong glance, beheld her, rapidly as thought, take up the night glass standing on his table, and for the glass containing clear cold water, which it was his custom to swallow every morning upon first awakening, substitute one which, he had seen from the first, she carried in her hand. This done, the stealthy figure moved away, gently drew back the door, and would have passed; but no—the spell was broken. A hand was on her shoulder—a hand of iron. Back it dragged her—into the room just left, shut the door and locked it, held her in its sinewy strength till other doors were locked, then bore her to the bed, placed her upon it, and then released her. And there she sat, white and silent as the grave, whilst before her stood Aubrey, pale as herself, but no longer silent.

Taking the glass which she had substituted, he held it to her lips, and pronounced one word—"Drink!" But one word; but O, what a world of destiny, despair, and agony hung on that word; again and again repeated. Her wild and haggard eyes, her white, speechless lips, all, alas! bore testimony to her guilt—to a mind unbalanced, but only added determination to Aubrey's deep, unflinching purpose.

"Drink! deeper yet! Pledge me to the last drop; drink deep; drink all!"

"Aubrey, Aubrey! mercy, as you look for it! let me explain——" The shrinking woman was on her knees, the half-drained glass in her hand.

"Drink!" shouted Aubrey. "Drain the glass to Reuel!"

"To Reuel!" gasped Dianthe, and set the glass down empty. Once more Aubrey led his bride of three months back to the door of her room. Once more before her chamber door he paused; and once again, but now in mockery, he stooped and kissed her hand.

"Farewell, my love," he said. "When we meet, 'twill be——"

"In judgment, Aubrey; and may God have mercy on our guilty souls!"

(To be continued.)

CHAPTER XXIII

'Twas a cold gray morning; the dawn of such a day as seems to wrap itself within the shroud of night, hiding the warm sun in its stony bosom, and to creep through time arrayed in mourning garments for the departed stars. Aubrey was up by the earliest glimpse of dawn. Uncertain what to do or where to go, he made a pretence of eating, sitting in solemn state in the lonely breakfast room, where the servants glided about in ghostly silence, which was too suggestive for the over-wrought nerves of the master of all that magnificence. Fifty times he asked the maid for Mrs. Livingston. The woman told him she was ill,—not alarmingly so; no physician's services were needed, neither his own nor another's. He did not ask to see her, yet with a strange and morbid curiosity, he kept on questioning how she was, and why she kept her chamber, until the knowing laugh and sly joke about the anxiety of bridegrooms over the welfare of brides made the servants' quarters ring with hilarity. At length, tired of his aimless wandering, he said he'd go. His valet asked him where. He could not tell. "Pack up some things."

"For how long a time, sir?"

"I cannot tell, James."

"Shall I order the carriage?"

"Anything, something! A horse; yes. I'll have the swiftest one in the stable. A valise—no more; no, you need not come. I must be alone."

In Dianthe's room the attendants tread noiselessly, and finally leave her to enjoy her feigned slumber. She waits but the closing of the door, to spring from her couch with all the seeming energy of life and health. First she went to the window and flung wide the hangings, letting in a flood of light upon the pale, worn face reflected in the mirror. What a wondrous change was there! The long white drapery of her morning robe fell about her like a shroud, yet, white as it was, contrasted painfully with the livid ash-hue of her skin. Her arms were thin and blue, her hands transparent; her sunny hair hung in long dishevelled, waving masses, the picture of neglect; the sunken, wan brow, and livid lips, the heavy eyes with deep, black halos round them—all these made up a ruined temple.

"When he comes he will not know me," she murmured to herself; then sighing deeply, turned and paced the room. What she thought of, none could say. She spoke not; never raised her eyes from off the ground, nor ceased her dreary walk for two long hours. She sometimes sobbed, but never shed a tear.

Here we drop the veil. Let no human eye behold the writhings of that suffering face, the torture of that soul unmoored, and cast upon the sea of wildest passion, without the pilot, principle, or captain of all salvation, God, to trust in,—passion, adoration of a human idol, hereditary traits entirely unbalanced, generous, but fervid impulses, her only guides. She knew that her spiritual person must survive the grave, but what that world was where her spirit was fast tending, only the dread tales of fear and superstition shadowed truth; and now, when her footsteps were pressing to it, horror and dread dogged every footprint.

Hour after hour elapsed alone. O, 'twas agony to be alone! She could not bear it. She would call her maid; but no, her cold, unimpassioned face would bring no comfort to her aching heart, aching for pity, for some cheering bosom, where she might sob her ebbing life away. The door opens,— and O joy! old Aunt Hannah's arms enfold her. For hours the two sat in solemn conference, while the servants wondered and speculated over the presence of the old witch.

At last night fell. "Mother," murmured the dying girl, raising her head from off her damp pillow. "A very golden cloud is printed with the fleecy words of glory. 'I will return.' " She pointed to the golden clouds banking the western sky. "O, will our spirits come, like setting suns, on each tomorrow of eternity?"

For answer, the old woman raised her hand in warning gesture. There sounded distinct and clear—three loud, yet muffled knocks on the panel directly above the couch where Dianthe lay.

" 'Tis nothing, mother; I'm used to it now," said the girl with indifference.

"You say 'tis nuffin, honey; but yer limbs are quiverin' wif pain, and the drops ob agony is on yer po' white face. You can't 'ceive me, chile; yer granny knows de whole circumstance. I seed it all las' night in my dreams. Vengeance is mine; I will repay. One comes who is de instrumen' ob de

Lord." And the old woman muttered and rocked and whispered.

Whatever was the cause of Mrs. Livingston's illness, its character was unusual and alarming. The maid, who was really attached to the beautiful bride, pleaded to be allowed to send for medical aid in vain. The causes for her suffering, as stated by Dianthe, were plausible; but her resolve to have no aid, inflexible. As evening advanced, her restlessness, and the hideous action of spasmodic pains across her livid face, became distressing. To all the urgent appeals of her servants, she simply replied she was waiting for some one. He was coming soon—very soon and then she would be quite well.

And yet he came not. From couch to door, from door to window; with eager, listening ear and wistful eyes the poor watcher traversed her chamber in unavailing expectancy. At length a sudden calm seemed to steal over her; the incessant restlessness of her wearied frame yielded to a tranquil, passive air. She lay upon cushions piled high upon the couch commanding a view of the broad hallways leading to her apartments. The beams of the newly risen moon bathed every object in the dim halls. Clear as the vesper bell, sounding across a far distant lake, strains of delicious music, rising and falling in alternate cadence of strong martial measure, came floating in waves of sound down the corridor.

Dianthe and Aunt Hannah and the maid heard the glorious echoes; whilst in the town the villagers heard the music as of a mighty host. Louder it grew, first in low and wailing notes, then swelling, pealing through arch and corridor in mighty diapason, until the very notes of different instruments rang out as from a vast orchestra. There was the thunder of the organ, the wild harp's peal, the aeolian's sigh, the trumpet's peal, and the mournful horn. A thousand soft melodious flutes, like trickling streams upheld a bird-like treble; whilst ever and anon the muffled drum with awful beat precise, the rolling kettle and the crashing cymbals, kept time to sounds like tramping of a vast but viewless army. Nearer they came. The dull, deep beat of falling feet—in the hall—up the stairs. Louder it came and louder. Louder and yet more loud the music swelled to thunder! The unseen mass must have been the disembodied souls of every age since Time began, so vast the rush and strong the footfalls. And then the chant of thousands of voices swelling in rich, majestic choral tones, joined in the thundering crash. It was the welcome of ancient Ethiopia to her dying daughter of the royal line.

Upspringing from her couch, as through the air the mighty hallelujah sounded, Dianthe with frantic gestures and wild distended eyes, cried: "I see them now! the glorious band! Welcome, great masters of the world's first birth! All hail, my royal ancestors—Candace, Semiramis, Dido, Solomon, David and the great kings of early days, and the great masters of the world of song. O, what long array of souls divine, lit with immortal fire from heaven itself! O, let me kneel to thee! And to thee, too, Beethoven, Mozart, thou sons of song! Divine ones, art thou come to take me home? Me, thy poor worshipper on earth? O, let me be thy child in paradise!

The pageant passed, or seemed to pass, from her whose eyes alone of all the awe-struck listeners, with mortal gaze beheld them. When, at length, the last vibrating echoes of the music seemed to die away in utter vacant silence to the terrified attendants, Dianthe still seemed to listen. Either her ear still drank in the music, or another sound had caught her attention.

"Hark, hark! 'Tis carriage wheels. Do you not hear them? Now they pass the railroad at the crossing. Hasten, O hasten!

Still they have a long mile to traverse. O, hasten! They call me home."

For many minutes she sat rigid and cold as marble. The trembling maid wept in silent terror and grief, for the gentle bride was a kind mistress. Old Aunt Hannah, with a fortitude born of despair, ministered in every possible way to the dying girl. To the great relief of all, at last, there came to their ears the very distant rumbling of wheels. Nearer it came—it sounded in the avenue—it paused at the great entrance, some one alighted—a stir—the sound of voices—then footsteps—the ascent of footsteps on the stairs. Nearer, nearer yet; hastily they come, like messengers of speed. They're upon the threshold—enter. Then, and not till then, the rigid lady moved. With one wild scream of joy she rushed forward, and Reuel Briggs clasped her in his arms.

For a few brief moments, the wretched girl lived an age in heaven. The presence of that one beloved—this drop of joy sweetened all the bitter draught and made for her an eternity of compensation. With fond wild tenderness she gazed upon him, gazed in his anxious eyes until her own looked in his very soul, and stamped there all the story of her guilt and remorse. Then winding her cold arms around his neck, she laid her weary head upon his shoulder and silently as the night passed through the portals of the land of souls.

CHAPTER XXIV

'Twas midnight. The landscape was still as death. Hills, rocks, rivers, even the babbling brooks, seemed locked in sleep. The moonbeams dreamt upon the hillside; stars slept in the glittering sky; the silent vales were full of dreaming flowers whose parti-colored cups closed in sleep. In all that solemn hush of silence one watcher broke the charmed spell. 'Twas Aubrey Livingston. Now he moves swiftly over the plain as if some sudden purpose drove him on; then he turns back in he self-same track and with the same impulsive speed. What is he doing in the lonely night? All day, hour after hour, mile on mile, the scorching midday sun had blazed upon his head, and still he wandered on. The tranquil sunset purpled round his way and still the wanderer hastened on. In his haggard eyes one question seems to linger—"I wonder if she lives!"

Many, many dreary times he said this question over! He has a secret and 'tis a mighty one; he fears if human eye but look upon him, it must be revealed. Hark! suddenly there falls upon his ear the sound of voices, surely some one called! Again! His straining ear caught a familiar sound.

"Aubrey! Aubrey Livingston!"

"By heaven, it is her voice!" he told himself. And as if to assure him still more of who addressed him, close before his very eyes moved two figures. Hand in hand they passed from out a clump of sheltering trees, and slowly crossed his path. One face was turned toward him, the other from him. The moon revealed the same white robe in which he had last beheld her, the long, streaming hair, her slippered feet—all were there. Upon his wondering eyes her own were fixed in mute appeal and deepest anguish; then both figures passed away, he knew not where.

" 'Twas she, and in full life. God of heaven, she lives!"

Pausing not to think he was deceived, enough for him, she lived. He turned his steps toward his home, with flying feet he neared the hall. Just as he reached the great entrance gates, he saw the two figures lightly in advance of him. This time Dianthe's face was turned away, but the silver moonbeams threw into bold relief the accusing face of Molly Vance!

With a sudden chill foreboding, he entered the hall and passed up the stairs to his wife's apartments. He opened wide the door and stood within the chamber of the dead.

There lay the peaceful form—spread with a drapery of soft, white gauze around her, and only the sad and livid, poisoned face was visible above it; and kneeling by the side of her, his first love and his last—was Reuel Briggs.

Rising from the shadows as Aubrey entered, Charlie Vance, flanked on either side by Ai and Abdadis, moved to meet him, the stern brow and sterner words of an outraged brother and friend greeted him:

"Welcome, murderer!"

Dianthe was dead, poisoned; that was clear. Molly Vance was unduly done to death by the foul treachery of the same hand. All this was now clear to the thinking public, for so secluded had Aubrey Livingston lived since his return to the United States, that many of his intimate associates still believed that he had perished in the accident on the Charles. It was quite evident to these friends that his infatuation for the beautiful Dianthe had led to the commission of a crime. But the old adage that, "the dead tell no tales," was not to be set aside for visionary ravings unsupported by lawful testimony.

Livingston's wealth purchased shrewd and active lawyers to defend him against the charges brought by the Vances— father and son,—and Reuel Briggs.

One interview which was never revealed to public comment, took place between Ai, Abdadis, Aunt Hannah, Reuel Briggs and Aubrey Livingston.

Aubrey sat alone in his sumptuous study. An open book was on his knees, but his eyes were fixed on vacancy. He was changed and his auburn locks were prematurely grey. His eyes revealed an impenetrable mystery within into whose secret depths no mortal eye might look. Thus he sat when the group we have named above silently surrounded him. "Peace, O son of Osiris, to thy parting hour!"

Thus Ai greeted him. There was no mistaking these words, and gazing into the stern faces of the silent group Aubrey knew that something of import was about to happen.

Aubrey did not change countenance, although he glanced at Reuel as if seeking mercy. The latter did not change countenance; only his eyes, those strange deep eyes before whose fixed gaze none could stand unflinching, took on a more sombre glow. Again Ai spoke:

"God has willed it! Great is the God of Ergamenes, we are but worms beneath His feet. His will be done." Then began a strange, weird scene. Round and round the chair where Aubrey was seated walked the kingly Ai chanting in a low, monotone in his native tongue, finally advancing with measured steps to a position directly opposite and facing Livingston, and stood there erect and immovable, with arms raised as if in invocation. His eyes glittered with strange, fascinating lights in the shaded room. To the man seated there it seemed that an eternity was passing. Why did not these two men he had injured take human vengeance in meting out punishment to him? And why, oh! why did those eyes, piercing his own like poinards, hold him so subtly in their spell?

Gradually he yielded to the mysterious beatitude that insensibly enwrapped his being. Detached from terrestrial bonds, his spirit soared in regions of pure ethereal blue. A delicious torpor held him in its embrace. His head sank upon his breast. His eyes closed in a trancelike slumber.

Ai quitted his position, and approaching Aubrey, lifted one of the shut eyelids. "He sleeps!" he exclaimed.

Then standing by the side of the unconscious man he poured into his ear—speaking loudly and distinctly,—a few terse sentences. Not a muscle moved in the faces of those standing about the sleeper. Then Ai passed his hands lightly over his face, made a few upward passes, and turning to his companions, beckoned them to follow him from the room. Silently as they had come the group left the house and grounds, gained a waiting carriage and were driven rapidly away. In the shelter of the vehicle Charlie Vance spoke, "Is justice done?" he sternly queried.

"Justice will be done," replied Ai's soothing tones.

"Then I am satisfied."

But Reuel spoke not one word.

*   *   *   *   *

One day not very long after this happening, the body of Aubrey Livingston was found floating in the Charles river at the very point where poor Molly Vance had floated in the tangled lily-bed. The mysterious command of Ai, "death by thine own hand," whispered in his ear while under hypnotic influence, had been followed to the last letter.

Thus Aubrey had become his own executioner according to the ancient laws of the inhabitants of Telassar. Members of the royal family in direct line to the throne became their own executioners when guilty of the crime of murder.

*   *   *   *   *

Reuel Briggs returned to the Hidden City with his faithful subjects, and old Aunt Hannah. There he spends his days in teaching his people all that he has learned in years of contact with modern culture. United to Candace, his days glide peacefully by in good works; but the shadows of great sins darken his life, and the memory of past joys is ever with him. He views, too, with serious apprehension, the advance of mighty nations penetrating the dark, mysterious forests of his native land.

"Where will it stop?" he sadly questions. "What will the end be?"

But none save Omnipotence can solve the problem.

To our human intelligence these truths depicted in this feeble work may seem terrible,—even horrible. But who shall judge the handiwork of God, the Great Craftsman! Caste prejudice, race pride, boundless wealth, scintillating intellects refined by all the arts of the intellectual world, are but puppets in His hand, for His promises stand, and He will prove His words, "Of one blood have I made all races of men."

THE END.